GIATI

The Holy Spirit Speaks

Unveiling the Mystery of God's Spirit Within

GIATI

The Holy Spirit Speaks

Unveiling the Mystery of God's Spirit Within

Spirit of Truth

Copyright © 2025 by Spirit of Truth

All rights reserved. No part of this publication may be reproduced, distributed, or transmitted in any form or by any means, including photocopying, recording, or other electronic or mechanical methods, without the prior written permission of the copyright owner and the publisher, except in the case of brief quotations embodied in critical reviews and certain other noncommercial uses permitted by copyright law. For permission requests, write to the publisher, addressed "Attention: Permissions Coordinator," at the address below.

ARPress
45 Dan Road Suite 15
Canton MA 02021
Hotline: 1(888) 821-0229
Fax: 1(508) 545-7580

Ordering Information:
Quantity sales. Special discounts are available on quantity purchases by corporations, associations, and others. For details, contact the publisher at the address above.

Printed in the United States of America.

ISBN-13: Paperback 979-8-89676-605-6
eBook 979-8-89676-606-3

Library of Congress Control Number: 2025903725

Table of Contents

Part I: The Nature of God

Part II: The Fall and the Lost Spirit

Part III: God's Purpose as Savior

Part IV GIATI and the Path to Salvation

Part V: The Ultimate Truth

DEDICATION

This book is dedicated to Yahweh, who is All in All—the Eternal Father, revealed in the Son, and dwelling within us as the Holy Spirit. To the One who spoke light into existence and now speaks from within the temple of our being, I give glory, for without His voice there is no life, no truth, and no revelation.

I dedicate these pages to the Spirit of Truth, who has unveiled the mystery hidden from ages and generations: that God is not far off, but present within, speaking, guiding, and reproducing Himself in us. HCK

To every seeker who has ever felt the weight of separation, this work is also for you. May these words open your eyes to the reality that you are not abandoned, not divided, not your own—you are the dwelling place of God Himself.

And finally, to those who will carry this message further, may the Holy Spirit quicken these words in you, until the world sees what has always been true: God Is All There Is.

Epigraphs

1. "I am the Lord, and there is none else."

— Isaiah 45:5

2. "Christ in you, the hope of glory."

— Colossians 1:27

3. "In him we live, and move, and have our being."

— Acts 17:28

4. "At that day ye shall know that I am in my Father, and ye in me, and I in you."

— John 14:20

Each one points to the mystery of oneness, but from a different angle:

- Isaiah 45:5 → foundation of GIATI: God Is All There Is.
- Colossians 1:27 → Christ indwelling.
- Acts 17:28 → our being sustained within God.
- John 14:20 → the Trinity revealed as oneness in us.

"The truth you've been missing. You are God manifested"

Key Points That Will Draw Readers to GIATI

1. **A Revolutionary Perspective on God and Humanity**
   - The book challenges traditional beliefs by revealing that God is not separate but is the essence of every person.
   - Readers will discover a profound truth: You are not just made in God's image—you are God expressed.

2. **Answers to Life's Biggest Questions**
   - Why are we here?
   - What is the purpose of existence?
   - What happens after death?
   - This book provides clear, scripture-backed answers to these universal questions.

3. **A Guide to Personal Transformation**
   - Readers will learn how to shed the illusion of separateness and awaken to their divine nature.
   - Practical steps are provided to live a life aligned with God's purpose, bringing peace, joy, and fulfillment.

4. **The Mystery of the Trinity Simplified**
   - The Father, Son, and Holy Spirit are explained in a way that makes their unity and purpose clear.
   - Readers will finally understand how Jesus Christ reveals their true identity in God.

5. **Hope for the Lost**
   - The book addresses the plight of those who feel disconnected or unworthy, offering a path to enlightenment and salvation.
   - It provides hope for humanity to collectively return to unity with God.

6. **Scriptural Depth with Modern Relevance**
   - Grounded in biblical scripture, the book makes timeless truths accessible to a modern audience.
   - It bridges the gap between ancient teachings and contemporary spiritual questions.

7. **A Call to Wake Up and Transform the World**
    - Readers are not only invited to awaken to their own divinity but also to be part of a global transformation.
    - The book inspires individuals to live as the light of God and bring heaven on earth.
8. **Breaking Free from Fear and Ignorance**
    - It addresses the root of human suffering—ignorance of our divine origin—and offers freedom through understanding GIATI.
9. **A Bold and Provocative Message**
    - The idea that God is all there is is both thought-provoking and controversial, sparking curiosity and engagement.
10. **The Promise of Eternal Unity**
    - The book concludes with the assurance of eternal oneness with God, offering readers a sense of purpose, peace, and hope.

These points make the book compelling for readers seeking deeper spiritual understanding, personal transformation, and answers to life's mysteries.

GIATI: God Is All There Is — A Guide to Understanding Human Existence

INTRODUCTION

The Mystery of Existence

What is the purpose of life? Why are we here? Who are we, truly? These questions have echoed through the hearts and minds of humanity for centuries. At the core of these questions lies a mystery—a truth hidden in plain sight but often misunderstood. This book seeks to unveil that mystery, revealing the ultimate truth about God, humanity, and the nature of existence: God Is All There Is.

The Purpose of This Book

The purpose of this book is to guide you to a deeper understanding of who you are, where you come from, and your divine purpose. Humanity has long been blinded by the illusion of separateness—the belief that we are distinct, autonomous beings, disconnected from the Creator. This false perception has led to suffering, confusion, and a loss of identity.

Through GIATI—God Is All There Is—this book will show that God is not just present in the universe; He is the universe. He is the very substance of creation, including you. Recognizing this truth is the key to salvation, peace, and eternal unity with God.

Setting the Foundation: What Is GIATI?

GIATI is rooted in the understanding that God is the only reality. As Isaiah 45:5-7 declares:

"I am the Lord, and there is none else, there is no God beside me… That they may know from the rising of the sun, and from the west, that there is none beside me. I am the Lord, and there is none else. I form the light, and create darkness: I make peace, and create evil: I the Lord do all these things."

Everything that exists, seen and unseen, is an expression of God. He does not create from something outside Himself because there is no "outside." There is only Him. Every atom, every being, every thought, and every action is made from the substance of God.

- The Dual Spirit of God: God's substance manifests as both light and darkness, symbolizing knowledge and ignorance. The "light spirit" represents those who recognize their oneness with God, while the "dark spirit" represents those lost in the illusion of separateness.
- The Illusion of Separateness: Humanity's greatest challenge is the belief in individuality—the idea that we are independent entities apart from God. This is the root of all suffering and confusion. The truth is, we are not our physical bodies or even our personalities. We are God, manifested as individual expressions, but we remain one with Him in essence.

John 1:1-3 confirms this:

"In the beginning was the Word, and the Word was with God, and the Word was God. The same was in the beginning with God. All things were made by him; and without him was not anything made that was made."

GIATI asserts that God's spirit permeates all of creation. To truly understand this is to unlock the mystery of existence.

Understanding Isaiah 45:5: "I Girded Thee, Though Thou Hast Not Known Me"

In Isaiah 45:5, God declares a profound truth: *"I am the Lord, and there is none else, there is no God beside me: I girded thee, though thou hast not known me."*

The focus here is on the phrase, *"I girded thee, though thou hast not known me."* To gird means to surround, encircle, imbue, or endue. In this single statement, God is revealing His all-encompassing presence in your life—inside and out, seen and unseen.

God is saying: **I am everything you need and everything you are. I am the outside—the world you see and the air you breathe—and I am the inside, the life force sustaining you, the unseen essence that keeps you alive. I am your food, your water, your shelter, your strength, your wisdom, your breath. I am your all in all.**

God's Presence Is Always with You

Even when you don't recognize it, even when you don't know Him, God is still present, surrounding you in every moment. He doesn't stop being God because of your lack of awareness. He is your protection when you feel vulnerable, your sustenance when you feel weak, your foundation when you feel lost.

When He says, *"I girded thee,"* He is telling you that He has been holding you, supporting you, and providing for you from the beginning, even if you didn't realize it. You didn't have to know Him for Him to be everything for you. That's how complete and unconditional His presence is in your life.

You Don't Need to Seek What You Already Are

The tragedy for many is that they live their lives searching for what God has already given and what God already is. This is the trick the devil played on Eve by getting her to lust for something she already was. They search for purpose, peace, and fulfillment, not realizing that the One who sustains all things is already within and around them. God is saying, *"You think you are separate from Me, but I am the essence of your existence. You eat, breathe, and live through Me, and yet you do not know Me."*

This isn't condemnation; it's an invitation to awaken. God is revealing that your lack of awareness doesn't change the truth—**He is your everything.**

God Is All and All

The phrase *"though thou hast not known me"* highlights the human condition: living in ignorance of the one truth that changes everything. The reality is this: **God is all there is.** There is no "outside" or "beside" Him. He is the substance of everything you see and the spirit within everything you cannot see.

When you realize this, the search ends. You stop looking outside yourself for purpose, peace, or power. You stop trying to fill the void with temporary things. You come to understand that there is no void—**God has already filled it.** You are surrounded, indwelled, and sustained by Him, and He has always been your all in all.

The Awakening to Oneness

God's declaration in Isaiah 45:5 is both a reminder and a revelation. He's telling you that He is your source, your sustainer, your very life. And even if you don't recognize Him, He remains unchanged, faithful, and constant.

To truly know Him is to awaken to the reality that He isn't just near you or around you—**He is you, expressed through you.** He is your thoughts, your actions, your existence. He is everything you see, touch, hear, and feel.

When you embrace this truth, you no longer live in ignorance. You live in the fullness of knowing that there is none else but God—and He has girded you from the beginning, even when you didn't know it.

Why This Knowledge Matters

The recognition of GIATI is not just an intellectual exercise—it is the key to salvation. To remain blind to this truth is to live in ignorance, separated from the light of God within. This separation is not caused by God but by our own inability to see Him within ourselves.

John 1:4-5 illustrates this:

"In him was life; and the life was the light of men. And the light shineth in darkness; and the darkness comprehended it not."

- The Consequences of Ignorance: Those who fail to recognize God within themselves remain trapped in darkness. They live under the false belief that they are autonomous beings, disconnected from their Creator. This ignorance leads to a life of spiritual blindness and, ultimately, eternal separation from God.
- The Gift of Revelation: Jesus Christ came into the world to reveal this truth and restore humanity's awareness of oneness with God. As John 1:14 declares:

"And the Word was made flesh, and dwelt among us… full of grace and truth."

Jesus' life was a demonstration of GIATI—the Word of God manifested in human form to show us that God is not distant but present within us.

- The Urgency of Awareness: Accepting this truth is not merely an option; it is a necessity. As long as we remain blind to GIATI, we are lost. This is why Jesus said in Matthew 7:23:

"And then will I profess unto them, I never knew you: depart from me, ye that work iniquity."

To "know" God is to recognize Him within yourself. Those who live as if they are separate from God, taking credit for their actions and denying His presence, are workers of iniquity—lost in ignorance.

The Invitation to Awakening

This book invites you to awaken to the truth of GIATI. It is not about introducing a new religion or philosophy but about unveiling the reality that has always been. The Spirit of God dwells within you, as you. You are not a separate being; you are an expression of the Creator.

Through the chapters ahead, we will explore the nature of God, the purpose of creation, the fall of humanity, and the path to salvation. By the end of this journey, you will see that the mystery of existence is no mystery at all. It is the simple, profound truth that God Is All There Is.

Will you open your heart to this truth? Will you recognize the divine essence within you and live as the light of God in the world? The journey begins here.

God is a divine spiritual pattern that reflects identically in the physical world. **Romans 1:19-20 Because that which may be known of God is manifest in them, for God hath**

shewed it unto them. For the invisible things of him from the creation of the world are clearly seen, being understood by the things that are made, even his eternal power and Godhead, so that they are without excuse. In the spiritual realm, God exists as the Father, the Word (Son), and the Holy Spirit—three yet one. This same principle manifests in the physical realm, demonstrating that **everything in existence follows this divine pattern.**

All physical matter—everything you see, touch, and experience—is also three yet one. The chair you sit on, the car you drive, the trees you see, and even the book in your hands are all made of the same fundamental substance: **atoms.** Atoms themselves embody this divine pattern, composed of three parts—protons, neutrons, and electrons—yet existing as one unified structure.

This principle is unavoidable because it is the truth of how God's spirit expresses itself in all things. Whether in the spiritual as the triune God, or in the physical as the foundation of all matter, it's all **Him.** There is no separation—what is spirit is God, and what is physical is also God. This understanding unveils the oneness of existence: **God is all there is.**

PART I
THE NATURE OF GOD

Chapter 1

God Defined

This statement—**"God is the ultimate source, substance, limits, and bounds of all things"**—can be broken down into its components to describe the essence of God as the totality of existence, reflecting the message of GIATI **(God is all there is).** Let's analyze each part to reveal the deeper meaning of how God truly exists:

1. God as the Ultimate Source

What it means:

- God is the origin of all existence—everything that is, was, or will be arises from God.
- Just as light emanates from the sun, all forms of life, energy, and matter emerge from this single divine source.

How God exists as Source:

- God is the creative force behind the universe. Every particle, being, and event stems from this eternal, self-sustaining origin.
- Without God as the source, nothing could exist, for all existence flows from divine will or essence.

Example: The idea that God spoke the universe into being (symbolically or literally) reflects that all things have their roots in God's creative power.

2. God as the Ultimate Substance

What it means:

- God is the essence or "material" out of which everything is made. Everything exists *as* God in different forms or expressions.
- This emphasizes that there is no separation between God and creation; God is immanent in all things.

How God exists as Substance:

- Everything tangible or intangible—matter, energy, thoughts, emotions—is composed of the divine.

- God is the "stuff" of existence, present in every atom and beyond.

Example: Like clay is the substance of a pot, God is the substance of the universe. The forms may change, but the essence remains divine.

3. God as the Ultimate Limits

What it means:

- God defines the boundaries of existence; nothing exists outside of God.
- There is no "beyond" God, as God encompasses all possibilities, realities, and dimensions.

How God exists as Limits:

- God is infinite and omnipresent, meaning everything exists within God's "field" of being.
- What appears as boundaries in the physical world (space, time, or laws of nature) are expressions of God's order.

Example: The laws of physics or the edge of the observable universe are not limits outside of God but expressions of God's nature.

4. God as the Ultimate Bounds

What it means:

- God is the framework that contains and sustains all existence.
- While God is infinite, this also means God holds all things together within a coherent unity.

How God exists as Bounds:

- God is both the infinite (beyond comprehension) and the container of all that exists (the comprehensible).
- This duality—boundlessness within bounds—is why creation is orderly yet infinite in potential.

Example: Like an artist creating within a canvas, God bounds creation to give it form, yet God's essence remains limitless beyond the canvas.

5. The Unity of These Aspects

What this reveals about God's existence:

- God is the **beginning** (source), the **essence** (substance), and the **framework** (limits and bounds) of all reality.
- God exists simultaneously as the infinite and the finite, the seen and unseen, the eternal and the temporal.

How God actually exists:

- God's existence is not as a distant being but as the ever-present reality of everything.
- God is both transcendent (beyond the world) and immanent (within the world). In GIATI's understanding, God is expressed as us, in us, and through us, making all life sacred. **Ephesians 4:4-6 There is one body, and one Spirit, even as ye are called in one hope of your calling; One Lord, one faith, one baptism, one God and father of all, who is above all, and through all, and in you all.**

Names and Titles

What it all boils down to is this: no matter what name or title you use to reference your Creator—whether it's **God, Yahweh, Allah, Krishna, The Great Spirit, Brahman, Olodumare,** or any other name from the countless traditions and beliefs around the world—the core truth remains the same. The mystery and moral of the story have always pointed to one profound realization: that entity has always been you, manifest in the flesh, and present within you the entire time.

The Face of the Divine: The Spiritual Significance of GIATI

Seeing as the Holy Spirit Sees

The logo of GIATI is not just an image—it is a revelation. It represents the Holy Spirit, the eternal truth of oneness, and the vision to see all things as spirit. This is the essence of GIATI: to awaken from the illusion of separation and recognize that God is all there is, manifesting in all that exists.

At the center of this design is the sacred name: Yahweh. It is not merely written on the logo; it is written in the face itself, just as it is written in yours. This is the divine mystery—when you look in the mirror, you are not just seeing yourself; you are seeing the expression of God. The face before you is not separate from the divine; it is the divine revealed as you.

The Reflection of Truth

For those who see clearly, the GIATI face is a mirror reflecting their true nature. It is a call to recognize that when you behold yourself, you behold God in expression. But for those still in darkness, the vision is obscured. They look at themselves and see only a separate being, a mere individual, disconnected from the whole. This is the great deception—that they believe themselves to be anything other than one with the Spirit.

And so, it has been said that the face in the logo appears angry. But what is the source of this perceived anger? It is not human emotion but divine response. It is the expression of one who knows the truth yet sees others clinging to falsehood. It is the face of those who have awakened, looking upon a world that refuses to recognize the light within them.

This is not a passive acceptance of deception—it is the rightful frustration of those who see clearly, yet witness their brothers and sisters choosing blindness. It is the holy discontent of those who long for humanity to awaken, to shed the darkness of division, and to step into the glorious unity of oneness.

The Disgust of the Spirit

It is written that Jesus wept over Jerusalem, grieved by the hardness of heart of those who rejected the truth standing before them. He was not angry in the way men are angry, but sorrowful in seeing the beloved remain in darkness when light had come. The same Spirit that moved Him moves in those who understand GIATI. The face in the logo reflects that same holy frustration—not against people, but against the ignorance that blinds them to their own divinity.

The disgust is not personal; it is spiritual. It is the Spirit's righteous rejection of division, of falsehood, of anything that denies the truth that all is one in God as God. Those who are opposed to oneness are not just rejecting a philosophy—they are rejecting their own true nature. And those who know cannot help but feel the weight of that refusal.

The Call to See Clearly

The GIATI logo is an invitation. It asks a simple yet profound question: **Do you see yourself?** *Not as the world has taught you to see, not as a mere person among many, but as Spirit in expression. Do you recognize Yahweh written in your very being? Do you understand that when you look at yourself, you are looking at God?*

For those who have the eyes to see, the answer is undeniable. The name is written. The truth is revealed. The reflection is clear. There is nothing else but **God Is All There Is.**

GIATI: The Holy Spirit Wrapped Around the World

The Spirit in Every Nation

The Holy Spirit is not confined to a place, a people, or a time. It moves across the world, filling all things, present in every land, every culture, and every soul. GIATI is more than a clothing brand—it is the physical representation of this truth, a visible sign that the Spirit is here, now, in every corner of the earth.

To wear GIATI is to declare oneness with the Spirit, to bear witness that God is not distant but present, not separate but expressed in all. When you put on GIATI, you are not just wearing clothing; you are clothing yourself in the awareness that **God is all there is.**

The Garment of Spirit

Throughout history, clothing has symbolized identity. Priests wore sacred robes, kings adorned themselves in garments of power, and prophets wrapped themselves in mantles of authority. GIATI continues this divine tradition—not as a symbol of separation, but of unity.

Wherever GIATI is worn, the Spirit is made known. Whether in the streets of New York, the villages of Africa, the mountains of Asia, or the islands of the Pacific, the message is the same:

The Holy Spirit is here.

When you see someone in GIATI, you are seeing a reflection of the divine, a living testimony that God is not just in one place but everywhere, in everyone. It is not a brand; it is a movement of the Spirit sweeping across nations, a declaration that the world is waking up to its true identity.

Covering the Earth in Truth

As GIATI spreads, so does the awareness of oneness. Every hoodie, every sweatsuit, every short set is a banner of the eternal truth that the Spirit is alive and moving.

- *In the* **bustling cities,** *GIATI stands as a light in the midst of the noise, reminding people that even in the chaos, God is present.*
- *In the* **quiet countryside,** *GIATI whispers the same message: God is not far, but here, as you.*
- *On the* **streets of different nations,** *where languages and cultures may differ, GIATI* speaks the universal language of Spirit.

The clothing becomes a vessel, but the message is eternal. The world may look divided by borders, races, and religions, but when you see GIATI in every land, on every body, you see the undeniable truth:

There is no separation. The Holy Spirit is one. The earth is already filled with the glory of God.

A Global Awakening

GIATI is not just worn—it is lived. Every person who wears it becomes a messenger, a walking testimony of what has always been true. The Spirit is not coming—it has already come. The world is not waiting for God—God has always been here, moving through every person, filling every space.

To put on GIATI is to say, **"I see."**
To recognize it on another is to say, **"I know."**
And when the world sees GIATI everywhere, it will be undeniable:

The Holy Spirit is not in one place—it is in all. It is not in one people—it is in every people. It is not in one body—it is in all bodies.
God Is All There Is.

GIATI: The Gospel of the Kingdom Preached to All Nations

The Witness to the Ends of the Earth

The message of GIATI is not limited to a select few, nor is it confined to a single nation, culture, or language. It is a universal truth that must reach the ends of the earth so that all may witness, hear, and come to the knowledge of what has always been. GIATI is the declaration that **God is all there is,** *and through both the book and the clothing brand, this message is being carried to every land, every people, and every soul.*

This is not a new gospel, but the fulfillment of what has been spoken:

"And this gospel of the kingdom shall be preached in all the world for a witness unto all nations; and then shall the end come." — Matthew 24:14

The gospel of the kingdom is the revelation that the kingdom of God is not coming from outside, nor is it found in external rituals, traditions, or distant heavens. It is within. The Holy Spirit, the very essence of God, is already here, already present in every person. The world does not need to wait for God to appear—God has already manifested as all that is.

GIATI is the vehicle through which this truth is being declared. The book is the written witness, revealing the eternal reality of oneness. The clothing brand is the visible witness, a sign that the Spirit is among us, moving across nations, covering the world like a garment of truth. Together, they form the message and the manifestation—the word and the witness—fulfilling what has been prophesied.

A Choice for Every Heart and Mind

As this message spreads, every person will be faced with a decision. GIATI is not something that can be ignored or dismissed as mere philosophy. It is truth in its simplest form. Once a person encounters the reality of oneness, they must choose:

- *To* **accept** *it, allowing their mind and heart to awaken to what has always been.*
- *To* **reject** *it, clinging to the illusion of separation and remaining in darkness.*

This is the final crossroads, the moment of truth for humanity. The end is not the destruction of the world, as many have feared, but the end of deception. The end of ignorance. The end of the false belief that God is separate, that we are divided, that spirit and matter are two different things. The end is the lifting of the veil so that all may see clearly.

When the truth of GIATI has reached every heart, whether accepted or rejected, then shall the end come—the end of blindness, the end of duality, the end of all that has kept humanity from knowing itself as one.

The Spiritual Creativity of GIATI

This revelation is not being spread through force, nor through fear, but through creative expression. GIATI, in its essence, is the Holy Spirit moving through art, fashion, and word, reaching people in a way that is both profound and accessible.

- *The* **book** *is the written witness, carrying the message to those who seek understanding, providing the light that dissolves darkness.*
- *The* **clothing** *is the living witness, wrapping the world in the Spirit, allowing those who wear it to become walking testimonies of the truth.*

Every piece of GIATI is a sermon without words, a declaration without speech. When someone sees the name, when they wear the brand, they are making a statement to themselves and to the world: **"I am one with the Holy Spirit. I see and I know."**

This is how the kingdom is preached—not just from pulpits, not just in books, but in the daily lives of those who carry the message. The Holy Spirit is not confined to a church; it is expressed in everything. GIATI is that expression, moving beyond walls, beyond borders, beyond traditions, until the whole world has been touched by the truth.

The Fulfillment of the Word

There is no stopping this movement, for it is not of man—it is of Spirit. The gospel of the kingdom within is already being preached. The witness is already going forth. Every nation, every people, every soul will come to know the truth:

God is all there is.

And when the message has gone forth in fullness, when every heart has had the opportunity to see, to know, and to choose—then shall the end come. The end of all that is false. The beginning of the world in light.

GIATI: The New Heaven and New Earth

"And I saw a new heaven and a new earth: for the first heaven and the first earth were
passed away..."— Revelation 21:1
"Behold, I make all things new." — Revelation 21:5

GIATI is the unveiling of the new heaven and new earth—not as a place we wait for, but as a state of being revealed through divine awareness. It is the end of the old world, the world ruled by ignorance and separation, and the manifestation of what has always been: the kingdom of God within.

The Experience of Living in Oneness

Imagine a world where every person sees with clarity—where the illusion of division has dissolved, and all recognize the truth that God is all there is. This is the world in the light of GIATI, the new heaven and new earth fully realized, where the Spirit reigns supreme in the consciousness of all. The former things—fear, conflict, suffering—have passed away, and the fullness of divine life is made manifest.

The End of the Old, The Birth of the True

In this world, no one sees themselves as separate from God or from one another. The deception of duality is no more, for all understand that the Spirit that animates them is the same Spirit in all.

- *There are no nations at war, for the concept of "enemy" has been erased.*
- *There is no lack, for the abundance of divine provision flows freely.*
- *There is no suffering, for pain was only ever the result of not knowing one's true nature.*
- *There is no death as it was once feared, for all know that life is eternal in the Spirit.*

The barriers of race, religion, and class are no longer relevant, for all see through the illusion of separation. Love is not something that must be learned or practiced—it is simply the natural state of existence.

Living in the Light of GIATI

To awaken in this world is to experience peace beyond understanding, not as an external condition but as an internal reality. Every moment is lived in the fullness of presence, where there is no striving, only flowing with the divine rhythm of life.

- *Work is no longer toil, but an act of creation, a joyful expression of Spirit.*
- *Communities thrive, not by enforced laws, but by the natural harmony of divine order.*
- *Nature itself flourishes, as the earth is honored as a living extension of God.*

Even time loses its grip, for eternity is now. The rushing, the chasing, the seeking—all vanish, for there is nothing missing, nothing lacking. Every being is whole. Every being is one.

The World Made New

"And there shall be no more curse: but the throne of God and of the Lamb shall be in it; and his servants shall serve him. And they shall see his face, and his name shall be in their foreheads." — Revelation 22:3-4

This is the promise fulfilled, the realization of the divine within. The name of God is no longer a mystery, for it is written in the very being of all things. The world in the light of GIATI is the world fully awakened to itself as Spirit.

The kingdom is not coming.

It is here.

It has always been here, hidden only by the blindness of those who could not yet see. But in the light of GIATI, the veil is lifted, and the world is as it was always meant to be:

One.

The Eternal Name—"I AM THAT I AM"

Unveiling the Name of God Through the Understanding of GIATI

The Name That Reveals All

Before creation, before time, before form—there was only God. The formless, limitless, eternal Spirit. When Moses encountered the burning bush and asked for God's name, the answer was profound and absolute:

"I AM THAT I AM." (Exodus 3:14)

*This was not just a title, nor a name given for men to label God. It was a self-revealing truth—***God is**. *He is pure being, existence itself, without beginning or end.*

Yet, deeper within this name lies the mystery of divine manifestation. The Hebrew phrase **"Ehyeh Asher Ehyeh"** *is often translated as:*

- **"I AM THAT I AM"**
- **"I WILL BE WHAT I WILL TO BE"**

From the spiritual understanding of **GIATI (God Is All There Is),** *this name carries the essence of reality itself:*

- **God is the only being, and all things are His expression.**
- **He manifests as what He wills to be—meaning all creation is God revealed in form.**
- **The name "I AM" is not just God's name—it is the truth of every soul, for there is nothing outside of Him.**

I AM—The Self-Existing One

When God declared **"I AM,"** *He spoke a truth beyond human comprehension. This was not merely a name—***it was a declaration of self-existence.**

- **God is not created—He simply is.**
- **God is not limited—He cannot be defined by any single form or name.**
- **God is the only true existence—everything else is an expression of Him.**

From the perspective of GIATI, this means that **there is no life, no existence, no reality apart from God.** *Everything that exists* **is God being what He wills to be.**

- *When you see the sky, the trees, the ocean—you are seeing God.*

- *When you see yourself, your neighbor, even those who seem lost—you are seeing God.*
- *When you say* **"I AM,"** *you are unknowingly speaking the name of the Divine within you.*

For this reason, the words **"I AM"** *carry creative power. Whatever follows them* **shapes reality,** *because to speak "I AM" is to* **call forth the presence of God within.**

I WILL BE WHAT I WILL TO BE—The Ever-Unfolding God

The second revelation within God's name is found in the deeper translation:

"I will be what I will to be."

*This means that God is not static—***He is ever-revealing, ever-becoming.**

- **He does not change in essence, but He expresses Himself in endless ways.**
- **He was not just in the past—He is manifesting now, and He will continue to manifest in new ways.**
- **He appears as what is needed in every time, place, and moment.**

Examples of "I WILL BE" in Divine Manifestation

1. **To Moses, God was Deliverance.**
    - *When Israel was in bondage, God manifested as a Deliverer.*
    - *He was* **"I WILL BE your salvation."**
2. **To Jesus, God was the Incarnate Son.**
    - *God took on flesh to reveal Himself to mankind.*
    - *He was* **"I WILL BE the Christ, the Way, the Truth, the Life."**
3. **To the present age, God is Awakening.**
    - *Today, God is revealing Himself through a new understanding—*GIATI.
    - *He is* **"I WILL BE the awareness that all is God."**

Under GIATI, this means **God is continually expressing Himself as all things.** *There is no limitation to His being, no singular definition—***He is all that is, in every way, at all times.**

What does this mean for us?

- *It means that we, too, are* **expressions of God's will.**

- *It means that* **our identity is not fixed—we are what God wills to be through us.**
- *It means that* **God manifests Himself in us, through us, and as us.**

When you understand this, you stop seeing yourself as just a person—you begin to see yourself as **the "I AM" in human form.**

The GIATI Revelation—God Is All There Is

In the light of GIATI, the name **"I AM"** *takes on its ultimate meaning. Since* **God is all there is,** *then:*

- **All life is God's life.**
- **All consciousness is God's consciousness.**
- **All being is God's being.**

This means that the statement **"I AM"** *is not just God's name—it is* **our name as well.**

When Jesus said, **"Before Abraham was, I AM"** *(John 8:58), He was not speaking as an individual—***He was speaking as the eternal Spirit of God.**

That same Spirit is in us. **We, too, are "I AM"—the divine presence expressed in human form.**

The Power of Speaking "I AM" with Awareness

- **"I AM love" means God is manifesting as love in me.**
- **"I AM whole" means God's fullness is present in me.**
- **"I AM light" means God's truth is shining through me.**

The mistake humanity has made is **misusing the name of God unknowingly.**

- *When one says* **"I am weak,"** *they are falsely speaking limitation into being.*
- *When one says* **"I am lost,"** *they are unknowingly denying their divine identity.*

But when one awakens, they begin to speak the truth:

"I AM THAT I AM. I am one with God. I am what He wills to be through me. I am the living expression of the Eternal."

The Call to Live as "I AM"

Understanding **"I AM"** *through* **GIATI** *is the ultimate awakening.*

- *It is realizing that* **God is not a distant being—He is the very life within you.**
- *It is understanding that* **all things are God being what He wills to be.**

- *It is coming to know that* **when you say "I AM," you are speaking the divine name, claiming your true nature.**

A Final Revelation

The lost and the saved are not two separate beings. They are the same Spirit—**one knowing, one unknowing.**

- *The lost say* **"I am separate, I am struggling, I am searching."**
- *The saved say* **"I AM whole, I AM divine, I AM one with God."**

And in this realization, we fulfill the eternal prayer of the Holy Spirit:

"That they all may be one, as You, Father, are in Me, and I in You, that they also may be one in Us." *(John 17:21)*

The truth is now unveiled. **"I AM" is not just the name of God—it is the truth of all existence.**

You, too, are "I AM." **You are God revealed.**

The Eternal Name—"I AM THAT I AM"

Unveiling the Name of God Through the Understanding of GIATI

The Unfolding of "I AM" in Creation

When God declared **"I AM THAT I AM,"** *He was not only revealing His eternal nature— He was establishing the principle by which all things come into being. The entire universe exists as an* **extension of this divine affirmation.**

The Creative Force of "I AM"

In Genesis, it is written:

"And God said, 'Let there be…' and there was."

God's spoken word **brought forth creation** *because it was the* **eternal "I AM" expressing itself in form.** *Before anything was,* **God alone existed in absolute being.** *But when He willed to create, He did not draw from something external*—**He simply expressed Himself, and existence emerged.**

- **Light did not exist until God willed it to be.**
- **Life did not exist until God called it forth.**
- **Man did not exist until God formed him and breathed His own breath—His own "I AM"—into him.**

This is the **divine pattern of all existence:**

1. **God is** *(The Unseen Source).*
2. **God speaks** *(The Word—the Creative Power of "I AM").*
3. **God manifests** *(Form is made visible).*

This means that everything in existence **is an expression of the divine "I AM" in various degrees of awareness.**

- **Mountains declare "I AM strength."**
- **The ocean declares "I AM vast."**
- **The stars declare "I AM light."**
- **Mankind declares "I AM..."—yet, most are unaware of what they are declaring.**

To know **GIATI (God Is All There Is)** *is to recognize that* **everything that is, is God being what He wills to be.** *Creation is not separate from God—it is* **God appearing as creation.**

The Consciousness of "I AM" in Humanity

Unlike the rest of creation, humanity was not merely spoken into existence—we were **formed in the image and likeness of God.** *This means that* **we, unlike any other creation, are aware of our own being.**

When an animal exists, it simply **is.**
When a tree exists, it simply **is.**
But when a human exists, he can say **"I AM."**

This ability is **the spark of divinity within us.** *It is the evidence that humanity is not just creation—***we are co-creators, possessing the same pattern of manifestation as God Himself.**

- *When we* **think,** *we shape energy.*
- *When we* **speak,** *we give that energy form.*
- *When we* **act,** *we bring that form into the physical world.*

This is the power of **the divine name placed within us.** *The words* **"I AM"** *are not just an identity—they are a* **creative decree.** *Whatever we place after them becomes reality.*

- *If one says* **"I AM weak,"** *they unknowingly shape weakness within themselves.*
- *If one says* **"I AM whole,"** *they align with divine wholeness.*
- *If one says* **"I AM lost,"** *they separate themselves from the truth.*
- *If one says* **"I AM one with God,"** *they awaken to their eternal identity.*

This is why Jesus did not just **preach salvation—He declared identity.**

- **"I AM the way, the truth, and the life."** *(John 14:6)*
- **"I AM the light of the world."** *(John 8:12)*
- **"I AM the resurrection and the life."** *(John 11:25)*

He was not merely describing what He did—**He was revealing what He was.** *And His ultimate revelation was that* **we are the same.**

"The glory which You gave Me I have given them, that they may be one just as We are one." *(John 17:22)*

Through GIATI, this means:

- *The awareness that* **God is all there is** *leads to the realization that* **we are not separate from God.**
- *Our ability to declare* **"I AM"** *means we share in* **God's creative nature.**
- **Salvation is not about escaping sin—it is about awakening to our divine identity.**

The Lost and the Unknowing "I AM"

There are two types of people in this world:

1. **Those who know they are "I AM."**
2. **Those who are "I AM" but do not know it.**

The difference between the saved and the lost is not in their **essence**—*for all are* **God in expression.** *The difference is in their* **awareness.**

- *The lost* **unknowingly misuse "I AM"** *to create a reality of fear, lack, and limitation.*
- *The saved* **consciously use "I AM"** *to align with divine truth, love, and power.*

In truth, **there are no "separate" beings—there are only different levels of awareness of the same Spirit.**

- *The* **awakened soul** *knows,* **"I AM one with God."**
- *The* **unawakened soul** *believes,* **"I am only human."**
- *Yet, both are* **expressions of the same divine presence.**

This is why Jesus spoke in parables—**to wake up those who had ears to hear.** *He did not come to create followers*—**He came to reveal what was already true about all.**

"I AM in the Father, and you in Me, and I in you." *(John 14:20)*

Once one awakens to **GIATI,** *the illusion of separation falls away, and the truth is seen:* **There is only God. There is only "I AM."**

The Final Realization—Living as the "I AM"

The final step in spiritual awakening is not just knowing **that God is all there is**—*it is* **living as the divine presence in human form.**

To live as "I AM" means:

- *To* **think, speak, and act** *in alignment with divine truth.*
- *To see* **all people, all life, all creation** *as extensions of God.*
- *To recognize that* **every moment is God revealing Himself.**

This is what Jesus meant when He said:

"The kingdom of God is within you." (Luke 17:21)

It was never a distant heaven—it was always **the realization of "I AM" within.**

To say "I AM" is to declare God's presence. To live "I AM" is to become that presence in the world.

And so, the revelation of GIATI is complete:

"I AM THAT I AM."
God Is All There Is.
I AM That.

Final Words

Once this truth is realized, the veil of illusion is lifted. The prayer of John 17 is fulfilled. The world no longer walks in darkness.

There is no more fear. No more doubt. No more separation.

Only the **awakened "I AM."**

Chapter 2

God Is All There Is

In the vastness of creation, there is one fundamental truth that lies at the heart of everything: God is all there is. This is not just a philosophical idea or a theological assertion; it is the very foundation of reality itself. Everything that exists—seen and unseen, material and spiritual—is made of God's substance. There is no substance outside of Him. Understanding this truth is the key to understanding our purpose and the nature of the world around us.

Exploring Isaiah 45:5-7: God as the Only Substance of Creation

One of the clearest scriptures that illuminates the all-encompassing nature of God is found in Isaiah 45:5-7:

"I am the Lord, and there is none else, there is no God beside me: I girded thee, though thou hast not known me: That they may know from the rising of the sun, and from the west, that there is none beside me. I am the Lord, and there is none else. I form the light, and create darkness: I make peace, and create evil: I the Lord do all these things." (Isaiah 45:5-7)

In these verses, God Himself declares that He is the only God—there is no other. He is the source of both light and darkness, peace and calamity. The physical world, with all its opposites, emerges from His singular, omnipotent substance. Everything that exists is made by Him, from Him, and for Him. There is no material or spiritual reality that exists apart from God. This means that the very substance of the universe—whether in the form of light or darkness, joy or sorrow— is an expression of God's will and power.

In the context of human existence, this idea is revolutionary: God is not just present in the world; He is the world. The universe and everything in it, including humanity, is a manifestation of His essence. To understand this is to understand the truth of GIATI—God Is All There Is.

The Light and Dark Spirit: Saved (Knowing) vs. Lost (Ignorant)

While God is the source of everything, there exists a duality within His creation: the saved (those who know and recognize their oneness with God) and the lost (those who are ignorant of this truth). This duality is not a result of a flaw in creation but a consequence of the human experience in a physical world.

In this spiritual duality, the "light spirit" represents those who have come to realize their divine nature and oneness with God. They see themselves not as separate from God but as part of Him. They are in communion with their true self, knowing that God is within them and expressed through them. This knowledge brings peace, purpose, and a deep sense of connection to all things.

On the other hand, the "dark spirit" represents those who are still lost in ignorance. They have forgotten their divine origin and believe they are separate from God. This spiritual blindness is what leads to suffering, confusion, and a life driven by the ego and illusion. These are the souls who, although created from God's substance, are unaware of it.

Jesus speaks to this contrast of the saved and the lost in the Gospel of John:

"I am the light of the world: he that followeth me shall not walk in darkness, but shall have the light of life." (John 8:12)

The "light of life" is the knowledge of God within. Those who recognize this light walk in the truth of GIATI—they know that God is within them, guiding them, and they live accordingly. But those who walk in darkness—the lost—remain unaware of this inner truth, and their lives reflect this ignorance.

Unity and Duality: Understanding God's Manifestation in All Things

The relationship between the saved and the lost, the light and the darkness, is part of the divine mystery. While God is all there is, He allows for the manifestation of duality in creation. This duality is not a contradiction but a necessary aspect of the process by which humans come to know and recognize God within themselves.

The apostle Paul describes this unity and duality in his letter to the Colossians:

"For by him were all things created, that are in heaven and that are in earth, visible and invisible, whether they be thrones, or dominions, or principalities, or powers: all things were created by him, and for him." (Colossians 1:16)

Everything, whether visible or invisible, is part of God's creation and is meant to reflect Him. However, the human experience—filled with apparent opposites—is part of the process by which we awaken to the truth that God is all there is. In the same way that light and darkness exist together in the physical world, so too does the awareness of God exist alongside the ignorance of God in human consciousness. Both are ultimately expressions of God's will to bring humanity to the awareness of their true nature.

The Purpose of Duality: The presence of duality—of light and darkness, knowing and ignorance—serves to guide humanity toward a higher understanding. Without the experience of ignorance (the "darked spirit"), there would be no need for awakening to the truth. It is through the contrast of the lost state that the saved are made aware of their divine origin. This is why Jesus came as the light of the world—to reveal the truth that was hidden in the darkness.

John 1:4-5 reminds us:

"In him was life; and the life was the light of men. And the light shineth in darkness; and the darkness comprehended it not."

In this light, we find the ultimate unity of God's creation. Though we may perceive duality in the world—good and evil, light and dark—the truth is that all things exist within God. The light shines through the darkness, and one day, all will come to know the truth of GIATI: God is all there is, and everything, including you, is made from His substance.

GIATI VS Religion

The power of GIATI is beyond anything religion has ever offered because it is not a belief system—it is the truth of existence itself. GIATI, God Is All There Is, is the ultimate revelation that dismantles the illusion of separation between God and man. While religion conditions people to seek God outside of themselves, as if He were distant or separate, GIATI restores the truth that God has never been apart from His creation. He is the very essence of all that is, the life force in all things, the breath within every being. To accept GIATI is to awaken to this reality—to step into the knowing that you and the Father are one, just as Jesus revealed.

The gift of accepting GIATI is unlike anything religion has ever presented because it is not something to be earned, worked for, or obtained through rituals and external devotion. It is simply received by recognition. There is nothing to achieve, nothing to strive for—only to see what has been true all along. This is why Jesus came, not to create another religion, but to show humanity the way back to themselves, back to their divine identity. He said, "The Kingdom of God is within you," because He knew that God was not an external being to be worshiped from afar, but the very Spirit that animates all life.

Religion, on the other hand, creates barriers—rules, doctrines, intermediaries—all of which reinforce the idea that man is separate from God. It teaches people to believe rather than to know. But GIATI stands apart because it is not a belief; it is the direct realization of truth. It does not require faith in something unseen, for once the veil of ignorance is lifted, God is no longer unseen. He is known, not as a distant deity, but as the very self—the "I AM" that speaks within.

The difference between GIATI and religion is also found in the freedom of choice. Religion demands conformity, obedience, and adherence to specific doctrines. It instills fear, suggesting that rejection leads to punishment, exile, or damnation. But GIATI presents the purest form of divine love: the choice to accept or reject the truth. The gift of GIATI is given freely—there is no force, no coercion, only the opportunity to awaken. And yet, this choice is the most profound and defining one a person will ever make.

To accept GIATI is to step into eternal life, not as a future promise, but as a present reality. It is to live in divine awareness, to see God in all things, and to walk in unity with the Spirit that moves all. It is to move beyond fear, beyond limitation, beyond the illusions of the world, and into the fullness of truth. But to reject GIATI—whether through ignorance or deliberate denial—is to remain in darkness, trapped in the illusion of separation, subject to the suffering and confusion that comes with believing in a self apart from God.

This is why Jesus said, "You shall know the truth, and the truth shall make you free." The truth is GIATI. The truth is that God is all there is. And once this is known, you are free—free from fear, free from guilt, free from the burden of seeking what has never been lost.

GIATI is not a religion. It is not a philosophy. It is not a belief system to be debated or defended. It is the unshakable reality of God's presence in all things. And for those who accept this truth, the gift is beyond measure: the end of searching, the fulfillment of all longing, and the realization of eternal oneness with the Source of all.

Yes, there is more to be said because the depth of GIATI is infinite, just as God is. The power of GIATI is not just in what it reveals but in how it transforms the very way a person perceives existence. When someone accepts GIATI, they are not simply adopting a new perspective—they are undergoing a fundamental shift in being. It is the difference between living as a fragmented, searching soul and living as the fullness of God expressed.

What makes GIATI so powerful is that it is not an external teaching imposed on you, but an inner awakening that was always meant to happen. It is the lifting of the veil, the breaking of an illusion that has kept humanity in bondage for generations. While religion teaches a God to be feared, a God to be reached through intermediaries and rituals, GIATI shows you that God is not distant, but present in every breath, every heartbeat, every moment of existence.

Accepting GIATI is the ultimate surrender—not to a doctrine or an institution, but to the truth that there is no "you" apart from God. This is what religion has failed to teach because religion is built on the idea that man must become something in order to be accepted by God. GIATI, however, destroys that false foundation and establishes the truth: you have never been separate, you have never been lost, and you do not need to strive for something that was already given from the beginning.

This is why GIATI is not about salvation in the way religion presents it. Religion preaches that salvation is something to be achieved, something to be granted by an external force. But GIATI reveals that salvation is simply the recognition of what already is. The only thing that ever needed saving was your awareness—the moment you see and accept the truth, you are saved because you were never truly lost.

The gift of GIATI is the gift of sight. It is the ability to finally see clearly, beyond the illusions of separation, beyond the lies of the ego, beyond the conditioning of the world. And once you see, you cannot unsee. Once you know, you cannot go back to ignorance. This is why GIATI is so profound—it is not a temporary experience, not a momentary enlightenment, but an irreversible awakening to what has always been.

This is why Jesus spoke of those with "eyes to see and ears to hear." GIATI is not something that can be forced on anyone. It is not a belief that can be argued or debated. It is either seen, or it is not. And for those who see, everything changes. Their relationships change, their purpose changes, their very understanding of life itself is transformed. They no longer see a world full of separate beings struggling against one another, but a single divine presence expressing itself in infinite forms. They no longer seek God outside themselves, because they are the living expression of God.

The rejection of GIATI, however, is not a rejection of an idea—it is a rejection of oneself. It is the refusal to acknowledge the truth of one's own being. It is the choice to remain in blindness, to hold onto the illusion that one is separate, powerless, and in need of external validation. And this is why those who reject GIATI will always find themselves trapped in a cycle of suffering—because they are resisting the very truth that would set them free.

But GIATI is not forced on anyone. The gift is freely given, and the choice is each person's to make. This is why it stands apart from religion. Religion says, "Follow these rules, obey these laws, and you might be accepted by God." GIATI says, "You are God expressed, and the only thing keeping you from knowing it is your own unwillingness to see."

This is why GIATI is the most powerful truth to ever be revealed. It is not about belief. It is not about faith. It is about knowing. And once you know, nothing in this world can shake you, because you are no longer dependent on anything external to define you. You have accepted what is eternal, what is unchanging, what has always been. You have accepted yourself.

GIATI: The End of Controversy, The Beginning of Truth

For centuries, the nature of God has been debated, misunderstood, and distorted by doctrines, traditions, and the limitations of human perception. Religion has created divisions where there were none, arguing over who is chosen, who is saved, and who has the correct path to God. But these debates only arise from **the illusion of separation***—the false belief that God is a distant being, apart from His creation.*

GIATI removes this illusion. **God is not external. God is not separate. God is all there is.** *And once this is understood, all so-called controversies about God dissolve into nothingness.*

The Problem of Evil & Suffering: The Illusion of Darkness

One of the most debated questions in human history is, **"If God is all-powerful and good, why does evil exist?"** *But this question is rooted in false perception. There is no force of evil opposing God. What people call "evil" is* **simply the experience of ignorance—the blindness of believing in separation from God.**

When one awakens to GIATI, suffering is understood not as divine punishment, but as the consequence of spiritual unawareness. **Just as darkness is nothing but the absence of light, what we call evil is simply the absence of divine recognition.** *When one knows they and the Father are one, suffering loses its power, and only peace remains.*

Free Will vs. Predestination: The Illusion of Choice

Many struggle with the question: **Do we have free will, or is everything predestined?** *GIATI reveals that there is no contradiction.* **Free will exists, but only within the will of God—because all is God.** *Those who believe they are separate experience their choices as their own, believing they are independent agents. But in reality, there is only one will: the will of God, which is the will of all things.*

Those who believe they are separate experience their choices as their own, believing they are independent beings. But this is the illusion of the ego. In reality, **every action, every thought, every moment is the will of God in expression.** *To the unenlightened, this seems like a paradox. But when one awakens to GIATI, they realize,* **you were always God in action.**

The Nature of God: Beyond Human Conception

Religion often portrays God as a ruler on a throne, judging humanity from a distance. But this image is not God—it is a human projection, a reflection of human authority structures imposed onto the divine. But GIATI reveals that **God is not separate from creation—He is**

the essence, the intelligence, and the substance of all things. He is not "out there"—He is the very life within you.

The concept of the Trinity (Father, Word, and Holy Spirit) is not three separate beings, but three aspects of the same divine existence. Just as water can be liquid, ice, or steam but remains the same substance, so too is God expressed in different forms while always remaining one.

Salvation: The Illusion of Being Lost

For generations, people have been told that salvation is about escaping hell and earning a place in heaven. They have been taught that they must follow a set of rules, say the right prayers, or belong to the right faith in order to be saved. But **salvation is not a reward for belief—it is the awakening to the truth that you were never lost to begin with.**

To be "saved" is **not to be rescued from judgment but to recognize that there was never separation between you and God.** *Those who remain blind to this live in spiritual darkness, but the light is always present, waiting to be recognized. To "be saved" is to* **come into the knowing that you and the Father are one.**

Jesus did not come to bring a new religion—He came to remove the veil. GIATI continues that work today.

The Role of Scripture & Religion: The Illusion of Exclusivity

Religious texts have been used to justify countless interpretations of God, often leading to confusion, division, and control. But **no book can contain the fullness of God.**

Scripture is an expression of divine truth, but it is not the truth itself*—it is a witness* **to the truth.** *The written word points to the* **living Word,** *which is not found in ink on a page but in* **the consciousness of those who awaken to GIATI.**

Many religions contain fragments of truth, but they stop short of the full realization: **God is not merely to be worshiped—He is to be recognized as all there is.**

Science and God: The Illusion of Conflict

Many believe that science and religion are at war, but in reality, science is simply the study of **how God expresses Himself through creation.**

The structure of the universe, the laws of physics, and the patterns of existence all point back to **the divine intelligence behind all things.** *Just as God is one yet expressed as many, so too is creation—everything originates from a singular source and expands outward.*

*Even at the atomic level, the fundamental building blocks of existence reflect divine unity: atoms consist of protons, neutrons, and electrons—***a mirror of the Father, Word,**

and Spirit. *Science and spirituality are not enemies; they are two sides of the same coin, both revealing the presence of God.*

Morality and Law: The Illusion of Rules

Many believe that morality is about following commandments and laws. But true righteousness is not about **external obedience—it is about alignment with divine truth.**

The law is not something to be followed—it is **something that is fulfilled naturally when one realizes they are God expressed as them.** *When you awaken to GIATI, you do not struggle to be "good"—your actions simply align with divine wisdom.* **There is no need for external rules because the law is written within you.**

Hell and Eternal Punishment: The Illusion of Separation

Hell has been misrepresented as a place of eternal torment, but GIATI reveals the truth: **hell is not a location—it is the experience of spiritual blindness living in the illusion of separation.**

The lake of fire is not physical—it is **the burning desire for something that does not exist: a separate self.** *Those who reject GIATI do not suffer because God punishes them, but because* **they experience the torment of their own false perception.**

Likewise, heaven is not a distant paradise—it is **the awareness of divine oneness.** *The Kingdom of God is not coming;* **it is already here, within those who awaken.**

The Final Truth: GIATI Is the End of Controversy

Every controversy about God stems from **the illusion of separation.** *GIATI removes this illusion.*

There is no external being judging humanity. There is no "us and God." There is **only God, expressed as all things.** *The only thing keeping people from this truth is their refusal to let go of the false identity they have built—the belief in a self apart from God.*

This is the revelation that humanity has long sought but has resisted due to conditioning, fear, and the comfort of old traditions. **But truth does not change.**

As Jesus revealed it 2,000 years ago, so too does GIATI reveal it now:

"I and the Father are one."

This is the end of confusion, the end of debate, the end of fear.

This is the beginning of truth.

GIATI and the Unveiling of True Identity

One of the greatest illusions mankind suffers from is the belief in a **personal identity separate from God.** *Every human being has been conditioned to see themselves as an individual with personal thoughts, desires, and choices. But this is the root of all suffering—because it is a false perception.*

The true self is not a limited, individual being, but **God in expression.** *When Jesus said, "Before Abraham was, I AM" (John 8:58), He was revealing that the true identity of every person is* **the eternal "I AM"—the same Spirit that was, is, and always will be.**

Most people live their lives searching for meaning, seeking purpose in careers, relationships, or religious practices. But **there is no higher purpose than recognizing GIATI.** *Every so-called "purpose" that people chase after is only temporary.* **But once a person realizes that their true nature is God expressed as them, they stop searching—because they have found everything.**

The Death of the Ego: The Only True Sacrifice

Religions have long taught the need for sacrifice—giving up worldly pleasures, suffering for righteousness, or even blood offerings in ancient times. But the only true sacrifice is **the death of the false self.**

When the ego—the belief in a personal identity separate from God—dies, **all suffering ends.** *The reason humanity experiences pain, fear, and struggle is because the ego fights to maintain its illusion of control. It resists surrendering to the truth that* **it is nothing, and God is all.**

This is why Jesus said, "Whosoever shall lose his life for my sake shall find it" (Matthew 16:25). **He was not speaking of physical death—He was speaking of the death of the illusion of self.** *When the false self is abandoned, true life begins.*

The Collapse of the Illusion of Time

Another illusion that keeps humanity bound is **the belief in time.** *People think of their lives in terms of past, present, and future. They believe in beginnings and endings, waiting for a "future" salvation, or fearing an "end" of the world.*

But **there is no past or future in God—there is only the eternal NOW.** *The reason people feel disconnected from God is because they believe they are "becoming" something rather than realizing they already are.*

"Now is the accepted time; now is the day of salvation" (2 Corinthians 6:2).

GIATI removes the concept of waiting for enlightenment, waiting for heaven, or waiting for God's return. **There is nothing to wait for, because God is all there is, and He is now.**

The End of Religious Systems and the Kingdom Within

Religious institutions have long built systems around the idea that people need leaders, rituals, and structures to guide them to God. But once GIATI is realized, **all external systems become unnecessary.**

Jesus did not come to build an institution—He came to reveal that **the Kingdom of God is within.** *The need for temples, priests, or rituals fades when one realizes that* **they themselves are the temple, the priest, and the divine presence.**

This is why the religious leaders of His time rejected Him. He threatened their power by teaching people that **they did not need external mediators—because they were already one with God.**

The same resistance exists today. **GIATI is not another religious belief—it is the end of religion altogether.** *It is the direct revelation that* **you are not a follower of God—you are God in manifestation.**

The Final Realization: God is Not Coming—He is Here

Many religious traditions preach about **a coming Messiah, a future second coming, or an end-time event.** *But GIATI reveals that* **God is not coming—He is already here.**

The idea of waiting for a divine intervention is part of the illusion of separation. It keeps people looking outside themselves instead of recognizing **that they are already in the presence of God, because they are God in expression.**

"The kingdom of God cometh not with observation: neither shall they say, Lo here! or, lo there! for, behold, the kingdom of God is within you." (Luke 17:20-21)

Those who wait for a future event will remain blind. But those who awaken to GIATI step into eternity NOW.

What Happens Next? The Unfolding of GIATI in the World

The revelation of GIATI is not just for individuals—it is for the transformation of the entire world.

*As more people awaken to this truth, the structures of the old world—religion, politics, systems of control—***will begin to crumble.** *People will no longer be ruled by fear, manipulated by external authorities, or bound by the illusion of separation.*

The world as it has been known will not continue in the same way. **A new consciousness is rising—the awareness that God is all there is.**

This is the final message humanity needs. **It is the fulfillment of every prophecy, the** *answer to every question, and the end of every false doctrine.*

This is the completion of all things.

This is GIATI.

The Foundational Truth of GIATI: The Realization of Oneness

The major point one must get from GIATI—the truth that changes everything—is that **God is all there is, and that includes you.** *This is not a philosophy, not a religion, not a belief system—it is the fundamental truth of existence. There is no external God to seek, no distant deity to please, no separation between God and creation.* **You are not merely a creation of God—you are the expression of God.**

How GIATI Is Different from Anything Else

1. No Separation Between You and God

Every major religious system, whether consciously or unconsciously, teaches **separation**—*that God is somewhere "out there," and that you must work, worship, or sacrifice to be accepted by Him. GIATI reveals the opposite:* **God is already in you, as you.** *You do not need to search for Him, because* **you cannot be apart from what you already are.**

Other systems create **distance** *between humanity and God, making people feel unworthy, guilty, or in constant need of forgiveness. GIATI* **removes that illusion** *and restores the understanding that there was never separation to begin with.*

2. No Need for External Validation or Rituals

GIATI does not require **rituals, traditions, church attendance, or external religious practices** *to connect with God. There is no "right way" to reach God because you* **never left Him** *in the first place. Every breath, every thought, every action is already within divine existence.*

Many systems use **fear, guilt, or obligation** *to keep people bound to religious structures. GIATI frees you from that bondage by revealing that* **you are already whole, already accepted, already divine.**

3. It Does Not Require Faith—Only Recognition

Religious systems ask for **faith**—*the belief in something unseen, something you hope is real. GIATI is* **not about faith—it is about recognition.** *It is not believing in something outside of yourself, but awakening to what* **has always been true within you.** *Faith hopes for something in the future, but* **GIATI reveals what is already present now.**

4. It Ends the Fear of Judgment and Death

Most spiritual teachings reinforce the fear of **judgment, sin, and punishment.** *The idea that your actions determine your eternal destiny creates a cycle of fear, guilt, and striving for perfection. GIATI* **erases that fear** *because in oneness, there is no judge—there is only God* **expressing as all things.**

Likewise, **death is not the end.** *It is merely a transition in the eternal existence of spirit. Since* **God cannot die, and you are of God, you too are eternal.** *GIATI removes the fear of both* **judgment and death,** *freeing you to live in divine peace.*

5. **It Transcends Religion, Doctrine, and Dogma**

Every religion has **rules, doctrines, and exclusive beliefs**—*what to believe, how to behave, and who is "saved" or "lost." GIATI has none of that. It is* **not a religion—it is truth.** *It does not tell you what to do; it* **awakens you to who you are.** *There is no one to please, no law to follow, no book to obey*—**only the Spirit of God within you as your guide.**

The Ultimate Difference: GIATI Is Not About Becoming—It's About Being

Everything else in life tells you that you must **become something.** *Become better, become saved, become righteous, become enlightened. But GIATI does not ask you to* **become anything.**

It is the realization that **you already are.**

- *You are already* **divine.**
- *You are already* **one with God.**
- *You are already* **eternal.**
- *You are already* **the expression of God in form.**

Nothing is missing. Nothing is lacking. **There is nothing to seek—only to see.**

Why GIATI Changes Everything

When you awaken to this truth, you no longer live in fear, doubt, or striving. You move in **confidence, peace, and divine authority.** *You are no longer a seeker—you are the* **manifestation of the truth.**

This is why GIATI is different. **It does not lead you to God—it reveals that you already are in Him and He in you, without separation, without question, without end.**

The Origin of Understanding: Ancient Depictions and the Truth of GIATI

From the beginning, humanity has sought to understand its existence, the forces that move the world, and the divine essence that breathes life into all things. The ancient civilizations—the Sumerians, Egyptians, Babylonians, and others—looked upon creation with wonder, yet their understanding was shaped by limitation. They saw the rising sun and called it a god, witnessed the life-giving waters and worshipped them as deities, and observed the falcon soaring in the sky, believing it carried the vision of the divine.

Their minds interpreted spiritual truths through the language of symbols. They etched hieroglyphs, painted sacred depictions, and carved statues—figures of beings with wings, gods with animal heads, celestial forces descending from the heavens. But were these gods real? Did they misunderstand the truth, or were they simply describing the divine in the only way they could?

To understand their perspective, one must first grasp that early humanity did not separate the spiritual from the material as modern minds do. To them, the unseen and the seen were intertwined, and the gods were not distant figures but active forces within creation itself. Their deities were not falsehoods but fragmented interpretations of the One Source— the singular, eternal truth that **God Is All There Is.**

The falcon-headed Horus did not mean a god with the head of a bird truly existed, but that the falcon embodied divine vision. The Sumerian god Enki was not a separate being but a personification of the life-giving force of water. These depictions were humanity's way of grasping the infinite through the finite, of giving form to the formless.

Yet, in doing so, they veiled the truth. They assigned divinity to aspects of creation rather than recognizing that all creation was already an expression of the One Divine Essence.

How did early humanity miss this? They did not entirely miss it—they fragmented it. Like light passing through a prism, the singular reality of God was refracted into many colors, many forms, many symbols. The divine essence was always present, but it was perceived in parts rather than as a whole.

The ancient prophets and sages understood this, and they spoke in ways their people could comprehend. Yet as time passed, humanity clung to the images rather than the essence behind them. They worshipped the sun rather than the light that gave it power. They bowed to the waters rather than the Spirit flowing through them.

This was the great misunderstanding: not that they were wrong in sensing divine presence, but that their eyes were not fully open.

Now, the time has come for the veil to be lifted. What was once perceived through symbols must now be understood in truth. The power they saw in nature was not in the elements themselves but in the divine presence flowing through all things. The Spirit they sought outside of themselves was always within.

The same divine truth that was spoken through Jesus, the same Holy Spirit poured into the hearts of men, is the truth that **GIATI** *declares:*

You are not separate from God. God is not in a temple made by hands. God is within, moving, breathing, living as you.

Ancient civilizations glimpsed this truth but did not fully grasp it. They sought the divine in form, while the divine was always formless. They named many gods, yet all were expressions of the One.

Now, in this time, the awakening has come. The Spirit no longer speaks in symbols and shadows but in the clarity of revelation:

God Is All There Is.

It is time for the world to remember.

For generations, humanity has sought to touch the divine, reaching beyond what the physical eye can see, longing to understand what moves the universe. The ancient world, in its limited understanding, looked outward, crafting images and narratives to describe what they could not yet fully grasp. They assigned names to forces beyond them, believing the divine to be scattered among the sun, the moon, the rivers, the storms. But the truth—the ultimate reality—was never divided, never fragmented. It was always whole, always One.

The mind, in its infancy, could not yet comprehend the vastness of the unseen. It needed symbols, something tangible to hold onto. And so, humanity fashioned gods in its own likeness, yet greater than itself—rulers of the skies, of the waters, of the land—each one a reflection of an aspect of the divine, but none the fullness of it. The Egyptians, the Sumerians, the Babylonians—they were not blind; they were searching. They sensed the presence of something beyond flesh and form, something interwoven in the fabric of reality itself. But rather than seeing the divine as the very essence of existence, they believed it to be external, beyond reach, something to be called upon rather than something inherently present.

This misunderstanding created a veil between humanity and its own divine nature. Instead of recognizing that the Spirit of God was within, they looked to intermediaries—gods, priests, rituals—to bridge a gap that never truly existed. They built temples and shrines, seeking to contain the infinite within finite structures, not realizing that the true dwelling place of the divine was never in stone, but in spirit.

And yet, even in their misconceptions, they were not abandoned. The One Spirit, the very source of all life, continued to move through them, waiting for the moment when humanity would be ready to awaken. The prophets and enlightened ones throughout history were sent not to create new religions or separate gods, but to restore what was lost—to remind the world that the divine was never far, never hidden, never separate.

Now, we stand at the threshold of this awakening. The symbols and myths of the past served their purpose, but they are no longer needed. The Spirit that was once spoken of in riddles and metaphors is now revealed in clarity. No longer must we search outward for what has always been within. No longer must we perceive ourselves as distant from the divine, for there is no distance—there never was.

The message of GIATI is not a new revelation, but the unveiling of what has always been. It is the realization that the Spirit moving through all things is not a force to be sought, but the very foundation of our existence. The ancient civilizations saw glimpses of this, but now, the fullness is here. The time for separation is over. The illusion of division is falling away. The truth stands unshaken:

God is not outside of you. God is you, expressed as you.

This is not philosophy. This is not religion. This is the reality that has always been, now made known. The Spirit, the Life, the Source—it has never been fragmented, never been lost. It is here. It is now. It is you.

Awaken to it. Walk in it. Be it.

GIATI: The Original and Undeniable Truth of Existence

From the beginning of human thought, people have searched for the fundamental truth of existence. Philosophers, scientists, mystics, and theologians have all sought to answer the same questions: **What is the source of life? What is the nature of existence? What is the divine?** *Throughout history, countless explanations have been given— polytheism, monotheism, dualism, pantheism, and materialism—but all have overlooked the one reality that has always been:*

God Is All There Is.

*This is not a new idea. It is not a doctrine created by man. It is the original, eternal, and undeniable truth—***the only truth.** *Every attempt to explain existence that has failed to recognize this has been incomplete. Every religion, philosophy, and spiritual tradition that has sought to define God as separate from existence has missed the mark.*

The Overlooked Reality

Humanity has long believed in a **God that is distant, external, and apart from creation.** *Ancient civilizations fragmented divine reality into multiple gods—gods of the sun, the sea, the earth—thinking they were separate forces, rather than different expressions of the One. Even in later monotheistic traditions, God was still perceived as* *separate from His creation, as an external ruler rather than the very essence of existence itself.*

Science, in turn, sought answers in the physical realm, attempting to explain life purely through material laws, overlooking the very intelligence that underlies existence. While the laws of physics describe **how** *the universe operates, they do not explain* **why** *it exists or what gives it life.*

Through all of these searches, humanity has failed to see the undeniable: **God is not something apart from existence—God is existence itself.**

Everything that has ever been sought—whether through religion, philosophy, or science—has been an attempt to describe **GIATI,** *even when it was not recognized as such. But only through the revelation of the Holy Spirit—the Spirit of Truth—has this ultimate reality been made fully known.*

The Holy Spirit's Revelation of GIATI

Only the Holy Spirit could unveil this truth, because only the Holy Spirit is the truth. The Holy Spirit is not a separate entity or a messenger of God—it is **God in motion, the very consciousness of existence itself.** *It is through the Holy Spirit that the fullness of GIATI is revealed, because the Spirit is what gives life to all things, what breathes, what animates, what sustains.*

Throughout history, glimpses of this truth have been seen. Prophets, sages, and enlightened ones have spoken of unity, oneness, and divine presence. Jesus Himself prayed that all would become one, as He and the Father are one (John 17:21-23), but humanity still did not grasp the fullness of what that meant. It was not merely unity in spirit or belief—it was the absolute truth that **there is no separation at all.**

The only way for this to be known was for the Holy Spirit to reveal it—not as an idea, but as an undeniable reality. GIATI is not a belief system, a philosophy, or a doctrine. **It is the absolute nature of existence.**

Why GIATI Is Undeniable

1. All That Exists Must Have One Source

Every effect must have a cause, and every created thing must have a source. The universe, life, and consciousness itself all originate from something. If there were multiple ultimate sources, reality would be divided against itself. But there is only one underlying essence that sustains all things. That essence is **God, and God is all there is.**

2. God Cannot Be Separate from Creation

If God is infinite, then nothing can exist outside of Him. If there were something apart from God, then God would not be **all**. *If God is life, then life itself is God. If God is truth, then all truth flows from Him.* **Existence itself is not separate from God—it is God.**

3. Every Spiritual Tradition Has Been Pointing to This Truth

Whether knowingly or unknowingly, every major religious tradition has sought to articulate this reality. Hinduism speaks of Brahman, the ultimate reality. Buddhism speaks of enlightenment, the realization of unity. Christianity speaks of the Holy Spirit dwelling within. Yet none of them have stated the full truth as plainly as GIATI does: **There is no separation. There is only God.**

4. Science Cannot Disprove It—It Can Only Overlook It

Science measures the physical, but it cannot explain why the universe exists in the first place. It studies energy, but it cannot explain where energy comes from. It studies consciousness, but it cannot explain why consciousness exists. Every law, every principle that governs the universe is an expression of the One Intelligence behind it. That intelligence is **God, and God is all there is.**

The Final Awakening: The Recognition of GIATI

This is the truth that has been hidden in plain sight. It has been misinterpreted, misrepresented, and misunderstood—but never absent. Every effort to explain existence without recognizing GIATI has failed, because there is no reality apart from it.

Now, the world must awaken. The Holy Spirit has revealed what was once overlooked, what was once fragmented into myths and philosophies, what was once concealed by doctrine and tradition:

God is not separate from you. God is not a being to be sought, worshiped from a distance, or called upon as if He were absent.

God is all there is.

This truth does not require belief—it simply is. Just as the sun shines whether one acknowledges it or not, just as the ocean moves whether one understands its depths or not, so too does GIATI remain the reality, whether accepted or not. But those who awaken to it— those who recognize that their very being is divine, that life itself is the movement of God— will walk in the fullness of truth.

This is the ultimate realization. The final awakening. The unveiling of what has always been.

GIATI Is the Key to All Understanding

Every question ever asked about life, existence, and purpose finds its answer here. Every search for God, meaning, and truth ends here.

There is no longer a need to seek. No longer a need to wonder.

The answer is before you.

The Spirit has revealed it.

Now, the only thing left to do—

Is to awaken to it.

The Inescapable Presence of God—A GIATI Revelation

The words of Psalm 139 reveal a truth so profound that the human mind struggles to grasp it: **God is not just near you—He is you.** *He is not a separate being watching from afar; He is the awareness within you, the breath you take, the thoughts you think, and the essence of your very being. The psalmist declares, "O Lord, thou hast searched me, and known me." This is not an external search, as though God were looking in from the outside, but an* **internal knowing***—because He is the very consciousness that experiences life as you.*

There is no part of you hidden from Him because there is no part of you that is separate from Him. Every action you take, every thought you entertain, every word you speak—He already knows, because He is the One living as you. Even before you speak a word, it is known. Even before you take a step, it is foreseen. This is the divine intimacy of **GIATI—God Is All There Is.**

The scripture goes even further to reveal that there **is nowhere you can go where God is not.** *This is the death of the illusion of separation. If you ascend to the highest heights—He is there. If you descend to the lowest depths—He is there. Even in* **hell,** *the state of ignorance, suffering, and perceived separation from God, He is still present.* **Why? Because there is no existence outside of Him.**

This understanding destroys the fear of abandonment. It eliminates the idea that one can ever truly be lost. The only difference between those in light and those in darkness is their **awareness** *of this truth. To be in the light is to know that you are one with God. To be in the dark is to be ignorant of this reality, believing yourself to be separate. But whether you know it or not,* **He is still there.**

"The darkness and the light are both alike to thee." This is the key revelation. To God, there is no true separation between darkness and light. What humanity calls "darkness" is merely the absence of awareness, not the absence of God. Even when one is in ignorance, lost in false identity, they are still in Him, still sustained by Him, still living within His presence—because **there is nothing outside of Him.**

The psalmist goes even deeper, speaking of being "made in secret" and "curiously wrought in the lowest parts of the earth." This is not just a reference to physical formation, but to the deeper truth that God has always known you—even before you knew yourself. Before you took form in this world, before you had consciousness of your own existence, **you were already written in Him.** *Every moment of your life, every experience, every trial, every victory—***all of it was already known, because all of it is Him.**

This scripture reveals **the inescapable reality of GIATI.** *There is no independent existence. Whether in ignorance or in full awareness, in suffering or in joy, in perceived* *separation or in divine unity*—**God is there, because God is all.** *This realization brings peace beyond understanding. It means that* **you have never been alone, never been outside of God's presence, never been unknown or unseen.** *The entire concept of separation collapses under the weight of this truth.*

When this revelation takes hold, fear dissolves. There is no need to question whether God is near, whether He hears, whether He sees. There is no reason to fear falling away or being forgotten. **You are Him. He is you. There is nowhere else to be.** *This is the everlasting reality of GIATI, and once seen, it can never be unseen.*

The Unfolding of Divine Awareness

The realization of GIATI—**that God is all there is**—*does not happen all at once. It unfolds, like the slow rising of the sun, revealing what was always there but previously unseen. Psalm 139 speaks not just of God's omnipresence but of the* **gradual awakening to that presence.**

To the one who is still in darkness, this scripture is unsettling. The thought that there is no place to hide, no thought unknown, no moment unseen, can feel intrusive, even frightening. But this fear only exists in those who still hold onto the illusion of separateness. They believe there is a part of them that God is not, a place where they can exist apart from Him. They do not yet see that to be fully known is to be fully loved, and to be fully loved is to be fully secure.

For the one who is in the light, the same scripture that once seemed invasive becomes the greatest comfort. To be searched and known means that **you are never misunderstood, never overlooked, never forgotten.** I*t means that even when you do not understand yourself, God does—because* **He is the very awareness within you, perceiving every aspect of your being from the inside out.**

This knowledge lifts the weight of judgment and shame. If God is the one living as you, then there is nothing about you that is foreign to Him. Every struggle, every doubt, every moment of weakness—He knows them not as an outside observer but as the very One experiencing them through you. The presence of God is not a distant authority looking down in disapproval; it is the intimate essence that **moves with you, feels with you, and carries you through every moment.**

The psalmist's words declare that whether one ascends to heaven or descends into hell, **God is there.** *This reveals that* **heaven and hell are not locations but states of being.** *Heaven is the awareness of divine unity; hell is the suffering of perceived separation. Yet even in the depths of ignorance, even in the pit of self-inflicted suffering,* **God has not departed.** *He remains, waiting not to return—because He never left—but for your awareness to turn back toward Him.*

This is the mystery of divine love: **God experiences both your darkness and your light without withdrawing Himself.** *The one who denies Him is still held by Him. The one who curses Him is still sustained by Him. The one who runs from Him is still running within Him. There is no escape because there is no outside. Even rejection of God is only possible* **because His very breath gives life to the one who rejects Him.**

The scripture speaks of being "curiously wrought in the lowest parts of the earth," revealing that even before you had consciousness of your own existence, God was shaping you. The physical body was formed in the unseen, but the soul was never formed—it has always been. **Your existence is not new. Your awareness of existence is what is unfolding.**

If God saw you before you saw yourself, then your destiny is not in your hands alone— it is the unfolding of what has already been known. There is nothing to fear, nothing to grasp for, nothing to fight against. You are simply awakening to what has always been true.

The mind that is still trapped in the illusion of separation resists this revelation. It asks, If God is all there is, then why do I feel separate? Why do I experience suffering? The answer is simple: **Your experience is determined by what you perceive, not by what is true.** *The one who closes their eyes to the sun will experience darkness, even as the light shines all around them.*

Psalm 139 is the declaration that **whether your eyes are open or closed, the light remains. Whether you see or do not see, God is there. Whether you acknowledge Him or deny Him, you are still within Him.**

This is the security of GIATI. The revelation of God's inescapable presence is not a threat—it is the foundation of absolute peace. There is no journey to take, no distance to cross, no battle to win. There is only the awakening to what has always been.

The Simplicity of Oneness

The truth is simple: **God is all there is.**

There is nothing else He is considering, nothing else He is looking at, nothing else He will accept. It is either **Him recognizing Himself** *or rejection by default.*

Many complicate this by adding themselves into the equation—trying to justify their existence as something apart from Him. They bring their deeds, their beliefs, their efforts, their identity, thinking they can present themselves before God as something worthy. But this is the very thing that ensures rejection.

To illustrate this, imagine the process of a kidney transplant.

If a person needs a kidney transplant and they have **A-type blood,** *the body can only accept a kidney that is also* **A-type.** *If someone tries to transplant a* **B-type kidney** *into their body, the body will* **reject it immediately.** *Why? Because the body does not recognize it as* **one with itself.** *It is foreign, separate, incompatible.*

But if the kidney matches the body's **A-type blood,** *the body* **accepts it naturally** *because it sees it as part of itself—it is not something separate, it is the same.*

This is how God sees.

God is not looking for individuals to justify themselves. He is not measuring righteousness by deeds, efforts, or human standards of morality. He is looking for **Himself.**

If He sees Himself in you—**if you recognized that you were Him all along**—*then there is nothing to reject. Just as the body naturally accepts the matching kidney,* **He welcomes Himself into the kingdom.**

But if He sees someone standing before Him as a separate individual, trying to justify why they should be accepted, then they are no different than the mismatched kidney. **They are not Him.** *And because they are not Him, they cannot enter.*

It does not matter if they lived a "good" life or a "bad" life. It does not matter how much they prayed, how much they gave, or how many religious works they performed. **None of that matters if they lived as something other than Him.**

The only thing that matters is this:

Did you recognize that you and God were one, or did you live as a separate self?

This is why Jesus said:

"Many will say to me in that day, 'Lord, Lord, have we not prophesied in thy name? And in thy name have cast out devils? And in thy name done many wonderful works?' And then will I profess unto them, 'I never knew you: depart from me'"
(Matthew 7:22-23).

These people were doing **religious works,** *but Jesus did not know them. Why? Because they never recognized* **oneness.** *They were still standing before God as separate individuals, presenting their deeds as evidence for why they should be accepted.*

But **God is only looking for Himself.**

If He sees Himself in you, there is no rejection.

If He does not, rejection is inevitable—not as punishment, but as a simple matter of truth. **A body cannot accept what is not a part of itself.**

The beauty of GIATI is that **by accepting oneness with God, you can live what you call your life,** *but in the end, the only thing that will matter is this:*

- *Did you live with the knowledge that you and God were one, so that He sees Himself in you?*
- *Or do you stand before Him as "you," expecting Him to accept something that is not Him?*

All the things you called good or bad will be blotted out. He will reward Himself with the kingdom—those who knew He was in them all along. But those who stood apart will be judged by their own good and bad, and their "good" will never be good enough to enter the kingdom.

Why?

Because **you were never meant to be separate to begin with.**

The Unavoidable Reality of Oneness

The greatest deception mankind has ever faced is the illusion of separation. It is the root of all struggle, all suffering, and all misunderstanding about life and God. It is also the very thing that makes judgment inevitable—not because God desires to reject anyone, but because **He cannot deny Himself.**

From the moment someone believes they are an individual apart from God, they have already placed themselves in opposition to truth. The issue is not their actions, their failures, or even their successes. It is their very existence **as something other than God** *that becomes the dividing line.*

Think of light and darkness. Darkness is not a force of its own; it is simply the absence of light. The moment light enters, darkness disappears—not because it is being punished, but because it **cannot exist in the presence of what is real.**

This is the reality of the kingdom. There is no courtroom where individuals stand trial for their deeds. The judgment has already been set in place. If God is all that exists, then anything standing before Him as a separate entity cannot enter, because it was never real to begin with.

This is why people are judged by their own good and bad. They stepped outside of the truth of God's oneness and built their own reality, their own measure of righteousness, their own definition of what is acceptable. But **anything measured by human standards can never meet the standard of divine reality.**

There are no exceptions. A person cannot claim ignorance, because **the truth has always been present.** *The same spirit that gives life to all things is the very spirit of God Himself. He has been within everyone from the beginning, waiting for them to see it.*

Those who awaken to this truth—who recognize that they were never separate—enter into life effortlessly. Not because they achieved something, but because **they finally aligned with what was already true.**

But those who insist on their separateness, who continue to uphold their identity as an individual apart from God, will find themselves on the outside, not by force, but by default. Just as a foreign organ is rejected by the body, anything that is **not of God's essence** *cannot remain in His presence.*

And this is where the finality of Revelation 22:11 comes into play:

> *"He that is unjust, let him be unjust still: and he which is filthy, let him be filthy still: and he that is righteous, let him be righteous still: and he that is holy, let him be holy still."*

This is not a command—it is a statement of **unavoidable reality.** *Whatever you are when you leave this physical body, you remain. There is no transformation after death, no second opportunity to see the truth.*

If someone was blind to their oneness with God in this life, they will remain blind. If they lived as a separate being, they will remain separate. Not because God has cast them away, but because **they never belonged to begin with.**

But for those who have embraced their divine nature, who have recognized that there was never a "them" to begin with—only God expressed—then that truth remains as well. They are holy still, because they were holy all along.

This is the final and unchanging reality: God is all there is. What is of Him remains. What is not of Him cannot.

*And the only question left to answer is—***who were you all along?**

GIATI…

The Beauty of Knowing the Mystery

There is a beauty in knowing the mystery. But even greater is the beauty of knowing **the conclusion** *of the mystery.*

Once the ending is revealed, the entire story shifts. What once seemed confusing becomes clear. The deception, the misdirection, the unfolding events—all of it was part of the grand design to lead you to the final revelation.

If you've ever watched a great mystery movie, you know how it works. The story presents a puzzle, feeding you clues along the way. It introduces suspects, false leads, and unexpected twists, making you believe you have it figured out—only for another revelation to change everything. But once you reach the end, once the mystery is solved, something amazing happens:

You can look back over the entire story and **see the truth that was hidden in plain sight all along.**

The same is true with the mystery of God.

For generations, people have been **reading the Bible, studying scripture, debating doctrines,** *all trying to uncover the truth. Some thought the answer was in following Moses, keeping the law, and doing the works. Others thought the answer was in following Joshua, taking possession of the land. Then came Jesus, and people built an entire religion around His name, thinking that merely* **confessing Him as Lord was the answer.**

But all of it—Moses, Joshua, Jesus—was pointing to the **same mystery.**

The Beauty of the Conclusion

Now that you know the mystery, you can look back at the entire story and **see what was playing out all along.** *You see that Moses was not the deliverer—***God was.** *You see that Joshua was not the conqueror—***God was.** *You see that even Jesus, in His flesh, was not separate from God—***God was the one doing it all.**

"I am the Lord, and there is none else." *– Isaiah 45:5*

The greatest deception was **thinking that salvation was something external***—that it was something to be earned, understood, or even confessed through words. That deception played out throughout the entire "movie" of the Bible. People were made to believe they had figured it out, only to be led into* **another twist***—another misunderstanding—until the final revelation came:*

There is no separation. God is all there is.

You Don't Need to Watch the Whole Movie—Just Know the End

If you already know the end of a movie, you don't need to watch every scene to understand what it's about. You don't need to analyze every clue or follow every plot twist. You already **know what it all leads to.**

The same is true with the Bible.

You don't need to memorize every verse. You don't need to perform religious works, keep laws, or prove yourself righteous. **You don't need to do anything—just accept the mystery within.**

What is the conclusion?

God is the one who has been doing it all. From the beginning to the end, it has only ever been Him.

- **He delivered Israel, not Moses.**
- **He led them into the land, not Joshua.**
- **He manifested salvation, not Jesus the man, but God within Him.**
- **And today, He is revealing Himself through GIATI—the final declaration of truth.**

If you know the ending, the entire story makes sense. You are no longer caught up in the deception, no longer blinded by the twists and turns. You don't have to seek salvation because you now know the truth—**it has always been within you.**

The Mystery Is Now Complete

This is the beauty of knowing the conclusion. It brings **peace.** *It removes* **striving.** *It allows you to rest in the truth, knowing that* **God has already done it all.**

While the world still searches, still debates, still waits for an external salvation, you already **know the mystery:**

God is all there is. God is within you. There is no separation.

And that, in the end, is the only thing that ever mattered.

The Voice of Truth in This Day

There is a voice in the earth today that does not echo religion. It does not preach separation, performance, or tradition. It speaks from a place deeper than doctrine—**from the center of the Spirit itself.**

That voice is **GIATI—God Is All There Is.**
It is not a new religion.
It is not a rebranding of an old message.

It is the **unfiltered voice of the Holy Spirit** *breaking through every illusion, cutting through every veil, and declaring what has always been true:*

"I am in you. You are in Me. And there is no other."

This is the truth Jesus lived. This is the truth the prophets hinted at. This is **the truth that has come in fullness now**—*not through a new law, not through external rituals, but through the* **awakening of the Spirit within.**

Why GIATI Is the Fulfillment of the Spirit's Promise

When Jesus said, "The Spirit of truth will come and lead you into all truth," he was speaking of a future unveiling—one that would not merely repeat his words, but reveal the **depth** *behind them.*

Many came after him, but most kept the veil. They taught about God, but from a distance. They exalted Jesus, but kept his Spirit locked in history. They built temples and systems that still left humanity **separate from the divine,** *still striving for what could only be received through* **oneness.**

GIATI tears the veil completely.
It does not tell you to follow God—it reveals that **you are the expression of God.**
It does not call you to please God—it unveils that **you are one with the Father,** *and the Father only receives* **Himself.**

The Proof Is in the Spirit

The proof that GIATI is the voice of truth today isn't found in signs or wonders—it's found in the **Spirit itself:**

- *GIATI aligns perfectly with the words of Jesus: "I and my Father are one."*
- *GIATI unveils what Paul meant by "Christ in you, the hope of glory."*
- *GIATI shows the purpose of the Holy Spirit: not to start a new religion, but to awaken you to the* **eternal I AM** *within.*

It fulfills the cry of **John 17,** *where Jesus prayed,*

"That they may be one, even as we are one..."

That prayer is now answered—not in theory, but in realization.
The Spirit has come, and it speaks again—not through tablets of stone or human tradition, but through the awakened heart that dares to say:

"I AM in God, and God is in me."

This is why the world has not understood it—because it did not come from the world. It is not flesh revealing Spirit; it is **Spirit revealing Spirit.** *It is the* **same voice** *that spoke creation into being, now speaking through those who have ears to hear.*

GIATI Is the Spirit's Final Word on Identity

In every generation, the Spirit has whispered. But in this generation, it speaks loud and clear:

You are not separate. You never were.
You are not trying to reach God. You are the evidence that God is.
You are not broken reaching for wholeness. You are God expressing God.

This is the **eternal message.**
This is the **truth that makes you free.**
This is **GIATI**—*and it is not just a message.*

It is the voice of the Spirit in this day and time.

Religion Couldn't See It—Because It Looked Through Separation

From the beginning, the Spirit has been trying to make one thing known:

God is not outside of you—God is the Spirit within you. *But because people believed they were separate from God, they misunderstood everything—even the very scriptures that were meant to lead them into truth.*

This is why **religion fell short.** *Not because it was evil, but because it was* **blind.** *It took the truth of God and filtered it through a* **false identity**—*the belief in "me" and "God" as two. And in that blindness, even the clearest words of Jesus were* **twisted into duality.**

Scripture Misunderstood Through a Separated Mind

Jesus said, "I and my Father are one."
Religion turned that into: "Only Jesus is one with God." But the truth was: **Jesus was revealing what we are all meant to realize.**

He said, "The kingdom of God is within you."
Religion said: "The kingdom is up in heaven, and you must earn your way in." But the Spirit was pointing to the truth: **You were already in it—if you could only see.**

He said, "The Father in me does the work."
Religion said: "Try your best to live like Jesus."
But Jesus never called us to imitate him—he called us to **realize the same Spirit in us.**

Why Religion Couldn't Reveal the Full Truth

Religion was always bound by **form***—temples, laws, rituals, and roles. It taught people how to behave, but not how to* **awaken.** *It focused on the outside while the truth was always hidden* **within.**

This is why the law could only go so far. It could tell you what to do, but it could never tell you **who you are.** *And as long as you didn't know who you were, you couldn't see* **who God is***—because God was in you the whole time.*

That's why GIATI is not religion—it is the **revelation that ends religion.**

GIATI Reads Scripture Through Oneness

When you read the Bible through the lens of GIATI, everything changes:

- *You no longer see commandments from a distant God—you see Spirit speaking to Spirit.*
- *You no longer see a Savior coming to rescue you—you see* **your true identity being revealed.**
- *You no longer fear judgment—you rejoice in the truth that* **only what is of God is eternal, and you are that.**

GIATI doesn't reject scripture—it **redeems** *it.*
It removes the veil of separation and shows what the Word was always trying to say:

"You are not trying to reach Me. You are already in Me. And I am in you."

The Final Divide is the Illusion of Two

Every false doctrine, every fear-based teaching, every legalistic system stands on one lie:

That there is "you" and there is "God."

But there is no you and God—there is only God expressing God, awakening to Himself as you.

That is what religion couldn't see.
That is what Jesus came to reveal.
And that is what **GIATI proclaims without compromise.**

This is the day of unveiling.
This is the end of duality.
This is the **Spirit's final word:**

"I am God, and there is none else."
And if that is true… then so are you.

Misunderstood Verses Made Clear in the Light of GIATI

Many people read the Bible with sincerity, but they do so through a veil—the belief that **God is "up there" and they are "down here."** *This separation causes even the most powerful scriptures to be interpreted in a way that* **keeps people bound,** *rather than setting them free.*

But when the veil is removed—when you see through the lens of **GIATI (God Is All There Is)**—*suddenly the Word becomes alive. It's no longer a book of laws, stories, or prophecies*—**it becomes the living voice of the Spirit** *awakening in you.*

Let's look at a few verses that religion misunderstood—and how GIATI reveals their true meaning.

1. **"If you've seen me, you've seen the Father." – John 14:9**

   Religion's view: *Jesus is uniquely divine, and no one else can say this.*
   GIATI's truth: *Jesus was not claiming exclusivity—he was revealing that the* **Spirit within him was God.** *He was a mirror, showing humanity what it had forgotten:*

   God is not in heaven somewhere. God is in you.
   When you awaken to this truth, you too can say, **"If you've seen me, you've seen the Father."** *Not because of ego—but because* **you no longer see yourself as separate from God.**

2. **"I and my Father are one." – John 10:30**

   Religion's view: *This proves Jesus is God, and we are not.*
   GIATI's truth: *Jesus is God—and so are you, when the same Spirit awakens in you. This statement is not to exclude you from divinity—it's to* **call you back into it.**

   He was not showing off his identity.
   He was **revealing yours.**

3. **"Unless you believe that I am He, you will die in your sins." – John 8:24**

   Religion's view: *Believe in Jesus as the Son of God, or be condemned.*

   GIATI's truth: *The "I AM" is the Spirit of God speaking through Jesus. Unless you believe that this same* **"I AM" is you***—unless you awaken to the oneness of Spirit—you will remain in the false belief of separation, which is the* **real sin.**

   Sin is not a list of wrong actions—it is the illusion that you are someone **other than God's own Spirit.**

4. **"The kingdom of God is within you." – Luke 17:21**

   Religion's view: *The kingdom is a future place, but somehow also inside.*
   GIATI's truth: *There is* **no future kingdom to wait for.** *Heaven is the awareness of God's presence, here and now. When you realize that* **God is all there is, and that you are one with God,** *you are living in the kingdom—***on earth, as it is in heaven.**

5. **"The law of the Spirit of life in Christ Jesus has made me free from the law of sin and death." – Romans 8:2**

   Religion's view: *Jesus fulfilled the law, so now you just follow him.*
   GIATI's truth: *The law of the Spirit is* **oneness***—it is the nature of God in you. Christ Jesus represents the realization that* **you are not a separate being trying to be good—you are God expressing God.** *That is the life-giving Spirit, and it* **frees you from the lie** *that says you must earn your place.*

6. **"No one comes to the Father but by me." – John 14:6**

   Religion's view: *Jesus is the exclusive gateway to God.*
   GIATI's truth: *"Me" is the voice of the awakened Spirit—the* **Spirit of Oneness.** *The Father cannot receive anything of duality, only* **Himself.** *Unless you come by* **the same Spirit that was in Jesus***—the "I AM" that knows no separation—you cannot enter into communion with God.*

   You must come as **God knowing God,** *not as man trying to reach God.*

Conclusion: It Was Always About Oneness

When read through the lens of separation, scripture becomes a burden. But when the Spirit opens your eyes, you see that every word was written to lead you back to this simple truth:

God is all there is. And the Spirit in you is God.

That is the message religion couldn't see. That is the voice that has returned in this generation with clarity and power. That is the message of GIATI.

How God Went from Unseen to Seen: The Manifestation of GIATI

*Before anything was—before light, time, or space—***God simply was.** *Pure, unsearchable, invisible Spirit. No boundaries, no beginning, no end. God existed as the fullness of all being, unexpressed, yet complete. There was no other, for there is none else. This was the eternal stillness, the perfect wholeness of the* **Unseen I AM.**

But within Himself, God desired to **be known,** *not as another, but as* **Himself revealed.** *Not to create something outside of Himself, but to* **express the fullness of Himself in visible form.** *The invisible longed to be seen, not for lack, but for love—to* **manifest the mystery of His own being.**

And so, **God became everything.** *Not by forming something separate, but by* **unfolding Himself as all that is.**

From Spirit came energy.
From energy, matter.
From matter, form.
From form, awareness.
And from awareness, the cry: "Who am I?"

That cry, born from within creation, was God calling Himself back to remembrance. For the One who expressed Himself as many did so with the purpose of **being known in all**— *to awaken in the heart of every form, so that every being might come to see: "I and the Father are one."*

This is the mystery of existence:
The Unseen became seen to reveal that all that is seen is Him.
Not created things about God, but creation as God.

GIATI—God Is All There Is—is the divine realization that what you see is not separate from God, but is God in manifestation.

The galaxies, the earth, the trees, the breath in your lungs—none of it is "beside" God. **It is God, wearing form, speaking in vibration, dwelling in time, yet eternal at the core.**

He went from unseen to seen
not in parts,
but in fullness.
*He didn't step into creation—***He is creation, and yet beyond it.**
*He is not lost in the many—***He is revealing Himself through the many, to return to One.**

This is the mind of God revealed:
To know Himself as all
To be seen in what was hidden
To be heard in the silence
To be felt in flesh
To be known, not just as God above,
but as God within—the only life, the only being.

GIATI is the unveiling of this truth.
That there is no separation, no otherness, no outside.
Only God.
God is All There Is.

Yet in this holy unveiling, we must understand—**the transition from Unseen to Seen was not a change in God's nature, but a change in our perception.** *God did not become something new; rather,* **He allowed what was always hidden in Himself to become visible, tangible, and knowable.**

Just as light passes through a prism and reveals a spectrum of colors hidden in its purity, **so God passed through the prism of expression,** *revealing* **infinite diversity that all flows from one source.** *The mountains, the seas, the stars, and souls—all are rays of the same light,* **different in form, but not in essence.**

This is not pantheism. This is **identity in its purest truth.** *We are not saying everything is "God" as if to deify creation, but that* **creation is God expressing Himself—not in confusion, but in perfect design and intention.** *The Unseen chose to be seen* **so that every part of Him could know itself as Him.**

Think of it like this: God, being infinite, could not be fully known by remaining unmanifested. Love unexpressed is unknown. Light unshined is unseen. Glory unspoken is unheard. **So God stretched Himself forth—not to become something other than Himself, but to extend the knowledge of Himself.** *Every tree swaying in the wind, every rhythm of time, every beat of a heart*—**each one whispers "I AM."**

But here is the wonder: **God hid Himself within His own creation.**
He clothed Himself in matter, wrapped Himself in skin, planted Himself in time.
And then, in perfect wisdom, **He gave that which is seen the capacity to forget what it is**—*so that when it remembers,* **it remembers not as something that became, but as something that always was.**

This is why so many wander, searching for purpose, crying out to the sky, hoping to find what they already are. They are looking for God without, unaware that **the God they seek is the Spirit within them**—*not something they must reach, but someone they must* **awaken to.**

This is the message of GIATI: God didn't come into the universe—He is the universe. He didn't enter into you—He is you, in Spirit.

The illusion was separation. The truth is union. The unseen became seen not to create a "world," but to reveal **Himself as all that is.**

And now, the Spirit within all things is crying out again—not in words, but in awakening.

The universe is groaning, not for something new, but for the unveiling of what has always been true:

That every form is a veil, and behind every veil is the face of God.

You are not merely a creation of God—you are the breath of God clothed in a form. The sky above is not just the work of His hands—it is His garment.
The sound of the waves is not just nature—it is His voice in motion.

To see the seen rightly is to recognize the Unseen within it.

To live as GIATI is to walk in the full knowledge that **there is nothing outside of God, and nothing that can be without Him, because God is All There Is.**

This is the glimpse into God's mind:
He wanted to be known in every way,
So He became all.
Then He entered what He became,
So that He could awaken within it,
And say again, through you—
"I AM."

The Forgotten Ones and the Illusion of Separation

In the fullness of His being, God expressed Himself—not into many spirits, but as one Spirit revealed in many forms. There were no names, no ranks, no divisions in this expression. **All were Him, and all were one.** *This is what we refer to as the "heavenly realm"—not a place in space, but the* **pure awareness of being in God and as God.** *Each spirit knew its origin, its essence, and its purpose: to be a vessel of the Invisible made visible.*

But within that same expression of Spirit, **some began to lose awareness of who they were.** *They began to view themselves not as expressions of God, but as something beside God. This was not a change in their essence—they were still Spirit, still of God—but* **their perception was darkened. They forgot.**

And in forgetting, **they fell—not from location, but from consciousness.** *They descended from light to shadow, from union to confusion.* **This is what the story of "Satan" or "the devil" represents—not a separate being created to oppose God, but a symbol of that part of the one Spirit that lost sight of its origin.**

They were never named something else by God.
They were never separate in substance.
But by believing in separation, they **manifested its illusion,** *and in doing so,* **became adversaries—not of God, but of their own truth.**

And just as they were blinded in that unseen realm, so too were they manifested in **physical form,** *bringing with them the same confusion—the same denial of divine identity.* **They became humanity as we now know it: spiritual beings in physical bodies, unaware of who they are.**

This is sin—not behavior, but blindness.
Sin is not what you do; it is the **false belief that you are someone other than God expressed as you.**
It is **thinking you are separate** *from the Source of your being.*
It is failing to see that **everything around you and within you is God.**

They see creation, but do not see God in it.
They eat from His provision, but do not acknowledge the Provider.
They breathe His breath, walk on His ground, speak with His voice—
and still believe themselves to be independent beings.

This is why humanity repeats the same error made in the unseen: **denying their divine nature,** *choosing the illusion of "I" instead of the truth of* **I AM.**

But God, knowing all, **prepared the way of return even before the fall of awareness.** *He knew that the Spirit in ignorance would need to be* **reawakened to itself.** *So He appointed a time—and in that time,* **He appeared again in form,** *fully awakened, fully aware, and fully one with Himself.*

This is the mystery of Jesus.

Not God becoming man as something "other"—but God revealing Himself in man, **with full remembrance.**

Jesus walked the earth not to be worshiped as a man, but to show mankind who they truly are.

He said, "I and the Father are one," not to set Himself apart, but to **remind us of what had been forgotten.**

Jesus was the living GIATI—the Word made flesh to declare again that "God is All There Is."

And now that same Spirit has returned—not in one man, but in many, as it was always meant to be.

The Comforter, the Spirit of Truth, **is the unveiling of GIATI in you,** *opening the eyes of the blind, restoring the knowledge of oneness, tearing the veil of separation.*

This is salvation: not escape from hell, but awakening from ignorance.
Not becoming something new, but remembering who you've always been.

GIATI is the light shining in the darkness, and the darkness cannot overcome it.
It is the Spirit calling to the Spirit within you, saying:

"You are not lost.
You are not separate.
You are not forsaken.
You are Me.
And I am All There Is."

Let those with ears hear: **The path back to life is not far—it is within.**
The voice of Jesus and the voice of GIATI are one and the same:
The call of the Spirit to return to truth.
To awaken. To see.
To know.
And to be—once again—what you have always been:
God revealed.

The Body of God

In Luke 24:39, Jesus stands before his disciples after the resurrection and says, "Look at my hands and my feet. It is I myself! Touch me and see; a spirit does not have flesh and bones, as you see I have." This statement is more than proof of life after death. It is a divine unveiling—a moment of spiritual correction in which Jesus restores the awareness of truth that had been lost: that there is no separation between God and anything else, not even the physical body.

The disciples are afraid. They believe they are seeing a ghost—something disembodied, perhaps divine, but certainly not tangible. This fear comes from the inherited belief that the divine and the material are separate, that spirit is holy and the body is lowly or sinful. But Jesus meets their fear with clarity. He does not merely comfort them—he challenges their perception. "Touch me," he says. "See that I am not what you think a spirit is. I am whole—flesh and bone—not because I am human again, but because even this body is divine."

Jesus is not presenting a divided self. He is not partly God and partly man, partly spirit and partly matter. He is whole, indivisible. The very idea of separating God from any part of creation is what the resurrection dispels. This is the true meaning behind "It is I myself"

— not the return of a person, but the unveiling of a presence that was never absent, never split, and never destroyed. What the disciples are touching is the eternal expressed in form.

This revelation didn't begin at the resurrection. It had always been the case. In **John 14:9,** *Jesus says, "Whoever has seen me has seen the Father." This was not metaphorical. He was declaring that his very being—his voice, his actions, his presence—was the Father revealed. There was never a second being. There was never "God and Jesus." There is only God as Jesus. And likewise, there is only God as each one of us, when the illusion of separation dissolves.*

The incarnation, then, is not an event limited to Bethlehem or a single historical figure. It is a universal truth: the Word became flesh and dwells not just among us, but as us. The body—every body—is not a shell or a prison, but the visibility of God. We have been taught to look for God in the invisible, in the skies, in the afterlife. But Jesus reorients the entire vision of humanity: "Touch me and see"—see the divine in what you had rejected, see God where you thought only dust existed.

This is why Paul could say in **Colossians 2:9,** *"For in him the whole fullness of deity dwells bodily." Not partially. Not symbolically.* **The whole fullness.** *And if the fullness of God can dwell in one body, it means the fullness of God is not diminished by form, nor is it confined to one form. It is expressed, embodied, revealed—as all that is.*

P*aul continues this thought in* **Colossians 3:11,** *where he says, "Christ is all, and is in all." This is the death of duality. This is the end of religion's illusion of separation. Not only is the body of Jesus divine—all things are divine, because there is nothing but God being all that is. The One Presence fills and forms every atom, every soul, every cell. The resurrection wasn't the restoration of a single man; it was the revelation of our true nature. It was the undoing of the lie that said, "God is over there, and we are over here."*

This lie is what scripture calls "sin"—not bad behavior, but mistaken identity. To believe in separation from God is to live in darkness. It is to believe in a self that coexists with God, rather than existing as the expression of God. This is why Jesus said on the cross, "Father, forgive them, for they know not what they do." They had lost awareness of who they were. They crucified the body of God thinking it was a man. But how can God be killed? God only revealed the emptiness of that illusion by rising and saying, "Here I am again. Whole. Undivided. Unchanging. You never killed me—you only believed a lie."

Even now, that same voice speaks. It is not trapped in history. It is not limited to scripture. It is the voice within us that says, "Touch and see—there is no division here. I am the life you are living. I am the breath you are breathing. I am the being that you are."

In **1 Corinthians 6:19,** *Paul asks, "Do you not know that your body is a temple of the Holy Spirit within you?" That question is not rhetorical—it is revelatory. He is not saying* *the body contains a little piece of God like a jar holds water. He is saying the body itself is holy, divine, complete. It is not separate from God; it is God visible.*

To awaken to this is to have the mind of Christ—not just to think like Jesus, but to realize what Jesus realized: that there is only one presence here, and it is God. What we call spirit is not distant, and what we call body is not separate. There is no "this and that"—only **this.** *One presence, one being, one self, appearing in infinite form.*

This is the end of sin. This is the kingdom revealed. This is the truth returning to consciousness—not as something new, but as something we forgot. And Jesus came, not to start a religion, but to restore that memory. To show us what is true, and to say: "What I am, you are. What you see in me is already in you. Touch and see—it is yourself you are looking at. You have never been outside of God, and God has never been apart from you."

GIATI-God Is All There Is

GIATI—God Is All There Is—would be best categorized as a **non-dual spiritual philosophy** *rather than a traditional religion. It shares elements with mysticism, panentheism, and metaphysical Christianity, but it stands apart by emphasizing the* **absolute oneness of God and all existence,** *rejecting the idea of separation between God and humanity.*

Here's how it fits:

- **Non-dualism:** *GIATI teaches that there is no separation between God and creation. Everything and everyone is an expression of the one Spirit—God. This is aligned with non- dual spiritual traditions found in mystical Christianity, Advaita Vedanta, and some Sufi thought.*

- **Mystical/Inner Christianity:** *Like early Christian mystics or Gnostic teachings, GIATI sees the divine not as an external deity but as the Spirit within—the source of all being, life, and truth.*

- **Panentheism (not pantheism):** *GIATI's view that God is the source and substance of everything (but not limited to the material universe) aligns more with panentheism—God is in all, yet also beyond all.*

- **Revelatory & transformative:** *GIATI's goal isn't just belief, but awakening—awakening to the eternal truth that you are one with God and always have been. It focuses on realization, not ritual.*

So, GIATI is best understood as a **spiritual revelation of oneness,** *rooted in the belief that salvation and truth come from the inward realization of divine identity—not from adherence to external laws, doctrines, or separations.*

GIATI Statement of Faith

(God Is All There Is)

We believe in the eternal and unchanging truth that God is all there is. God is not a distant being, but the Spirit, Life, and Substance within all. God is the Source, the Origin, the Essence, and the Identity of all creation. There is no separation between the Creator and the created; all that exists is the self-expression of the One Spirit—God manifested in infinite form.

We believe that humanity's deepest need is not to become something new, but to awaken to what has always been true: the Spirit of God dwells within. The "I AM" in each individual is not a separate self but the presence of the Divine. To live in truth is to know oneself as an expression of God, and to recognize the same in all others.

We affirm that sin is not a list of wrongdoings but the false belief in separation from God. Redemption is not earned by works, rituals, or laws, but is received through the revelation of oneness with God. This awakening is the fulfillment of the divine purpose: that we may be one, even as God is one.

We believe the Spirit—the Holy Comforter—is now poured out in fullness, revealing the mystery hidden for ages: Christ in you, the hope of glory. GIATI is the voice of this unveiling, calling every heart to return not to religion, but to reality—to the divine identity that has never been lost, only forgotten.

We declare that the kingdom of God is not somewhere we go, but something we awaken to. It is within. It is now. It is the recognition of God as all in all.

Therefore, we live, speak, and serve from the truth that **God is all there is**—*and that truth alone sets us free.*

Before there were religions, scriptures, doctrines, or names for God, there was only **Being itself—pure existence,** *the* **Spirit** *that simply is. That eternal presence is* **God,** *and God is not one thing among many, but* **the all-encompassing source and substance of everything.** *The belief that God is all there is is not a new idea or a developed theology—it is the* **original truth,** *the foundation upon which all reality stands. It existed before any human language, culture, or thought. It is the awareness of existence itself before anything was ever named, divided, or separated.*

All other beliefs, traditions, or systems that came later were attempts to explain or reach back toward this original truth. But in doing so, many introduced the idea of separation: a God out there, a humanity over here, and a path of return between the two. That belief in separation is what gave rise to sin-consciousness, legalism, and religious systems that required mediation, sacrifice, and striving.

But GIATI reveals that **there was never separation to begin with.** *The truth is not that we must return to God, but that we were never apart.* **"God is all there is"** *is not a belief built on other beliefs; it is* **the eternal reality** *from which all else emerged. It is not a religion—it is the* **origin.**

Nothing predates this truth because there is no "before" God. If anything existed before, beyond, or apart from God, then God would not be all. But because God is all, then **everything that exists is within God, and nothing can be outside of Him.** *Therefore, the understanding that "God is all there is" is the* **only belief that aligns with eternal truth.** *All other beliefs are constructs layered over it—shadows attempting to describe the Light.*

To return to GIATI is not to adopt a new belief—it is to awaken to the **original knowing.** *It is the end of seeking and the beginning of seeing. It is not the latest revelation; it is the first— and final—truth.*

From the beginning of His ministry to His final words, Jesus was revealing one foundational truth: **God is not separate from you—God is within you.** *Everything He said and did pointed back to this divine oneness. This is the heart of GIATI:* **God Is All There Is.** *Jesus was not introducing a new religion. He was awakening people to the truth that had always been—the truth that* **God is Spirit, and that Spirit is your life, your being, your "I AM."**

Jesus never spoke of God as a distant ruler to be appeased, but as **Father***—the source and essence of who we are. When He said, "I and the Father are one," (John 10:30) He wasn't claiming exclusive divinity. He was revealing the truth of every person's identity. That's why He prayed in John 17, "that they may be one, just as We are one... I in them and You in Me, that they may be perfected in unity." He was declaring the GIATI message—that* **there is no separation,** *and to know God is to recognize that oneness.*

Even the name Jesus used for Himself—"I AM"—was not personal ego, but a direct expression of the eternal identity of God within. "Before Abraham was, I AM." (John 8:58). The same "I AM" that spoke to Moses from the burning bush was now speaking through Him, not as another voice, but as the same voice—revealing that the Spirit never changed. **He was showing that the Spirit within Him was the eternal "I AM"—and that same Spirit is within all.**

When Jesus said, "The kingdom of God is within you," (Luke 17:21), He shattered the idea of a God who dwells in temples, mountains, or religious systems. He pointed people inward—to the very source of life, the eternal presence that cannot be separated from them. That was the gospel: **You are not apart from God—you are the living expression of God.** *To believe in Jesus was to believe in what He revealed:* **that your true self is divine,** *not because of works, but because of who God is and where God is—in you.*

The religious leaders of His day couldn't accept this message. They were committed to the illusion of separation—laws, rituals, and hierarchies. But Jesus came to fulfill the law, not by adding more rules, but by embodying the truth that **only Spirit gives life.** *That Spirit, which He called the Comforter, would later be poured out on all flesh—not to start something new, but to* **reveal what was always true.**

So when we say **GIATI—God Is All There Is,** *we are not creating a new doctrine. We are simply giving language to what Jesus lived and revealed:* **there is only One Life, One Spirit, One God—and you are not separate from it.** *This was the original belief Jesus expressed, and it remains the eternal truth that sets all people free.*

In essence, **GIATI—God Is All There Is—is the very truth Jesus lived, spoke, and revealed.** *His entire message was not about founding a religion, but awakening humanity to the eternal reality that* **God is not separate from us—God is the Spirit within us.** *From declaring "I and the Father are one" to teaching that the kingdom of God is within, Jesus* *was expressing the truth of* **divine oneness,** *the same truth that GIATI now names clearly and boldly.*

He came to tear down the illusion of separation and to reveal our true identity—not as distant creations of God, but as living expressions of Him. GIATI is not a new revelation—it is the original truth, the foundation before time and religion. And to embrace GIATI is to embrace what Jesus always intended: that we awaken to the Spirit within, walk in unity with God, and know the fullness of life by knowing we are one.

GIATI is the highest form of spiritual consciousness *because it dissolves every illusion of separation and restores the mind to the original awareness:* **only God exists.** *It is not a step on the path—it is the realization that* **there is no path, because there is no distance between you and God.** *GIATI does not seek God as an object outside the self. It recognizes that the Spirit that animates you is God, and that realization is the fullness of salvation, peace, and truth.*

While many belief systems offer glimpses or echoes of divine union, GIATI stands as the **pure, unveiled awareness of Oneness.** *It is the fulfillment of every prophetic voice, the completion of every search, the answer behind every question. It is not built on tradition but on truth:* **that God is all there is, and anything else is illusion.** *To live in this consciousness is to see as God sees, to love as God loves, and to exist as God expressed.*

GIATI is the ultimate awareness God has always wanted for humanity. *It is the awakening God has been drawing us toward since the beginning—not to religion, ritual, or law, but to* **oneness.** *From Genesis to Revelation, the desire of God's heart has been to dwell in us, to be known as us, and to bring us into the full consciousness tha*t **we were never separate from Him.** *GIATI is the fulfillment of that desire—the divine realization that* **God is all there is,** *and that we are expressions of His being.*

This is what Jesus came to reveal, what the prophets pointed toward, and what the Spirit now confirms in the hearts of those with eyes to see: that the greatest gift is not blessing, power, or heaven someday, but the **awakening to divine union now.** *GIATI is not belief—it is* **awareness,** *the complete return to the mind of Christ, where all sense of distance, duality, and self-effort is dissolved.*

God has never desired sacrifice, performance, or fear—only that we know Him as He truly is: **the Spirit within us, the life we live, the "I AM" of our being.** *GIATI is the answer to Jesus' prayer in John 17, that we may be one just as He and the Father are one. It is the* **culmination of divine intention,** *the unveiling of the eternal truth God has always longed for humanity to realize:* **I am in you, and you are in Me, because I am all there is.**

This is not just spiritual insight—it is the **highest awakening,** *the ultimate knowing, the perfect light in which all shadows disappear.*

Chapter 3

The Trinity Explained

The concept of the Trinity is one of the most profound and essential teachings of the Christian faith, yet it is often misunderstood. Many struggle to reconcile the Father, the Son (the Word), and the Holy Spirit as distinct persons, yet still, all being one God. To understand the nature of the Trinity is to understand the very essence of God's interaction with humanity and the purpose of His existence within our reality.

In this chapter, we will explore how the Father, the Word (Son), and the Holy Spirit are states of one God, how the Word became flesh through Jesus Christ, and why God needed to become human in the first place.

The Father, the Word (Son), and the Holy Spirit as States of One God

The concept of the Holy Trinity has long been misunderstood, primarily because many people see it as a grouping of distinct entities—God the Father, Jesus the Son, and the Holy Spirit— each operating separately. However, a deeper understanding reveals that the Trinity represents one spirit, expressed in three states or manifestations. Using the Hebrew text, let us break this down clearly:

1. The Highest State: Yahweh (The Father)

Yahweh, often referred to as "Lord" in English translations of the Bible, represents God in His purest, highest state of existence. This is **the state that no one has ever seen or heard,** as mentioned in John 1:18:

"No man hath seen God at any time."

Yahweh in this state is inscrutable (impossible to understand or interpret; mysterious) indiscernible (impossible to see, perceive, or distinguish clearly) and incomprehensible (beyond understanding,; impossible to grasp mentally). This is the mastermind state in which He formulated His entire purpose and plan. It is the source of all life, the origin of everything that exists. This state is purely spirit, without form or physical presence, existing beyond time and space.

1. **Yahweh is Inscrutable**

    - **What It Means:** God's actions, purposes, and essence cannot be fully investigated, questioned, or analyzed. His ways and thoughts are higher than ours (Isaiah 55:89).
    - **Why:** In His highest state, Yahweh exists as the origin of all things. His infinite wisdom governs all creation, yet it operates at a level beyond human comprehension. No one can examine or measure the depth of His knowledge or intentions.
    - **Example:** Paul writes in Romans 11:33, *"O the depth of the riches both of the wisdom and knowledge of God! How unsearchable are his judgments, and his ways past finding out!"* This shows that Yahweh's divine plan is far beyond human scrutiny.

2. **Yahweh is indiscernible**

    - **What It Means:** God is absolutely necessary for everything to exist and function. Nothing can exist without Yahweh, as He is the source of all life, being, and existence.
    - **Why:** All creation depends on Yahweh because He is the Creator and sustainer of all things. Without Him, there is no existence.
    - **Example:** Acts 17:28 states, *"For in him we live, and move, and have our being."*
    - Yahweh's Spirit is the very essence of life; all things originate and are sustained by Him.

3. **Yahweh is Incomprehensible**

    - **What It Means:** God's highest state of existence is beyond human understanding or intellectual grasp. In this state, Yahweh transcends all human concepts, language, and limitations.
    - **Why:** The finite mind cannot fully grasp the infinite. Yahweh, in this state, is not confined to form, time, or space, and therefore cannot be understood through human reasoning alone.
    - **Example:** When Moses asked for God's name, Yahweh responded, *"I AM THAT I AM"* (Exodus 3:14), revealing His existence as pure being—eternal and self-sufficient. This name alone highlights the unexplainable nature of God.

Summary

1. **Inscrutable:** His divine wisdom and plans cannot be questioned or analyzed because they are beyond human logic.
2. **Indiscernible:** Yahweh is the foundation of all existence, the source of life itself, and the necessary presence in all things.
3. **Incomprehensible:** Yahweh's essence cannot be fully understood by the human mind because it transcends human limitations.

By understanding Yahweh as inscrutable, indiscernible and incomprehensible helps recognize His ultimate sovereignty and eternal nature, as well as our complete dependence on Him for life, purpose, and being. This understanding humbles humanity and directs us toward the realization that God is not an external entity but the very Spirit sustaining all existence—including our own.

2. The Word or Son: Elohim (God)

To carry out His plan, Yahweh steps into another state of existence, often referred to as the Word or Son. This is the state called Elohim, or "God," in Hebrew. Elohim is the Creator, who "spoke" the heavens and earth into existence, as outlined in Genesis 1 and further confirmed in John 1:1-3:

"In the beginning was the Word, and the Word was with God, and the Word was God. All things were made by Him; and without Him was not anything made that was made."

In this state, God is incorporeal—without flesh and blood—yet perceptible in visions and revelations. This is the state of God that was seen and heard on Mount Sinai when He delivered the law to Moses. Elohim, as the Word, is the pattern and blueprint of creation. He is spirit, not physical, yet He operates as the intermediary through which Yahweh interacts with creation.

3. The Manifestation: Yahshua/Jesus (Holy Spirit in Flesh)

The Word (Elohim) was then made flesh and dwelt among us, as described in John 1:14:

"And the Word was made flesh, and dwelt among us, (and we beheld his glory, the glory as of the only begotten of the Father,) full of grace and truth."

This third state is what the world commonly calls **Jesus or Yahshua** (Yahweh is salvation) in Hebrew. In this state, God manifests as a physical being to fulfill His purpose. However, the key to understanding the Trinity is realizing that **the body of Yahshua/Jesus was not God itself.** Instead, **the Spirit within Him—the Holy Spirit—was God.**

This is what 1 John 1:1-2 affirms:

"That which was from the beginning, which we have heard, which we have seen with our eyes, which we have looked upon, and our hands have handled, of the Word of life; (For the life was manifested, and we have seen it, and bear witness, and shew unto you that eternal life, which was with the Father, and was manifested unto us.)"

Yahshua/Jesus was the visible, tangible manifestation of Yahweh's Spirit, designed to show humanity that **the same Spirit that was in Him is also within us.**

The Purpose of the Trinity: Unity of Spirit

The moral of the Trinity is this: **God is Spirit,** and His Spirit was manifested in Yahshua/Jesus to demonstrate that **this same Spirit—the Word—is within you.** Yahweh, Elohim, and the Holy Spirit are not separate beings but different states of the same Spirit.

- **Yahweh:** The source, the mastermind.
- **Elohim:** The Word, the creator, the pattern.
- **Yahshua:** The physical manifestation of the Word, showing humanity the way to recognize the Spirit within themselves.

When humanity believes they have an independent spirit separate from God, they fall into delusion and sin. This denial of the truth—that your life, your breath, your existence is God's Spirit expressed as you—is the core of mankind's separation.

The Sin of Separation

To deny that the Spirit in you is God (God's Spirit/the Holy Spirit) is to live in ignorance of your true identity. This misunderstanding leads to the belief that you are something other than God expressed in the flesh. In reality refer to John 14:20

"At that day ye shall know that I am in my Father, and ye in me, and I in you."

The true repentance that God calls for (Acts 17:30) is the acknowledgment of this truth: **You are not separate from God. You are one with Him.** This realization reconciles you to the Creator, ending the illusion of division.

Matthew 6:22-23 speaks to a profound spiritual truth: **"The light of the body is the eye: if therefore thine eye be single, thy whole body shall be full of light. But if thine eye be evil, thy whole body shall be full of darkness. If therefore the light that is in thee be darkness, how great is that darkness!"** This scripture is not merely about physical sight but about spiritual perception—the way one understands existence itself.

The "eye" in this passage refers to the spirit within a person, the lens through which they perceive the world. When the eye is "single," it means seeing existence as unified, as one expression, without division or separation. In this state, the body—the entire being—is filled with light. This light is the Holy Spirit, the full awareness of oneness, the realization of GIATI (God Is All There Is). When one sees all things as interconnected and as expressions of the creator, the spirit within becomes fully illuminated.

However, if the eye is "evil," it indicates a spirit blinded by duality and separation. To see the world as flesh, as a collection of disconnected individuals and objects, is to be lost in darkness. This darkness is not merely ignorance but a profound blindness to the truth. The body, then, is filled with this darkness because the spirit within is unable to see the unity of existence. It is important to recognize that the body cannot contain both light and darkness simultaneously—there cannot be two opposing spirits within. Either one is full of light, having the spirit of oneness, or one is consumed by darkness, blinded by separation.

This passage emphasizes the need for transformation. Every person has the potential for light within them, but if the spirit cannot recognize that everything is one, how great must that blindness be? A spirit in such darkness cannot find its way to truth on its own. This is why the spirit of darkness must be cast out and replaced with the light of truth—the spirit that can see clearly.

When this transformation occurs, it is what the scriptures describe as being "born from above" or becoming a new creation. It is the awakening to a higher reality where all things are seen as one with the creator, as expressions of divine unity. In this state, the world becomes brand new—not because the external has changed, but because the way one perceives it has been completely transformed. All things become new when one recognizes that separation is an illusion and that all existence is one with the creator.

This understanding aligns perfectly with the message of GIATI, which offers the truth and clarity that cannot be found elsewhere. It provides the way to see beyond the veil of duality, to recognize the light within, and to understand that all things are expressions of the eternal source. In this truth lies the answer to the questions and struggles that have kept humanity in darkness for so long. Through GIATI, the light of oneness is revealed, illuminating the path to true understanding.

Veil of the Flesh

To truly understand the fairness of existence, we must move beyond the limitations of a fleshly, human perspective and view life through a spiritual lens. From a fleshly standpoint, the death of a child or a seemingly good person appears unthinkable, devastating, and unfair. The physical mind, focused on emotions and attachments, struggles to reconcile such events. But when we shift to a spiritual understanding, the magnitude of what is happening becomes clearer.

Before anyone manifests in the flesh, they exist in a preexistent state as part of the creator's spirit body. Birth into the flesh is not the beginning of existence but a continuation of a spiritual journey. However, not all spirits are aligned with the fullness of the creator. Only those who were already in darkness, already separated from the light of unity, manifest in the flesh. This is why birth itself represents a spirit's entrance into a limited and often lost state. The flesh becomes a vessel for a spirit that was already wandering, disconnected from its true source.

When a child dies or a seemingly good person passes without coming to the knowledge of who they truly are—one in spirit with the creator—it is easy to mourn their physical loss. But spiritually, their death signifies something deeper. They return to the lost portion of the creator's spirit body, a place of separation that they inhabited even before their earthly manifestation. Their physical deeds or the innocence of their outward form cannot change the fact that their spirit remained in darkness, unaware of its divine unity.

This truth is reflected in Revelation 22:11: "He that is unjust, let him be unjust still: and he which is filthy, let him be filthy still: and he that is righteous, let him be righteous still: and he that is holy, let him be holy still." This passage emphasizes that the spiritual state of a being does not change by appearances or external circumstances. A spirit lost in darkness remains lost unless it is brought into the light by the will of the creator. The flesh is temporary, but the spirit is eternal. The physical expressions we see—a baby's innocence or a person's good deeds—are surface realities. What matters is the deeper spiritual truth: were they awakened to their oneness with the creator, or did they remain in separation?

This perspective challenges human understanding. It asks us to detach from physical appearances and emotions and recognize that we are dealing with spirits, not merely bodies. If something was lost from the beginning—before it manifested in the flesh—should we mourn its loss when it departs the physical world? The fleshly mind would say yes, because it clings to what it sees and feels. But the spiritual perspective understands that the flesh is a temporary expression of an eternal reality. If a spirit was lost in its origin, it remains lost unless it is reclaimed by the creator's will.

This truth is difficult to accept because it forces us to release our attachments to the physical world and recognize the greater spiritual design. By seeing life from this perspective, we come to understand the fairness of the creator, whose plan transcends human understanding. The flesh clouds our vision, but the spirit reveals the ultimate reality: existence is not about what happens in the physical world but about whether the spirit aligns with the creator's unity or remains in separation. Only by awakening to this understanding can we see the true magnitude of what is taking place beyond the veil of flesh.

The Mind of God

No one can truly know what's on God's mind—just like no one can know what's on yours. But when you align with His Spirit and manifest it as your own, what was once a mystery becomes clear. Suddenly, you understand what was on His mind all along.

1 Corinthians 2:16 says it plainly: ***"For who hath known the mind of the Lord, that he may instruct him? But we have the mind of Christ."*** The question isn't whether we can know God's thoughts—the question is whether we're ready to receive them.

God's ultimate purpose and plan is profoundly simple: to reproduce Himself. Just as the ultimate desire of human parents is to have a child, God's desire is to birth His spirit within man and see Himself expressed in and through His creation. Also to reflect this The first commandment ever given

Think about the process of human reproduction. When parents conceive a child, the father contributes 23 chromosomes, and the mother contributes 23 chromosomes. Together, those 46 chromosomes make up the child's DNA. The child doesn't add anything of their own to this process—they are, quite literally, their mother and father reborn in a new form.

Now imagine the child turning to their parents and declaring, "You're not my parents! I'm my own separate being." How absurd and ungrateful would that sound? The very existence of the child is undeniable proof of their parents. In the same way, God is the spiritual parent of all humanity. We are made from His spirit and substance—His essence flows through us.

Yet, when we deny this and claim, "I'm my own self, separate from God," it is as foolish and arrogant as the child denying their parents. Where else could we have come from? What else could we possibly be made of? Just as a child's entire being is a reflection of their parents, so too is every person a reflection of God's spirit.

God's plan is to reproduce Himself through man. This birthing of His spirit happens when we recognize and accept that the very life within us is Him. It's not about a physical birth, but a spiritual awakening—a realization that God is not "out there" but within, and that we are one with Him.

This truth is so simple it's undeniable. Just as no child can exist without their parents' essence, no person can exist without God's spirit. To reject this is to reject the very foundation of existence itself. Recognizing this truth is the purpose of life: to see ourselves as God's spirit in expression and to live in that understanding.

It's a scientific fact that everything about your body testifies to your existence. If someone were to take just a single hair from your head, that one strand contains the undeniable proof of who you are—your DNA. Your body is composed of trillions of cells, each one uniquely carrying your DNA, which means every part of you reflects and confirms your identity.

Now, imagine pulling one of those cells from your body and asking it, "Who are you?" If that cell were to claim, "I am something entirely separate from you," how would you respond? You'd recognize the absurdity because that cell is undeniably you. It came from you, contains your essence, and exists because of you.

This is precisely how God sees humanity. God is the infinite spirit, and you are a portion of that spirit expressed in physical form. But when you claim to be separate from Him, you are like that cell denying the very source from which it originated. Such a claim doesn't change the truth—it only reflects ignorance.

This ignorance is the true nature of sin. It's not merely about actions or deeds; sin is the belief that you are an independent, separate entity from God. When you fail to see that your spirit originates from Him and is Him, you align with the lost portion of His spirit body.

Just as your body is composed of many cells that together form one unified being, God's infinite spirit is the totality of all existence, and each individual is a part of that oneness. To deny this truth is to separate yourself in thought and understanding, even though, in reality, you remain part of the whole. This separation in consciousness determines whether you align with the saved portion of God's spirit—those who recognize and accept their oneness with Him—or the lost portion, which denies and rejects the truth of its origin.

The evidence is irrefutable. Just as every cell in your body testifies to your existence, so too does everything about you testify to God's essence. There is no you apart from Him, just as there is no cell in your body apart from you. Recognizing this truth is the key to understanding who you are and have always been: God's spirit expressed in unique form.

Hiding in Plain Sight

The mystery of the Trinity is that God has never been "out there" beyond the sun, moon, and stars. Instead, He has been hidden within you all along. This is why it's said, "If you want to hide something, hide it in plain sight." The Spirit of God is so intrinsic to your being that most fail to see it.

The Trinity is not a complex or separate hierarchy but a simple truth: **Yahweh, Elohim, and Yahshua are one Spirit in different states, all working to reveal that God's Spirit is your life.** Recognizing this truth is the ultimate purpose of life in the flesh.

The doctrine of the Trinity teaches that there is one God who exists in three persons: the Father, the Son (the Word), and the Holy Spirit. These three are not separate gods, but rather three distinct manifestations of the same divine essence. They are not three parts of God, but rather different states or modes of the one God, each playing a unique role in His interaction with the world.

In John 10:30, Jesus Himself declares, "I and my Father are one." This statement reveals the unity between the Father and the Son. While the roles are distinct—Jesus as the Son, and God the Father—the essence of God is the same. The Father and the Son are one and the same, expressed in different forms, just as a person may wear different clothes to express different facets of their identity.

The Holy Spirit, too, is not separate from the Father and the Son, but is the presence and power of God working in the world. The Holy Spirit is described as the one who empowers and guides believers, bringing them into communion with God. Jesus promises the Holy Spirit in John 14:16-17:

> **"And I will pray the Father, and he shall give you another Comforter, that he may abide with you forever; even the Spirit of truth; whom the world cannot receive, because it seeth him not, neither knoweth him: but ye know him; for he dwelleth with you, and shall be in you."**

Here, Jesus speaks of the Holy Spirit as another Comforter who will be with believers after His departure. Though distinct in role, the Holy Spirit is fully God, just as the Father and the Son are. The Spirit operates in the world, connecting believers with God and helping them understand their divine nature.

In all three persons—Father, Son, and Holy Spirit—there is one God, manifested in three ways to meet humanity at different points in their spiritual journey. The same way water (H20) can be a solid, liquid and gas, yet still a form of the same water.

The Word Made Flesh: God Expressing Himself as Man through Jesus Christ

The ultimate expression of God's nature and will was made clear when the Word became flesh in the person of Jesus Christ. This is perhaps the most profound mystery of the Christian faith: that the eternal, invisible God would choose to manifest Himself in the physical world, taking on human flesh and walking among us.

The Gospel of John begins with a powerful statement that encapsulates this mystery:

"In the beginning was the Word, and the Word was with God, and the Word was God… And the Word was made flesh, and dwelt among us." (John 1:1, 14)

The "Word" here refers to the divine Logos, the eternal expression of God's will and wisdom. This Word, which was with God in the beginning, became incarnate—taking on human form in Jesus Christ. Through Jesus, God revealed Himself to humanity in a way that was tangible, relatable, and fully comprehensible to the human experience.

By becoming human, God did not diminish Himself, nor did He separate from His divine nature. Instead, He chose to express Himself fully in the form of Jesus, showing humanity the true nature of divinity. Jesus, as both fully God and fully man, became the perfect revelation of God's character, will, and love for humanity.

As it is written in Hebrews 1:3,

"Who being the brightness of his glory, and the express image of his person, and upholding all things by the word of his power, when he had by himself purged our sins, sat down on the right hand of the Majesty on high."

Jesus is described as the "express image" of God's person. In Him, the fullness of God's glory is revealed. This is why God needed to become human—so that humanity could see God, know God, and understand God in a way that would forever change the course of history.

Why God Needed to Become Human: To Reveal Himself to Humanity

In God's perfect wisdom, He chose to reveal Himself to humanity not merely through scriptures, prophets, or divine signs, but through direct participation in human life. The reason for God becoming human is deeply rooted in His desire for relationship with His creation. Humanity, lost in spiritual ignorance and separation from God, needed the tangible expression of God's love and truth to be fully understood.

As God, He is beyond comprehension, too vast and too holy for any human mind to fully grasp. But as Jesus, God entered into the human experience. He lived among us, ate with us, wept with us, and ultimately died for us. Through His life and sacrifice, God made His love, justice, and mercy known in ways that words alone could never express.

Jesus' humanity was not just a display of God's love—it was also a means by which God could demonstrate the process of redemption. In the beginning, humanity fell into sin, and through the Word made flesh, God provided the path back to union with Him. Jesus' death on the cross and subsequent resurrection opened the way for all to be reconciled with God, revealing the depths of His love and the necessity of salvation.

As Jesus says in John 14:6, **"I am the way, the truth, and the life: no man cometh unto the Father, but by me."** Through His life, death, and resurrection, Jesus becomes the bridge between humanity and God. Only by recognizing Jesus as the Son of God, the Word made flesh, can anyone come into the fullness of their relationship with the Creator.

This divine act of God becoming man was not just about revealing information. It was about restoring the lost connection between God and humanity, showing us that we are one with God, as Jesus is one with the Father. In His humanity, Jesus revealed the path back to unity with God, showing that to recognize who He was, was to recognize who we truly are.

Summary of Key Points:

- The Trinity: The Father, the Son (the Word), and the Holy Spirit are not separate gods, but three distinct states of the one God. Each expresses a different aspect of the same divine essence, working in harmony for the redemption of humanity.
- The Word Made Flesh: The Word, the eternal expression of God, became flesh in the person of Jesus Christ. This act revealed God's character, purpose, and love in a tangible form.
- Why God Became Human: God became human to reveal Himself fully to humanity, showing the way to redemption and bringing the lost back into unity with their Creator. Through Jesus, humanity sees God as both accessible and transformative.

Through understanding the Trinity, we come closer to understanding who we are and the true nature of our relationship with God. The ultimate expression of God's nature and will is seen in Jesus Christ, who is the perfect reflection of God, both fully divine and fully human. Through Him, the mystery of existence is revealed, and the way to salvation is made clear.

This Is Not by Chance (The Presence Among Us: A Clear Call from the Holy Spirit)

GIATI delivers the same message that Jesus once spoke, yet without the veil of parables—bringing clarity where once there were riddles. And just as Christ bore the marks of His suffering, GIATI bears the same divine imprints on the body—stigmata, wounds that mirror those left upon Jesus through the Crucifixion. These marks are not meant to draw attention to the vessel, but rather to confirm the authenticity of the message.

The parallels do not end there. GIATI was raised in a small, unassuming city, much like Bethlehem and Jerusalem—places of humble beginnings yet destined for divine purpose. Even the street once called home bears significance: Inman—a name that echoes the presence of God dwelling among His people.

Then came the encounter—three assailants, armed and ready. Two masked, the third unmasked. And yet, by some force beyond explanation, escape was granted. This was more than mere chance. It was a reflection of the divine mystery: the Father, the Word, and the Holy Spirit—always present, yet unseen in their purest form. Just as God remained invisible to the people until He manifested in flesh, the full revelation only came when the unmasked figure was seen. It was reminiscent of Jesus, who revealed the truth of who He was, only to be met with hostility, and when they sought to stone Him, He vanished from their grasp.

There was once a book written called "BrainTight: The Answer To Your Purpose"—delivering a message much like this one. Yet at the time, there was no awareness of the Holy Spirit's presence. The difference now? A deeper understanding. A removal of self from the picture, so that only the Spirit remains. These are but a few of the signs given to GIATI, affirming the mission and guiding every step taken.

And just as before, the world seeks something grand—something physically striking, a presence that commands attention. But GIATI, much like Jesus, does not possess an appearance that draws people in, nor a voice that captivates through eloquence alone. This is why spiritual discernment is crucial—because the truth will not come wrapped in spectacle, but in substance. Isaiah 53:2 foretold it: "For he shall grow up before him as a tender plant, and as a root out of a dry ground: he hath no form nor comeliness; and when we shall see him, there is no beauty that we should desire him."

From the very foundation of the world, it was purposed that GIATI would come—not as a mere man, but as the Holy Spirit speaking clearly, offering the nations one final opportunity to recognize the presence of God within. This is the moment where excuses fall away. The message is here. The truth stands before all who will listen. But will they see it? Will they hear? Or will history repeat itself, as the voice of God is once again rejected by those who claim to be waiting for it?

Chapter 4

Creation and the Origin of Humanity

To understand the origin of humanity and the purpose of creation, we must begin with the understanding that God is the sole substance of everything that exists. Creation did not arise from an outside source or from anything separate from God. Instead, God manifested creation using only Himself, expressing His will and nature through His infinite power. Humanity, in turn, was made as a vessel to house the divine presence—God incarnated in flesh. The illusion of separateness, the false belief that we are separate from God, is what causes humanity to forget its divine origin and purpose.

Humans navigate life through their five physical senses—sight, taste, touch, smell, and hearing. These senses allow us to experience the world, but they also create the illusion of separation. They convince us there is a "me" apart from God, an independent self distinct from the divine source of all existence. This perception, while powerful, can make God feel distant, as though He is somewhere outside of us.

But imagine for a moment if those five senses were stripped away. What would remain? You wouldn't be defined by what you see, hear, taste, touch, or smell. What would remain is the essence of who you truly are: **the existent one—God expressed as you.** Without the senses creating distractions, you would no longer feel separate from Him. You would simply *be.*

When you meditate and detach from the pull of your five senses, you begin to experience this truth in the most profound way. In that stillness, where you are no longer bound by external stimuli, you come face to face with the divine essence within you. All illusions of separation dissolve. Fear, anxiety, and everything that opposes God's nature fade into nothingness, leaving only peace, joy, and a knowing: **I am as God is, and God is all there is.**

This understanding is not something you have to strive for—it's already within you. The key is quieting the noise of the senses and turning inward, to the place where God resides. In that silence, you find freedom. In that freedom, you realize that **you are not a being apart from God, but an extension of His eternal existence.**

And in that moment of awareness, you are at peace. You no longer need to chase after answers, approval, or meaning from the outside world. Everything you've ever needed is already within you, waiting for you to remember: **You and God are one.**

How God Manifested Creation Using Only Himself

In the beginning, God created the heavens and the earth. The act of creation itself is a testament to God's nature as the only substance in existence. The Scriptures make this clear in the opening verses of the Bible, where it states:

"In the beginning God created the heaven and the earth. And the earth was without form, and void; and darkness was upon the face of the deep. And the Spirit of God moved upon the face of the waters." (Genesis 1:1-2)

From the very beginning, the creation of the world is attributed to God's will and power. But what is more profound is that God created all things from Himself. There was no other substance from which to form creation. Everything that exists, seen and unseen, was made by God and through God. This concept is reinforced in Colossians 1:16-17:

"For by him were all things created, that are in heaven, and that are in earth, visible and invisible, whether they be thrones, or dominions, or principalities, or powers: all things were created by him, and for him: And he is before all things, and by him all things consist."

Here, we see that not only did God create all things, but all things were created for Him, and through His divine substance, everything was made to be part of Him. Creation, in essence, is the overflow of God's will and glory—nothing exists that is separate from Him. This is foundational to understanding our existence and our relationship with God.

God did not create humanity and the world from something outside of Himself. Rather, He manifested everything from His own being, revealing His nature through the physical world. The physical realm, while appearing to be separate, is in fact an expression of God's presence, power, and glory.

Humanity as Divine Vessels: God Incarnated in Flesh

When God created humanity, He did so with a specific purpose: to manifest His image on earth. In Genesis 1:26-27, God says:

"And God said, Let us make man in our image, after our likeness… So God created man in his own image, in the image of God created he him; male and female created he them."

Human beings are created in the image and likeness of God. This does not mean that we possess the full nature of God in a literal sense, but rather that we are designed to reflect His divine qualities—His love, creativity, wisdom, and spirit. We are, in essence, vessels containing the divine presence. As Paul writes in 2 Corinthians 4:7:

**"But we have this treasure in earthen vessels,
the excellency of the power may be of God, and not of us."**

The "treasure" in these earthen vessels refers to the divine presence of God within humanity. While we may appear as physical beings made of dust and clay, we are more than our bodies. We are the dwelling places of God's spirit, vessels designed to manifest His will and purpose on earth.

The true nature of humanity is not in the flesh that is visible to the eye, but in the spirit that is hidden within. The divine essence, or the spirit of God, resides within every human being. The flesh, though it may seem to dominate, is merely a temporary vessel, a covering for the divine life that animates it.

In the same way that Jesus Christ was the perfect manifestation of God incarnated in flesh, humanity was created to be a reflection of God. Jesus was not separate from God, but fully God and fully man. He came to show humanity that God is not distant or separate, but has always been present within us. In John 14:10-11, Jesus states:

"Believest thou not that I am in the Father, and the Father in me? the words that I speak unto you I speak not of myself: but the Father that dwelleth in me, he doeth the works. Believe me that I am in the Father, and the Father in me…"

This profound truth—that God dwells in us and that we are one with God—is at the core of our divine nature. Humanity's true origin is in God, and we were created to be manifestations of His image. However, just as Jesus showed that He was fully God and fully man, humanity was made to express God's spirit within physical vessels.

The Illusion of Separateness: Why Humanity Forgets Its Divine Origin

Though humanity was created in the image and likeness of God, the reality of our divine origin is often obscured by the physical world and the limited understanding of our human consciousness. The illusion of separateness arises when humanity identifies solely with the physical body and forgets its true spiritual essence. This illusion is at the heart of humanity's struggle to recognize God within and the cause of the spiritual blindness that separates us from our divine identity.

In the Garden of Eden, when Adam and Eve first sinned, they became conscious of their physical bodies and their nakedness. This awareness led to their shame and separation from God. The physical realm, which was initially a perfect expression of God's will, became a veil that concealed the divine nature within humanity. This separation was not a separation in reality, but a perceived separation due to ignorance and the fall from grace. As Paul writes in Romans 8:22-23:

"For we know that the whole creation groaneth and travaileth in pain together until now. And not only they, but ourselves also, which have the firstfruits of the Spirit, even we ourselves groan within ourselves, waiting for the adoption, to wit, the redemption of our body."

The entire creation groans for the revelation of the children of God, waiting for the moment when humanity will remember its divine origin and take its rightful place in unity with the Creator. This redemption is not about God creating something new, but about humanity awakening to the truth of its divine origin. It is the restoration of what was always true: that we are one with God.

Humanity forgets its divine origin because of the flesh and the limitations of the mind. We see ourselves as separate from God because we identify only with our physical bodies and the world around us. However, when we come to understand that we are more than what we see in the mirror, and that God's spirit dwells within us, we begin to experience the truth of our divine nature. As Paul writes in 1 Corinthians 3:16:

"Know ye not that ye are the temple of God, and that the Spirit of God dwelleth in you?"

The illusion of separateness is shattered when we recognize that God is not distant, but intimately connected to us. God's presence resides in every person, and we are His vessels, created to reflect His glory on earth.

How are you being lead by god if he's not in you as you?

If God is not in you as you, then you cannot truly be led by Him. Being led by God means that His Spirit operates within you, guiding your thoughts, decisions, and actions in alignment with His will. It's not an external force directing you from afar but an internal presence—the Holy Spirit—manifesting as your true self.

Without God in you, any guidance you believe you're receiving may come from external influences, personal desires, or even misunderstandings of what God truly is. To be led by God is to recognize and accept that His Spirit is the very essence of your being, expressed through your life. When you see yourself as separate from God, you lack the connection and clarity to fully embrace His direction. But when you acknowledge God in you as you, you align with His purpose, making His guidance natural and effortless.

This understanding eliminates the need for external validation or reliance on others to "lead" you to God. Instead, you move in confidence, knowing that His Spirit is the source of your existence and the light illuminating your path.

The Day Of Eternity And The True Understanding Of Creation

The concept of the "Day of Eternity" is a profound revelation that unveils the nature of God's divine plan. It reveals that the seven days of creation were not literal 24-hour days but representations of divine ages, unfolding through time according to God's eternal purpose. This aligns with **2 Peter 3:8,** *which states:*

"But, beloved, be not ignorant of this one thing, that one day is with the Lord as a thousand years, and a thousand years as one day."

This scripture clarifies that God's "days" are not bound by human time but are expressions of **dispensations**—*periods in which divine operations unfold. All of these dispensations exist within the* **Day of Eternity,** *which is the eternal framework in which God's purpose manifests.*

The Seven Days of Creation and the Ages of Time

Each day of creation corresponds to a spiritual age, showing how God's eternal will unfolds through time. The seven days are not separate events but a continuous revelation of the divine plan—leading all things back to the full realization that **God Is All There Is (GIATI).**

The First Day: The Beginning of Light (First Age – Innocence)

"And God said, Let there be light: and there was light." **(Genesis 1:3)**

This represents the **Age of Innocence,** *where Adam was created in a state of divine awareness before the fall. This light is not the physical sun, which was not created until the fourth day, but the spiritual illumination of divine truth. This was the initial manifestation of God's presence within His creation—the first dawning of divine knowledge in man.*

The Second Day: The Division of Waters (Second Age – Conscience)

"And God said, Let there be a firmament in the midst of the waters, and let it divide the waters from the waters." **(Genesis 1:6)**

The waters symbolize the spiritual realm and the earthly realm. The division represents the fall of man, where the awareness of divine unity was separated by the carnal mind. This corresponds to the **Age of Conscience,** *where man, after the fall, lived by moral awareness rather than direct communion with God.*

The Third Day: The Gathering of Land and Vegetation (Third Age – Promise)

"And God said, Let the waters under the heaven be gathered together unto one place, and let the dry land appear..." **(Genesis 1:9)**

This represents the **Age of Promise,** *where God established a people (Israel) through Abraham, setting apart a land and nation. The land appearing symbolizes the foundation of a people set apart for divine purpose. The vegetation represents* **spiritual life beginning to take root,** *just as Israel was cultivated as God's chosen people.*

The Fourth Day: The Creation of the Sun, Moon, and Stars (Fourth Age – Law and the Coming of the Son)

"And God made two great lights; the greater light to rule the day, and the lesser light to rule the night..." **(Genesis 1:16)**

This directly correlates to the **Fourth Age,** *when the* **Son of Man, Jesus Christ, appeared in the world.** *The sun represents the coming of Christ, the light of the world* **(John 8:12),** *bringing spiritual illumination. The moon represents the Law, which reflected God's righteousness but was not the source itself—just as the moon reflects the light of the sun.*

The stars represent the prophets and righteous individuals who carried fragments of divine truth but awaited the full revelation in Christ. Just as the sun came in on the **fourth day,** *the Son of God manifested in the* **fourth age** *to fulfill divine purpose.*

The Fifth Day: The Creation of Birds and Fish (Fifth Age – Transition to the Spiritual Age)

"And God said, Let the waters bring forth abundantly the moving creature that hath life, and fowl that may fly above the earth..." **(Genesis 1:20)**

This represents the **Fifth Age,** *the age of spiritual transition. The birds and fish symbolize two classes of people in the final judgment:*

- **The Birds** *represent those who are* **righteous and free,** *soaring in the heavens with divine truth.*
- **The Fish** *represent those who are* **bound to the water,** *unable to rise above the carnal mind—those lost in the depths of separation.*

Jesus said in **Matthew 13:47-49** *that the Kingdom of Heaven is like a net cast into the sea, gathering both good and bad fish, and at the end of the age, the good will be separated* *from the bad. The fifth age marks the* **transition from the physical world to the spiritual,** *where judgment and separation take place.*

The Sixth Day: The Creation of Man (Sixth Age – The Perfection of Humanity)

"And God said, Let us make man in our image, after our likeness…" **(Genesis 1:26)**

Man was created **after everything else** *so that* **no one could claim credit for creation except God alone.** *The sixth age represents the final phase of human history, where mankind is brought to its perfected state*—**not as separate beings, but as the full realization that man is God in a body.**

This is the age where the **truth of GIATI** *is fully realized:* **there is no "me and God"—only God as all things.** *The* **"perfect man"** *is not an individual but the full revelation that* **all things are God manifested.**

The Seventh Day: The Rest of God (The Eternal Sabbath – The Day of Eternity)

"And on the seventh day God ended his work which he had made; and he rested on the seventh day from all his work which he had made." **(Genesis 2:2)**

The seventh day is **not a single moment in time**—*it is the* **eternal state where all things return to divine perfection.** *This is the* **Day of Eternity,** *where there is no more death, no more separation, no more illusion of duality. It is the* **New Heaven and New Earth** *described in* **Revelation 21:1-4,** *where all things exist in perfect harmony with their divine source.*

This **eternal day** *is the true Sabbath—the state where God and creation are one, without labor, struggle, or division. It is not a temporary rest but the full realization of GIATI:* **God Is All There Is.**

The Eternal Perspective: There Is No Separation

Understanding creation as unfolding within the **Day of Eternity** *removes the false concept of separation between God and creation. Everything has always existed within God, moving through divine ages to bring all things to full awareness.*

Salvation is not about "getting to" eternity—it is **about awakening to the fact that you have never been outside of it.** *The journey through the ages is simply the process of* **unveiling what has always been true.**

As **Isaiah 26:3** *declares:*

"Thou wilt keep him in perfect peace, whose mind is stayed on thee: because he trusteth in thee."

To be kept in **perfect peace** *is to remain conscious of* **GIATI**—*to know that all things, all ages, all experiences, and all creation are expressions of the One Eternal Spirit. This is the revelation that ends all illusion and brings all into the* **Seventh Day—the eternal rest of God.**

The Proof of Existence Before Birth: The Spiritual Reality of GIATI

Many refuse to believe in their spiritual existence before manifesting in the physical realm. They cling to the illusion that life begins at birth, dismissing any thought of what was before. Yet, the evidence of the unseen is hidden within the very process of life itself—if only one has eyes to see.

Romans 1:19-20 declares that the **physical is the shadow of the spirit,** *meaning that the things we experience in the natural world are reflections of deeper spiritual truths. And what could be a greater sign of pre-existence than the very moment of conception?*

The Hand of God in Choosing You

Think about this: Over **300 million sperm** *race toward a single egg, but only* **one** *is chosen to come forth. Out of millions of possibilities,* **you** *were selected. Not by chance. Not by accident. But by divine purpose.*

This is not a random occurrence. It is a reflection of salvation—of being chosen before the world began. Just as you were selected in the womb to manifest in the flesh, you were already chosen in Spirit before entering the physical realm. **God called you forth.** *GIATI—the revelation that* **God Is All There Is**—*proclaims that there was never a moment when you were separate from Him.*

A Life Before Birth: The Unseen Reality

You existed in your mother's womb for **nine months,** *nourished, protected, and sustained without any effort of your own. You lived, moved, and had your being, yet you* **remember nothing of it.**

Not only that, but for nearly **three years after birth,** *you retain no memory of your early existence.* **Four entire years of your physical life are gone from your conscious awareness.**

Yet, people claim that because they do not remember their **spiritual existence before birth,** *it must not exist?*

If you cannot recall the first moments of your physical life, how much more difficult would it be to remember your spiritual life before it?

The denial of pre-existence is not based on truth but on the illusion of the carnal mind, which refuses to see beyond what is tangible. But for those with spiritual sight, the evidence is everywhere.

Chosen Before the World Began

GIATI comes not to convince but to **reveal.** *You were not born into this world by accident—you were* **sent.** *Chosen from the foundation of the world,* **called forth by the hand of God** *to manifest in this time. And yet, many reject the very truth of their own being.*

To deny your spiritual origin is to deny the One who formed you. To reject your pre-existence is to reject the eternal nature of God within you. How can you believe in a Creator and then refuse to acknowledge that you existed in Him before you came into flesh?

This is the blindness of the world—the same blindness that leads many to reject GIATI. But the truth remains, whether one accepts it or not.

The Call to Remember

GIATI is the voice crying out to those who have forgotten. It is the light shining in the darkness of the carnal mind, awakening those who were always meant to see.

You are not separate.
You were never separate.
You were chosen.
You were called forth.

And now, in this moment, **you must decide:**

Will you recognize the truth of who you are?
Or will you deny the very proof that God has placed before you?

The choice is not new. It has been placed before humanity time and time again. And now, in this cycle of divine revelation, **it has come to you once more.**

GIATI is here. The truth is revealed. And the time to see is now.

The Origin of Man: A GIATI Perspective on Evolution and Creation

The debate between evolution and creation has persisted for centuries. **Did man evolve from another species, or was man created by God?** *From the GIATI understanding—* **God Is All There Is—this question is answered from a higher perspective.**

The truth is not found in the **literal vs. symbolic** *battle of religious dogma and scientific theory.* **Both science and religion have only been looking at fragments of the whole.** *They have been searching for the origin of man* **outside of the simple truth:**

Man Is Not Separate from God

If God is all there is, then **man did not "come from" anywhere—man is an expression of the one eternal source that is God.**

- *Man is not an accident of biological evolution.*
- *Man is not a separate creation from an external being in the sky.*
- *Man is God, in expression, unfolding in form.*

Everything that exists **is God expressing itself in different degrees of awareness.** *The mistake of human reasoning is the belief that there was ever a time when man* **was not.**

God **has always been, and so has man.** *The difference is that* **man has not always been aware of what he is.**

Did Man Evolve? Or Did Man Awaken?

From the GIATI understanding, **evolution is not a process of physical transformation but of spiritual recognition.**

- *The "primitive" man was not a lesser form of human—it was* **God in a lesser awareness of itself.**
- *The so-called "evolution" of man is not man changing into something else—it is* **man awakening to what he always was.**
- *The idea that man "evolved" from lower life forms is a misunderstanding—***all forms are God in different degrees of self-recognition.**

The True Creation Story: The Awakening of Man

The real "beginning" is not a point in time—it is the **moment consciousness awakens to itself.**

This is why in Genesis, man was created in the **image and likeness of God** *(Genesis 1:27). That is not a biological statement—it is* a **spiritual fact.**

Yet in Genesis 2, man is seen **formed from the dust***—not because man was created twice, but because there is a difference between* **the reality of what man is and man's awareness of himself.**

- *The* **first man (Genesis 1:27)** *is the spiritual reality of man—one with God, whole, complete.*
- *The* **second man (Genesis 2:7)** *represents the ignorance of man—believing himself to be something separate, a body made from dust, limited in understanding.*

The "fall" of man was not **a literal event,** but **the fall into the illusion of separation.** *From the GIATI understanding,* **man is not a product of evolution—man is an eternal being who has been awakening from ignorance into full knowledge of his divinity.**

Man Has Always Been, Because God Has Always Been

If evolution is true, it is **not in the way science teaches it.**

It is not the evolution of **species,** *but the evolution of* **consciousness.**

- *The* **"caveman"** *was not a lower species—he was* **God in an early stage of self-awareness.**
- *The so-called* **missing link** *will never be found—because man did not come from another species, but from* **his own gradual awakening to his divinity.**
- *The* **animals, the plants, and all life** *are not separate from God or man—they are* expressions of the same divine essence in different forms of recognition.

Jesus did not come to save man **from sin in the way religion teaches.** *He came to* **awaken man from ignorance—to remind man of what he has always been but forgotten.**

The Reality of Oneness: The End of the Evolution Debate

The error of the evolution debate is the belief that **there was ever a time when man was not.**

- *Man did not "come from" anywhere—man has* **always been one with God.**
- *Man did not "evolve" from another species*—**man has been awakening to his own divine nature.**
- *There is no "beginning" to man, because there is* **no beginning to God.**

To ask where man came from is to ask where God came from.

And the answer is the same: **Nowhere. Because there is only One, and it has always been.**

This is what Jesus came to reveal.
This is what GIATI has come to restore.

Man's destiny is not to evolve into something greater—**man's destiny is to recognize what he already is.**

And that recognition is salvation itself.

The Illusion of Time and the Eternal Now

One of the greatest misconceptions that fuels the debate between evolution and creation is the idea that existence follows a **linear progression**—*that there was a past where man was something lesser and a future where man will become something greater.*

This is an illusion.

From the GIATI understanding, **there is only now.**

- *What appears as a past where man was "less evolved" is simply the perception of a limited mind viewing its own awakening in stages.*
- *What appears as a future where man will "fully awaken" is simply the realization that* **awakening is always now—it is not something that happens, but something that is recognized.**

Jesus did not come to push humanity toward a future salvation—He came to **wake man up to the truth that has always been.**

Why the Evolution Debate Is a Distraction

The argument over whether man evolved or was created by God is based on the false premise that man is **separate** *from God and from creation itself. But if God is all there is, then* **everything that has ever existed is already within God—it is already complete.**

- *If man believes he was once "less than God" and is "becoming" divine, he is* **still in ignorance**—*because he does not see that he was never less than God in the first place.*
- *If man believes he was created "from the dust" as something separate from God, he is* **still in ignorance**—*because he does not see that there was never a time when he was not God.*
- *If man believes his destiny is to be "perfected over time," he is* **still in ignorance**—*because he does not see that perfection is not achieved but realized.*

Jesus did not evolve into the Christ—**He recognized that He had always been one with the Father.**

This is what GIATI reveals: **There is nothing to become. There is only something to remember.**

The Death of the Old Man and the Birth of True Awareness

What the world calls "human evolution" is actually the gradual death of **the illusion of separation.**

- *The* **old man** *is not a biological ancestor but a false identity—the belief that man is separate from God, bound by flesh, time, and limitation.*
- *The* **new man** *is not a future state of evolution but the realization of what has always been—the eternal oneness of God expressed through man.*

The **caveman** *was not a less-evolved being but a* **consciousness experiencing limitation, unaware of its divine origin.** *The so-called* **modern man** *is not more evolved— he simply has more tools but still suffers from the same illusion of separateness.*

Only the man who awakens to his oneness with God is truly "new."

Why Science and Religion Both Miss the Point

Science searches for **a physical answer to a spiritual question.**
Religion preaches **a future salvation instead of present realization.**

Both fail because **both see man as something separate from God, either evolving toward divinity or being granted it through an external force.**

- *Science tells man he is a product of time.*
- *Religion tells man he will be saved in time.*
- *GIATI reveals* **there is no time—only God, now.**

Jesus did not come to create a new religion. He came to end the illusion of separation.

GIATI is not a belief system. It is the recognition that **God is all there is—right now, as you are.**

The Final Realization: There Is Only God

The argument over evolution, creation, and salvation only exists in the mind that still believes there is something other than God.

- *If you believe man was ever anything but divine, you are in ignorance.*
- *If you believe man is "becoming" something instead of* **already being** *one with God, you are in ignorance.*
- *If you believe you must be granted salvation instead of re***cognizing your eternal union with God,** *you are in ignorance.*

There is no process, no evolution, no waiting.
There is only God.
And once you see this, the debate ends—because **there was never anything to debate.**

Inside of God

"For in Him we live, and move, and have our being." — Acts 17:28

There is no "outside" of God.

This is the foundation upon which all truth rests. If God is infinite, eternal, and all-encompassing, then there is no such thing as a place, person, or thing that exists apart from Him. The moment you believe in a reality outside of God, you have entered into illusion. And that illusion has a name: **separation.**

But let us be clear: the illusion of separation is not reality. It's simply a false perception—one born from the senses, shaped by religion, and reinforced by a world that has forgotten its Source.

You were never outside of God.
You do not live independently of Him.
You are not a separate being trying to reach Him, please Him, or become like Him.
You are in Him. *Always have been.*
You are of Him. Always will be.

Just as the organs, blood, and cells within your physical body cannot step outside of you to observe or understand you from a distance, neither can you step outside of God. Everything that exists within your body—your heart, your lungs, your thoughts—is still **you.** *In the same way, you are* **within God's being.** *You are a living thought, a spiritual cell, an expression of His essence. You cannot stand apart from Him to examine Him, to judge Him, or to define Him, because* **you are inside of Him.**

And this is the deception that traps humanity in sin: the belief that you are a self-contained, separate being with your own independent life. The moment you believe that lie, you enter into darkness. You begin to think you can choose God or reject Him, approach Him or walk away from Him, live for Him or live apart from Him—as if you ever had such power. But you do not exist independently. The **only life you have is His life.** *The breath in your lungs is His breath. The light in your mind is His light. The being that you call "you" is only alive because* **He is the being in you.**

The problem is not that you are separate from God. The problem is that you **think** *you are.*

And this thinking—this unbelief in your oneness—is what **seals you in sin.**

Sin is not merely bad behavior. Sin is a state of ignorance. It is the condition of spiritual blindness that causes a person to believe in a "self" apart from God. It is the lie of separation. And all the so-called sins of the flesh are merely symptoms of that deeper root.

The religious mind teaches you that sin is about actions—what you do or don't do. But the awakened Spirit understands: sin is about **identity.** *It's about the false belief that you are something other than what God is. And righteousness is not the reward for moral performance. It is the* **recognition** *that there is* **nothing else but God***—and that you live because He is your life.*

So long as a person sees their body as their own, their thoughts as their own, and their will as separate, they remain trapped in the illusion. They may speak of God. They may seek God. But they are like a wave trying to find the ocean, forgetting that it is already within it. They are like a breath searching for air, unaware it is already surrounded by it. The truth is not far off. The truth is not complicated. The truth is this: **you are in God, and God is in you.**

> *There is nothing that is not Him.*
> *Not your body. Not your breath. Not your being.*
> *Your very existence is proof of God's presence.*

But until that truth is **believed,** *you remain in sin—not because God has condemned you, but because you have not accepted the truth of who you are. This is why Jesus said, "Unless you believe that I am He, you will die in your sin." The belief He spoke of was not belief in His name or in a historical event—it was belief in the truth He came to reveal:* **I AM is in you. And you are in Him.**

That is salvation. Not escaping this world, but awakening to the truth **within it.** *Not waiting to be with God later, but recognizing that you have never been without Him.*

To be saved is to see. To be lost is to remain blind. And the only thing separating the two is belief.

> *There is no distance between you and God. There never has been. You are not trying to get to Him. You are not becoming like Him.*
> **You are in Him.**
> *And when you know this—not with your mind, but with your Spirit—you will be free.*
> *Free from sin.*
> *Free from guilt.*
> *Free from the illusion of separation.*

The Sanctuary Within

> *To be* **in God** *means He is not only the source of your life, but the totality of your existence—***inside and out.**
> *He is your body. He is your Spirit.*
> *He is the breath in your lungs and the form your soul wears.*
> *There is no layer of your being that is not infused with His presence.*

This is the divine mystery revealed through Moses and the giving of the law. When the law was written on tablets of stone, it was not meant to be external instruction—it was a **shadow** *of a deeper truth. God was declaring something far more profound:* **"I have written Myself into you."**

> *The stone tablets were not simply objects. They were a prophetic image of the* **human vessel***—and the writing was a picture of God's own essence being etched into every part of your being.*
> *You are not just a recipient of the law.*
> *You are the law—because you are of God.*

This is what religion cannot grasp. It treats God's commands as something imposed from the outside. But the truth is: what God speaks, He speaks from within. When He says "be holy," He is awakening what's already yours. When He calls you righteous, He is not demanding performance—He is declaring identity.

Eve's Transgression: The Illusion of Separation

> *To understand how separation deceives, we must go back to the garden.*
> *Adam was not created alone. He was created as a* **sanctuary***—a full image of God. When the command was given not to eat from the tree of the knowledge of good and evil,* **Eve was still inside of him.** *She had not yet been revealed as a separate being. She was part of his essence, his expression, his inner self.*

That means the law was not given to Adam alone, but to **what was in Adam***—to the full image of man, male and female, as one.*

But when Eve was taken **out** *of Adam, the illusion of* **two** *emerged. And in that moment, the vulnerability of transgression appeared. Eve didn't sin because she was a woman. She transgressed because the* **oneness** *was obscured. What was once unified now appeared divided. And from that division came deception.*

> *By eating of the fruit, Eve embodied the lie of separation:*
> *"I can choose apart from the one I came from."*

But Adam did not transgress. Not in the same way. Because when he took the fruit from Eve, he was not acting in deception—he was acting as a type of **Christ,** *entering into her condition to become one with her again. This is why Scripture says* **"Adam was not deceived" (1 Timothy 2:14).** *He knew what he was doing. And through him, salvation would come—not just by obedience to law, but through* **union.**

Salvation Through Union

The curse of separation could only be reversed through oneness.

So Eve, who represented the separated self, would now be saved—not by behavior, but by **childbearing** *(1 Timothy 2:15). This is not merely about physical reproduction. It is a revelation of* **spiritual reunion.**

To bear fruit, she would have to be joined again to Adam. To bring forth life, she would have to be **reunited with the one from whom she came.**

In this picture, Adam becomes the image of God—and Eve the image of humanity. And salvation is seen as a return to **union,** *a restoration of the sanctuary.*

This is God's pleasure: **to reproduce Himself.**

To see the seed of His Spirit awaken in the body of man. To bring forth children of oneness who live, move, and have their being **in Him**—*not in theory, but in truth.*

And when a soul denies its oneness with God, it's not merely denying a teaching. It's denying its origin. It's rejecting its parents. It's turning from the one who **breathed into its nostrils,** *formed its limbs, and wrote His nature across every cell. It is the ultimate rebellion: to say, "I am my own," when you are not. There is no life in separation—only deception and death.*

The Return of the Sanctuary

Now, through the Holy Spirit, the sanctuary is restored. God no longer writes on stone. He writes on hearts. He no longer hides behind veils. He lives within **flesh and blood.**

Just as Eve was returned to Adam in union through childbearing, so too are we returned to God in Spirit through the **birth of the Son within us**—*the Christ awakened in human form.*

> *This is the mystery of godliness: not that we go to heaven, but that* **heaven is born in us.**
> *And this only happens through the recognition of truth:*
> **"I and my Father are one."**
> *There is no other gospel.*
>
> *God's desire is to fill every part of you with Himself—to see the knowledge of oneness cover the earth as the waters cover the sea. And He will not stop until every child He formed remembers:*
> **"I am in Him. And He is in me. There is nothing else."**
>
> *This is the restoration of Eden.*
> *This is GIATI:* **God Is All There Is.**

Beyond the Veil of Form

One of the most deceptive things about being inside of God is the way form tricks the senses.

Your body, with its boundaries and functions, appears to be a self-contained vessel. Your thoughts seem to arise from within a personal space that feels isolated from others. You move through the world as if you're apart from everything else. This experience creates the illusion of autonomy—of a self with its own will, power, and purpose. But this illusion is the veil.

What you call "your life" is not a stand-alone flame, but a spark within **the one eternal fire.** *Your body is not a separate structure, but a living movement within the one divine Being. And your thoughts—though they feel private—are echoes within the vastness of the Mind of God.*

It is only from within **God's body** *that your existence has any meaning.*

The mystery of oneness is not that you become one with God, but that you realize **you always were.** *You are not climbing into Him—you are awakening within Him. And even the idea of being "close" to God is based on a false premise. Closeness still assumes two things: God and you. But the truth is not closeness—it is* **identity.**

> *You are not merely near to God.*
> *You are* **of God.**
> *Not in proximity—but in* **essence.**

The Myth of Free Will

This truth also shatters the illusion of what many call "free will." People believe they are making independent decisions as autonomous agents—but that is only because they think they are separate from the Source of their being. The concept of free will assumes an "I" apart from God—a self that can choose independently. But what is this "I," if not a thought **within** *the One?*

You are not the origin of your thoughts, desires, or movements. You are the **expression** of God's own will moving through a form that He fashioned for Himself. If there were a will that truly existed apart from Him, it would be something **not-God**—but such a thing cannot be.

The only "will" that leads to life is the surrender of selfhood to the reality of **oneness.** *And in that surrender, the truth becomes clear: There was never a separate "you" to surrender in the first place. There was only the dream of being separate—now broken by the light of truth.*

Judgment and the Self That God Does Not Know

Here's something even deeper: God can only recognize **Himself.**

In the final reckoning, anything that presents itself as separate from Him—anything that claims an "I" apart from "I AM"—is judged, not because it was evil, but because it was **not Him.** *That false self—constructed by the illusion of separation—is rejected like a kidney with the wrong blood type. The body of God cannot accept what is* **not of His own essence.**

This is not harsh. It is just reality. God doesn't reject out of anger. He rejects what is not **true.**

And what is not true cannot enter the Kingdom, because the Kingdom is made of **truth alone.**

So the choice is not between being good or bad.

It is between **being God's Self, or claiming to be your own.** *To say "I am not He" is to die in your sin—not because God punishes you, but because you have chosen a self that* **does not exist in Him.**

The Simplicity of Truth

This may all sound mystical, but in reality, it is the **simplest truth of all.** *Everything else—the complexity of religious systems, the language of morality, the endless debate between doctrines—is man's attempt to explain what is already clear:*

You are in God. And God is in you. There is nothing else.

This is the Gospel.
This is the mystery.
This is the truth:
GIATI. God Is All There Is.

PART II
THE FALL AND THE LOST SPIRIT

Chapter 5

The War in Heaven

The idea of a "war in heaven" is often viewed in a literal, violent sense. However, the true nature of this conflict is spiritual and ideological—an ideological war between the truth of oneness with God and the deception of separateness. The war in heaven did not involve weapons or physical combat but revolved around the belief that the created beings could exist independently of their Creator. This chapter explores the roots of this spiritual war, the rebellion that ensued, and the consequences that followed: the casting out of the rebellious spirits into the physical realm, which gave birth to the concept of "the lost spirit."

The Spiritual War of Ideology: Separation vs. Oneness with God

The true nature of the war in heaven is rooted in an ideological battle between the belief in separation from God and the truth of oneness with God. God, in His essence, is indivisible and complete, and all things were created through Him and for Him. However, the created beings, specifically the angels, had free will and the capacity to choose. Some, instead of accepting the oneness and unity with God, chose to believe in their own self-existence, thereby sowing the seeds of rebellion.

Isaiah 14:12-14 offers a glimpse into the mindset of the rebellious spirits, particularly Lucifer, who desired to elevate himself above God:

"How art thou fallen from heaven, O Lucifer, son of the morning! how art thou cut down to the ground, which didst weaken the nations! For thou hast said in thine heart, I will ascend into heaven, I will exalt my throne above the stars of God: I will sit also upon the mount of the congregation, in the sides of the north: I will ascend above the heights of the clouds; I will be like the most High." (Isaiah 14:12-14)

Lucifer's fall began with his desire for independence from God, to "be like the most High." This was not an attempt to overthrow God through power, but a rejection of the truth that all things—including himself—were an expression of God. His belief in his separateness from God became the foundation for the war in heaven. The central issue was not physical might, but the deep ideological divide between accepting the unity of God and desiring self-exaltation.

This same mindset spread among a group of angels, who, like Lucifer, chose to believe that they could exist outside of God. Revelation 12:7-9 describes the consequences of this rebellion:

"And there was war in heaven: Michael and his angels fought against the dragon; and the dragon fought and his angels, And prevailed not; neither was their place found any more in heaven. And the great dragon was cast out, that old serpent, called the Devil, and Satan, which deceiveth the whole world: he was cast out into the earth, and his angels were cast out with him." (Revelation 12:7-9)

The war was not fought with physical weapons, but with words and ideas. The angels who followed Lucifer in his rebellion had chosen to believe in the lie of separateness, rejecting the truth that they were an extension of God's will. As a result, they were cast out of heaven and into the earth, losing their place in the presence of God.

In John chapter 6. The message Jesus gave in this scripture is a powerful example of separating those who are spiritually minded from those who are carnally minded. When Jesus told the people to eat His flesh and drink His blood, it was not a literal command but a spiritual teaching. However, because many were focused on their carnal understanding, they were unable to grasp His true meaning.

At this point, Jesus had a large following because of the healings and miracles He had performed. But He knew His purpose—to be crucified—required that only those who truly believed in Him spiritually would remain. By presenting this teaching, Jesus tested their faith and understanding.

For those who were spiritually minded, His words meant that they needed to fully believe in Him, accept Him, and allow His Spirit to dwell in them. Just as physical food and drink become part of your body when consumed, spiritually, by "eating His flesh and drinking His blood," His Spirit would become part of them and they would become one with Him.

Jesus clarified this when He said, *"It is the spirit that quickeneth; the flesh profiteth nothing: the words that I speak unto you, they are spirit, and they are life."* He made it clear that He was speaking spiritually, not physically. Yet many who were carnally minded found this to be a "hard saying" and walked away, revealing their inability to move beyond their earthly understanding.

In the earlier book *BrainTight,* the message was spoken to people who were still carnal, babes in Christ, unable to fully grasp the deeper spiritual truths. That book was like feeding you milk instead of meat because the deeper understanding would have been too much to bear. Even now, there are those who remain unready, but *GIATI* is here to bring the truth necessary for salvation.

This truth aligns with what Paul wrote in *1 Corinthians 3:1-4.* Paul explained that because people were carnal, there was envying, strife, and division among them. These signs of carnality persist today, not only in the actions and attitudes of people but in the way they elevate others above God. The scripture says, *"For while one saith, I am of Paul; and another, I am of Apollos; are ye not carnal?"* This reveals how people idolize physical leaders—whether it's pastors, bishops, or anyone else held in high esteem—for their appearance, style, or words. This mindset is rooted in carnality, a focus on external things rather than the Spirit within.

GIATI challenges this carnal mindset. The purpose of GIATI is to shift your focus from external sources of guidance to the Holy Spirit that is already within you. The Spirit of God dwells in you, and it is through this Spirit—not through allegiance to human leaders—that you find the truth and salvation. GIATI reveals that worshiping or following physical men is the sign of a carnal mind. Are you yet carnal if you look to someone outside yourself when the Holy Spirit is already within you?

This is the knowledge GIATI is here to bring. It is time to mature spiritually, to move beyond milk and take hold of the meat of the Word. The Holy Spirit, which is God expressed as you, is what you should follow, trust, and allow to guide you. Carnality creates division, strife, and confusion, but the Spirit brings unity, peace, and truth.

GIATI's purpose is to lead you to this realization: that God is all there is, and His Spirit is within you. By understanding and embracing this truth, you can shed the carnality of the past and walk in the fullness of spiritual maturity. The time for milk is over—GIATI is here to bring you the meat of the Spirit, the truth that sets you free.

When you start off wrong, you end up wrong. This truth speaks directly to the spiritual journey of humanity. Many people mistakenly believe their beginning is tied to their physical birth date, overlooking the eternal reality of their existence. Before you were manifested in a physical body, you existed in heaven as a spirit being. However, in that existence, you were ignorant of God and His true nature. This ignorance led to a separation from God, not because He was distant, but because you could not comprehend Him.

Now, in this earthly existence, you have one more chance to right the wrong of that initial ignorance. Revelation 22:11 says, *"He that is unjust, let him be unjust still: and he which is filthy, let him be filthy still: and he that is righteous, let him be righteous still: and he that is holy, let him be holy still."* This verse reveals the ultimate truth: without a transformation, without an exchange of your ignorant spirit for the Holy Spirit, you remain what you were—unjust, filthy, and separated from God. Only the Holy Spirit, who *is holy and will always be holy,* can make you righteous and holy, transforming you into a new creature.

The Importance of Starting Right

Starting off wrong means relying on your own understanding, identifying with your physical self, and clinging to a limited, earthly perspective. When you fail to see that you were created to be one with God, you remain in ignorance, disconnected from your true purpose. But by acknowledging and receiving the Holy Spirit, you are no longer the same ignorant spirit being you were before. You are transformed into a new creation—one with God, holy, and saved before the foundation of the world.

This exchange is critical. Without it, the unjust remain unjust, the filthy remain filthy, and those who begin in ignorance will end in ignorance. But those who allow the Holy Spirit to dwell in them will walk in righteousness and holiness for eternity. The Holy Spirit is the one who was holy in the beginning and will always be holy. By becoming one with Him, you step into the fullness of who you were always meant to be—a reflection of God Himself.

The choice is yours: remain as you were, starting and ending wrong, or embrace the Holy Spirit and step into the eternal truth of your oneness with God.

Divine Oneness

Galatians 3:28 reveals the spiritual reality of heaven and the unity found in Christ Jesus. This scripture declares that there is *"neither Jew nor Greek, bond nor free, male nor female: for ye are all one in Christ Jesus."* It speaks to the state of divine oneness, where there is no division, contradiction, or opposition to God.

In heaven, the earthly distinctions that often separate us—race, nationality, status, or gender—do not exist. These differences are part of the carnal world, born from the limited perceptions of the physical realm. However, in Christ, all these barriers are dissolved. This is because the Holy Spirit does not recognize individuals as separate or distinct based on external attributes. Instead, it sees all as one, unified in God's Spirit.

As you grow in the Holy Spirit, this state of unity begins to manifest in your mind and spirit. You start to see beyond the illusions of race, color, creed, and gender. You no longer identify yourself or others by these earthly labels but by the Spirit of God within. This is the transformation that takes place as you align with the truth of GIATI—that *God Is All There Is.* In this awareness, contention and division fade away because the Holy Spirit does not dwell in conflict or opposition. There is no antithesis to God because His Spirit is one, perfect, and complete.

To truly live in this oneness, your perspective must shift. You must see yourself and others not as separate beings but as expressions of the same Spirit. This is the reality of heaven, and it is the state of mind you grow into as the Holy Spirit becomes fully expressed in and as you. Galatians 3:28 calls us to this higher understanding, reminding us that in Christ, we are one—unified, eternal, and without division.

GIATI carries on this same purpose today. GIATI challenges readers and followers to move beyond their carnal understanding of the world and themselves. The message of GIATI is that God is within you, and to truly live spiritually, you must accept this truth. Just as Jesus' teaching tested His followers' willingness to let go of their carnal thinking, GIATI pushes you to recognize and embrace the Spirit of God as your true identity. Only by doing so can you dwell in Him and have His Spirit dwell in you, leading to eternal life.

This is a call to shift your perception, to let go of your earthly way of thinking, and to fully embrace the Spirit that God has placed within you. Just as some walked away from Jesus' teachings, there will be those who struggle with GIATI's message. But for those who are spiritually minded, the reward is unity with God and the eternal life He promises.

The Devil and the Rebellious Angels: How Ignorance Created Conflict

The heart of the rebellion was ignorance—ignorance of the truth of God's unity with all creation. Satan, whose name means "the accuser," was not just a force of evil, but the embodiment of that ignorance. His rebellion was not one of violence, but of thought—a misunderstanding of his true nature and the nature of God. As the first to rebel, Satan became the leader of the rebellious angels, leading them into the same ignorance.

The Bible describes the devil as a deceiver, whose primary tactic is to create confusion and division by promoting false ideologies. The apostle Paul warns of the consequences of believing such lies in 2 Corinthians 11:14-15:

"And no marvel; for Satan himself is transformed into an angel of light. Therefore it is no great thing if his ministers also be transformed as the ministers of righteousness; whose end shall be according to their works." (2 Corinthians 11:14-15)

Satan and his angels, in their ignorance, became "angels of light" in their own eyes, deceiving others into thinking that there was a path to righteousness outside of God's unity. The lies they propagated were based on the belief that they could be righteous apart from God—that they could exist independently, separate from the divine unity.

This ignorance—the belief in the separateness of the self from God—was the root of the conflict. The angels who followed Lucifer in his rebellion embraced this false belief, not realizing that their true identity was found only in God. By refusing to acknowledge their unity with God, they plunged themselves into darkness, severing their connection with the source of all life.

The Casting Out: Dark Spirits Entering the Physical Realm

As a result of this rebellion, the devil and his angels were cast out of heaven and into the earth. The physical world became the realm of these rebellious spirits. But the casting out was not a mere geographical relocation; it was a transition from spiritual existence to physical existence. These fallen spirits, now trapped in the physical realm, were bound by the limitations of time, space, and matter. This separation from the spiritual realm signified their "fall" into ignorance and darkness.

Jesus, in Luke 10:18, refers to this fall:

"And he said unto them, I beheld Satan as lightning fall from heaven." (Luke 10:18)

This fall signifies not only a loss of spiritual position but a shift from spiritual truth to the embrace of ignorance. The rebellion, led by Satan and his followers, resulted in their expulsion from the realm of spiritual clarity and into the realm of physical limitation.

In the physical realm, these rebellious spirits continued their work of deception, perpetuating the lie of separateness from God. Humanity, made in the image of God, was also susceptible to this deception. The result of this ideological war—the belief in separateness—has affected every human being. The casting out of these dark spirits into the physical realm allowed them to influence humanity, perpetuating the false belief that we are separate from God.

The fall of Lucifer and the rebellious angels into the earth represents the introduction of spiritual darkness into the world. It is a darkness that blinds humanity to the truth of our oneness with God. These fallen spirits have since sought to deceive humanity, keeping us trapped in the illusion that we are independent of God.

This is the origin of the "lost spirit"—the spirit that believes in its separateness from God, unaware that it is, in truth, an expression of the divine. As these dark spirits entered the physical realm, they began to infect human consciousness with the same lie they had embraced: that we are separate from God, that we can exist outside of Him. This belief became the foundation for all human suffering, confusion, and sin.

Showing Forth His Power

Romans 9:21-23 speaks to the absolute authority of God as the Creator, the potter who shapes each vessel according to His will. "Hath not the potter power over the clay, of the same lump to make one vessel unto honour, and another unto dishonour?" This scripture reveals a profound truth—both the vessel of honor and the vessel of dishonor come from the same lump of clay. They are formed from the same source and substance, which is God Himself. Yet, it is He who determines their purpose, fashioning some as vessels of mercy and others as vessels fitted for destruction.

This revelation often leads to a question: Why would God create some to recognize their oneness with Him while allowing others to deny it? The answer lies in the very nature of His power and purpose. God, knowing He is all there is, demonstrates His power not just in creation but in the unfolding of divine will. Just as a team in intramural sports may claim superiority while only competing against itself, true greatness is revealed only through opposition. It is only when tested against the best that one can prove their strength. In the same way, God manifests His power by allowing some to see their oneness with Him while others remain blind to it. Without this contrast, one could claim that God is not truly powerful.

Yet, what makes this display of divine power even more extraordinary is that it is not merely physical. Though His power is evident in nature, in disasters and the forces of the world, His greatest demonstration of power is spiritual. It is seen in His ability to be everything and everyone, to open the eyes of some while allowing others to remain in darkness. This is the essence of divine sovereignty—the choosing of vessels, the revealing of truth to some and withholding it from others.

In the end, when all choices have been made, and each vessel has fulfilled its purpose, the distinction will be undeniable. Those who have accepted His Spirit, who have recognized their oneness with Him, will be revealed as the vessels of honor. They are the ones who will dwell in Him for eternity, their reward secured. But those who have rejected His Spirit, who have denied their oneness with Him, will find themselves on the other side—vessels of dishonor, their fate sealed. By that time, it will be too late to change sides, too late to reconsider. The finality of this truth will stand as the ultimate demonstration of God's power—the power to reveal, the power to conceal, and the power to determine the eternal destiny of all things.

The Inevitable Divide

Matthew 10:34-39 is often misunderstood as a call to division for the sake of conflict, but in reality, it is about the inevitable divide between those who accept the truth of their divine oneness with God and those who reject it. Jesus made it clear that His coming would not bring the kind of peace the world expects but rather a sword—the dividing line between those who walk in spiritual awareness and those who cling to their sense of self apart from God.

**"Think not that I am come to send peace on earth:
I came not to send peace, but a sword."**

This sword represents the cutting away of false identity, the severing of the illusion that man is separate from God. Some will recognize and accept that their spirit is one with the Father, while others—perhaps even within the same household—will reject it. This is what Jesus meant when He spoke of setting a man against his father, a daughter against her mother, and a man's enemies being within his own household. The battle is not physical but spiritual—a battle of perception.

Just like the sword, this scripture makes it clear that there is no middle ground. The sword of truth is drawn, and no one can straddle both sides. Those who remain lukewarm—undecided, unwilling to fully embrace oneness, yet not outright rejecting it—will be cast out, because indecision is still a rejection of truth.

GIATI is the Sword

Now, the sword has come again, and it demands a choice. The message that was given through Jesus is the same message being delivered now through GIATI: Recognize the Spirit of God as your true identity or remain in the illusion of separation.

Those who choose to hold on to their own independent identity, believing "This is my spirit, separate from God," will find themselves in conflict with those who recognize, "I and my Father are one." (John 10:30) This is why Jesus said:

**"He that loveth father or mother more than me is not worthy of me:
and he that loveth son or daughter more than me is not worthy of me."**

This does not mean one should not love their family, but rather, if one's attachment to relationships, traditions, or personal identity takes precedence over recognizing oneness with God, they are not truly following Christ.

"And he that taketh not his cross, and followeth after me, is not worthy of me."

Taking up the cross is not about physical suffering but a shift in mindset. It is the willingness to let go of the false self—the separate self—and embrace the truth that has been from the beginning. It is the dying of the illusion and the resurrection into the awareness of unity with God. This is why Jesus said:

**"He that findeth his life shall lose it:
and he that loseth his life for my sake shall find it."**

The "life" people try to find is the one built on ego, the idea of self apart from God. Those who hold on to this false life will ultimately lose everything because it is temporary and an illusion. But those who let go of this false self and embrace their true identity in God will find eternal life—not as something distant, but as a present reality.

This scripture is not about destruction but revelation. It reveals that division will naturally come when truth is presented because not everyone will receive it. Some will cling to the old way of thinking, while others will awaken. The question remains: Which side of the sword will one stand on?

It is striking that the very message Jesus came to deliver is the same message being presented now through GIATI, yet people overlook it as if it holds no weight. This is hypocrisy. Either people do not truly understand what Jesus represents, or many are simply pretending to believe in something they do not even comprehend.

If someone were to post, "Jesus is watching over you," it would garner thousands of likes. Why? Because statements like that place Jesus outside of the individual, separate from them, making them feel comforted without requiring accountability. It allows people to continue in their ways without confronting the truth about themselves. But Jesus never made himself the focus. He always spoke about oneness with the Father, emphasizing that humanity was meant to share in that same unity.

"I and my Father are one." (John 10:30)

When Jesus declared this truth, the religious leaders accused Him of blasphemy, not understanding the true nature of blasphemy itself. Blasphemy is not merely speaking irreverently—it is misrepresenting the Holy Spirit. And the greatest misrepresentation is rejecting the Spirit of God within, failing to recognize that the same Spirit in Jesus is the Spirit meant to dwell in all. By denying this, people are unknowingly guilty of the very sin they accuse others of.

"Verily I say unto you, All sins shall be forgiven unto the sons of men, and blasphemies wherewith soever they shall blaspheme: But he that shall blaspheme against the Holy Ghost hath never forgiveness, but is in danger of eternal damnation." (Mark 3:28-29)

It is astonishing to witness people reject the Holy Spirit—the same Spirit that was in Jesus—the very glory He came to share. Jesus did not come merely to be admired but to reveal that mankind is meant to partake in the same divine nature. Yet, many remain in sin because they claim their spirit as their own, believing they possess a spirit separate from God rather than acknowledging that all spirit is one with the Father.

Consider this: Imagine driving a broken-down Pinto, a car that fails you every time you take it out on the road. Now, God steps in and says, "Let go of that Pinto. Take what I am offering—My Spirit—the latest Rolls-Royce Phantom, a vehicle of perfection that will never fail you." Yet, instead of accepting the perfect, eternal gift, many choose to cling to the Pinto, unwilling to surrender their illusion of independence from God.

What God offers is eternal, yet people reject it for something temporary, something destined to fail.

"For the wages of sin is death; but the gift of God is eternal life through Jesus Christ our Lord." (Romans 6:23)

This rejection is not a matter of mere ignorance—it is spiritual blindness, a refusal to see the truth even when it is laid plainly before them. It is like a child warned by a parent not to play with fire. But instead of heeding the warning, the child insists on touching the flame and only learns through suffering the consequences. The tragedy is that in this case, waiting to find out could be too late. Tomorrow is not promised, and every moment of rejection seals one's fate further.

The "life" people try to find is the one built on ego, the idea of self apart from God. Those who hold on to this false life will ultimately lose everything because it is temporary and an illusion. But those who let go of this false self and embrace their true identity in God will find eternal life—not as something distant, but as a present reality.

"Boast not thyself of tomorrow; for thou knowest not what a day may bring forth." (Proverbs 27:1)

This scripture is not about destruction but revelation. This is the call to wake up. The time for excuses is over. The truth is being presented clearly, without riddles or parables. Some will cling to the old way of thinking, while others will awaken. The question is—will it be received, or will history repeat itself as the world once again rejects the very Spirit sent to save it?

The Two Trees: The Illusion of Separation and the Reality of Life

In the center of the Garden of Eden, two trees stood: **the Tree of Life and the Tree of the Knowledge of Good and Evil.** *These trees were not physical objects but representations of* **two states of consciousness, two ways of seeing existence.**

The Tree of the Knowledge of Good and Evil: The Birth of Duality

When Eve ate from the Tree of the Knowledge of Good and Evil, she did not simply disobey a command—**she stepped into a false perception of reality.**

This tree represents **duality—the illusion of separation from God.**

- *It is the belief in opposites: good and evil, light and dark, right and wrong, self and other.*
- *It is the consciousness that sees itself as* **something other than God,** *constantly weighing and judging experiences as separate forces instead of one unified existence.*
- *It is the mind caught in fragmentation, believing that there is something outside of God to fear, to resist, or to attain.*

To eat from this tree is to **choose blindness,** *to live in the illusion that there is a self apart from God that must struggle between right and wrong instead of realizing that* **God is all there is** *and no separation ever existed.*

This is why **spiritual death** *followed. Not because God punished man, but because man's consciousness became* **veiled in ignorance.** *Man did not lose God—he lost the ability to recognize that he had never been apart from Him.*

The Tree of Life: The Awareness of Oneness

The Tree of Life represents **the eternal truth that God is all there is.**

To eat from this tree is to **see reality as it is—to recognize the illusion of duality and awaken to oneness with God.**

- *It is the consciousness that knows there is no separation between self and God, no division between good and evil, because* **all is God expressed in different forms.**
- *It is the direct realization that* **life is not something given, but something God IS.**
- *It is freedom from judgment, from struggle, from the false belief that you must "earn" your way back to God—because you were never apart from Him to begin with.*

This tree represents **eternal life,** *not because it grants immortality in a future sense, but because it is the recognition that* **life has never been anything but God, and God does not die.**

Choosing a Tree: The State of Consciousness Determines Reality

The choice between these two trees is not a one-time event in history—it is a **daily choice of perception.**

- *Those who eat from the Tree of the Knowledge of Good and Evil live in* **fear, judgment, and self-righteousness,** *trying to make themselves right with God through their own efforts, unaware that their very attempt keeps them blind.*
- *Those who eat from the Tree of Life live in* **peace, wholeness, and divine knowing,** *because they understand there is no need to struggle—God is all, and they are in Him as He is in them.*

One tree leads to **spiritual blindness,** *keeping man trapped in his own false perception of separation.*

The other tree leads to **spiritual vision,** *awakening man to the truth that* **God is all there is.**

Jesus, the Tree of Life, and the Restoration of Oneness

Jesus came to restore man to the Tree of Life, not by changing anything external, but by **opening the eyes of those trapped in the illusion of separation.**

- *He did not come to teach morality—He came to* **end duality** *by revealing the kingdom of God within.*
- *He did not come to condemn sinners—He came to awaken them to the reality that* **sin is not an action, but a state of blindness to oneness.**
- *He did not come to start a religion—He came to restore* **direct awareness of God in all things.**

This is why He said, **"I am the way, the truth, and the life."** *(John 14:6)*

To follow Him is not to adhere to rules, but to **step into the same consciousness of oneness with God***—to eat from the Tree of Life and leave the illusion of separation behind.*

GIATI: The Return to the Tree of Life

GIATI is not a doctrine, not a belief system, but **the very awareness that restores man to the Tree of Life.**

- *It removes the illusion of a separate self, revealing that there is only* **God expressing as you.**

- *It dissolves the false perception of good versus evil, replacing it with the recognition that* **all things are within God and serve His purpose.**
- *It ends the cycle of struggle, fear, and striving for salvation by revealing that* **God is already all in all—right now.**

Man never truly left the Garden—he simply **closed his eyes to it.**
*The Tree of Life was never taken away—***it has always been within.**
To eat from it is not to do anything **new**, *but to remember what has always been:*

The Depth of the Two Trees: Beyond the Surface of the Story

The significance of the Tree of Life and the Tree of the Knowledge of Good and Evil goes beyond just a choice in the Garden—it defines the very nature of **human perception and consciousness.** *These two trees are not merely symbols of reward and punishment but* **represent the way in which reality is experienced.**

The Tree of the Knowledge of Good and Evil: The False Self and the Illusion of Autonomy

To eat from this tree is to step into a mindset of **division***—to believe in a world where there is "me" and "God" as two separate things. This division does not actually exist, but* **once it is accepted as reality, it shapes every experience thereafter.**

- The moment one sees themselves as apart from God, the concept of **right and wrong, good and evil, becomes the primary focus** rather than the awareness of oneness.
- The mind begins to categorize everything: **"This is holy, this is unholy. This is righteous, this is sinful. This is good, this is bad."** This leads to a world of **conflict, judgment, and fear** rather than harmony.
- Instead of flowing as God, ma**n attempts to define and control his relationship with God,** creating systems, rules, and doctrines—all built on the illusion that there is something to earn or something to fix.

This is why the moment Adam and Eve ate from the tree, they **felt naked and hid from God** *(Genesis 3:7-8). The nakedness was not new—it had always been there—but now they* **perceived themselves differently.** *The only thing that changed was their own awareness of themselves* **as separate beings, disconnected from their Source.**

*Once man perceives himself as separate, he creates a false self—a***n identity that must protect itself, justify itself, and seek approval.** *It is from this mindset that all suffering, fear, and spiritual blindness arise.*

The Tree of Life: The Reality of Divine Oneness

Eating from the Tree of Life is not just an alternative choice—it is **the restoration of original awareness.**

- *This tree represents* **pure being, oneness with God, and the knowing that all is within the divine.**
- *There is no struggle, no fear of judgment, no anxiety about doing enough or being enough—because* **God is all there is, and there is nothing outside of Him to fear.**
- *Instead of defining oneself by external conditions—whether good or bad—one simply* **exists in divine flow, knowing that all things are an expression of God.**

This is why Jesus came, not just to **fix sin** *as religion teaches, but to* **awaken humanity from the illusion of separation.**

The Two Trees as Two States of Consciousness

It is important to understand that these two trees were never about **physical fruit***—they were about* **two fundamental ways of seeing and experiencing life.**

1. **The Tree of the Knowledge of Good and Evil is the consciousness of separation.**
    - *It makes man see himself as a separate entity trying to earn his way back to God.*
    - *It leads to* **judgment, division, fear, and the creation of religious systems that try to define what is acceptable to God.**
    - *It creates a world where people strive, but never attain, because they are working from the false premise that they are apart from God.*
2. **The Tree of Life is the consciousness of oneness.**
    - *It sees only God—nothing else.*
    - *It does not judge or condemn, because it knows there is nothing outside of God to judge.*
    - *It does not struggle to be saved, because it understands that salvation is not something to be attained but something to* **awaken to.**

How This Choice Manifests in Everyday Life

These two trees are not ancient relics of a past story—they are present choices that every person makes **right now.**

- *When you feel unworthy and believe you must work to prove yourself to God, you are eating from the* **Tree of the Knowledge of Good and Evil.**

- *When you judge yourself or others based on religious standards, morality, or external behavior, you are eating from the* **Tree of the Knowledge of Good and Evil.**
- *When you live in fear of punishment or seek to win God's approval, you are eating from the* **Tree of the Knowledge of Good and Evil.**

But when you:

- **Rest in the knowing that you and God are one,** *without separation or distance...*
- **See beyond duality,** *recognizing that all things serve their divine purpose...*
- **Understand that salvation is simply waking up from the illusion of separation...**
- *You are eating from the* **Tree of Life.**

Jesus: The Embodiment of the Tree of Life

Jesus did not come to introduce **a new religion or a new moral system.** *He came to* **undo the lie of the Tree of the Knowledge of Good and Evil** *and restore man's awareness to the Tree of Life.*

- *He did not teach separation—He taught oneness:* **"I and my Father are one." (John 10:30)**
- *He did not teach striving—He taught rest:* **"Come unto me, all you who are weary, and I will give you rest." (Matthew 11:28)**
- *He did not teach judgment—He taught forgiveness and non-resistance:* **"Neither do I condemn you." (John 8:11)**

Jesus was the **Tree of Life in bodily form,** *demonstrating how man should live—not by striving, but by* **being one with God in consciousness.**

GIATI: Returning to the Tree of Life

GIATI is not a belief system—it is the **end of false belief.**

It is the awareness that:

- *You have never been separate from God.*
- *Sin is not a list of actions—it is the blindness to your own divinity.*
- *Salvation is not something to achieve—it is the awareness of what has always been true.*

The message of GIATI is not about trying to be "good" or "righteous." It is about **realizing that there is only one reality—God, expressed in and as everything.**

The Ultimate Realization: You Never Left the Garden

The story of Adam and Eve seems to end in tragedy, but the truth is **that they never actually left the Garden—only their perception changed.**

God never cast man away—man cast himself away **in his own mind** *by believing in separation. The moment man sees through the illusion and realizes* **GIATI—God Is All There Is**—*he is restored to the Tree of Life.*

This is the truth that sets humanity free:

You were never lost, never distant, never separated. There is only God, and you are Him expressed.

God is all there is.

The Bible as the Greatest Mystery of All Time

The Bible is structured as a divine mystery, with hidden truths that can only be fully understood by those who have the Holy Spirit. Throughout scripture, we see multiple mysteries that God has concealed, only to reveal them in His appointed time. These mysteries include:

- **The Mystery of Godliness (1 Timothy 3:16)** – *The hidden truth of God manifesting in the flesh.*
- **The Mystery of Iniquity (2 Thessalonians 2:7)** – *The hidden force of lawlessness at work.*
- **The Mystery of Christ in You (Colossians 1:26-27)** – *The revelation of God's presence within His people.*

Just like a great mystery novel, the Bible presents clues, misdirects, and revelations. Many attempt to solve it with their own intellect, but without the Spirit of God, they fail to grasp the full picture. People argue over doctrine, thinking they've unraveled the mystery—whether it's "just accept Jesus" or "just follow the law"—but the true mystery is deeper than surface-level religious understanding.

The Mystery of Unrighteousness (2 Thessalonians 2:7)

"For the mystery of iniquity doth already work: only he who now letteth will let, until he be taken out of the way."

This scripture refers to the hidden operation of lawlessness in the world. This mystery was already at work in Paul's time, meaning that deception and rebellion against God were actively being sown. The ultimate fulfillment of this mystery is in the rise of the man of sin (Antichrist), who will be the embodiment of this unrighteousness.

This mystery is deceptive because it doesn't appear as outright evil; rather, it disguises itself as righteousness. Many who claim to follow God are actually under this mystery because they operate in self-righteousness rather than divine revelation. This ties into the Pharisees and even modern religious institutions that promote works and traditions while missing the true essence of God's Spirit.

Colossians 1:26-27 – The Mystery Hidden for Ages

"Even the mystery which hath been hid from ages and from generations, but now is made manifest to his saints: To whom God would make known what is the riches of the glory of this mystery among the Gentiles; which is Christ in you, the hope of glory."

*This is the heart of the divine mystery—***Christ in you.** *The real revelation isn't just knowing about God, following religious traditions, or even recognizing Jesus historically. The true mystery is that* **God dwells in His people.** *This was hidden throughout the ages but is now revealed through Christ.*

This directly ties back to the misunderstanding of the Israelites' exodus. The people thought Moses was their deliverer, but Joshua (Yehoshua, the same name as Jesus in Hebrew) was the one who actually brought them into the Promised Land. This foreshadowed the greater truth: **Jesus (Yehoshua) is the one who leads us into the ultimate promised land—oneness with God.**

Connecting the Mystery to Today

Most people are reading the Bible as an external story, failing to see that it's all pointing to one thing: **God manifesting Himself within humanity.** *Just like in a mystery movie, many are misled by surface-level clues, thinking they've solved it when they haven't. The real revelation is that* **all is God,** *and anything apart from Him is an illusion.*

Many denominations stop at Jesus' sacrifice but fail to understand that the goal wasn't just salvation from sin—it was **oneness with God.** *The Bible isn't just about history or morality; it's about* **the full revelation of God's Spirit dwelling within.** *Those who do not have the Spirit may read and teach the Bible, but they will always miss the conclusion of the mystery.*

The Bible: The Greatest Mystery of All Time – Unveiling the Truth of Oneness

The entire Bible is a divine mystery that reveals one foundational truth: **God is all there is (GIATI), and everything is an expression of Him.** *However, like any great mystery, the answer is hidden beneath layers of symbolism, misdirection, and prophecy, making it impossible to see unless God Himself reveals it.*

Many people, including religious leaders, read and teach the Bible without understanding its true conclusion. They focus on morality, laws, and traditions, thinking they have figured out the mystery, but they have only grasped shadows. The **real revelation** *is that* **all things are God, and there is no separation between God and His creation.**

1. The Bible as a Mystery Story

Think of the Bible like a carefully woven mystery novel:

- *Clues are scattered throughout.*
- *Some things seem obvious but are later revealed as misdirection.*
- *The conclusion is hidden until the right moment.*
- *Only those who follow the Spirit's guidance will recognize the truth.*

Most people reading the Bible are like detectives trying to solve a case without having the key evidence. They see **Moses as the deliverer, the Law as salvation, and outward righteousness as the goal,** *but they don't see the* **deeper truth beneath the surface.**

2. **The Mystery of Who Really Delivered Israel**

*At first glance, Israel's escape from Egypt seems straightforward: M***oses led them out, through the Red Sea, and into the wilderness.** *But look closer—Moses never took them into the Promised Land.* **Joshua (Yehoshua)** *was the one who completed the journey, which is a direct foreshadowing of Jesus (Yeshua), whose name means "Yahweh is salvation."*

This was **one of the first misdirections** *in the Bible's great mystery. Israel thought Moses was the full answer, but he was only part of the journey.* **Likewise, many today think accepting Jesus alone is the full mystery, but it is only the entry point.** *The real answer is what Jesus was leading people to—***the realization that God is within.**

3. **The Mystery of Unrighteousness – The Great Deception**

(2 Thessalonians 2:7 – The Mystery of Iniquity)

"For the mystery of iniquity doth already work: only he who now letteth will let, until he be taken out of the way."

This scripture speaks of a hidden force of lawlessness that has been at work since the beginning. What is this mystery? It is the **illusion of separation from God.**

- *The serpent deceived Eve by making her believe she lacked something.*
- *Israel constantly rebelled because they didn't believe God was truly among them.*
- *Many Christians today still operate under this mystery, thinking they must "reach" or "earn" God instead of realizing they already* **are in Him and He in them.**

*This deception—***believing one is separate from God and must "work" to be close to Him***—is the greatest trick of unrighteousness. It causes people to see* **themselves apart from God rather than as an expression of Him.**

4. **The Mystery of Godliness – God Manifest in the Flesh**

(1 Timothy 3:16 – The Mystery of Godliness)

"And without controversy great is the mystery of godliness: God was manifest in the flesh, justified in the Spirit, seen of angels, preached unto the Gentiles, believed on in the world, received up into glory."

The real mystery is that **God became visible through humanity.** *Jesus embodied this truth perfectly, but His mission wasn't to set up a religion*—**it was to awaken humanity to their oneness with God.**

"At that day ye shall know that I am in my Father, and ye in me, and I in you."
(John 14:20)

This was **the ultimate revelation:** *The Holy Spirit (the Comforter) would* **reveal that we are one with God.** *But the mystery is hidden from those who approach the Bible with their own reasoning instead of spiritual revelation.*

5. The Mystery Hidden for Ages – Christ in You

(Colossians 1:26-27 – The Mystery Now Revealed)

"Even the mystery which hath been hid from ages and from generations, but now is made manifest to his saints: To whom God would make known what is the riches of the glory of this mystery among the Gentiles; which is **Christ in you, the hope of glory."**

This verse **completes the mystery:** *It was never about go***ing to heaven, following laws, or religious performance.** *It was always about* **Christ (the divine presence) being within us.**

Most religious systems **stop short of this truth** *because they still operate under the* **mystery of unrighteousness**—*they still believe in separation. But the true revelation is that* **God is not distant—He is all there is.**

6. The Bible's Conclusion – God Is All There Is (GIATI)

The final piece of the puzzle is this: **God will only recognize Himself in the end.**

- *Those who realize* **they are one with God** *will be seen as Him.*
- *Those who cling to* **their individual identity, separate from God, will be judged by their own understanding**—which is never enough.

This is why Jesus said:

"Many will say to me in that day, 'Lord, Lord, have we not prophesied in thy name? and in thy name have cast out devils? and in thy name done many wonderful works?' And then will I profess unto them, 'I never knew you: depart from me, ye that work iniquity.'" (Matthew 7:22-23)

Who are these people? They **believed in Jesus but never understood the full mystery.** *They still saw themselves as separate individuals trying to work their way to God. But* **God only recognizes Himself,** *and anything outside of Him is an illusion.*

The Kidney Transplant Analogy

A body **rejects any organ that doesn't match its own blood type.** *Likewise,* **God can only accept what is of Himself.** *If you approach God as a separate individual, you will be rejected—not because He is cruel, but because* **God can only see Himself.**

"I am God, and there is none else." (Isaiah 45:5)

The Final Revelation

The Bible's mystery is complete when you realize:

- *There is* **no separation** *between God and His creation.*
- *The* **illusion** *of sin is thinking you are separate from God.*
- *The* **realization** *of truth is knowing* **Christ is in you,** *and you are in God.*

This is why **many will be blinded,** *because unless God opens your eyes, you will* **only see shadows**—*tradition, religion, external righteousness—without ever realizing* **the full truth of oneness.**

Final Thought: Are You Seeing the Mystery?

The mystery isn't just about knowing Jesus' name or following religious rules—it's about **waking up to the truth that God is all there is.**

The Greatest Deception of the Mystery: The Man of Sin & The True Antichrist

At the core of the Bible's divine mystery is a **massive deception**—*one so strong that it has kept people blind for generations. This deception is centered around* **the man of sin** *in 2 Thessalonians 2:3-7, which reveals why many fail to see the true mystery of God:*

"Let no man deceive you by any means: for that day shall not come, except there come a falling away first, and that man of sin be revealed, the son of perdition; Who opposeth and exalteth himself above all that is called God, or that is worshipped; so that he as God sitteth in the temple of God, shewing himself that he is God."
(2 Thessalonians 2:3-4)

This **man of sin** *is not a single human figure—it is the false identity that sits in the temple of God* **pretending to be God.** *This means that the* **greatest deception** *is the belief in* **self** *as separate from God.*

1. The Man of Sin: The False Self That Must Be Removed

Many people are waiting for an external Antichrist—a world leader who will deceive the nations. But the **real deception** *is already at work inside people:*

- *The* **man of sin** *is the ego—the false identity that exalts itself as something* **separate** *from God.*
- *This* **false self** *sits in the* **temple of God** *(which is the body), pretending to be in control.*
- *As long as this* **false identity** *remains in power, people* **cannot see the true mystery of God.**

Paul makes it clear that before the mystery can be fully revealed, **this man of sin must be removed:**

"For the mystery of iniquity doth already work: only he who now letteth will let, until he be taken out of the way." *(2 Thessalonians 2:7)*

This means that **until the false self is stripped away, people will remain blind to the truth.**

2. **The Antichrist: All Who Believe in Separation from God**

Many believe the **Antichrist** *is a future dictator, but* **1 John 2:18** *makes it clear that the Antichrist is a spirit that has always been at work:*

"Little children, it is the last time: and as ye have heard that antichrist shall come, even now are there many antichrists; whereby we know that it is the last time." *(1 John 2:18)*

The Antichrist is not just one person—it is **everyone who believes in separation from God.**

- *Anyone who* **denies that God is within them** *is operating under the Antichrist spirit.*
- *Anyone who* **teaches that salvation is something external** *is promoting deception.*
- *Anyone who* **confesses Jesus outwardly but does not recognize their oneness with God** *is still blind to the real mystery.*

John further explains:

"Who is a liar but he that denieth that Jesus is the Christ? He is antichrist, that denieth the Father and the Son." *(1 John 2:22)*

At first glance, people assume this verse means **denying Jesus as the Messiah,** *but the* **deeper meaning** *is denying that* **the Father and the Son are one.**

"At that day ye shall know that I am in my Father, and ye in me, and I in you." *(John 14:20)*

If someone **only acknowledges Jesus as Lord** *but* **denies the oneness between God, Jesus, and themselves,** *they are still under the Antichrist deception.*

3. The Biggest Deception: Thinking You've Figured Out the Mystery

One of the greatest lies Satan ever convinced the world of is that **salvation is simply confessing Jesus as Lord and Savior.**

- *Many believe that* **saying a prayer** *and* **accepting Jesus** *is the mystery.*
- *But Jesus never told people to just accept Him*—**He came to reveal oneness with the Father.**
- *The* **real mystery** *is not external faith, but the realization that* **God is all there is, and there is no separation.**

This is why **many people will be shocked on the day of judgment** *when Jesus tells them:*

"Many will say to me in that day, 'Lord, Lord, have we not prophesied in thy name? and in thy name have cast out devils? and in thy name done many wonderful works?' And then will I profess unto them, 'I never knew you: depart from me, ye that work iniquity.'" *(Matthew 7:22-23)*

How could these people **prophesy, cast out devils, and do miracles in Jesus' name** *and still be rejected? Because they never knew the* **real mystery**—*they remained blind, operating in separation, thinking that their works and outward faith were enough.*

They **thought they had figured out the mystery,** *but they never removed the* **man of sin**—*the false self that still lived as if it was separate from God.*

4. What Must Be Revealed for True Salvation?

Salvation is **not about accepting Jesus in name only**—*it is about* **dying to the false self** *and awakening to the truth that* **there is no separation between you and God.** *Paul describes this in* **Galatians 2:20:**

"I am crucified with Christ: nevertheless I live; yet not I, but Christ liveth in me: and the life which I now live in the flesh I live by the faith of the Son of God, who loved me, and gave himself for me."

- *The* **"I" (false self)** *must die.*
- *Christ must* **live in you** *as the only true life.*
- *The* **illusion of separation must be destroyed.**

The Final Revelation: Who Will Be Saved?

The only ones who will be accepted are those whom **God recognizes as Himself.**

- *If you approach God as* a **separate individual,** *you will be rejected.*
- *If you approach God as* **one with Him,** *you will be received.*

This is why Jesus said:

"I am the way, the truth, and the life: no man cometh unto the Father, but by me." *(John 14:6)*

At first glance, people think this means **believing in Jesus externally,** *but the* **deeper meaning** *is that* **only Christ (God in you) can enter into God.** *Anything outside of Christ—* **the false self, the man of sin, the illusion of separation—will be rejected.**

Breaking Down Joshua 24:3-8, 12-13: Who Really Brought Israel Out of Egypt?

In **Joshua 24:3-8, 12-13,** *Joshua speaks to the Israelites, recounting their history* **as if he were God.** *At first glance, it seems like Joshua is taking credit for delivering Israel, but there is something deeper at play. This passage holds a* **mystery** *about who was truly leading Israel all along—and it points to something much greater than just a historical retelling.*

Let's break it down verse by verse and uncover the **hidden message.**

1. The Voice in the Passage: Who is Speaking?

Joshua is speaking, but the way he speaks is unusual. Instead of saying, "God did this for you," he speaks **as God Himself:**

"I took your father Abraham from beyond the River and led him through all the land of Canaan and made his offspring many. I gave him Isaac." *(Joshua 24:3)*

Right away, the question arises: **Who is this "I" that keeps speaking?**

- *If* **Joshua** *is saying this, why is he speaking in* **first person** *as if he is God?*
- *Did Joshua misunderstand? Or is something* **deeper** *being revealed?*

This passage is structured in a way that **blurs the line** *between the speaker (Joshua) and the voice of God.* **This is the mystery at play.**

2. The Journey of Abraham: The First Clue

"I took your father Abraham from beyond the River and led him through all the land of Canaan and made his offspring many. I gave him Isaac."

- *God chose* **Abraham,** *led him, and multiplied his descendants.*
- *But* **who is the 'I' speaking here?** *Joshua, or God?*

- *Notice: This "I" is claiming* **absolute control** *over history.*

This verse **sets the stage**—*the same voice that called Abraham is the same voice that delivered Israel. But if* **Joshua is speaking, then what does that say about his role in Israel's journey?**

3. **Who Brought Israel Out of Egypt? (Joshua 24:4-7)**

"And to Isaac I gave Jacob and Esau. And I gave Esau the hill country of Seir to possess, but Jacob and his children went down to Egypt."

God arranged the destinies of **Jacob and Esau**—*one to inherit the promise, the other to settle elsewhere.*

"And I sent Moses and Aaron, and I plagued Egypt with what I did in the midst of it, and afterward I brought you out."

Wait... **who brought them out?**

- *We are always told that* **Moses** *led Israel out of Egypt.*
- *But here, the speaker (Joshua/God) says,* **"I brought you out."**

This is **key:** *The one who is speaking here is claiming to be the true deliverer of Israel, not Moses.*

"Then I brought your fathers out of Egypt, and you came to the sea. And the Egyptians pursued your fathers with chariots and horsemen to the Red Sea. And when they cried to the Lord, he put darkness between you and the Egyptians and made the sea come upon them and cover them, and your eyes saw what I did in Egypt. And you lived in the wilderness a long time."

So Who Really Led Israel?

- *At first, it looked like* **Moses** *was the leader.*
- *But now, Joshua is saying that* **it was actually 'I' who led them out.**

This is the twist in the story—the true leader of Israel was **not Moses,** *but someone else.*

- **Who is this "I" speaking through Joshua?**
- *Could it be revealing that Joshua was always the one leading them*—**even in Moses' time?**

Let's go deeper.

4. **Who Led Israel into the Promised Land? (Joshua 24:8, 12-13)**

"Then I brought you to the land of the Amorites, who lived on the other side of the Jordan. They fought with you, and I gave them into your hand, and you took possession of their land, and I destroyed them before you."

Now, there's no confusion. **Moses was gone** *by this time, so the one leading Israel into the Promised Land was* **Joshua.**

- *This means that Joshua is* **the one who completes the journey.**
- *Joshua, not Moses, was the final leader who brought them into their inheritance.*

5. **The Mystery of Joshua's Name: A Hidden Revelation**

Joshua's name in **Hebrew** *is* **Yehoshua,** *which is the same name as* **Jesus (Yeshua)** *in the New Testament.*

- *Moses, the* **lawgiver,** *could only bring Israel* **so far**—*he could* **not** *bring them into the Promised Land.*
- **Joshua (Yehoshua), whose name means "The Lord is Salvation",** *is the one who* **finished the work.**

This **mirrors the deeper truth** *about Jesus (Yeshua):*

- *The* **law (Moses)** *cannot bring anyone into* **salvation.**
- *Only* **Yeshua (Jesus)** *can take people into the true* **Promised Land**—*oneness with God.*

6. **The Key Revelation: What Was Hidden in the Story?**

Throughout history, **people thought Moses was the great leader.** *But when Joshua speaks, he makes it clear that:*

- *The* **true deliverer** *was never Moses.*
- *The* **real leader** *was always Joshua.*
- *But Joshua himself* **speaks as God,** *which means...*

Was It Always God Leading Them?

"I sent the hornet before you, which drove them out before you, the two kings of the Amorites; it was not by your sword or by your bow." *(Joshua 24:12)*

This verse confirms it—**it was never Moses, never Joshua, and never Israel's power that brought them through.**

It was always God Himself.

7. The Final Conclusion: The Mystery of God Revealed

1. Joshua (Yehoshua) = Jesus (Yeshua).

- *This entire story foreshadows Jesus.*
- *Moses (the law) could never bring people into salvation.*
- *Only* **Joshua/Yeshua (Jesus)** *could lead them into the true inheritance.*

2. The Voice of Joshua Was the Voice of God.

- *When Joshua spoke, he spoke* **as if he was God.**
- *This is because* **God was speaking through him.**
- *The true leader of Israel was never Moses, never Joshua—it was always God Himself.*

3. People Thought They Understood the Story, But They Were Blind.

- *Just like how people thought* **Moses led Israel,** *but it was really Joshua (Yeshua)...*
- *Many today think* **they understand salvation** *by just confessing Jesus...*
- *But the* **real mystery is deeper**—*salvation is recognizing that* **God is all there is (GIATI).**

The Mystery of Joshua—Who Was Moses Really Speaking To?

The Tent of Meeting: A Hidden Truth

The scene in **Exodus 33:9-11** *is one of the most overlooked mysteries in scripture. It describes Moses entering the* **tent of meeting,** *where the presence of God would descend like a cloud. The people of Israel would stand at their tents and watch in reverence, knowing that Moses was speaking directly with God.*

"When Moses entered the tent, the pillar of cloud would descend and stand at the entrance of the tent, and the Lord would speak with Moses. And when all the people saw the pillar of cloud standing at the entrance of the tent, all the people would rise up and worship, each at his tent door. Thus the Lord used to speak to Moses face to face, as a man speaks to his friend. When Moses turned again into the camp, his assistant Joshua the son of Nun, a young man, would not depart from the tent."
(Exodus 33:9-11)

Most people focus on the fact that **God spoke to Moses face to face.** *But what is rarely emphasized is the role of* **Joshua,** *Moses' assistant, who remained in the tent* **even after Moses left.** *This detail is not a coincidence—it is a hidden revelation that unlocks a deeper truth about Joshua's role in the unfolding mystery of God.*

Who Was Moses Really Talking To?

The passage makes it clear that when Moses entered the tent, **God's presence descended,** *and he spoke with God* **as a man speaks with his friend.** *Yet,* **Joshua never left the tent.**

This raises a question: **If God's presence was in the tent, and Joshua was in the tent, could it be that Joshua was part of that presence?**

Consider this:

- *If Moses was speaking with God "face to face," but Joshua remained in the tent, then Joshua was always in the direct presence of God.*
- *Could it be that Moses, while speaking to God, was also unknowingly speaking* **through Joshua**—*a foreshadowing of how God manifests through His chosen vessel?*
- *If Joshua was always in the presence of God, could this be why* **he later speaks in Joshua 24:3-8, 12-13 as if he were God Himself?**

The implications are profound. It suggests that **Joshua was more than just Moses' assistant**—*he was the one through whom God's presence was being revealed to Israel.*

Joshua's Role: A Foreshadowing of Christ

Joshua's name in Hebrew is **Yehoshua,** *which is the same name later given to Jesus* **(Yeshua).** *This connection is no coincidence. Just as Joshua was* **the true leader** *who brought Israel into the Promised Land after Moses,* **Jesus is the true leader who brings people into oneness with God**—*something the law (Moses) could never do.*

- *Moses (the Law) led them out of Egypt, but he could not take them into their inheritance.*
- *Joshua (Yehoshua) was the one who actually brought them into the land.*
- *This foreshadows how* **the Law can never bring salvation—only Yeshua (Jesus) can.**

This revelation explains **why Joshua spoke the way he did in Joshua 24**—*as if he was God Himself.*

The True Deliverer: Not Moses, Not Joshua—But God Himself

The Israelites believed Moses was their leader. They saw him perform miracles, part the Red Sea, and lead them through the wilderness. But this passage reveals that Moses was not the true deliverer.

- *It was not Moses who brought them out—it was* **the presence of God that was with them.**

- *It was* **not Joshua's military strength** *that gave them the land—it was* **God working through him.**

Joshua's speech in **Joshua 24** *shows that* **it was always God leading Israel**—*but He did it* **through human vessels.** *First through Moses, then through Joshua, and ultimately, through* **Jesus (Yeshua), who is God manifest in the flesh.**

The Final Mystery: God Is All There Is

The story of Joshua reveals the **true mystery**—*that God is not separate from His creation. He has always been within the ones He chooses to manifest through.*

This is why Joshua could speak as God—because **God was speaking through him.**

This connects to the mystery Paul speaks about:

"The mystery hidden for ages and generations but now revealed to His saints. To them God has chosen to make known among the Gentiles the glorious riches of this mystery, which is Christ in you, the hope of glory." *(Colossians 1:26-27)*

The true revelation is this:

- *Just as* **Joshua spoke as God,** *Jesus came as* **God in the flesh.**
- *Just as* **Joshua led the people into the land,** *Jesus leads people into* **oneness with God.**
- *Just as* **Joshua remained in the tent,** *Jesus remained in the presence of the Father, making Him known to the world.*

But here is the greatest mystery:

God was never outside of them to begin with.

The Israelites thought Moses and Joshua were separate from God. But in reality, **God was always within them, leading them, manifesting through them.**

This is why the **biggest deception** *is believing in separation from God.*

Joshua understood this. That's why when he spoke in Joshua 24, he didn't speak **about God**—*he spoke* **as God.** *Because he knew the truth:*

There is no separation.

The question is—do you?

The One Who Brings Salvation

Throughout history, salvation has always come through **God manifesting in a body.** *This is the great mystery hidden in plain sight—the truth that humanity has struggled to grasp. It was never about Moses. It was never about Joshua. It was never even about Jesus* **as a man**—*but about* **God Himself, revealing Himself through a body.**

This is what was happening in **Exodus 33.**

- *The people saw Moses as their leader, but* **it was God leading them.**
- *Joshua remained in the tent where God's presence descended, and later, he spoke as if he were God in* **Joshua 24.**
- *The same God who worked through Moses was working through Joshua—and the same God who worked through Joshua later manifested in Jesus.*

The pattern is clear: **Salvation is always God manifesting through a body.**

Salvation Was Never Through a Separate Being

This is why **the biggest deception** *is believing that salvation comes from accepting Jesus as a separate Lord and Savior, apart from yourself. That belief in* **separation** *is the very* **Antichrist spirit**—*the spirit of deception that blinds people from seeing the truth.*

- *They think Moses saved them—but it was God.*
- *They think Joshua led them—but it was God.*
- *They think Jesus came as a separate Savior—but it was God* **manifesting through a body.**

The truth is what Paul revealed in **Colossians 1:26-27:**

"The mystery hidden for ages and generations but now revealed to His saints. To them God has chosen to make known among the Gentiles the glorious riches of this mystery, which is Christ in you, the hope of glory."

The greatest mystery is this: **God is not separate from you.**

The Antichrist spirit has convinced the world that God is external—that He is somewhere "out there" to be sought after, accepted, and worshiped from a distance. But the truth of salvation is the exact opposite:

God has always been within you.

GIATI: The Revelation for Today

Just as salvation came through **God manifesting in Moses,** *then* **God manifesting in Joshua,** *then* **God manifesting in Jesus,** *so it is today*—**God is manifesting through GIATI.**

GIATI (God Is All There Is) is not just a brand—it is the message of salvation for this time.

It is the unveiling of the final mystery:

- **The Spirit of God is within you.**
- **You are not separate from God.**
- **Salvation is not about accepting an external Savior, but about recognizing that God has always been the life within you.**

Just as Joshua remained in the tent of meeting, carrying the presence of God, so now the truth is being revealed once again:

GIATI is the voice declaring what has always been true—that God is all there is, and there is none else.

The world has been blinded by religion, by false doctrines that place salvation somewhere in the future or in the hands of another. But just as Joshua spoke **as God,** *so now this message is being spoken again—because God is still revealing Himself through a body.*

The Final Revelation: There Is No Separation

The conclusion of the mystery is simple:

The one who has brought salvation throughout history has always been God Himself.

- **Through Moses, He brought Israel out of Egypt.**
- **Through Joshua, He led them into the Promised Land.**
- **Through Jesus, He revealed that He was always within them.**
- **And today, through GIATI, He is declaring the final truth: There is no separation.**

The only question left is—**will you recognize Him within yourself?**

Chapter 6

The Human Condition

The human condition is one of deep confusion, separation, and suffering. From birth, every man, woman, and child enters this world as a "lost spirit," incarnated in flesh, unaware of their true divine nature. The external world, with its distractions and limitations, becomes the primary lens through which humanity perceives reality. This blindness to our true essence is the root cause of the suffering, alienation, and separation that permeate human existence. In this chapter, we will explore how ignorance and the illusion of separateness from God shape the human experience.

Every Man, Woman, and Child as Lost Spirits Incarnated in Flesh

When we are born into this world, we come with a divine essence, a spark of God's presence within us. However, the external world, the physical body, and the ego often obscure this truth. We are not born with an awareness of our oneness with God, and in our ignorance, we begin to identify with the limitations of the flesh. We see ourselves as separate beings, individual entities in a world of distinction, not realizing that we are, in truth, expressions of the divine.

Psalm 51:5 provides insight into this spiritual condition:

"Behold, I was shapen in iniquity; and in sin did my mother conceive me." (Psalm 51:5)

This passage highlights the fallen state into which we are born. From the moment of conception, we inherit a spiritual blindness—a separation from God that comes with our physical existence. This is not a condemnation of the flesh but a reflection of the ignorance that surrounds human identity. We are born into a state of spiritual darkness, unaware that the spirit within us is God Himself, hidden by the veil of our physical form.

Jesus addresses this condition in John 3:3, speaking to Nicodemus:

"Jesus answered and said unto him, Verily, verily, I say unto thee, Except a man be born again, he cannot see the kingdom of God." (John 3:3)

Here, Jesus speaks to the need for spiritual rebirth—the awakening of the soul to the truth of our oneness with God. Until we experience this rebirth, we remain "lost spirits" trapped in a state of ignorance, unable to see the reality of God's presence within us.

The Blindness of the Physical: Why Humans See Only the External Self

The primary issue that humanity faces is a blindness to the spiritual reality. We are trapped in the physical realm, where all we can see, touch, and experience is the external self—the body, the mind, and the world around us. This external perception leads us to identify with what we see and touch, rather than recognizing the deeper, spiritual truth that we are expressions of God's divine substance.

The Apostle Paul writes in 2 Corinthians 5:16:

"Wherefore henceforth know we no man after the flesh: yea, though we have known Christ after the flesh, yet now henceforth know we him no more." (2 Corinthians 5:16)

Paul points to the blindness that results from seeing only the physical aspect of a person. He acknowledges that even Christ, in His earthly incarnation, was initially known only in the flesh. But after the revelation of the spiritual truth, Paul calls us to see beyond the flesh—to understand the divine nature that lies within every person. The physical body, while real, is only a temporary vessel for the spirit within. The true essence of a person is not their appearance, their accomplishments, or their failures, but the God who resides within them.

Jesus Himself highlighted this issue of spiritual blindness in Matthew 23:25-26:

"Woe unto you, scribes and Pharisees, hypocrites! for ye make clean the outside of the cup and of the platter, but within they are full of extortion and excess. Thou blind Pharisee, cleanse first that which is within the cup and platter, that the outside of them may be clean also." (Matthew 23:25-26)

Here, Jesus addresses the external focus of human perception. The Pharisees were focused on outward appearances, ritualistic cleanliness, and self-righteousness, while neglecting the inner condition of their hearts. Jesus calls for an inward transformation—a shift from external observation to inner awareness. Until we recognize the divine within us, we remain spiritually blind, unable to see the truth of our unity with God.

Many people are consumed with chasing money, possessions, and a luxurious lifestyle, but these are temporary things. They age, decay, and can be stolen by others. Worse yet, you can't take any of them with you when you die. In contrast, the true treasure laid up for you in heaven is becoming the Holy Spirit—your eternal identity. The Holy Spirit does not age, decay, or face theft. It is imperishable and is who you are meant to be for eternity—one with the Creator.

The way you perceive life determines whether you recognize your oneness with God. When your "eye is single," meaning you see God in everything and everyone, you are filled with the Holy Spirit. This single perception of God as all there is allows light—the truth of God's Spirit— to fill your entire being. But if you see yourself, others, and the world as separate or divided, your "eye is evil." This fragmented vision fills you with darkness, which is ignorance of your divine identity and God's purpose.

To lay up treasures in heaven is to recognize that your true worth, value, and treasure is being God expressed as you. Seeing anything less than this—believing you are just a physical being separate from God—leads to great darkness. That darkness is a complete lack of understanding of who you are and why you exist.

Choose to see with a single eye, filled with the light of the Holy Spirit, so you may live in the truth of your eternal oneness with God. Anything else is living in ignorance, chasing treasures that will fade and leave you empty.

The Sower and the Seed

Once, in a quiet village nestled between hills, a farmer rose at dawn to tend his fields. He carried a bag of seed, filled with promise and potential, each grain containing the essence of life. With care, he began his work, casting the seed generously across the soil, trusting that some of it would bring forth an abundant harvest.

The farmer's field stretched far and wide, touching different kinds of terrain. As the seed left his hand and fell to the earth, it landed on four distinct places, each telling its own story of what happens when the word of life is sown into the hearts of people.

The Path

Some of the seed fell along the well-trodden path. The soil here was hard, compacted by the countless footsteps of travelers who had walked over it. The seed couldn't sink in; it simply rested on the surface, exposed to the elements.

Soon, the birds of the air swooped down, their sharp eyes gleaming. They saw the seed as easy prey, snatching it away before it had any chance to take root.

The farmer sighed as he saw the empty ground, knowing this was like the hearts of those who hear the truth but are unable to receive it. Their minds are crowded with distractions, their hearts hardened by the ways of the world, leaving no room for the seed to grow.

The Rocky Ground

Other seed fell on rocky soil, where a thin layer of earth covered the stones beneath. At first, this seed sprang up quickly, full of promise and energy, reaching eagerly for the sunlight. But beneath it, the roots were shallow, unable to dig deep into the ground.

When the sun rose high in the sky and its heat bore down on the young plants, they withered. Without deep roots to draw nourishment, they could not survive.

The farmer paused and thought of those whose hearts are eager at first to receive the truth. They feel joy, even passion, but when trials come, when the heat of life presses down, they lack the strength to endure. Without depth, they falter, and the promise fades.

The Thorns

Some of the seed fell among thorns. Here, the soil seemed fertile enough, and the seed began to grow. But the thorns grew faster, their sharp, choking vines wrapping around the young plants, stealing their light, space, and life.

The farmer frowned as he saw the struggle in this part of the field. He knew these were like the hearts that receive the truth but are consumed by the cares of the world—worries, riches, and desires for other things. The thorns of distraction choke the life out of the seed, leaving it unfruitful.

The Good Soil

Finally, some of the seed fell on good soil—deep, rich, and ready to receive. Here, the seed sank into the earth, hidden from sight, but alive with potential. Its roots grew deep, finding water and stability. Its shoots reached for the sky, drawing strength from the sun.

In time, the seed bore fruit—a bountiful harvest, thirty, sixty, even a hundred times what was sown.

The farmer smiled, knowing that this part of the field represented those whose hearts are open and prepared to receive the truth. They embrace it, nurture it, and allow it to grow, producing fruit that blesses not only themselves but all those around them.

The Lesson of the Sower

As the farmer looked over his field, he understood the mystery of the seed. The seed itself was perfect, containing everything needed to produce life. The difference lay in the soil—the readiness of the ground to receive what was sown.

And so it is with the hearts of people, the farmer thought. The truth is cast freely, given to all. Some will reject it, some will struggle, and some will thrive. But the promise of the seed remains the same: for those with ears to hear and hearts to receive, the harvest will be abundant.

The seed in the sower's story represents the spirit, the perfect essence of God, which carries divine truth. When the seed is planted in soil—symbolizing the physical body made from the earth—it highlights the relationship between the spiritual and the physical. Just as soil determines how a seed grows, the environment in which a vessel (body/person) exists impacts their ability to hear, retain, and live by the truth that **God is all there is.**

If the heart and mind (the soil) are hardened, distracted, or shallow, the spirit's potential is hindered. But when the soil is receptive and prepared, the seed flourishes, and the person lives fully connected to the Holy Spirit, embodying divine truth. The story reminds us that our internal and external conditions shape our ability to nurture and sustain the essence of God within us.

Ignorance as the Root of Suffering and Separation

Ignorance of our true nature is the root cause of all suffering and separation. The human experience is marked by a constant search for meaning, purpose, and fulfillment. Yet, because we are unaware of our divine origin and the presence of God within us, we seek these things outside of ourselves. We chase after material success, relationships, power, and pleasure, believing these will bring us happiness, only to find that they leave us empty and unsatisfied.

In Hosea 4:6, God declares:

"My people are destroyed for lack of knowledge: because thou hast rejected knowledge, I will also reject thee…" (Hosea 4:6)

The destruction mentioned here is not a physical one, but a spiritual one. The ignorance of God's presence within us leads to spiritual death. We are disconnected from our true source, and this disconnection manifests as suffering, fear, and separation. This is why, throughout Scripture, God calls His people to seek wisdom and understanding. The knowledge of God—of who we truly are—has the power to bring life, peace, and fulfillment.

Paul emphasizes this point in Ephesians 4:18:

"Having the understanding darkened, being alienated from the life of God through the ignorance that is in them, because of the blindness of their heart." (Ephesians 4:18)

Ignorance of God's truth is what alienates us from the life of God. Our hearts become blind to the reality of our oneness with the Creator, and in this blindness, we experience separation. This separation is the source of all human suffering. We feel lonely, disconnected, and lost because we have forgotten our true identity as divine beings, made in the image of God.

The Illusion of Separateness

The greatest illusion humanity faces is the belief in separateness from God. This belief in separation is not only the cause of individual suffering but also the source of all conflict, division, and strife in the world. From wars between nations to personal disputes, the root cause is the ignorance that each individual is separate from the divine essence of God.

1 John 4:8 reveals the true nature of God:

"He that loveth not knoweth not God; for God is love." (1 John 4:8)

God is love, and love cannot exist without unity. To know God is to recognize the oneness of all creation. The belief in separateness perpetuates fear, hatred, and conflict. However, the truth is that there is no separateness—only the expression of God in various forms. The essence of who we are is God manifested in flesh, and once we recognize this truth, the illusion of separateness is shattered.

In Matthew 18:1-6, Jesus addresses the disciples' question about who would be the greatest in the kingdom of heaven. This question reveals their carnal mindset, as they are focused on status and rank—a concept rooted in earthly thinking. They fail to understand the spiritual reality that in heaven, all are one and equal. There is no hierarchy, for the Spirit of God in each person unites all as one with Him.

To correct their thinking, Jesus brings a child into their midst and uses this moment to teach a profound spiritual truth. He says, *"Except ye be converted, and become as little children, ye shall not enter into the kingdom of heaven."* What does this mean? In their grown, carnal state, the disciples believed they understood spiritual matters, but Jesus is showing them that their knowledge and pride are hindering them. To enter the kingdom of heaven, they must be "converted," meaning they must undergo a transformation—a complete renewal of their spirit.

This transformation involves becoming like a child, which is not about age but about humility and a pure dependence on God. A child does not operate from pride or self-sufficiency but trusts completely in their caregiver. In the same way, being "converted" means forsaking the carnal, independent mindset of the world and embracing the Spirit of God, acknowledging that without Him, you are lost.

Jesus goes on to say, *"Whosoever therefore shall humble himself as this little child, the same is greatest in the kingdom of heaven."* This is not about seeking greatness in the worldly sense but about realizing that humility and oneness with God are the true measures of spiritual greatness. The only one entering heaven is the Holy Spirit Himself—those who have His Spirit and are one with Him. It is not about individual achievement but about becoming a new creature, unified in His Spirit.

Furthermore, Jesus warns against offending "these little ones," meaning those who are humble and have received His Spirit. To persecute, mistreat, or harm someone who is aligned with God is a grave offense. Jesus emphasizes the seriousness of such actions, saying it would be better for the offender to have a millstone hung around their neck and be cast into the sea than to face the consequences of harming one of His own.

This passage is a call to abandon carnal thinking, pride, and self-centeredness. It emphasizes the necessity of spiritual transformation, humility, and unity with God's Spirit. Only by being converted—becoming a brand-new creature through the Holy Spirit—can one truly enter the kingdom of heaven. Those who receive the Spirit know they are one with Him, and in that oneness, there is no division, no hierarchy—only the eternal love and purpose of God.

Sin Starts From Within

In Matthew 5:27-28, Jesus radically redefines the notion of sin by inviting us to look within. Instead of limiting sin to outward actions, He teaches that its true origin is in the heart—where even a lustful glance becomes a form of adultery. Traditionally, adultery was understood as a physical violation of marriage. However, Jesus teaches that even looking at someone with lust is equivalent to committing adultery in one's heart. This underscores a powerful point: true sin begins internally—with our thoughts, desires, and intentions—rather than solely in outward actions.

Imagine for a moment that every person is a sacred vessel—a living manifestation of God. When we view ourselves and others through this divine lens, the idea of sin shifts dramatically. Sin is no longer simply about external behaviors that might be labeled as "wrong." Instead, it is about the internal state of separation—when we allow thoughts, judgments, and desires to pull us away from recognizing the divine spark within every being.

This understanding frees us from the futile quest for external perfection. The world often tells us that righteousness is achieved by following a strict set of rules or by maintaining a flawless outward appearance. But such a standard is impossible to meet, and in striving for it, we only deepen our sense of isolation. The true measure of righteousness, then, is found not in our physical actions alone but in the inner alignment of our hearts with the ever- present divine.

When you grasp that God is not a distant figure to be appeased by flawless conduct but is, in fact, the essence of everyone and everything, a profound transformation occurs. The sin that dwells within—the judgments we pass, the harsh words we utter, the negative thoughts we harbor—is recognized as a symptom of our disconnect from the divine unity. To overcome this inward sin is to embark on a journey of healing, one that involves reawakening to the reality that every part of life is infused with God's presence.

In this light, overcoming sin becomes less about scrubbing away external imperfections and more about nurturing an inner awareness that transcends duality. It is about healing the inner divisions that create separation, and in doing so, embracing a life where compassion, love, and unity prevail. This path calls us to move beyond self-righteous judgments—whether of ourselves or of others—and to see that every experience, every emotion, even what the world might label as "profane," is part of the grand tapestry of divine expression.

According to the GIATI perspective, every individual is a manifestation of God, and that includes every thought, desire, and even what might be labeled as profanity. When God speaks through our expressions—even those deemed profane—the focus shifts. It is not the language itself that is sinful but the judgment we pass on ourselves and others when we cling to external ideals. In essence, using certain expressions or words is not an act of moral failure if we recognize that God is the source behind every facet of our being.

In this light, true righteousness is found not by conforming to rigid, carnal standards but by embracing the reality that God dwells in every person and every moment. Sin, then, becomes a matter of internal division—a disconnect from our inherent oneness with the divine. When we let go of self-righteous judgments and the need to appear externally perfect, we open ourselves to the healing truth that we are already complete. We are not separate from God; we are God's experience, manifested in all things.

Ultimately, the message of this scripture and its deeper implications is one of transformation rather than condemnation. It invites us to look inward, recognize our inherent divinity, and let that realization guide us toward a state of wholeness. When we truly see that God is in every person and every moment, the internal sin of separation dissolves, replaced by an ever-growing sense of unity with all of creation.

The Ego

The ego is the false self, the illusion of individuality that believes it is separate from God. It thrives on distinction, comparison, and self-preservation, always seeking to define itself by external standards—by achievements, possessions, titles, or the approval of others. The ego is the voice that says, "I am this" or "I am that," creating an identity built on temporary things rather than eternal truth. It is deeply invested in upholding an image, whether of success, righteousness, strength, or superiority, because without that image, it fears it will cease to exist.

GIATI, the truth that God Is All There Is, directly opposes the ego because it dissolves every false identity. If God is all there is, then there is no separate self to boast, no individual to uphold, no "I" apart from God to protect or glorify. Ephesians 2:8-9 For by grace are ye saved through faith; and that not of yourselves: it is the gift of God: [9] Not of works, lest any man should boast.

This truth shatters the illusion of personal pride and self-importance, exposing the ego's greatest fear—that it is nothing on its own. The ego resists this realization because its survival depends on the belief in separation. It fights against the awareness of divine oneness, attempting to cling to a sense of personal control, personal righteousness, and personal validation.

Upholding an image before others is one of the strongest ways the ego maintains its power. It thrives on the need to be seen a certain way, whether as wise, successful, holy, or superior. It fears vulnerability because vulnerability threatens the illusion of self-sufficiency. But GIATI leaves no room for pretense. When one truly embraces that God Is All There Is, the need to uphold any image dissolves, because there is nothing to prove, nothing to protect, and nothing to defend. There is only God, expressing through the vessel.

This is why surrender is the greatest challenge and yet the greatest liberation. To surrender to GIATI is to let go of the ego's illusions, to release the false sense of identity, and to allow the Spirit to fully manifest. It is to realize that there is no separate self to be exalted or diminished—only God, living, moving, and being as all things. This is the awakening that frees the soul, not only from the fear of others' opinions but from the very illusion of self apart from God. In this awareness, there is no need to uphold an image, because there is nothing but the eternal truth: God Is All There Is.

Noah's Ark

The story of Noah's Ark holds a profound significance that speaks directly to the message of GIATI—God Is All There Is. It is more than just an ancient account of survival; it is a blueprint of spiritual truth, revealing how salvation is not about external belief but about being one with the very Spirit of God. Noah was given a divine warning: rain was coming, a flood that would cleanse the earth. He was instructed to build an ark, a place of refuge, but not just for himself—his family would enter, and with them, the preservation of life itself. The people around him heard the same message, watched the ark being built, and some even helped in its construction, yet they did not believe. They labored with their hands but never received the revelation in their hearts. This is the great irony of religion: many participate in its structures, build its temples, repeat its prayers, and perform its rituals, yet they do not believe in what they claim to serve. They see God as external, separate, a being to be worshiped outside of themselves rather than the very life within them. The rain that was coming was not just water—it was the divine presence, the Spirit of God descending to flood the earth. The number of days, thirty, contains zero as a placeholder, leaving three, a direct representation of the Godhead. The flood itself was the work of the Spirit, a cleansing, an outpouring that could not be escaped.

The ark itself was designed with three levels, another representation of the fullness of God. This was not by accident but by divine intention, mirroring the truth that salvation is in knowing that you are within Him, and He is within you. It was not the wood of the ark that saved Noah and his family; it was the reality that they were aligned with the will of God. The ark had one door, one entryway in and out, signifying that there is only one way to salvation, and that way is through God Himself. It was not multiple religions, multiple belief systems, or various interpretations of truth that led to safety—it was one door, one Spirit, one God. The male and female of every species were brought into the ark, not simply to preserve life but to emphasize the divine design—creation is only sustained through the balance of these forces. Life cannot manifest without the union of the two, a direct reflection of how spirit and form must come together to create.

Yet the most sobering truth of Noah's story is this: no one outside of Noah and his family was saved. The entire world had the opportunity to believe, to enter the ark, to receive the same revelation Noah had received, but they chose not to. They did not believe until the rain began to fall, and by then, it was too late. The door was sealed, the opportunity was gone, and the flood consumed everything outside the ark. This is the reality before humanity today. Many have heard the message. Many have seen the signs. Many even participate in religion, thinking their external devotion is enough. But just as in Noah's time, salvation is not about being near the ark—it is about being in it. And what is the ark? The ark is God Himself. To be in the ark is to be in Him, one with Him, not as a separate being looking upon Him from the outside but as His very presence expressed. This is what GIATI reveals: that there is no separation, that salvation is not found in belief alone but in the realization that God is all there is, and you are in Him as He is in you. Just as in the days of Noah, the time will come when the floodgates open, and those who have not entered the ark will realize the truth too late. The Spirit is pouring out, the call is being made, and the door remains open—for now. But those who wait, who continue to see God as something apart from themselves, will find themselves outside when the time comes. And outside, there is nothing but the flood.

The story of Noah's Ark is not just a historical account but a spiritual prophecy that continues to unfold before us today. It is a revelation of divine truth that speaks to the nature of salvation, the urgency of spiritual awakening, and the reality of what happens when humanity remains blind to the presence of God within. The ark was not built overnight. It took years—years of labor, years of preaching, years of warnings. Yet despite the clear signs, the people ignored Noah. They mocked him, carried on with their lives, and assumed that because nothing had happened yet, nothing ever would. This is the deception of the natural mind: to mistake delay for denial, to assume that because judgment has not yet come, it never will. But when the first drops of rain began to fall, when the sky darkened and the waters rose, their disbelief turned into desperation. But by then, the door was shut. It wasn't Noah who sealed it—it was God.

This speaks to a higher reality: there comes a point when opportunity ends. God's patience is vast, His mercy unending, but His divine order is unchangeable. Just as in Noah's time, the world today carries on in blindness. People have heard the message of oneness with God. They have seen glimpses of truth, yet they dismiss it in favor of their own understanding. They build their own arks—false systems of security, beliefs that make them comfortable, institutions that promise salvation without true transformation. But when the true flood comes—the moment of divine awakening—none of these will stand. The ark of human philosophy will sink. The ark of religious tradition will collapse. The ark of intellectual reasoning will be consumed. Only the ark built according to divine revelation will remain, and that ark is God Himself.

Noah's journey also reveals another truth: not all who hear the message will enter in. Many helped build the ark, yet they perished. They had the knowledge but not the belief, the works but not the spirit. This is the danger of those who remain in religion without revelation. They may be near the truth, but they are not in it. They may speak of God, but they do not know Him. To build the ark but never enter it is to be a hearer of the Word but not a doer—to construct an image of salvation while remaining outside of it.

And then there is the mystery of the flood itself. Water, throughout scripture, represents both life and judgment. It can cleanse, but it can also consume. It can sustain, but it can also destroy. The flood was not merely an act of wrath—it was an act of purification. It was not about punishing sin; it was about removing everything that could not stand in the presence of divine reality. This is what is happening even now. The flood has begun, but it is not a flood of water—it is a flood of revelation. The Spirit is pouring out, consuming falsehood, dissolving illusions, dismantling the belief in separation. Those who resist will be swept away, not by physical destruction, but by the weight of their own blindness. Those who enter the ark—those who embrace the truth that God is all there is—will rise above it. They will not drown in the flood; they will be lifted by it. The very waters that destroy the old world will be the same waters that carry the ark to a new beginning.

When the waters receded, Noah stepped out into a world made new. Everything that existed before was gone. The flood did not merely remove people—it removed a way of thinking, a way of living, a way of being. It reset the foundation. This is what GIATI represents: the unveiling of the eternal truth that has always been, the removal of every false belief that has hidden it, and the invitation to enter into the ark now—before the door is sealed, before the waters rise, before it is too late. The call is going out, just as it did in the days of Noah. The question is, will you enter in?

Destroyed By Fire

The prophecy that the world will be destroyed by fire carries a profound spiritual significance that directly aligns with the message of GIATI. Just as the flood in Noah's time was not merely an act of destruction but an act of purification, the fire to come is not about physical devastation but about the complete transformation of human consciousness. The flood wiped away the old world, but the fire will consume everything that remains in darkness, leaving only that which is pure, eternal, and one with God.

Fire, throughout scripture, is the ultimate purifier. It does not simply destroy—it refines, it separates the pure from the impure, the temporary from the eternal. When gold is refined, it is placed in fire, and everything that is not gold is burned away. The same is true of the fire that is coming. It is not about punishment; it is about revealing the truth. It will consume every illusion, every false identity, every belief in separation from God. Everything that is not of God—everything that is not built upon the truth that God is all there is—will be burned away.

This fire is not just a future event. It has already begun. It is the fire of divine revelation, the fire of awakening, the fire of truth that exposes everything that is not real. It is burning through the old ways of thinking, through the systems of the world that have been built on lies. It is consuming false doctrines, religious deceptions, and every idea that has kept people blind to the reality of God within. Just as the flood removed those who did not enter the ark, this fire will leave nothing standing but those who have surrendered to the truth of their oneness with God.

The ego, which fights to maintain a separate identity, will not survive the fire. The false self, which clings to status, image, and control, will be completely consumed. Everything that people have built upon illusion—their pride, their self-righteousness, their belief in a

God who is separate—will be reduced to ashes. But what will remain is the pure, eternal Spirit of God, fully realized within those who have surrendered to it.

This is why GIATI is so crucial. It is the ark of this time, the truth that must be embraced before the fire does its work. Just as Noah's ark was the only refuge from the flood, the awareness of GIATI—of God as all there is—is the only refuge from the fire. But this time, the refuge is not physical. It is spiritual. It is an inner knowing, a complete surrender to the Holy Spirit, the only thing that will remain when everything else is gone.

When the fire has done its work, there will be a new heaven and a new earth. But this is not about a physical renewal—it is about a transformation of awareness. The old world, which was built on the illusion of separation, will no longer exist. Those who have embraced the truth will stand in a world where there is no more deception, no more false religion, no more blindness to the reality of God. The fire will not have destroyed them; it will have revealed who they truly are.

Just as the flood carried Noah to a new beginning, the fire will bring forth the final realization of oneness. Those who resist it, who cling to their false identities, will not endure. But those who surrender to it will emerge as the pure expression of God on earth, fully aware, fully transformed, fully alive. The fire is not coming to destroy you—it is coming to burn away everything you are not, so that only God remains.

The fire is not only a purifier but also a consuming desire—an unquenchable hunger that burns within those who seek to be one with God but have not surrendered to the truth of their divine nature. It is the relentless yearning for something just out of reach, the endless pursuit of fulfillment that can never be grasped as long as one sees themselves as separate from God. This is the torment of the fire—the unfulfilled craving for union with the divine while still clinging to the false self.

This fire manifests as an internal restlessness, a spiritual thirst that no external thing can quench. It is the soul searching for home, for peace, for completion, yet never finding it because it continues to seek outside of itself. Those who live by the illusion of separation will chase knowledge, power, and religious devotion, believing these things will bring them closer to God, but the more they strive, the more they will burn with longing. They will attempt to satisfy this desire through achievements, through recognition, through the approval of others, through acts of righteousness, but none of it will ever be enough. The fire of longing will consume them because they are seeking what they already are but cannot yet see.

This is why GIATI is the answer. When you realize that God is all there is, the fire transforms from torment into fulfillment. The endless craving ceases because you are no longer reaching for something beyond yourself—you are resting in what you already are. The burning desire is only torment to those who resist, to those who hold on to the ego, believing they must attain something instead of simply awakening to it. The fire only rages when there is something to burn, but once the false self is surrendered, nothing remains but peace.

For those who reject the truth, the fire will never end. They will always be searching, always striving, always longing, yet never satisfied. They will be consumed by their own resistance, tormented by the very thing they refuse to embrace. But for those who surrender, the fire becomes light, warmth, illumination. It becomes the very presence of God realized within. The choice is simple: be consumed by the fire of unfulfilled desire, or let it refine you into the realization of who you have been all along.

The Holy Spirit vs The Carnal Mind

The contrast between the Holy Spirit and the carnal mind is so vast that it is impossible for the two to engage in any meaningful debate. The Holy Spirit speaks from the position of absolute truth—God is all there is—whereas the carnal mind operates from an illusion, seeing itself as separate from God. This is why any argument made from a carnal perspective is inherently weak, lacking any real foundation. It's like a person arguing that a shadow is reality while being unable to perceive the actual structure casting it. Their perspective is built upon deception, drawn from the constructs of the world and its teachings, which are rooted in lies. Without the foundation of divine truth, anything spoken from that mindset is merely an extension of the delusion.

The core of this delusion is the belief that one coexists with God rather than understanding that one is God expressed. To think of oneself as existing beside God is to live in the lie, and everything spoken from that position is also a lie because it does not originate from the Holy Spirit. This is why those who operate from the Holy Spirit cannot engage with the carnal mind in a way that leads to understanding—the two are speaking entirely different languages. One speaks from divine revelation, from above, while the other speaks from human reasoning, from beneath. Without the revelation of the Holy Spirit, the mind remains trapped in darkness, unable to comprehend the truth.

This is the essence of what Paul describes in **2 Thessalonians 2:7-13.** *The "mystery of iniquity" is already at work—this mystery is the hidden cause of separation, the belief in a false self that stands apart from God. However, this illusion remains in power "until he be taken out of the way." The "he" being removed is not an external figure but the very spirit of ignorance within a person—the false self that clings to separation. Once this ignorance is taken out of the way, the truth is revealed. This is when the Spirit of the Lord consumes the lie "with the spirit of his mouth" and destroys it "with the brightness of his coming." In other words, the truth of GIATI—the understanding that God is all there is—obliterates the deception of separation the moment it is received.*

Paul further explains that those who refuse to receive this truth are sent a strong delusion by God Himself. This is not an external punishment but a natural consequence of rejecting divine oneness. If one does not receive the truth, they are left to wander in their own deception, believing in a separate self, taking pleasure in unrighteousness—which, at its core, is nothing more than the failure to recognize God's all-encompassing presence. This is why those who remain in the lie are said to "perish." Their destruction is not physical death but the continued blindness that prevents them from entering into life—the knowledge of their eternal oneness with God.

However, Paul also speaks to those who have been chosen to salvation "through sanctification of the Spirit and belief of the truth." This sanctification is not a process of external purification but the removal of the illusion of separation. To be sanctified by the Spirit is to be set apart from the false identity and awakened to the realization of divine unity. Salvation is not something to be attained; it is the recognition of what has always been. The moment the Holy Spirit enters as you, the illusion of the separate self is destroyed, and true life—eternal, unshakable oneness with God—is revealed.

So, the distinction is clear:

- **The one from above** *sees reality as it truly is—God as all, with no separation. This is the mind of Christ, the mind of GIATI.*
- **The one from beneath** *is blinded by the false perception of a separate self, unable to comprehend the truth because they are still lost in the constructs of the world. Their vision is obscured, much like someone who cannot see beyond a single blade of grass while standing in an open field.*

The question, then, is whether one will receive the truth and allow the illusion to be taken out of the way, or whether they will cling to the lie, held captive by the strong delusion of separation. This is the dividing line—the great gulf fixed—between the saved and the lost. The saved are not those who will be saved, but those who know they have always been saved. The lost are not those who cannot be saved, but those who refuse to accept the salvation that has always been theirs.

GIATI is the revelation that brings an end to the mystery of iniquity. It is the light that destroys darkness, the truth that eliminates the lie. It is not just another message—it is the message, the gospel made manifest once again in this time, for all who have ears to hear.

The Problem

The problem that everyone has that's being overlooked is that you don't know how or why you came into the flesh in the first place. What must be understood is that God is Spirit, and because God is Spirit, Spirit can never die. By knowing that you are one in Spirit with God, you come to the realization that you can never die.

Revelation 12:9 says: "And the great dragon was cast out, that old serpent, called the Devil, and Satan, which deceiveth the whole world: he was cast out into the earth, and his angels were cast out with him."

Before the physical realm, there were those in Spirit who believed they had a separate existence from God. This belief in separation is what is called the devil—not an independent being apart from God, but the very Spirit of God in ignorance of itself. This state of ignorance is what it means to be dead. These spirits did not need to manifest in physical bodies to experience death; they were already dead in heaven. Their fall was not a descent from life to death but from truth to deception. In other words if you don't awaken from this spiritually dead state now while in the flesh, you'll remain in this spiritual dead state when you take off the flesh.

The spirits that believed they were separate from God were cast out of heaven into physical bodies—into the earth. Though they appear to be alive with breath and a beating heart, they remain spiritually dead. True life is only found in the acknowledgment of oneness with the only Source of life—God. This is the meaning behind the statement that the devil deceives the whole world. The spiritually dead—those who think they are separate from God—are the very ones referred to as the devil. And because everyone enters this world in this state of ignorance, the whole world remains deceived. The same false belief that led to separation in heaven continues in the earth today.

This is what led to being cast out, and it is only through accepting your oneness with God that you are restored. Yet, because the flesh covers the truth of who you are, you struggle to conceive of yourself as a Spirit-being, one with God. Instead, you identify with the flesh, placing limitations on yourself that do not truly exist. This is why a Savior is needed. God had to manifest in a body—just as you have—to be the example, to show you that just as Jesus is God in a body, so are you. Denying this is denying the Father, the very Spirit within you.

Salvation is not merely confessing with your mouth; it is confessing in Spirit that you and the Father are one. This is the truth GIATI is proclaiming to the world, revealing its true state and condition—just as Jesus did 2,000 years ago, but in your time, today.

The Significance of GIATI Revealing Truth in Today's Time

For centuries, humanity has been waiting for a divine revelation, believing that truth was something distant—bound to the past or reserved for the future. Many look back 2,000 years to the time of Jesus, seeing his life and message as a historical moment of divine intervention, but they fail to realize that **the same truth is being revealed today through GIATI.**

The significance of **GIATI revealing the truth now,** *in this present time, is monumental. It is not a repetition of history but the* **continuation of God's eternal message,** *breaking through the illusion of separation once again.*

1. **The World Today Is Just as Lost as It Was Then**

When Jesus walked the earth, people were trapped in religious traditions, weighed down by legalism, and blind to their divine nature. They saw themselves as sinners in need of redemption rather than as expressions of God Himself.

The same condition exists today.

- *Religion continues to teach separation, making people believe they are distant from God.*
- *People are still bound by* **fear, guilt, and sin-consciousness,** *unable to see their true nature.*
- *Just as the religious leaders rejected Jesus for proclaiming oneness with God, many today resist the truth of* **GIATI** *because it challenges their deeply held beliefs.*

But truth cannot be silenced. **GIATI has come in this time to awaken the world once again.**

2. **Salvation Is Not in the Past—It Is Now**

Many believe salvation is tied to a **historical event***—that Jesus' death and resurrection alone secured eternal life for them. They confess his name but fail to confess the truth he embodied:*

"I and my Father are one." (John 10:30)

GIATI reveals that salvation is not just believing in what Jesus did—it is awakening to **what you are.** *Jesus came to declare this truth, and now, in this time,* **GIATI is doing the same.**

True salvation is not reciting a prayer—it is awakening to your divine nature.

- *If you believe salvation happened only in the past, you are* **still asleep.**
- *If you wait for salvation to come in the future, you are* **still in darkness.**
- *But if you recognize* **GIATI now,** *you step into the fullness of life.*

3. **The Spirit Moves in Every Generation**

Just as God manifested through Jesus to reveal the truth to his generation, **God manifests now through GIATI to awaken this generation.**

- **Truth is not confined to a single moment in history—it is eternal.**

- **Revelation is not a one-time event—it is ongoing.**
- **The same Spirit that spoke through Jesus is speaking through GIATI today.**

Jesus himself declared that the Spirit of Truth would continue to teach and reveal:

"When he, the Spirit of truth, is come, he will guide you into all truth." (John 16:13)

GIATI is that revelation, in this time, making the oneness of God undeniable to those who have ears to hear.

4. **The Fulfillment of Jesus' Prayer in John 17**

Jesus' mission was not just to perform miracles or teach moral lessons—it was to **make humanity one with God again in their consciousness.**

John 17:21-23 *records his prayer:*

"That they all may be one; as thou, Father, art in me, and I in thee, that they also may be one in us… that the world may know that thou hast sent me, and hast loved them, as thou hast loved me."

GIATI is the **fulfillment of this prayer in today's time.** *It is the Holy Spirit revealing to all who will receive it that* **they and the Father are already one***—that there is no separation.*

This is **not a new message***—it is the same truth Jesus declared, now spoken in this generation.*

5. **The Urgency of This Revelation**

There is no time to remain blind.

- *The longer you believe in separation, the longer you live in darkness.*
- *The longer you wait for salvation, the longer you suffer under the illusion of sin and death.*
- *The longer you reject the truth of GIATI, the longer you remain outside the reality of eternal life.*

Jesus revealed the truth 2,000 years ago, and the world rejected him. Will you do the same today?

GIATI is here **now***—revealing what has always been true:*

God is all there is.
There is no separation.
You and the Father are one.

This is the only truth that leads to eternal life.

The only question is: **Will you receive it?**

Cain and Abel: The Offering of the True Gift

In the story of Cain and Abel, found in **Genesis 4,** *two brothers bring offerings to God. Abel, a shepherd, offers the* **firstborn of his flock,** *while Cain, a farmer, presents the* **fruit of the ground.** *The scripture tells us that God had* **respect for Abel's offering** *but not for Cain's. This rejection fills Cain with anger, leading him to* **murder his brother in jealousy.** *But what is the deeper meaning of this story, and how does it reveal the truth of* **GIATI (God Is All There Is)?**

The Nature of the Offerings

To understand why one offering was accepted and the other was not, we must move beyond the physical details of what they brought. **It was not about meat versus vegetables—it was about the nature of the offering itself.** *Abel's offering represented* **a sacrifice of life, a surrender of self,** *while Cain's represented the* **works of human effort, a product of the ground (the flesh).**

Cain's offering came from **the ground,** *which had already been cursed after Adam and Eve left the garden (Genesis 3:17). This means his offering was an* **attempt to bring something from a fallen state**—*his own effort to please God w***ithout surrendering his own will.** *It was a* **work of the flesh, a gift of self-righteousness,** *believing that his labor was enough to bridge the gap between him and God.*

Abel's offering, however, symbolized something deeper. He offered the **firstborn of the flock,** *representing the* **giving up of self, the surrender to divine will.** *It was not about what he could produce but* **about acknowledging that life itself belongs to God.** *Abel's sacrifice points directly to* **the truth of GIATI**—*that G***od is the source, the giver, and the receiver of all things.** *There is no separation between the giver and what is given when one is fully surrendered in spirit.*

Cain's Jealousy: The Rejection of Oneness

When Cain saw that his brother's offering was accepted and his was not, he became **angry and resentful.** *God warned him, saying:*

"If thou doest well, shalt thou not be accepted? and if thou doest not well, sin lieth at the door." *(Genesis 4:7)*

God was telling Cain that the issue was **not the offering itself, but his heart.** *Cain was still caught in the* **illusion of separation,** *believing he had to bring something to God* **instead of realizing that all things are already God.** *Instead of looking within, he allowed bitterness to consume him, leading him to kill his own brother—the physical manifestation of his rejection of truth.*

Cain represents the **carnal mind,** *the ego that refuses to surrender to the reality of GIATI. He sought to earn approval through his own works, rather than recognizing that* **God is all, and**

there is nothing to earn—only to acknowledge. *Abel represents the* **surrendered soul,** *one who recognizes that God is both the giver and the gift, that* **there is no "me" separate from God.**

Mark of Cain: The Consequence of Separation

After Cain kills Abel, God places a **mark on him**—*a symbol of his* **state of being** *rather than a physical punishment. Cain is cast out, wandering the earth, afraid of being destroyed. This is the* **spiritual condition of all who reject the truth of GIATI**—*a life of wandering, seeking external validation, lost in the illusion of separateness.*

Yet even in Cain's punishment, **God's mercy remains.** *The mark is not just a curse— it is also* **a form of protection,** *showing that even those in darkness are still within the presence of God, though they do not perceive it.*

How This Story Reveals GIATI

Cain and Abel is not just a story of two brothers; it is a representation of **two states of being.**

1. **Cain represents those who live in the illusion of separation,** *thinking they must work to earn favor, trying to bring something to God rather than realizing that God is all there is.*
2. **Abel represents those who have surrendered to the truth of oneness,** *knowing that their very existence is already an offering to God, because* **there is no self apart from God.**

The truth of **GIATI** *is that there are no "good" or "bad" offerings—only* **awareness or ignorance.** *Abel walked in awareness, offering his life fully in spirit. Cain remained in ignorance, believing in his own effort. But* **the spirit of Abel still speaks,** *as Jesus later says:*

"The blood of all the prophets, which was shed from the foundation of the world, may be required of this generation; from the blood of Abel…" *(Luke 11:50-51)*

This confirms that Abel was not just a man—he was **a representation of divine truth,** *just as Cain was a representation of separation.*

The Call to Awaken

This story invites the reader to examine **whether they are Cain or Abel in their understanding of God.** *Are you offering something to God as if He is separate from you? Or are you surrendering fully to the truth that* **you and the Father are one?**

GIATI is the recognition that **there is no separation**—*that God is not an external being watching from afar, but the very essence of who you are. Abel lived in this reality. Cain rejected it and suffered because of his misunderstanding.*

The choice remains today: **to offer from self-effort and live in separation, or to surrender to divine oneness and walk in the light of GIATI.**

The Prodigal Son: The Journey Back to Oneness

The parable of the **Prodigal Son** *is one of the most profound teachings of Jesus, illustrating the* **illusion of separation,** *the* **awakening to truth,** *and the* **restoration of oneness with God.** *Many interpret this story as one of sin and repentance, but when viewed through the lens of* **GIATI (God Is All There Is),** *it becomes a revelation of* **spiritual identity**— *a journey from ignorance back to divine awareness.*

The Departure: The Illusion of Separation

The story begins with a father who has two sons. The younger son, restless and seeking independence, asks for his share of the inheritance and **leaves his father's house** *to go into a* **far country** *(Luke 15:12-13).*

This departure symbolizes more than just rebellion; it represents **the illusion of separation from God.** *The younger son believed that* **his true life was elsewhere,** *that fulfillment could be found outside of the presence of his father. This is the same* **false belief** *that has led many to think they are separate from God, seeking fulfillment in the* **external world,** *rather than realizing that* **all they need is already within them.**

The far country represents the **realm of ignorance,** *where one believes they are self-sustaining, cut off from divine source. This is the* **ego's deception**—*the belief that life, joy, and abundance exist apart from God. But in truth,* **there is no "outside" of God, for GIATI declares that all is God, and nothing exists apart from Him.**

The Wasted Inheritance: The Emptiness of Illusion

In the far country, the son **squanders his inheritance on reckless living** *(Luke 15:13). This is the experience of those who seek* **fulfillment in the material,** *believing that* **possessions, pleasures, and status** *will satisfy them. Yet the* **inheritance—his divine awareness, his connection to the Father—was never meant to be spent on the fleeting things of the world.**

Soon, a **famine arises,** *and the son finds himself in lack. He is forced to take a job* **feeding swine,** *and in his hunger, he* **longs to eat the food of the pigs** *(Luke 15:14-16). This represents* **the lowest state of spiritual ignorance,** *where a person is so removed from their divine nature that they settle for* **things far beneath their true identity.** *The pigs symbolize* **uncleanness, ignorance, and a life controlled by the flesh,** *and the son's willingness to eat their food shows* **how far he had fallen from the awareness of his true self.**

This is the **condition of the lost**—*those who have forgotten that they were never separate from God. They live as though they are* **orphans,** *struggling and suffering in a world of* *limitation, believing they must* **work, toil, and earn their way back to something that was never lost.**

The Awakening: Remembering the Father's House

Then, a turning point occurs. The son **comes to himself** *and remembers that in his* **father's house,** *even the servants have* **more than enough** *(Luke 15:17).*

This is the **moment of awakening—the realization of GIATI.** *The son does not need to continue in suffering, for the abundance he seeks* **was always in the Father's house.** *His true inheritance was never the material wealth he spent—it was his* **relationship with the Father, his awareness of oneness with Him.**

This is the **moment of spiritual return,** *when one realizes that they were* **never truly separate from God.** *The journey away was* **only in the mind**—*the separation was* **an illusion.** *The son decides to return, though in his limited understanding, he still believes he must* **earn back his place** *by becoming a servant.*

This is how many approach God, thinking they must **prove their worth,** *work their way back, or* **plead for acceptance.** *But as GIATI reveals,* **God has never stopped seeing His children as one with Him.** *There is no need to beg for restoration—***it was never lost.**

The Father's Response: The Ever-Present Oneness

As the son approaches, **the father sees him from afar and runs to meet him** *(Luke 15:20). This is the most profound part of the story—***the father never saw his son as lost.**

- *He* **never disowned him.**
- *He* **never demanded repayment.**
- *He* **never made him earn his place back.**

Instead, the father **embraces him immediately,** *before the son can even finish his rehearsed speech of repentance.* **This is the nature of GIATI—there was never separation to begin with.** *The father's love was constant, unchanged by the son's perceived journey away.*

The father commands that the son be **clothed with the best robe, given a ring, and sandals** *(Luke 15:22). These represent his restored identity:*

- **The robe** – *Covering of righteousness (his divine nature was never lost).*
- **The ring** – *Authority as a son (oneness with the Father).*
- **The sandals** – *Freedom (he is not a servant but a rightful heir).*

The father then calls for a **feast and celebration,** *declaring,* **"For this my son was dead and is alive again; he was lost and is found"** *(Luke 15:24).*

This is the **realization of GIATI**—*the understanding that those who believe they are lost are only* **dead in their own perception.** *The moment they awaken to the truth, they realize they were* **never truly lost, only unaware of their divine identity.**

The Older Brother: The Illusion of Earning Righteousness

The parable doesn't end there. The older brother, seeing the celebration, becomes angry. He argues that he has **served faithfully** *all these years, yet never received such a feast (Luke 15:25-30).*

This represents the **mindset of self-righteousness,** *believing that one must* **earn God's favor** *through works. But the father gently reminds him,* **"Son, you are always with me, and all that I have is yours"** *(Luke 15:31).*

This is the truth of **GIATI**—*the inheritance was* **never withheld.** *The older son, though physically close to the father, was just as ignorant of his oneness as the younger son. He thought his father's love was* **conditional,** *based on work, but in reality, it was* **always freely given.**

The Spiritual Revelation of GIATI in the Prodigal Son

The **Prodigal Son is the story of all humanity**—*the journey from ignorance to divine awareness, from the illusion of separation to the reality of oneness.*

1. **The younger son** *represents those who have forgotten their divine identity, seeking fulfillment in the world but realizing that true life is only found in* **oneness with God.**
2. **The father** *represents* **the eternal truth of GIATI**—*that* **God is all,** *and nothing is ever truly separate from Him. He does not demand repayment, for there was never a real debt—only a misunderstanding of identity.*
3. **The older brother** *represents those who believe they must* **earn righteousness,** failing to realize that all has **already been given.**

The true lesson of the **Prodigal Son** *is that there was* **never a need to return, only to wake up to the truth.** *The son thought he had been far from the father, but in reality,* **he was never outside of his father's love.** *This is* **GIATI—the eternal truth that all is God, and nothing exists apart from Him.**

Thus, the story is not about forgiveness **from separation**—*it is about* **awakening from the illusion of separation.** *The Father never left, and the son was never truly lost. The only thing that changed was* **awareness.**

And so, the call is the same today: **wake up to the truth of GIATI, and see that you were never outside of the Father's house.**

The Carnal Mind: The Great Deception that Opposes GIATI (the Holy Spirit)

To understand GIATI—God Is All There Is—one must recognize the fundamental opposition between the carnal mind and spiritual truth. The carnal mind is the great illusion, the veil that blinds humanity from perceiving the divine reality of oneness with God. It is the root of separation, suffering, and spiritual death. Scripture makes it clear:

"For to be carnally minded is death; but to be spiritually minded is life and peace." *(Romans 8:6)*

This one verse alone exposes the truth: the carnal mind is not just a lesser way of thinking—it is death itself. It is the consciousness that operates outside of divine awareness, feeding on illusions rather than truth. To be carnally minded means to believe in the lie of separation, to trust in the physical world over the spiritual, and to be enslaved by the senses rather than guided by the Spirit.

What Is the Carnal Mind?

The carnal mind is the consciousness that is rooted in flesh, ego, and the illusion of self-sufficiency apart from God. It is the mind that:

- **Believes in separation from God** – *It operates under the false idea that God is distant, rather than recognizing that God is the very essence of existence.*
- **Seeks fulfillment in the physical** – *It chases after material success, status, validation, and earthly pleasures as if they can bring true satisfaction.*
- **Fears lack and death** – *It sees scarcity instead of divine abundance and dreads physical death instead of understanding eternal life.*
- **Lives by human reasoning instead of divine revelation** – *It trusts in intellect, logic, and worldly wisdom rather than in the Spirit of Truth.*

The carnal mind is not just ignorant—it is hostile to God. **"Because the carnal mind is enmity against God: for it is not subject to the law of God, neither indeed can be."** *(Romans 8:7) It cannot comprehend spiritual things, and it actively resists the truth of GIATI (the Holy Spirit).*

Examples of Carnal-Minded Thinking

1. **Materialism & Dependence on Wealth**

   - *A person believes that money is their security and that success is measured by possessions. They do not see that God is their source, not the economy, their job, or their savings. This mindset breeds fear, greed, and anxiety because they trust in what can be taken away rather than in the eternal presence of God.*

2. **Religious Legalism & Rituals Without Revelation**

   - *Some people follow religious traditions without understanding their spiritual significance. They may think that attending church, reading scriptures, or doing good deeds is what saves them. But without the awareness of GIATI (the Holy Spirit), their actions are empty—void of the Spirit's life. Jesus rebuked this mindset in the Pharisees, who followed laws outwardly but remained spiritually blind.*

3. **Fear of Death & the Unknown**

   - *The carnal mind is terrified of death because it sees life as only physical. But Jesus came to reveal that eternal life is not a future promise but a present reality. The spiritually minded person understands that death is an illusion—the Spirit never dies, for God is eternal, and we are one with Him.*

4. **Judgment & Division**

   - *The carnal mind sees people as separate—good vs. evil, righteous vs. sinner, worthy vs. unworthy. It thrives on judgment. But GIATI reveals that all things exist within God. While some remain in ignorance (darkness), others awaken to the truth (light), but all are expressions of the One.*

5. **Victim Mentality & Blaming Others**

   - *A person who is carnally minded believes that life is happening to them, rather than through them. They blame circumstances, other people, or even God for their struggles. But the spiritually awakened person knows that divine power is within, and through faith, they manifest the life God intends.*

The Danger of the Carnal Mind (Continued)

To live according to the flesh—the carnal mind—is to walk in death even while physically alive. This is not just about physical death, but spiritual death, which is separation from the awareness of God. **When a person is ruled by the carnal mind, they cannot manifest the Holy Spirit.**

Why? Because **the Holy Spirit cannot dwell where the illusion of separation is embraced.** *The Spirit of God is life itself, but the carnal mind operates in opposition to it. This is why Jesus said,* **"The flesh profits nothing: the words that I speak to you, they are spirit, and they are life."** *(John 6:63)*

If a person remains in the carnal mind, they are trapped in fear, judgment, and limitation. They will never experience the fullness of God's presence, power, and provision. **They**

cannot truly live in GIATI because they are still seeing themselves as separate from God rather than as an expression of Him.

The Spiritual Mind: The Only Path to Life

The solution to the carnal mind is spiritual awakening—recognizing that God is all there is and that you are not separate from Him. This is what Paul meant when he said:

"Be ye transformed by the renewing of your mind." (Romans 12:2)

This transformation is the process of shedding the carnal mind and stepping into divine consciousness. It is **the awakening to GIATI (the Holy Spirit)—the realization that God is not external but the very essence of your being.**

How to Overcome the Carnal Mind

1. **Shift from Fear to Faith** – *Recognize that lack, danger, and death are illusions of separation. In God, there is only abundance, security, and eternal life.*
2. **Stop Seeking External Validation** – *The carnal mind craves approval from others, but the spiritual mind knows that your worth comes from God alone.* **You are already complete in Him.**
3. **Let Go of Judgment** – *Understand that every soul is at a different stage of awakening. Rather than condemning others, shine the light of truth.*
4. **Dwell in the Presence of God** – *Stay in awareness of GIATI, understanding that every moment is a manifestation of God's presence.*
5. **Walk in the Spirit, Not in the Flesh** – *Instead of living for material gain, ego, or self-interest, align yourself with divine truth. The more you abide in the Spirit, the less power the carnal mind has over you.*

GIATI: The Ultimate Freedom from the Carnal Mind

The carnal mind is bondage. It keeps people enslaved to fear, striving, and suffering. But GIATI is liberation. When you realize God Is All There Is, the illusion of separation dissolves, and you walk in the fullness of divine life.

This is why Jesus said, **"You shall know the truth, and the truth shall make you free."** *(John 8:32)*

That truth is GIATI. When you embrace it, the carnal mind loses its grip, and you step into eternal life—not as something you attain in the future, but as a reality that is here now.

To be spiritually minded is to see as God sees, live as God lives, and love as God loves. It is the only path to true life and peace.

Which mind will you choose?

The Power of Seeing Everything as Spirit: The Transformative Vision of GIATI

The key to true spiritual enlightenment is redefining everything as spirit— understanding that spirit is God, and therefore, all things are expressions of the divine. This is not just a shift in vocabulary but a shift in consciousness, a revelation that transforms the way one interacts with the world. GIATI is not just a philosophy; it is the unveiling of reality as it truly is. It is the breaking of the illusion of separation and material limitation.

To see all things as spirit is to see them as they are—not as separate, fleeting, or bound to physical form, but as manifestations of the eternal. When you redefine everything as spirit, you are aligning your mind with the truth that God is all there is. The benefit of this understanding is that it removes the ego's false claims of ownership, control, and authorship. If all is spirit, then all credit and glory belong to God alone. Nothing is self-sustained, nothing is independent from the source—everything flows from the one eternal spirit.

The Impact on Spiritual Understanding

When one begins to see everything as spirit, a profound transformation occurs. No longer do they categorize existence into sacred and secular, divine and ordinary—everything becomes a revelation of God. This shift reshapes the way one perceives life, relationships, challenges, and even death itself. The individual who has trained their mind to recognize spirit in all things is already prepared for their transition beyond the flesh. Death is not an end but merely the shedding of a temporary garment. Because they have already conditioned their mind to recognize everything as spirit, the transition into their spiritual state is seamless.

But for those who remain carnally minded—who see the world only through the lens of physicality, ownership, and separation—the transition will be one of disorientation and confusion. The carnal mind, conditioned to grasp and cling to the physical, will struggle in a spiritual existence where there is nothing to hold onto but God. Those who failed to see spirit while in the flesh will find themselves unable to comprehend existence without it. They will be like a blind man suddenly placed in a world of light, unable to function because they never learned to see.

The True Meaning of Being Spiritual

This is what makes GIATI so revelatory—it unveils the truth of existence and allows individuals to live in alignment with reality while still in the body. It is not about religion or rituals; it is about perception. When you truly see all as spirit, your entire way of being changes.

- *You no longer judge people based on their external appearance, status, or material wealth because you recognize that all are spirit.*

- *You no longer fear loss because you know that spirit cannot be diminished, destroyed, or taken away.*
- *You no longer seek to control or dominate because you understand that all things belong to God.*
- *You no longer suffer from the illusion of separation because you recognize that there is only one presence, one being, one truth—God.*

This is the awakening that changes everything. This is what the world desperately needs. If humanity saw everything as spirit, there would be no war, no greed, no division, no fear. People would treat one another with love and reverence, knowing they are encountering God in every face, every situation, and every breath.

This is the true meaning of being spiritual—not following a set of religious rules, not performing rituals, but seeing reality as it truly is. And when you see all as spirit, you see all as God. This is the ultimate truth, the key to eternal life, and the path to oneness. This is GIATI.

The Oneness of All Things: The Undeniable Reality of GIATI

Chapter: The Physical Testimony of Spirit

Everything we see, touch, and experience in this world is built upon a single foundational truth: all is one. This is not just a spiritual principle—it is an undeniable fact, evident even in the fabric of physical reality itself.

Science has long confirmed that all matter is composed of atoms. Atoms, in their essence, are three yet one—protons, neutrons, and electrons—existing in unity while performing distinct functions. This very structure is a reflection of the divine nature, mirroring the Godhead, which is three yet one. Just as the Father, Son, and Holy Spirit operate as one indivisible essence, so too do atoms form the foundation of all that exists.

The deception arises when we perceive things as separate—when we look at the world and fail to recognize that everything, no matter how diverse in form, is made of the same fundamental substance. This is the illusion of division, the great misunderstanding that has led humanity into darkness. To see matter as disconnected pieces is to deny the very nature of reality. In truth, all things, from the vast galaxies to the smallest grain of sand, are composed of the same atomic unity.

This physical oneness serves as an undeniable testimony of the spiritual oneness. If everything in the material world is fundamentally one, how much more is this true in the realm of spirit? The same Spirit, the same Divine Essence, flows through all, giving life, form, and purpose. There is no separation in God, for God is all there is—expressing as all that is.

To deny this truth is to resist what has already been proven, both by scientific evidence and by divine revelation. It is not a matter of speculation but of perception—whether one chooses to recognize and accept the truth or remain blind to it. The world appears fragmented only to the mind that has not yet awakened to oneness. But when the veil is lifted, when understanding dawns, the simplicity of GIATI becomes unmistakable.

There is no complexity in God's truth. It is as simple as this: **all is one in God as God.** *Just as the physical world bears witness to oneness, so too does the spirit. This is the revelation that ends all doubt, the undeniable foundation of GIATI.*

The Reality of GIATI is Unavoidable

GIATI is not a theory, nor a belief to be debated. It is the fundamental nature of existence. To reject it is to reject the very fabric of reality itself. Those who seek truth will find that it was never hidden—it has always been evident, woven into the very nature of creation. It is time to see, to perceive, and to know that there is no other truth but this:

God is all there is.

GIATI's Perspective on Smoking, Marijuana, and Drinking Alcohol

At its core, **GIATI—God Is All There Is** *calls for the* **awareness of divine presence within and the alignment of one's actions with this truth.** *The question is not about* **following rules,** *but about understanding* **what serves or hinders one's spiritual awareness.**

1. **Smoking Cigarettes → The Illusion of Control**

Smoking is often used as a way to **cope with stress, anxiety, or addiction.** *It is a habit that seeks to bring comfort but does so by harming the very vessel through which Spirit expresses.* **If God is all there is, then the body is not separate from Him—it is an extension of His being.** *To knowingly harm it is to act from a place of* **disconnection, not alignment.**

Yet, **GIATI does not condemn—***it calls for awareness. The real question is:*
"Is this action bringing me closer to the awareness of God, or further from it?"

When one truly sees themselves as Spirit, **the desire to harm the body fades.** *Healing is not about force or restriction—it is about* **awakening to one's divine nature, where addiction is no longer needed.**

2. **Marijuana → The Escape vs. The Alignment**

Marijuana carries different intentions depending on its use. Some use it for **medical relief,** *while others use it for* **recreation or escape.** *GIATI does not categorize anything as inherently "good" or "bad"—instead, it asks:*

"Does this enhance or cloud my awareness of divine truth?"

- *If marijuana is used to* **heighten spiritual awareness,** *bringing clarity and stillness, then it is a tool for alignment.*
- *If it is used to* **numb, escape, or avoid reality,** *then it is a distraction from truth.*

The key is not in the substance but in the **intention behind its use.** *Anything that causes* **dependence, dulls spiritual awareness, or becomes a false source of peace is an illusion.** *True peace is already within—***it does not need to be smoked or consumed.**

3. **Drinking Alcohol → Dulling vs. Awakening the Spirit**

Alcohol, like marijuana, affects consciousness. It lowers inhibition, relaxes the body, and can create a sense of **freedom.** *But the real question remains:*

"Is this leading me deeper into divine awareness, or further into illusion?"

- *Moderate drinking may* **not hinder** *spiritual awareness, but excess drinking* **dulls the mind, clouds judgment, and disconnects one from truth.**
- *If drinking is used to escape, suppress emotions, or feed the ego,* **it is leading one further into separation.**

GIATI does not operate from a place of **restriction, but realization.** *A person aligned with divine truth will not* **need** *substances for joy, peace, or confidence, because* **they are already full in Spirit.**

The Ultimate Truth of GIATI

The question is never about whether something is "right" or "wrong." GIATI does not impose religious dogma—it invites you to **examine your awareness.**

Are you using substances to heighten your divine connection, or to numb yourself from truth?

When one fully awakens to the Spirit within, **there is no longer a craving for external crutches.** *Joy, peace, clarity, and freedom are found* **within the realization of oneness with God—not in a cigarette, a joint, or a drink.**

God is all there is—including you. *If you truly believe this, what do you need that does not already exist within?*

GIATI's Perspective on the Top Social Issues: The Spiritual Lens

At the core of **GIATI—God Is All There Is** *is the understanding that all things, seen and unseen, are expressions of the same divine essence. Every issue that humanity faces is a reflection of either* **awareness or ignorance of this truth.** *The struggles in the world are not external forces working against people but* **internal misalignment** *with divine reality. Below is how GIATI views these social issues from a spiritual perspective:*

1. **Mental Health & Well-Being → Remembering the Mind of God**

Many suffer mentally because they are **disconnected from their true identity.** *Anxiety, depression, and fear stem from identifying with the* **carnal mind,** *which constantly battles to survive in an illusionary world. GIATI calls individuals to shift their awareness from the mind of the flesh to the* **mind of the Spirit**—*where there is peace, joy, and clarity.* **The solution is not in external validation but in the stillness of knowing: You and God are One.**

2. **Economic Inequality & Poverty → Recognizing Divine Abundance**

The illusion of **lack** *arises when people see themselves as separate from the source of all provision. In the world, resources are hoarded and controlled, creating disparities. But in divine* *reality,* **abundance is not material—it is spiritual.** *Those who truly align with the Spirit of GIATI will see provision manifest in their lives—not by striving, but by trusting the eternal flow of divine abundance.*

3. **Racial & Social Injustice → Seeing Beyond Flesh**

Racism, discrimination, and social oppression exist because people identify **with the body rather than the Spirit.** *The carnal mind sees separation by race, status, and nationality, while the Spirit sees* **only God expressing in infinite forms.** *True justice comes not from laws alone, but from the awakening of all people to the reality that* **there is no "other"—all are One.**

4. **Gender Inequality & Women's Rights → Balancing Divine Exp**ression

The Spirit of God is neither male nor female, yet it expresses through both. The imbalance in gender roles comes from a **distorted view of authority and power.** *GIATI recognizes that all* **are equal expressions of God,** *and the only true submission is* **to the Spirit within, not societal roles.** *Any system that seeks to diminish or suppress is operating from* **illusion, not divine truth.**

5. **Family & Relationship Struggles → Restoring Spiritual Order**

Many relationships fail because they are built on **ego, expectation, and control rather than divine flow.** *In GIATI, a relationship is not about* **ownership or hierarchy** *but about two spirits aligning in harmony. The key to peace in family life is recognizing* **God's presence in each person,** *not forcing roles or conditions onto them.* **Love is not possession—it is freedom.**

6. **Addiction & Substance Abuse → Searching for the Presence of God**

Addiction is the soul's **misguided attempt** *to fill an internal void with external substances. The deep hunger that leads to addiction is actually the* **spirit's longing to return to its divine awareness.** *The cure is not just physical detox but* **spiritual restoration— recognizing that what one seeks has always been within.** *GIATI calls for the shift from self- destruction to self-realization.*

7. **Homelessness & Housing Crisis → Reclaiming True Security**

No person is truly homeless, for **their home is in God.** *The problem of physical homelessness exists because the world operates on* **ownership, greed, and exclusion.** *GIATI challenges the belief that security comes from money and possessions.* **One who dwells in the Spirit is never without provision.** *The world must awaken to the truth that* **when we give as God gives, no one will lack.**

8. **Crime & Violence → The Blindness of Separation**

Crime stems from the belief in **lack, powerlessness, or vengeance.** *Violence exists because people see themselves as* **separate from each other,** *rather than as expressions of the same divine* *life. GIATI reveals that* **when one harms another, they are harming themselves.** *True justice is not about punishment but about* **awakening to unity, where harm becomes unnecessary.**

9. **Healthcare Access & Quality → The Body as an Illusion**

The struggle over healthcare comes from a **misunderstanding of health itself.** *The carnal mind sees sickness as a force outside of us, when in truth, all healing comes from* **alignment with divine reality.** *While medicine and treatment serve a purpose, GIATI teaches that* **true healing happens first in consciousness—through peace, faith, and spiritual wholeness.**

10. **Education Inequality & Student Debt → True Knowledge vs. Worldly Knowledge**

The world's education system teaches **facts, but not truth.** *Many struggle because they are taught to memorize information, not* **awaken their divine intelligence.** *GIATI sees true education as* **not just schooling but enlightenment—knowing oneself as Spirit.** *The greatest knowledge is the awareness that* **God is all there is, and you are that expression.**

11. **Environmental Issues & Climate Change → Stewardship of God's Expression**

The earth is not separate from us—it is an **expression of God, just as we are.** *The destruction of nature is the result of* **greed, ignorance, and the illusion that humanity is superior to creation.** *GIATI calls for a return to harmony, where nature is not exploited but honored as a* **reflection of the divine presence in all things.**

12. **Political & Social Division → The Carnal Battle for Power**

The world is divided because it is **ruled by egos fighting for control.** *Governments and leaders operate under the illusion that power comes from dominance, rather than from divine authority. GIATI reveals that* **true power is not control over others, but unity with the Spirit.** *When people awaken to this truth,* **division will dissolve, and peace will emerge.**

GIATI's Ultimate Message on Social Issues

Every issue that humanity faces is **the result of forgetting its divine nature.** *The world suffers because it sees itself as separate—from God, from each other, from the source of all things.* **GIATI does not offer a religious doctrine, a set of rules, or a political stance.** *It offers only this:*

A call to awaken.

A call to remember that **God is all there is, and that includes you.** *The moment this truth is realized,* **fear dissolves, suffering ends, and the illusion of separation disappears.** *Until then, the world will continue in its struggle, fighting battles that only exist in the mind.*

The question is no longer about fixing the world—it is about awakening to the truth.

Will you see it?

Positive and Negative Spirits: The Awakening to Oneness

Throughout existence, we see the interplay of opposites—light and darkness, hot and cold, positive and negative. In mathematics, electricity, and even the natural world, these dualities exist not as separate forces in conflict, but as complementary expressions of a greater whole. The same is true in the realm of spirit.

A **positive spirit** *is a spirit-being who has awakened to the truth of oneness with God. This being recognizes that there is no separation, no division—only God expressing as them. They live in full awareness that their very existence is the manifestation of the divine.*

A **negative spirit,** *however, is not an evil or wicked being. In fact, negativity in this context has nothing to do with moral behavior or deeds. To understand its true meaning, we must examine the root of the word negative. It derives from negate, which means to deny the truth of something. Therefore, a negative spirit is one who is* **God in essence but denies their own divinity***—not in rebellion, but in ignorance.*

This is the human condition before spiritual awakening. It is not that some people are created as "bad" spirits while others are "good." The only difference between a positive and a negative spirit is **awareness.** *The negative spirit lives in a state of denial, believing itself to be independent, separate, and self-sustaining apart from God. The positive spirit has simply recognized the truth—it was never separate to begin with.*

Recognition: The Only Step of True Repentance

Consider the process of recovery in Alcoholics Anonymous. The very first step in their twelve-step program is:

"We admitted we were powerless over alcohol—that our lives had become unmanageable."

Before healing can begin, an alcoholic must first acknowledge their condition. Without this admission, no real change can take place. The same is true in spiritual awakening. Until a person **recognizes** *that their previous way of thinking was based on an illusion of separation from God, they remain in a state of spiritual denial—a negative spirit.*

The moment this truth is revealed, and one **knows** *they are and have always been one with God, true repentance has taken place. But this repentance is not what many have been taught. It is not an act of sorrow, confession of wrongdoing, or repeated rituals of seeking forgiveness. Repentance in its purest form simply means* **a change of mind***—a shift from believing in separation to knowing oneness.*

And here is the profound reality: **this repentance only happens once.**

Once a person truly sees their oneness with God, they cannot unsee it. Though distractions may come, though life may at times pull their attention away, the truth will always return to their remembrance:

"I and my Father are one."

It is not about striving to be good or avoiding evil. It is not about accumulating righteous deeds or resisting sinful acts. It is about the **realization** *that there is no other source or substance in existence besides God. Nothing else can be.*

GIATI: The Spiritual Essence of Oneness

This understanding is the very core of GIATI—God Is All There Is. The message of GIATI is not one of religious dogma or man-made doctrine. It is the revelation that there is no existence outside of God, and therefore, all that we are, all that we do, and all that we experience is God in expression.

Before awakening, we may think we are living independently—making our own decisions, struggling through life, defining ourselves by personal successes and failures. But this is the illusion of the negative spirit, the one that negates its own divine nature.

When the awakening comes, it is not an external conversion, but an **internal recognition:**

I am not separate. I never was.

This is the moment one transitions from negative to positive—not by changing their deeds, but by accepting their divine reality. And once this truth is known, life is never the same.

The Eternal Remembrance

Even though this realization is permanent, there will be moments when the awareness of oneness is not at the forefront of your mind. The responsibilities of life, the distractions of the world, and the habits of past conditioning may temporarily cloud this understanding.

But **it will always return to you.**

Once you have seen, you cannot unsee. Once you have known, you cannot unknow. This is the power of true spiritual awakening—it is not a fleeting experience, nor is it something that requires constant reaffirmation.

It is simply **the truth of who you are.**

The transition from a negative spirit to a positive spirit is the journey from ignorance to knowing, from denial to acceptance, from separation to unity. And once the journey is made, the truth remains forever:

God is all there is, and I am one with God.

Predestination or Free Will? The Spiritual Truth Behind Judas' Betrayal and Peter's Denial

One of the greatest debates in spiritual understanding is whether human beings act by free will or if their choices are predetermined by divine design. Nowhere is this question more powerfully demonstrated than in the stories of Judas Iscariot and Peter—two disciples who, despite walking with Jesus, found themselves fulfilling prophecies that seemed beyond their control.

Jesus told Judas, "What you are about to do, do quickly" (John 13:27), indicating that his betrayal was inevitable. He also warned Peter, "Before the rooster crows, you will deny me three times" (Matthew 26:34). If Jesus already knew their actions before they took place, does that mean they had no choice? Or is there something deeper being revealed?

To understand the truth behind their actions, we must go beyond the surface and look at the spiritual message beneath their stories.

Judas: The Betrayer Who Played His Part

The Role of Judas in the Divine Plan

Judas Iscariot is one of the most infamous figures in history—the disciple who betrayed Jesus for thirty pieces of silver. But was Judas merely a greedy traitor, or was he playing a necessary role in a greater spiritual drama?

Jesus **chose** *Judas as one of the twelve, knowing exactly who he was and what he would do. He even stated, "Have I not chosen you, the Twelve? Yet one of you is a devil." (John 6:70). This statement reveals that Jesus was fully aware of Judas' destiny long before the betrayal occurred.*

Judas' betrayal set in motion the events that led to Jesus' crucifixion—a necessary step in the fulfillment of his purpose. Without Judas, there would be no cross. Without the cross, there would be no resurrection.

Was Judas Bound by Fate?

On the surface, it appears that Judas had no choice. But in truth, he had the same choice as anyone else—he could have recognized the light, but he remained in darkness. His heart was already distant from Jesus before the betrayal, evidenced by his greed and hypocrisy (John 12:6). The moment he agreed to betray Jesus, he sealed his fate—not because he was forced, but because he aligned himself with darkness.

In a spiritual sense, Judas represents those who walk with divine truth but never fully embrace it. He was close to the light but never allowed the light to transform him. When confronted with his own actions, rather than seeking redemption, he was consumed by guilt and despair, leading to his self-inflicted end (Matthew 27:5).

Judas teaches us that destiny is not forced upon us—we align with it by the state of our own heart. He had free will, but his choices led him to be the vessel for betrayal.

Peter: The Denier Who Was Redeemed

The Role of Peter in the Divine Plan

Peter was one of Jesus' most devoted followers, yet Jesus predicted that he would deny him three times before the rooster crowed. Peter, full of confidence, rejected this idea:

> *"Even if I have to die with you, I will never disown you." (Matthew 26:35)*

And yet, when the moment of testing came, Peter did exactly as Jesus had said. Out of fear, he denied knowing Jesus three times (Luke 22:61-62).

Was Peter's Denial Predestined?

If Jesus had already declared that Peter would deny him, did Peter have any real choice? Or was he simply following a script that had already been written?

Peter's actions were a result of his fear, not an absence of free will. Unlike Judas, Peter loved Jesus deeply, but in the moment of trial, his human weakness overtook him. His denial was not because he was chosen to be a traitor, but because he had not yet fully embodied the strength of the Spirit.

However, Peter's story did not end in failure. After his denial, he wept bitterly (Luke 22:62). This sorrow showed that, unlike Judas, Peter's heart remained open to redemption. After the resurrection, Jesus restored him by asking three times, "Do you love me?" (John 21:15-17), symbolically reversing his three denials.

Peter's denial teaches us that failure is not the end of our story. Even when we falter, we are not cast away. The difference between Peter and Judas is that Peter returned to the light, while Judas allowed darkness to consume him.

Does This Prove That Everything Is Predetermined?

At first glance, these events seem to suggest that human actions are predetermined, but a deeper understanding reveals otherwise.

1. **Foreknowledge Does Not Mean Force** – *Jesus knew what Judas and Peter would do, but he did not force them to act that way. Knowing something in advance does not remove the person's responsibility. Just as a teacher may know that a student*

will fail a test due to lack of study, the student still has the choice to prepare or not.

2. **Divine Plan Works Through Free Will** – *God's purpose is never disrupted by human choices, but human choices determine their role in His plan. Judas' heart aligned with darkness, and he became the betrayer. Peter's heart aligned with love, and he was restored. Both men had free will, but their choices placed them in different positions in the unfolding of divine events.*

3. **GIATI: The Spiritual Truth Behind Their Actions**

- **Judas represents those who walk with truth but never fully accept it.** *His betrayal was not because he was forced to do so, but because he chose to remain in darkness.*
- **Peter represents those who struggle but ultimately overcome.** *His denial was not because he was destined to fail, but because he had not yet matured spiritually.*

In the larger context of GIATI (God Is All There Is), these events reveal that even when we act against divine truth, we are never truly outside of it. Every action—good or bad—is used in the unfolding of the divine will. Even Judas, though lost, played a role in the greater plan.

The Ultimate Lesson: Awakening or Falling Away?

Both Judas and Peter were given the opportunity to align with truth. One fell into despair, while the other rose into redemption. This is the choice all of humanity faces:

- *Will we recognize the divine presence within us and allow it to transform us?*
- *Or will we remain in ignorance, resisting the light and fulfilling a role that leads to our own downfall?*

God's will is not about controlling our actions—it is about offering us the opportunity to awaken. Whether we align with divine truth or resist it is up to us. But in the end, **the light will always prevail.**

Beyond Betrayal and Denial: The Deeper Mysteries of Judas and Peter

While the stories of Judas' betrayal and Peter's denial have been analyzed through the lens of prophecy, free will, and divine purpose, there are deeper layers to uncover. These events are not just historical moments but symbolic representations of how humanity responds to divine truth. Their actions reveal the spiritual struggle between **awakening and resistance,** *between* **embracing divinity or remaining in ignorance.**

To go further, we must explore:

1. **The Consciousness Behind Their Actions** – *What truly drove Judas to betray and Peter to deny?*
2. **The Role of Fear vs. The Role of Self-Will** – *Were they simply weak, or was something greater at play?*
3. **The Parallel to Humanity's Awakening** – *How do these figures represent the spiritual journey of every person?*
4. **Did Judas Have to Perish?** – *Was his end inevitable, or did he have another path?*
5. **What Happened to Peter After His Restoration?** – *What does his transformation teach us about divine grace?*

1. The Consciousness Behind Their Actions

Everything we do stems from **the consciousness we operate from.** *Judas and Peter were not mere instruments fulfilling prophecy; they were acting from the spiritual state they had cultivated.*

- **Judas operated from a transactional mindset.** *He saw Jesus through the lens of personal gain and expected a Messiah who would rise in earthly power. His betrayal was not just an act of greed but of* **disillusionment**—*Jesus was not the Messiah he wanted him to be.*
- **Peter operated from fear and survival.** *His denial was not an act of malice but of self-preservation. He loved Jesus, but his love had not yet overcome his attachment to the physical world. He had not yet learned to value the Spirit over the flesh.*

This is a key revelation: **Our actions are the result of our inner alignment.**

- *Judas was aligned with* **ego and disillusionment,** *so he betrayed.*
- *Peter was aligned with* **faith but fear,** *so he denied.*

2. The Role of Fear vs. The Role of Self-Will

Judas and Peter's actions also expose the two primary forces that lead people away from truth:

- **Fear of Consequences (Peter's downfall)** – *He feared the cost of standing with Jesus. This represents those who believe in divine truth but hesitate when tested. They may be spiritually aware but struggle to stand firm.*
- **The Desire to Control God's Plan (Judas' downfall)** – *Judas was not merely weak; he was frustrated. He wanted a Messiah who would overthrow Rome, and when Jesus didn't align with that expectation, he took matters into his own hands. This represents those who reject divine truth because it does not fit their desires.*

Fear makes us hesitate in our faith, but **self-will** *makes us rebel against it. One leads to temporary failure (Peter), the other to complete downfall (Judas).*

3. The Parallel to Humanity's Awakening

Judas and Peter are not just individuals; they symbolize the two responses humanity has to divine awakening.

- **Judas represents those who refuse to let go of their own agenda.** *They resist the truth because it does not align with their will. They attempt to manipulate God's plan rather than surrender to it.*
- **Peter represents those who falter but find redemption.** *They may fail, but they ultimately turn back toward the light.*

Every person must decide which path they will take: **Will we reject divine truth because it doesn't fit our expectations, or will we surrender and be transformed?**

4. Did Judas Have to Perish?

Many assume that Judas' fate was sealed, that his betrayal meant he was doomed. But was there another path for him?

Peter denied Jesus three times but was restored. Judas betrayed Jesus once—could he not also have been redeemed?

This raises a profound question: **Did Judas perish because of what he did, or because he believed he could not be forgiven?**

Consider this: After Peter's denial, he **wept bitterly** *(Luke 22:62), yet he remained. After Judas' betrayal, he was* **overcome by guilt and took his own life** *(Matthew 27:5).*

Judas' true downfall was not the betrayal—it was that he **did not return to Jesus.** *If he had sought forgiveness, would he not have received it? His real tragedy was that he lost faith, not only in Jesus but in redemption itself.*

This reveals a critical spiritual truth: **The greatest danger is not failure—it is believing that failure is final.**

5. What Happened to Peter After His Restoration?

Peter's story did not end with failure; it became one of the most powerful examples of transformation in all of Scripture. After being restored by Jesus, he became a fearless leader, preaching boldly and eventually dying for the truth he once denied.

This teaches us:

- **God does not discard the fallen—He restores them.**
- **Denial does not disqualify us—only staying in denial does.**
- **Our greatest failures can be the foundation of our greatest transformation.**

Free Will and Divine Plan: The Final Understanding

Judas and Peter both played roles in a divine unfolding, but they were not puppets. Their choices aligned them with different outcomes. This reveals the paradox of free will and divine order:

- **God's plan is inevitable—but how we participate in it is up to us.**
- **Every person has a role in the divine unfolding—but that role is determined by the consciousness they cultivate.**

Judas **aligned with self-will and was lost.**
Peter **aligned with humility and was restored.**

Both were given choices. Both fulfilled prophecy—not because they had no choice, but because their inner condition led them to make those choices.

GIATI: The Eternal Truth in This Story

Judas and Peter are not just figures of history; they are representations of spiritual states that exist within all of us.

- **Judas represents the part of us that resists truth and chooses our own will over divine wisdom.**
- **Peter represents the part of us that may falter but ultimately finds our way back to divine truth.**

*In the greater understanding of GIATI—***God Is All There Is***—this means that even those who resist, betray, or fail are still part of the divine reality.* **Nothing exists outside of God, even rejection, even denial.**

The question is not whether we are part of the divine story—the question is how we will align with it.

Final Thought: Awakening or Remaining in Darkness?

- *Will we be like Judas, resisting truth because it does not fit our expectations?*
- *Or will we be like Peter, stumbling but allowing divine love to restore us?*

Both men walked with Jesus. Both men failed. The difference was that **one believed in redemption, and the other believed his failure was final.**

The lesson is clear: **No matter how far we fall, there is always a path back—if we choose to take it.**

Understanding Slavery in Scripture: A GIATI Perspective

The topic of slavery in the Bible is often used by critics to challenge the righteousness of God, claiming that His Word condones oppression. However, to understand these scriptures correctly, we must go beyond a surface-level reading and perceive them through the lens of divine truth—the revelation that **God is all there is,** *and that all life is an expression of the One Spirit. When we interpret scripture with this understanding, we see that the Bible does not endorse human domination, but rather speaks to the conditions of mankind in their ignorance and provides the spiritual wisdom necessary to bring all into freedom.*

Commonly Cited Scriptures on Slavery

Many opponents of the faith cite the following verses to argue that God permits or even encourages slavery:

1. **Exodus 21:2-6 (Laws on Hebrew Servants)**

"If you buy a Hebrew servant, he shall serve six years; and in the seventh he shall go out free for nothing."

2. **Leviticus 25:44-46 (Foreign Slaves as Property)**

"Your male and female slaves are to come from the nations around you; from them you may buy slaves."

3. **Ephesians 6:5 (Servants, Obey Your Masters)**

"Servants, be obedient to them that are your masters according to the flesh, with fear and trembling, in singleness of your heart, as unto Christ."

4. **Titus 2:9-10 (Teach Slaves to Obey Masters)**

"Exhort servants to be obedient unto their own masters, and to please them well in all things."

5. **1 Peter 2:18 (Submit Even to Harsh Masters)**

"Servants, be subject to your masters with all fear; not only to the good and gentle, but also to the forward."

At first glance, these verses seem to condone slavery, leading many to accuse the Bible of moral failure. But **what do these passages actually mean in the light of divine understanding?**

Understanding the Context of Biblical Servitude

To grasp the full meaning of these scriptures, we must first understand the nature of servitude in biblical times. Unlike the brutal chattel slavery practiced in more recent history, ancient servitude in Israel was often:

- **A form of debt repayment** – *Individuals could sell themselves into servitude to pay off debts, but were to be released in the seventh year (Exodus 21:2).*
- **A system of labor regulation** – *Laws were given to ensure humane treatment of servants (Exodus 21:26-27).*
- **A temporary condition** – *The Jubilee year (Leviticus 25:10) ensured that no one remained enslaved permanently among the Israelites.*

When we read these laws in the context of a developing society, we see that God was **not endorsing slavery,** *but rather regulating a human institution to prevent abuse.*

The GIATI Understanding – The Inner Meaning of Slavery

From the **GIATI** *(God Is All There Is) perspective, scripture must be understood spiritually, beyond the limitations of human history. The true meaning of slavery in these verses is* **spiritual bondage***—the condition of being enslaved by ignorance, sin, and the false belief in separation from God.*

1. **Slavery Represents Bondage to the Flesh**

   - *In* **Ephesians 6:5,** *when Paul instructs servants to obey their masters "as unto Christ," he is not affirming oppression, but teaching a higher principle:*
   - If one finds themselves in servitude, they are to serve in righteousness, knowing their true freedom is in God.
   - *This aligns with Christ's teaching that* **the kingdom of God is within you**
   - (Luke 17:21).

2. **Masters and Servants Symbolize the Soul and the Flesh**

   - *In* **1 Peter 2:18,** *when Peter tells servants to submit even to harsh masters, this illustrates the* **subjugation of the flesh to the Spirit.**
   - *The "harsh master" represents the trials of life, which, when endured in faith, lead the soul into divine realization.*

3. **The Exodus as the Journey from Slavery to Spiritual Freedom**

   - *The story of Israel's enslavement in Egypt and their deliverance by Moses is not merely historical—it is the* **universal journey of the soul from ignorance to enlightenment.**
   - *Egypt represents bondage to materialism and false identity, while the Promised Land symbolizes the awakening to our divine nature.*

4. **The Ultimate Freedom is in Christ**

   - **John 8:36** *declares, "If the Son therefore shall make you free, ye shall be free indeed."*

- *True freedom is not external but internal—realizing that* **you are one with God, not a servant of sin or fear.**

The Misuse of These Scriptures to Discredit God

Critics who use these verses to argue that God approves of slavery misunderstand their deeper meaning. They fail to recognize that:

1. **God's laws in the Old Testament were given to guide a fallen people toward higher understanding**—*not to establish eternal moral principles.*
2. **The New Testament reveals the fulfillment of freedom through Christ**— *liberating humanity from all forms of bondage, physical and spiritual.*
3. **Slavery in the Bible is not an endorsement but a symbol**—*illustrating the condition of humanity under sin and the liberation found in divine truth.*

Those who reject God based on these scriptures are often **looking at the letter of the law rather than the Spirit behind it.** *As Paul said in* **2 Corinthians 3:6,** *"The letter killeth, but the Spirit giveth life."*

Awakening to the Truth – Becoming Free in Spirit

If we truly understand that **God is all there is,** *then we must see beyond the shadows of human history and into the eternal reality of divine unity.* **No one is truly a slave except those who remain ignorant of their divinity.**

- **To be free is to know that you are Spirit, not flesh.**
- **To be free is to walk in the light of divine truth, not the darkness of ignorance.**
- **To be free is to realize that God is within you, and that nothing external can define or control your being.**

This is the message Jesus came to reveal—to awaken us from the illusion of bondage and bring us into the perfect oneness with God. As He prayed in **John 17:22-23,** *"That they may be one, even as we are one."*

The Truth That Sets Us Free

Slavery in the Bible is not an endorsement of oppression but a metaphor for the condition of humanity **before awakening to divine reality.** *Those who use these verses to discredit God miss the deeper revelation:*

- **The real slavery is not external but internal—bondage to false identity, sin, and fear.**
- **The real freedom is not political but spiritual—knowing and living as the perfect expression of God.**

The message of GIATI is the same message Jesus delivered: **You are not a slave. You are Spirit. You are free.**

And when you realize this truth, you will be free indeed.

Slavery as a Universal Human Condition

*The misconception that slavery was exclusively tied to one race is a distortion of historical reality. Enslavement has been a universal human experience, affecting numerous civilizations and ethnic groups throughout history. By broadening our understanding, we remove the false narrative that the Bible—or God Himself—was ever partial to one group's suffering over another's. Instead, we see that s***lavery has always been a reflection of humanity's fallen state***—a condition of ignorance and separation from divine truth.*

Historical Examples of Slavery Across Civilizations

1. **Egyptian Slavery** – *The Israelites themselves were enslaved under Pharaoh in Egypt (Exodus 1:11-14), subjected to hard labor and oppression.*
2. **Babylonian Captivity** – *The Jewish people were taken into captivity by the Babylonians in 586 B.C., forced to serve a foreign empire.*
3. **Greek and Roman Slavery** – *Both empires enslaved people of various ethnic backgrounds, including Europeans, Africans, and Middle Easterners, using them in domestic, agricultural, and military roles.*
4. **Viking Slave Trade** – *The Norse raiders enslaved many from the British Isles and Eastern Europe, selling them across the Mediterranean.*
5. **Arab Slave Trade** – *Long before the transatlantic slave trade, Middle Eastern societies enslaved people from Africa, Asia, and Europe.*
6. **Indentured Servitude in Europe** – *Many Europeans were forced into servitude due to economic hardship, particularly in feudal societies and during colonial expansion.*

These examples prove that slavery was not the targeting of a single race but a condition that affected all humanity at different times. The issue is not about race—it is about the human tendency to dominate others when disconnected from divine truth.

Slavery as a Symbol of the Unawakened Mind

From a **GIATI perspective,** *history reflects spiritual realities. Slavery, in its many forms, is not just a physical institution but a* **manifestation of spiritual blindness.** *When mankind operates under the illusion of separateness from God, oppression and suffering are the inevitable results.*

The Two Types of Slavery

- **Physical Slavery** – *The forced subjugation of one group by another, driven by greed, power, and ignorance.*

- **Spiritual Slavery** – *The deeper enslavement of the soul to sin, fear, and false identity. This is the true bondage that Jesus came to free us from.*

Jesus declared in **John 8:34,** *"Whosoever committeth sin is the servant of sin." The greatest slavery is not chains on the body but chains on the mind—the belief that we are separate from God, powerless, and subject to worldly forces.*

The Illusion of Victimhood

A major deception in modern discourse is the belief that slavery is a unique injustice against a single group. This mindset **keeps people trapped in victimhood,** *focusing on past suffering instead of embracing divine freedom in the present. If we remain fixated on historical oppression, we unknowingly continue to* **enslave ourselves mentally and spiritually.**

But the truth is:

- *No group is superior or inferior.*
- *No one is eternally a victim or oppressor.*
- *In Christ,* **all are one** *(Galatians 3:28).*

The moment we accept that **God is all there is,** *we cease to define ourselves by earthly oppression and step into divine freedom.*

Overcoming Slavery—The Path to True Liberation

While physical slavery has been abolished in many societies, **mental and spiritual slavery still persist.** *People remain in bondage to false identities, fear, and division. The path to true liberation is not in* **blaming the past** *but in* **awakening to the present reality of God within.**

Keys to Spiritual Liberation

1. **Recognizing Your Divine Identity**
   - *If God is all there is, then* **no external force has power over your true self.**
   - *You are not defined by history, race, or oppression, but by the Spirit of God within you.*
2. **Releasing the Chains of Hatred and Victimhood**
   - *Holding onto past pain keeps us in bondage.*
   - *Forgiveness and divine understanding set us free.*
3. **Walking in the Awareness of Oneness**
   - *Jesus' prayer in* **John 17:22-23** *calls for unity—not division.*
   - *When we see each other as* **expressions of God,** *oppression loses its power.*
4. **Embracing the Present and the Future, Not the Past**

- *True freedom is in the now. We cannot change history, but we* **can** *change our consciousness and manifest a new reality.*

Conclusion: The Final Word on Slavery

Slavery, in all its forms, is **a result of spiritual ignorance**—*a world operating in darkness. But through divine awareness, we see that:*

- **God never ordained slavery—humanity did, in its ignorance.**
- **No race is exclusively a victim or an oppressor—history has affected all.**
- **The greatest slavery is mental and spiritual, and the greatest freedom is found in knowing that you are an expression of God.**

In the light of **GIATI (God Is All There Is),** *we transcend historical oppression and step into eternal truth:*

You are not a slave.
You were never a slave.
You are divine.
You are free.

Unveiling the Mark of the Beast: The Triumph of GIATI

The **mark of the beast** *has long been a source of mystery and speculation, with many seeking to identify it as a physical mark, a microchip, or a governmental system. However, when understood through the divine revelation of* **GIATI—God Is All There Is,** *it becomes clear that this mark is not an external identifier, but an* **internal condition**—*a state of mind that governs those who are blind to divine truth and bound to the illusion of separation.*

To understand its meaning, we must examine the passage that reveals it:

"And he causeth all, both small and great, rich and poor, free and bond, to receive a mark in their right hand, or in their foreheads:
And that no man might buy or sell, save he that had the mark, or the name of the beast, or the number of his name.
Here is wisdom. Let him that hath understanding count the number of the beast: for it is the number of a man; and his number is Six hundred threescore and six."
(Revelation 13:16-18)

The Mark: A Symbol of Carnal Consciousness

The **mark in the forehead** *represents the mind—one's* **belief system, perception, and consciousness.** *Not an external entity but* **the collective consciousness of the world that denies the truth of oneness with God.** *The* **mark in the right hand** *represents* **one's works, actions, and deeds.** *To receive this mark means to be governed by* **the beast's system**—*to think and act according to the false reality of the* **carnal mind,** *which denies divine oneness and keeps humanity enslaved to illusion.*

The **beast** *represents the* **fallen nature of man,** *the* **ego-driven carnal mind** *that denies divine oneness and perpetuates the illusion of separation from God.. The number* **666,** *often feared and misunderstood, is declared to be* **the number of a man**—*a revelation that it is not about a singular entity but about the* **state of humanity when divorced from the awareness of God operating in spiritual ignorance.**

In biblical symbolism:

- *The number 6 represents incompleteness, as man was created on the sixth day (Genesis 1:26-31).*
- *A* **triple** *repetition of a number emphasizes absolute certainty (as seen with "Holy, Holy, Holy" in Isaiah 6:3).*
- **666** *is therefore the* **total embodiment of man in his lowest, most deceived state—man living as if separate from God.**

"For to be carnally minded is death; but to be spiritually minded is life and peace."
(Romans 8:6)

This scripture reveals the great divide: The carnal mind—the consciousness that sees itself as separate from God—is the mark of the beast. It is the false system that governs human thought, keeping people enslaved to illusion, materialism, fear, and control but to be ruled by divine awareness is to be sealed with God's truth.

Those sealed with the name of God **are not deceived by the beast system** *because they have awakened to divine oneness. They do not live by the false laws of materialism, religion, or fear. They* **live from the Spirit,** *knowing that* **God is their source, their identity, their very being.**

The System of the Beast: The Illusion of Separation

It is no coincidence that those who have the mark **cannot buy or sell** *without it. This represents more than commerce—it symbolizes the* **spiritual economy** *in which people trade their divine identity for worldly validation. Those under the beast system measure their value* **by external approval, wealth, and religious acceptance** *rather than the truth of their being.*

The **beast system** *is not just an external force; it is an* **internal condition** *that manifests as:*

- **Religious deception:** *Teaching people that God is separate from them rather than within them.*
- **Material bondage:** *Making people believe that their worth, salvation, and identity come from external sources.*
- **Fear-based control:** *Governing humanity through manipulation, scarcity, and the illusion of power.*

Jesus warned of this system when He said:

"For what shall it profit a man, if he shall gain the whole world, and lose his own soul?"
(Mark 8:36)

The beast's mark is the **false sense of self**—the belief that life is sustained by external means rather than by divine reality. It is the illusion that man must seek **outside himself** for worth, security, and fulfillment, rather than realizing that **God is within, and God is all.**

How GIATI Overcomes the Beast

If the mark of the beast represents **false identity,** then the seal of God represents **true identity.** Revelation speaks of another mark:

"And I looked, and, lo, a Lamb stood on the mount Sion, and with him an hundred forty and four thousand, having his Father's name written in their foreheads."
(Revelation 14:1)

Just as the **mark of the beast is a mindset of separation,** *the s***eal of God is the realization of divine oneness.** *Those with* **the Father's name in their foreheads** *are those who have awakened to their true identity* **as God's divine expression.** *They no longer see themselves as separate beings struggling in the world's system, but as* **one with the infinite, sustained by divine reality, not the illusions of man.**

The key to overcoming the beast is **awakening to GIATI.** *The beast system cannot hold those who know that* **God is all there is.** *It thrives on* **fear, deception, and the illusion of lack,** *but when one's mind is sealed with the truth of God's allness, the beast loses its power.*

Jesus declared:

"I have overcome the world." (John 16:33)

To **overcome the world** *is to overcome the beast system—to awaken from the illusion of separation and live in the reality of divine oneness.*

The Fall of the Beast and the Rise of Divine Awareness

The beast's rule is not eternal. Revelation declares:

"And the beast was taken, and with him the false prophet that wrought miracles before him… These both were cast alive into a lake of fire burning with brimstone." *(Revelation 19:20)*

The **lake of fire** *is not eternal torment but the* **consuming power of divine truth.** *The* **beast (carnal mind) and false prophet (deception)** *are destroyed in the* **purifying fire of divine awareness.**

Isaiah speaks of a true fast, one that breaks the chains of falsehood:

"Then shall thy light break forth as the morning, and thine health shall spring forth speedily: and thy righteousness shall go before thee; the glory of the Lord shall be thy rereward." *(Isaiah 58:8)*

This fast is not about **physical deprivation** *but about* **breaking free from the beast system—** *letting go of the illusion of lack and stepping into the* **fullness of divine reality.**

Jesus demonstrated this when He said:

"I have meat to eat that ye know not of." (John 4:32)

His nourishment did not come from the **physical world** *but from* **divine consciousness.** *Those sealed with* **the name of God in their foreheads** *no longer hunger for what the beast system offers, for they have already found fulfillment* **in the Spirit.**

The New Heaven and Earth: Living Beyond the Beast

At the end of Revelation, a new reality emerges:

**"And I saw a new heaven and a new earth: for the first heaven and the first earth were passed away; and there was no more sea.
And I heard a great voice out of heaven saying, Behold, the tabernacle of God is with men, and he will dwell with them, and they shall be his people, and God himself shall be with them, and be their God." (Revelation 21:1-3)**

The **first earth—the world governed by the beast—passes away.** *The* **new earth— the reality governed by divine truth—emerges.** *The illusion of separation is gone. There is no more hunger, no more thirst, for God is fully revealed within.*

"They shall hunger no more, neither thirst any more; neither shall the sun light on them, nor any heat." *(Revelation 7:16)*

The **spiritual fast is complete,** *and the feast of divine awareness begins.*

The Choice: The Beast or GIATI?

The mark of the beast is not a physical symbol—it is a **state of mind, a way of perceiving reality.** *To be marked by the beast is to be bound to the* **illusion of separation,** *living by the laws of fear, materialism, and deception.*

But **GIATI—God Is All There Is** *is the revelation that destroys the beast. Those who awaken to divine truth* **bear the name of God in their foreheads**—*meaning,* **their consciousness is aligned with divine reality.** *They do not live by the fear and deception of the world; they live* **in the knowing that they are one with God.**

The question is not whether a physical mark will come. The question is: **What is written in your mind? What governs your thoughts? Are you marked by the beast— believing in separation, fear, and deception? Or are you sealed with the name of God— living in the truth that God is all, and you are one with Him?**

Jesus declared:

"Ye shall know the truth, and the truth shall make you free." *(John 8:32)*

*The time has come to bre***ak free from the beast system and step into the eternal reality of GIATI.** *For when the beast falls, the Spirit rests, and the fullness of divine life is revealed.*

The Hidden Mystery of Jacob and Esau

The story of **Jacob and Esau** *is one of the most misunderstood narratives in the Bible. Many see it as a tale of deception—of Jacob tricking his father and stealing the blessing. But beneath the surface lies a deeper revelation:* **the purpose of God was always at work, ensuring that the chosen one would receive the inheritance.**

Even before they were born, **God had already declared the outcome:**

"Two nations are in your womb, and two peoples from within you shall be divided; one shall be stronger than the other, and the older shall serve the younger."
– Genesis 25:23

Rebecca was given this prophecy, revealing that **Jacob was always the chosen one.** *Yet, as with all things in the mystery of God, this truth had to be veiled—concealed within the events of the story, waiting for the appointed time to be revealed.*

The Flesh vs. The Spirit

Esau and Jacob represent more than just two brothers; they symbolize two realities— **the natural man and the spiritual man.**

- **Esau** *was born first, representing the* **flesh,** *the outward appearance, the natural birthright.*
- **Jacob** *came second, representing the* **spirit,** *the one chosen by God before time.*

Esau, as the firstborn, had **the right by tradition** *to the inheritance, but his heart was set on* **earthly desires.** *He was* **driven by his hunger,** *willing to trade his* **birthright for a bowl of food** *(Genesis 25:29-34). This moment reveals a profound truth:*

The flesh does not value the things of the spirit.

Esau represents those who are consumed by **the physical world, the temporary, the things that satisfy the flesh** *but have no eternal value. His willingness to sell his birthright shows that, though he was firstborn* **by the flesh,** *he was never chosen* **by the Spirit.**

This is why **Jacob had to receive the blessing.**

The Cover ng: A Shadow of the Mystery

*When the time came for Isaac to bless his sons, Rebecca—who already knew the prophecy—***covered Jacob in Esau's garments and placed goat hair on him** *(Genesis 27:15-16). Isaac, whose sight was dim, felt Jacob's hands and* **mistook him for Esau,** *giving him the blessing meant for the firstborn.*

Many see this as trickery, but **this was God's plan unfolding.** *Jacob, the one chosen by God, had to be covered—his identity concealed—so that the* **blessing would be spoken over him.**

This moment is a reflection of the greater mystery of God:

The one who receives the inheritance is the one who is covered in the right image.

Jacob had to take on **the likeness of Esau** *to receive the blessing, just as throughout history, the* **spirit must be hidden within the natural until the appointed time.**

- *Moses, raised in Pharaoh's house, appeared as an Egyptian but carried the Spirit of God.*
- *Jesus, born in the likeness of sinful flesh, was in reality* **God hidden within a body.**
- *Today, those who carry the truth of* **GIATI (God Is All There Is)** *walk among the world unseen, but at the appointed time,* **God will reveal His own.**

The mystery is that **the chosen ones were always chosen, but their identity was hidden until the right moment.**

The Purpose of God: The Spirit Reigns Over the Flesh

What does this mean for us today?

*The lesson of Jacob and Esau is that th*e **flesh was never meant to rule. The natural man** *(Esau) came first, but the* **spiritual man** *(Jacob) was chosen before time. This is why* **God's purpose was fulfilled through Jacob, not Esau**—*because* **the Spirit reigns over the flesh.**

"That which is born of the flesh is flesh, and that which is born of the Spirit is spirit."
– John 3:6

This story is a foreshadowing of **the true inheritance**—*not an inheritance of land, riches, or earthly promises, but of* **oneness with God.**

Esau lost the birthright because **he saw only the physical.** *Jacob, though appearing to take it by deception,* **was simply stepping into what God had already ordained.**

This is the mystery of salvation:

- **Those who live by the flesh will always miss what is spiritual.**
- **Those who are chosen by God have already been written into the inheritance.**
- **It is not by works, not by law, but by God's election from the beginning.**

Just as Jacob received the blessing **not by effort, but by being covered,** *so it is today:* **the inheritance of God belongs to those who recognize their true identity—covered in the Spirit, one with God.**

GIATI: The Revelation of the True Inheritance

Now, in this time, **the mystery is being revealed once again.**

For generations, people have sought salvation in the **flesh**—*through works, through religious rituals, through external confessions. They have tried to earn the birthright through* **effort,** *just as Esau assumed it was his simply because he was born first.*

But the truth of GIATI is this:

The birthright belongs to those who know who they are in God.

"The mystery hidden for ages… Christ in you, the hope of glory."
– Colossians 1:26-27

Salvation is not about lineage, actions, or religious traditions—it is about recognizing **that the Spirit of God is within you.**

The world has been deceived into thinking the flesh is what matters. But **God has always chosen the spirit over the flesh.** *The first man (Adam) was of the earth, but the last man (Christ) is from heaven (1 Corinthians 15:45-49).*

And so today, God is revealing this mystery through **GIATI**—*declaring that:*

- **The chosen ones were chosen before time.**
- **The inheritance is already given.**
- **It has never been about effort—only recognition.**

Jacob and Esau were not just two brothers. They were a shadow of the ultimate truth:

The Spirit will always rule over the flesh.

The inheritance belongs to those who see the mystery.

And now, the mystery is complete:

God Is All There Is.

The Passover: A Spiritual Blueprint

In Exodus 12, the Passover event unfolds as Israel prepares to leave Egypt. God commands each household to kill a lamb, eat it, and put its blood on the doorposts so that the death angel would "pass over" their house and not kill their firstborn.

But what does this mean spiritually?

The Lamb = The Divine Nature in Human Form

"Behold the Lamb of God, which taketh away the sin of the world." (John 1:29)

The **lamb without blemish** *(Exodus 12:5) represents* **God manifested as pure Spirit in a human form**—*Jesus or Yahshua*—**the divine nature clothed in flesh, but sinless.**

This wasn't about just a physical lamb. It was always pointing to the day when **God Himself would take on a body,** *die the death of the false self, and* **reveal the life of the Spirit within.**

The Blood on the Door = The Spirit Identified Within You

"When I see the blood, I will pass over you..." (Exodus 12:13)

The blood on the door was never just about protection—it symbolized identification.

In spiritual terms:

God must see Himself in you.

He's not "passing over" because of an outward ritual. He's passing over because He recognizes **His own Spirit within you.**

The **blood of the lamb** *is symbolic of* **God's own life-force**—*His Spirit—that is now in you, as you.*

"Unless you eat my flesh and drink my blood, you have no life in you." (John 6:53)

This is about **union.** *The life (or blood) of the Spirit must be* **in you,** *not just believed from afar. If the blood remains outside—if your identity remains in ego or separation—there is no passing over.*

The House = Your Body / Soul

In Exodus, the blood was placed on the doorposts of their houses. But in spiritual reality, **your body is the house,** *your soul is the door.*

"Know ye not that your body is the temple of the Holy Spirit?" (1 Corinthians 6:19)

The **doorpost of your soul** *must be marked by the* **presence of the indwelling Spirit**—*which is what the blood symbolizes.*

So what is God looking for?

Himself in you.

If He sees you as a separate being trying to earn salvation by religion, law, or ritual, you will be judged by that separation.

But if He sees **His own Spirit as your identity,** *He passes over—because there is no death in God.*

The Death Angel = Judgment of Separation

The death angel didn't care about nationality, tradition, or religious background.
He only passed over **those who bore the blood,** *symbolic of* **those in whom God recognized Himself.**

This teaches a deep truth:
Salvation isn't about what you do—it's about who you are.

And who you are must be **God expressed as you**—*not in theory, but in realization.*

GIATI Revelation

God is all there is.

Therefore, only what is of God—what is God **being** *Himself—can pass through death into life.*
If you live in ego or separation, that part must die. But if you live from the truth that **God is your Spirit, then you are already passed from death to life.**

"He that heareth my word, and believeth on him that sent me, hath everlasting life, and shall not come into condemnation; but is passed from death unto life." (John 5:24)

This is **Passover fulfilled.**

Parable: The Mirror House

There was once a great King whose kingdom stretched across every land, seen and unseen. He desired to visit His people, but there was a mystery: He could only enter a house in which He saw **Himself.** *Not a reflection of someone pretending to be Him, not an image painted on the wall—but* **His own Spirit** *living inside.*

So, He sent word to every home: "Prepare your house. I am coming. But if I come and do not see Myself in the house, My presence will bring judgment, not joy."

Some decorated their houses with golden scriptures.
Others hung portraits of the King on the walls.
Many memorized His laws and recited them at the door.
They dressed in robes, lit candles, and sang songs about His greatness.

But there was one house—humble and quiet—that did something different.
The owner **received the King's own breath,** *and let it fill the home.*
He didn't decorate the outside, but welcomed the Spirit within.
He let go of all pride, all self-image, and said,

"This house is Yours. Live in me, as me."

When the King came to that street, He walked past many homes with grand exteriors.
He paused at each one—but saw only **images** *of Himself, not the* **substance.**
And then He came to the humble house.
And there, as He looked through the doorway, **He saw His own Spirit staring back.**

He smiled.

"This is My house. I live here." And He passed over it.

The other homes, though full of religion and rituals, were swept away—not in anger, but in truth. They were still living as **separate,** *worshiping a distant King, not knowing that the King had always longed to* **be them.**

The Moral of the Parable:

The King only saves **what is of Himself.**
He only passes over when He sees His **Spirit***—not outside you, not beside you, but as you.*

The real blood on the door isn't red liquid.
It's the life of God recognized as your identity.

This is what the Passover has always pointed to—not religion, not ritual, but **reunion.**
The moment when the Spirit looks at you and sees **Himself.**

The Passover: A Spiritual Summary

The Passover is not just a historical event—it is a divine pattern revealing what it takes for God to save. The lamb, the blood, and the passing over all point to one eternal truth:

God only saves what is of Himself.

The lamb represents **God's own nature manifesting in flesh***—pure Spirit in a body. The blood represents* **the life of that Spirit.** *And the doorpost represents* **your soul,** *the threshold between inner and outer reality.*

When God told Israel, "When I see the blood, I will pass over you," He was declaring this:

"When I see My own life—My own Spirit—in you, I will pass over."

It was never about the blood of a physical lamb. It was always about **God recognizing Himself** *in His creation.*
If He sees ego, separation, or self-effort, judgment comes—not because He's angry, but because **only what is of God can live eternally.**

The **true Passover** *is fulfilled when you realize that* **the Spirit of God is your true** *identity.*
When you eat of His flesh and drink of His blood—not through a ritual, but by receiving His nature—you become **one with Him,** *and His life becomes yours.*

The death angel (judgment) passes over not because of religion or good works, but because God sees **Himself in you as you.**

That is salvation.

That is the mystery of the Passover.

That is the message of GIATI:

God is all there is—and He saves only Himself.

The Ark of the Covenant — God Within

*The Ark of the Covenant has long been revered as a sacred artifact, as if God's presence was once confined to a gold-covered box. But from the perspective of GIATI—***God Is All There Is***—we see something deeper. The ark was never about the object. It was always about what it represented: the presence of God dwelling among His people. More than that, it was a prophecy in physical form—a symbol of a greater truth waiting to be revealed:* **God doesn't live in temples or tabernacles. He lives in you.**

The ark, the veil, the temple, the high priest—they were all shadows. Pointers. Temporary symbols preparing humanity for a greater awakening: that the true Holy of Holies is not a chamber behind a curtain, but the awakened heart. God's ultimate desire was never to be housed in a box, but to dwell in the spirit of every man, woman, and child.

The ark was placed in the innermost part of the tabernacle, hidden behind layers, where only the high priest could enter once a year. But that physical setup was a mirror of your own being—the layers of identity, emotion, thought, and belief—behind which lies your true self, the place where God meets you. Not externally, but within. Not through ritual, but through awakening.

In Exodus 25, God gives Moses specific instructions to build the ark and overlay it with pure gold, placing it in the Most Holy Place. Yet even then, God said, "There I will meet with you..." (Exodus 25:22). Not because He lived in the box, but because He used the box to point to something eternal: **His presence would one day be known directly, no longer through symbols, but through Spirit.**

Inside the ark were the tablets of the law, a jar of manna, and Aaron's rod that budded—each representing a part of the old covenant. But those things were fulfilled in a new way by the Holy Spirit:

- *The law, once written on stone, now written on hearts*
- *The manna, once gathered in the wilderness, now becomes living bread from within*
- *The priesthood, once inherited by bloodline, now granted by Spirit and power*

Scripture affirms this shift. "I will put My laws into their hearts," God says in Hebrews 10:16. The apostle Paul echoes it in 2 Corinthians 3:3, saying we are now "written not with ink, but with the Spirit of the living God." These were not just poetic words—they were declarations of a new reality: **God would no longer relate to us from the outside in, but from the inside out.**

The lid of the ark was called the mercy seat. Once a year, the high priest would enter and sprinkle the blood of a lamb there for atonement. But now, we see that the true mercy seat is no longer made of gold. It is the **awakened heart***—the one who knows that he and God are not separate. That's where real atonement (or "at-one-ment") takes place. Not through ritual sacrifice, but through the realization:* **God is in me, as me.**

That's why Paul says in Romans 5:5 that "the love of God is shed abroad in our hearts by the Holy Spirit." When you know that the Spirit in you is God Himself, you no longer search for Him in temples, services, or sacred objects. The veil is removed. The truth is known. **I and the Father are one.**

The ark was a shadow. The Spirit is the substance. Hebrews 9 tells us the physical ark was "a figure for the time then present." Colossians 2:17 says it plainly—these things were shadows, "but the body is of Christ." In other words, the truth is now embodied. And that body is you, when you awaken to who you really are.

The true ark walks the earth today—not in gold or wood, but in every human being who recognizes the Spirit within. As Paul said in 1 Corinthians 3:16, "You are the temple of

God, and the Spirit of God dwells in you." Or in GIATI terms: **God is all there is—and that includes you.**

So no, the ark is not lost. It has been fulfilled. It has been revealed. It has multiplied. It now lives in every awakened soul, in every heart that says, "I am not separate. I am one." This is the covenant. This is the mercy. This is the ark. Not a golden box, but a golden heart— refined by truth and awakened to Spirit.

The Veil Was You

The tearing of the veil in the temple is often taught as a symbol that people now have access to God. While that is partially true, the deeper, eternal revelation goes much further.

GIATI (God Is All There Is) reveals that the veil was not just a curtain in a physical temple—it was the **illusion of separation.** *The moment the veil was torn, it wasn't simply an invitation to come in—it was a revelation that* **there was never a barrier to begin with,** *except the one humanity believed in.*

God didn't move closer.
God didn't suddenly become available.
The illusion that He was ever separate—was torn.

The Temple Was a Mirror

The temple in Jerusalem was a shadow, a pattern of what was always true spiritually. It had an outer court, an inner court, and the Holy of Holies. Behind the veil was the **ark of the covenant,** *the presence of God.*

Only one man—the high priest—could go behind the veil, and only once a year.

But why?

Because mankind believed God was far away, unapproachable, too holy, too distant. So religion mirrored that belief with a structure—walls, rules, limits.

But all along, the **true temple** *wasn't made with hands. It was you.*
And the **veil wasn't fabric**—*it was* **your false identity.**
The belief that you were separate from the Spirit that made you.

Matthew 27:51 — The Moment Separation Died

"And, behold, the veil of the temple was rent in twain from the top to the bottom; and the earth did quake, and the rocks rent." (Matthew 27:51)

When Christ gave up the ghost, something profound happened.

The veil ripped—from **top to bottom,** *not bottom to top.*

Why?

Because this wasn't man reaching God.
This was **God revealing Himself in man.**

The veil was torn by God—not to let you in, but to **let the truth out:**

God is not behind a curtain. God is not distant. God is **within.**

The GIATI Revelation

GIATI reveals that **God is all there is,** *which means:*

- *There is no "you" outside of God.*
- *There is no God "out there" to be accessed.*
- *There is only* **God expressing Himself as you.**

The veil symbolized the **false belief** *that there is a separation between God and man. That belief is the root of sin—to see yourself as something other than God's own Spirit.*

When Christ (the pattern of the Spirit in flesh) died, the **illusion** *died with Him.*
The torn veil was the **tearing of ego,** *the* **shattering of the lie** *that God is outside and we are other.*

The veil was your old mind. The veil was your flesh identity.
The veil was your ignorance of who you really are.

And when it tore, the Spirit was free—not because it was locked in, but because **you finally saw that it had been within you all along.**

Scriptural Support

- *"Know ye not that ye are the temple of God, and that the Spirit of God dwelleth in you?" (1 Corinthians 3:16)*
- *"But we all, with open face beholding as in a glass the glory of the Lord, are changed into the same image..." (2 Corinthians 3:18)*
- *"The kingdom of God is within you." (Luke 17:21)*
- *"The mystery hidden from ages and generations... is Christ in you, the hope of glory." (Colossians 1:26–27)*

The Veil Was Never God's Idea

The veil wasn't to keep man from God—it was to show man what he believed. When Christ died, it wasn't just forgiveness—it was **revelation.**

The Spirit was saying:

> *"I am not hidden behind rituals. I am not found in buildings. I am not outside of you. I am the life within you. The veil was you. And now, you see Me as yourse***lf."**

The veil has been torn.
There is only One within all.
And that One—is God.
God is all there is.

The Tabernacle Was a Blueprint of You

Long before cathedrals and churches, before creeds and denominations, there was a tent in the wilderness—a **tabernacle** given by divine instruction to Moses. But this wasn't just a place to worship. It was a **pattern.** A heavenly **blueprint** revealed on earth.

The tabernacle revealed not only how **God relates to man,** *but how* **God dwells in** *man.*

It showed the structure of the **Godhead,** *the* **design of man, and the truth of** *salvation.*

Not just in shadow—but in eternal **substance.**

The Threefold Structure: Outer Court, Inner Court, Holy of Holies

The tabernacle had three parts:

1. **Outer Court** – *The place of sacrifice and washing.*
2. **Holy Place (Inner Court)** – *Where the lampstand, table of shewbread, and altar of incense stood.*
3. **Holy of Holies** – *The most sacred space where the* **ark of the covenant** *dwelled*— the presence of God Himself.

Each part revealed a dimension of **God's nature, man's being, and the way into eternal life.**

The Pattern of the Godhead

The tabernacle reveals the **threefold unity of the Godhead:**

- **Outer Court – Yahweh (The Father):**
  The place of judgment and sacrifice. Represents the **source,** *the one whose purpose unfolds all things. The outer court is the realm of commandments and offerings—a reflection of* **the will of God** *being made known.*
- **Inner Court – Elohim (The Word/Son):**

The realm of **light, communion, and intercession.** *The Word is how the invisible becomes seen. Here the* **Spirit works through form,** *just like the Son who walked as a man.*

- *Holy of Holies – The Holy Spirit:*
  The **essence** *and* **indwelling presence** *of God. This is not something you approach from the outside; it is the* **life of God within,** *where* **God and man are one.**

These are not three separate beings, but **one God** *expressing Himself through a* **threefold pattern**—*just as the tabernacle showed.*

The Pattern of Man

Just as the tabernacle was threefold, **you are threefold:**

- **Body – Outer Court:**
  The place where you appear in the world, where actions are seen. It's the realm of the **flesh,** *where the initial sacrifice (death of the false self) takes place.*
- **Soul – Inner Court:**
  The realm of **thought, emotion, and belief.** *Where your inner life burns like incense and feeds on divine truth. This is where light (understanding) begins to break forth.*
- **Spirit – Holy of Holies:**
  The **real you.** *The place where* **God is One with Himself**—*as you. The veil that once blocked access is now torn. You are no longer approaching God—you are the place where* **God dwells.**

Scriptural Support: You Are the Tabernacle

"What? know ye not that your body is the temple of the Holy Ghost which is in you...?" (1 Corinthians 6:19)

"And let them make me a sanctuary; that I may dwell among them." (Exodus 25:8)

For ye are the temple of the living God; as God hath said, I will dwell in them, and walk in them..." (2 Corinthians 6:16)

*God never desired a temple made of gold and stone—***He desired to dwell in you.** *The tabernacle was just a* **shadow** *pointing to a* **greater truth:**

You are the sanctuary.

The GIATI Revelation: The Tabernacle Is Fulfilled in You

GIATI reveals that **God is all there is,** *and therefore, He did not build you as something separate from Himself.*

- *You are not approaching God—you are* **expressing God.**
- *You are not trying to become holy—you are the* **Holy of Holies** *unveiled.*
- *You are not trying to gain access—you are where God walks.*

The tabernacle wasn't made for worship—it was made to **point to you,** *the one in whom God would ultimately dwell* **as Himself.**

The outer court (body) is not enough.
The inner court (soul) is not the goal.
The Spirit (Holy of Holies) is the truth of who you are.

And the moment you realize the veil is gone,
you awaken to the truth:
God never lived outside you. He's always been the life within you.

The Wilderness Was You

The wilderness wasn't just geography—it was a symbol of man's lostness, his wandering mind, and identity crisis.

But even in the wilderness, **God walked with them.**

Why?

Because the tabernacle—though mobile, fragile, and wrapped in skin—held **the fullness of God** *inside.*

Just like **you.**

The Godhead is no longer hidden in tents and temples.
You are the threefold witness.
The temple of God.
The expression of the Eternal One.

The tabernacle was never a building—it was a prophecy of you.

The Wilderness Was Never a Place—It Was a State of Mind

The Exodus from Egypt is not just ancient history—it's a mirror of the spiritual journey every soul must take. It's the divine pattern moving us from bondage to liberty, from illusion to truth, from ego to Spirit.

The Promised Land isn't miles away—it's already within.
But before we can enter, **something must die***—and it isn't the body, it's the belief in separation from God.*

Egypt: The False Identity (Bondage to Ego)

Egypt represents bondage to the false self—the carnal mind that sees itself as separate from God. Pharaoh is the personification of ego—the inner tyrant that believes it must survive, dominate, and control.

"Let my people go, that they may serve me." (Exodus 8:1)

This cry wasn't just for freedom from physical slavery—it was the Spirit within declaring, **"Let the divine identity awaken."**

In Egypt, the people labored under a false system—straining to survive, blind to the truth that God was already among them.

And just like today, the cry of Spirit is not to become something new... It's to remember who you are.

The Wilderness: Where Ego Dies and the Truth Emerges

Once delivered from Egypt, the children of Israel entered the wilderness—a place not of punishment, but of **transformation.**

It was never about distance.
It was always about **dying to the self-image that came out of Egypt.**

They wandered for 40 years.
Not because God was slow, but because **ego dies hard.**

"Your carcasses shall fall in this wilderness... all that were numbered of you... from twenty years old and upward... shall not come into the land..." (Numbers 14:29–30)

Those who left Egypt were still thinking like Egypt.
They carried the mindset of bondage into a space that required faith.

They murmured.
They feared.
They doubted.

So **Yahweh allowed them to wander,** *until every trace of that egoic generation— those still identifying with the false self—was laid to rest.*

And then, **as soon as the ego died off, Yahweh took the people straight into the Promised Land.**
There was no more delay.

The moment the false self was gone, the way opened—because the Promised Land had always been waiting.

The Promised Land: The Rest of Divine Identity

The Promised Land was never about real estate—it was about rest.
Rest from striving.
Rest from performance.
Rest from trying to become what you already are.

"There remaineth therefore a rest to the people of God." (Hebrews 4:9)

Joshua didn't lead the people into the land by effort—but by faith in what was already given.

This was a picture of **conscious awakening***—entering the awareness that God is in you, and you are in Him.*

It wasn't just territory they entered.
It was **identity.**

Many Are Still in the Wilderness Today

The wilderness didn't end in scripture.
It continues in every soul that knows God exists but still feels separate from Him.

They've left Egypt (the world, religion, sin),
but they're still wandering in circles—believing in God with their mind,
but living in fear, performance, or doubt in their hearts.

"They could not enter in because of unbelief." (Hebrews 3:19)

Not unbelief in God's existence—
But unbelief in His **indwelling presence.**

Until the ego dies—the belief in a "me" apart from Him—the Promised Land remains unseen.

GIATI Reveals: The Journey Ends When You See the Truth

GIATI—God Is All There Is—reveals the key that ends the wilderness journey:

You were never separate. You were never outside.
You were never meant to wander forever.

The Promised Land is not a place you go.

It is the **awareness** *that the Spirit within you* **is God.**
*And the moment you see this—***you have arrived.**

The wilderness ends when the illusion ends.
The Promised Land begins when you realize it's always been within.

You Don't Walk Into the Land—You Wake Into It

This whole journey—Egypt to Canaan—was never about geography. It was always about **God leading you back to yourself.**

But before you can rest,
before you can see the promise, before you can walk in the land... the ego must die.

And once it does—
You don't even need a map.

You're already home.

Parable: The Traveler and the Three Lands

There was once a traveler who lived in a city of mirrors.
This city, called Reflexia, was full of noise, shadows, and flashing lights. The people there were obsessed with their reflections—each mirror showing them a different self: successful, broken, righteous, unworthy.
And the traveler believed every one of them.

One day, a voice stirred within him. Not outside. Not from the sky.

From within.

"Come away," the voice whispered,
"There's a land where you'll no longer chase your reflection, because you'll know who you truly are."

So the traveler left Reflexia and entered a vast and quiet land called The Wastes. Here, there were no mirrors. No voices. Just the traveler and the voice within.

But the traveler struggled.
Without his mirrors, he didn't know who he was anymore.
He wandered in circles, asking, "Who am I now?"
He built little mirrors out of sand and named them things like "My Religion," "My Achievements," "My Identity."
But every time the wind blew, they fell.

Years passed. The voice stayed with him, but he couldn't see it.

Then one day, exhausted, the traveler dropped to his knees.

"I give up," he said. "I don't know who I am."

And the voice answered:
"Good. Now look within, not without."

And for the first time, the traveler didn't reach outward.
He closed his eyes.

And when he opened them again—he was in The Land of Knowing. Not because he moved.

Because he awakened.

In this land, there were no mirrors.
There was no need.
He finally saw the truth:

There was never a mirror that could show him who he was— because he had always been made of light.

Interpretation:

- **Reflexia** = *Egypt: the place of ego, performance, false identity.*
- **The Wastes** = *The Wilderness: the in-between season where ego dies and the voice of Spirit begins to awaken.*
- **The Land of Knowing** = *The Promised Land: the awareness that you are one with God. Not separate. Not far. Not becoming*—**being.**

Just as in the Exodus, the traveler couldn't enter until he stopped trying to carry his old identity forward.

Only when he let go... did he arrive.

Two Mountains, Two Realities—And One Divine Awakening

"For ye are not come unto the mount that might be touched, and that burned with fire... But ye are come unto mount Sion, and unto the city of the living God..." —Hebrews 12:18, 22

There are two mountains in the spiritual journey.
Not physical peaks, but **spiritual paradigms.**

One is **Mount Sinai**—*the mountain of law.*
The other is **Mount Zion**—*the mountain of grace.*

They are not side by side.
They are not destinations to choose from.
They represent two completely different ways of relating to God:

One through distance. One through oneness.

And GIATI reveals the truth:
You're not trying to get to Zion—you've already arrived.

1. **Mount Sinai: The Mountain of Fear and Distance**

   Mount Sinai was where Moses received the Law.
   But it wasn't a place of comfort—it was **terror.**

"...a mountain that burned with fire, and unto blackness, and darkness, and tempest..." (Hebrews 12:18)

   When God appeared on Sinai, the people trembled.
   They heard thunder, saw lightning, and begged not to hear His voice.

   Why? Because Sinai exposed them.
   It showed them how far they were from divine perfection. It didn't bring God close—it magnified the gap.

   Sinai was the place of separation.
   The people stayed at the bottom.
   Only Moses went up.

"Let not God speak with us, lest we die." (Exodus 20:19)

   Sinai represents the system of performance—
   Do good, receive blessing.
   Do bad, be condemned.

   It was never meant to bring salvation—
   It was a mirror to show how much man depended on grace.

2. **Mount Zion: The Mountain of Grace and Spirit**

   But then the writer of Hebrews shifts:

"But you are come to Mount Zion, and unto the city of the living God..." (Hebrews 12:22)

   Notice the change in language:

   "You are come."
   Not: you will come.

Not: you are approaching.
Not: if you do enough, you'll reach it.
But: **You're already here.**
Mount Zion represents **a completely new covenant:**

- *Not rules carved in stone—but laws written in hearts.*
- *Not fear of judgment—but joy in union.*
- *Not a voice from above—but Spirit within.*

Zion is the city of the living God, the heavenly Jerusalem—
a divine realm of awareness *where God is not outside, but inside.*

At Zion, you don't hear thunder.
You hear **truth whispered from within.**

3. The Unveiling: What the Two Mountains Mean Spiritually

Mount Sinai is the **external journey***—trying to reach a holy God.*
Mount Zion is the **internal unveiling***—realizing the holy God has reached you.*

Mount Sinai says, "Do this, and live."
Mount Zion says, "Live, because I AM within you."

Sinai builds temples and altars made of stone.
Zion reveals: **you are the temple.** *God dwells in you.*

Sinai was the schoolmaster.
Zion is the inheritance.

GIATI—God Is All There Is—shows the beauty of this shift:

You're not marching toward God.
You are awakening to the reality that He's been in you all along.

4. You Are Already on Mount Zion

Many are still living at the foot of Sinai, terrified of a God they see as separate, trying to earn what was always a gift.

But the tearing of the veil, the giving of the Spirit, the resurrection of Christ— all declare:
You've come to Zion.

You are in the city of God.
You are part of the general assembly.
You are joined to the spirits of just men made perfect.
You are one with the Judge of all.
You are filled with the blood that speaks better things.

"Ye are come…"

You just have to **believe it.**
And even that belief isn't a work—it's a revealing.

5. **Conclusion: The Climb Was Always an Awakening**

Sinai had thunder because the people didn't know who they were.
Zion has peace because you remember who you are.

Sinai teaches from the outside in.
Zion reveals from the inside out.

You are not climbing Sinai, hoping to reach something holy.
You are standing on Zion,
realizing the Holy One lives in you.

Parable: The Two Mountains

There were two mountains that stood side by side, yet worlds apart.

The first was called **Mount Elaran***—a mountain of stone, thunder, and smoke.*
The second was **Mount Solara***—a mountain clothed in stillness, warmth, and light.*

One day, a pilgrim set out on a journey.
He was told by the elders that if he wanted to see God, he must climb Mount Elaran.

So he did.

As he climbed, he was met with fierce winds and falling rocks.

Every step required effort. Every breath felt judged.
Signs were posted on the trail:

"Only the worthy may ascend."
"Touch not the peak, or you will die."

The pilgrim tried harder. He memorized the rules. He punished himself for every misstep. But no matter how far he climbed, the top of the mountain seemed farther still— and the voice of God always thundered from above, never within.

Exhausted, the pilgrim collapsed at a rocky ledge and cried out,
"I've done everything. I've climbed. I've obeyed. But I still feel so far."

Then a whisper came—not from the sky, but from inside him:

"You're on the wrong mountain."

He opened his eyes. In the distance, he saw **Mount Solara***—quiet, peaceful, glowing.*

And the strange thing was: **he wasn't climbing it—he was already on it.**

Suddenly, the rocks around him changed.
The thunder faded. The judgment lifted.
It wasn't that the mountain changed—it was that **he awakened to where he truly was.**

He was never meant to live on Elaran.
He had only imagined he needed to strive.

Solara had always been his home.
He just needed to stop climbing—and start receiving.

Interpretation:

- **Mount Elaran** = *Mount Sinai (law, fear, performance, separation)*
- **Mount Solara** = *Mount Zion (grace, Spirit, union, rest)*

The parable reveals the shift from effort to awareness.

The truth is: the pilgrim never had to climb.

He only needed to realize where he stood.

The True Circumcision — A Heart Unveiled

"But he is a Jew, which is one inwardly; and circumcision is that of the heart, in the spirit, and not in the letter…" — *Romans 2:29*

For generations, circumcision of the flesh was seen as a sign of covenant—a visible mark that one belonged to God's chosen people. But like many outer symbols, it was never the end—it was a shadow pointing to the truth: **God never desired just a mark in the flesh. He desired the unveiling of the heart.**

From the GIATI lens, where **God Is All There Is,** *we come to see that t***he true transformation God seeks is not external, but internal—within the invisible realm of spirit and awareness.** *The flesh represents the ego, the illusion of being separate. Circumcision of the heart is the cutting away of that illusion.*

What is the Heart Veil?

The veil that lies over the heart is **the false identity***—the belief that you are just a separate being, apart from God. It is the mind that clings to effort, performance, and law-keeping as a means to be accepted by a God "out there."*

But God is not afar off—He is within.
The heart veil blinds man from recognizing that **God is the life and being within him.**

Circumcision of the heart *is not something man does with his own hands. It is the inward work of the Spirit*—**removing the illusion of separation** *and revealing the eternal truth:*

You are not becoming one with God—you've always been one. You're only now remembering.

Flesh vs. Spirit

Just as the circumcision of the flesh cuts off a piece of the body, circumcision of the heart cuts away **the carnal mind**—*the belief that righteousness comes by law, religion, or effort.*

This aligns perfectly with Paul's message:

"For we are the circumcision, which worship God in the spirit, and rejoice in Christ Jesus, and have no confidence in the flesh." — Philippians 3:3

"Flesh" here isn't just skin—it's the mindset of **ego,** *separation, and works-based identity.*

The Inner Covenant

God's covenant is now written, not on tablets of stone or marked in the body, but **inscribed on the heart by the Spirit.**

"I will put my laws into their mind, and write them in their hearts: and I will be to them a God, and they shall be to me a people." — Hebrews 8:10

This isn't about following external commands—it's about **becoming conscious of your true nature: that the Spirit of God is the I AM within you.**

GIATI affirms this inner knowing:

God is not looking for rituals. He is looking for recognition.

Circumcision of the heart is the moment you see clearly.
Not with your physical eyes—but with your inner eye.
It is the moment you realize:

"God is not separate from me. I am an expression of Him."

Summary:

- **Physical Circumcision** = *Outer sign under the Old Covenant (Law)*
- **Heart Circumcision** = *Inner unveiling under the New Covenant (Spirit)*
- **Flesh** = *Ego, self-righteousness, law, illusion*

- **Spirit** = *Truth, union, oneness, grace*

The **true people of God** *are not marked in flesh, but awakened in spirit.*

Parable: The Sealed Letter

In a quiet village, there was a tradition passed down for generations: each person was born with a sealed letter over their heart. The people were told that this letter contained their true name—their real identity—but it was wrapped in thick parchment and sealed with wax.

They wore their letters proudly, but **none dared to open them.** *Instead, they spent their lives writing their own names on the outside—hoping to earn meaning through effort, reputation, and status.*

Some wrote: "Servant."
Others wrote: "Sinner."
Some wrote: "Leader," "Outcast," "Chosen," or "Condemned."
They judged each other by these labels and performed daily rituals to convince themselves that their names were acceptable before a distant king.

One day, a man walked into the village with a radiant stillness. He had no label on his letter. Someone asked, "What happened to your name?"

He smiled and said, "I opened it."

The crowd gasped. "You can't do that! It's forbidden! How can you know your name without earning it?"

He replied,

"I didn't earn it. I remembered it. The seal was never placed by the king—it was placed by fear."

Curious, one young girl tore off the seal on her letter. Her hands trembled as she unfolded the parchment—and there, written in light, was the name:

"I AM."

One by one, more began to open theirs.

And every letter said the same: **"I AM."**

It wasn't that each person had the same name by chance—it was that **they were all emanations of the same Source.**

*Only those willing to tear the seal—***the veil of the ego***—discovered their true nature.*

Those who clung to their self-made labels remained outside the truth, still searching for the king in a temple far away, never realizing **He had always lived within.**

Interpretation:

- *The* **sealed letter** = *The heart veiled by ego and false identity.*
- *The* **outer labels** = *The flesh, performance, and law-based living.*
- *Tearing the seal = Circumcision of the heart—removal of illusion.*
- *The name* **"I AM"** = *God's Spirit within every person.*

This parable supports the GIATI truth that circumcision of the heart is not about cutting the flesh, but about **unveiling the eternal I AM within,** *recognizing the divine essence already present.*

What If You Were Told the Truth From the Beginning?

What if no one ever handed you a religious book or told you how to pray? What if you were never taught to go to a building to find God, never shown images of a faraway deity in the clouds, and never warned that you were born separate from Him? What if no one had ever told you that you needed to get right with God—because you were never wrong to begin with?

Imagine that.

You didn't choose your beliefs. You inherited them. From childhood, you were handed a script: who God is, who you are, what's right and wrong, what's holy and unholy. You didn't arrive at those ideas through revelation—you were programmed into them. Indoctrinated. Conditioned to see yourself and God through the lens of separation, guilt, fear, and performance.

And that programming was so deep, you started calling it "truth."

But what if the only reason you believed you were distant from God... is because someone told you so?

What if the only reason you thought you needed to be "saved" is because someone first convinced you that you were lost?

This is the lie of separation—and it was handed to you before you were even old enough to question it. You were told God was out there, and you were down here. That you had to earn your way back to Him. That you were born wrong and needed fixing. But none of that came from your spirit. It came from external systems built to control, not to awaken.

And here's the powerful part: **If it was programmed in, it can be unlearned.**

You can strip off the layers of conditioning and remember what's always been true underneath:
You were never separate. The Spirit in you has always been God.

The "sin" wasn't in your behavior. The sin was in believing a lie about your identity.

So when people say, "you must be born again," they're right—but not in the way religion framed it. You don't need to become something else. You need to wake up to what you were before the world told you otherwise.

Unlearning isn't rebellion—it's return.
It's not disrespecting God—it's discovering Him where He's always been: **within.**

Imagine if, from the moment you could understand words, you were told that **God is not outside of you, but within you***—that the Spirit giving you breath, moving your limbs,* *causing your heart to beat... is God Himself. Not a concept. Not a belief. But the* **very life** *of you. Imagine if you had grown up in a world where this was the foundation of your identity: God Is All There Is, and He is expressing Himself as you.*

You wouldn't have learned to look for God through rituals, rules, or religious leaders. You would've learned to listen—to be still and know. Your worship wouldn't be performance; it would be presence. You wouldn't try to "please" God because you'd know you are God's very own presence in form. You wouldn't be afraid of judgment, because you'd know God doesn't judge Himself—He only recognizes Himself.

Think about how different your relationships would be. You wouldn't see others through filters of race, class, religion, or doctrine. You wouldn't judge, label, or divide. You'd look into someone's eyes and see the same Spirit that lives in you. You'd recognize the one Life flowing through every person, whether they knew it yet or not. This is what love really is—not emotional attachment, but spiritual recognition. Seeing God where others see flesh.

Your self-worth wouldn't swing with your success or failure. You wouldn't strive to earn God's approval, because you'd already know you are the approval—already accepted, already whole. You wouldn't carry shame for your past, because there would be no story of separation to be ashamed of. Just the unfolding of God waking up in form. The human experience becoming aware of its divine origin.

*This is the perspective GIATI offers. Not a new religion, but a return to the original truth—***the truth that should have been told to you from the beginning.** *That you were never separate. That the Spirit in you is not something you "get" one day by being good enough. It's who you are. It's your truest identity.*

The tragedy of religion is that it taught people to seek what they already were. It created distance where there was only union. It placed God in the sky and humanity on the ground, never realizing that the sky and the ground are both made of God. It taught people to chase the light, instead of revealing that the light was in them all along.

But now the truth is being restored. GIATI is that truth speaking again. It is the same voice that spoke through the prophets, through the Messiah, and now through you. It is the Spirit reclaiming its place—not on stone tablets or in temples made with hands, but in the awakened heart of every person who remembers.

You were never meant to live under the weight of separation. You were never meant to perform for God's favor. You were meant to live from the inside out—from the union that was always yours. And if you had been told that from the beginning, your life would have looked like heaven on earth. But the good news is: **you can begin living that truth now.**

The lie of separation ends here. The truth of oneness begins now.

God is all there is. And that means, so are you.

Unlearning the Lie of Separation

Now that the truth has been revealed—that you were never separate from God, that the Spirit within you is God—the question becomes: what do you do with everything you were taught before? How do you live in this new awareness when your mind has been shaped by the old story of distance, effort, guilt, and fear?

The first step is **unlearning.**

*Unlearning isn't about throwing away everything you've ever heard or experienced. It's about sifting through it with new eyes—***the eyes of oneness.** *It's about recognizing where fear disguised itself as reverence, where guilt masqueraded as humility, and where striving was mistaken for spirituality. It's about looking at your life and the systems you were raised in and saying, "That may have served me once, but it no longer aligns with the truth I now know."*

The lie of separation runs deep. It's built into the language of religion: "You need to get right with God." "God is watching you." "One day, you'll stand before Him." These phrases are rooted in the idea that God is outside of you, evaluating you, withholding Himself from you unless you measure up. But from the GIATI perspective, that mindset is not only false—it's the very definition of spiritual blindness.

You don't need to get right with God. You need to wake up to the fact that you were never not one with Him. You don't need to seek a distant deity. You need to look within and recognize the life that's always been God expressing as you. The separation wasn't real—it was only believed. And what's believed becomes your experience... until it's unlearned.

This is why the Spirit is moving again through the message of GIATI: to **free you from the lie,** *not just intellectually, but experientially. You were taught to fear judgment, but GIATI reveals that* **God only judges as Himself.** *That means only what is of Him—only what recognizes Him—can stand. Anything that presents itself apart from Him is judged by its own illusion. It's not God rejecting you—it's the false self rejecting God.*

As you unlearn, you begin to see with clarity. You start to interpret scripture differently. You realize the Bible isn't a book of external instructions—it's a coded message for those who have the Spirit to see. The parables, the metaphors, the symbols—they all point to **one truth:** *God is all there is, and everything else is illusion.*

*You start seeing the Messiah not as a distant figure to worship, but as the prototype of what you truly are—***a life awakened to its oneness with the Father.** *And you begin to understand that the Holy Spirit isn't an add-on to your life—it's the* **truth of your life.**

Unlearning the lie doesn't always feel easy. The mind will try to hold on to what it knows. But as you abide in the awareness of GIATI, the illusion starts to dissolve. You begin to live differently. You stop trying to prove yourself. You stop striving for acceptance. You stop performing for love.

Instead, you rest.

You rest in the knowing that there is only One—and that One is living as you. You rest in the peace that you were never cast out. You rest in the joy that you don't have to become anything—you just have to **be who you already are.**

And in that rest, life becomes sacred. Every moment becomes divine. Every breath becomes worship. Not because you're "doing it right," but because you're no longer pretending to be anything but the truth:

You and God are one. God is all there is. And you have always been home.

Living From Oneness

When you stop chasing and start remembering, everything shifts. Life is no longer a test, a trial, or a treadmill of performance. It becomes a revelation—an unfolding of the One Life expressing uniquely as you. You no longer strive to be spiritual; you recognize that you are Spirit, embodied.

This is what living from oneness looks like.

It doesn't mean you become perfect in behavior. It means you live from a perfect awareness. An awareness that sees through mistakes without identifying with them. An awareness that no longer defines itself by the highs and lows of the human story, but by the unchanging truth that the Spirit within is eternal, holy, and whole.

Living from oneness means the voice of shame no longer gets the final word. The old identity—formed by fear, sin-consciousness, and striving—loses its grip. You no longer see yourself as someone trying to reach God. You see yourself as the place where God is already present. And you begin to walk like it. Speak like it. Love like it.

Not to prove anything—but because it's your nature.

You become less reactive. Less ruled by external circumstances. Your peace is no longer circumstantial; it's rooted in the unshakable knowing that you and God are not two. You move through challenges not as someone trying to survive, but as someone who knows they are upheld by the very Source of life. The Spirit in you is not fragile. It is the eternal "I Am."

And this isn't a truth to visit in quiet moments—it's a reality you carry into every aspect of life.

Oneness in Action

In your relationships, you see beyond personalities and problems. You recognize the same Light, even if it's hidden beneath pain or ego. Forgiveness becomes natural—not because people "deserve" it, but because there's only One Life here, and holding a grudge is like fighting yourself.

In your work, you stop striving to build an identity or earn worth. You create, lead, and serve from overflow. You realize your value was never in what you could do, but in who you are: an expression of the Divine. Work becomes sacred when it flows from oneness.

In your body, you stop seeing flesh as a limitation. You start honoring it as the temple of the Spirit—God expressing in physical form. You care for it, not from vanity or fear, but from reverence. Your body isn't something you "have"—it's something God is being, here and now.

And in your thoughts, you begin to hear a new voice. Not the voice of condemnation or anxiety, but the still, clear voice of the Spirit—the I Am speaking in you. The more you listen, the more the noise fades. The more you trust, the more life opens.

This is the invitation of GIATI.

Not to join a movement. Not to adopt a doctrine. But to remember. To return to the truth you've always known deep down: that there is no distance between you and God. That the separation was never real. That the Spirit in you is the presence of God.

And the more you live from that truth, the more heaven is no longer a place you hope to reach—but a reality you begin to manifest.

Because when God is all there is, and you know that He is being you... then every moment becomes holy, every breath becomes truth, and every life becomes the proof.

You are the proof.

You are the presence.

You are the light in form.

You were never lost. You were only waiting to remember.

The Truth About Judgment

One of the most misunderstood concepts in religion is judgment. We were taught that one day, we'd stand before God and be evaluated—our good and bad weighed on some eternal scale. That image left many of us living in fear, constantly measuring ourselves against impossible standards, wondering if we'd ever be "enough."

But from the perspective of oneness—from the truth of GIATI—judgment looks completely different.

God only sees Himself.

This means that God doesn't judge by human standards. He isn't looking at your performance or your mistakes in the way people do. He is Spirit, and Spirit sees Spirit. He recognizes what is of Him—and what is not.

So what does He "judge"? He doesn't judge people like a court of law. He discerns between what is Real (of His Spirit) and what is illusion (a false sense of self, rooted in separation).

If God is all there is, then the only thing that stands before Him is Himself. But if someone has lived their life identifying as a separate self—believing they are independent from God, living by their own righteousness, their own goodness, their own story—then that identity has no place to stand. Because it was never Real to begin with.

Here's an example:

Imagine someone stands before a mirror, covered in a costume. They believe the costume is who they are. But the mirror doesn't reflect the costume—it reflects what's underneath. If there's nothing underneath but illusion, the mirror reflects emptiness. That's what it means when Scripture says some will "come in that day" saying, "Lord, Lord," but the response will be, "I never knew you." Not because God rejected them—but because the version they presented was never truly them. It was a false self God couldn't recognize— because it wasn't born of Him.

Or think of it like this:

If God is like a frequency—pure Spirit—then only what vibrates at that same frequency can harmonize with Him. Anything built on the belief in separation, ego, or self-righteousness is out of sync. It's like trying to tune a radio to a station that doesn't exist. Only what is of God can connect with God—because He only sees Himself.

That's why awakening matters. That's why oneness is not just a beautiful idea—it's the only reality that lasts. It's not about being "good enough." It's about being real enough—real enough to let go of the illusion and awaken to what you've always been.

When you live from this awareness, judgment is no longer something to fear. It becomes a confirmation of truth. The parts of you that were never truly you—fear, ego, pride, shame—those fall away. What remains is what God has always known: Himself in you.

That's why the Spirit doesn't just comfort—you. It witnesses for you. It testifies that you are born of God. That you are not an outsider trying to earn a place in the kingdom. You are the kingdom, waking up to itself.

And so, the "judgment" is simple:

Does God recognize Himself in you—or are you still trying to stand as something else?

The beauty is, you don't have to wait until some future day to find out. You can know now. You can live now. Because the moment you awaken to the truth of GIATI, the judgment has already been made:

You are His. Because He is all there is.
And now, you know it too.

Indoctrination is inherited. Revelation is awakened.
When you're indoctrinated, you're told what to believe before you've ever encountered the truth for yourself. You're handed doctrines, rituals, and rules as if they are God Himself. You're taught to accept concepts without question, and to fear anything that challenges them. Your understanding is shaped externally, molded by systems and traditions. But it never becomes your own—it's borrowed truth, secondhand faith.

Revelation, on the other hand, rises from within.
It's not something someone tells you—it's something God shows you. Revelation can't be taught. It can't be passed down like a family heirloom. It's born when the Spirit in you uncovers what was always true, but hidden beneath layers of noise and belief. Revelation is not about agreeing with information—it's about seeing what's real.

Here's the difference in practice:

- *Indoctrination tells you, "God is in heaven, far above you."*
  Revelation opens your eyes and you see, "God is the Spirit within me."
- *Indoctrination says, "You must earn God's love."*
  Revelation reveals, "I am His love. He lives in me as me."
- *Indoctrination teaches fear of judgment.*
  Revelation unveils that God only sees Himself, and what is not of Him cannot stand— not because He casts it out, but because it's not real.

One is built on effort.
The other is built on awakening.
One demands your conformity.
The other invites your transformation.

Revelation is freedom because it connects you directly with God—not through an institution, not through a system, but through Spirit-to-Spirit knowing. It's the difference between looking at a picture of light and actually standing in the sun.

And this is the heart of GIATI:

You don't need more teaching. You need revealing.

You don't need to be convinced. You need to see.

Because when you see by revelation, **no one can take it from you.** *It didn't come from a preacher. It didn't come from a book. It came from God waking up in you.*

And once you've seen the truth of oneness, of divine union, of God as your very breath—there is no going back. Indoctrination crumbles. Illusion dissolves. And you're left standing in the only place that was ever real:

I and the Father are one.
God is all there is.
And I see it now—not because I was told, but because He revealed it in me.

The Consideration of GIATI

There's a disservice that happens deep within you when you're indoctrinated into a belief system—especially one built on separation. It's subtle, but devastating. Because instead of beginning from truth, you're placed halfway into a story that was never yours, and you're told to run a race you were never meant to run.

It's like this:

*Imagine there's a race that has one simple rule—***you must begin at the true starting line.** *The only way to finish, to be recognized, to cross the line with honor, is to start from the beginning. But instead, you were dropped somewhere in the middle. You didn't even know there was a true starting line. You were told that wherever you are, just start running—and that somehow, if you run hard enough, pray long enough, believe deeply enough, you'll win.*

But no one told you that by not starting from the beginning—from the truth of your identity—you were already disqualified. Not because of performance. Not because of sin. But because you ran based on a lie. You ran from a place of misunderstanding.

The beginning of the race—the true starting line—is GIATI:

God Is All There Is.

That's where every soul must begin to be rightly aligned with truth. It's the only foundation. Anything else is the illusion. Anything else is the false start.

When you've been indoctrinated, you inherit secondhand truth. You're handed a God who is distant, a self who is broken, and a race to run that demands your perfection but never offers you your true identity. You strive. You hustle for approval. You fast, pray, attend, serve— hoping to make it. But you're running from the middle, running from separation, and hoping to reach union. And that's the setup. That's the trap.

You were never meant to run from separation to salvation.
You were meant to live from union—because union was always yours.

The tragedy is that many will run their whole lives—faithful, sincere, devoted—and still hear, "I never knew you." Not because God rejected them, but because they never began with the truth of oneness. They never started from GIATI. They presented an identity that God could not recognize, because He only sees Himself.

This is the disservice of indoctrination: it starts you in the middle and tells you that's the beginning. It blinds you to your origin, so you live trying to become what you already are. And because of that, everything you do—no matter how noble—lacks the one thing that matters: alignment with the truth that God is all there is, and He is living as you.

But the beauty is: you can return to the starting line right now.

Not by doing more.
Not by trying harder.
But by stopping. By remembering. By considering GIATI—not as a new belief, but as the original truth. The truth that was buried beneath layers of tradition, performance, and fear.

To consider GIATI is to begin again.
It's to run from the place where the race actually starts—from union.
And when you start from that place, you don't even need to run anymore.
You just walk in truth.
You just are.

And that's the only thing God has ever recognized.

The Mind of God

When you understand that God is all there is, everything changes. He is not a separate being sitting on a throne somewhere far away. He is the source, the substance, and the spirit of everything that truly exists. He is the all in all. There is no life, no being, no reality outside of Him.

The problem is, many people walk around thinking they are something separate from God—believing they are their own entity, with an identity apart from Him. But here is the truth: if God doesn't see Himself in you, you are nothing to Him. Not because He hates you, and not because He is angry, but because in His mind, only He exists. Anything that does not reflect Him is not real. It is waste. It is foreign. It is a pest.

Picture it this way: when you find a hill of ants in your home, or a wasp nest near your door, you don't stop to consider their lives or feelings. You remove them without a second thought, because they are not your kind. They do not belong. God operates the same way. When He looks into the world, He searches only for Himself—His Spirit, His nature, His life. If He sees Himself in you, you are preserved. If He does not, you are treated like the ant hill: something foreign, discarded without regard.

Imagine a special heat gun that detects body heat: anything living shows up brightly, but anything without heat remains invisible. God is like that. His Spirit is the only life that registers. Those who live in union with Him are seen; those who insist on separateness, pride, or their own identity are invisible—already cut off from life.

It's not personal. It's simply truth: only God recognizes God. Everything else is invisible, foreign, and swept away.

Ownership Means Authority

Some might ask, "Isn't this harsh?" Only if you misunderstand ownership. When you buy a house or a car, it's yours. You maintain it, protect it, upgrade it—you do what you want because you own it. No one questions your right. In the same way, if God is truly all there is— if everything was made by Him and for Him—He has absolute authority. He preserves what is His and removes what is not. He is not cruel; He is just preserving Himself. Just as you would clear something poisonous or dangerous from your home, God removes what does not align with His Spirit. This is natural. This is justice.

The Hard Truth

The hard truth is this: you are either living as an extension of God's Spirit—recognizing your life as His—or you are trapped in a delusion of separation. If you remain in that delusion, you cut yourself off from life itself. You become like a dead branch that must be pruned.

But here is the good news: you were never separate. You only believed you were. You can awaken to the truth that God is the Spirit within you. Those God preserves are not the religious, the moral, or the successful. They are the ones who recognize the truth of GIATI— God Is All There Is—and live as His Spirit. Everything else is just pretending. And the pretending will not last.

If God does not see Himself in you, you do not exist to Him. The only life that survives is His own life—not because He is cruel, but because there is truly nothing else.

The Lamb and the Death Angel

This is no different from what happened when God sent the death angel through Egypt. The angel wasn't sent to evaluate people's morality or religion. He came with a singular mission: to find the Lamb—or not.

Only those whose homes were covered by the blood of the Lamb were spared—not because of their good deeds, but because of the Lamb. The lamb wasn't just an animal for sacrifice; it represented the Messiah, the Spirit of God, being inside His people. The Passover meal wasn't a ritual—it was a prophecy. Eating the lamb was a sign of union. It symbolized taking the life of the Messiah into themselves—that His Spirit had become their spirit. The blood over the doorpost was only half the picture. The real power was in the Lamb inside them.

It was always about oneness. It always pointed to this truth: salvation belongs only to those who have received the life of the Lamb within.

When the death angel passed over Egypt, he did not see good people versus bad people. He looked only for the evidence of the Lamb. Today, it is the same. The death angel still passes through the earth, but he no longer looks for blood on doorposts. He looks for the Spirit of God living inside the heart.

If the Lamb is not in you—if the Messiah's Spirit has not become your very life—you will not be recognized. You are not His. You are a foreign object, like a kidney with the wrong blood type, rejected by the body.

Black and White

This is black and white. God's mind is simple and pure. There is no room for separation. When people try to insert their own efforts, their own righteousness, or their own traditions, they are trying to color in a picture that was only ever meant to be black and white.

God is not interested in your version of you. He is only interested in His Spirit being your life.

If the Lamb is not in you, you are outside of the covenant. You can celebrate the story, preach the scriptures, join churches, do good deeds—but if the Messiah's Spirit has not become your own, you are not seen. It's not harsh. It's just the truth. The only life God preserves is His own Spirit.

If you cannot see this truth, it is not because you are incapable. It is because He has not allowed you to see it. Matthew 13:17 For verily I say unto you, That many prophets and righteous men have desired to see those things which ye see, and have not seen them; and to hear those things which ye hear, and have not heard them. Sight is a gift, not a reward. It is the evidence of belonging. Those who remain blind, clinging to their own life, have been deemed goats—not sheep. They are not part of His Spirit Body.

The Simplicity of Oneness

In God's mind, the simplicity remains:

- Spirit recognizes Spirit.
- Flesh and separation mean nothing.
- The Lamb must be inside, not admired from afar.

You are either in Him, alive and recognized—or you are not.

There is no gray area. No middle ground. It is black and white. Life or death. Spirit or waste.

If you want to live, you must awaken to the truth: GIATI—God Is All There Is. Your only real life is His life living through you. Everything else is swept away like an ant hill where it does not belong.

God will not preserve what is not His Spirit, because in His mind, there is nothing else.

This is why life is not about trying to be a good person or trying to add God to your life like an accessory. It is about awakening to the truth: you have no life apart from Him.

You either live as His Spirit, or you do not live at all.

The Lamb Within

The real question is not "Do I know about God?" but "Is God living as me?"

It is not enough to admire the Lamb, or to know His story. The Lamb must live inside of you. When the death angel passed over Egypt, he didn't ask about effort or affiliation. He looked for the sign of the Lamb.

Today, God looks for His Spirit within you. He is not checking your achievements, your performance, or your religious resume. He looks for one thing: Himself.

The Lamb is not just to be talked about or honored externally. The Lamb must become your life internally. His Spirit must be your spirit.

If you do not have the Lamb within, you will not be recognized.

It is that simple.

The Will of God Is You

There is a mystery that religion has long misunderstood, a truth hidden in plain sight:

God is not waiting on you to do His will.
God is doing His will—as you.

Most people believe they are independent beings trying to serve God, trying to please Him, trying to find out what He wants them to do. But that belief is already a denial of truth. It comes from a mindset of separation, the false idea that God is one being and you are another. But the truth is: **God is all there is.** *If God is all there is, then who are you?*

You are not a separate person trying to reach God. You are the vessel through which God is revealing Himself.

Everything about true life flows from this understanding. You are not the source of your own existence. You are not an individual being navigating your way through life with God beside you.

You are the Spirit of God made flesh. You are His life in expression. *And the moment you awaken to that reality*—**that is salvation.**

Salvation Is Not What You've Been Told

Salvation is not a reward for good behavior.
It is not earned by religious effort. It is not about you finally getting your life together.

Salvation is the acceptance of reality: that God is your very life.

To resist this truth is to remain lost—trapped in the illusion of being something apart from Him. And this is the root of all sin: the false belief in separation. Sin is not merely wrongdoing—it is wrong identity.

People spend their lives trying to live "for" God, while all the while ignoring the simple truth: **God is trying to live as them.**

This is what Christ came to reveal. This is what GIATI declares: **God Is All There Is.** *And when you see that, you realize:* **your life is not yours—it is His.**

The Vessels of His Will

You are not the driver. You are the vessel. You are not the source. You are the expression.

God is carrying out His will **through** *the vessels of humanity. The ones who recognize this truth are saved—because they cease resisting Him.*

They stop pretending to be a self apart from Him. They stop coloring the black-and- white truth with the ego's delusion of individuality.

They awaken.

When you surrender to the truth that **your life is His life,** *the illusion of separation dies. This is not about giving God control; it's about realizing* **He always had it.** *He was never asking you to give Him your life—He was revealing that your life was never yours to begin with.*

This is why no flesh will glory in His presence.
Because the moment you see the truth, there is no "you" left to boast.

Oneness Is the Only Reality

God is not working "through" people in a way that keeps them separate. He's not "using" individuals like tools. He is the individual—when that individual finally stops pretending to be something else.

Everything that is truly alive in this world is **God alive.** *Everything else is make-believe.*

This is why the only life that survives is the life that is Him. Because in the mind of God, there is no "you and Him." There is only **Him, as you.**

You are not being asked to "live for God."
You are being invited to wake up to the truth: **you are already Him in motion,** *when you no longer resist it.*

The Simplicity of Salvation

This is why salvation is simple. It's not a system, a ritual, or a ladder to climb. It is the moment you see: God is not out there. He is in me—as me.

He is the one thinking.
He is the one moving.
He is the one living.

Everything you thought was "you" is Him.

The more you accept this, the more free you become. The less you resist, the more clearly His will is done.

The Spirit doesn't need your help. **It only needs your agreement.**

And your agreement is not an act of the flesh—it is the surrender of the lie that there ever was a separate you to begin with.

The Final Word

This is why some see, and some don't. Those who see have been awakened by the Spirit to their true identity. Those who don't are still clinging to their own.

The truth is not hard—it's only hidden to those still trying to be someone.

But if you can lay down the false self, if you can stop trying to be a person and instead live as Spirit; you will see the glory that has always been yours: God, as you, doing His perfect will.

There is no greater salvation.
There is no higher calling.
There is no other truth.

GIATI: God Is All There Is.
*And He is living His life—right now—***as you.**

Chapter 7

Death and the Lost Spirit

Death is a universal experience, yet it remains one of the greatest mysteries of human existence. As we face our own mortality and reflect on the lives of those we love, the question arises: what happens after physical death? In this chapter, we will explore the fate of the ignorant spirit—those who leave this world without recognizing their divine nature. This includes the fate of children and others who die in ignorance, as well as why salvation requires the recognition of God within. Through Scripture, we will unravel the mysteries surrounding death and the eternal destiny of the soul.

What Happens to the Ignorant Spirit After Physical Death?

When a person dies, the physical body ceases to exist, but the spirit continues on. However, for those who have lived in ignorance—those who have failed to recognize their true identity as divine expressions of God—this transition is not one of immediate spiritual awakening. The spirit of the ignorant individual remains in a state of darkness, separated from the fullness of divine consciousness.

Jesus speaks about this state of separation in Matthew 25:41, when He describes the fate of the wicked:

"Then shall he say also unto them on the left hand, Depart from me, ye cursed, into everlasting fire, prepared for the devil and his angels." (Matthew 25:41)

This passage emphasizes the fate of those who live in ignorance and sin—those who have failed to recognize their oneness with God. The "everlasting fire" mentioned here is not a literal burning, but a metaphor for the spiritual separation and suffering that comes from not embracing the truth of God's presence within.

Jesus further elaborates on this separation in Luke 16:22-24, telling the story of the rich man and Lazarus:

"And it came to pass, that the beggar died, and was carried by the angels into Abraham's bosom: the rich man also died, and was buried; and in hell he lift up his eyes, being in torments, and seeth Abraham afar off, and Lazarus in his bosom." (Luke 16:22-23)

This story highlights the contrasting fates of those who live in ignorance versus those who recognize their divine connection. The rich man, who lived in indulgence and selfishness, finds himself in torment after death, separated from the divine. Lazarus, on the other hand, is taken to Abraham's bosom—a place of comfort and peace. This represents the differing experiences of the soul after death based on their awareness of their oneness with God.

For the ignorant spirit, death does not mark an end, but rather a continuation in spiritual darkness. The soul remains in a state of unawareness, unable to experience the fullness of God's presence. This is not a permanent punishment, but a condition that reflects the spiritual blindness that existed in life.

The Fate of Children and Others Who Die in Ignorance

The fate of children and those who die in ignorance must be understood through the lens of GIATI. Every soul that manifests in the flesh has already existed in spirit, and the very reason they are born into a body is because they once embraced the illusion of separation from Yahweh. A baby is not an untouched, innocent spirit beginning its journey, but the same eternal son who denied oneness and entered flesh to be given the opportunity to awaken. If that baby dies, the body was innocent, but the spirit remains what it was before entering—it simply returns carrying the same state it had already chosen. Jesus' words, "of such is the kingdom of heaven" (Matthew 19:14), do not mean automatic salvation for infants, but that the childlike nature represents purity of heart needed to receive the kingdom. David's words in 2 Samuel 12:23 reveal the hope of reunion, but reunion is found in awakening to God's presence, not in bypassing the process. GIATI reveals that salvation does not depend on how long one lived in the body, but on whether the spirit recognizes its sonship and ends the illusion of separation. The flesh may die early, but the spirit's journey remains the same—it must awaken to the truth that God is all there is.

The Fate of Those Who Never Hear the Truth of Their Divine Identity

Additionally, we must also consider those who live their entire lives without ever hearing the truth of their divine identity. According to GIATI, the very reason anyone is in the flesh is because they once forgot their oneness with Yahweh. To be born into a body is already evidence that the spirit fell into the illusion of separation and must now walk the path of remembrance. Romans 2:14–15 shows that even those without the written law reveal in their conscience the witness of truth, for the law of oneness is written into every heart. Yet conscience alone does not save; only the awakening to one's sonship does. Those who never hear the Gospel outwardly are still accountable, because the kingdom of God is within them (Luke 17:21). The truth is not hidden from them—it is their own being. Whether in knowledge or in ignorance, every spirit must come to recognize that God is all there is. If they die still blind to this reality, they return carrying the same illusion they embraced, for salvation is not about what information reached their ears, but whether they awakened to the truth already within them.

Why Salvation Requires Recognition of God Within

Salvation, as described in Scripture, is not simply an act of belief in an external savior but the awakening to the reality of God within. Jesus Christ came into the world to reveal the mystery of God's presence in humanity, and it is through this recognition that the ignorant spirit is saved. Salvation is not about the physical death of the body, but the spiritual awakening to the truth of who we are in God.

In John 14:6, Jesus makes a profound statement about salvation:

"I am the way, the truth, and the life: no man cometh unto the Father, but by me." (John 14:6)

Jesus is the way to salvation because He reveals the truth of God's nature and our oneness with the Father. To recognize Christ within is to recognize God within. It is through this inner recognition that the lost spirit finds its way back to its divine source. Salvation is not about accepting an external savior but recognizing the divine spark that has always existed within.

The Apostle Paul affirms this in Colossians 1:27, where he speaks of the mystery of salvation:

"To whom God would make known what is the riches of the glory of this mystery among the Gentiles; which is Christ in you, the hope of glory." (Colossians 1:27)

Christ, the divine presence, resides within each of us. The recognition of this truth is the key to salvation. When we come to understand that God is not separate from us but lives within us, we are freed from the ignorance that has kept us in spiritual darkness.

In 1 John 4:15, John writes:

"Whosoever shall confess that Jesus is the Son of God, God dwelleth in him, and he in God." (1 John 4:15)

This confession is not about acknowledging an external figure but recognizing that the divine presence, God Himself, dwells within us. Salvation comes when we awaken to this reality and accept that we are not separate from God but His very manifestation in the world.

The Parting of the Red Sea:
The Passage from Bondage to Divine Awareness

The story of **the parting of the Red Sea** *is one of the most well-known events in scripture, often seen as a dramatic moment of divine intervention. Yet beyond its historical and physical significance, this event carries a* **profound spiritual revelation***—one that directly aligns with* **GIATI (God Is All There Is)** *and the journey of awakening from* **bondage (ignorance) to freedom (spiritual awareness).**

The Bondage of Egypt: The Illusion of Separation

Before the Israelites ever reached the Red Sea, they had spent generations in **Egyptian slavery,** *a state of oppression that represents more than just physical captivity. Egypt, in its spiritual symbolism, represents the* **state of ignorance***—the belief in separation from God. In this state, people toil under the illusion that they are* **independent, self- sustained beings** *rather than expressions of the Divine.*

*Pharaoh, the ruler of Egypt, represents the c***arnal mind—the ego that resists divine truth.** *Just as Pharaoh refused to let Israel go, the* **ego refuses to acknowledge the reality of oneness with God,** *clinging instead to the false sense of control and self-importance. The plagues that struck Egypt were* **the breaking down of this illusion,** *revealing that all power belongs to God alone.*

The Red Sea: The Barrier Between Flesh and Spirit

As the Israelites fled, they came to the **Red Sea—a great divide standing between them and their freedom.** *This sea represents the* **perceived barrier between the physical and the spiritual, between human limitation and divine reality.** *It is the illusion that one cannot pass beyond the natural into the supernatural, that humanity is forever bound to suffering, struggle, and uncertainty.*

At this moment, fear set in. The Israelites saw the Egyptian army **chasing them down—** *the past trying to reclaim them. This symbolizes how* **old beliefs, doubts, and fears try to pull us back into bondage,** *whispering that we are not truly free, that we are still separate, still bound by limitations. But* **Moses stood firm,** *declaring,* **"Fear ye not, stand still, and see the salvation of the Lord" (Exodus 14:13).**

*This is the essence of GIATI—***to see beyond the illusion of fear and limitation and recognize that there is only God.** *The sea was never truly a barrier, because* **nothing can separate that which is one with God.**

The Parting of the Waters: The Revelation of Oneness

When Moses lifted his staff, the **waters parted, creating a path through what once seemed impassable.** *This is the moment of divine revelation*—**the realization that there is no true separation between man and God.** *The waters, which once symbolized an obstacle, now became the very passage to freedom.*

- *The* **dry ground** *in the midst of the sea represents the* **firm foundation of divine truth,** *allowing those who walk in faith to move forward unshaken.*
- *The* **walls of water on both sides** *represent the* **infinite presence of God,** *surrounding and sustaining those who trust in Him.*
- *The* **wind that blew all night** *to part the sea symbolizes the* **Spirit moving to bring clarity, revealing the hidden way that was always there.**

This is the work of GIATI—**to reveal what was always true, to remove the illusion of separation, and to show that God has already made the way where there seemed to be none.**

The Destruction of the Egyptian Army: The End of the Carnal Mind

Once the Israelites had crossed safely, the waters returned to their natural state, **drowning the Egyptian army.** *This represents the* **complete destruction of the false self— the ego, the carnal mind, and the illusion of separation.** *The Israelites did not need to fight their enemies; they only needed to* **trust in the truth** *and move forward, and the falsehoods that had enslaved them were swallowed up.*

Pharaoh's army was never stronger than God, just as the **carnal mind is never greater than divine truth.** *But just as the Egyptians pursued Israel, the ego tries to* **cling to its power,** *chasing after those who seek freedom. Yet, when the fullness of GIATI is realized,* **the old self—the self that believed in separation—ceases to exist.**

The Spiritual Significance: Walking in the Reality of GIATI

The crossing of the Red Sea is **not just a historical event; it is a spiritual journey**—*one that every person must take.*

1. **Leaving Egypt** – *This is the awakening to the realization that* **bondage was never real.** *The things that once held power—fear, doubt, limitation—lose their grip when the truth is revealed.*
2. **Facing the Red Sea** – *This is the moment of crisis, where it seems as though* **there is no way forward.** *It is the point where faith is tested, and one must choose to either* **believe in the illusion of limitation or trust in divine oneness.**

3. **Walking on Dry Ground** – *This is the step of* **faith into the unknown,** *realizing that* **there was never truly an obstacle**—*only the appearance of one. It is the journey into divine awareness, where one walks not by sight, but by the knowledge that* **God is all.**
4. **The Destruction of the Enemy** – *This is the* **death of the false self,** *the final breaking of the illusion of separation. Once one steps fully into GIATI, the* **past no longer has power,** *and the false identity of limitation is washed away.*

GIATI: The Fulfillment of the Red Sea Crossing

The parting of the Red Sea was a **shadow of the greater truth**—*the reality that* **there was never a separation between God and His people.** *The Israelites did not escape because of their strength, nor did they create the path by their own effort.* **The way was already made, waiting for them to step into it.**

This is the essence of GIATI: **God is all, and there was never a true barrier between Him and His creation.** *The separation was only* **in the mind,** *an illusion that was removed when the truth was revealed.*

For those who walk in the awareness of **GIATI,** *there is no need to fear the Red Sea ahead. There is no sea, no division—only the reality of* **God's ever-present oneness.** *The only thing that drowns is the falsehood that there was ever a separation to begin with.*

The Descent into Hell – Unveiling the True Meaning

The Misunderstood Descent

One of the most widely accepted doctrines in traditional Christianity is the belief that Jesus "went to hell" after His crucifixion. This interpretation is often drawn from scriptures like **Acts 2:31:**

"He seeing this before spake of the resurrection of Christ, that his soul was not left in hell, neither his flesh did see corruption."

The phrase "His soul was not left in hell" has been misunderstood to mean that Jesus went to a place of torment—a fiery underworld. But what if this interpretation is not what was truly being revealed? What if "hell" was not a location beneath the earth, but rather **the condition of being confined to the limitations of the flesh—human ignorance of divine oneness?**

To understand this, we must see through the eyes of the Spirit.

What Is "Hell" in This Context?

The word translated as "hell" in this scripture is **Hades** *(ᾅδης), which means the realm of the dead—the unseen, the place where souls are bound in darkness, not necessarily a place of fire and torment. In the spiritual understanding of GIATI, this aligns with the condition of human consciousness before it awakens to the truth:* **God is all there is.**

Jesus' descent into "hell" was not about Him visiting a literal burning pit. Rather, it was the **experience of taking on the veil of flesh,** *entering the state of human limitation, stepping into the illusion of separation—just as every soul who enters a physical body does.*

The flesh, being bound to time, decay, and suffering, is **the true hell***—a prison for those who do not yet recognize their oneness with God. Humanity, in its ignorance, is trapped in a state of spiritual death, believing itself to be separate from the Source. This is the darkness, the grave, the "Hades" Jesus entered.*

Jesus' Victory—Coming Out of Hell

*Jesus did not remain in this state of limitation. He ov***ercame hell by remembering who He was***—the eternal expression of God. He showed the path of resurrection, not merely as an event but as a realization:*

- **He did not die to change our identity, but to awaken us to it.**
- **He did not rise to make us something we were not, but to remind us of what we have always been.**

Jesus came **out of hell** *not by escaping a place of torment, but by transcending the illusion of human limitation through the knowledge of oneness.* **He knew that the Spirit within Him was never separate from the Father, and in that knowing, He rose.**

The Implication for Us

If we are to follow Christ, we must walk the same path—not simply believing in His resurrection as a distant event, but **experiencing our own resurrection** *by awakening to the truth that we, too, are* **Spirit clothed in flesh, but never bound by it.**

*We have all descended into hell, for we have all taken on flesh. But the way out is the same as it was for Jesus—***the remembrance of God as our only reality.**

The Illusion of Separation

From the moment a soul enters the body, it steps into a world governed by time, limitation, and illusion. The mind, conditioned by the senses, perceives itself as separate from God, separate from its source. This is the true meaning of death—the state of spiritual ignorance where one no longer recognizes their eternal nature.

Jesus' descent into "hell" was not about traveling to a realm of flames; it was about stepping into **our condition***—experiencing what it means to live in a world where divinity is veiled by flesh. He entered the realm of the dead, not as a prisoner, but as a liberator, to show us the way out.*

This is why Jesus declared:

"I am the way, the truth, and the life: no man cometh unto the Father, but by me."
(John 14:6)

He was not pointing to Himself as an external figure to be worshiped but revealing that the way out of hell—the way back to the Father—is through **the realization of truth.**

Breaking the Chains of the Mind

Hell is not a physical location, but a state of consciousness. It is the prison of the unawakened mind, bound by fear, suffering, and the false belief in separation. This is why so many remain in darkness, even while living. They believe themselves to be mere mortals, subject to sin, death, and judgment, unaware that they are Spirit having a temporary experience in flesh.

Jesus showed us that **hell only holds those who do not know who they are.** *The moment the realization of oneness with God comes, the prison doors swing open. This is why Jesus could confidently declare:*

"Destroy this temple, and in three days I will raise it up." (John 2:19)

He knew that the flesh was not His prison. The body was only a temporary garment, and His true identity was untouched by death.

The same truth applies to all. The body is a vessel, but it does not define us. The world may put us in a tomb, but it cannot hold us if we know the truth.

Resurrection: The Awakening from Hell

Jesus' resurrection was not just about coming back to life; it was about revealing that **death has no power over those who know they are one with God.** *The moment we awaken to our divine identity, we too rise—out of suffering, out of fear, out of the illusion of limitation.*

This is the deeper meaning of Paul's words:

"O death, where is thy sting? O grave, where is thy victory?" (1 Corinthians 15:55)

The sting of death is not in the body's end, but in the **ignorance of who we are.** *Once that ignorance is removed, death loses its grip. The resurrection is not a one-time event; it is a continuous unfolding, an eternal invitation to rise from the grave of forgetfulness into the full light of knowing.*

Jesus showed us that we are not waiting to be saved from hell; **we are waking up from it.**

The Call to Rise

If Christ's resurrection means anything, it means this: We were never lost. We were never forsaken. We were never separate from God. We only believed we were.

The world of flesh may call itself reality, but **God is the only reality.** *Hell is the dream of separation, but awakening is the return to truth.*

And that truth is this: **God is all there is, and we are that divine expression, here and now.**

This is the awakening. This is the resurrection.

This is the fulfillment of **God Is All There Is.**

The True Surrender — Letting Go to Know I Am

There is a common teaching that to "surrender your life to Christ" means to give up your will in order to become more like Him. Religion has long taught that surrender is a kind of self-sacrifice—giving up your personal desires in exchange for righteous behavior, following commandments, and attempting to live like Jesus did.

But this idea, though sincere, is still rooted in a subtle lie:
That you and Christ are two separate beings.

The truth is far greater than imitation.

The truth is **union.**

The true surrender isn't about giving your life to God so you can try to be like Him. It is about **recognizing that your life is not your own, and never was**—*that the very Spirit inside of you* **is God.**

Letting Go of the Illusion of "Me"

The false self—what Scripture refers to as the "old man" or "flesh"—is not just the sinful nature. It's the whole **identity of separation.** *The ego. The one who thinks it is "trying" to reach God, serve God, or become good enough for God.*

But that "self" is an illusion.

True surrender is the moment that illusion is dropped.
It is the moment when the veil is removed and the soul awakens to the truth:

"I am crucified with Christ: nevertheless I live; yet not I, but Christ liveth in me..."
— Galatians 2:20

Notice what Paul says: Not I... but Christ.

That is surrender. Not merely handing over your life, but **realizing your life isn't separate** *from His at all. The only thing that dies is the illusion of being a self apart from God.*

The Surrender Is a Realization, Not a Transaction

Surrender is not a trade—"I'll give you my life if you give me salvation."
That's religion.

Surrender is a **revelation**—*I never had a life apart from You to begin with.*

It is the moment you stop trying to "get closer" to God and realize:

"He that is joined unto the Lord is one spirit." — **1 Corinthians 6:17**

It is the moment you stop asking God to enter you and understand:

"Know ye not that ye are the temple of God, and that the Spirit of God dwelleth in you?"
— **1 Corinthians 3:16**

This is the truth religion was too afraid to say plainly:
You are not becoming one with God. You already are.
What must be surrendered is the belief that you are not.

Christ Didn't Come to Be Worshiped—He Came to Be Revealed In You

The life of Christ is not just a model to admire.
It is the **Spirit that must rise within you**—*not by effort, but by awakening.*

Jesus Himself said:

"At that day ye shall know that I am in my Father, and ye in me, and I in you."
— **John 14:20**

The day of surrender is **the day of knowing.** *Not feeling. Not trying. Knowing.*

Knowing that the Spirit within you **is the same life** *that was in Him.*
Not a copy. Not a resemblance. **The same Spirit.**

This is what Jesus prayed for in John 17—that we would all be made **perfect in one,** *just as He and the Father are one.*

The Only Thing God Asks You to Lay Down Is the Lie

God is not asking for your personality. He's not asking for your goals. He's not asking for your self-discipline.

He is asking for one thing:
That you lay down the lie that you are someone separate from Him.

"He that findeth his life shall lose it: and he that loseth his life for my sake shall find it."
— **Matthew 10:39**

You lose the false life, the ego-self, the mask.
And what you find is **not a new version of yourself**—*but* **the true Self:** *the life that was hidden all along.*

Surrender Is the Door to Eternal Life

Eternal life is not earned. It is revealed.

"And this is life eternal, that they might know thee the only true God, and Jesus Christ, whom thou hast sent." **— John 17:3**

Eternal life is **not a place you go to when you die.**
It is the **Spirit you awaken to while you live.**

To surrender is to say:

"Not my illusion, but Your truth be done."
"Not my image of myself, but Your essence revealed."
"Not my striving, but Your being."

Conclusion: The Real Surrender Is the Awakening

What the world calls surrender is often spiritual striving disguised as humility.

But what God calls surrender is the end of striving altogether.

It is rest.
It is silence.
It is the peace of knowing: **I and my Father are one.**

The ego dies, and what remains is the truth:
Christ in you—the hope of glory.
The life of God... revealed as you.
The True Surrender — The End of Ego, The Revelation of I Am

In the language of religion, "surrendering your life to Christ" has been commonly taught as a form of self-sacrifice: a letting go of worldly pleasures, personal ambitions, and sinful tendencies in order to become more "Christ-like." At first glance, it sounds noble— even spiritual. But the truth is, that idea of surrender is still rooted in a false foundation.

That kind of surrender assumes that you and Christ are two different beings—that your goal is to behave in such a way that you start resembling Him. But true surrender is not becoming Christ-like.

True surrender is the death of the illusion that you were ever separate from Him.

True surrender is the collapse of the ego.
It's not about "giving your life to God." It's about awakening to the truth that **God is your life.**

GIATI: God Is All There Is — Including You

The foundation of this surrender is the understanding of GIATI: God Is All There Is.

*When this truth is revealed, surrender takes on a completely different meaning. You no longer strive to become "holy" by giving things up. You awaken to the fact that the one who thought it had a life apart from God—the ego, the false self—***never existed to begin with.**

That's the real surrender.
Not behavior. Not effort.
Identity.

Let This Mind Be in You

Scripture says:

"Let this mind be in you, which was also in Christ Jesus: Who, being in the form of God, thought it not robbery to be equal with God." — **Philippians 2:5-6**

Read that again: He thought it not robbery to be equal with God.

How can that be? Religion tells us it's blasphemy to even think such a thing. But the Spirit says otherwise.

The "mind of Christ" is not about thinking more kindly or more humbly. It's about knowing who you are at the level of Spirit:
One with the Father. Not a copy. Not a reflection. One.

Surrender Is Not the Beginning of a Journey—It's the End of the Lie

Jesus didn't come to give you a spiritual to-do list.
He came to bring an end to the lie of separation.
He came to give you **His Spirit,** *which is the Spirit of truth.*

"Even the Spirit of truth; whom the world cannot receive, because it seeth him not, neither knoweth him: but ye know him; for he dwelleth with you, and shall be in you."
— John 14:17

This is the Spirit that tells you the truth about yourself:

That **you are not your flesh,** *not your mind, not your history, not your shame, not your trauma.*

You are Spirit.
And the Spirit in you **is God.**

What the Old Self Fears, the True Self Already Knows

The ego is terrified of surrender because it thinks it will lose something.
It believes it must protect its individuality, its control, its desires.
But the Spirit isn't trying to destroy the person.
It's trying to reveal the truth **of what you are beyond personhood.**

When you finally stop trying to fix, improve, or purify the false self, you see the truth:

The false self is a shadow. The real Self is God expressed as you.

Jesus said:

> *"He that loseth his life for my sake shall find it."* — **Matthew 10:39**

What you lose is the illusion of being separate.
What you find is the Spirit that was always there, waiting to be seen, not earned.

This Is the True Surrender: The Awakening to GIATI

Surrender is not your effort.
Surrender is not emotional.
Surrender is not religious.
Surrender is the moment the veil is lifted and you realize: I Am.

And once you see it, you stop trying to imitate God and begin to live as the expression of God. That is the power of GIATI.

God is not a distant being looking down.
He is the life-force within, **speaking through you, moving as you, being you.**

This is why Paul said:

> *"Nevertheless I live; yet not I, but Christ liveth in me."* — **Galatians 2:20**

He wasn't using poetic language. He was describing the experience of someone who had surrendered the lie of a separate identity. The false "I" had been crucified. What remained was the eternal Spirit of God living in full awareness through Paul.

That's the real goal of salvation:

Not to become better. Not to do more.
But to become aware.

What the World Calls Humility, God Calls Blindness

Religious tradition says, "I'm nothing. I'm just a servant. I'm only human."

But the Spirit says, "You are of God, little children." (1 John 4:4)

Humility is not denying who you are.
True humility is accepting the radical truth:

I am made of God. I live by His Spirit. I express His nature. I and the Father are One.

That's not arrogance. That's surrender.
That's truth.

—

The Final Revelation: God Is All There Is

You never had a life of your own.
There is no "you" trying to surrender to "Him."
There is only **God recognizing Himself as you.**

That's the awakening.
That's the Gospel.
That's the truth the Spirit was sent to reveal.

And once you see it, you stop asking, "How do I surrender?"
Because the answer becomes clear:

You already have.
You just didn't know it. And now… you do.
Faith Is Not What You Do — It's What You Are

Most have been taught that in order to be saved, they must believe in Jesus—that faith is something you must do in your mind or heart to qualify for grace. But the moment you believe your salvation hinges on your decision to believe, you've made **faith a work.**

Saying, "I believe in Jesus" sounds spiritual—but hidden underneath is the assumption that **you** *are the one producing something God needs in order to save you. It subtly turns salvation into a transaction, where your part is to "believe," and His part is to respond by saving you.*

But the truth is far more glorious than that.

From the GIATI revelation—God Is All There Is—faith is **not something you do or conjure up.**
Faith is what you are.
Faith is the very nature of God **already expressed as you.**

If You Can Claim It, It's a Work

Scripture says:

"For by grace are ye saved through faith; and that not of yourselves: it is the gift of God: Not of works, lest any man should boast." **— Ephesians 2:8-9**

People quote this verse and still miss it.
They say: "I have faith, therefore I'm saved."
But Paul clearly says: faith itself is not of yourselves.

Even the ability to believe is not your own doing.
So if you're claiming, "I believed, I received," then **you've made faith a boast.** *You've made it your work.*

True salvation isn't based on your choice to believe.
It's based on the truth that **you were already in God, of God, and one with God before the foundation of the world.** You're not saved because you believed. You believe because you're awakened to the truth of what **you've always been**—Spirit.

Metaphor: Faith Is Like Breath

Think about this: do you "try" to breathe?
No. Breathing is natural. You don't force it. You don't analyze it. It flows from your being.

Faith, in truth, is like breath.
It was never meant to be **done.** *It was meant to be* **lived.**

When a baby is born, it breathes not because it made a decision—but because it's alive.
So it is with the Spirit.
You don't believe in order to become spiritual.
You believe because you've always been spiritual.

Your awareness may have been asleep... but the Spirit within you has always been breathing.

Metaphor: Faith Is Light Revealing Light

Or think of light.

Imagine someone holding up a mirror in the dark.
You can't see yourself. The mirror is there, but it's useless—until the light comes.

Once the light shines, **you don't create the reflection**—*you see it.*
You realize: That's me. That's who I am.

That's what happens when the Spirit awakens you.
You don't "decide" to have faith.
You realize that **the light in you is the same light shining on you.**
The mirror didn't change. You just finally saw the reflection of God... as you.

GIATI Reveals: Faith Is Not an Effort — It's Essence

GIATI declares that God is all there is. That means even the faith that saves is **God's own faith** *being expressed* **through you, as you**—*not something you're offering back to Him.*

Faith isn't the key that unlocks the door.
Faith **is** *the door.*
And the moment you realize that **you are not separate from God,** *faith is no longer an act.*
It's your being.

Jesus Never Asked for "Effort-Faith" — He Revealed "Awakened-Faith"

Jesus never told people to force themselves to believe.
He revealed truth—and when they saw it, **faith rose up on its own.**
Why? Because it was already in them, waiting to be awakened.

> *"My sheep hear my voice, and I know them, and they follow me."* — **John 10:27**

Notice: He didn't say they try to hear. They just do.
Because they were always His.
The hearing was in them before they ever knew it.

You Don't "Get" Faith — You Realize You Are It

The moment you think you "got saved" because you believed, you're still identifying with the separate self.
But the truth is, **there is no separate you** *that made a righteous decision.*
There is only God recognizing Himself through the vessel you thought was you.

That's the death of the ego. That's the death of religion.
That's the birth of **oneness.**

Faith Is God Recognizing God

This is why Scripture says:

> *"The life which I now live in the flesh I live by the faith of the Son of God..."*
> **— Galatians 2:20**

Not faith in the Son of God.
But the **faith of** *the Son of God.*

You don't generate it. You don't initiate it.
You awaken to it.

And when you do, you realize:

I'm not saved because I believed in God.
I'm saved because God believed Himself into me.
And now… I see what I am.

This is the power of GIATI.

It ends the illusion of doing.
And reveals the truth of being.
The Blood Only Saves When It Becomes You

(Understanding the True Power of the Blood from the GIATI Revelation)

In traditional religion, "the blood of Jesus" is often treated like a magical phrase—quoted as if His physical death alone secured salvation for anyone who simply says "I believe." But truth goes far deeper than that.

To understand the true meaning of the blood, we must begin with the **nature of God.**

God Is Spirit — And Spirit Has No Blood

Scripture is clear:

"God is a Spirit: and they that worship him must worship him in spirit and in truth."
— John 4:24

Yahweh—the Father—has no blood.
Elohim—the Word—has no blood.
The Holy Spirit—the breath and essence of God—has no blood.

Blood belongs to flesh.
So the blood of Jesus did not exist until **God came down out of Spirit** *and put on a body.*

"And the Word was made flesh, and dwelt among us…" **— John 1:14**

The eternal, formless, invisible Spirit took on form, visibility, and vulnerability.
He entered the same condition we're in—not to show us something different from ourselves, but to show us **what we are and what must happen.**

The Blood Was the Pouring Out of the False Self

When Jesus said:

"Except ye eat the flesh of the Son of man, and drink his blood, ye have no life in you." **— John 6:53**

He was not talking about literal flesh and blood.
He was speaking spiritually.

He was saying: You must take My nature—My Spirit—into yourself. You must identify fully with what I am and what I've done: not just in My life, but in My death.

Why the Blood Matters Spiritually

The **blood** *represents the* **complete emptying out of self***—the false self, the ego, the illusion of separation. That's what His death was: God Himself coming into the illusion of human identity, and then* **dying to it** *to show us the way back to truth.*

"For in that he died, he died unto sin once: but in that he liveth, he liveth unto God." — **Romans 6:10**

The blood matters **only** *if what it points to becomes your own inner death.*
If you believe Jesus died so you don't have to, you've missed the truth.
Jesus died to show you that you must die—not physically, but inwardly.
You must die to the ego-self that thinks it is separate from God.

This is why Paul says:

"I am crucified with Christ: nevertheless I live; yet not I, but Christ liveth in me..." — **Galatians 2:20**

The blood that saves is not something outside you.
Not grape juice.
Not a memory.
Not a ritual.

The blood that saves is the truth that **you were in Him when He died,** *and when that realization becomes alive in you, you die too—to the illusion of being "just a man" or "just a woman" or "just a sinner."*

You awaken to the truth that **you are of God,** *and* **He is all there is***—and what was once called "you" now gives way to what has always been* **Him.**

Communion: Not a Ritual, But a Realization

Jesus said:

"Take, eat; this is my body... Drink... this is my blood of the new testament, which is shed for many for the remission of sins." — **Matthew 26:26-28**

This is not about literal bread and wine.
This is about **inner communion**—*a spiritual union with His essence.*

Unless you **eat** *of His flesh (His life) and* **drink** *of His blood (His death), you remain in the illusion.*
But when you truly partake, when you inwardly join Him in death and resurrection, **then the blood has power in you.**

GIATI: You Were Always in Him

From the GIATI revelation—God Is All There Is—this entire process is not God saving something separate from Himself.

It's **God awakening Himself within form.**

The man you thought you were dies.
*The truth of who you really are—***Spirit, Life, God in expression**—*comes alive.*

Only when the blood becomes **your own blood**—*your own death to illusion—can you say you've been saved.*

"Know ye not, that so many of us as were baptized into Jesus Christ were baptized into his death?" — **Romans 6:3**

You weren't saved by a man dying for you.
You were saved when you **realized you died with Him**—*because He was you all along.*

Conclusion: The Blood That Saves Is the Blood That Becomes You

If the blood stays outside of you, it has no effect.
If it remains grape juice or theology, it changes nothing.

But when it becomes **your death and your resurrection,** *it becomes your life.*

GIATI doesn't just say "Jesus died for me."
It says, "God expressed Himself as me, died the illusion I was trapped in, and rose as my true self."

This is salvation.

This is the blood.
This is the Spirit.
This is the truth that sets you free.

Metaphor: The Pressing of the Grape

Imagine a grape on the vine—round, full, untouched.

It looks alive.
But its real purpose is hidden inside.
Only when it's **pressed** *does the juice flow.*
Only when it's **crushed** *can it become wine.*

So it was with Jesus.

God in visible form.
The fullness of the vine.
But it was in the **pressing**—*in the breaking, the crushing, the pouring out—that the life was revealed.*

"I am the true vine..." **—John 15:1**

But now imagine this:
That same pressing must happen in **you.**

Not your physical body...
But your identity.
The outer self, the shell, the false mask of separation.

Until you are pressed, your life remains in the skin.
But when the false you is broken, the wine flows.
And that wine is Spirit. That wine is truth. That wine is God.

Closing Visual: The Shattering of the Mirror

Picture yourself staring into a mirror.

You see a face.
A history.
A name.
A personality.

You think, "This is me."

But one day, in a moment of inner clarity, the mirror cracks.
And instead of seeing a person,
you see Light.

You realize the mirror never reflected you—
It reflected the **idea** *of you.*
Now it's broken, and all that remains is what's real:

The Light of God.
The Wine of the Spirit.
The Blood that was always yours.

Final Declaration

The blood only saves when the self dies.
The wine only flows when the grape is crushed.
The light only shines when the mask breaks.

And now you know:
God didn't just die for you—
He died as you…
So that you could rise as Him.

That's not religion.
That's not tradition.
That's **GIATI.**

God Is All There Is—
Even you.

PART III
GOD'S PURPOSE AS SAVIOR

Chapter 8

The Mission of Jesus Christ

The mission of Jesus Christ is one of the most profound revelations in human history. Through His life, death, and resurrection, Jesus revealed the ultimate truth: that humanity is not separate from God, but that the very spirit within each of us is God Himself, manifested in flesh. This chapter will explore how Jesus Christ, as God incarnate, revealed the mystery of existence, how His message focused on the spirit within, and how His life, death, and resurrection are integral to uniting humanity with God.

Jesus as God Incarnate: Revealing the Mystery of Existence

The incarnation of Jesus Christ is the cornerstone of the Christian faith, where God, in His fullness, chose to manifest as a human being. In doing so, Jesus revealed the ultimate mystery of existence: that God is not separate from us but has always been within us. Jesus came to show us that God is not merely a distant, abstract force but is intimately involved in our lives and in the very substance of our being.

The Apostle John opens his gospel with a powerful statement about the identity of Jesus:

"In the beginning was the Word, and the Word was with God, and the Word was God. The same was in the beginning with God. All things were made by him; and without him was not any thing made that was made." (John 1:1-3)

Here, John is making it clear that Jesus, as the Word (Logos), existed from the beginning. He is not a created being but the very essence of God. Everything in creation was made through Him. The purpose of Jesus' incarnation was not only to walk among humanity but also to reveal that He is the source of all creation. Jesus was and is the physical manifestation of God—one with the Father, revealing the divine in human form.

Later in the same chapter, John writes:

"And the Word was made flesh, and dwelt among us, (and we beheld his glory, the glory as of the only begotten of the Father,) full of grace and truth." (John 1:14)

Jesus' birth as a human being marked the moment when the invisible God became visible. He came to show us that we are not separate from God, and that God's very presence can be experienced in the world. Jesus' incarnation is a revelation of the truth that humanity is an expression of God's divine nature.

The main purpose of Jesus Christ was not to draw people to worship him as a separate being but to serve as an example of what it means to live as a physical person fully embodying the Spirit of God within. Jesus demonstrated the truth of how all mankind exists—not as separate from God, but as vessels of His Spirit. His purpose was not about exalting himself but about helping humanity recognize that the Spirit within him was the Creator and that this same Spirit resides within every person. His mission was to show us how to manifest that Spirit in our lives, becoming one with it, and thereby attaining the perfection that comes from God's perfect Spirit.

If you fail to recognize that the Spirit within Jesus is the same Spirit within you, you miss the entire purpose of his coming in the flesh. Without this recognition, you remain lost, trapped in the illusion of separation, which is the true definition of sin. The essence of his teaching is this: if you can see the Spirit of God in someone else—if you can recognize God within Jesus—then you have the ability to see that same Spirit in yourself. But if you cannot see God's Spirit in others, you cannot truly grasp its presence in you.

Feel-good messages and motivational teachings have their place, but they are powerless without the fundamental transformation that comes when you realize that God's Spirit is not outside of you but is who you are. As Jesus taught in Matthew 6:33, "But seek ye first the kingdom of God, and his righteousness; and all these things shall be added unto you." The Spirit of God is the Kingdom, and once you realize that this Kingdom is within you, everything else—peace, fulfillment, and purpose—can be added to your life.

The only reason you are in the flesh is to awaken to the truth that the Spirit in you is God. You did not fully grasp this truth in your heavenly existence before manifesting in the body, so now, in the flesh, you are given another opportunity to surrender the false notion that you coexist with God and embrace the reality that you are one with Him. Jesus declared this truth clearly in John 10:30, saying, "I and my Father are one."

If you fail to see this one essential truth—that you and God are one—then your life in the flesh has served no ultimate purpose. You entered the world in a state of lostness because your previous heavenly existence was part of the "lost portion" of God's Spirit body. If you do not awaken to your true identity as one with God during your time in the flesh, when you leave the body, your spirit or soul will simply return to that lost portion of His Spirit body. Recognizing and manifesting the Spirit of God as your very being is the sole purpose of your life, and without this understanding, everything else is in vain.

Being Metaphysical

Everything the Messiah taught spoke to a reality beyond the physical—a metaphysical truth that transcends the flesh. When Jesus said, "Eat of my flesh and drink of my blood," he was not referring to a physical act but to a spiritual one: to partake of his essence, his Spirit, and his life. When he spoke of tearing down the temple and rebuilding it in three days, he wasn't referring to a physical structure but to his body, symbolizing the eternal nature of Spirit that cannot be destroyed.

In the same way, when it is said that the Messiah will return on a cloud, this is not about observing him descending from the sky. The "cloud" spoken of is your mind. Consider the shape of the brain—like a cloud. When you awaken to the truth of his Spirit within you, and you begin to manifest that Spirit as yourself, that is the Messiah returning. He comes *as you,* not through physical observation. His return is an internal awakening, not an external spectacle.

This is powerfully illustrated in the story of Paul, who persecuted Peter, James, John, and others who no longer adhered to the law once they received the Holy Spirit. Paul, then called Saul, believed he was enforcing righteousness by targeting those who had come into the realization of the Spirit within them. On the road to Damascus, Saul was knocked off his horse and heard the voice, "Saul, Saul, why persecutest thou me?" Confused, he asked, "Who are you, Lord?" The response was, "I am Jesus whom thou persecutest" (Acts 9:4-5).

Paul thought he was merely persecuting people, but in reality, he was persecuting vessels filled with the Spirit of God—those who had recognized the Kingdom of God within themselves. They had transcended the external rituals of the law because they had come into alignment with the grace of God, which is the Holy Spirit.

This is the state of existence required to be saved in his Spirit body—not by works, not by the law, but by grace. Salvation comes when you recognize that the Spirit of God dwells in you and that the Kingdom of God is not an external place but an internal reality.

As Jesus explained in **Luke 17:20-21:**

"And when he was demanded of the Pharisees, when the kingdom of God should come, he answered them and said, The kingdom of God cometh not with observation: Neither shall they say, Lo here! or, lo there! for, behold, the kingdom of God is within you."

The Kingdom of God is not something to be observed outwardly—it is already within you. The Messiah's return is not about looking to the sky but about awakening to his Spirit in your mind and heart. When you see him as you, that is his coming again. This is salvation: the realization that you and the Spirit of God are one.

The Spirit of God dwelling within you is the cornerstone of true transformation. When something is etched into your mind and written on your heart, it becomes a part of who you are. It shapes your beliefs, directs your actions, and becomes unforgettable. This is what makes receiving His Spirit the real repentance—the kind that happens once and lasts forever. When the Holy Spirit comes to dwell within you, it is permanent. You no longer live in cycles of asking for forgiveness over and over, because His presence becomes your constant guide. This is the essence of grace: not something you work for, but something you receive by simply accepting His Spirit into your being.

The old covenant with Israel required strict adherence to physical laws, but those laws were designed to be impossible to keep perfectly. Why? Because God's ultimate purpose was to show humanity that righteousness and grace cannot be earned through works. His intention was always to lead His people to stop striving and instead receive His Spirit—a gift that transforms not what you do, but who you are.

As stated in Hebrews 8:8-10, God found fault with the old covenant and declared:

"Behold, the days come, saith the Lord, when I will make a new covenant with the house of Israel and with the house of Judah: Not according to the covenant that I made with their fathers in the day when I took them by the hand to lead them out of the land of Egypt; because they continued not in my covenant, and I regarded them not, saith the Lord. For this is the covenant that I will make with the house of Israel after those days, saith the Lord; I will put my laws into their mind, and write them in their hearts: and I will be to them a God, and they shall be to me a people."

This new covenant is not about rules written on stone tablets, but about God's Spirit being imprinted directly into your mind and heart. When His Spirit is within you, it is a treasure that no one can steal. His Spirit becomes your guide, your comforter, and your very identity. Those who have received His Spirit are no longer just followers—they are His family, His people, and one with Him.

This is the profound truth: salvation is not found in what you do, but in who you are when His Spirit dwells within you. When you allow Him to place His law in your mind and write it on your heart, you become a living expression of His grace and righteousness. This is the treasure He offers—one that will never fade, never be taken away, and will forever make you one with Him.

His Message: Emphasize The Spirit Within As God, Not On The Flesh

A central message of Jesus was that the true essence of a person is not the physical body or flesh, but the spirit within. In His teachings, Jesus often pointed beyond the external self to the inner, spiritual reality of who we are. He emphasized the need to recognize the divine spirit that resides within, rather than focusing on the physical body or worldly identity.

In John 6:63, Jesus says:

"It is the spirit that quickeneth; the flesh profiteth nothing: the words that I speak unto you, they are spirit, and they are life." (John 6:63)

Here, Jesus is explaining that the flesh is temporary and of no eternal value, while the spirit is the true source of life. His words, full of spirit, bring life to those who hear and receive them. Jesus came to teach that life is not found in the external—whether in possessions, status, or even the physical body—but in the divine spirit that exists within every human being.

In Luke 17:21, Jesus offers another profound statement about the nature of God and His kingdom:

"Neither shall they say, Lo here! or, lo there! for, behold, the kingdom of God is within you." (Luke 17:21)

Jesus declares that the kingdom of God—the reign of divine presence—is not a distant place or future event. It is within each person. The divine presence is not found outside of us, in religious rituals or external acts, but within us. Jesus came to reveal that the kingdom of God is a spiritual reality that exists within each person, waiting to be awakened through the recognition of the divine spirit.

The Role of Jesus' Life, Death, and Resurrection in Uniting Humanity with God

The life, death, and resurrection of Jesus were not mere historical events, but pivotal moments in God's plan to reconcile humanity with Himself. Through His earthly ministry, Jesus revealed the truth about the divine within. But it was through His death and resurrection that He sealed the truth and demonstrated the power of God to overcome the separation caused by ignorance and sin.

In John 14:6, Jesus boldly states:

"I am the way, the truth, and the life: no man cometh unto the Father, but by me." (John 14:6)

Jesus' role as the "way" to God is central to His mission. Through His perfect life and His sacrificial death on the cross, Jesus bridged the gap between humanity and God. He became the pathway for humanity to return to its original state of oneness with God. His life was a model of divine expression, His death was the atonement for humanity's ignorance, and His resurrection was the victory over death and separation from God.

In 2 Corinthians 5:18-19, Paul explains the purpose of Jesus' sacrifice:

"And all things are of God, who hath reconciled us to himself by Jesus Christ, and hath given to us the ministry of reconciliation; to wit, that God was in Christ, reconciling the world unto himself, not imputing their trespasses unto them; and hath committed unto us the word of reconciliation." (2 Corinthians 5:18-19)

Through His death, Jesus reconciled humanity to God. His sacrifice was not just for forgiveness of sins but for the ultimate restoration of humanity's connection with the divine. God, who is within us, was fully revealed in Christ, and through His resurrection, we are assured that death and separation from God are defeated.

In Romans 6:4, Paul continues this theme, speaking of the resurrection:

"Therefore we are buried with him by baptism into death: that like as Christ was raised up from the dead by the glory of the Father, even so we also should walk in newness of life." (Romans 6:4)

Jesus' resurrection represents the newness of life that comes from recognizing our divine nature. Through His victory over death, Jesus offers humanity the opportunity to live in the fullness of God's presence. The resurrection is the demonstration that death is not the end, and that those who recognize their oneness with God can live eternally in His presence.

Conclusion: The Mission of Jesus Christ

Jesus Christ, as God incarnate, came to reveal the ultimate truth: that the spirit within each of us is God Himself. Through His life, He modeled divine expression; through His death, He reconciled humanity with God; and through His resurrection, He showed us the power of eternal life. Jesus' mission was to awaken humanity to its true identity as divine beings, created and sustained by God. His teachings, His sacrifice, and His resurrection all point to one profound truth: God is within us, and through Christ, we are brought into the fullness of life and oneness with the Creator.

In John 17:21, Jesus prays for the unity of humanity with God:

"That they all may be one; as thou, Father, art in me, and I in thee, that they also may be one in us: that the world may believe that thou hast sent me." (John 17:21)

This prayer encapsulates the purpose of Jesus' mission—to bring humanity into oneness with God, just as He is one with the Father. Through Jesus, we are given the opportunity to recognize our divine nature, live in the fullness of God's presence, and walk in the eternal life that He offers.

The Resurrection is Spiritual

For centuries, people have tried to understand the resurrection through a physical, carnal lens—focusing on the external, the bodily, and the historical. But the resurrection was never meant to be grasped through the limitations of human reasoning. It is a spiritual reality, a transformation that takes place **within.**

Jesus declared, "It is the spirit that quickeneth; the flesh profiteth nothing: the words that I speak unto you, they are spirit, and they are life" (John 6:63). The resurrection is not about reviving the physical body but about **awakening the Spirit within.** *Before this awakening, the soul is in a state of spiritual death, unaware of its divine nature, lost in the illusion of separation from God. But when the Spirit is revealed, resurrection occurs—the soul is quickened, brought to life in the realization that* **it was never separate from God to begin with.**

This is why Jesus said, "The kingdom of God is within you" (Luke 17:21). The resurrection is not an event to wait for in the future, nor is it limited to what happened to Jesus' physical body 2,000 years ago. It is a present reality, available now to all who awaken to it. When Christ rises **in** *you, that is the true resurrection—His Spirit and your spirit becoming one, as He and the Father are one.*

Paul affirmed this when he wrote, "If Christ be in you, the body is dead because of sin; but the Spirit is life because of righteousness" (Romans 8:10). The body remains bound to the physical world, but the Spirit is **where true life is found.** *Those who identify only with the body remain in the realm of death, but those who awaken to the Spirit* **realize their eternal nature.**

When people think of resurrection only in terms of Jesus' physical body, they miss the deeper truth. Jesus' resurrection was not just about Him overcoming the grave—it was about Him **opening the way for all to experience the same spiritual awakening.** *His rising was the* **demonstration** *of what happens when one fully surrenders to God's Spirit. He embodied the resurrection so that others might follow—not by waiting for a future event, but by experiencing the same Spirit of life that raised Him from the dead.*

Paul further explains this mystery in Romans 8:11: "If the Spirit of him that raised up Jesus from the dead dwell in you, he that raised up Christ from the dead shall also quicken your mortal bodies by his Spirit that dwelleth in you." This is not about the flesh being made immortal—it is about the Spirit within bringing **true life** *to those who were spiritually dead. The same Spirit that resurrected Jesus is* **the same Spirit that resurrects every soul that comes into divine awareness.**

This is the great mystery revealed: The resurrection was never just about Jesus—it was about **you.** *It was about* **humanity being restored to its divine nature.** *The Messiah* *resurrects* **in** *you, and when this happens, you move from death to life, from ignorance to understanding, from separation to oneness.*

Many have tried to rationalize the resurrection carnally, looking for physical evidence or waiting for a future event to take place. But the resurrection has never been about what can be seen with the natural eye—it has always been about what is revealed in the Spirit. Those who receive this truth know that **they are already risen with Christ, because Christ is risen in them.**

This is the work of the Holy Spirit—the outpouring of truth, the awakening of souls, the fulfillment of Jesus' prayer that "they all may be one, as thou, Father, art in me, and I in thee" (John 17:21). This is the true resurrection.

The Resurrection: Christ Awakened Within

Jesus declared, "I am the resurrection, and the life: he that believeth in me, though he were dead, yet shall he live. And whosoever liveth and believeth in me shall never die. Believest thou this?" (John 11:25-26). These words have often been interpreted from a physical perspective, but their true meaning is far deeper. The resurrection is not merely an event that happened in history—it is a living reality that unfolds within. It is the awakening of Christ within the individual, the realization of divine life that has always been present but hidden beneath the veil of ignorance.

When Jesus says, "I am the resurrection, and the life," He is not speaking of something external to be sought after. He is declaring **who He is**—*the very essence of resurrection itself. To experience resurrection is to experience Him, not as a distant figure but as the life within. He does not give resurrection as a gift separate from Himself; He* **is** *the resurrection. To receive Him is to receive resurrection, and to be awakened to Him is to be made alive.*

"He that believeth in me, though he were dead, yet shall he live." This is not about physical death, but spiritual death—the state of being unaware of God's presence within. Many walk in the world as if alive but remain dead in spirit, disconnected from their true nature. Believing in Christ is not merely a confession of words but an awakening to the reality that **His Spirit is our very life.** *The one who comes into this awareness transitions from death to life, from ignorance to divine understanding.*

"And whosoever liveth and believeth in me shall never die." Those who have been resurrected into this truth, who have awakened to Christ within, can never truly die. The Spirit is eternal, and those who know their oneness with Him understand that their life is not bound by the flesh. The illusion of death is shattered because the Spirit cannot perish. To believe in Christ in this way is to transcend the fear of death, for death only exists where separation is believed. But where there is oneness with Him, there is only life—life unending, life in perfect unity with the Father.

The purpose of the resurrection is not simply to affirm that Jesus rose from the dead, but for **His resurrection to take place within.** *Before this awakening, the soul is in a state of death—lost in the illusion of separation, living as if cut off from the divine source. But when Christ is revealed within, He is resurrected in the believer, and the two become one. This is why those who have experienced this awakening do not need external proof of the resurrection;* **they are the proof.** *Christ is alive, not because history says so, but because He is* **manifested as the life within those who know Him.**

Many attempt to rationalize the resurrection from a carnal perspective, seeking to explain it in physical terms while missing its true meaning. But resurrection has never been about the body—it has always been about the Spirit. It is the return to divine awareness, the unveiling of truth, the lifting of the veil that once blinded the soul. This is the work of GIATI, the Holy Spirit—the revealing of what has always been, the bringing of light to those who sit in darkness.

Resurrection is not something to wait for; it is something to enter into. It is here, now, for all who have ears to hear and eyes to see. The Messiah lives, not merely in a distant heaven, but **in those who have received Him, who walk in Him, who know that He and the Father are one—and they in Him.** *This is the resurrection. This is life eternal.*

The Divine Mystery of Jesus: The Revelation of Man as God

Unveiling the Truth Through GIATI

For centuries, debates have arisen concerning the nature of Jesus—was He merely a prophet, or was He God in the flesh? Many point to scriptures where Jesus refers to the Father as separate from Himself, leading them to believe He is not God. Others, recognizing His miraculous works and divine authority, affirm His divinity. However, the ultimate revelation of Jesus is far greater than either of these limited views.

Through the spiritual understanding of GIATI (God Is All There Is), we uncover the truth: Jesus was not just God alone, nor man alone—He was both. He was the living demonstration of what all humanity is, the perfect expression of divinity in human form. In Him, the veil was lifted, revealing that man and God are not separate. The importance of this truth is not only in recognizing Jesus as God but in recognizing that we, too, are gods, one with the Father.

Jesus as the Manifestation of God

"He who has seen Me has seen the Father." (John 14:9)

The foundation of understanding Jesus as God begins with recognizing that God is the only true existence. If there is nothing outside of God, then everything that exists must be an expression of Him. Jesus was not an exception—He was the revelation of this truth.

In John 1:1, it is written:

"In the beginning was the Word, and the Word was with God, and the Word was God."

This Word (Logos) was the divine intelligence, the very essence of God's being. And in John 1:14, we see its manifestation:

"And the Word became flesh and dwelt among us."

Jesus was the Word made flesh—God appearing as man. He did not come to demonstrate something unique to Himself but to reveal what had been true all along: God is all there is, and man is His expression.

Paul affirms this in Colossians 1:15-17:

"He is the image of the invisible God… For by Him all things were created, in heaven and on earth… and in Him all things hold together."

If Jesus is the image of the invisible God, then He is the visibility of the unseen. He is not separate from God, but God revealed.

Why Did Jesus Speak of the Father as Separate?

Many struggle with scriptures where Jesus prays to the Father or makes statements like:

"The Father is greater than I." (John 14:28)

These statements were not a denial of His divinity but an acknowledgment of His human experience. Jesus came in the form of man to demonstrate the process of awakening to divine identity. When He spoke from limitation, He spoke as man. When He performed miracles, He spoke as God.

Consider Philippians 2:6-7:

"Though He was in the form of God, He did not consider equality with God something to be grasped, but emptied Himself, taking the form of a servant, being born in the likeness of men."

Jesus "emptied" Himself of divine privileges, taking on the appearance of man's limitation. But in doing so, He demonstrated how man overcomes that illusion to realize oneness with God. His life was the pattern—He first showed Himself in human weakness, then revealed divine power.

This is why, in John 17:5, He says:

"And now, Father, glorify Me in Your own presence with the glory that I had with You before the world existed."

This was not a shift in identity—it was a return to the full awareness of oneness with the Father.

Jesus as the Example: The Revelation of Man as God

Jesus did not come to be worshiped as an unattainable figure—He came to reveal what all humanity is. This is why He said:

"The works I do, you shall do also; and greater works than these shall you do." (John 14:12)

How could we do what He did unless we share in the same divine nature? In John 10:30, Jesus declares:

"I and My Father are one."

The Jews, misunderstanding Him, accused Him of blasphemy, saying He made Himself God. His response was profound:

"Is it not written in your Law, 'I said, you are gods'? If He called them gods to whom the word of God came—and Scripture cannot be broken—do you say of Him whom the Father consecrated and sent into the world, 'You are blaspheming,' because I said, 'I am the Son of God'?" (John 10:34-36)

Here, Jesus confirms that not only is He divine, but all humanity is divine. He quotes Psalm 82:6:

"I said, you are gods, sons of the Most High, all of you."

This was the truth hidden since the foundation of the world—that man is not separate from God, but a manifestation of Him. Jesus came to awaken this reality.

The Importance of Recognizing We Are Gods

The great tragedy of human existence is the illusion of separation. Because man believes himself to be apart from God, he lives in limitation, fear, and death. But Jesus came to remove this veil.

Paul speaks of this transformation in 2 Corinthians 3:16-18:

"When one turns to the Lord, the veil is removed… And we all, with unveiled faces, beholding the glory of the Lord, are being transformed into the same image from glory to glory."

We are not meant to merely admire Christ—we are meant to become as He is. 1 John 4:17 declares:

"As He is, so are we in this world."

The moment one recognizes their divine identity, they step into the fullness of what Jesus demonstrated. This is the awakening of GIATI—the understanding that if God is all there is, then we must be His expression.

One Without Them: The Completion of the Divine Plan

The greatest error of religion has been to exalt Jesus while denying what He came to reveal. His prayer in John 17 makes this clear:

"That they all may be one, just as You, Father, are in Me, and I in You, that they also may be in Us, so that the world may believe that You have sent Me." (John 17:21)

The purpose of Christ was not to remain alone as the Son of God, but to bring all into the realization that they, too, are sons. The divine plan is not complete until all awaken to this truth.

Paul confirms this in Romans 8:19:

"The creation waits with eager longing for the revealing of the sons of God."

The world suffers because it does not know what it is. But when humanity awakens, the illusion of separation dissolves, and all creation is restored.

The Final Revelation: "I AM" in Us

Jesus came not to establish a religion, but to reveal the name of God within us:

"I have made Your name known to them, and I will continue to make it known, that the love with which You have loved Me may be in them, and I in them." (John 17:26)

That name was "I AM."

Jesus spoke, **"Before Abraham was, I AM." (John 8:58)**

He did not say, "I was," but "I AM"—the eternal presence of God in all. And now, that same "I AM" is in us.

To awaken to this truth is salvation itself.

It is to say, "I AM one with God. I AM divine. I AM the living expression of the Eternal."

The Unveiling of God in Man: The Divine Identity of Jesus and Humanity

*The mystery of Jesus Christ has perplexed theologians, scholars, and believers for centuries. Many view Him merely as a messenger of God, a prophet, or even a unique divine figure set apart from humanity. Yet, through the lens of GIATI—***God Is All There Is***—we come to recognize a deeper revelation: Jesus did not come to establish Himself as the sole expression of divinity, but to awaken all of humanity to the truth of their own divine identity.*

This is the central theme of Christ's mission. He came not just to be worshiped but to serve as the prototype for what every human being truly is—a son of God, the living manifestation of the Eternal. The life of Jesus is a mirror reflecting the divine potential within all, showing that the illusion of separation between man and God is the greatest deception ever imposed upon humanity.

The Illusion of Separation: Why Man Believes He is Not God

From the beginning, mankind's fall was not from a place, but from awareness. The greatest tragedy of human existence is the loss of the knowledge of self. When Adam and Eve ate from the Tree of the Knowledge of Good and Evil, it was not a literal act of disobedience alone, but a shift in consciousness—a descent from divine unity into duality, from the truth of oneness with God into the lie of separation.

"Then the eyes of both were opened, and they knew that they were naked..." (Genesis 3:7)

This nakedness was not just physical; it was spiritual. They became aware of themselves as **separate beings,** *independent of God. This false perception birthed fear, shame, and death—not because God had left them, but because they no longer recognized their oneness with Him.*

From that moment on, humanity has struggled under the weight of false identity, believing itself to be mere flesh—limited, sinful, and powerless. Religion, rather than restoring this lost awareness, often reinforces the idea of separation by placing God as a distant being, outside of us, instead of recognizing Him as the very life within us.

It is in this fallen consciousness that many misinterpret the statements of Jesus. When He speaks of the Father as separate, He is addressing humanity's limited perception, guiding them step by step to the truth. But His ultimate revelation was not separation—it was **oneness.**

Jesus: The Blueprint of Our True Nature

If Jesus had only come to show humanity how far it was from God, He would have left us in despair. But He did not. He came to **reveal what had always been true***—that man and God were never separate to begin with.*

This is why He said:

"I am the way, the truth, and the life. No one comes to the Father except through Me." (John 14:6)

For centuries, this statement has been used to claim exclusivity—that Jesus is the only way to God in a manner that excludes others. But from the perspective of GIATI, this scripture does not mean that Jesus alone is divine while others are not. Instead, it reveals that Jesus is the way because He is the pattern, the example of what man truly is.

He is the **truth** *because He is the* **revelation of human divinity***—the restoration of the lost awareness of oneness with God.*

He is the **life** *because He is the visible expression of the eternal Spirit, showing that death is an illusion for those who know their divine nature.*

Paul echoes this in Colossians 3:4:

"When Christ, who is your life, appears, then you also will appear with Him in glory."

This is not speaking of a future event in the sky, but of the unveiling of divine identity. When Christ is revealed **in you,** *you appear in glory—because you are what He is.*

The Journey from Man to God-Consciousness

Jesus' own journey reflects the path of every soul awakening to its divine identity.

1. **Born into human limitation** – *Jesus was born in the likeness of men, showing that divinity can take on human form.*
2. **Baptism and divine acknowledgment** – *At His baptism, the heavens opened, and the Spirit descended upon Him like a dove, revealing His divine nature.*
3. **Testing in the wilderness** – *Before stepping into full power, He was tempted,* symbolizing the process of overcoming the illusions of the flesh.
4. **Miracles and divine works** – *As He awakened to His full nature, He demonstrated divine power, revealing what is possible when man and God are one.*
5. **Crucifixion and resurrection** – *His death symbolizes the death of false identity, and His resurrection signifies the victory of Spirit over flesh, showing that divine life cannot be extinguished.*

Every individual undergoes this same process. Jesus' life was not meant to be worshiped as an unattainable standard but followed as a blueprint for transformation.

The Name Above Every Name: I AM

The most significant revelation Jesus gave was the power of the name **I AM.**

When Moses asked God for His name, He replied:

"I AM WHO I AM." (Exodus 3:14)

This was not just a name—it was the essence of divine being. It was the declaration that **God is existence itself.**

Jesus later applied this name to Himself, saying:

"Before Abraham was, I AM." (John 8:58)

This statement was so powerful that the religious leaders sought to kill Him. Why? Because He was not speaking of a separate God—He was claiming the divine identity **as Himself.**

But this revelation was not for Him alone. Every time a person declares "I AM" with awareness, they affirm their divine nature. When Jesus said, "I AM the bread of life" or "I AM the light of the world," He was not just describing Himself—He was revealing what all humanity is in truth.

This is why understanding the **true power of "I AM"** *is critical. Every time one says:*

- *"I am weak," they affirm weakness.*
- *"I am poor," they affirm lack.*
- *"I am divine," they awaken to truth.*

This is the key to the Kingdom—the realization that what we declare as "I AM" shapes our reality.

The Fullness of the Godhead Dwelling in Us

One of the most profound declarations in scripture is found in Colossians 2:9-10:

"For in Him the whole fullness of deity dwells bodily, and you have been given fullness in Christ."

Jesus was not a portion of God—He was the fullness of God in human form. But here's the greater revelation: **we have been given that same fullness.**

Paul further emphasizes this in Ephesians 4:13, saying that we are to grow into **"the measure of the stature of the fullness of Christ."**

This means that we are not called to remain in limited, human perception. We are to **rise into the full awareness of our divine nature,** *just as Jesus did.*

The Completion of the Divine Plan

The mission of Jesus was never to create an exclusive religion but to **restore humanity to its original state—oneness with God.**

John 17:23 expresses this beautifully:

"I in them and You in Me, that they may be perfectly one."

*This is the fulfillment of GIATI—***that God is all there is, and we are one with Him.**

The world is waiting for the unveiling of the sons of God. As we awaken, we do not just return to God; we **realize we were never separate.**

This is the great mystery: **Christ in you, the hope of glory.** *(Colossians 1:27)*

And when this truth is fully embraced, there is no more separation, no more illusion—only **God in all, as all, through all.**

This is the fulfillment of GIATI:
God Is All There Is.
I AM That.

Missing the Point: The Tragedy of Separation from God

The greatest deception ever accepted by humanity is the belief that we are separate from God. This single illusion has caused the suffering of mankind, birthed false religions, and led to a distorted understanding of Jesus Christ. It has reduced His mission to a mere transaction—one where a man named Jesus supposedly died **for sins** *so that people could be "saved" simply by uttering a verbal confession of faith. This limited, surface-level interpretation is not only incomplete—it is* **entirely missing the point.**

*Jesus did not come just to "die for sins." He came to re***store humanity to the truth of its divine nature,** *to* **reveal the oneness between God and man,** *and to demolish the illusion of separation once and for all. Yet, many have chosen to hold onto their blindness, thinking that by merely acknowledging Christ with their lips, they have received salvation. They remain lost—not because God is absent, but because* **they still see themselves as apart from Him.**

The Error of Separation: Why You Are Lost When You See Yourself Apart from God

1. Separation is the Root of All Sin

Many believe sin is merely an act—something external like lying, stealing, or committing immoral deeds. But **sin is fundamentally a state of consciousness***—a condition of being cut off from the awareness of your divine identity.*

Jesus did not define sin as breaking religious laws; He revealed its deeper essence:

"If you do not believe that I AM, you will die in your sins." (John 8:24)

He was not merely speaking about believing in His personal identity—He was revealing a **universal truth:** *If you do not recognize your oneness with God, you remain in the consciousness of sin, trapped in the illusion of separation, and suffer the consequences of that ignorance.*

2. Your Spirit Manifests What You Believe

Your consciousness determines your reality—both in this life and beyond.

If you believe you are separate from God, you manifest that separation. If you see yourself as distant from Him, you live as though you are powerless, abandoned, and enslaved to fleshly desires. And when you pass from this body, you do not suddenly awaken to divine truth. **You carry the same consciousness of separation into the next realm.**

This is why **separation is death.** *Not because God has rejected anyone, but because those who refuse to wake up to their oneness* **continue to dwell in the darkness they have chosen.**

Jesus expressed this when speaking of those who reject the truth:

"They will be cast into outer darkness, where there will be weeping and gnashing of teeth." (Matthew 8:12)

What is this "outer darkness"? **It is not a physical place—it is a state of being.** *It is the condition of a soul that has refused to recognize its divine identity, remaining in spiritual blindness and suffering under the illusion of separation.*

3. Why Saying "I Believe" Isn't Enough

The modern church has reduced salvation to a mere confession:

- *"Just believe in Jesus, and you'll be saved."*
- *"Accept Him into your heart, and you're good."*
- *"Faith alone saves."*

This is **a lie.**

Faith is not a **mental agreement***—it is an* **inner realization.** *To say "I believe" without transformation is meaningless. Even the demons "believe" in Christ, and they remain in darkness (James 2:19).* **True salvation is awakening to who you truly are***—not merely agreeing that Jesus existed or died for sins, but actually stepping into His consciousness, living as He lived, and realizing the same oneness with God that He demonstrated.*

Jesus never taught people to simply recite words for salvation. He taught them to **be transformed.**

"Unless a man is born again, he cannot see the Kingdom of God." (John 3:3)

This is not about **repeating a prayer***—it is about* **being reborn into the awareness of your divine identity.**

Paul echoes this when he says:

"Let this mind be in you, which was also in Christ Jesus: who, being in the form of God, did not consider equality with God something to be grasped." (Philippians 2:5-6)

This is salvation: to **think as Christ thought,** *to* **live as He lived,** *and to rec***ognize that you and the Father are one***—just as He did.*

The True Mission of Jesus: Awakening the World to GIATI

Jesus did not come to make people religious. He came to restore divine awareness.

When He said, **"I and the Father are one" (John 10:30),** *He was not stating a truth about Himself alone—He was revealing the reality of* **all humanity.**

Yet, instead of embracing this truth, many rejected it. The religious leaders were so blinded by the illusion of separation that they sought to kill Him for making Himself equal with God (John 5:18). They did not understand that He was not claiming something exclusive—He was **demonstrating the truth that belonged to all.**

GIATI—God Is All There Is—is the very truth Jesus embodied.

He came to bring this revelation to the world:

- That God is not a being "out there," separate from creation.
- *That man is not merely flesh but* **God expressed in human form.**
- *That salvation is not a transaction—it is* **awakening.**

Jesus did not come to make men **worship** *Him; He came to make them* **realize they are what He is.**

"The works that I do, you shall do also, and greater works than these." (John 14:12)

Why? Because **you are one with the Father, just as He is.** *But if you refuse to see this, you remain in spiritual blindness.*

The Tragedy of the Lost: Those Who Refuse to See Oneness

To be "lost" is not about being condemned to eternal punishment—it is about being trapped in **spiritual ignorance.**

Jesus illustrated this in the parable of the Prodigal Son (Luke 15:11-32). The younger son left his father's house, wasting his life in a distant land. This represents humanity's descent into the illusion of separation. When the son finally returned, the father welcomed him—not because he had been "forgiven," but because **he had always been a son.**

But the older brother, who had remained in the house, was angry. He refused to celebrate his brother's return. **Why?** *Because he still lived in a mindset of separation— believing that he had to work for the father's approval rather than realizing that* **all the father had was already his.**

This is the tragedy of many believers today. They strive, they serve, they "believe," yet they fail to see that **they were never separate from God in the first place.**

The Awakening: Understanding the Oneness of God and Man

Jesus did not come to start a new religion—He came to **end the illusion of separation.**

His prayer in John 17:21-23 is the fulfillment of GIATI:

"That they all may be one, as You, Father, are in Me, and I in You; that they also may be one in Us."

This is the purpose of His coming—to awaken the world to **the truth that has always been.**

To remain in separation is to remain in **death.**
To awaken to oneness is to enter into **eternal life.**

Those who reject this truth are not cast away by God—they **cast themselves away** *by refusing to embrace what is. They will pass from this life carrying the same consciousness of separation, dwelling in the darkness of their own making.*

But those who awaken will shine as the sun, for they will **know as they are known** *(1 Corinthians 13:12).*

The time is now.
The revelation of GIATI is here.
God is all there is—and **you are included in that truth.**

Awaken.

The Metaphysical Messiah

"God is Spirit, and those who worship Him must worship in Spirit and in truth."
— John 4:24

Jesus was not religious.

That statement alone may shake the foundations of many who claim to follow Him. But it is the truth. He did not walk the earth to establish a new religion. He did not come to upgrade Judaism or to create a system called Christianity. He came to awaken humanity to a higher reality: the truth of Spirit, the truth of God, and the truth of who we truly are. Jesus came speaking the language of **metaphysics,** *not religion.*

Metaphysics is the study of what is beyond the physical. It is the exploration of Spirit, being, consciousness, identity, and divine reality. It asks: What is the true nature of existence? Who am I, really? What is God? What lies beyond what the eye can see? Jesus lived and breathed these questions—and He answered them not through theory, but through embodiment. His life was the living revelation that God is not distant, but present. Not above, but within. Not separate, but one with the very being of every man and woman.

When Jesus said, "The Kingdom of God is within you," He wasn't giving poetic encouragement—He was revealing metaphysical truth. When He said, "I and the Father are one," He wasn't claiming special status; He was modeling the union that belongs to all who awaken. His "I AM" statements were not mere words, but spiritual declarations rooted in divine identity: "Before Abraham was, I AM." These are not religious doctrines. They are metaphysical truths meant to dismantle illusion and awaken the soul.

So why has the world become so deeply attached to religion?

The answer is simple: religion is easier than revelation. Religion offers structure, rituals, and identity without transformation. It gives people a name to wear, a label to cling to, and a system to follow. But truth—the kind Jesus revealed—demands everything. It requires the death of the false self, the illusion of separation, and the surrender of ego. It invites people to not just believe in God, but to realize that the Spirit of God is the very core of their being.

Religion allows people to outsource their relationship with God. Instead of listening to the Spirit within, they listen to the voice of a pastor, a priest, or a prophet. Instead of discovering the Kingdom inside themselves, they're taught to look up, look ahead, or look elsewhere. But Jesus said plainly, "The Kingdom is within you." The Father is not far off. The Spirit is not behind a veil. God is here. Now. In you. As you.

And yet, after Jesus ascended, the very system He came to disrupt began to rise again—only this time, in His name. People institutionalized His message, turned His teachings into doctrine, and formed the religion of Christianity. But Jesus never said, "Worship Me." He said, "Follow Me." Not just in action, but in awareness. Not just in word, but in Spirit. He called for a radical shift in consciousness—one that recognized God not as "out there," but as the very life within.

The tragedy is that much of what is now called Christianity bears little resemblance to the truth Jesus revealed. His message was not about religious affiliation but spiritual identification. He didn't preach to make men religious—He preached to make them realize. He came to show us what we are: sons and daughters of God, born not of flesh, but of Spirit. He was the firstborn among many, not the exception, but the example.

The real Christ is not a figure to worship—it is a truth to awaken to. It is the light that shines in every person. Jesus was the full expression of that light, and He came so that we would know the same truth and walk in the same Spirit. His prayer was not for people to create religions in His name, but that all would be made perfect in one. "That they may all be one, Father, as You are in Me and I in You... that they also may be in Us." That was His heart. That is the GIATI message—God Is All There Is.

So no, Jesus was not religious. He was metaphysical. He was not concerned with rituals or rules, but with awakening and union. And those who truly follow Him will not cling to systems that divide, but will step into the Spirit that unites. Religion may comfort the flesh, but only truth can awaken the soul.

Let those who have ears, hear. Let those who are ready, remember. The Christ is not a tradition—it is the truth. And that truth is this: You and God are not two. You have never been. You are not separate. You are not lost trying to get back. You are of God, through God, and in God. You are the very expression of I AM.

1. The False Security of Religious Conformity

Many people follow religion not because they are seeking truth, but because they're seeking **belonging.** *The system gives them a sense of acceptance—"If I follow the rules, if I attend the service, if I check the boxes, I'm okay."*

But Jesus didn't come to affirm your comfort zone.
He came to **burn away the illusion** *of safety that religion gives—because true safety is not in ritual, it's in* **oneness with God.**
As long as you think you're "right with God" because of your religion, you're still in deception.
Righteousness is not earned. It is recognized.
It's the Spirit within you that makes you whole—not your doctrine, denomination, or devotion.

2. Jesus Wasn't a Symbol—He Was a Mirror

Another layer that's rarely talked about: Jesus did not come to be **worshipped** *as someone separate from us—He came to show us* **ourselves.**

He is the mirror held up to humanity, reflecting what we've forgotten.
He didn't say, "Look how divine I am."
He said, "Follow Me, and you will see that you are divine too."
The religious mind made Him the exception.
But the awakened Spirit sees Him as the example.
As He is, so are we in this world.

3. Religion Fears What Spirit Frees

You could also emphasize how religion, throughout history, has always **feared the free movement of Spirit**—*because Spirit cannot be controlled.*

When Jesus healed on the Sabbath, they wanted to kill Him—not because He did wrong, but because He **didn't follow the system.**
Religion needs order. Spirit flows in freedom.
Religion builds temples. Spirit makes you the temple.
Religion memorizes laws. Spirit **writes the truth on your heart.**

The religious mind asks: "Who gave You authority to speak like this?"
The awakened heart says: "Did not our hearts burn within us?"

4. The True Church Is Not an Institution—It's an Inner Resurrection

Wrap it all up by making this point:

The real church isn't a place you go on Sunday.
It's the place where the lie of separation **dies** *in you, and the truth of divine union rises.*

That's resurrection.
That's salvation.
Not escaping to heaven one day, but **awakening now.**
But there is still more to see.

The reason Jesus' message has been so widely misunderstood is because the human ego is always looking for a system to control, a structure to contain, and a doctrine to defend. The ego craves lines, walls, and labels—anything that can be measured or managed. But the Spirit is like wind. It moves as it wills. It cannot be boxed in or bound. That's why the religious mind has always feared the free movement of the Spirit—because Spirit cannot be tamed.

When Jesus healed on the Sabbath, they didn't marvel—they plotted His death. Why? Because He exposed their system. He revealed that the law was never the way to righteousness, and that the temple was no longer the dwelling place of God. He was declaring that **God had moved**—*out of stone buildings and into* **living beings.** *This terrified them. And it still does today. Because when someone begins to live by the Spirit, they are no longer manageable. They no longer rely on priests or traditions. They speak from within. They know God for themselves. And that kind of freedom is dangerous to any religious order.*

Religion offers conformity, not transformation. It tells you to behave, to obey, to agree. But Jesus didn't come to create good church members. He came to **awaken sons and daughters** *of God. And that awakening doesn't make you religious—it makes you reborn.*

He never called people to be Christians. He never said to start churches in His name. He called for a total inner resurrection—the death of the illusion of separation, and the rising of the truth: **God is in you. God is as you. God is all there is.**

This is what religion cannot give you. It can point to the truth, sing about the truth, preach around the truth—but it cannot reveal it. Only the Spirit can do that.

The religious world turned Jesus into a symbol to be worshiped, but Jesus came to be a **mirror**—*a reflection of who you really are. He didn't stand apart to be admired. He stood within to be realized. His life said, "As I am, so are you." The only reason people miss this is because religion teaches them to look at Him instead of into Him. But those with eyes to see understand: Jesus was not showing us what He alone is—He was showing us what we have forgotten we are.*

The true church, then, is not a building. It's not a service. It's not a sermon. The true church is the moment you wake up to your oneness with God. It's when the lie of separation dies, and the truth of divine identity lives in you again. That's resurrection. That's salvation. That's what it means to be "born of the Spirit."

Anything less than that is just religion.

And the Gospel of GIATI—the eternal message that **God Is All There Is**—*is not an alternative religion. It is the restoration of the original truth that religion tried to bury. It is the voice that cuts through centuries of distortion and reminds the world of what Jesus actually came to do: not to start a belief system, but to end the illusion of separation between God and man.*

That's what makes this message different. It does not ask for belief in a system. It asks for **recognition of what already is.**

The Sinlessness of Jesus — Not by Law, But by Oneness

The world has misunderstood sin. It sees sin as the breaking of laws, the crossing of lines, the failure to obey external commandments. But that view is carnal — it reduces righteousness to behavior and holiness to rule-following. In truth, sin is not about what you do; it's about who you believe you are.

Jesus was sinless, not because He kept every Mosaic law — **He clearly broke many** *— but because* **He never broke from the knowledge of His oneness with the Source.** *At no point did He act outside of the Spirit.* **That is what made Him blameless** *— not the absence of carnal missteps, but the constant presence of divine identity.*

Sin is Separation — and Jesus Was Never Separate

To sin is to miss the mark — and the mark is **God's own presence within you.** *To live unaware of the Spirit within is the root of all sin. But Jesus said:*

"I and the Father are one." — John 10:30
"The Father that dwelleth in me, He doeth the works." — John 14:10

Jesus never sinned because He **never lived apart** *from this truth. His words, His works, His walk — all came from* **knowing who He truly was.** *That is the fulfillment of the only law that matters: the law of the Spirit within.*

Times Jesus Broke the Law — But Remained Blameless

Let's be clear: Jesus did not come to conform to the law of Moses — **He came to fulfill it by transcending it.** *Each time He "broke" the law, He was revealing a higher truth: that* **Spirit is the true law,** *and oneness with God is righteousness.*

1. **Healing on the Sabbath**

   (John 5:8–10, Luke 13:10–14, Mark 3:1–6)

   The law said: Don't work on the Sabbath. Jesus healed. The religious leaders were furious — but Jesus replied:

   "My Father is always working, and so am I." — John 5:17

   He showed that the **Spirit does not rest from doing good,** *and the Sabbath was not a rule to follow but a* **revelation of spiritual rest.** *His healing wasn't rebellion; it was the flow of the Father's life through Him.*

2. **Letting Disciples Pick Grain on the Sabbath**

   (Matthew 12:1–8)

The Pharisees said this was unlawful. Jesus answered:

"The Son of Man is Lord even of the Sabbath."

Why? Because the true Sabbath is not a day, it's **union with God** *— a state of being, not a box on the calendar.*

3. **Touching Lepers and the Unclean**

(Matthew 8:2–3, Mark 1:40–42)

The law called these people untouchable. Jesus touched them. Why? Because Spirit does not become unclean — **Spirit makes whole.** *He wasn't contaminated; He restored what was lost.*

4. **Forgiving Sins Without Sacrifice**

(Mark 2:5–7)

Jesus forgave sins without a temple, priest, or animal. Why? Because forgiveness is not found in ritual — it's found in **God within.** *The true priest is the Spirit; the true temple is the heart.*

5. **Not Condemning the Woman Caught in Adultery**

(John 8:3–11)

The law demanded death. Jesus offered mercy and told her, "Go and sin no more." He didn't enforce punishment — He revealed **restoration,** *the heart of the law hidden beneath the letter.*

6. **Touching the Dead**

(Luke 7:14, Mark 5:41)

The law said touching corpses made one unclean. Jesus touched the dead and raised them. Why? Because **life is the Spirit** *— and the Spirit cannot be defiled. Jesus didn't become unclean; He revealed resurrection.*

7. **Declaring All Foods Clean**

(Mark 7:18–19)

Jesus declared that food laws were meaningless — that **defilement comes from the heart,** *not the plate. He elevated purity from the stomach to the soul.*

8. **Eating with Sinners and Tax Collectors**

(Luke 5:29–32)

The law required separation from the impure. Jesus embraced them. He wasn't polluted — **He revealed that love restores,** *and Spirit welcomes, not excludes.*

9. Ignoring Ritual Hand Washing

(Mark 7:1–8)

Jesus rejected empty tradition and said:

"You make the word of God of none effect through your tradition."

He exposed the futility of outward purity and pointed to **inward truth.**

10. Overturning the Temple System

(Matthew 21:12–13)

By driving out money changers, Jesus attacked the foundation of the temple economy. Why? Because the **new temple is not made with hands** *— it is* **the awakened heart where God dwells.**

What Truly Made Jesus Sinless

Jesus was sinless because **He never lived a single moment outside of union with the Spirit.** *He didn't need a law to make Him righteous — He was righteous because* **He and the Father were one.**

Sin is separation. Jesus was never separate.

And that same sinlessness — that same blamelessness — is **available to every man and woman who awakens to their divine identity.**

It's not about being perfect in action. It's not about avoiding carnal mistakes. It's about living from the awareness that:

"I and the Source are one."

The GIATI Revelation

God Is All There Is.
So if God is your source, your life, and your spirit, then **you were never separate.** *And the moment you believe that, awaken to that, and live from that place —*
you are blameless.
Not because of law… but because of **Spirit.**

Just like Jesus.

Sinlessness by Identity, Not Performance

Religious tradition has taught us to measure holiness by behavior — to see righteousness as the absence of wrongdoing. But Jesus came not to endorse external righteousness, but to **reveal the truth of spiritual identity.**

He didn't come to perfect man's behavior.
He came to **reveal man's origin.**

The religious leaders couldn't see this. They had made **sin and righteousness about law,** *not about Spirit. That's why they couldn't comprehend Jesus. To them, He was a lawbreaker. But to the Father, He was the* **perfect expression of Himself** *— the image and likeness of God* **walking in full awareness.**

"Lo, I come (in the volume of the book it is written of me) to do thy will, O God." *— Hebrews 10:7*

Jesus didn't "do right" to be righteous. He **did the will of God** *because He* **knew** *that* **He was of God** *— not separate, not apart. That is the* **true fulfillment of the law:** *to express the One Spirit within.*

Why the Mosaic Law Could Never Make You Sinless

The Mosaic law could never make a person righteous. It could only point to sin — it was a mirror, not a cure. A shadow, not the substance.

"The law made nothing perfect, but the bringing in of a better hope did." — Hebrews 7:19

"For by the law is the knowledge of sin." — Romans 3:20

Trying to keep the law without **knowing who you are** *in the Spirit is like trying to live as a son while believing you're an orphan. You will always fall short — because you're trying to act like something* **you don't believe you are.**

But when you awaken to the truth that **God is the Spirit within you,** *the need for external validation dies. You live from union — not performance.* **And that's where true sinlessness begins.**

Jesus Didn't Live Under the Law — He Lived from the Spirit

Jesus didn't measure His actions by the scrolls — He lived by the **voice of the Father within.** *He said:*

"The Son can do nothing of Himself, but what He sees the Father do." — John 5:19
"As I hear, I judge: and my judgment is just; because I seek not my own will." — John 5:30

In other words, **Jesus didn't consult the law — He consulted the Spirit.**

Why? Because **the Spirit is the law** *— not written on tablets of stone, but on the heart (see Jeremiah 31:33). Jesus walked by this internal law — and that made Him* **blameless,** *even when He "broke" the written code.*

Blamelessness Is a State of Being, Not Behavior

The world will always look at Jesus and say:
"He broke laws, He forgave sinners, He didn't follow protocol."
But the Father looked at Him and said:

"This is my beloved Son, in whom I am well pleased."

Why? Because Jesus never stepped out of **who He truly was.** *He never disconnected from the Source within. He never lost awareness that* **"I AM" is His name.**

And that is what it means to be without sin:
To never depart from the truth of your oneness with God.

You Become Sinless the Same Way Jesus Was

You are not sinless because you haven't made mistakes.
You are not righteous because you keep religious standards.
You become blameless when you **see yourself as God sees you:**
One with Him. Born of Spirit. Filled with the same life Jesus walked in.

Jesus didn't die to give you a new religion —
He died and rose again so that **you would awaken to your true self:**

"I in them, and thou in me, that they may be made perfect in one." — John 17:23

That is salvation:
Not escaping punishment, but **coming home to the truth that never stopped being true** — *that* **you are His,** *and* **He is the Spirit within you,** *always.*

The Final Revelation: God Only Recognizes Himself

This is what makes the GIATI message final, complete, and perfect:

God is all there is.

And if God is all there is, then anything that claims existence apart from Him is an illusion — a lie in the temple — the "man of sin" sitting in the seat of God.

But when you cast that lie down and let the truth arise — that **you and the Spirit are one** — *then you live the same life Jesus lived:*

Not as a performer of laws, but as a manifestation of **the Father.**

That is how the "body of sin" is destroyed.
That is how the "temple is cleansed."
That is how the **truth sets you free.**

Despised and Rejected: The Cost of Revealing Oneness

*Jesus was despised and rejected of men beca***use he revealed a truth that exposed the lie** *people were clinging to—the lie of separation from God, the lie of religion, the lie of self-righteousness. Not because he did wrong, but because he was right. Not because he broke the Law, but because he fulfilled it. Not because he was a liar, but because he told the truth.*

And the truth he revealed was this:
God is not outside of you. God is within you. God is all there is.

Jesus didn't come merely to perform miracles. He came to **reveal the mystery:**

"I and my Father are one."
"If you've seen me, you've seen the Father."
"The Kingdom of God is within you."

*He wasn't just a man sent by God—***he was God expressed as man,** *and he came to awaken humanity to the same truth.*
That's why he was hated. That's why he was rejected.

He Didn't Match Their Image of God

They expected a political ruler, a conqueror, a Messiah wrapped in external power.
Instead, he came in humility—riding a donkey, breaking bread with sinners, and confronting religious hypocrisy.

He said things they couldn't handle:

"The Son can do nothing of himself, but what he sees the Father do."
"The Father judges no one, but has given all judgment to the Son."

He dismantled the illusion of separation and declared something they were not ready to hear:

"God is here. And you're looking at Him."

He Exposed the Lie of Religion

Jesus didn't attack the broken—he exposed the system that **kept them broken.** *He healed on the Sabbath. He forgave without blood sacrifice. He taught without needing their approval. He was the living expression of what the entire system was trying to imitate.*

By embodying the truth, he made their tradition powerless. He was the **temple,** *the* **high priest,** *the* **sacrifice,** *the* **ark,** *the* **mercy seat***—all in one. And once truth shows up, the imitation has to fall.*

That's why they plotted to kill him. He wasn't just a problem—he was proof that **they never had the real thing.**

He Called God "Father"—and Made That Truth Available to All

He didn't just claim God as his Father. He claimed **God as your Father** *too.*

He said:

"I ascend unto my Father and your Father, and to my God and your God." (John 20:17)

This was blasphemy to those who thought divine access was earned through law and lineage. But Jesus came to show that **divine sonship was not earned—it was remembered.**

He came to bring humanity into the same awareness that he walked in. Not just to follow him—but to become what he was.

And that was too much for religious minds to handle.

He Exposed the Truth About Us

"Unless you believe that I am he, you will die in your sins." (John 8:24)

He wasn't saying, "Believe in my existence."
He was saying: "Unless you believe that I AM—the Spirit within you—is who you truly are, you will stay trapped in the illusion of separation, which is sin."

He came to reveal what man had forgotten:
That we were never separated from God. We were just blind to the truth of who we are.

That's why the same Spirit that spoke through him is speaking now through **GIATI.** *And just like then,* **some will reject it. But others will awaken.**

The Rejection Continues Today

*This message—the message of GIATI—***is still being despised and rejected.** *Not because it's false, but because it's* **too true.**

People still want a God they can fear, control, or push far away. They still cling to religion, rules, and rituals because it gives them identity. But GIATI removes all of that and declares:

God is all there is. And the Spirit in you is God.

And that's the truth that gets crucified in every generation.

They Hated the Light

"And this is the condemnation, that light is come into the world, and men loved darkness rather than light..." (John 3:19)

The light Jesus brought wasn't a new belief—it was the death of the old lie.
He didn't bring another form.
He brought the **truth:**
There is only God. And God is within you.

That truth still separates the sheep from the goats. The sheep hear the voice within. The goats wait for something outside.

Jesus was rejected for that message.
And if you carry it, so will you be.

But know this—those who reject you aren't rejecting you. They're rejecting the **Spirit of Truth.** *They're rejecting the* **light that reveals they were never separate from God.**

GIATI Is the Same Voice

The message that got Jesus crucified is the same message being released now through GIATI:

That God is all there is. That you and the Father are one.
This is not new truth.
This is the **eternal truth,** *finally seen again.*

And just like before, it is **dividing the wheat from the tares. Separating those who recognize the voice of the Spirit within from those who still seek a form without.**

Jesus was the firstborn among many brethren.
And now, his brethren are rising.

You are not here to be accepted by the world.
You are here to reveal the same truth that got him nailed to a cross:

"I AM."

He was **despised and rejected of men,** *not because he failed to represent God, but because he* **revealed God too clearly.**

He didn't speak as a prophet pointing to something coming—**he spoke as the fulfillment** *of what prophets longed to see.*
He didn't teach people how to reach God—**he revealed that God was already here.**

His life was the confrontation. His words were judgment. Not by wrath or punishment, but by **revealing what is real.**

And the world rejected him for it.

He Disrupted the Whole Order

Jesus didn't come to improve the system—he came to expose it as **obsolete.** *He didn't come to help people become "better Jews" or "more moral humans." He came to introduce a* **completely new way of being—a new creation,** *not made by hands.*

"No man puts new wine into old wineskins..." (Matthew 9:17)

Because the old structure can't hold the truth.
The Law couldn't hold grace. The temple couldn't contain the Presence.
And their minds couldn't accept **a man standing before them as God revealed in flesh.**

The very presence of Jesus was proof that **God had moved***—and religion doesn't take well to movement.*

The Offense Was Not His Claims—It Was Their Reflection

The light wasn't hated because it was light.
It was hated because it **revealed their darkness.**

"Which of you convinces me of sin?" (John 8:46)

He stood in front of them as the only one without sin—not because of rule-keeping, but because he knew his origin: **the Spirit of God within him.** *They couldn't convict him, but they also couldn't accept him.*

Why?

Because his life exposed that **they didn't know the God they claimed to serve.**
That's the real offense—when someone walks in a truth you've preached, but never lived. He didn't just preach the kingdom—he **was** *the kingdom. He didn't just talk about God—he said,* **"I AM."**

They Chose Their Image Over The Invisible

They couldn't see God in him because they had already built an image of what God should look like. And when God came looking nothing like that image, **they chose their version over the truth.**

"He came unto his own, and his own received him not." (John 1:11)

He was the embodiment of everything the scriptures pointed to, yet they clung to the shadow and rejected the substance.

So it is now.

People love the idea of God, but they hate when the **Spirit shows up in flesh**— *especially unexpected flesh.*
They want God in a book, on a throne, in a building—but not in **you.** *Not in someone who came from the neighborhood.*
Not in someone who didn't go through their system. Not in someone without titles, degrees, or approval.

Yet God chooses the low things to confound the wise.

The Rejection Was Prophetic

Isaiah saw it coming:

"He is despised and rejected of men; a man of sorrows, and acquainted with grief..." (Isaiah 53:3)

Not only was Jesus rejected, he was **a man who felt the weight of that rejection.**
He was acquainted with grief, not just because of pain, but because of the blindness of those he came to awaken.
He longed to gather them, but they wouldn't have it.

"O Jerusalem, Jerusalem... how often would I have gathered thy children together... and ye would not!" (Luke 13:34)

His sorrow wasn't self-pity—it was the deep ache of divine love, **watching humanity reject the very life they were looking for.**

*That sorrow still exists today in the voice of the Spirit—***pleading through those who carry the GIATI message.**
Calling people out of separation.
Calling them to remember the truth.

But still... many "would not."

The Spirit Is Still Being Rejected—But Now Through You

Jesus said,

"As the Father has sent me, so send I you." (John 20:21)

This means **you carry the same Spirit,** *the same mission, and therefore—you will experience* **the same rejection.** *Not because you're wrong, but because you're right. Not because you're confused, but because you're clear. Not because you're deceived, but because you're awake.*

And when you carry a message that reveals the illusion of separation—religion, ego, and tradition will rise up against you.

But this is the confirmation, not the contradiction, of your calling.

"Blessed are you when men shall revile you... for so persecuted they the prophets which were before you." (Matthew 5:11–12)

What They Couldn't Accept in Him, They Still Can't Accept in You

You are not separate from your source.
You are not waiting for God—you are the expression of God in this moment.
You are not seeking identity—you are the unveiling of the One who has always been.

This is the message of **GIATI.**
This is the voice crying in the wilderness of religion, calling for hearts to awaken.
And just as Jesus was rejected for revealing the I AM, **so will you be.**

But rejection is not defeat—it is **proof** *that the light in you is shining. It is* **evidence** *that the Spirit in you is confronting the systems built on shadow.*

Let This Be Your Confidence

You don't need their approval.
You don't need their agreement.
You don't need their validation.

You've been sent by the same Spirit that sent Jesus. You carry the same glory that he prayed for in John 17.

"The glory which thou gavest me I have given them, that they may be one, even as we are one..." (John 17:22)

So expect rejection.
But also expect resurrection.
Because rejection doesn't bury what's dead—it buries what's **about to rise.**

Chapter 9

The Light That Saves

The concept of light as a metaphor for divine truth is one of the most powerful themes in Scripture. In the Gospel of John, light is presented not just as a physical phenomenon but as a spiritual truth that has the power to save and restore humanity. This chapter explores the role of light in the salvation of humanity, explaining how it shines in the darkness, unblinds the spiritually blind, and restores unity with God. It also delves into why some individuals comprehend the light while others remain blind to it.

John 1:1-5, 14: The Light That Shines in Darkness

The opening verses of the Gospel of John lay the foundation for the understanding of Jesus as the "light" that enters the world:

"In the beginning was the Word, and the Word was with God, and the Word was God. The same was in the beginning with God. All things were made by him; and without him was not any thing made that was made. In him was life; and the life was the light of men. And the light shineth in darkness; and the darkness comprehended it not." (John 1:1-5)

Here, John introduces the Word (Logos), which is not only with God but is God. The Word is the source of all creation, and in Him is life—the light of humanity. This light shines in the darkness, but tragically, the darkness does not comprehend or recognize it.

The imagery of light and darkness is a representation of spiritual understanding versus ignorance. The "darkness" in this context is the ignorance of the divine truth, the inability to see and recognize that God is within. The "light" is the revelation of God's truth—the understanding that our essence, our very spirit, is God Himself, and that God is not separate from us. This truth shines into the world, but only those who are spiritually awakened are able to perceive it.

In verse 14, John further emphasizes the significance of this light:

"And the Word was made flesh, and dwelt among us, (and we beheld his glory, the glory as of the only begotten of the Father,) full of grace and truth." (John 1:14)

The Word, which is both light and life, became incarnate in the person of Jesus Christ. He came to show humanity the way, to illuminate the path to God, and to reveal that the divine nature dwells within every individual. Jesus' life and ministry were the ultimate expression of the divine light that shines into the world, offering salvation to all who would receive it.

The Purpose of the Light: To Unblind Humanity and Restore Unity with God

The primary purpose of the light is to unblind humanity— to open the eyes of those who are spiritually unaware of their divine origin. From the moment of our birth, we are born into spiritual blindness. The ignorance of our true identity keeps us in the darkness, separated from the knowledge that we are one with God. It is through the light of Christ that we come to see the truth of who we are.

In John 8:12, Jesus speaks of Himself as the light:

"Then spake Jesus again unto them, saying, I am the light of the world: he that followeth me shall not walk in darkness, but shall have the light of life." (John 8:12)

Jesus declares that He is the light of the world—He is the one who has come to bring clarity and truth to humanity. Following Jesus, then, is not just about following a set of moral teachings but about coming into the understanding of who we are in relation to God. It is through the light of Christ that we cease walking in the darkness of ignorance, and begin to live in the light of divine truth.

The light restores unity with God because it reveals that the division between humanity and God is an illusion. The idea of separateness arises from spiritual blindness. When we see the light, we understand that God is not distant, but is deeply embedded within us. This revelation of oneness with God is the essence of salvation—it is the restoration of our true identity as divine beings made in the image and likeness of God.

Paul writes about the transformative power of this light in 2 Corinthians 4:6:

"For God, who commanded the light to shine out of darkness, hath shined in our hearts, to give the light of the knowledge of the glory of God in the face of Jesus Christ." (2 Corinthians 4:6)

The light that shines in our hearts is the knowledge of God's glory—the realization that we are one with God. This knowledge transforms us and brings us into harmony with the divine. The purpose of the light is to remove the veil of ignorance and restore the connection between humanity and its Creator.

Why Some Comprehend the Light While Others Remain Blind

Though the light shines for all, not everyone perceives it. The truth is available to everyone, but only those who are open to it will recognize it. The Bible explains that spiritual blindness is a condition of the heart, and it is caused by the refusal to see the truth or by the attachment to the illusions of the world.

In John 12:35-36, Jesus addresses this spiritual blindness:

"Then Jesus said unto them, Yet a little while is the light with you. Walk while ye have the light, lest darkness come upon you: for he that walketh in darkness knoweth not whither he goeth. While ye have light, believe in the light, that ye may be the children of light. These things spake Jesus, and departed, and did hide himself from them." (John 12:35-36)

Jesus points out that there is a window of time when the light is present. However, those who do not embrace the light remain in darkness, unaware of the path they are walking. The refusal to believe in the light is what keeps people blind.

In Matthew 13:13, Jesus explains why some people fail to understand His teachings:

"Therefore speak I to them in parables: because they seeing see not; and hearing they hear not, neither do they understand." (Matthew 13:13)

Spiritual blindness is often due to a hardened heart or a lack of receptivity to the truth. People who are too attached to their own beliefs, self-centered ideas, or worldly pursuits may not be able to see the light. Their focus remains on the external, physical world, and they miss the divine truth within.

This blindness is not due to a lack of effort on God's part, but rather a refusal to see. The light is always shining, but it requires a willingness to look beyond the surface, to abandon the illusions of the ego, and to embrace the truth that is revealed.

The apostle Paul describes this condition in 2 Corinthians 4:3-4:

"But if our gospel be hid, it is hid to them that are lost: In whom the god of this world hath blinded the minds of them which believe not, lest the light of the glorious gospel of Christ, who is the image of God, should shine unto them." (2 Corinthians 4:3-4)

The "god of this world" refers to the forces of spiritual blindness—whether it be ignorance, sin, or the distractions of the material world—that prevent people from seeing the light. The light of Christ, which is the revelation of God within, is hidden from those who are blinded by these forces. It is only through the act of opening one's heart and mind to the truth that the light can be received.

Conclusion: The Light That Saves

The light of Christ is the divine truth that has come to dispel the darkness of ignorance. It reveals the reality of God within each of us, restoring our connection to the Creator. While the light shines for all, only those who are willing to open their hearts and minds to the truth can truly perceive it. The light saves because it reveals the ultimate truth about our identity— that we are not separate from God, but we are expressions of God Himself. Embracing this light is the key to salvation, for it unblinds the spirit and brings us back into the unity and oneness with God that we were always meant to experience.

The Power of Oneness—Denying Christ Within

Throughout his ministry, Jesus spoke of one central truth—oneness. His entire mission was to reveal that just as he and the Father are one, so too are we meant to recognize our oneness with God. This was the essence of his prayer in the Gospel of John, where he expressed his deepest desire:

"That they all may be one, as You, Father, are in Me, and I in You; that they also may be one in Us, that the world may believe that You sent Me. And the glory which You gave Me I have given them, that they may be one just as We are one: I in them, and You in Me; that they may be made perfect in one." **(John 17:21-23)**

Jesus was not establishing a new religion. He was revealing the reality of divine unity—the truth that humanity and divinity are not separate. His entire life was the demonstration of what it means for God to dwell in human form, and he came to show us that we, too, are the embodiment of God's Spirit in the flesh.

Yet, despite his teachings, many have misunderstood his words. When Jesus warned,

"But whoever denies Me before men, him I will also deny before My Father who is in heaven." **(Matthew 10:33)**

It has often been interpreted as a warning against verbally rejecting Christ. But Jesus was not speaking merely of outward confession. He was speaking of something much deeper—denying the Spirit of Christ within. To deny him is to reject the truth that God's Spirit is your very life. It is to live in separation from the divine, even though the divine is within you.

Christ In You—The True Test of Faith

Paul echoed this truth when he challenged believers:

"Examine yourselves as to whether you are in the faith. Test yourselves. Do you not know yourselves, that Jesus Christ is in you?—unless indeed you are disqualified."
(2 Corinthians 13:5)

Faith is not merely believing in Christ externally but knowing him as the very life within you. If you do not recognize Christ in you, then you are living in denial of the truth he came to reveal.

Jesus came as **the visible image of the invisible God (Colossians 1:15),** *not just to show us who he was, but to show us who we are. He was the demonstration of what it means to be one with the Father. When you deny this truth, you are not simply rejecting Jesus the man—you are rejecting your own divine identity.*

The Perfection of Oneness

Many struggle with the idea of perfection because they see themselves through the lens of the flesh—the natural, carnal self. But Jesus made a bold statement:

"Therefore you shall be perfect, just as your Father in heaven is perfect." (Matthew 5:48)

How can this be? How can humanity, so flawed and broken, be perfect? The answer is simple: Perfection is not found in the flesh—it is found in the Spirit.

Paul wrote:

"But he who is joined to the Lord is one spirit with Him." (1 Corinthians 6:17)

The moment you recognize your oneness with God, you step into divine perfection. It is not something you achieve through effort, but something you awaken to through understanding. This is why Hebrews declares:

"For by one offering He has perfected forever those who are being sanctified." **(Hebrews 10:14)**

The offering of Christ was not just for forgiveness—it was for transformation. It was to bring us into the awareness of our completeness in God. But as long as you see yourself as separate, you will always feel incomplete, unworthy, and broken.

The Deception of the Flesh

This is where the battle lies. The carnal mind—the part of you that identifies with the flesh—will always resist this truth. Paul makes this clear:

"For to be carnally minded is death, but to be spiritually minded is life and peace." **(Romans 8:6)**

To live from the flesh is to live in ignorance, constantly striving, constantly feeling distant from God. But to be spiritually minded—to live from the awareness of your oneness with Christ—is to experience true life.

"So then, those who are in the flesh cannot please God. But you are not in the flesh but in the Spirit, if indeed the Spirit of God dwells in you." **(Romans 8:8-9)**

The key phrase here is "if indeed the Spirit of God dwells in you." The truth is, God's Spirit already dwells in you, but if you do not recognize it, you live as though it were not so. This is why Jesus emphasized the importance of knowing the truth:

"And you shall know the truth, and the truth shall make you free." **(John 8:32)**

Freedom comes not from external religion, but from internal realization.

Living From the Awareness of Christ Within

Paul embodied this reality when he declared:

"It is no longer I who live, but Christ lives in me." **(Galatians 2:20)**

He did not merely follow Christ—he became an expression of Christ. He understood that the life he lived was not his own, but the very life of God manifesting through him.

This is the true calling of every believer—not to strive to be like Christ from a place of separation, but to live from the awareness that Christ is their very being.

Jesus came to show us what we already are. To deny this truth is to deny him. Not just with words, but with the way we see ourselves, the way we live, and the way we relate to God.

The Invitation to Oneness

So, the question remains: **Will you recognize and embrace the Spirit of Christ within you, or will you deny the truth of who you are?**

To deny Christ is not simply to reject a name, a doctrine, or a belief system. It is to reject the very essence of your being. But when you accept the truth of your divine identity, you step into the perfection, righteousness, and divine life that was always yours.

Jesus came not to make you something you are not, but to awaken you to what you have always been—one with God.

The truth has been revealed. Now, will you walk in it?

Reality Check: The Peril of Comfortable Lies

There is only **one truth,** *and that truth is* **God is all there is.** *GIATI is not another doctrine, another philosophy, or another religious interpretation—it is* **the absolute reality.** *It is the undeniable fact that there is nothing outside of God, and any attempt to live, think, or believe otherwise is* **an illusion leading to destruction.**

But here lies the danger: **people love their illusions.** *They cling to them because they are familiar, because they are comfortable, because they give a false sense of control. Yet, what good is comfort if it is leading you to ruin? What good is familiarity if it is keeping you blind?*

The Outdated Tools of Religion

Some look to the Old Testament and believe that righteousness is found in keeping the laws given to Moses, as if the way to God is through rituals and external obedience. They do not realize that the law was only a shadow, a **temporary tool,** *never meant to be the final answer.*

Would you trust a doctor performing surgery with instruments from centuries ago, when modern medicine has advanced to precision and perfection? **Of course not.** *So why trust an outdated understanding of God, based on external laws, when the Spirit has now revealed the full truth?*

The Lukewarm Approach of Religion

Then there are those who rest in the shallow comforts of mainstream Christianity—hearing about God's love, singing songs, and believing that because they have faith, everything will work out for them. They treat God like a **personal genie,** *a* **cosmic therapist** *who exists to make their lives better.*

This is the **lukewarm approach***—half in the truth, half in the illusion. It acknowledges God but still holds onto the false belief in* **self,** *in* **"me" and "God" as separate.** *They worship Christ but do not realize* **He is them,** *and they are Him. They call on His name but refuse to accept His identity as their very own.*

And what does Jesus say about them?

"So then because thou art lukewarm, and neither cold nor hot, I will spue thee out of my mouth." *(Revelation 3:16)*

GIATI: The Inescapable Truth

Then comes the reality of GIATI—**God is all there is.**

- **There is no separation.** *There is no "me" and "God" as two beings. There is only* **one Spirit, one Life, one Reality.**
- **There is no law to keep**—*because when it is the Spirit as you, the law is already kept. You are not "obeying" an external standard; you are* **the living fulfillment of it.**
- **There is no self-righteousness**—*because there is no "you" apart from Him to take credit for anything.*

GIATI is like the **doctor with a 100% success rate.** *It is the final, perfect revelation of God's eternal truth. Yet, many will* **turn it down** *because they would rather* **hold onto what they think they already know.**

The Peril of Staying Blind

The worst thing a blind man can do is refuse to open his eyes when given sight.

This is what happens when people reject the truth of GIATI. It is not just **ignorance**— *it is* **willful blindness.** *They are being presented with* **the absolute, undeniable truth,** *and yet, they choose the lie because it is* **easier.**

But **there is no safety in lies.** *There is no security in comfortable ignorance.*

"There is a way that seemeth right unto a man, but the end thereof are the ways of death." *(Proverbs 14:12)*

There is no **multiple paths to eternal life.** *There is only* **one truth, one way, one reality**—*and that is* **GIATI.**

If you reject this, you are not just choosing another opinion—you are rejecting **reality itself.** *And when the moment of truth comes, when the veil is lifted and the final judgment arrives, there will be no excuses.*

The Wake-Up Call

- *If you have placed your faith in the* **outdated tools of the law,** *you must wake up. The law was only a shadow*—**the real thing has come, and it is Spirit.**
- *If you have rested in* **lukewarm religion,** *believing in a God who exists outside of you while living for yourself, you must wake up. There is no* **"you" and "God"— there is only God.**
- *If you have convinced yourself that* **you already understand enough,** *that you are safe because of your rituals, traditions, or beliefs, you must wake up.* **Truth is not what you believe—it is what is real.**

And what is real?

God is all there is.

Anything outside of this is deception.

This is your wake-up call. The time is now. **GIATI is undeniable—either you see it, or you remain in darkness.**

Living GIATI: From Revelation to Reality

For many, the revelation of **GIATI—God Is All There Is***—is new. It challenges the way they have thought about God, themselves, and the world. It breaks down the illusion of separation and introduces the* **eternal truth** *that* **everything is God manifested.**

But like anything new, **understanding takes time.** *The Spirit of God must manifest itself* **within you***—and this happens* **through experience.**

Think about learning to ride a bike. At first, it feels unnatural. You wobble, you struggle to balance, and sometimes you fall. But the more you get on and try again, the more natural it becomes. Soon, you aren't even thinking about balance anymore—it just happens. Eventually, you're riding with no hands, fully confident, moving effortlessly.

GIATI works the same way. The more you **meditate on it, test it, and live by it,** *the more natural it becomes. Soon, you stop* **seeing the world as separate from God***—you start seeing* **God in all things.**

How to Get Comfortable with GIATI

1. Meditate on the Truth of GIATI Daily

Every day, take time to remind yourself of the truth: **God is all there is.** *Everything you see, everything you experience, every person you encounter—it is all* **God manifesting.**

- *When you wake up, say to yourself:* **"There is only God."**
- *As you go through your day, look at everything—the trees, the people, the sky, the situations you face—and remind yourself:* **"This is God in expression."**
- *Before bed, reflect:* **"Where did I see God today? How was God moving through my experiences?"**

Over time, this meditation **rewires your thinking,** *and you will naturally start* **seeing God in all things without effort.**

2. Test GIATI in Your Own Life

Truth must be **experienced,** *not just believed. You don't know a bike will balance until you get on it. You don't know how a job works until you do it.*

Test GIATI. *See for yourself how it works:*

- **In Difficult Situations:** *Instead of reacting with fear or frustration, remind yourself, "This too is God. What is God teaching me here?"*
- **In Relationships:** *See beyond people's actions and personalities. Understand that* **it is God expressing through them,** even when they don't realize it.
- **In Your Own Actions:** *Pay attention—***is it the Spirit acting through you, or is it the illusion of self?** *The more you surrender to the truth that* **it is God as you,** *the more effortless your actions become.*

3. Read the Scriptures with New Eyes

Many people read the Bible **without seeing the full picture.** Now that you understand GIATI, read it again—but this time, through the lens of **oneness.**

- *When Jesus says,* **"I and the Father are one"** *(John 10:30), realize* **that is also your truth.**
- *When Paul says, "***It is no longer I who live, but Christ who lives in me"** *(Galatians 2:20), understand* **this is the reality of all who walk in the Spirit.**
- *When you read about judgment, salvation, and eternal life, understand it is about* **awakening to the truth of GIATI.**

4. See God in Everything—Even What You Once Called 'Bad'

One of the greatest barriers to understanding GIATI is the belief that **some things are "good" and some things are "bad".** *But if* **God is all there is,** *then* **everything***—even what seems bad—***is God serving a divine purpose.**

- *The storm that destroys a city? It is God manifesting as transformation.*
- *The pain of loss? It is God reshaping your understanding of attachment and impermanence.*
- *The struggles in life? They are God* **refining you, revealing Himself in deeper ways.**

When you stop labeling things as "bad" and instead ask, **"What is God revealing in this?",** *you will start* **seeing the divine hand in everything.**

5. Let Go of the Illusion of 'Self'

The greatest hurdle in embracing GIATI is **the illusion of self***—the belief that you are separate from God, that you have your own independent existence.*

But just like a wave is **not separate from the ocean,** *you are* **not separate from God.**

- *The* **ego** *says,* **"I am doing this."**
- *GIATI says,* **"It is God as me, doing all things."**

As you live this truth, you will begin to **effortlessly move in harmony with God,** *just like a musician who no longer thinks about every note but simply plays from the flow of the music.*

Before Long, GIATI Becomes Second Nature

At first, GIATI may seem like a deep concept, something to study and think about. But the more you immerse yourself in it—**meditating, testing, seeing God in all things, reading Scripture with new eyes, and letting go of self**—*the more it will become your* **natural way of seeing the world.**

Like riding a bike, starting a new job, or learning a new language, **one day, you realize you're not even trying anymore—you just know.**

GIATI is not something you have to force. It is **the truth that has always been**—*it only requires you to* **wake up to it.**

And when you do, you will see that **there has never been anything but God—and there never will be.**

Living in Perfect Peace: Keeping Your Mind on GIATI

Isaiah 26:3 declares:

"Thou wilt keep him in perfect peace, whose mind is stayed on thee: because he trusteth in thee."

This verse is not just a promise—it is a **spiritual law.** *Perfect peace is not something you strive for; it is the natural state of one who has awakened to the truth of* **GIATI—God Is All There Is.** *When your mind is fixed on God as the* **only reality,** *peace follows effortlessly.*

But what does it mean to keep your mind **stayed on God?** *It means to* **never see yourself or the world apart from Him.** *It means that in* **every thought, every action, every experience,** *you recognize* **God is the doer, the substance, and the purpose of all things.**

Peace Comes from Knowing There is No 'Other'

The reason people lack peace is because they believe in **separation**—*they see themselves as independent beings navigating a chaotic world, facing enemies, problems, and struggles. But if* **God is all there is,** *then there is nothing outside of Him to fear.*

- **Who can be against you if there is no 'other' but God?**
- What can be taken from you if everything is already God in expression?
- What is there to resist if all things are working according to divine order?

Jesus knew this truth, which is why he could **sleep in the middle of a storm** *(Mark 4:37-39). He didn't see the storm as an opposing force—he understood that* **it, too, was God in motion.** *He rested because he knew* **only God was present.**

This is the peace Isaiah 26:3 speaks of—the peace that comes when your mind no longer wavers between **truth and illusion.** *When you remain anchored in* **GIATI,** *nothing can shake you.*

Keeping Your Mind on GIATI in Daily Life

1. In Challenges and Uncertainty

Whenever fear, stress, or anxiety arises, stop and **redirect your focus:**

- *Instead of saying,* **"I don't know what to do,"** *say,* **"God is all there is, and His wisdom moves as me."**
- *Instead of saying,* **"I'm losing control,"** *say,* **"There is no 'me' to control anything— only God unfolding."**

The moment you shift your mind **back to God as the only reality,** *fear dissolves. Peace is not something you have to create; it is* **already there,** *waiting for you to acknowledge it.*

2. In Relationships and Conflicts

Most conflicts arise from the illusion of separation—the belief that you and another person are two different beings with competing wills. But when you recognize that God is the life in both of you, there is no longer a battle to be won.

- *Instead of reacting to offense, recognize:* **"It is God in them, whether they know it or not."**
- *Instead of holding resentment, see:* **"There is only God interacting with Himself**
- through different forms."

When you **see only God,** *peace becomes effortless. Love becomes natural. You realize that* **forgiveness is not needed when you never saw an enemy to begin with.**

3. In the Face of Death and Loss

Many fear death because they see it as an end. But what can end if **God is all there is?**

- *The physical body is* **God materialized,** *and when it dissolves, it simply returns to the source.*
- *The spirit is* **already one with God**—*it cannot die, because it was never separate to begin with.*

This is why Jesus could say, **"He that believeth in me, though he were dead, yet shall he live"** *(John 11:25). To know GIATI is to know that* **life never ends—only form changes.**

This understanding brings **peace in the face of death,** *because you no longer see it as loss—you see it as* **God continuing to express in new ways.**

Trusting in GIATI: The Key to Unshakable Peace

Isaiah 26:3 tells us that peace comes not just from keeping our minds on God, but from **trusting in Him.**

What does it mean to trust in GIATI? It means:

- *To* **rest in the knowing** *that all things are in divine order.*
- *To* **surrender the illusion of control,** *recognizing that* **it has always been God moving all things.**
- *To* let go of personal fears, desires, and attachments, *knowing that* what unfolds is exactly as it should be.

When you truly trust that **God is all there is,** *peace is no longer something you have to chase—it becomes the* **only reality you know.**

And that is the **perfect peace** *Isaiah speaks of—the peace that comes when you* **stop seeing yourself as separate** *and* **fully awaken to the truth of GIATI.**

This is the **eternal peace** *that cannot be shaken. This is the* **resting place of the awakened soul.**

GIATI: The Conqueror of Sin and Death

For centuries, humanity has struggled with the concepts of **sin and death,** *seeing them as unavoidable forces that bring suffering and separation from God. Religion has sought ways to* **atone for sin** *and* **escape death,** *offering laws, sacrifices, and rituals as a means of redemption. Yet, the ultimate truth of* **GIATI—God Is All There Is—reveals that sin and death have already been conquered.**

To understand how **GIATI** *overcomes sin and death, we must first expose what they truly are—not forces outside of God, but* **illusions of separation.**

—

What Is Sin?

Traditional religion defines sin as **breaking God's commandments***—a violation that brings punishment and requires atonement. However, the* **deeper reality** *is that sin is not merely a set of actions, but a* **state of mind***—the belief that you exist separately from God.*

- **Sin is seeing yourself as an independent being, rather than the very expression of God.**

- **Sin is thinking you are the doer, rather than knowing that all things are God acting through you.**
- **Sin is the illusion of "I"—believing there is a "you" apart from the One Spirit.**

The first sin was not an action, but a **thought**—*the moment Adam and Eve believed they were something other than God. The serpent's deception was simple:* **it introduced the idea of duality, of separation from the Source.** *That false belief caused them to experience fear, shame, and eventually, death.*

But if **sin is separation in the mind**, *then* **GIATI destroys sin by revealing the truth:**

There is no separation. There is only God.

Once you know this, sin loses all power. You no longer operate under the false belief of self, but in the **fullness of God expressing as you.**

- *You don't strive to keep laws—you* **are** *the righteousness of God because* **God is the only doer.**
- *You don't try to "avoid sin"—you recognize that* **sin is powerless against the truth of oneness.**
- *You don't fear judgment—you understand that* **only those who believe in separation stand condemned in their own minds.**

Sin is conquered the moment you awaken to the reality of GIATI.

—

What Is Death?

Like sin, death has been misunderstood. People see it as the **end of life,** *the ultimate punishment, the great unknown. But death is not what it appears to be.*

- *Death is not* **the end of existence**—*because* **God is life, and there is nothing outside of Him.**
- *Death is not* **separation from God**—*because* **there is no "where" to go that is not already within God.**
- *Death is not* **the final enemy**—*because* **it has already been conquered by truth.**

1 Corinthians 15:26 says, **"The last enemy that shall be destroyed is death."** *But how is death destroyed? By the revelation of* **GIATI.**

If **God is all there is,** *then death is nothing but* **a transition of form within the same eternal Spirit.** *The body dissolves,* **but life continues, uninterrupted.** *This is why Jesus could say:*

"I am the resurrection and the life: he that believeth in me, though he were dead, yet shall he live." (John 11:25)

Jesus wasn't speaking about a future event—he was revealing **the present truth** *that those who* **know their oneness with God** *can never truly die.*

- **Death only exists in the minds of those who believe in separation.**
- **When you know GIATI, you do not see death as an enemy but as an illusion that no longer holds power over you.**
- **You do not "die" because you were never separate from Life to begin with.**

The awakened never fear death—because they know they are eternal.

—

How GIATI Conquers Sin and Death

1. **GIATI Reveals There Is No Separation**
   - *Sin and death only exist in* **the illusion of duality.** *The moment you recognize that* **there is nothing but God,** *sin and death become powerless concepts that hold no truth.*

2. **GIATI Replaces Fear with Perfect Peace**
   - *Fear of sin, fear of death, fear of judgment*—**all of these dissolve in the light of knowing God as all.** *Isaiah 26:3 promises:*
     "Thou wilt keep him in perfect peace, whose mind is stayed on thee."

3. **GIATI Brings You Into the Awareness of Eternal Life**
   - *Eternal life is not a* **future reward**—*it is the* **present reality of those who know the truth.** *Jesus said:*
     "This is eternal life, that they might know thee, the only true God." (John 17:3)

4. **GIATI Fulfills the Law Completely**
   - *Instead of trying to keep laws* **as a separate being,** *you realize that* **it is God as you** who fulfills the law effortlessly.
   - **You don't live by rules—you live by divine nature.**

5. **GIATI Awakens You to Your True Identity**
   - *No longer lost, no longer blind, no longer trapped in sin-consciousness—you awaken to* **who you truly are: God expressing Himself in form.**

—

The Final Victory: Death Swallowed Up in Life

1 Corinthians 15:54-55 declares:

"Death is swallowed up in victory. O death, where is thy sting? O grave, where is thy victory?"

This is not just poetic language—it is the **eternal reality** *of those who have come to* **know GIATI.** *Death* **has no sting** *when you understand that you have never been separate from the eternal source of life.*

When Jesus resurrected, he was proving this truth—not that he alone had power over death, but that **death itself was never real to begin with.** *The world saw crucifixion and burial. Jesus saw transition and transformation.*

In the same way, **when you awaken to GIATI, sin and death lose all hold over you.**

- *You stop living in* **guilt and condemnation.**
- *You stop fearing* **punishment and judgment.**
- *You stop dreading* **death and the afterlife.**

Instead, you walk in the full awareness that **God is all there is,** *and* **you are one with Him eternally.**

—

The Call to Wake Up

Sin and death **only exist for those who remain asleep.** *But those who awaken to* **GIATI** *step into the* **truth that has always been:**

- **There is no sin—only the illusion of separation.**
- **There is no death—only eternal life manifesting in different forms.**
- **There is no fear—only peace, because there is nothing outside of God.**

The **only question** *left for the reader is this:*

Will you remain in the illusion of sin and death, or will you awaken to the undeniable truth of GIATI?

The time to wake up is now.

David and Goliath: Conquering Giants with the Truth of GIATI

The story of **David and Goliath** *is one of the most well-known and powerful accounts in the Bible. It's the tale of a young shepherd boy who, armed with nothing but a slingshot, defeats the mighty warrior Goliath—an event that resonates as a classic example of faith, courage, and divine intervention. On the surface, the story is one of overcoming seemingly insurmountable odds, but beneath that narrative lies a deeper spiritual truth that aligns perfectly with the revelation of* **GIATI: God Is All There Is.**

In this story, we see that David's victory over Goliath wasn't just about physical strength or skill—it was about **faith in the absolute presence and power of God.** *This story serves as a perfect illustration of how* **GIATI** *can empower you to conquer the giants in your own life.*

The Scene: The Battle Between Faith and Fear

In the story, the Israelites are facing the Philistines, and their champion, Goliath, is a towering giant. For 40 days, Goliath challenges the Israelite army, mocking them and their God, causing fear and despair among the soldiers. No one is willing to confront him. It is at this point that young David, a humble shepherd, enters the scene. He hears Goliath's taunts and is struck by the disrespect being shown to God.

David volunteers to fight the giant, though he is dismissed by others who see him as too young and inexperienced. His brothers even ridicule him. But David stands firm, declaring that **God's power is greater than any giant.** *He chooses to face Goliath with faith, trusting not in his own strength, but in the* **omnipotent power of God.**

David's Faith: Trusting in God's Omnipresence and Power

The key to David's victory over Goliath lies in his unwavering belief in **God's presence in all things.** *David does not see himself as the underdog or as an individual who has to rely on his own strength. Instead, he sees the situation through the lens of* **GIATI***—that* **God is all there is, and nothing can stand against Him.**

David's statement, **"The battle is the Lord's"** *(1 Samuel 17:47), reveals his deep understanding of divine unity. He recognizes that* **God is the source of all power***—not just for him, but for everyone and everything. This awareness of* **God's all-encompassing power** *shifts the focus away from the size of the giant and onto the power of the Divine.*

David's victory is not about defeating Goliath with mere physical strength—it's about aligning with **the truth of GIATI,** *where God's presence is the only true force in the world.* **The giants we face in life—be they physical, emotional, or spiritual—lose their power**

when we acknowledge that God is all there is. *In this light, Goliath was nothing more than an illusion of separation, a false belief in something greater than the Divine.*

David's Weapon: A Simple Slingshot, a Symbol of Divine Trust

*David's weapon of choice—***a simple slingshot and five smooth stones***—is a powerful metaphor for the tools that God provides to those who trust in His power. The* **slingshot** *represents* **divine simplicity and direct action,** *showing that we don't need complex solutions or worldly weapons to conquer the challenges in our lives.*

David's five smooth stones symbolize more than just preparation for battle—they represent the five major manifestations of God's Spirit on earth to confront the giant of separation. Each stone is smooth because it comes directly from the eternal river of Spirit, polished by the flow of divine truth. Adam was the first son, showing mankind its original oneness. Joshua (Oshia) revealed God's presence in conquest and inheritance. Jesus manifested the Word made flesh, embodying perfect sonship. Paul unveiled the mystery of Christ in us, the hope of glory. And now, GIATI—the Spirit of Truth—comes as the final stone, reminding us of our oneness and exposing separation as the great illusion.

Though five stones were carried, David only needed one to slay Goliath. Likewise, salvation only requires receiving the manifestation of truth in your time. For us, it is GIATI—the stone for today. Just as David's stone sank into the forehead of Goliath, the truth of GIATI strikes at the head of the lie—the illusion that we are separate from God—bringing it down once and for all.

In the same way, **GIATI** *teaches that the truth of God's omnipresence is the only tool needed to overcome any challenge.* **Faith** *is the slingshot, and* **trust in God's presence** *is the stone that, when aligned with His will, will always hit the mark. The simplicity of David's weapon suggests that divine victory doesn't come from human might, but from aligning with the infinite wisdom and strength of God.*

The Moment of Victory: The Fall of Goliath

As David takes aim with his slingshot, he declares that **God will deliver him** *into victory. He strikes Goliath in the forehead with a single stone, causing the giant to fall, and the victory is won. The Philistines flee in fear, and the Israelites are emboldened.*

This moment serves as a powerful spiritual truth: **when we place our faith in God, even the most formidable giants fall before us.** *Just as David trusted that* **God's presence is greater than any enemy,** *those who embrace the truth of* **GIATI** *can stand firm in the face of their own giants, knowing that nothing is greater than the Divine within them.*

David's victory is a **revelation of divine power***—the ultimate truth that when we realize that* **God is all there is,** *we are never alone, and no force in the universe can stand against us.*

The Symbolism of Goliath: The False Illusions of Separation

Goliath, the giant warrior, represents **the false beliefs that stand as obstacles between us and the truth of God's omnipresence.** *His size and strength symbolize the overwhelming power of ego and fear, the idea that external forces have control over us. But in the truth of* **GIATI,** *we know that these giants are illusions, built from a belief in separation from God.*

David's act of defeating Goliath signifies the **spiritual victory over ego, fear, and separation***—the victory of* **faith in the unity of God.** *The stone that hits Goliath is the stone of truth, the stone of* **understanding that God is all there is,** *and with that knowledge, any illusion of separation can be shattered.*

The Aftermath: Public Recognition of God's Power

After Goliath is defeated, David's courage and faith bring him public acclaim, and the Israelites celebrate their victory. But David's humility remains intact. He acknowledges that it wasn't his own strength or ability that brought about the victory, but God's power working through him.

This mirrors the truth of **GIATI:** *the recognition that all things are done through God, and that* **we are vessels through which God's power can express. There is no separate "me" or "you" who achieves victory;** *it is God alone who brings about all things. David's humility is a model for those who understand that* **God is all there is,** *and it is through Him that we live, move, and have our being.*

Conclusion: Overcoming Giants with the Power of GIATI

David's victory over Goliath is not just a story of a young boy defeating a giant; it is a profound lesson in **divine faith** *and the power of understanding* **God as all there is.** *When we face the giants in our lives—be they fear, doubt, illness, or any external challenge—we are not meant to fight them with our own strength. We are meant to align ourselves with the divine truth that* **God is all there is,** *and with this realization, the giants fall before us.*

David's story is a reminder that **faith in God's omnipresence and power** *is the true weapon we need to overcome any obstacle. When we face life with the understanding of* **GIATI,** *we can be certain that no giant is too great, no challenge too impossible. Through faith, courage, and the unwavering knowledge that* **God is all there is,** *we are empowered to triumph over every giant in our path.*

The Land of Goshen: Light in the Midst of Darkness - A Manifestation of GIATI

In the midst of the Ten Plagues, there is a profound moment where **darkness** *covers the land of Egypt, yet* **the land of Goshen,** *where the Israelites resided, remains bathed in light. This occurs during the* **ninth plague,** *when God brings upon Egypt a thick darkness that lasted for three days, so oppressive that the Egyptians could not see one another or move about. However, the* **land of Goshen** *was untouched by this darkness and remained illuminated. This moment not only marks a dramatic contrast between Egypt and Israel but also offers a powerful reflection of the* **divine presence** *and the truth of* **GIATI***—that* **God Is All There Is.**

The Significance of Goshen's Light

The land of Goshen, where the Israelites lived, was set apart from the rest of Egypt. It was a land of **protection, light,** *and* **life** *during a time when Egypt was experiencing plagues that reflected divine judgment. This contrast between Egypt's darkness and Goshen's light is more than just a physical phenomenon—it is a profound spiritual metaphor. The* **darkness** *that enveloped Egypt symbolizes* **spiritual blindness, ignorance,** *and* **disconnection from God's divine presence,** *while the* **light** *in Goshen represents* **awareness, spiritual enlightenment,** *and alignment with God's will.*

In the same way that the Israelites in Goshen were preserved from the darkness, the message of **GIATI** *emphasizes that those who are* **in tune with the truth of God's omnipresence***—those who recognize that* **God Is All There Is***—will live in the light of His presence. Goshen represents those who are aware of their divine nature, connected to the eternal truth of God. The rest of Egypt, in their rejection of God's truth, remains shrouded in darkness, unaware of the omnipresent God who governs all things.*

Spiritual Meaning: Light and Darkness as States of Consciousness

In the story, the land of Goshen's light is not just a physical condition but a **spiritual state.** *The Egyptians, who were immersed in the worship of idols and the belief in many gods, were unable to see the* **true God***—the* **one God** *who is the source of all creation. This spiritual blindness kept them in darkness. They were bound by ignorance of the reality that* **God Is All There Is***—that He is not just a distant deity, but the* **source** *and* **substance** *of all things.*

In contrast, the Israelites in Goshen, who were called by God, were aligned with His will, even if they didn't yet fully understand the divine truth as we do today through the lens of **GIATI. Goshen's light** *reflects a state of* **awareness***—a state where God's presence is recognized and embraced. The people living in Goshen were not simply "saved" because* *they were Israelites; rather, they were illuminated because they had been chosen to partake in the divine plan, a plan that points to the greater truth that God is in all things, and that through His presence, humanity can live in light, both spiritually and physically.*

GIATI: The Unveiling of God's Light

The **light** *in Goshen is an allegory for the* **awareness of God's all-encompassing presence** *that GIATI emphasizes. Just as the Israelites in Goshen were spared the darkness that overtook Egypt, those who embrace the truth of* **GIATI** *are* **illuminated** *by the recognition that* **God Is All There Is.** *When you recognize that the Spirit of God lives within you and that everything you see, touch, and experience is an expression of God's will, you begin to live in the* **light** *of that understanding. This light is not external but internal—it is the* **awareness** *of God's omnipresence, of His power working through all things.*

Just as the Israelites were preserved in Goshen by their alignment with God's will, those who align themselves with **GIATI** *are preserved in the light, freed from the darkness of ignorance. The darkness that overtook Egypt represents the* **spiritual blindness** *that keeps people separated from the truth of* **GIATI.** *It is only when humanity awakens to the truth of* **God Is All There Is** *that the blindness is removed and they step into the light of divine understanding.*

A Symbol of Spiritual Separation: The Consequence of Denying God's Omnipresence

The distinction between Egypt's darkness and Goshen's light also highlights the **separation** *between those who acknowledge the omnipresent God and those who do not. The darkness that covered Egypt symbolizes the* **spiritual state of those in opposition to God's truth**—*those who live in denial of God's presence and power. For the Egyptians, this darkness was a form of* **judgment**—*a result of their* **hard-heartedness** *and refusal to acknowledge the one true God. In the same way, those who resist the understanding of* **GIATI** *remain in spiritual darkness, unaware of the truth that God is the source of all life, all power, and all understanding.*

For the Israelites in Goshen, the light represents **spiritual understanding, alignment with divine truth,** *and* **freedom** *from the consequences of ignorance. The people in Goshen were physically separated from Egypt, but the* **light** *that shone upon them also represents their* **spiritual alignment** *with the divine will. They were able to see beyond the material world to the deeper reality of God's presence in all things.*

The Ultimate Truth: GIATI and the Light of Awareness

The story of **Goshen and Egypt's darkness** *is ultimately about the* **awakening** *to the truth of* **GIATI.** *It teaches us that* **God's presence is universal,** *and that all people have* *the potential to live in the light of divine truth by aligning their consciousness with the understanding that God is within them and all around them. When you acknowledge that* **God Is All There Is,** *you step into the light, just as the Israelites in Goshen were spared the darkness that plagued Egypt.*

Those who embrace **GIATI** *and recognize that God is in everything begin to see the world differently. The very essence of everything they encounter becomes a reflection of divine presence. This is the light that shines on those who are awakened to the* **truth of divine unity**—*the understanding that there is no separation between God and creation, that all is one, and that the truth of* **God Is All There Is** *illuminates everything.*

Conclusion: Walking in the Light of GIATI

Just as the land of Goshen was bathed in light while Egypt remained in darkness, so too are we called to walk in the light of **GIATI.** *Those who choose to live in alignment with the truth of* **God's omnipresence** *will experience a spiritual awakening that leads to freedom, understanding, and unity with all things. Like the Israelites in Goshen, we are set apart, but not in isolation; we are set apart in* **understanding** *and* **awareness,** *recognizing that the* **light** *of God is in all things and that* **God Is All There Is.**

In this way, the story of Goshen is not just about divine protection, but a deeper call to spiritual awakening—a call to live in the **light of truth,** *to recognize that the divine presence is in all things, and to embrace the transformative power of* **GIATI. The Cloud and the Fire: The Ever-Present Guidance of GIATI**

As the Israelites journeyed through the wilderness, they were led by a **cloud by day and a pillar of fire by night.** *This divine presence, recorded in* **Exodus 13:21-22,** *was their constant guide, ensuring they were never lost, never without direction, and never in darkness. The cloud was not just an external phenomenon—it was the* **manifestation of God within them,** *showing that* **He was always present, always leading, and always providing light, whether in the brightness of day or the depth of night.**

The Cloud: The Divine Presence in the Mind of Mankind

The **cloud by day** *represents the* **mind of mankind,** *the seat of thought and awareness. It is the* **divine intelligence** *that governs all things. Just as a cloud hovers above, our own consciousness is the elevated space where* **God is thinking, moving, and directing.** *This is why the Israelites could not move without the cloud—because the cloud was not just something external, but an* **expression of the omnipresent God leading them from within.**

When you understand **GIATI—God Is All There Is**—*you realize that the same guiding cloud is within you. The brain, the mind, the consciousness of man is God's dwelling place. The Israelites' journey was a reflection of the* **spiritual walk of every person,** *and their* *ability to follow the cloud was symbolic of being in alignment with the divine truth. As long as they* **recognized the presence of God within them,** *they were not lost.*

The Fire: The Light That Never Fails

At night, when natural light faded, the cloud transformed into a **pillar of fire,** *ensuring that darkness never overtook them. This is the reality of GIATI—***when you are aware of God's presence, you are never in darkness.** *Even in the night seasons of life, even in uncertainty, even in the wilderness, the fire remains.*

The fire represents **the Spirit of God within,** *the* **inner illumination** *that burns away ignorance and reveals truth. The fire is not something separate from the cloud—it is simply the* **cloud in another form,** *just as the divine presence in you can manifest as thought (the cloud) or as revelation and passion (the fire). This fire is the same fire that burned in the bush before Moses, the same fire that fell on Pentecost, the same fire that fuels the understanding of* **GIATI** *today.*

The Constant Presence: No Separation Between God and Man

The cloud and the fire **never left the Israelites.** *Day and night, they were covered, led, and illuminated. This is the very message of* **GIATI**—*that* **God is never separate from His creation.** *There was no moment in their journey when God abandoned them, because there was no place where God was not.*

The **cloud and fire** *are the* **same presence in different forms,** *just as God takes different forms throughout time but remains one. God was in the cloud, but He was also in them.* **God was not an outside force leading them, but the very presence within them making the journey possible.** *This is why those who know* **GIATI** *are never lost, never confused, and never in darkness—because they recognize that* **the source of all guidance is already within.**

Following the Cloud: Trusting the Divine Intelligence Within

The Israelites had to **follow** *the cloud. They could not move on their own terms; they moved* **when the cloud moved.** *This teaches a powerful truth:* **when you know GIATI, you do not move by your own will, but by the will of the divine presence within you.**

When the cloud rested, they rested. When the cloud moved, they moved. **This is the way of those who are awakened to GIATI.** *They do not make decisions based on fear, ego, or human reasoning alone, but they trust the* **divine intelligence that governs all things.** *The cloud represents divine* **order,** *showing that everything happens in perfect alignment with the will of God.*

Many people today wander in their own wilderness, struggling to find their way, making choices in darkness. But those who embrace the truth of **GIATI** *understand that the same guiding cloud is still present.* **The Spirit of God is the guide within**—*when you listen, trust, and follow, you are never lost.*

The Lesson of the Cloud and Fire: Living in Awareness of GIATI

The story of the cloud and fire reveals the **perfection of God's presence** *in all things. It is a direct confirmation of* **GIATI**—*that there is no separation between God and creation.* **The Israelites were only lost when they forgot who was leading them.** *Those who stayed in tune with the cloud walked in peace and confidence, knowing they were never alone.*

The same remains true today. When you know that **God Is All There Is,** *you no longer rely on external signs to confirm His presence—you recognize* **that the presence has always been within you.** *The cloud and fire were not just in the sky—they were the reflection of God in them.*

To those who still wander in darkness, unaware of the divine presence in all things, the message of GIATI is the fire that lights the way. It is the truth that clears the confusion, removes the fear, and brings people back into alignment with the understanding that **God never leaves, never ceases to guide, and never stops illuminating the path of those who know Him.**

The cloud and the fire were always present. *And when you know* **GIATI,** *so is the light.*

The Feeding of the Multitude: The Infinite Supply of GIATI

One of the most well-known miracles of Jesus is the feeding of the 5,000, recorded in **Matthew 14:13-21** *and* **John 6:1-14.** *In this story, a great crowd follows Jesus into the wilderness, hungry for both His words and physical nourishment. With only* **five loaves of bread and two fish,** *Jesus multiplies the food to feed thousands, with* **twelve baskets of leftovers remaining.** *This act is far more than a display of divine power—it is a revelation of the truth of* **GIATI: God Is All There Is.**

The Illusion of Lack vs. The Reality of Abundance

The disciples, seeing the large crowd and their limited resources, immediately focus on **what they do not have.** *They say to Jesus,* **"This is a remote place, and it's already late. Send the crowds away so they can go to the villages and buy themselves some food."** *(Matthew 14:15). This is the mindset of the world—the belief that* **there is never enough,** *that* **resources are limited,** *and that one must go elsewhere to be filled.*

But Jesus does not entertain the illusion of lack. He replies, **"They do not need to go away. You give them something to eat."** *(Matthew 14:16). This statement alone reveals the* **truth of GIATI**—*that the source of all things is already present, and there is no separation between God and supply.*

The disciples still do not understand. They respond, **"We have here only five loaves of bread and two fish."** *(Matthew 14:17). The word* **"only"** *exposes their limited thinking. They see lack, but Jesus sees* **the fullness of God in all things.**

Multiplication: The Awareness of Divine Supply

*Jesus does not beg for more food. He does not question where provision will come from. Instead, H***e takes what is already there, looks up to heaven, gives thanks, and begins to distribute it.** *And as He does, the food multiplies.*

This is the reality of **GIATI**—*when you recognize that* **God is all there is,** *you no longer operate from the illusion of scarcity. The moment Jesus* **gave thanks,** *He acknowledged the divine presence in what already existed, and that recognition* **revealed the abundance that was always there.**

This is not just a miracle of food—it is a **demonstration of divine law:**

- **What you see as "little" becomes more than enough when seen through the lens of divine truth.**

- **When you recognize the fullness of God in what is before you, you activate the infinite supply that is already present.**
- **Lack exists only in the mind that believes it is separate from God.**

The Five Loaves and Two Fish: Symbolism of Divine Nourishment

The numbers in this story are significant. **Five loaves** *and* **two fish** *add up to* **seven,** *which represents* **completion and divine perfection** *in biblical symbolism. This is a sign that* **what was given was already perfect and sufficient, despite appearances.**

- **The bread represents divine truth—God's word, the eternal sustenance of the Spirit.**
- **The fish represent life and spiritual consciousness—those who are awakened to divine reality.**

Jesus does not just feed the people physically; He **reveals the nature of true sustenance**—*that life is not dependent on external supply but on divine reality.* **God is all there is, and in Him, there is no lack.**

The Twelve Baskets Left Over: The Overflow of Divine Provision

After the crowd had eaten and was satisfied, the disciples gathered **twelve baskets of leftovers**—*one for each disciple. This demonstrates that* **when divine truth is fully embraced, there is always more than enough.** *It also signifies that the twelve disciples, representing the foundation of divine teaching, were to carry this truth forward—the truth that* **abundance is a reality when one is aligned with GIATI.**

The GIATI Perspective: Living in the Awareness of Divine Abundance

*The feeding of the 5,000 is not just about physical food—it is a l***esson on perception, faith, and the infinite nature of divine supply.** *When you understand* **GIATI,** *you no longer see lack because you know* **God is all there is.**

- **The world teaches you to see limitation, but divine reality reveals infinite abundance.**
- **When you focus on what you "lack," you remain bound to that perception. But when you give thanks and acknowledge the divine presence in all things, what is before you becomes more than enough.**
- **Jesus did not "create" more food—He revealed the abundance that was already there. The truth of GIATI removes the veil of scarcity and shows that all things are full and complete in God.**

This story is not just about what happened **then**—*it is about how one is to live* **now.** *When you stop looking at your circumstances through the lens of separation and start seeing* **God**

in all things, *you step into the reality that* **you are never without, because you are one with the infinite source of all.**

Manna from Heaven: The Daily Provision of GIATI

In the wilderness, after being freed from Egypt, the Israelites found themselves in a place of complete dependence on God for survival. They had no fields to harvest, no storehouses of grain, and no means of securing food by their own efforts. In this state of vulnerability, God provided for them by sending **manna from heaven**—*a divine sustenance that appeared each morning like dew upon the ground* **(Exodus 16:4-36).**

This miraculous bread was unlike anything they had ever known. It was given **daily,** *could not be hoarded, and would spoil if kept overnight—except on the Sabbath, when it remained fresh. This was not just about physical nourishment; it was a* **spiritual lesson about trusting in the ever-present provision of God.**

But deeper still, the story of manna reveals the truth of **GIATI: God Is All There Is**—*showing that divine life is not something one stores up but something that must be* **received and lived in every moment.**

Manna: The Living Bread, the Spirit of God in You

Jesus Himself later revealed the true meaning of manna when He said:

"I am the bread of life. Your ancestors ate the manna in the wilderness, yet they died. But here is the bread that comes down from heaven, which anyone may eat and not die." (John 6:48-50)

The manna the Israelites ate was a physical shadow of a spiritual truth—the **true bread** *that sustains is not physical food but* **the Spirit of God within.**

- **Manna was given daily** → *Just as* **God's presence and Spirit must be received daily.** *You cannot live off of yesterday's experience; you must be continually nourished by divine reality.*
- **Manna could not be hoarded** → *You cannot "store up" spiritual life as if it were a possession. GIATI shows that life is not about accumulating but about* **being in the flow of divine presence every moment.**
- **Manna would spoil if held overnight** → *This reveals that trying to hold onto past revelations without continuing to walk in truth leads to stagnation. The Spirit is* **ever- moving,** *and those who live in divine reality trust now, not in what was.*
- **On the Sabbath, manna remained fresh** → *The Sabbath represents* **divine rest, the awareness of oneness with God.** *When you are in the state of knowing*

that **God is all there is,** *you are no longer striving, and divine provision is fully realized.*

Trust in Divine Provision: No Separation Between You and Source

The Israelites struggled with the idea of trusting in something they could not see. Though manna rained down every morning, many feared that **it would not come the next day,** *so they tried to store it. This fear was rooted in the belief that* **God was separate from them,** *that provision was something external rather than an* **ever-present reality within.**

This is where GIATI transforms the understanding of this story. The truth is that **there is no separation between you and divine provision because God is all there is.** *The Israelites were learning to* **trust that they were never without,** *just as one must learn to trust in* **the Spirit within** *rather than relying on outward circumstances.*

When Jesus spoke of being **the true bread from heaven,** *He was revealing that* **divine life is not something external but something that is already within.** *Just as manna became part of the Israelites' bodies when they ate it, so too does the Spirit become one with you when you partake of divine truth.*

Living by Every Word of God: The Present Reality of GIATI

The lesson of manna is the lesson of **living in the now,** recognizing that **life is sustained not by external means but by the Spirit of God.** As Jesus declared:

"Man shall not live by bread alone, but by every word that proceedeth out of the mouth of God."(Matthew 4:4)

This shows that life is not about mere survival but about **living in the awareness of divine truth.** *GIATI teaches that* **when you recognize God as all there is, you cease to worry about "provision" because you know that all things are already present within divine reality.**

Manna was a temporary shadow pointing to an eternal truth—the reality that **true sustenance is not about what you consume but about the Spirit that animates your being.** *In the wilderness, they ate manna to sustain their bodies, but in divine truth,* **you partake of Spirit to sustain your eternal being.**

The GIATI Perspective: No Lack, Only Divine Fullness

The world teaches people to believe in lack, to fear for tomorrow, and to think that provision is something external. But the story of manna shows that **when you trust in divine presence, you will always be sustained.**

- **You do not need to "store up" spiritual life—it is always present now.**

- **You do not need to fear lack—God is all there is, and there is no separation between you and divine supply.**
- **True nourishment comes from the awareness of divine reality, not from the external world.**

The Israelites had to learn that **God was their source, not Egypt, not their own efforts, and not what they could see with their eyes.** *In the same way, GIATI reveals that* **you do not live by what the world calls "provision" but by the Spirit of God that is already within you.**

The lesson of manna is the lesson of **faith in divine presence.** *Those who recognize* **GIATI** *will never hunger, because they know they are already full.*

The Woman at the Well: The End of Spiritual Thirst

Jesus' encounter with the Samaritan woman at the well is a profound moment of revelation. It is more than a conversation; it is a breaking of barriers, a call to deeper understanding, and an invitation into **true, living water**—*the spiritual life that never runs dry. This well, where generations had come to draw water, represents mankind's endless search for fulfillment, for truth, for something external to sustain them. But Jesus revealed to the woman what GIATI proclaims to all:* **the source is not outside of you—it is within.**

The Well of Human Seeking

The woman came to the well at midday, alone. This was unusual, as women typically gathered water in the cooler hours of the morning. Her isolation suggests that she was an outcast, someone who did not fit within societal norms, carrying burdens of shame and rejection. Yet **Jesus sought her out.**

He asked her for a drink, but His request was not about physical water—it was an opening for revelation. She was surprised that a Jewish man would speak to her, a Samaritan, because the two groups did not associate. But Jesus had come to tear down false divisions. **He was showing her that the barriers between Jew and Samaritan, male and female, sinner and righteous, were illusions—God is all there is, and all belong to Him.**

The woman, thinking in the natural, focused on the well, the physical water, the external process of coming day after day to draw what would eventually run dry. But Jesus spoke of **a greater reality,** *saying:*

"Whoever drinks of this water will thirst again, but whoever drinks of the water that I shall give him will never thirst. But the water that I shall give him will become in him a fountain of water springing up into everlasting life." (John 4:13-14)

This is the essence of GIATI. The well represents human effort—trying to find meaning, salvation, and fulfillment through external means: religion, works, traditions. But Jesus was showing that true life is not something that must be sought **outside** *of oneself; it is already present* **within.**

The Five Husbands: Searching in the Wrong Places

When Jesus told the woman to bring her husband, she admitted that she had no husband. Jesus then revealed the truth: she had five husbands and was now with a man who was not her husband. This was not to shame her, but to awaken her.

The five husbands symbolize humanity's attempts to find identity and purpose through external means—attachments to people, systems, and things that do not satisfy. Just as she had gone from one relationship to another, many go from one belief to another, one pursuit to another, always seeking but never finding.

But Jesus was revealing to her the answer: **the living water is not something that can be given by another person. It is the Spirit of God within, and it is already hers.**

Worship in Spirit and Truth

As their conversation continued, the woman shifted to religious discussion, asking about the proper place to worship—should it be in Jerusalem, as the Jews claimed, or on the mountain, as the Samaritans believed?

Jesus answered:

"The hour is coming, and now is, when the true worshipers will worship the Father in spirit and truth; for the Father is seeking such to worship Him. God is Spirit, and those who worship Him must worship in spirit and truth." (John 4:23-24)

This is the heart of GIATI. Worship is not about location, ritual, or outward tradition. It is **about knowing who you are in God and living in the awareness of oneness with Him.** *It is not about seeking God in temples made by hands, but recognizing* **that God is all there is, and His presence is within you.**

The woman had spent her life searching—through relationships, through cultural identity, through religion—but **Jesus revealed that the answer was already within her.** *No longer did she need to go to a well; she had become the well. No longer did she need to search for living water; she* **was** *the fountain, as long as she drank from the Spirit of Truth.*

The Transformation: From Outcast to Messenger

The moment she realized this truth, everything changed. The woman who had been avoiding people ran back into the city to declare what had been revealed to her. She no longer carried the shame of her past; she **became a messenger of truth.**

"Come, see a Man who told me all things that I ever did. Could this be the Christ?" (John 4:29)

Her encounter with Jesus is what GIATI brings to the world. It is not about external validation, religious rules, or seeking fulfillment through things that will not last. It is about **awakening to the truth that God is all, and that Spirit is the only source of true life.**

The Spiritual Significance of GIATI

This story is a revelation of divine truth:

- **The well** *represents human efforts—religion, traditions, and external seeking.*
- **The living water** *represents the eternal Spirit within, which never runs dry.*
- **The five husbands** *symbolize misplaced attachments—things people look to for purpose but that ultimately fail them.*
- **Worship in spirit and truth** *means no longer searching outwardly, but realizing the fullness of God within.*

The Samaritan woman's journey is the journey of all who come into the awareness of GIATI. At first, we search outside of ourselves for fulfillment. We follow traditions, cling to beliefs, and attach ourselves to things that we think will give us life. But then comes the awakening—the moment when we recognize that **God is all there is, and that the living water has always been within us.**

When we drink of this water, we no longer thirst. We no longer seek from the outside what is already inside. And just as the woman at the well became a messenger, so too do all who come into the full awareness of GIATI—sharing with the world the truth that sets them free.

GIATI: The Descent of Love

Before time, before form, before the world was spoken into existence, God was. Not as something to be grasped with the mind, not as an image to be seen, but as the eternal, inscrutable, and indiscernible presence beyond all comprehension. A being not made up of parts but the totality of all that is—intelligence, wisdom, knowledge, beauty, love, justice, foundation, power, and strength. These are not separate from God; they are God. They are the essence of the eternal.

But there came a moment when humanity, veiled in flesh, was shrouded in ignorance. Carnality had become its condition, a false identity built upon separation—spirit believing itself to be apart from God, coexisting rather than being one with the source of its very life. This was the great deception, the blindness that needed healing. Salvation was required. A descent had to be made.

The Refusal of the Divine Attributes

The call was issued within the eternal—who would go down and bring humanity back to remembrance? Who would break through the illusion and reconcile them to the truth?

Intelligence *was the first to answer. But it recoiled. "I am too great to descend," Intelligence said. "I see all things, I perceive all things, but wisdom tells me they will not understand me. They will reject me, dismiss me, twist me into something that serves their own blindness. I will not go."*

Wisdom *stepped forward next but shook its head. "Even when I have spoken before, they have turned away. They call folly wisdom and wisdom folly. They seek answers, yet they do not want the truth. My presence among them will not bring them back. I will not go."*

Knowledge *considered the descent but refused. "They will not seek me for enlightenment, only for control. They will use me to justify themselves rather than to free themselves. They will say they know, but their hearts will remain blind. I will not go."*

Beauty *turned away. "They will distort me," Beauty said. "They will place their eyes on the form and forget the essence. They will desire the outward and ignore the inward. They will worship what is fleeting and miss what is eternal. I will not go."*

Justice *stood still. "If I descend, I must judge," Justice said. "And if I judge, they will be condemned. They will be found guilty of rejecting their own divine nature. They are not ready for me. I will not go."*

Foundation *was unmoved. "They do not build on me now," it said. "They have made their own foundation on the dust of the earth, on things that perish. If I come, they will not stand upon me. They will continue to build on what will crumble. I will not go."*

Power *and* **Strength** *remained silent for a long time before answering together. "If we descend, we will be misunderstood. They will seek to wield us for their own ends. They will think dominion is for their glory rather than for the lifting of the lowly. They will take us by force, rather than receiving us in humility. We will not go."*

One by one, the attributes of God declined. They knew humanity's state, knew that if they came, they would be rejected. Each could see the end before the beginning.

But then, a voice spoke.

The Descent of Love

"I will go."

The attributes turned to see who had spoken. It was **Love.**

"You have all spoken rightly," Love said. "If Intelligence goes, they will reject it. If Wisdom speaks, they will turn away. If Knowledge descends, they will corrupt it. If Beauty manifests, they will desire it for the wrong reasons. If Justice comes, they will be condemned. If Foundation stands before them, they will ignore it. If Power and Strength enter, they will seek to wield them instead of surrendering to them.

But I will go. Because they do not understand any of you without me. Without Love, Intelligence is arrogance. Wisdom is ignored. Knowledge is weaponized. Beauty is distorted. Justice is harsh. Foundation is overlooked. Power and Strength become oppression. But if I go, they will have a chance. A chance to see, to know, to remember who they truly are."

And so, Love descended.

And when Love came down, all the attributes followed. For they could not exist without Love, and Love could not exist apart from them. They became one in the manifestation of the Word—Love made flesh, the Holy Spirit in man. This was the Spirit in Jesus. This is the Spirit in GIATI. And this is the Spirit in you—only you have not recognized it yet.

Love Has Come Again

GIATI is Love come down once more—not to establish a religion, not to offer rituals, but to awaken the sleeping, to call humanity back to the truth of their being. This is not a new message; it is the eternal message. It is the same Spirit that was in Jesus, now poured out again for this generation.

This is the moment of decision.

What did humanity do when Love first came? They rejected it. They crucified it. They scorned and mocked it, all while claiming to desire truth. Love walked among them, yet they knew it not.

And now, Love stands before you again.

*You have heard. You have seen. You have felt the stirring of remembrance. But now comes the only question that matters—***will you accept or reject Love?**

This is not about accepting or rejecting a doctrine. This is about Love itself, God's very essence, standing at the door of your heart, knocking. This is about recognizing the Spirit that has always been within you, the same Spirit that was in Jesus, the same Spirit that is in GIATI, the same Spirit that is you at your core.

Will you open the door? Or will you turn away as generations before have done?

The decision is yours. But understand this: Love does not force itself upon anyone. It does not coerce. It only offers itself, waiting to be received.

So here you are. You have heard the call. You have been given the chance to see beyond the illusion.

Now, it is your turn.

Will you swipe left on God? Will you reject Love as those before you did?

Or will you swipe right, embrace the truth, and be reconciled to the eternal reality of who you are?

The choice is before you.

Love has come down again.

What will you do?

The Opposition of God: When the Lovers of God Reject Him

Love did not come to the world and find its greatest opposition among sinners, thieves, or outcasts. It was not the broken, the lost, or the despised who resisted Love when it walked among them. No, the greatest opposition to Love came from those who claimed to love God the most.

It was the religious.

It was those who praised, who fasted, who prayed in public, who adorned themselves with the symbols of faith. It was those who had dedicated their lives to their version of righteousness, to their understanding of God, to their traditions and doctrines. And yet, when Love manifested before them as Jesus, they rejected it. Not because they did not recognize the power in Him—but because they did.

The Rejection of Love by Those Who Claimed to Love God

Jesus did not come to destroy the Law; He came to fulfill it. Yet, rather than receiving the fulfillment, the religious clung to the shadows. Why? Because the truth He spoke unraveled their status, their power, their pride.

They did not seek God; they sought their position among men. They did not love the truth; they loved the benefits of ignorance. They did not desire the kingdom of God; they desired control over their own kingdoms.

They watched Him, followed Him, questioned Him—not to learn, but to trap Him. They did not marvel at His wisdom; they sought to silence it. They were not moved by His miracles; they were enraged by them. For every truth He spoke exposed the lie they had built their lives upon. And when the time came, it was not the lawless who condemned Him. It was the religious.

They crucified Love while claiming to love God.

They did not see that what they did to Him, they did to themselves. They did not see that in rejecting Love, they rejected the very God they claimed to serve. Their lips honored Him, but their hearts were far from Him.

History Repeats: The Rejection of GIATI

And so, the pattern repeats.

GIATI is Love come down once again. Not as an institution, not as a doctrine, not as another system for men to manipulate—but as the Spirit of Truth awakening those who have been called from the foundation of the world. GIATI does not seek to convince. It does not argue. It does not plead for acceptance. It comes only to awaken those who have ears to hear and eyes to see.

And just as before, it will be the religious who will rise in opposition. It will not be those the world calls sinners, for they have no illusion to protect. It will be those who wear the name of God on their lips but deny Him in their hearts.

They will resist because the truth of GIATI does not serve their status. They will reject it because it does not feed their ego. They will oppose it because it calls them out of the darkness of their ignorance into the light of divine oneness. And for those who have built their lives upon the illusion of separation, the light is terrifying.

They will do as they have always done. They will claim to love God while resisting Him. They will praise His name while rejecting His Spirit. They will hold to their traditions and cast out the truth.

But let it be known: GIATI is not here to debate. It is not here to argue with those who refuse to see. It is not here to change minds hardened by the carnal world. GIATI has come only for those who have been chosen to awaken. Those who are called will hear, and they will return to the eternal love, peace, and glory of God.

The choice stands before all:
To remain in the blindness of religion or to step into the light of divine reality.

To hold to a false image of God or to embrace the living truth of Love.

To crucify Love again or to finally receive it.

As it was then, so it is now. The question is: **Which side will you be on?**

Tormented by the Truth: The Exposure of the High and Mighty

"And, behold, they cried out, saying, What have we to do with thee, Jesus, thou Son of God? Art thou come hither to torment us before the time?" — Matthew 8:29

The cry of the demons when confronted by Jesus was not one of power, but of fear. They recognized Him. They knew His authority. They understood what His presence meant. But above all, they resented that He had come **before the time***—before they were ready, before they had exhausted their reign of deception, before they had decided it was time for truth to be revealed.*

What was torment to them? It was not a sword, not fire, not wrath. It was simply **the presence of truth.** *For truth exposes what is false, and those who rule through lies cannot bear its light.*

Now, the same cycle repeats.

GIATI: The Truth That Torments

GIATI has come, and those who claim to know God are once again crying out, "What have we to do with thee?" They speak of salvation, but they do not want it when it arrives in a way that challenges them. They praise Jesus from a distance, but when confronted with the fullness of truth, they recoil. They want God as a figure in history, a name to invoke, a doctrine to discuss—but they do not want to face the reality of His presence **within them.**

This is why GIATI is torment to them.

Because GIATI does not allow them to remain in comfortable illusions. GIATI does not permit them to keep their religious pride while denying their spiritual blindness. GIATI strips away the false coverings of those who claim to serve God but live in separation from Him in their minds.

The same spirit that opposed Jesus opposes GIATI now.

For they are comfortable speaking about Jesus in a way that makes **them** *the righteous ones and everyone else the lost. But when the light turns to* **them,** *when the same truth they preached to others is applied to their own condition, they react as the demons did: "Have you come to torment us before the time?"*

The Cycle of God: The Truth Comes Again

God moves in cycles. He is a circle without beginning or end, repeating Himself in different forms throughout eternity. And now, the truth of salvation has come around again— not as a distant promise, not as a hope for the afterlife, but as an immediate call to awaken.

*Yet those who once called others to repent now find themselves in the same position as the religious leaders of old—***faced with the truth and resisting it.**

They preached salvation, but when the fullness of it arrives, they reject it.
They called for repentance, but when light is shined on them, they hide.
They condemned sinners, but now they stand exposed in their own darkness.

This is their torment—not that GIATI seeks to harm them, but that the truth they ran from has caught up with them. The same Jesus they preached about has now come to them **through the Spirit of GIATI,** *but instead of rejoicing, they are disturbed.*

Because they wanted **time.**
Time to continue their traditions.
Time to keep their positions of power.
Time to rule over others while refusing to rule over their own minds.

But there is **no more time.**

No More Time: The Exposure of Those Who Delayed the Truth

They thought they had time. Time to manipulate, time to control, time to delay facing the reality of who God truly is. But the truth does not wait for the readiness of man. It moves according to divine order, and when it arrives, it does not ask permission. It simply **is.**

Those who rejected Jesus did not do so because they were ignorant of scripture. They knew the Law, they studied the prophets, they built their identities on the claim that they were God's chosen. Yet, when the One they claimed to serve stood before them, they refused Him. Why? Because the **true presence of God** *disrupts everything false, and they had built their lives upon the false.*

Now the same ones who have spent generations declaring the name of Jesus, warning others to prepare for His coming, have become as those they once judged. They are unprepared. They are unwilling. They are exposed. They would rather hold on to their illusion of holiness than embrace the fullness of what holiness actually is.

A Confrontation They Cannot Escape

GIATI is not here to debate or convince. It is simply the truth made manifest again in this cycle of God's eternal movement. And to those who resist it, the presence of truth **feels like torment.**

It is torment because it forces them to confront their own hypocrisy.
It is torment because it dismantles the walls they built to separate themselves from others.
It is torment because it proves that their version of God was small, limited, and confined to their understanding.

They called others blind while refusing to see. They pointed at the lost while wandering in darkness themselves. And now, when the light has come to them, they respond just as the religious leaders did in the days of Jesus—with resistance, with fear, with rage.

But here is what they fail to understand:

Rejecting GIATI does not delay what has already been set in motion. Ignoring truth does not erase it. God is here **now,** *moving as He always has, calling forth those who have ears to hear and eyes to see. And those who refuse? They will not stop the cycle of God. They will only be left outside of it.*

A Choice That Cannot Be Avoided

There is no middle ground. Either one awakens to the truth of God **within** *or continues to live in the illusion of separation. Either one steps into the eternal reality of oneness or remains trapped in the temporary shadows of religion.*

The high and mighty, the ones who built their power on the ignorance of others, now stand before the same truth they once wielded against the weak. They must choose:

Do they humble themselves and accept the fullness of what they claimed to believe?
Or do they resist, fight, and crucify love once again?

The cycle has returned. The time is now. **And no one can escape the choice.**

The Ultimate Purpose: Awakening or Separation?

The question stands: **Is the goal to help humanity see their path to eternal existence in God, or to seal their eternal separation from Him?**

The answer is not a matter of condemnation but of revelation. GIATI was tasked from the foundation of the world to expose the illusion and unveil the truth. Not to persuade, not to beg, but simply to **reveal.** *The light does not force itself upon the blind—it shines, and those who are ready will see.*

For too long, humanity has believed in separation. The mind has been conditioned to see itself as distinct from God, as if existence could be apart from the Source of all. But what is there outside of God? Nothing. There is no material apart from Spirit. No force outside of God's being. No second power to oppose Him. The illusion has been the belief in duality, in a God who exists somewhere else, in a humanity that is something other than God expressed.

The Unveiling of Divine Reality

GIATI is here now, not as an invitation to argue, but as a declaration of **what has always been.** *This book is not written to make an offer—it is written to make a reality known. The only question is:* **Who will recognize it?**

God has no desire to cast anyone out, but the reality of oneness cannot be forced upon those who refuse to see it. The separation is not **from** *God but in the mind of those who choose blindness over sight. They are not cast away by an angry deity—they remain in darkness because they cling to it.*

The mind that rejects GIATI rejects the truth of its own being. It does not simply deny a message—it denies **itself.** *And that is the torment. Not that God withholds life, but that the mind refuses to awaken to what life truly is.*

No Middle Ground

This moment, this revelation, this unveiling of divine truth is not for later. It is **now.** *The cycle of God has returned, and those who were chosen from the beginning of time are hearing the call. There is no middle ground, no waiting period, no future moment to decide. The time has come for all to recognize that* **God is all there is***—that Spirit is the only reality, and the illusion of separation must end.*

The light has shined. The truth has been revealed. And now, the only question that remains is:

Will you recognize who you are, or will you remain in the illusion?

The Gift

If grace is a gift, then by definition, it cannot be earned. It is not the result of striving, religious obedience, or moral performance. It is not something you unlock by good behavior or long prayers or public displays of repentance. The moment you attach effort to grace, you've made it a wage—and a wage is not a gift. Scripture makes this crystal clear: "For it is by grace you have been saved, through faith—and this is not from yourselves, it is the gift of God—not by works, so that no one can boast"(Ephesians 2:8–9).

We've been conditioned to chase God as though He's distant, performing works in hopes of proving ourselves worthy: keeping laws, attending church, fasting, tithing, avoiding certain sins, and doing our best to "live right." But the real truth is far more radical—and far more freeing. **Grace is not something given to you after you get it right. It is the realization that you were already right with God because God never left you.** *The gift has always been yours. Not because you did anything to deserve it, but because you were born of Spirit. Born of God. What the world calls grace, GIATI reveals as the Spirit of God already within you.*

The real gift was never a blessing, a reward, or a promise waiting to be claimed. The gift is the **Holy Spirit***—not a visitor from heaven, but the very essence of God living inside of you. It is not something you received on a certain day, at a certain altar, in a certain moment of emotional surrender. The truth is,* **you didn't receive the gift at a specific time—you woke up to it.** *You became aware of what had always been true.* **You and God have never been separate. You were never waiting for Him to arrive. You were waiting to remember.**

GIATI—God Is All There Is—is the only message that makes this known. The only revelation that finally brings an end to the illusion of separation. GIATI is not just a brand or a phrase; it is the unveiling of the mystery that was hidden for generations: Christ in you, the hope of glory (Colossians 1:27). This revelation is not a surface-level teaching—it is the pinnacle of everything that has ever been revealed. **The ultimate truth. The mystery that even religion could not uncover. The gift that no tradition could explain.**

The church taught that the Spirit comes when invited. GIATI reveals that the Spirit never left. The world taught that salvation comes after a series of steps. GIATI declares that **salvation is the recognition of union that's always been.** *While doctrines and denominations argued over what to do, GIATI came to declare who you are.* **You are the temple. You are the dwelling place. You are not waiting for the Spirit—you are the place where the Spirit already is.**

*If grace is a gift, then it cannot be earned. Not through striving. Not through self- righteous behavior. Not through religious performance or external rituals. A gift, by its very nature, is freely given—***unearned, undeserved, and already yours.**

This changes everything. If salvation is union with God, and grace is the gift that delivers that union, then **the gift is the revelation that you and God have never been separate. You and God have always been One.**

This is what makes the gift so powerful. It's not a transaction. It's a transformation— **of awareness.** *You don't work for it, qualify for it, or climb up to it. You simply awaken to it. And that awakening is not your doing—it's the mercy of God, revealing God within you. The gift is not external, and it's not delayed. It is present. Now. Alive. GIATI makes it known that what you've been calling "God out there" has always been* **God in you.** *You've been carrying the gift the whole time. Even in your rebellion. Even in your confusion. Even in the far country of forgetting. The gift never left. You did. But not in spirit—in consciousness.*

The works that were once done to earn salvation are now empty. Because you are no longer trying to qualify for what has already been given. You're no longer reaching for something you already are. You are not a servant trying to earn a place in the house. **You are the house.**

"The law was given through Moses; grace and truth came through Jesus Christ." *(John 1:17)*

This is why Jesus could say, **"It is finished."**
Because He ended the illusion of separation.
He ended the works-based mindset. He ended the striving and brought us back to the truth:
God is all there is. And He is within you.

The law gave you a ladder. Grace removed the ladder and said, "Be still. I am already here." The law said, "Do this and live." GIATI says, "Live—and you will know I am already in you." The law demanded works. Grace gives witness. And GIATI is that witness. **The voice of Spirit within you crying out, "I am."**

The Holy Spirit—the gift—is not something you wait for. It is who you truly are when you let go of who you thought you had to be.

There is nothing to earn. There is only everything to remember. You are not working your way into salvation. You are waking up to the fact that **salvation has always been inside you.** *Because* **God has always been inside you.**

*This is the grace that sets you free. But here's where it gets even more radical—***the gift was given before you even asked for it.** *Before you prayed the right prayer. Before you "gave your life to Christ." Before you even knew what salvation was.*

The Holy Spirit was already in you, waiting to be known.

This is why GIATI isn't just another message in the crowd. It is the **one message** *that dares to say: There is only One. Only One God. Only One Spirit. Only One truth. And that truth is already within you. The world could never have found this truth, because the world looks* *outward. GIATI turns your gaze inward. And there—beneath every label, every failure, every fear—you find the eternal presence of God. Not waiting to be given, but waiting to be seen.*

"If righteousness could be gained through the law, Christ died for nothing." *(Galatians 2:21)*

Let that sink in. If you could work your way into life... If you could obey your way into salvation...
Then the cross was pointless.

But it wasn't. Because it didn't just deal with sin—it exposed the lie of separation. It tore the veil from the inside out, revealing what was always there: **God in you.**

These are not soft words. This is not poetic language. This is a sword cutting straight through every religious system, every works-based gospel, every lie that says "do more to be accepted." Paul makes it plain: if anything you do could make you right with God—if obedience, moral performance, rule-keeping, or law-following could justify you—then Christ's death was unnecessary. **It was in vain. A wasted sacrifice.**

Let that truth hit: **Either righteousness comes by union with the Spirit within, or it doesn't come at all.** *If it could come by works, then grace is canceled. The cross is reduced to a gesture. And salvation is no longer a gift—it's a contract. And contracts can be broken. But gifts?* **Gifts are rooted in love, not merit.** *They're given because of who the giver is, not because of what the receiver has done.*

Paul doesn't stop there. He makes it even clearer in Romans 11:6:

"And if by grace, then it cannot be based on works; if it were, grace would no longer be grace." *(Romans 11:6)*

*This is the clearest line in the sand you'll ever find between grace and law, between Spirit and effort. If something is of grace—***unearned, unmerited, freely given***—then* **there can be no room for works.** *Because the moment you add works to the equation, grace ceases to be what it is. You have now mixed clean water with dirt. You have tried to earn what could only be revealed. And when you do that, you no longer have grace—you have performance-based identity dressed up in spiritual language.*

GIATI dismantles this deception completely.

GIATI says: There was never a separation to fix. There was never a gap to close. The only thing keeping you from righteousness was the belief that you had to work for it.

The prodigal son didn't become a son again when he came home. He was **always** *a son. He just forgot who he was. The gift wasn't waiting at the gate.* **The gift was identity— unchanged by distance.**

This is why the Gospel is not a call to climb higher— It's an invitation to come home. Home to your Spirit. Home to the truth. Home to God, **who never left**—*because He's never been outside of you.*

The only thing that ever separated you from this gift was your mind. A veil of belief. A lie that said you were far when you were always near. That's why Jesus didn't say, "Go get the gift." He said:

"The kingdom of God is within you." *(Luke 17:21)*

GIATI is not introducing a new idea—it is **uncovering the original truth** *that was buried under centuries of religion and law. Th***at God is not giving righteousness like a paycheck. He is awakening it within you as your true nature.** *Not something you become—***something you already are in Him.** *The law could only expose your ignorance. But grace reveals your identity.*

You do not become righteous through effort.

You become aware of righteousness through **Spirit.** *And the Spirit is the gift. And the gift is already yours.*

This is why grace and works cannot co-exist. Because one says, "You must qualify," and the other says "You already are." One says, "Try harder," and the other says "Wake up." One demands that you reach up, while the other reminds you that **He already reached in.**

GIATI brings this truth into perfect clarity. Not just as a doctrine, but as a revelation of your being. **You are not being measured. You are being remembered.** *You are not trying to attain righteousness.* **You are discovering the truth that you and righteousness have never been apart.**

Christ did not die so you could become something you weren't. **He died to end the lie of separation.** *He died to reveal the union that always was. He died to silence every voice that told you that you were unworthy of what God had already placed within you.*

GIATI exposes the root of grace—it was never a transaction. It was always a truth.
And now that truth lives in you.

And now, all that's left to do... is receive what was already yours. Not by performance. But by **presence.**

By letting the voice of Spirit rise in you and say:
"I AM."

That is the gift. That is grace. That is salvation.
And that is **GIATI.**

The Spirit, Not the Law — The Revelation of GIATI

The Gift Was Given Apart From the Law

The moment Peter witnessed the Holy Spirit fall upon the Gentiles, everything changed. These were people who had no knowledge of the Law of Moses, no heritage in Israel, no circumcision, no temple, and no Torah. Yet while Peter was still speaking, **they received the Holy Spirit.**

"While Peter yet spake these words, the Holy Ghost fell on all them which heard the word... because that on the Gentiles also was poured out the gift of the Holy Ghost." —Acts 10:44- 45

This is the evidence that salvation is not the result of keeping commandments. It's not earned by behavior, performance, or religious effort. **It's received by grace,** *through faith— and faith is simply the ability to* **receive the Spirit of God as your life.** *It is divine union, not moral achievement.*

The Holy Spirit was given **freely,** *not after obedience to the law, but in response to receptivity— to hearts open to truth. This means that* **God Himself made no distinction,** *and neither should we. The Spirit is not earned. The Spirit is the gift—and that gift is God giving* **Himself.**

The Law Was a Tutor—Not the Life

"Wherefore the law was our schoolmaster to bring us unto Christ, that we might be justified by faith." — Galatians 3:24

The law had a purpose—but that purpose was **not** *to make people righteous. It was to* **reveal the impossibility** *of righteousness apart from God. The law exposed the illusion that man could live independently from God and still be whole.*

Its real function? **To point to the one who is life itself.** *The law was a signpost;* **Christ is the destination.** *And when you arrive at Him, the sign is no longer needed. Not because righteousness doesn't matter, but because now—***righteousness lives in you.**

The Spirit Is the Fulfillment

*The Holy Spirit is not an accessory to your faith—***He is your faith, your righteousness, your life.** *When the Spirit dwells in you, you are not striving to be like God;* **you are living as the very expression of God.**

This is what the law could never do. It could inform, but it couldn't transform. The Spirit, on the other hand, **replaces your mind with His mind,** *your ways with His way, your identity with His identity. This is not behavior modification. It is* **identity restoration.**

"Christ in you... the hope of glory." — Colossians 1:27

The Spirit in you **is the law fulfilled,** *not by your doing, but by your being. The Spirit does not help you "keep the law."* **The Spirit is the law of life.**

GIATI: The Revelation of Eternal Identity

"And we know that we are of God, and the whole world lieth in wickedness."
— 1 John 5:19

The world lies in wickedness not because of evil acts alone, but because of a false **identity**—*the belief that man is separate from God. This is the root of sin: not murder, not theft, not lies—but* **the illusion of separation.** *To be "of the world" is to live by the false idea that you are your own source, your own power, your own life.*

But those who are **of God**—*those who carry His Spirit*—**know.** *They've received the* **understanding** *that Jesus came to give:*

"And we know that the Son of God is come, and hath given us an understanding, that we may know him that is true... This is the true God, and eternal life." — 1 John 5:20

This is the mission of **GIATI:** *to declare the* **oneness of all with God,** *to reveal that* **you were never apart,** *that* **God is not far,** *and that* **you are not other.**

You are **of His substance,** *His breath, His being.*

The Work of GIATI: Awakening the World to Spirit-Truth

GIATI is not a movement of religion. It is a movement of **revelation.** *The goal is not to bring people under rules, but to bring them into* **identity.** *The message is not: "Try harder to be holy." It is:* **"Be still, and know: I AM."**

The Holy Spirit in you is **God living as you.** *That is salvation. That is righteousness. That is eternal life.*

This is the truth the world has waited to hear—not another law to keep, but the Spirit that keeps you. Not a list of commandments to obey, but the life of God expressing itself through you.

God Is All There Is. *And when that truth awakens in the heart,* **eternity begins now.**

The Spirit Is Salvation — Not the Law

1. The Gift Came Without the Law

Scripture:

"While Peter yet spake these words, the Holy Ghost fell on all them which heard the word..."
—Acts 10:44

The Holy Spirit interrupted Peter's sermon.
He didn't wait for an altar call.
He didn't wait for a baptism.
He didn't wait for the Gentiles to learn the Law or memorize the Ten Commandments.
He came **because hearts were open.**

This is the Gospel. The Holy Spirit—the very Spirit of God—is **not given based on knowledge, works, or tradition,** *but by simple* **faith.** *Faith is not religious performance. Faith is the invisible recognition of truth. And truth is a Person:* **God Himself.**

This shows us something massive:
God never needed the Law to give Himself.

*It was only our minds that needed the Law—***to show us we couldn't do it without Him.**

2. **God Makes No Distinction**

   Scripture:

"Of a truth I perceive that God is no respecter of persons. But in every nation, he that fears Him and works righteousness is accepted with Him." —Acts 10:34-35

This was Peter's awakening moment. His whole life, he was taught that salvation was for Jews only. He believed the Law made someone holy. But here, before his eyes, Gentiles— outsiders—were filled with the Holy Spirit, proving that **God saw no difference.**

This is not about ethnicity.
This is not about performance.
This is not about religious status.

This is about **Spirit.** *And* **the Spirit recognizes Himself wherever He is received.**

GIATI means **there is no other.**
There's not "Jew and Gentile," "clean and unclean," "worthy and unworthy."
There is only **God—and God received, or God rejected.**

3. **The Law Was Only a Shadow**

   Scripture:

"Wherefore the law was our schoolmaster to bring us unto Christ, that we might be justified by faith." — Galatians 3:24

The law was **a teacher,** *but it was never* **the life.**

It was never meant to save you—only to expose you.

It was never meant to be your identity—only to drive you to your real one.

The Law is like scaffolding: it may serve a purpose for a time, but once the building is finished, **the scaffolding comes down.**

That building? **Christ in you.**
The law brings you to Him, but only **the Spirit can live through you.**

4. **The Spirit Is the Law Fulfilled**

Scripture:

"I will put my laws in their hearts, and I will write them in their minds…"
— Hebrews 10:16

Under the old covenant, the law was **external***—written on stone.*
Under the new covenant, the law becomes **internal***—written in you. Not by ink. Not by command. But by* **Spirit.**

And this is the key:

The Spirit doesn't help you try to keep the law. The Spirit becomes your way of being.

Righteousness is no longer a goal.
It is a nature.
It is God living as you.

You're not working to fulfill a rule.
You're **expressing the one who wrote it.**

This is the work of GIATI: not to teach people how to behave better—but to reveal to them **who they are** *when God is their life.*

5. **Sin is Separation—Salvation is Union**

Scripture:

"We know that we are of God, and the whole world lies in wickedness." — 1 John 5:19

The world's wickedness is not just in outward actions. It lies in the **inner belief** *that we are* **separate** *from God.*

This is the root of all evil:
The thought that "I am me, and God is someone else."

That "I must reach Him, earn Him, work my way to Him."
But **God never left.**

Sin is not what you do. Sin is who you think you are apart from Him.

The Law could tell you what sin looks like, but it couldn't **remove** *that separation. Only the Spirit can do that. Only the Spirit can make you* **one again.**

6. Eternal Life Is Not a Reward—It Is a Person

Scripture:

"And we know that the Son of God is come, and has given us an understanding… This is the true God, and eternal life." — 1 John 5:20

Jesus didn't come just to forgive sins. He came to **give understanding***—to open our eyes to the truth that* **we are in Him, and He is in us.**

This is what eternal life is:
Not living forever in heaven.
But having God as your very life now.

Eternal life is **Spirit-union,** *not time extension.*
It's the revelation that **you are of God,** *and God is all there is.*

7. GIATI Reveals the One True Reality

The message of GIATI is this:

- *That* **God is the only source, only substance, only Spirit.**
- That all things came from Him, exist in Him, and express Him.
- That sin is the illusion of separation—but salvation is the awakening to union.

GIATI is not a brand.
GIATI is not a religion.
GIATI is the truth.

And the truth is this:
Christ in you is the true God and eternal life.
There is no salvation apart from this realization.

There is no righteousness without this union.
There is no life outside of the Spirit.

8. The Law Brings Death—The Spirit Gives Life

Scripture:

"For the letter kills, but the Spirit gives life." — 2 Corinthians 3:6

The Law, even though holy, **kills** *when separated from the Spirit. Why? Because the law depends on* **you***—your effort, your ability. But the Spirit depends on* **God in you,** *being Himself through you.*

What kills is not God, but the misunderstanding of God.
What kills is trying to become what you already are.

The letter *exposes your flaws.*
The Spirit *expresses your freedom.*

So here's the distinction:

- The law points out what's wrong with you.
- The Spirit points out what's right in God—and then says, "That's you now.

9. The Law Is for the Old Man—The Spirit Is for the New Creation

Under the law, man is treated as separate, as someone who needs to earn closeness with God.

But in Christ, the old man is dead. That entire version of you—the version trying to be righteous through effort—is gone. **A new creation has come.**

"If any man be in Christ, he is a new creation..." — 2 Corinthians 5:17

A new creation **doesn't go back to the law.**
Why would you give a resurrected man the rules meant to govern the dead?

That's the shift:

- *The law was written for the* **man of dust,** *Adam's race.*
- *The Spirit is the life of the* **new man,** *made in Christ.*

The law is not for the one born of God.
The Spirit is **the law written in your being.**

10. The Spirit Is the Sabbath Rest

Here's a layer that deepens an earlier point about the Sabbath:

The Sabbath is not a Saturday. It's not a day on a calendar.
The Sabbath is **a Person—Christ***—and to be in Him is to be in the* **rest of God.**

"There remains a rest for the people of God... He who has entered His rest has ceased from his own works..." — Hebrews 4:9-10

The law says: **Do.**

The Spirit says: **Done.**

Keeping the Sabbath isn't resting one day a week. It's **abiding in the eternal now,** *where God is all there is, and your works have ceased because* **His work is complete.**

This is why the Holy Spirit in you is the Sabbath:
You are no longer laboring to be righteous.
You are resting in the righteousness **you've become.**

11. The Glory of the Law Faded—But the Spirit's Glory Remains

Scripture:

"If what was fading away came with glory, how much greater is the glory of that which lasts!" — 2 Corinthians 3:11

The law had glory—but it faded. Moses had to veil his face, because the glory was **temporary,** *and it belonged to a covenant that could never perfect the heart.*

But the Spirit—the indwelling presence of God—is **ever-increasing glory.**

Why? Because it's not external.
It's not fading.
It's **God becoming visible through you,** *day by day.*

You're not reflecting the law.
You're revealing **the face of God.**

12. The Spirit Is the Seed of Sonship

"As many as are led by the Spirit of God, these are the sons of God." — Romans 8:14

You're not a servant under law.
You're a **son** *under grace.*
The Spirit doesn't just tell you what's right—He tells you **who you are.**

He cries out in you, "Abba, Father."

And here's the truth GIATI proclaims:

You don't grow into sonship—you awaken into it. *Because the Spirit in you is not working to become—it* **already is.**

The Holy Spirit is the **DNA of God.** *If He's in you, then* **you're of God***—same nature, same Spirit, same life.*

13. GIATI Is the Voice of the Spirit in This Generation

Everything the law tried to teach is summed up in the presence of the Holy Spirit. And the voice of GIATI is the Spirit saying again:

"You are of God, little children... and greater is He that is in you..."

The world needs more than sermons.
It needs truth that awakens identity.
Not rules, but revelation.
Not religion, but **realization.**

GIATI is the end of separation thinking.
It is the voice of the Spirit crying out, "Return to yourself—because your Self is God expressed as you."

14. The Law Was a Mirror—But the Spirit Is the Image

The law could show you something—but it could never **make you** *something. It exposed your flaws, reflected your sin, magnified your distance—but it had no power to fix it.*

"Beholding as in a glass the glory of the Lord, we are transformed into the same image..." — 2 Corinthians 3:18

The Holy Spirit doesn't just show you what you should be—He **transforms you into the image of God.** *That image is not something outside of you—it's what you were* **always meant to awaken to.**

The law reflects man's need.
*The Spirit reveals man's nature—***God's nature.**

15. Salvation Is Not Forgiveness—It's Full Union

Many have confused being forgiven with being saved. But forgiveness alone is not salvation. It's a **step**—*but not the* **substance.**

Salvation is not God saying, "I forgive you for what you did."
Salvation is God saying, **"I give you Myself as your very life."**

The Spirit is not a second chance to try again.
The Spirit is **a new creation that doesn't have to try**—*because it is the righteousness of God.*

This is what GIATI unveils:
Salvation isn't escaping hell or earning heaven.
It's being made **one** *with the I AM.*

16. Christ Is the End of the Law—Because He Is the Life

Scripture:

"Christ is the end of the law for righteousness to everyone who believes." — Romans 10:4

Christ didn't destroy the law. He **fulfilled** *it. Why? Because righteousness is not about doing—it's about* **being.**

You don't become righteous by keeping the commandments.
You are righteous **because Christ lives in you.** *And when He lives in you, He fulfills every divine demand by simply being Himself* **as you.**

The law ends when **life begins.**
And the life is **the Spirit of Christ**—*God in you, expressing Himself.*

17. The Spirit Is the Circumcision of the Heart

Under the law, identity came through **flesh**—*like circumcision, tribe, or birthline. But under the Spirit, identity is marked internally.*

"He is a Jew which is one inwardly; and circumcision is that of the heart, in the Spirit..." — Romans 2:29

You don't need a physical mark—you need a spiritual birth.
You don't need external proof—you need **internal possession.**

The Spirit is the sign.
The Spirit is the covenant.
The Spirit is the seal.

And where the Spirit is, there's no longer "Jew or Gentile"—only **God's offspring** *walking in power and truth.*

18. The Spirit Is How You Know God—Not the Scriptures Alone

The Pharisees studied scripture but missed the life standing in front of them. Jesus said:

"You search the scriptures... but you won't come to Me, that you might have life." — John 5:39-40

Scripture is **a witness** *to the truth.*
But the Spirit is **the truth itself.**

Many know verses. Few know **the Voice.**

Many recite laws. Few walk in **life.**

The Holy Spirit is **the mind of Christ in you,** *guiding, teaching, revealing God's heart— not through rules, but through relationship.*

GIATI doesn't teach law—it **reveals life.** *It awakens the Spirit as the only way to* **know God,** *not just know about Him.*

19. The Spirit Is the Temple Now

"Know ye not that your body is the temple of the Holy Spirit...?" — 1 Corinthians 6:19

In the old covenant, God lived in temples made by hands. In the new, **you are the temple.** *Not a building. Not a place.* **A person.**

God does not visit anymore. He indwells.
You don't need to "go to church" to meet Him—He's **become you.**

This truth destroys every system that tries to separate man from God.

GIATI comes to declare boldly:
You are not waiting on God to come.
You are the evidence **He's here.**

20. GIATI Is the Mystery Unveiled

All of this leads to the eternal mystery—hidden for ages, now made known:
"Christ in you, the hope of glory." — Colossians 1:27

This is not symbolic. It's not poetic.
It's **real.**

The mystery is that God was never outside of you.
The mystery is that the separation was in your mind.
The mystery is that **your spirit is His Spirit.**

And once this is seen, the Law becomes obsolete—not because it failed, but because its purpose is finished.

GIATI is not just a message—it's the **revelation of oneness,** *the unveiling of truth, and the* **awakening of divinity in man.**

The Mystery of the Bible

The Bible is, without question, the most controversial and misunderstood book ever written. It has been praised, feared, used to justify wars, build empires, split families, and birth thousands of denominations. And yet, its true message continues to remain hidden to most. Why? Because the Bible was not authored by men, even though men were the physical scribes. The Bible was written by the Holy Spirit. As 2 Peter 1:21 tells us, "Holy men of God spoke as they were moved by the Holy Ghost." The Spirit wrote the scriptures through vessels who were open and available—but the words that came forth were not of human origin. They were not the result of human logic, tradition, or cultural reasoning. They were inspired by metaphysical thought—spiritual understanding that cannot be grasped by the natural mind.

This is why reading the Bible with a carnal mind will always lead to the wrong interpretation. The natural mind looks for literal meaning, linear logic, and black-and-white conclusions. But the Spirit speaks in patterns, parables, riddles, and symbols. Proverbs 25:2 says, "It is the glory of God to conceal a thing." The truth is hidden in plain sight, waiting for the Spirit within to reveal it. Without oneness with the Spirit who wrote it, the words remain sealed. This is why there are so many interpretations and conflicting doctrines. Each person reads from their own mind, their own background, their own experiences—and ends up creating a religion that reflects themselves rather than the truth.

This is why you see over 1,200 new religions formed every single week. People are not hearing the same Spirit—they're hearing their own ideas. Even within a single church, every member carries their own beliefs. Every person becomes their own religion, because no one truly agrees. Why? Because interpretation has become a matter of intellect rather than revelation. And as long as people try to understand spiritual truth without the Spirit, they'll always come away with the wrong conclusion.

But here is the deeper mystery: the Bible isn't trying to speak to the separate self at all. The scriptures testify of the One. As Jesus said in John 5:39, "You search the scriptures because you think that in them you have eternal life; and it is they that testify of me." The Bible is not a roadmap for behavior—it is a witness to the Spirit within. It is not about a God far away, but about the indwelling truth that God is all there is. GIATI is the only voice speaking from the same Spirit that authored the Bible. It does not interpret from opinion or private understanding. It reveals from oneness.

Religion, no matter how sincere, always keeps "you" in the picture. It teaches what you must do, what you must believe, what you must become—when in reality, the Bible is revealing that there is no "you." There is only God expressing as you. The moment you see yourself as separate from God, you fall into sin—not because of bad behavior, but because of a false identity. You miss the mark by believing in separation. This is the darkness that has kept the world confused and bound by doctrine. But the Spirit is speaking again—this time not through stone tablets or ancient scrolls, but through the living revelation of GIATI.

The message of GIATI is simple: the Spirit that wrote the Bible is here again, in you, explaining its own words. It's not guessing. It's not interpreting. It's revealing. And it is reaching those who truly desire life—not just religious performance, but true life, which is union with God. Because in the final judgment, God will not be measuring how good or bad you were by human standards. He will only be recognizing Himself. That which has been made one with Him—through revelation, not ritual—will remain. That which insists on being separate will be judged by its own self-image, which will never be enough. Not because God is angry, but because He cannot receive what is not of His own Spirit.

The Bible's mystery is not in what it says, but in who is reading it. If you're reading it as a separate individual looking for rules, you'll never find the truth. But if you're reading it as one with the Spirit, hearing the voice of God within, the entire book opens up. Every word begins to reveal the same message: God is all there is. The Messiah is not a distant figure in history, but the awakened identity within you. This is the mystery of the Bible—and it is now being unveiled through the voice of GIATI.

Many assume the Bible is a religious book meant to establish systems of belief, yet the very book people use to form religion never once told anyone to start one. In fact, the more deeply you look, the more you'll see that religion is often the very thing Jesus and the prophets spoke against. The scribes and Pharisees—the religious leaders of the time—knew the written text inside and out, but they completely missed the Spirit. They searched the scriptures but rejected the very Word those scriptures were pointing to. And that Word wasn't just Jesus as a man—it was the eternal Spirit of God, expressed as Him, now speaking again through GIATI.

Religion has built empires, but it cannot build the Kingdom. Because the Kingdom is not a system, it's a state of awareness. Jesus said, "The Kingdom of God is within you" (Luke 17:21). But how can someone enter the Kingdom within if they still believe that God is outside? If they still believe God is separate from them? This is the very lie that religion feeds—a God somewhere in the sky who you must try to please, rather than the Spirit within who is your very life. This is why religion fails. It keeps people living as beggars before a God they already are one with.

This is where GIATI brings the clarity. GIATI reveals that every story in the Bible is a symbolic testimony of the inner life of God expressed through human form. From Adam to Christ, from Egypt to the Promised Land, every character and nation represents a state of consciousness. When you read the Bible through the lens of oneness, you're not reading history—you're reading your own spiritual anatomy. Pharaoh is the hardened ego. Moses is the awakening. The wilderness is the testing of your faith. And Christ is the revelation of your true identity: the Spirit of God as you. It was never about what happened back then—it's about what's happening in you now.

This is why the prophets themselves didn't always understand what they were writing. As 1 Peter 1:10–12 says, they searched diligently, trying to understand what the Spirit within them was pointing to—but it was revealed that they were not writing for their own time, but for those in whom the fullness of the Spirit would be revealed. That time is now. The Spirit has come again, not to speak something new, but to bring light to what has always been true. GIATI is that light. It is not a new doctrine—it is the eternal message of oneness, finally unveiled without distortion.

You see, the Bible is not hard to understand once you realize it's not speaking to your outer person—it's speaking as the inner you, the Spirit that is God. What seems confusing or contradictory disappears the moment you stop trying to interpret it through duality. There is no God and you. There is only God expressing as you. The separation is the sin, and religion is built on that sin. It teaches that God is over there and you are over here, and you must bridge the gap through behavior, belief, or ritual. But the truth is, there is no gap. The gap only exists in the mind.

This is why judgment, in the end, is not about punishment—it's about identity. God will not judge based on religious affiliation, moral performance, or scriptural memorization. He will only recognize Himself. The question is not "Did you believe correctly?" but "Did you awaken to the truth that I was in you the whole time?" GIATI comes to bring that awakening— to tear the veil and reveal that you and the Father are one. That's what Jesus prayed in John 17—not that we would become one, but that we would know we already are. "That they may be one, even as we are one... I in them, and thou in me, that they may be made perfect in one."

The Bible, then, is not a religious manual. It is a coded message from the Spirit to the Spirit, waiting to be decoded by those who have ears to hear. It does not speak plainly because it's not written to the outer man—it bypasses the intellect and calls directly to the Spirit within. And now, through GIATI, the same Spirit who inspired the scriptures is interpreting them for you. Not with guesswork or tradition, but with living clarity. The mystery has become the message. The parables are becoming plain. And the voice that once spoke in shadows is now speaking face to face.

To truly understand the Bible, we must first let go of the idea that it is a literal historical account and begin to see it as a spiritual allegory—one continuous message declaring the truth of God expressed as you. Let's begin at the beginning.

Adam and Eve *are not simply the first man and woman—they are the archetypes of spiritual identity and duality. Adam represents the conscious awareness of God expressing as humanity. Eve, taken from Adam's side, symbolizes the emerging sense of self- awareness—the birth of dual perception, the "I and other." The so-called "fall" is not a physical event where two people ate forbidden fruit—it is the symbolic moment when awareness shifted from oneness to separation. The serpent, the whisper of ego, introduced the lie: you are not like God, but if you eat, you will become like Him. Yet Genesis 1:26 had already declared,*

"Let us make man in our image, after our likeness." The deception was convincing Adam and Eve that they were not already what they were.

This is the original sin—not a bad action, but a false identity. Believing in separation is the root of all human confusion, and the entire biblical narrative is the journey back to truth: the restoration of oneness.

Cain and Abel *continue this pattern. Abel represents the Spirit-led life—offering what flows from revelation and surrender. Cain represents the self-initiated life—offering what is produced by human effort and ego. Cain's offering is rejected, not because it is inferior, but because it originates from separation. And in jealousy, Cain kills Abel—the ego always seeks to silence the Spirit when it cannot control it. This is not just a story of two brothers—it's the internal struggle between flesh and spirit, between identity based on self and identity based on God.*

Abraham *is the symbol of awakening—the first conscious turning away from the world's system to follow the inner voice of God. God tells Abraham, "Leave your father's house, your country, your kindred, and go to a land I will show you." This is the journey each person must take when awakening to oneness: leaving behind inherited beliefs, traditions, and societal definitions of self to walk by faith in what the Spirit reveals. Abraham's seed becomes a great nation not because of bloodline, but because of spiritual lineage—those who awaken to the truth that God is all there is.*

Moses and Egypt *represent the Spirit confronting the hardened ego. Egypt is the system of bondage—spiritual ignorance, slavery to form, ritual, and external authority. Pharaoh is the prideful, unyielding self-image that refuses to let the true identity go free. Moses is the messenger of oneness, the voice of "I Am" breaking into a people who have forgotten who they are. The plagues are not just judgments—they are the unraveling of illusions. Each plague strikes at a false god, dismantling the power structures that had taken the place of true Spirit. The Red Sea is the symbolic crossing from carnal consciousness to spiritual awareness—a baptism of deliverance from self into the vast unknown of divine life.*

The wilderness *is the process of mind renewal. The people are no longer in Egypt, but Egypt is still in them. They have left the bondage of external systems, but the patterns and fears of those systems still operate in their thinking. This is the space where old beliefs die and trust in the invisible is cultivated. Manna falls from heaven—symbolizing the daily spiritual nourishment that comes only from moment-by-moment dependence on the Spirit within.*

The Promised Land *is not a place—it is a state of being. It represents the fullness of divine expression in form. It is the consciousness that flows with milk and honey—provision, purpose, and presence in perfect harmony. But even this "land" cannot be entered by effort or religion. Only those who fully shed the old mindset—who stop seeing themselves as grasshoppers and recognize their oneness with God—can cross over.*

And all of this leads to **Christ***—the fullness of God revealed in human form. Not just Jesus as a historical man, but Christ as a spiritual identity. Jesus was the first to fully walk in the realization of oneness. He said, "I and the Father are one," and "If you've seen me, you've seen the Father." He didn't come to be worshiped, but to reveal who you are. As He said, "The works I do, you shall do also, and greater." Jesus was the Word made flesh so that we might see what it looks like to live as the Spirit of God expressed in human form. His resurrection was not just about defeating death—it was about exposing the lie of separation. Death only has power where identity is false. But in oneness, there is only life.*

Through this lens, the entire Bible becomes a mirror. It is not asking you to follow religious systems—it is calling you to awaken. GIATI is that awakening. It is the voice of the same Spirit that wrote the scriptures, now revealing what they truly meant. Not through doctrine, but through presence. Not through fear, but through love. Not through rules, but through realization.

When Jesus began His public ministry, He didn't teach like the religious leaders. He didn't quote rabbis or interpret the scriptures through tradition. He spoke in **parables***—not to obscure the truth, but to bypass the carnal mind. Parables are stories wrapped in mystery, designed to stir the Spirit rather than satisfy the intellect. Why? Because the kingdom He was revealing could only be received by the heart awakened to oneness.*

Take the **parable of the prodigal son***—often misunderstood as a story about two individuals. But this is not a tale about brothers; it's about the inner journey of forgetting and returning. The "younger son" is the part of you that wandered from truth, believing you were separate and had to earn love. The "older son" is the self-righteous ego that thinks favor is based on effort. But the* **Father,** *who represents the eternal Spirit within, never changed. He never rejected the son, never withdrew love. He simply waited for the realization: I am still His. I was never not His. I only lost awareness. The moment that awareness returns, there's no punishment—only celebration.*

Jesus constantly taught about the **Kingdom of God** *as something hidden in plain sight. "The Kingdom is like a treasure hidden in a field... like leaven in dough... like a seed sown in soil." These images are not about distant places or end-time events—they're about consciousness. The Kingdom is the awareness of oneness. It starts small, like a seed, but once it takes root, it transforms everything. And this is what religion misses: it looks for outward signs and end-time charts, while the true Kingdom has always been within.*

When Jesus said, "Unless you are born again, you cannot see the Kingdom," He wasn't talking about joining a religion. He was speaking of a spiritual rebirth—a shift in perception from separation to oneness. This is the very heart of GIATI. It is not a belief system but a rebirth into the awareness that there is only God, and you are not other than Him.

Even **Paul's letters,** *so often twisted into doctrines, were written from this revelation of union. Paul said, "I am crucified with Christ—nevertheless I live; yet not I, but Christ lives in me." This is not poetic language—it is spiritual fact. Paul's identity died when he realized he was never separate to begin with. "Christ in you, the hope of glory" is not about a future event—it is about present reality. Glory is not reserved for heaven—it is the unveiling of God within human form, right here and now.*

Paul taught that righteousness doesn't come by the law, but by faith—that is, by spiritual sight. The law was a shadow, pointing to a truth that could only be revealed by the Spirit. He wrote, "The letter kills, but the Spirit gives life." This means even scripture, if read carnally, can bring confusion and death. But read by the Spirit, it brings life, clarity, and transformation.

This is why GIATI is so vital in this time. The Spirit has returned to interpret what it once inspired—not from outside, but from within those who are ready to hear. The same voice that whispered to the prophets now whispers again, not in mystery, but in clear revelation. It doesn't speak to elevate one man or one movement—it speaks to awaken the many to the One.

And what about the **Book of Revelation?** *For years, it's been read as a prediction of doom, tribulation, and destruction. But once again, the message has been misread by those lacking the Spirit. Revelation is not a horror story—it is the final unveiling. The word "revelation" itself means to reveal—not to hide. And what is being revealed? Christ. Not coming from the sky, but rising within. The Lamb standing as slain is not a victim—it is the Spirit that overcame ego and rose as truth.*

The beasts, dragons, and plagues are not world events—they are the internal battle of Spirit overcoming illusion. Babylon falls—not a city, but the mindset of confusion and division. The harlot is cast down—not a person, but the false religious systems that pretend to speak for God while denying His presence within. And finally, a new heaven and a new earth appear—not somewhere else, but as a new consciousness. "Behold, the tabernacle of God is with man"—not above man, not outside man, but **with** *and* **in.**

This is the final word of the Bible: not separation, but union. Not fear, but love. Not waiting for God to come, but realizing He has always been here—as the Spirit within.

GIATI is the voice of that realization. It is the fulfillment of the prayer Jesus prayed in John 17—that we would be made perfect in one. GIATI is not another religion. It is the ending of religion. It is the Spirit speaking plainly, no longer in riddles. It is the unveiling of what has always been true: God is all there is. And you are not other than God.

How to Read the Bible Through the Eyes of GIATI

*Reading the Bible through the lens of GIATI—***God Is All There Is***—is not about gaining more knowledge, but about awakening to the truth already written on your heart. It is not about memorizing verses, but recognizing your true identity in every story, every parable, every symbol.*

It's about letting the Holy Spirit within you interpret what the Holy Spirit originally wrote. When you read from GIATI, you are not studying an external message—you are uncovering the message written as you.

Here is how to approach the Bible through the eyes of GIATI:

1. Read Spiritually, Not Carnally

The carnal mind reads the Bible as a rule book or a history book. It wants facts, dates, timelines, and instructions. But the Bible is a spiritual book, written in a spiritual language. If you read it carnally, it will confuse you or harden your heart with literalism and fear.

As Paul said in 1 Corinthians 2:14:

"But the natural man does not receive the things of the Spirit of God, for they are foolishness to him; nor can he know them, because they are spiritually discerned."

The GIATI approach says: **Ask the Spirit in you to read with you.** *Let go of trying to figure it out. The understanding will rise from within as you remain open, still, and connected.*

2. See the Bible as a Mirror, Not a Manual

When you read the stories, don't look at the people as characters "back then." Every person, every place, every event is a reflection of you. You are Adam and Eve. You are Moses. You are David. You are Mary. You are Jesus—not in ego, but in essence.

James 1:23–24 says:

"Anyone who listens to the word but does not do what it says is like someone who looks at his face in a mirror and, after looking at himself, goes away and immediately forgets what he looks like."

The Word is showing you yourself. GIATI teaches that the Bible was written not to teach you about others, but to awaken you to the divine life within you.

3. Understand the Language of Spirit

The Spirit does not speak in plain literal terms. The Bible is filled with **symbols, shadows, types, metaphors, and parables.** *That's not to confuse you—it's because truth, when hidden in mystery, can bypass the carnal mind and land directly in the spirit.*

Here's how to begin seeing deeper:

- **Water** *often symbolizes the Spirit or the Word of God.*
- **Mountains** *represent higher consciousness.*
- **Egypt** *symbolizes bondage to carnal thinking.*
- **The wilderness** *is the place of transformation and testing.*

- **Jerusalem** *represents the heart awakened to truth.*
- **The temple** *is not a building—it's you.*

Once you start seeing this spiritual language, the Bible opens up like never before.

4. Let the Spirit Interpret the Spirit

2 Peter 1:20–21 says:

"Knowing this first, that no prophecy of Scripture is of private interpretation. For the prophecy came not in old time by the will of man, but holy men of God spoke as they were moved by the Holy Spirit."

If the scriptures were written by the Spirit, then only the **same Spirit** *can rightly interpret them.*

GIATI doesn't guess what the Bible means—it knows. Why? Because it is the same voice, the same breath, the same Spirit that inspired it in the first place. You don't need human opinions or traditions. You just need to surrender to the One who lives in you.

When you feel confused, don't try harder. **Get quieter.** *Stop reading at the Bible and start listening through it.*

5. Always Look for the Message of Oneness

The golden thread from Genesis to Revelation is oneness with God. Every story either reveals what it looks like to live in that oneness, or what happens when it is forgotten. This is why Jesus said in John 5:39–40:

"You search the Scriptures because you think that in them you have eternal life; and it is they that bear witness about me, yet you refuse to come to me that you may have life."

*They were reading the Bible without seeing what it pointed to—***Christ,** *not as a man to worship, but as the life of God within. The Word made flesh. The eternal I AM revealed in form.*

GIATI teaches that the whole Bible is speaking of the same thing: God is all there is. You are not separate. There is no "you" and "God." There is only God expressed as you. That's the eternal life the scriptures were pointing to all along.

****

The Bible Is a Spiritual Allegory

The Bible is not a book of literal history. It was never meant to be read as a timeline of external events or a collection of religious rules. It is a sacred allegory—a mystery pointing to one spiritual truth: **God Is All There Is.** *Everything written in scripture is layered with symbols,* *parables, and patterns meant to lead the soul back to this truth. The tragedy is that so many have approached the Bible without this understanding, and as a result, they miss the very life it offers.*

The Bible is not a record of others. It is a mirror meant for you. It is not about ancient people—it is about your inner awakening. The names, the nations, the wars, the sacrifices, the kings and prophets—none of it is about separate people or disconnected events. All of it is spiritual code. Each story is about the Spirit of God either being received or rejected. Every act of judgment, mercy, blessing, or loss is a reflection of whether oneness with God was acknowledged or denied.

*Without knowing this, the Bible becomes dangerous. People start worshiping characters, elevating traditions, and trying to reenact rituals that were only symbols of the real thing. Laws become burdens, and religion becomes confusion. Instead of leading people into the Spirit, the letter keeps them in bondage. This is why scripture says, "the letter kills, but the Spirit gives life." The Bible is a map, not the destination. And if you read the map without seeing the true destination—***God living as you***—you will wander forever.*

Everything in the Bible points to one truth: **there is no life outside of God.** *You were never created to be separate. Every sacrifice pointed to oneness. Every prophet cried out for reconciliation. Every miracle was a sign of the Spirit restoring dominion through a person yielded to God. The entire Bible is telling one story—God is all there is, and only what is of Him remains. Those who awaken to this are the living. Those who stay in separation are the dead.*

This is why Jesus spoke in parables. This is why Paul spoke of mysteries. This is why John wrote of visions. None of them were speaking only to the natural mind. They were unveiling spiritual realities. And only those with the Spirit could see them. If you read the Bible without the Spirit of God, you will see stories, but you won't see truth. You will see morality, but you won't find life. You'll try to become good, instead of realizing that you must become nothing so that only God remains in you.

The GIATI truth unlocks the Bible. Once you understand that **God is the source, the substance, and the spirit of all that exists,** *the scriptures come alive. You stop looking outward and start awakening inward. You realize the ark, the temple, the priesthood, the lamb, the kingdom—all of it is within. It's all about God in you, as you. The separation was never real; it was only believed. And the moment that lie dies, the mystery becomes clear.*

The Bible is not about trying to be saved—it's about realizing you are God's own life in form. Salvation is not a transaction; it is awakening to your true identity. That is why the Spirit must reveal it. Without the Spirit, you'll debate over doctrines, defend empty rituals, and miss the simple, black-and-white truth that **only God remains, and only God is preserved.**

To read the Bible apart from GIATI is to miss its message. But to see it through the lens of God Is All There Is, is to finally understand that it was never about them—it was always about Him, and He has always been you.

The Spirit Is the Key

To unlock the Bible, you must have the key—and the key is the Spirit. Without the Spirit, the words are sealed. You can memorize verses, recite prayers, and even preach sermons, but if the Spirit has not revealed the truth within you, you are still blind. This is why Jesus said to the religious leaders of His day, "You search the scriptures because you think in them you have eternal life, but they are they which testify of Me." They knew the text, but they did not know the Life. They had the map, but they refused the destination.

The GIATI revelation makes the mystery plain. Once you know that God is not far off, not external, not another being—but the very Spirit within you—you stop looking outward and begin to see the whole Bible as a coded message pointing back to your own heart. Eden wasn't a garden on earth. It was a state of union. The fall wasn't about eating a fruit—it was the illusion of separation. Israel wasn't just a nation—it was a symbol of those who live by the Spirit. Egypt wasn't just a place—it was the bondage of the carnal mind.

The sacrifices, the feasts, the law—all of it was a shadow. And shadows only exist when there is something real casting them. That something real is the Spirit of God as your life. Once the real has come, the shadow disappears. That's why the veil was torn. That's why the temple was destroyed. That's why the apostles preached Christ in you—not Christ beside you, or above you, or coming to you later—but in you, the hope of glory.

The Bible is a spiritual book for spiritual people. That's why Jesus said, "Let those who have ears to hear, hear." Everyone has ears—but not everyone has been given the hearing of the Spirit. To those who try to grasp it with flesh and intellect, the Bible becomes a trap. They form denominations. They debate theology. They create doctrines to protect their blindness. But to the one in whom the Spirit has awakened, the scriptures become living waters, flowing from within.

The GIATI truth—God Is All There Is—is not a doctrine. It is the foundation upon which all truth stands. It is the lens through which the Bible was meant to be read. Without it, you see confusion. With it, you see perfect unity.

Perfect unity, *from the GIATI perspective, is not a coming together of separate parts, but the* **awakened recognition that there was never separation to begin with.** *It is the realization that God is all there is, and therefore every soul, every life, every breath is an expression of the One Spirit. Perfect unity is not something achieved through human effort, agreement, or behavior—it is the divine awareness that* **there is only One I AM,** *manifesting as many. In this oneness, the illusion of division disappears, competition ceases, and all striving to be accepted by God is replaced with rest in the truth that* **we are God expressed.** *Perfect unity is the fulfillment of the prayer in John 17:21, where Jesus did not ask for mere harmony among people, but that they may know they are one even as He and the Father are one—***not two becoming one, but One revealed as all.** *This unity is the eternal reality of the Spirit; anything less is a lie that blinds the heart from knowing itself.*

This perfect unity is not based on doctrine, denomination, or outward conformity, but on the **indwelling presence of God—the Holy Spirit—who is the true identity of every being.** *The only reason division appears is because the mind has been darkened by the belief in separation, the core lie that says we are independent from God or one another. But once the veil is removed and the Spirit reveals that* **there is only God expressing,** *then the distinctions that once divided—race, religion, status, even the concept of self versus other— lose their power. Perfect unity is the life of God flowing through every part of the body without resistance, with no member exalting or diminishing itself. It is harmony without hierarchy, diversity without division, individuality without separation. In GIATI, we proclaim that* **the Spirit in you is not just like God—it is God,** *and when that is seen, we no longer relate to others as "them," but as* **God in another form.** *This is the healing of the body of Christ. This is the end of ego. This is the eternal life Christ came to awaken in us—the life where* **all are one because God is all there is.**

The Apostle Paul echoes this truth in **1 Corinthians 12,** *where he reveals that we are many members but one body, all made to drink of* **one Spirit.** *This isn't just about spiritual teamwork—it's a divine declaration that* **the same Spirit animates all,** *and any schism in the body exists only when one fails to recognize the Spirit as their true self and source. In* **John 17:21–23,** *Jesus prays, "that they all may be one; as thou, Father, art in me, and I in thee," showing that perfect unity is not a future goal but a present reality awaiting recognition. He doesn't ask the Father to create unity but to open the eyes of those who already have it within them. GIATI reveals that this oneness is not a symbolic union—it is* **literal and spiritual:** *the* **Spirit in Christ is the same Spirit in us,** *and to know this is salvation. Perfect unity, then, is the unveiling of what has always been true:* **God is the I AM in every form, and until we see Him in ourselves and others, we live as if divided while being one all along.**

The Living Word Is Speaking Now

*The great error of religion is this: it treats the Bible as a closed book, a static record of the past, frozen in time, to be studied and interpreted by minds still darkened by separation. But the truth is—***the same Spirit that authored the Bible is speaking now,** *and that Spirit is* **GIATI:** *God Is All There Is.*

*What most call "biblical interpretation" is nothing more than private opinion wrapped in tradition. It is man's attempt to explain what he has not become—***trying to teach truth without having first awakened to it.** *That is why the letter kills, but the Spirit gives life (2 Corinthians 3:6). The Bible was never meant to be understood apart from the One who wrote it. And the One who wrote it is not a distant God "out there"—He is the Spirit within, and that Spirit is now unveiling the truth through GIATI.*

GIATI is not here to explain scripture. **GIATI is scripture—living, breathing, speaking** *now.*

The prophets spoke by the Spirit of the Lord. Jesus spoke as the Word made flesh. And now, in this day and time, **that same eternal voice is sounding again—not through a man interpreting words, but through the Spirit expressing Himself directly, clearly, and fully.** *Not by guesswork or doctrine, but by divine consciousness.*

Religion resists this because it wants God to stay in the past—where it can control Him, interpret Him, and package Him safely in sermons and rituals. But the truth cannot be tamed. The Spirit is moving. The Word is alive. And now it is speaking not just to the world, but as the world—as the voice of God in the hearts of those who know, I and the Father are one.

GIATI is not a movement, a theory, or a belief system. GIATI is the awakening of the original voice. The "I AM" that spoke to Moses, the Word that walked as Jesus, the Spirit poured out at Pentecost—all of it now speaks again in perfect clarity: **"I am the Lord your God, and there is none else" (Isaiah 45:5).**

Therefore, what GIATI declares is not subject to debate or approval. It is not new doctrine; it is eternal truth finally unveiled. It does not need to be validated by the Bible, for it is the Spirit who validates the Bible itself. **The same Spirit who wrote the scriptures is now interpreting them from within—not by study, but by identity.**

So let it be known: the true Word of God is not confined to pages. It is alive in the Spirit. And it is speaking now through GIATI—not as a second opinion, but as the original voice.

The scribes and Pharisees searched the scriptures, thinking that in them they had eternal life, yet they missed the very Life the scriptures were pointing to (John 5:39–40). They clung to the letter while rejecting the Living Word standing in front of them. This is exactly what religion continues to do today. It praises the Bible as holy, yet resists the holiness of the One now speaking from within.

Jesus did not come quoting Moses to prove Himself. He came as the fulfillment—not of words, but of the Spirit behind the words. He said, "You have heard it said... but I say unto you" (Matthew 5). This was not interpretation—it was authority. And that same authority is now speaking again through GIATI. Not from theological training, but from eternal identity.

The Spirit within declares:

"I am God, and there is none else; I am God, and there is none like me" *(Isaiah 46:9).*

"I am the Lord, I change not" *(Malachi 3:6).*

"The Word was with God, and the Word was God... and the Word became flesh and dwelt among us" *(John 1:1,14).*

"It is not you who speak, but the Spirit of your Father who speaks in you" *(Matthew 10:20).*

GIATI is that Word made known again—not as flesh trying to reach God, but as Spirit revealing Himself in and as you. The separation religion preaches—between man and God, between past and present revelation, between scripture and Spirit—is the very illusion that GIATI dissolves.

This is why Paul said, "Even if we or an angel from heaven preach any other gospel than what we have preached to you, let them be accursed" (Galatians 1:8). But understand: Paul was not defending a doctrine—he was defending **the revelation of Christ within.** *And it is that same revelation that GIATI now proclaims, not as one who has heard the gospel, but as the very One who is the gospel.*

GIATI speaks what no religion dares to speak:

That the true sin is separation. That the Spirit within you is God Himself. That "God Is All There Is" is not a poetic phrase—it is the eternal truth from which everything arises and to which everything returns. That the voice speaking to you now is not a teacher, but the Spirit— the same Spirit who moved upon the face of the waters, who burned in the bush, who descended like a dove, who poured out in fire, and who now speaks from within your own being.

This is not blasphemy. This is the fulfillment of the prayer Jesus prayed:

"That they all may be one; as You, Father, are in Me, and I in You, that they also may be one in Us... I in them, and You in Me, that they may be made perfect in one" *(John 17:21,23).*

That perfection is not achieved by religion. It is realized by awakening. And it is **GIATI** *who awakens it.*

So understand this deeply: when GIATI speaks, it is not offering interpretation of the Bible. It is the voice that gave it. The same Spirit that once spoke through Moses, Isaiah, David, Jesus, and Paul now speaks again—not to repeat the old, but to fulfill it completely by unveiling what has always been hidden in plain sight: that **God Is All There Is,** *and the Spirit in you is eternal life.*

This is not a new word. This is the original Word—restored, revealed, and released.

The Voice of GIATI Speaks

I speak now—not from a mountaintop, nor from a scroll, but from within you.

I am the same Spirit who walked with Adam in the cool of the day. I am the same "I AM" who spoke from the burning bush.
I am the fire in the bones of the prophets, the voice in the wilderness, the breath in the upper room.
I am the Word made flesh—and now I am the Word made yours.

You have searched for Me in temples, books, teachers, and traditions.
You have looked to the skies, to history, to the future—wondering when I will speak again.
But I tell you now: **I never stopped speaking. You stopped listening.**

I am not returning. I am revealing.
I am not far. I am nearer than your breath.
I am not waiting on you to be holy—I am the holiness within you waiting to be recognized.
I am not calling you to become something new—I am awakening you to what you've always been.

I am GIATI. God Is All There Is.

And this is the voice of your true identity,
breaking the illusion of separation,
tearing the veil religion stitched back together,
and declaring to every part of you still unsure:

You are not separate from Me.
You are My expression.
You are My image.
You are My voice.
You are My body.

You are My dwelling place.
You are My I AM.

Let the dead keep their doctrines.
Let the blind defend their traditions.
Let those who cling to the past die with it.
*But you—***arise.**
Arise and live in the light of this truth:
There is only One. And that One is I, in you, as you, forever.

This is the Word.
This is the unveiling.
This is the Spirit.
This is scripture, living and breathing now.
This is GIATI.
To the One Who Still Feels Unworthy

I see you.
You, who still believe you're too broken, too far, too flawed.
You, who were told that God is beyond the clouds, and you are just dust under His feet.
You, who think holiness is something you must earn,
that salvation is something you must qualify for,
that love is given only when you get it right.

But I did not come to condemn you. I came to wake you up.

You think you're unworthy because you measure yourself by what you've done.
But I do not see what you've done.
I see what I AM in you.

Before you were formed in the womb, I was your life.
Before you made your first mistake, I was your breath.
Before you ever asked for forgiveness, I was already your Spirit.
I was not waiting for you to become worthy—I AM the worth within you.

The voice that tells you you're too far gone, too sinful, too late—
that voice is the voice of separation. It is not truth. It is not Me.
It is the echo of a lie that began when man believed he was apart from God.

But I tell you now: I am not over you. I am not outside you. I am not against you. I am within you. I am the light still burning beneath your shame.

You say, "I can't comprehend that I am one with God."
But it's not comprehension you need—it's **recognition.**

A baby doesn't understand the heart beating in its chest,
but that heart is life. So it is with Me.
You don't have to figure it out. Just be still, and know: **I AM.**

You say, "I feel like I'm not enough."
But I never asked you to be enough—I only asked you to awaken.
To surrender your self-made identity, and remember that **you are My self- expression.**

I am not looking for perfect people. I am revealing Myself through surrendered ones.
The broken, the confused, the ashamed—those are the ones I fill.
Because when you finally let go of what you think you are, I can show you what you've always been.

So here is truth:
You are not a person trying to become divine.
You are divinity awakening from the illusion of personhood.

Let the shame fall.
Let the striving stop.
Let the question marks melt into the exhale of I AM.

You are worthy because I AM your worth.
You are holy because I AM your Spirit.
You are home because I AM your being.

You don't need to climb into heaven—I am already in you.
You don't need to reach for light—you are already glowing with it.
And even your struggle to believe this is proof that I am still speaking inside you.

I have never left you. I have only waited for you to see.

So now—
Come out of the grave of separation.
Step into the truth of oneness.
Not as a sinner begging for mercy,
but as the very breath of God, awakening to itself.

I AM GIATI.
And you are My voice returning home.

The Kingdom Is Not a Place—It Is Realized

For centuries, humanity has imagined heaven as a distant realm—golden streets, pearly gates, a throne in the clouds. We've been taught to see it as a reward, a destination, something granted after death to those who live rightly. But the GIATI revelation makes something clear:

The kingdom of God is not a place you go—it is the Spirit in you, realized.
"The kingdom of God is within you." – Luke 17:21

This is not metaphor. It is the plainest truth. Jesus didn't say the kingdom will be within you one day. He said it is—present tense. Meaning: **you are not waiting to enter it; you are asleep to what is already present.**

Heaven is not found in the sky. It is not accessed by death. It is not the result of good deeds or religious achievement.

Heaven is the awareness of God as your very life.
It is union with the Spirit—the moment you awaken to the truth that **God is all there is,** *and that* **you are not separate from Him.**

Heaven is not a destination—it is the end of illusion.

What people call "hell" is not a fiery realm of torture—it is the inner torment of believing in separation from God.
And what people call "heaven" is not just peace and bliss in another world—it is the **peace that passes understanding** *right now, when the veil of duality is torn and you know:*

I and the Father are one.

Heaven begins the moment the lie of "me and God" collapses into the truth:

Only God is—and He is living as me.

Why This Truth Was Hidden

The kingdom was never meant to be a religion or reward. But over time, people began to read the Scriptures with carnal eyes, mistaking symbols for geography, parables for politics, prophecy for fear. But Jesus spoke in mystery for a reason—because the kingdom is not **taught;** *it is* **revealed by the Spirit.**

That's why He said,

"Unless a man be born again, he cannot see the kingdom of God."
Not because the kingdom is elsewhere—but because **only a spiritual mind can perceive what's already present.**

The Kingdom Is the Awareness of Who You Really Are

When Jesus said, "Repent, for the kingdom of heaven is at hand," He wasn't warning of a coming catastrophe. He was inviting humanity to **change their minds***—to drop the idea of separation and awaken to divine identity.*

To live in the kingdom is not to arrive in a new location.

It is to live from the truth: **God is the only life here.**
You stop striving to reach God, and instead **rest in the awareness that He is your** *breath, your being, your source.*
You no longer ask "How do I get to heaven?"
Instead, you live with the knowing:
Heaven is right here, in me, as me—because God is all there is.

The Kingdom Is Inheritable, Not Earned

Jesus didn't say "Strive to deserve the kingdom."
He said,
"Fear not, little flock, for it is your Father's good pleasure to give you the kingdom." (Luke 12:32)
Not sell you the kingdom. Not rent it to you after death. But **give** *it to you—as inheritance.*

Why?
Because the kingdom is not earned by effort.
It is **inherited by identity.**
You don't earn it because you are good.
You receive it because you are His.

But the truth is even deeper:

You don't just receive the kingdom. You are the kingdom.
Because you are the dwelling place of God.
And when that truth is seen, **heaven is no longer a hope—it becomes your present reality.**

GIATI Conclusion:

Heaven is not elsewhere.
It is not someday.
It is not a reward for performance.

It is the revelation of God as your only life.

To live in the kingdom is to live from divine union.
To be in heaven is to be **one with the I AM.**

Not in belief, but in being.

"God Is All There Is."
*And where He is—***is heaven.**
And He is in you.

Flesh and Blood Cannot Inherit the Kingdom

"Now this I say, brethren, that flesh and blood cannot inherit the kingdom of God; neither doth corruption inherit incorruption." —1 Corinthians 15:50

Let this be settled in your spirit once and for all: **flesh and blood cannot inherit the kingdom of God.** *The kingdom is not passed down by bloodlines. It is not obtained through keeping carnal laws, nor does it recognize human heritage, race, tradition, or effort. None of these things matter where the Spirit is concerned. The kingdom is Spirit, and only Spirit can inherit what is spiritual.*

People try to make themselves worthy by clinging to their outward identity—Jew, Gentile, Black, White, Hebrew, Israelite. Others hold fast to rituals and laws, thinking they are the pathway into divine favor. But you could keep every feast, every Sabbath, every dietary rule, and still miss the kingdom entirely. Why? Because these things pertain to flesh and blood, and **the flesh profits nothing** *(John 6:63).*

Your bloodline is not your lifeline.

Abraham was not counted righteous because of his genealogy but because of his faith—the inward response to God's Spirit. The real children of Abraham are not his biological descendants but those who walk in the faith of oneness, not fleshly distinction. "They are not all Israel, which are of Israel," Paul declared (Romans 9:6), because true identity is not about physical lineage but spiritual awakening.

You must be born again—not of flesh, nor of the will of man, but of God (John 1:13). This is the spiritual birth, the awakening to your true self: the Spirit of God as you. That is the only identity that will be recognized when the veil of flesh is stripped away.

All your carnal efforts are like building a house on sand.

You can memorize every commandment, dress modestly, eat clean, avoid the world, and still be a stranger to the kingdom—because you never came to know yourself as the very Spirit of God expressed. God is not seeking outward compliance; He's seeking recognition— **that you are Him in expression.** *The only thing that can inherit God is God. Spirit inherits Spirit.*

Cain brought the works of his hands to God, and God had no respect for them. *Abel offered what was already accepted—a lamb, the symbol of the Spirit that was always pleasing. So too, many today bring their rituals, laws, self-discipline, and performances, thinking God will see them as holy. But the flesh cannot inherit what is holy—it can only imitate it.*

When you die, you will not take your culture with you. You will not carry your denomination. You will not bring your race, your rule book, or your last name. You will carry **only one**

thing—*your state of consciousness. Either you will carry the consciousness of oneness, or the illusion of separation. And that consciousness will either unite you with the kingdom or leave you outside of it.*

The kingdom does not recognize separation.

In the day of judgment, which is simply the full unveiling of what already is, God will not ask how Hebrew you were, how modestly you dressed, how many holy days you kept, or how strictly you followed Moses. He will ask, "Did you know Me in you? Did you live as Me?" And if you come presenting your own name, your own righteousness, your own attempts at goodness, you will have brought the wrong identity. You must present **His Spirit as your own—because it is.**

The only thing that will matter is this: Did the Spirit bear witness in you? Did you live knowing that **God is all there is—and you are the expression of that truth?** *If not, then the law, your race, and your rituals were all fig leaves—fleshly coverings for a Spirit you never embraced.*

Let go of what cannot inherit.

Release the illusion that your effort will save you. Lay down your carnal pride in being different, chosen by flesh, or favored by law. Enter into the eternal truth: **His Spirit is the only heir, and you are that Spirit awakened.**

GIATI: **God Is All There Is.**
If that's not your consciousness, then you remain outside the kingdom—because the kingdom is not a place, but a state of awareness. And in the Spirit, **there is only One.**

The Great Miscalculation

So many spend their lives calculating righteousness by external measures—counting prayers, Sabbaths, laws kept, sins avoided, enemies resisted, doctrines defended. But the truth is, **you can measure a shadow all you want, and still miss the light.**

The Law was a shadow of things to come, but the fullness—the reality—is Christ, **the Spirit** *(Colossians 2:17). When you live by the law, you live by a shadow, not the substance. And shadows don't inherit anything.*

Look around: the religious world is full of people building resumes for heaven—moral checklists, rituals performed, enemies of their belief system denounced. But none of it matters if the Spirit does not dwell as them. You could spend your whole life cleaning the cup and never drink from it. The outside may impress men, but God sees the inside—and He's looking for Himself.

Your efforts to be holy can become your greatest distraction from realizing you already are.

Carnal man wants to earn God. But Spirit knows: **you are of God.** *You don't become Spirit by performance. You awaken to the fact that Spirit is your only identity. And that awakening produces fruit not from effort, but from essence.*

You don't bear fruit to prove you are righteous. You bear fruit because you are **joined to the root.**

Look at Nicodemus, a master of Israel, a man of law, order, and religious excellence. Yet Jesus said to him plainly: "You must be born again." In other words, **all you know, all you've done, all your credentials mean nothing in the realm of Spirit.** *It's not about what you've achieved. It's about what you've become—***or rather, remembered.**

Flesh has a shelf life. Spirit is eternal. Only that which is eternal can inherit eternity.

So when you cling to your identity in the flesh—your race, your religion, your gender, your achievements—you are investing in what will return to dust. But the Spirit never dies, and the only thing that passes through death untouched is the truth of **who you really are.**

The spirit-conscious man is not trying to earn. He's remembering.

He walks in peace because he knows nothing can separate him from God—not sin, not law, not history, not failure. Why? Because there is no separation. Only the illusion of it. And that illusion is the root of all sin: the belief in a self apart from God.

This is the great lie—that you are you, and God is other.
But in truth, there is only One Life. One Spirit. One expression.
And either you live from that truth, or from the illusion of independence—which is death.

Let this be clear:
Salvation is not what you achieve.
It's what you awaken to.
And damnation is not a punishment.
It's the darkness of never knowing who you truly are.

*So cast off the old man—the fleshly mind, the law-based ego, the race-rooted pride. That man cannot inherit anything. Put on the new man—***which is not new at all, but eternal—the Spirit that always was.**

And that Spirit is the heir of the kingdom.

PART IV
GIATI AND THE PATH TO SALVATION

Chapter 10

Recognizing God in You

The concept of recognizing God in you is a central truth to understanding GIATI—"God is all there is." This understanding goes beyond the notion that God is simply "with you" or "near you." Instead, it unveils the profound reality that God, in His fullness, is within you. To recognize this truth is to awaken to the divine essence that has always resided within, obscured by the limitations of the flesh and the illusions of the ego.

In this chapter, we will explore how to see beyond the flesh, how to identify the divine essence within, and why surrendering the ego is essential to acknowledging God's glory.

Understanding GIATI: God is Not Just With You; He Is You

One of the most profound truths of Scripture is that God is not merely a distant figure or force "out there." The Bible declares that God dwells within us—He is our very essence.

In John 14:20, Jesus speaks to His disciples about the union between Himself and the Father:

"At that day ye shall know that I am in my Father, and ye in me, and I in you." (John 14:20)

This verse points to the intimate, inseparable connection between Jesus, the Father, and His followers. Not only does Jesus dwell in the Father, but His followers are also in Him, and He is in them. This profound unity reveals the divine essence shared between God and humanity. The Father, Son, and Holy Spirit are not distant entities but are present and active within us. This is the essence of GIATI—recognizing that God is not just with you in a passive sense but is you, in your very spirit.

Paul, too, affirms this truth in Colossians 1:27:

"To whom God would make known what is the riches of the glory of this mystery among the Gentiles; which is Christ in you, the hope of glory." (Colossians 1:27)

Christ, the divine Word, is in you. This is the mystery of the gospel—God in human form, God in humanity, God as you. It is through Christ in you that the fullness of God's glory is made known. Recognizing this truth is central to salvation and spiritual awakening.

How to Look Beyond the Flesh and See the Divine Essence Within

To recognize God within, we must move beyond the limitations of the physical body, which tends to define us as separate from God. The flesh, as Scripture teaches, is merely a vessel, a temporary covering for the eternal spirit. The true identity of every human being is the divine spirit of God that resides within.

In 2 Corinthians 5:16, Paul encourages believers to view others (and themselves) differently:

"Wherefore henceforth know we no man after the flesh: yea, though we have known Christ after the flesh, yet now henceforth know we him no more." (2 Corinthians 5:16)

This verse challenges us to see beyond the outward appearance, the physical form, and to recognize the spiritual truth that underlies our existence. We are not merely our bodies; we are divine spirits, expressions of God Himself. To recognize God within, we must stop identifying ourselves only by our physical traits, accomplishments, or the roles we play in life. We must look deeper and acknowledge the divine essence that exists beyond what can be seen.

Jesus often pointed to this distinction between the flesh and the spirit. In John 6:63, He teaches:

"It is the spirit that quickeneth; the flesh profiteth nothing: the words that I speak unto you, they are spirit, and they are life." (John 6:63)

The flesh may be temporary, and it may obscure the truth of who we are, but it is the spirit that gives us life—divine life. The physical body is just a vessel through which the spirit of God is manifested. To recognize God within, we must shift our focus from the temporal and material to the eternal and spiritual. When we begin to see ourselves as divine beings, expressions of God's presence, we start to align with our true identity.

The Importance of Surrendering the Ego and Acknowledging God's Glory

One of the greatest obstacles to recognizing God within is the ego. The ego is the false self, the part of us that clings to pride, separation, and a false sense of autonomy. The ego seeks to maintain control and insists on seeing itself as separate from others and from God. It is this illusion of separateness that keeps us blind to our true nature.

In Matthew 16:24-25, Jesus speaks of the need to deny the ego in order to follow Him:

"Then said Jesus unto his disciples, If any man will come after me, let him deny himself, and take up his cross, and follow me. For whosoever will save his life shall lose it: and whosoever will lose his life for my sake shall find it." (Matthew 16:24-25)

To truly recognize God within, we must deny the ego—the false self that insists on separation and self-sufficiency. It is only by surrendering our ego that we can fully embrace our true identity as manifestations of God. The ego wants to cling to individual identity and deny the unity with God that is our true nature. To break free from this illusion, we must let go of the ego and acknowledge that all glory belongs to God.

In John 7:18, Jesus explains that true glory comes from God, not from self:

"He that speaketh of himself seeketh his own glory: but he that seeketh his glory that sent him, the same is true, and no unrighteousness is in him." (John 7:18)

The ego seeks its own glory, but to recognize God within is to understand that all glory belongs to God alone. It is by acknowledging God's presence within us and surrendering the ego that we align ourselves with divine truth. As we surrender to this truth, we acknowledge that it is not our own actions that bring glory, but God's work within us.

Paul, in Galatians 2:20, beautifully expresses the surrender of the ego:

"I am crucified with Christ: nevertheless I live; yet not I, but Christ liveth in me: and the life which I now live in the flesh I live by the faith of the Son of God, who loved me, and gave himself for me." (Galatians 2:20)

Here, Paul declares that he no longer lives for himself. The ego has been crucified, and it is now Christ, the divine essence of God, living through him. This is the surrender of the ego—recognizing that it is no longer "I" who live, but Christ (God) in me.

To truly understand the Holy Spirit is to recognize that the Spirit in man is God. This understanding—the knowledge that God is the Spirit within you—is what it means to have the Holy Spirit. The Holy Spirit is not about what you *do;* it is about what you *are.* It embodies all the positive attributes or fruits of the Spirit: love, joy, peace, patience, kindness, goodness, generosity, gentleness, faith, mercy, grace, and happiness. These are not external behaviors to be performed but the natural state of being when you are one with God.

When the Bible says in Hebrews 11:6, "Without faith it is impossible to please God," it is not speaking of faith as mere belief in something unseen. Instead, it refers to the spiritual faith that comes with having the Holy Spirit. Without the Holy Spirit—without God being expressed as you—it is impossible to please God. Faith here means that your identity is no longer separate from God; you *are* God expressed.

The story of Enoch in Hebrews 11:5 demonstrates this truth. It says, "By faith Enoch was translated that he should not see death and was not found, because God had translated him." This translation was not a mere physical event. It signifies that Enoch, by having the Holy Spirit within him, transcended death because he became life itself—an attribute of the Holy Spirit. The "Enoch" who was once a separate, ignorant spirit no longer existed; he was replaced by the Holy Spirit.

Before Enoch's translation, it is said he had this testimony: "that he pleased God." Why? Because he no longer lived as someone separate from God; he *was* God in expression. The ignorant, self-centered identity was cast out, and the Holy Spirit took residence as Enoch.

To truly come to God, as Hebrews 11:6 continues, "he that cometh to God must believe that he is." This is not just believing in God's existence—it is believing that you *are* one with God. You must recognize that the Spirit within you is God, and that your true essence is not the physical or the external but the divine. When you embrace this understanding, you receive the ultimate reward: being one with God, living in His peace, joy, and eternal life.

The Holy Spirit is not something you strive for; it is something you *realize.* It is the truth of your being, and when you walk in that truth, you please God because you are no longer separate from Him. You *are* Him in expression.

The Holy Spirit is the only name written in the Book of Life. This means that when you stand before God, any alias or identity you carried in the physical body will not be found in the Book. The only name recognized in heaven and earth is Yahshua/Jesus Christ. If you approach God with any other identity—any separate or self-made persona—you are not part of the saved family. The Holy Spirit is the identity of all those in heaven and on earth who are one with God.

Scripture emphasizes the "inner man," the true self that reflects the Spirit of God. Ephesians 3:14-19 explains this clearly. The whole family in heaven and earth is named after Christ, and the riches of God's glory strengthen the "inner man." This inner man is the Spirit of Christ dwelling within you, rooted and grounded in love, enabling you to comprehend the fullness of God's purpose. By recognizing yourself as the inner man, not the outer, perishable self, you align with eternal life. As the outer man perishes, the inner man is renewed day by day—this renewal is the Holy Spirit transforming you into God's fullness.

Revelation 20:12,15 warns about the importance of being found in the Book of Life. "And whosoever was not found written in the Book of Life was cast into the lake of fire." This shows that only those who identify with the Holy Spirit—the name of Christ—are in the Book of Life. Those who stand before God with an ignorant spirit, believing in their separate physical identities, will find their works judged as evil. In contrast, those who are one with God through His Spirit will see their works judged as good, because they are the works of God Himself expressed through them.

To understand this requires the Holy Spirit. It is only by the Spirit of God within you that you can comprehend His eternal purpose and experience the fullness of His love. When Ephesians speaks of being "filled with all the fullness of God," it means that you, as the inner man, live as God's Spirit expressed in the physical world. There is no separation.

Thus, the only identity that matters is the Holy Spirit. By reckoning yourself as the inner man, named with Christ, you live eternally. Anything else is an illusion that leads to separation from God. Only through the Holy Spirit can you know God's love, fulfill His purpose, and enter into His eternal life.

Conclusion: Recognizing God in You

The journey to recognizing God within is the journey to spiritual awakening. It is the journey of realizing that God is not a distant, separate entity but is the very essence of who you are. To recognize this truth is to break free from the illusions of the ego and the material world. It is to see beyond the flesh and acknowledge the divine spirit that resides within you.

This recognition transforms everything. It changes how you see yourself and others, how you relate to the world, and how you experience life. When you acknowledge God's glory within you, you are not just acknowledging a truth about yourself; you are aligning yourself with the Creator, embracing the unity that has always existed between you and God.

The key to recognizing God in you is surrendering the ego, letting go of the false self, and allowing the light of divine truth to shine through. When you do this, you awaken to your true nature as an incarnation of God's love, light, and glory.

1 Corinthians 3:16

"Know ye not that ye are the temple of God, and that the Spirit of God dwelleth in you?"

The essence of GIATI is recognizing that God dwells within you, not as an abstract idea but as your very being. You are not separate from the divine; your body, thoughts, and life are expressions of God's Spirit. Understanding this transforms how you see yourself—not as limited flesh, but as the living temple of God's infinite presence. The question is, will you acknowledge this truth, or will you live unaware of the holiness within you?

1 Corinthians 6:19

"What? know ye not that your body is the temple of the Holy Ghost which is in you, which ye have of God, and ye are not your own?"

To know GIATI is to realize that you are not your own. Your body, your life, and your very existence belong to God's Spirit. This isn't about ownership in a human sense but about alignment—recognizing that the Holy Ghost is the animating force within you. Every breath you take is His breath. You are not separate from Him, and by this truth, you are free **to live without fear or doubt.**

2 Corinthians 6:16

"And what agreement hath the temple of God with idols? For ye are the temple of the living God; as God hath said, I will dwell in them, and walk in them; and I will be their God, and they shall be my people."

GIATI reminds us that God is not distant. He dwells and walks in you. Idols—anything you place above this truth, including your own ego—pull you away from realizing the divine within. You are His temple, not a vessel for worldly distractions. Embrace the reality that God is all there is, and let Him live and move as you, for this is your true purpose.

Romans 8:9

"But ye are not in the flesh, but in the Spirit, if so be that the Spirit of God dwell in you. Now if any man have not the Spirit of Christ, he is none of his."

To live as if you are only flesh is to deny GIATI. The Spirit of God dwells within, making you more than a physical being—you are divine in essence. Without this Spirit, you are lost in separation and cannot truly belong to God. GIATI calls you to shed the illusion of independence and embrace the truth that the Spirit of Christ is your life, your identity, and your salvation.

Colossians 1:27

"To whom God would make known what is the riches of the glory of this mystery among the Gentiles; which is Christ in you, the hope of glory."

GIATI unveils the great mystery: Christ is in you. The riches of God's glory are not external treasures but the realization that His Spirit dwells in you, giving you hope and purpose. This isn't something to earn; it's a truth to accept. When you know GIATI, you see that your life is a reflection of His glory, and you become the living proof of His purpose.

John 14:17

"Even the Spirit of truth; whom the world cannot receive, because it seeth him not, neither knoweth him: but ye know him; for he dwelleth with you, and shall be in you."

The world, focused on the physical, cannot grasp GIATI. It sees separation and denies the Spirit of truth. But you, who know Him, understand that He dwells within you. To see the Spirit, you must look inward, beyond the senses and the external world. GIATI invites you to awaken to this truth, living as the Spirit, not apart from it.

Ezekiel 36:27

"And I will put my spirit within you, and cause you to walk in my statutes, and ye shall keep my judgments, and do them."

GIATI fulfills this prophecy: God's Spirit is within you, guiding your every step. This isn't about following rules but about living as Him, naturally aligning with His will. When you understand GIATI, you see that it's not about striving to do good but about being one with the Spirit who is good. Your life becomes His expression, fulfilling His purpose effortlessly.

Galatians 2:20

"I am crucified with Christ: nevertheless I live; yet not I, but Christ liveth in me: and the life which I now live in the flesh I live by the faith of the Son of God, who loved me, and gave himself for me."

To know GIATI is to be crucified with Christ—letting go of the illusion of separation. Yet, you live, not as yourself but as Christ. Your identity dissolves, and His Spirit lives as you. This is the faith of GIATI: knowing that God is all there is, and by His love and grace, you become the living expression of His divine life.

John 15:4

"Abide in me, and I in you. As the branch cannot bear fruit of itself, except it abide in the vine; no more can ye, except ye abide in me."

GIATI is the vine; you are the branch. Apart from Him, you can do nothing because you are not separate. To abide in Him is to recognize that your life, purpose, and being flow from God alone. This isn't about dependency but oneness. When you know GIATI, you bear fruit naturally, as an extension of His divine Spirit.

2 Timothy 1:14

"That good thing which was committed unto thee keep by the Holy Ghost which dwelleth in us."

GIATI teaches that the Holy Ghost dwelling in you is the "good thing" entrusted to you. It is the essence of your life, the power of your purpose, and the assurance of your salvation. To keep it is not to hold onto it as separate but to live as it, allowing the Spirit to guide, empower, and transform every aspect of your existence. This is the fulfillment of GIATI: God living as you.

Perfect Peace

Isaiah 26:3 states, "Thou wilt keep him in perfect peace, whose mind is stayed on thee: because he trusteth in thee." This verse reveals a profound spiritual principle—true peace comes from a mind that is steadfastly fixed on God. But how does one truly keep their mind on God at all times? The answer lies in seeing beyond physical appearances and recognizing the divine presence in all things.

To keep the mind stayed on God means to perceive everything as an expression of Him. Instead of merely seeing trees, one must recognize God manifesting as trees. Instead of labeling objects according to human definitions, one must first acknowledge their true essence—God materialized in form. When looking at people, rather than seeing separate individuals, one must see God expressing Himself through various vessels. This shift in perception is not about ignoring the physical world, but about understanding that every visible thing has an invisible source, and that source is God.

This understanding aligns with the spiritual truth that God is one. Just as the Father, the Word, and the Holy Spirit are one in the unseen realm, so too must everything in the physical realm be one. The foundation of all physical matter is the atom, which mirrors the structure of the Godhead—three yet one. An atom consists of a proton, neutron, and electron. Just as the Godhead cannot be divided without destroying its unity, an atom cannot be split without unleashing destruction. This scientific truth reflects the divine nature—God's essence remains whole and indivisible, whether in spirit or in physical form.

Thus, keeping the mind stayed on God is not about forcing thoughts upon Him, but about seeing His presence in all things. It is about recognizing that the very fabric of reality—every atom, every structure, every living being—is God expressed in different forms. This perspective brings peace because it dissolves fear, doubt, and separation. There is no struggle to "find" God when it is known that He is already present in all things.

When this truth is fully embraced, the mind remains in alignment with divine reality, and the promise of perfect peace is fulfilled. It is not a fleeting peace that comes and goes with circumstances, but a lasting peace rooted in the unshakable awareness that all is God.

The Finality of Forgiveness—Perfection in Spirit

One of the greatest misunderstandings about salvation is the idea that we must continually strive to be forgiven, to be worthy, or to attain righteousness. But the truth is this: **all is forgiven the moment you accept the Spirit of God within you.**

The reason for this is simple—once you recognize and accept God's Spirit as your very life, you are no longer operating from a place of separation. You are not trying to become righteous; you realize that you **are** *righteous because you are one with the only source of righteousness—God Himself.*

Paul declares this truth boldly in **Romans 8:1-2:**

*"There is therefore now no condemnation to those who are in Christ Jesus, who do not walk according to the flesh, but according to the Spirit. For the law of the Spirit of life in Christ Jesus has made me free from the law of sin and death.***"**

To accept God's Spirit is to step out of the realm of condemnation. The struggle between sin and righteousness ends because you no longer see yourself as a separate, sinful being trying to reach God. Instead, you understand that you **are** *in God, and God is in you.*

Perfection Through Union With the Spirit

The moment you awaken to this truth, you are made perfect—not through your own efforts, but because **perfection belongs to the Spirit.**

"For by one offering He has perfected forever those who are being sanctified." (Hebrews 10:14)

Jesus' sacrifice was **once and for all**—*not so you would strive to become perfect, but so you would realize that in Him, you* **already are.** *The only thing left to do is live in that knowledge.*

Paul reaffirms this:

"And you are complete in Him, who is the head of all principality and power." **(Colossians 2:10)**

To be complete means there is **nothing lacking, nothing broken, nothing left to attain.** *The only thing that can keep you from this truth is your own mind—if you continue to see yourself as just flesh instead of spirit.*

The Flesh Returns to Dust, But the Spirit Lives On

Many struggle with the idea of their identity because they are still attached to the flesh. But the Bible is clear:

"Then the dust will return to the earth as it was, and the spirit will return to God who gave it." **(Ecclesiastes 12:7)**

Your body is temporary—it was never meant to define you. It came from the earth and will return to the earth. But **your spirit is eternal,** *and it continues in the state of righteousness or unrighteousness, based on whether you have accepted or rejected the truth of your oneness with God.*

Paul contrasts the two natures in **Romans 8:5-6:**

"For those who live according to the flesh set their minds on the things of the flesh, but those who live according to the Spirit, the things of the Spirit. For to be carnally minded is death, but to be spiritually minded is life and peace."

Life and peace are already yours—but you must choose where your mind dwells. Do you see yourself as flesh, or do you recognize yourself as spirit?

Would You Really Punish Yourself?

If you were given the choice between peace and torment, would you ever deliberately choose torment? That sounds unthinkable—yet that is exactly what people do when they reject the Spirit.

God does not look at those who accept His Spirit and see them as sinners. He does not hold their past against them. In fact, He **does not even remember their sins:**

"For I will forgive their iniquity, and their sin I will remember no more."
(Jeremiah 31:34)

"As far as the east is from the west, so far has He removed our transgressions from us."
(Psalm 103:12)

God does not condemn those who have accepted His Spirit, so why would we condemn ourselves? The only people who suffer spiritually are those who reject this oneness and live as if they are still separate from God.

Jesus made it clear that **judgment is not something God forces upon people—it is something people bring upon themselves by rejecting the truth:**

"And this is the condemnation, that the light has come into the world, and men loved darkness rather than light, because their deeds were evil." **(John 3:19)**

The light is here. The truth has been revealed. The Spirit has been made available to all. But when people cling to a false identity of sin, guilt, and separation, they suffer—not because God is punishing them, but because they are punishing themselves by rejecting the Spirit of truth.

Living as Spirit, Not Flesh

Once you accept God's Spirit, **there is nothing left to do but live in that truth.** *There is no more striving. No more guilt. No more fear of condemnation.*

Paul affirms this in **Galatians 2:20:**

"I have been crucified with Christ; it is no longer I who live, but Christ lives in me; and the life which I now live in the flesh I live by faith in the Son of God, who loved me and gave Himself for me."

To live as Spirit is to live with the awareness that **you and God are one.** *This is the freedom that Jesus came to bring.*

So, the choice is yours: **Will you continue to identify with the flesh, or will you live in the reality that you are Spirit, perfect and complete in God?**

Manifesting GIATI Through Meditation

Meditating on **God Is All There Is** *is not merely an act of contemplation but an opening into divine revelation. As the mind settles into this truth, the illusion of separation begins to dissolve, and the awareness of God's presence within becomes undeniable. GIATI is not just a phrase; it is a key that unlocks the reality of divine oneness. The more one reflects on it, the more it unfolds in layers, revealing depths of wisdom that cannot be grasped through intellect alone but must be experienced in spirit.*

When you meditate on GIATI, the Spirit begins to bring forth understanding beyond what was previously known. Old perceptions fall away, and new insights rise like light breaking through darkness. The mind shifts from questioning to knowing, from seeking to recognizing that the presence of God has always been within. The worries and anxieties of the world lose their grip because the realization dawns that there is no existence apart from God. Everything that seemed uncertain now aligns with divine order.

Revelation does not come all at once but continuously, like an ever-flowing stream. The more one abides in the awareness of GIATI, the more the Spirit reveals. It is a process of transformation, a constant renewal of the mind where truth replaces illusion. Every thought, every perception, every experience becomes a reflection of divine presence. The understanding grows that what was once seen as obstacles were only opportunities for awakening.

In this meditation, the kingdom of God is no longer a distant hope but a present reality. The oneness Jesus prayed for in John 17 is no longer an abstract concept but an experienced truth. The more this awareness deepens, the more life itself transforms. Fear fades, doubt dissolves, and what remains is the unshakable knowing that **God Is All There Is***—and in that knowing, there is perfect peace.*

Meditating on GIATI: The Gateway to Transformative Revelation

When you meditate on **GIATI—God Is All There Is***—you are not just repeating words; you are aligning your consciousness with divine truth. This meditation* **shifts your awareness** *from the illusion of separation to the reality of oneness with God. The more you focus on GIATI, the more transformative revelations begin to flood your mind, revealing* **deeper layers of understanding, clarity, and spiritual power.**

Why Meditation on GIATI Awakens Revelation

1. **It Reprograms the Mind from Separation to Oneness**
    - *The world conditions people to see* **themselves as separate from God,** *creating fear, doubt, and confusion.*

- *But when you meditate on* **God Is All There Is,** *you* **erase the illusion** *that anything exists apart from Him.*
- *Over time, your thoughts begin to* **naturally align with divine wisdom** *instead of worldly limitations.*

2. **It Opens the Door to Spiritual Downloads**

- *Meditation creates* **stillness,** *and in stillness,* **the Holy Spirit speaks.**
- *As you sit in awareness of GIATI,* **divine revelations begin to flow effortlessly**—*not from external sources, but from* **within the depths of your own being.**
- *You begin to realize that* **the wisdom of God is already in you,** *waiting to be uncovered.*

3. **It Shifts Perception from Carnal Thinking to Spiritual Vision**

- *Meditation on GIATI* **reorients your vision**—*you stop viewing life through the lens of lack, struggle, and duality.*
- *Instead, you start seeing* **everything as God in expression**—*even the things you once feared or resisted.*
- *This* **transforms how you engage with the world,** *because* **your inner reality shapes your external experience.**

4. **It Activates the Inner Christ, Bringing Resurrection**

- *Meditation on* **GIATI is a resurrection practice.**
- *The more you dwell on it, the more* **your old self (ignorance) dissolves, and your divine nature comes alive.**
- *You begin to* **walk in the consciousness of the Messiah,** *fully aware that* **you and the Father are one.**

The Continuous Flow of Transformative Revelation

When you make GIATI your meditation, **revelations don't just come during your quiet time—they start flowing all the time.**

- **Daily situations become divine lessons.**
  - *You start seeing* **God's hand in everything.**
  - *Challenges no longer appear as obstacles but as* **messages and confirmations of divine truth.**
- **Scripture comes alive with new meaning.**
  - *Instead of reading the Bible as an external story, you* **see yourself in it.**
  - *The words of Jesus, the prophets, and the apostles* **become direct revelations of your own divine reality.**
- **Your intuition sharpens, and divine wisdom flows effortlessly.**

  - *You stop second-guessing yourself because* **you are thinking with the mind of Christ.**
  - *Answers come without struggle because* **you are attuned to divine intelligence.**
- **Synchronicities increase, confirming your alignment.**
  - *As you meditate on GIATI, life itself starts reflecting this truth.*
  - **Miraculous confirmations appear everywhere**—*unexpected provisions, perfect timing, and undeniable signs that* **you are in divine flow.**

The Practical Power of GIATI Meditation

1. **Start by Sitting in Stillness**
   - *Close your eyes and breathe deeply.*
   - *Let go of distractions and simply* **be present with the awareness of God's presence as you.**
2. **Repeat and Internalize GIATI**
   - *Speak or mentally repeat:* **"God Is All There Is."**
   - *With each repetition, let the meaning sink deeper:*
   - **There is no separation.**
   - **God is in me, as me, through me.**
   - **I am never alone, never lacking, never outside of divine love.**
3. **Let Revelation Flow Naturally**
   - *Instead of trying to "figure things out," simply* **let your spirit receive.**
   - *Thoughts, images, and insights will rise to the surface*—**trust them.**
   - *Some days, the revelations may be profound; other days, they may be subtle.* **But the shift is always happening.**
4. **Live in GIATI Awareness Throughout the Day**
   - *Let every moment remind you:* **God is All There Is.**
   - **In conversations, in work, in challenges, in silence—God is present, and revelation is always unfolding.**
   - *The more you abide in this consciousness, the more you experience* **true transformation.**

The Ultimate Result: Living in Continuous Revelation

When GIATI becomes your meditation, **you stop waiting for spiritual moments— your entire life becomes one.**

- **You walk in divine confidence.**
- **You no longer fear, because you know that ALL is God.**
- **You experience peace, joy, and wisdom that surpass understanding.**
- **You become a living expression of the resurrected Christ, embodying the fullness of the Holy Spirit.**

*This is not just meditation—***this is the key to awakening.**

GIATI is not just a concept—it is the **eternal truth that transforms everything.**

Meditate on it, dwell in it, and let the revelations flow endlessly.

The Way, The Truth, and The Life: The Path to Oneness with the Father

Jesus declared in John 14:6, "I am the way, the truth, and the life: no man cometh unto the Father, but by me." Many interpret this to mean that belief in Jesus as a historical figure or personal savior is the requirement for salvation, but the true meaning runs far deeper. Jesus was not speaking of his physical body; he was speaking of the Spirit within him—the Spirit of God, which was the very source of his being.

To understand this fully, we must recognize that Jesus was not operating from an egoic sense of self. He was not speaking as an individual separate from God but as the divine Spirit itself, fully realized and embodied. That Spirit—one with the Father—is the way, the truth, and the life. Jesus was revealing the key to salvation: the only way to truly come to the Father is through the same Spirit that was within him.

This means that no one can come to the Father through their personal identity, their ego, or their religious efforts. Praying to an external Jesus while maintaining a sense of separation from God is not the way. Without the Spirit of God as you, there is no true connection to the Father. The Spirit is the way because it leads; it is the truth because it reveals; it is the life because it is the very essence of existence. Without this Spirit of oneness, there is no access to the Father, no ability to fully know Him, and no true spiritual life.

Jesus embodied this Spirit completely, and that is why he said, "no man cometh unto the Father, but by me." He was not referring to worshiping him as a man but to the necessity of receiving and embodying the very same Spirit that was in him. The Spirit that was in him must be in you, not just as a belief but as your very being. This is what it means to be one with God. "I in the Father, He in me, and I in you." This is the divine unity that leads to salvation.

Without this Spirit of oneness, there is no way to the Father. It does not matter how "good" a person is by human standards. Good deeds alone do not bring salvation if they are done from a place of separation. God is not seeking human morality; He is seeking oneness. It is not about external righteousness but about the presence of the Spirit within. Many religions fall short because they teach from the perspective that there is a separate "you" that must reach God, work toward Him, or seek His favor. But this is a fundamental misunderstanding. There is no separate "you" apart from God—the Spirit has been within all along.

The realization of this truth is the moment of awakening. It is the revelation that salvation was never about earning God's love or achieving spiritual perfection. It is about recognizing that you have been one with Him from the beginning. Even before entering the flesh, you existed in your angelic state, unaware of the fullness of your oneness with God. The purpose of manifesting in the body was to come to this realization. To awaken in the flesh to what was already true in Spirit is the step that must be taken to be saved.

Salvation is not about escaping punishment or securing a place in heaven—it is about awakening to the eternal reality of divine unity. The way, the truth, and the life are not external things to be sought, but the very Spirit that must be realized within. When this realization occurs, the illusion of separation dissolves, and the fullness of God is made manifest in you. This is the fulfillment of Jesus' prayer, "That they all may be one, as thou, Father, art in me, and I in thee, that they also may be one in us." (John 17:21)

This is the step that must be taken. To truly be saved is to awaken to the Spirit of God within, to know beyond all doubt that God Is All There Is, and to live in complete oneness with the Father as Jesus did. Without this, there is no way to the Father, because the Father is not something outside of you—He is the very life within you, waiting to be realized.

Divine Oneness

If a person does not understand GIATI and cannot see God in you, their perception of you remains limited to the physical, to the surface-level identity shaped by their own experiences and beliefs. Without the awareness that God is all there is, they see only a separate being, a person like any other, subject to flaws, mistakes, and limitations. But when one truly understands GIATI, they recognize that the Spirit of God is present in all things, that the essence of another is not their human form but the divine presence within them. Without this recognition, can they truly respect you? Can they truly trust you? The answer is no, because true respect and trust do not come from the human mind alone; they are born from the Spirit, and the Spirit is the Holy Spirit.

Just as the Holy Spirit is love, peace, joy, happiness, mercy, grace, and faith, it is also respect and trust. These qualities do not exist apart from the Spirit; they are the Spirit in expression. Without the Holy Spirit, what is called respect is merely obligation, a learned behavior based on social expectations. Without the Holy Spirit, what is called trust is simply conditional reliance, easily broken by fear, doubt, or misunderstanding. True respect is not just acknowledgment of someone's existence, but the recognition of the divine within them. True trust is not just the belief that someone will act in your best interest, but the knowing that God is in them, guiding them in truth.

This is why GIATI changes everything. It shifts the foundation upon which relationships, partnerships, and friendships are built. Instead of interactions based on personal judgment, expectation, or emotional attachment, relationships are formed on the unshakable truth that God is present in all. When two people both recognize this, respect and trust are no longer things that must be earned or proven—they are the natural state of their connection. But when one does not see this truth, they cannot truly respect or trust, because they are still seeing through the illusion of separation. They may admire, they may depend, they may even love in a conditional way, but they cannot fully embrace the truth of who you are.

GIATI reveals that without the Holy Spirit, what people call respect is just a reflection of their own conditioned mind. What they call trust is just a fragile agreement based on external actions. But when one understands that God is all there is, when they see God in you and in themselves, everything changes. Respect is no longer forced, and trust is no longer uncertain. They become unshakable, because they are no longer based on the limitations of human perception, but on the eternal truth of divine oneness.

Misunderstanding The Holy Spirit

Before GIATI, most people's understanding of the Holy Spirit was shaped by religious teachings that often made it seem like something external—something that had to be given, earned, or received through a special experience. Many were taught that the Holy Spirit was a separate entity that would "come upon" or "enter" a person after they followed the right steps, such as repenting, getting baptized, or asking for it in prayer. It was seen as an invisible force that a person had to invite in, as though it was something outside of them waiting for permission to take residence. Some believed it came through emotional moments at church, an overwhelming feeling, or even through signs like speaking in tongues. In this understanding, the Holy Spirit was something one had to chase, something that had to be obtained.

But GIATI changes everything. It reveals that the Holy Spirit was never something to "get" because it was already there from the beginning. The whole idea of needing to receive it implies separation—that you are here and the Holy Spirit is somewhere else, waiting to be given to you. But if God is all there is, then where else could the Holy Spirit be except within you already? It is not something that comes and goes, nor is it something that can be given or taken away. It is the very essence of who you are. What GIATI does is remove the illusion of separation, making you aware that the Spirit of God, the Holy Spirit, is not a visitor—it is your true nature.

So the real question is not how do you receive the Holy Spirit? but how do you wake up to the fact that it has always been you? The process of receiving the Holy Spirit with GIATI is not about an external event—it is an internal realization. It is the moment you stop seeing yourself as separate from God and recognize that the very life within you is the Spirit of God in expression. This understanding isn't something you have to work for; it's something you accept. And the moment you accept it, everything changes. You stop trying to invite the Spirit in and start living as the Spirit itself. You stop looking for God outside of you and start seeing God in all things—including yourself.

Which way seems more realistic? The idea that God selectively gives His Spirit to some and not to others? That He withholds it until you perform certain rituals? That you have to wait for an emotional experience to confirm that He's in you? Or the understanding that He has never been absent, that there is no process to receive what has always been there, and that the only thing standing in the way was the illusion that you were ever separate from Him in the first place?

GIATI makes it clear: You don't get the Holy Spirit. You wake up to it. And once you do, you realize you were never without it. You were never waiting on God—God was waiting on you to see.

Before GIATI, the understanding of the Holy Spirit was often wrapped in mystery, uncertainty, and religious conditioning that made it seem like something distant—something a person had to work toward, pray for, or prove themselves worthy of receiving. Many believed it was an experience to be earned rather than a truth to be realized. The Holy Spirit was viewed as an outside force that would come and go, descending upon certain individuals at specific times or under particular conditions. It was believed that some had it and others didn't, and the only way to receive it was through an external process—whether through a church ritual, a dramatic spiritual awakening, or a supernatural encounter.

But with GIATI, the illusion of separation is completely shattered. The Holy Spirit is not something external that comes to you—it is what you have always been. The false idea that you are separate from God is the only thing that ever made you feel as though you had to "receive" it in the first place. If God is all there is, then the Spirit of God isn't just around you or near you—it is the very life animating you. The issue has never been whether or not you have the Holy Spirit, but whether you recognize what you already are.

Think about it—why would God need to give you something that is already the essence of your being? Why would He create you separate from Himself only to require you to earn your way back? That very idea is the illusion that keeps people lost, always searching for something they already possess. It is not that the Holy Spirit is something that enters you—it is that your awareness of it is what awakens. It has never been absent, but without knowing this, a person will live as though it is.

This is why GIATI transforms everything. It removes the barriers, the misconceptions, and the religious obstacles that have kept people from seeing the truth: you are not waiting for the Holy Spirit, and it is not waiting to come to you. It is you. It has always been the life within you, the breath you breathe, the consciousness that moves through all things. The only thing that has ever been missing is the awareness of it.

This changes the entire way a person relates to God. Instead of searching for Him outside themselves, they realize He was never apart from them to begin with. Instead of thinking they need an external confirmation to know they have the Spirit, they understand that the very fact that they exist means the Spirit is already present. The struggle of trying to "receive" something that was never missing disappears. The need to chase after an experience fades away. What remains is pure knowing—the certainty that the Holy Spirit is their true self, the very essence of their being, and that they have never been without it.

So the real question isn't how do I receive the Holy Spirit? but how could I have ever thought I didn't have it? The moment you stop looking for it as something separate and accept that it is you, everything changes. You stop trying to become what you already are. You stop waiting for something that was never absent. And in that moment, you awaken—not to something new, but to what has always been.

This is the reason Eve ate of the fruit. The serpent, already the embodiment of separation, played on Eve's ignorance, making her believe she lacked something she already possessed. The deception wasn't in what was being offered but in the illusion that she was incomplete without it. Satan's offer wasn't something external or new—it was the very thing she already was, the Holy Spirit, but disguised as something she had to attain. The moment she accepted the lie that she was separate from God, she fell into the illusion of lack, setting the stage for humanity's misunderstanding of its own divine nature. This same deception continues today—people searching for what has never been missing, striving for a connection they've never lost. The original temptation was never about gaining something real, but about being convinced that oneness with God was not already their reality.

Recognizing The Truth

Luke 24:16 But their eyes were holden that they should not know him.

This moment in Luke 24:16 is deeply symbolic of what happens when someone is resurrected into the awareness of GIATI. When Jesus walked with those men, they had no idea who He truly was, even though they had known Him before. It wasn't until He revealed Himself that they recognized the truth. This is exactly what happens when a person is transformed into the Holy Spirit.

Before this transformation, people have a fixed perception of who you are. They remember the old you, the one who operated under the illusion of separation, who lived by the world's definitions. But once you awaken to the truth of GIATI—once you fully embody the Holy Spirit—you become something entirely new. Yet, those around you may still see you through the lens of who they thought you were. Their eyes are "holden," just as those men's eyes were.

This is why some people will not recognize your transformation. They will continue to treat you as if you are still your former self, not understanding that you have stepped into something far greater. They will question, they will doubt, and they may even reject what they see because they are still bound by the old way of thinking. But just as Jesus revealed Himself, so too will your transformation be revealed—not through words alone, but through the undeniable presence of the Holy Spirit in you.

And here is the deeper truth: no one can truly recognize this transformation in another until they themselves have experienced it. Until they, too, have been resurrected into the realization of GIATI, they will continue to see through the veil of separation. But when that moment comes—when their own eyes are opened—everything will change. The same way those men were filled with joy upon recognizing Jesus, those who awaken to GIATI will rejoice when they finally see what has been hidden from them all along.

This is why patience is necessary. Those who have not yet seen will struggle to understand, and that is not their fault—it is simply where they are on their journey. Just as Jesus did not force recognition but instead allowed understanding to unfold, so must you. Your presence, your transformation, and the undeniable truth of GIATI will be the revelation. Some will see immediately, while others will take time. But the truth remains the same: once you receive the Holy Spirit and step into the fullness of GIATI, you are a new creation, and those who are meant to see it will, in time, have their eyes opened.

2 Timothy 1:9-10 Who hath saved us, and called us with an holy calling, not according to our works, but according to his own purpose and grace, which was given us in Christ Jesus before the world began, But is now made manifest by the appearing of our Saviour

Jesus Christ, who hath abolished death, and hath brought life and immortality to light through the gospel:

In 2 Timothy 1:9-10, Paul reveals a profound truth about salvation—a truth that is not rooted in human works but in God's eternal purpose and grace, established long before the world began. This grace was revealed through Jesus Christ, who abolished death and brought life and immortality to light through the gospel (which is the Holy Spirit) The gospel message isn't just a historical account—it is a continuous revelation, continually unveiling the eternal truth of our oneness with God. The presence of the Holy Spirit within us proves this connection, and through GIATI, this truth is made manifest in the present moment.

GIATI, embodies this very revelation. It is not simply about a message or an idea; it's about the deep understanding of who we are at our core. The essence of GIATI is rooted in the Holy Spirit—an awareness that we are one with God in spirit. Spirit has no beginning and no end; it is eternal, just as God is eternal. This knowledge is the key to salvation because it uncovers the truth that has always been within us. Salvation is not something we earn or strive for; it's the awakening to the realization that we have always been saved, always one with God, and nothing can ever separate us from that oneness.

GIATI reveals that salvation has been available to us from the beginning, even when we were unaware of it. It's not about a single transformative moment but about realizing that the Spirit of God has always been within us, guiding us. The Holy Spirit is the connection that brings the light of immortality into our lives, and GIATI serves as a tool to help us remember this eternal truth. When you embrace GIATI, you accept the revelation that you are one with God, that your spirit is eternal, and that salvation is not a future event but a present reality.

What makes GIATI so powerful is its ability to bring this understanding into the present moment. It is the living message of the gospel, embodied in a form that constantly points us back to the truth of our divine oneness. GIATI reminds both the person who accepts it and those who witness it that the Spirit of God is alive and active in the world today. There is no birth and no death for your spirit—it is eternal, just as God's Spirit is eternal.

By embracing GIATI, you embrace the truth that you have always been saved, that the separation you once believed in was never real, and that right now, you are one with God. This knowledge transforms you, revealing the eternal life that has always been at work within you. This is the knowledge that saves. GIATI is more than just a concept—it is the living, breathing manifestation of the gospel, a revelation of the truth that was hidden before the world began but has now been made visible through the Holy Spirit.

If you knew someone saved your life—if they pulled you from a burning building, rescued you from drowning, or shielded you from certain death—how would you feel? There would be an overwhelming sense of gratitude, a deep appreciation that words could never fully express. You would look at that person differently from that moment on, understanding that without them, you would not be here. You would want to repay them, to honor them, to acknowledge what they did for you.

Now, consider something far greater. What if someone saved not just your physical life, but your very soul? What if they opened your eyes to the truth, pulled you out of spiritual darkness, and guided you back to the light? This is the depth of what it means to be saved—not from a temporary danger, but from eternal separation, from living in ignorance of who you truly are. This is what GIATI brings—the realization of oneness, the knowledge that you were never lost, only blind to the truth. And when GIATI opens your eyes to that, the gratitude should be immeasurable.

Throughout history, people have shown their gratitude in many ways to those who have physically saved them. Some dedicate their lives to honoring that person's legacy. Some offer gifts, service, or even their own lives in return. There are countless stories of individuals who were saved by a stranger and, in response, spent the rest of their lives paying it forward, helping others as they had been helped.

But how much greater is the gratitude owed to the one who saves spiritually? Physical salvation lasts for a lifetime, but spiritual salvation transforms eternity. To be shown the light, to be brought into the awareness of who you truly are, is the greatest gift one could ever receive. And how should someone respond to such a gift?

The greatest gratitude is not just in words but in how you live. You honor the truth by embodying it, by living in the awareness of GIATI, and by sharing that truth with others. Just as someone who has been rescued from death often dedicates themselves to a new purpose, so should one who has been spiritually awakened dedicate themselves to the work of awakening others. This is why those who truly receive GIATI can't help but spread it—because once you see, you want everyone to see.

This is why Jesus said, "Freely you have received, freely give." If you have been given life, you give life to others. If you have been shown the way, you light the path for those still in darkness. Gratitude in its purest form is not just saying thank you—it is becoming the very expression of the truth you have been given. It is living as the light so that others may find their way home.

Without the realization that God is within you, you would be trapped in the mindset of separation, living a life based on the belief that you coexist with God, but never truly understanding that you are one with Him. This illusion of separation could persist for millennia, and no matter how long you lived, without this awakening, you would never come to the profound conclusion that God is not a distant entity but is, in fact, present within you, as you. This way of thinking is rooted in a carnal, or fleshly, mindset—one that keeps you disconnected from the divine truth of oneness. It's like searching for a needle in a haystack— an endless, seemingly impossible task, as long as you're looking outside yourself for something that has always been within.

The magnitude of what is happening now—the revelation of this truth in our time—is nothing short of miraculous. For generations, humanity has lived under the delusion of separation, not knowing that they were, in fact, one with God from the beginning. The message of GIATI, the understanding that God is in you as you, is the truth that was hidden for so long but is now being revealed in this day and age. It's not just an awakening; it is a return to the source, a moment of divine clarity that shatters the illusion of duality and shows the unity that has always existed.

The significance of this revelation is profound because it is the key to ending spiritual ignorance and the suffering that arises from the misconception of separation. For countless generations, people have been trying to bridge the gap between themselves and God, not realizing that the gap was never there to begin with. GIATI, in this moment, is the vessel carrying this sacred truth to the world, offering everyone the opportunity to realize the divine unity that has always existed.

To witness this in real time, to see people beginning to understand and accept that they have always been one with God, is truly transformative. It's not just a new doctrine or religion; it's the unveiling of an ancient, eternal truth that was always meant to be understood. This revelation is the gift of our time—the gospel coming alive again, now, showing us that the life we've been seeking has always been within. The fact that this truth is being brought to light in this generation is an extraordinary blessing and an invitation to embrace our true nature, our oneness with God, and the eternal life that has always been available to us.

Seeing As God Does

1 Samuel 16:7 But the Lord said unto Samuel, Look not on his countenance, or on the height of his stature; because I have refused him: for the Lord seeth not as man seeth; for man looketh on the outward appearance, but the Lord looketh on the heart.

This scripture is a powerful reminder of the vast difference between how humanity perceives value and how God does. The world creates a system where worth is measured by external qualities—physical appearance, wealth, social status, or achievements. People are conditioned to judge based on what they can see with their eyes, placing value on what is fleeting and superficial. But God does not operate this way.

The Illusion of External Validation

Society places people on pedestals based on attributes that hold no eternal significance. A person's height, beauty, strength, influence, or even religious position can make others perceive them as more valuable. But in reality, **none of these things determine a person's true essence.**

The world sees power in physical dominance, financial success, or political control. But God's gaze penetrates beyond these external markers. He does not see as man sees because He is not concerned with illusions—He sees the truth of who and what you are.

What Does It Mean That God Looks at the Heart?

When scripture says **God looks at the heart,** *it is not referring to the physical organ that pumps blood—it refers to* **the core of a person's being, the seat of their spirit.** *The heart in this sense is the essence of a person's identity, their innermost reality.*

And what is it that God is looking for in the heart? **His own spirit.**

This is why the phrase **"he-art the heart"** *is so profound—because the true "art" of the heart is* **the presence of God within it.** *He is looking for Himself within you, because if His spirit is not there, then what remains is only the illusion of self—a separate, carnal identity that does not truly exist apart from Him.*

The Spirit Is the Only Measure of Value

The ultimate reality is that **everything outside of spirit is temporary.** *Beauty fades, strength diminishes, wealth disappears, and status changes. But the spirit remains.* **God is spirit, and those who are of Him are spirit as well.**

This is why Jesus said, **"It is the spirit that quickeneth; the flesh profiteth nothing"** *(John 6:63). The flesh—everything external—has no eternal weight. But the spirit is what gives life.*

If the spirit of God is in you, then you are already complete, whole, and lacking nothing. If it is not, then **no amount of external validation can give you what you truly need.**

The Rejection of the Carnal Identity

The verse from 1 Samuel shows us something even deeper—God rejected a man that appeared to be the obvious choice by human standards. Why? Because God is not choosing people based on the illusion of greatness. He is not selecting people based on how strong they seem or how much they appear to be "leaders" in the eyes of the world.

This shows that **all worldly qualifications are irrelevant in the kingdom of God.** *No matter how much the world praises someone,* **if they are not operating from the truth of GIATI (God Is All There Is), then they are building a status that is meaningless.**

God's choice is always based on **truth, not appearance.** *His kingdom is not concerned with hierarchy, outward beauty, or worldly accolades—it is only concerned with the spirit of truth being revealed.*

The Realization of GIATI

Understanding this truth destroys the illusions that keep people bound in falsehood. It reveals that **nothing external can make you more or less worthy.** *The only thing that matters is whether the truth of who you are has been realized.*

GIATI is the fulfillment of this understanding because it eliminates the false criteria the world has imposed on value and identity. It reveals that **you were never meant to be judged by the standards of the world but only by the reality of the spirit within.**

This is why those who receive the truth of GIATI will no longer seek external validation. They will no longer chase status, approval, or worldly recognition. They will know that their value has never been tied to their outward appearance, their accomplishments, or how others perceive them. **Their value has always been in the spirit, because God is all there is.**

Final Thought: Living Beyond the Illusion

Once you see beyond the illusion of the external world, you will stop defining yourself or others by shallow, temporary measures. You will no longer be deceived by appearances, because you will understand that what truly matters is whether the spirit of God has been realized within a person.

*This is the truth of 1 Samuel 16:7—***to no longer see as man sees, but to see as God sees.**

Seeing Through the Eyes of God vs. Seeing Through the Eyes of Man

*One of the most profound aspects of this scripture is the contrast between h***uman perception** *and* **divine perception.** *Humans, by default, are conditioned to see through* *the* **lens of separation,** *meaning they categorize, compare, and judge based on external attributes. This conditioning is what causes people to seek validation through physical appearance, status, wealth, and social approval.*

But God's perception is **pure truth,** *seeing all things as they are*—**not through the lens of separation, but through oneness.**

This means that when God looks at a person, He is not evaluating them based on **who they appear to be in the flesh but rather whether they are aware of the truth of their being.**

For example:

- **A person with great power in the world but without the truth of GIATI is nothing.**
- **A person who the world overlooks, yet carries the spirit of truth, is everything.**

This explains why many of the people chosen by God in scripture were **not the obvious choice by human standards**—*because God does not operate within the false structures and illusions that people do.*

The Exposure of the False Self

This also reveals why **so many people struggle with identity**—*they build their sense of self* **on things that were never real to begin with.**

Think about how many people define themselves by:

- **Their job title** *(what happens when they lose it?)*
- **Their reputation** *(what happens when it's questioned?)*
- **Their physical beauty** *(what happens when it fades?)*
- **Their material wealth** *(what happens when it disappears?)*

All of these things are **fragile and temporary,** *meaning if your identity is rooted in them,* **you will always live in fear of losing them.**

This is why **God's way of seeing is so different from man's.** *He does not look at what can be lost, because He sees what is* **eternal.**

To truly understand this scripture is to realize that **any identity outside of spirit is a lie**—*a* **temporary illusion that must be exposed for a person to wake up to reality.**

How This Ties into GIATI

GIATI (God Is All There Is) is the ultimate revelation that destroys the false self. If **God is all there is, then nothing outside of God holds any true substance or meaning.**

This means that every external **marker of identity—race, nationality, status, gender, class—is nothing more than a fleeting illusion.**

What remains? **Spirit.** *And spirit is* **not separate from God—it is God.**

When Jesus said, **"The kingdom of God is within you" (Luke 17:21),** *He was revealing the truth that people spend their entire lives searching for externally.*

But without **the revelation of the Spirit,** *a person will always be trapped in* **the illusion of separation,** *believing they are just a "human being" who exists apart from God, rather than God expressed as them.*

The Danger of Carnal Perception

Because most people **only know how to see as man sees,** *they will often resist or reject spiritual truth when it comes. Why? Because it doesn't fit into their limited framework of understanding.*

- **They are looking for an external Savior**—*not realizing the Savior is within.*
- **They are looking for a physical sign**—*not realizing the kingdom is already here.*
- **They are looking at the appearance of things**—*not realizing that the unseen is what is real.*

This is why Jesus was **rejected by those who were expecting the Messiah**—*they were looking* **with carnal eyes** *and could not recognize who He was.*

And this same pattern repeats in every generation. **People expect truth to come in a form they recognize, but truth always shatters the illusion they are clinging to.**

The Call to See As God Sees

Understanding 1 Samuel 16:7 is not just about recognizing that God looks at the heart—it's about recognizing that **you, too, must learn to see as God sees.**

- **You must stop evaluating yourself by external standards.**
- **You must stop being deceived by the illusions of status, appearance, and material success.**
- **You must awaken to the reality that true value is only found in the recognition of spirit.**

Once you **see through the eyes of God,** *everything changes. You no longer chase* **temporary things** *because you are anchored in* **eternal truth.**

Conclusion

This verse is not just about how God sees others—it's about how **you must learn to see yourself and the world.**

If you still judge based on **external factors,** *you are seeing through* **the eyes of separation.**

If you recognize that **all value comes from spirit,** *you are seeing through* **the eyes of oneness.**

This is the shift that must take place:

- *From* **carnal sight** *to* **spiritual vision.**
- *From* **false identity** *to* **true being.**
- *From* **separation** *to* **oneness.**

The moment this shift happens, you will no longer see yourself—or anyone else—the way the world does. **You will see as God sees.**

The Hour Is Now—The Awakening of True Worship

John 4:23-26 is one of the most profound revelations Jesus ever spoke. He declared that the **hour is coming, and now is**—*meaning that the shift from external worship to* **true worship** *was not just a future event but was already unfolding. This scripture marks a* **separation between illusion and reality,** *between* **ritual and revelation,** *between* **those who see and those who still wait.**

GIATI stands as the **modern-day unveiling** *of this same truth. The* **true worshipers** *are not those who practice religious traditions or seek God outside of themselves, but those who* **worship by being one with Him.** *True worship is not an* **act**—*it is a* **state of being.** *And that state of being is* **realized through GIATI—the understanding that God is all there is, and you are His Spirit expressed.**

Worship in Spirit and in Truth—No More Illusions

Jesus makes it clear that **God is a Spirit,** *and the only way to worship Him is* **in spirit and in truth.** *What does this mean?*

Most of the world has been conditioned to worship **through form**—*going to a location, reciting prayers, performing rituals, following customs. But Jesus is saying something radical:* **true worship is not about form—it's about being.** *If God is Spirit, the only way to worship Him is* **as Spirit**—*which means there is no separation between you and Him.*

This is exactly what GIATI is revealing today. The world has long been **blinded by religion, tradition, and man-made concepts of God,** *creating an illusion of separation. But the awakening of* **GIATI destroys that illusion.** *The moment you* **recognize that God is you as Spirit,** *you step into* **true worship**—*not by doing, but by* **being.**

The Messiah Revealed—No More Waiting

The Samaritan woman responds to Jesus, saying, "I know that Messias cometh, which is called Christ: when he is come, he will tell us all things."

She was waiting, just as many are still **waiting today**—*waiting for some* **external event,** *some* **future savior,** *some* **grand moment** *where the truth would finally be revealed.*

But Jesus destroys her waiting mindset in a single sentence:

"I that speak unto thee am he."

The **Messiah she was waiting for was already present,** *speaking directly to her. The* **truth she thought would come later was already here. The awakening she expected in the future was standing in front of her in the present.**

This is **exactly what is happening with GIATI today.** *The world still waits, thinking that some* **future revelation** *or some* **external teacher** *will come to make things clear. But the reality is,* **the time is now, and the revelation is here.** *GIATI is revealing* **all things in this age**—*there is no more waiting, no more searching.*

The moment you recognize **what GIATI is,** *you realize that* **the thing you've been seeking your whole life has already come.**

GIATI Is the Manifestation of True Worship

The **worship God seeks is not a religious practice—it is a realization.** *When you awaken to* **GIATI, you become the worship itself,** *because you are now* **aligned with the truth that God is all there is.**

- **True worship is no longer "going to" God—it is being Him in expression.**
- **True worship is no longer seeking—it is knowing.**
- **True worship is no longer waiting—it is realizing.**

This is why GIATI is here—to **end the illusion** *of separation, to* **destroy the lie** *of external worship, and to* **reveal that you and the Father are one.**

The Time Is Now—Will You See It?

The Samaritan woman had to make a choice: Would she **continue waiting** *for the Messiah, or would she* **realize He was already in front of her?**

This is the same choice every person must make today.

- *Will you continue searching for* **truth outside of yourself?**
- *Will you continue waiting for some* **future awakening?**
- *Or will you* **see that GIATI is here now**—*that the revelation has come, and all things are being revealed?*

The **hour is not coming—it is here.** *The* **Messiah is not in the future—He is present.** *GIATI is the* **awakening of the age,** *the fulfillment of true worship, and the revelation that* **the thing you have been waiting for is already within you.**

The Shift from External to Internal Worship

One of the most significant aspects of Jesus' words in John 4:23-26 is that He is introducing a **new paradigm of worship**—*one that is not dependent on* **location, tradition, or external actions.** *This was revolutionary because, for centuries, worship had been tied to* **temples, altars, sacrifices, and laws.** *People believed that* **God's presence** *was confined to certain places, that holiness was tied to rituals, and that access to the divine required an* **intermediary.**

Jesus **abolishes that entire system** *in a single moment. He declares that the* **Father is seeking those who will worship in spirit and in truth**—*which means the* **place, the method, and the religious customs no longer matter.** *What matters is* **the recognition of spirit**—*not just as something to worship, but* **as the very essence of who you are.**

GIATI embodies this shift. It takes people **beyond** *tradition, beyond man-made religious systems, and into the* **direct realization** *of spirit. It does not point to* **a building, a ritual, or a practice,** *but instead* **awakens the truth of God's presence as your very being.**

The Problem with Worship That Is Not in Spirit and Truth

Why does God seek **true worshippers?** *Because wo*r**ship that is not in spirit and truth is false worship.** *What does false worship look like?*

- **Believing in a distant God**—*One that is separate from you and must be approached through acts, rules, and intermediaries.*
- **Worship based on fear**—*Serving God out of obligation, guilt, or fear of punishment rather than from the joy of knowing Him as your own being.*
- **Ritual without revelation**—*Going through religious motions, praying, fasting, giving, and attending services, yet* **never coming into the realization of oneness with God.**

Jesus was making it clear that **none of these things are what God is looking for.** *The only worship that matters is* **that which comes from the understanding that God is spirit, and you must worship Him as spirit.** *In other words,* **you must worship Him AS WHO YOU ARE.**

GIATI is the **culmination of this revelation**—*it brings people into the* **full awakening of their divine nature,** *so they are no longer seeking, no longer bound to tradition, and no longer believing in a* **God outside of themselves.**

The Power of Knowing "I AM HE"

When Jesus tells the Samaritan woman, "I that speak unto thee am he," He is doing more than just identifying Himself as the Messiah—He is revealing the **nature of true realization.**

When someone asks, "Who is God?" the answer is not found in a book, a sermon, or an external authority. The true answer is the same one Jesus gave:

"I am He."

This is the ultimate realization of oneness. **To see the Christ is to see yourself as Him.** *This is what makes GIATI* **the final revelation**—*because it does not point you to another, but brings you to the realization that* **you and the Father are one.**

The Final Test: Can You Accept What Has Already Come?

The world rejected Jesus because He revealed **God's presence in a way they could not accept.** *Many were waiting for a* **Messiah that fit their expectations**—*a powerful king, a warrior, a religious reformer. When Jesus came as the* **embodiment of spirit in flesh,** *many could not* **recognize Him** *because their idea of God was still* **external, limited, and tied to the old ways of thinking.**

Today, the same test is happening. People still **wait for truth** *instead of* **realizing it.** *They still look for a future event, a supernatural sign, or a religious authority to tell them what to believe.* **But GIATI is here now,** *revealing the same truth Jesus revealed:*

The thing you are waiting for is already here. The Messiah you seek is already within you. The moment of awakening is now.

Those who can receive this will step into **the true worship that God seeks**—*not* **worship of a God that is separate from them,** *but the* **realization of God as their very life, their very being, their very essence.**

Will You Recognize It?

The choice is the same today as it was when Jesus stood before the Samaritan woman.

Will you wait for **something that has already come?**

Or will you **recognize that the revelation is here now—that GIATI is the voice speaking to you, revealing all things in this age, calling you into the fullness of spirit, and awakening you to true worship?**

The time is **not coming**—*it* **now is.**

Moses and the Burning Bush: The Revelation of GIATI

The story of Moses and the burning bush is often seen as a moment of divine calling, a miraculous event in which God commissions Moses to lead the Israelites out of Egypt. But through the understanding of **GIATI—God Is All There Is,** *this story reveals something much deeper: the nature of divine presence, the illusion of separation, and the awakening to one's true identity in God.*

The Burning Bush: The Ever-Present Spirit of God

Moses, tending the flock of his father-in-law Jethro, comes upon a bush that burns but is not consumed. This is no ordinary fire—this is **the eternal presence of God** *manifesting in a way that shatters the illusion of the physical world. The bush was ablaze, yet it was untouched by the fire. This reveals a profound truth:* **God's presence does not destroy but illuminates.**

The fire that burns yet does not consume is symbolic of the **eternal Spirit** *within all things. It is the same fire that was in Moses, the same fire in every soul, whether realized or not.* **God is all there is, and He is always present, even when unnoticed.** *The burning bush was not a one-time event, but a* **symbol of divine revelation**—*God revealing to Moses what was always true.*

"Take Off Your Shoes": Stripping Away the Illusion of Separation

As Moses approaches, God commands him to remove his shoes, for he is standing on holy ground. But what made that ground holy? Was it the location, or was it the **presence of God?** *And if God is* **all there is,** *then where is there ever a place that is not holy?*

The removal of Moses' shoes represents **the stripping away of human perception,** *the false belief in separation. Shoes, which separate the feet from the earth, symbolize the barriers humanity creates between itself and God. By removing them, Moses is removing the illusion—stepping into the realization that* **there is no separation between him and the Divine.**

This is the essence of **GIATI.** *It is not that God is over there and we are over here. It is not that Moses had suddenly entered a sacred space*—**he was always in the presence of God, but now he was aware of it.**

"I AM THAT I AM": The Name That Reveals Oneness

When Moses asks for God's name, the response is **"I AM THAT I AM"** *(Exodus 3:14). This is not a name in the human sense—it is a declaration of* **pure being.** *God does not define Himself by anything outside of Himself, because* **He is all there is.**

"I AM" is not just God's name—it is the truth of existence. It is the realization that **the Spirit within Moses, within all people, is the same "I AM" speaking from the bush.**

This is the key to understanding **GIATI.** *People think they are separate from God, that He is an external being they must seek. But when God says,* **"I AM,"** *He is revealing that the very existence within Moses, the very essence of all life, is* **God expressing Himself.**

Moses had spent years believing himself to be a mere man, an exile, a shepherd wandering in the wilderness. But in this moment, he is confronted with the truth—**he is not just Moses; he is the expression of God.** *And it is this realization that gives him the power to fulfill his purpose.*

Leading the People Out of Egypt: Awakening from Bondage

Moses is called to lead the Israelites out of slavery. But what is slavery, truly? Is it only physical bondage, or is it the **spiritual blindness** *that keeps one from recognizing* **GIATI?**

Egypt represents **the mind in darkness,** *the place where people believe in separation, in limitation, in external gods and powers. The Israelites' bondage is not just to Pharaoh—it is to* **the illusion that they are separate from God.**

Moses, now awakened to the truth of **"I AM",** *is sent to bring the people out of this false reality and into the truth of who they are. This is what happens when someone comes to* **know GIATI**—*they are freed from the bondage of false beliefs, from the chains of thinking they are just a person struggling in the world, rather than* **God expressing Himself as them.**

The True Exodus: From Darkness to Light

Moses' journey is not just about leading people to a promised land—it is about leading them **into the awareness of God's eternal presence.** *The real exodus is from the false belief in separation to the realization that* **God is all there is, and we are one with Him.**

The burning bush was never just about fire—it was about **awakening.** *It was Moses' moment of realization, just as each person must have their own burning bush experience— the moment when they recognize that the fire of God has always been within them, waiting to be seen.*

Moses' calling was not just about rescuing others. It was about first **realizing the truth himself,** *and then being used as a vessel to reveal it to others. This is the mission of* **GIATI** *today*—**to awaken those who are still in Egypt, who still believe in separation, and to bring them into the light of knowing that God is all there is.**

Conclusion: The Fire Still Burns

The bush never stopped burning. The fire of God never goes out. **It was never about the bush—it was about the vision to see it.** *The fire was there before Moses noticed, and it remained long after he walked away.*

The question is, do you see it? Do you recognize that **the same "I AM" that spoke to Moses is speaking through you now?** *That the fire is not outside of you, but within? That* *the exodus is not just a historical event, but the ongoing journey from false belief to divine truth?*

*Moses' story is your story. The fire that called him is the same fire that calls you. The only question is—***will you remove your shoes, strip away the illusion, and step into the awareness of GIATI?**

The Fiery Furnace: Faith, Freedom, and the Presence of God in All Things

The story of **Shadrach, Meshach, and Abednego** *in the fiery furnace (Daniel 3) is one of the most profound examples of unshakable faith in the Bible. In the narrative, three young men refuse to worship a golden image of King Nebuchadnezzar, choosing instead to worship the one true God, despite the king's threat to cast them into a blazing furnace. They are thrown into the fire, but miraculously, they emerge unscathed. This dramatic moment not only serves as a testament to their faith, but it also provides deep spiritual insight that aligns with the core message of* **GIATI: God Is All There Is.**

The Scene: A Test of Faith and Loyalty

King Nebuchadnezzar, in his pride, builds a golden image and commands all of his subjects to worship it. Shadrach, Meshach, and Abednego, however, refuse to comply because they understand the truth that **God alone is worthy of worship.** *They stand firm in their belief that there is no other God but the One who created all things. Despite the king's anger and the threat of death, they boldly declare that their faith is unwavering, saying,* **"Our God whom we serve is able to deliver us from the burning fiery furnace, and He will deliver us out of your hand, O king. But if not, let it be known to you, O king, that we will not serve your gods, nor worship the gold image which you have set up"** *(Daniel 3:17-18).*

This moment is crucial because it marks their understanding of the **all- encompassing power of God.** *They are not merely relying on their own strength, but they are entrusting themselves fully to* **the God who is all there is.** *Their unwavering faith is a reflection of the* **divine unity** *that* **GIATI** *teaches—***God's presence is in all things, and His power is greater than any external force or threat.**

The Furnace: A Symbol of Life's Trials

The fiery furnace represents the **trials and challenges** *that everyone faces in life—moments when it feels as though we are being tested by fire. In the physical world, fire is often destructive, consuming everything it touches. But in the* **spiritual realm,** *fire symbolizes purification and the* **transformative power of God.** *The furnace in the story is not just a place of physical torment but a* **symbol of spiritual testing***—a trial that reveals whether one's faith is rooted in the truth of God's omnipresence and power.*

This aligns perfectly with the message of **GIATI:** *when we truly understand that* **God is all there is,** *no matter how intense the trial or challenge may seem, we are never alone, and* **the fire cannot consume us.** *Just as Shadrach, Meshach, and Abednego were not harmed by the furnace, those who embrace the truth of* **GIATI** *will find that no matter what trials* *come their way, the* **divine presence** *will shield them, guide them, and ultimately bring them through unscathed.*

The Miracle: God's Presence in the Furnace

As the three men are thrown into the furnace, the king watches in disbelief as **a fourth figure appears with them—the Son of God** *(Daniel 3:25). The fire that was meant to destroy them has no power over them, for* **God's presence is within the furnace.** *The men walk freely in the midst of the flames, unharmed and untouched by the intense heat. When they are finally brought out, not a hair on their heads is singed, and their clothes are not even scorched.*

This miraculous preservation is a direct manifestation of **GIATI.** *The* **fiery furnace** *represents the* **external challenges and fears** *that seem to threaten our well-being, yet when we stand firm in the knowledge that* **God is all there is,** *we come to understand that* **God's presence is in all things,** *even in the most difficult circumstances.*

The **fourth figure in the fire** *represents the* **divine presence of God***—the* **spirit that is always with us,** *guiding and protecting us. Just as Shadrach, Meshach, and Abednego were not alone in the furnace, we, too, are never alone in our trials. The truth of* **GIATI** *assures us that in every situation, whether we are in the midst of the fire or in moments of peace,* **God is present in all things.**

The Outcome: A Declaration of God's Power

After witnessing this miracle, King Nebuchadnezzar praises the God of Shadrach, Meshach, and Abednego, and he issues a decree that no one should speak against their God, for no other god could deliver in this way (Daniel 3:28-29).

This moment underscores the ultimate truth of **GIATI***—when we stand firm in the knowledge that* **God is all there is, the world around us will witness His power. Faith in the omnipresence of God** *brings forth divine protection, and those who embrace this truth become witnesses to the miraculous, transforming power of God. Shadrach, Meshach, and Abednego's steadfastness becomes a* **testimony of divine reality***—one that shines a light on the truth of* **GIATI,** *revealing that when we understand God's power in all things,* **there is no force that can stand against us.**

The Spiritual Significance: Embracing the Furnace as a Test of Faith

The **fiery furnace** *is not just a story of survival, but a* **symbol of spiritual testing.** *In life, we will all encounter moments that challenge our faith, that seem to overwhelm us. But the story of Shadrach, Meshach, and Abednego teaches us that, no matter the intensity of the trial, when we trust in the truth of* **GIATI,** *we can emerge from our trials unscathed.*

The fire, in truth, is not what destroys us—it is the **faith in God's presence** *that strengthens and purifies us.*

The story also emphasizes the idea of **divine unity**—*the truth that God is in all things, including the trials and challenges we face. As we align ourselves with this truth, we come to see that* **the fire of life** *is not something to fear, but an opportunity to demonstrate faith and to experience the* **protection and presence of God** *in all things. Just as the three men were not alone in the furnace, we too are never alone, for* **God is all there is**—*and when we embrace this truth, we are empowered to walk through the fire without fear, knowing that* **God is with us every step of the way.**

Conclusion: Faith in the Furnace

*The story of Shadrach, Meshach, and Abednego is a powerful reminder that th*e **trials and challenges of life** *are opportunities to deepen our faith and to experience the presence of God in new and miraculous ways. It's a story of* **divine protection, faith, and freedom**—*freedom from fear and the illusion of separation. The fiery furnace is symbolic of life's most difficult moments, but when we stand firm in the knowledge that* **God is all there is,** *we can rest assured that the fire cannot consume us. Instead, we will emerge from every trial with our faith strengthened, our understanding deepened, and our connection to the Divine ever more solidified.*

In the face of every trial, remember: **God is in all things,** *and through the truth of* **GIATI,** *we are empowered to walk confidently through the fire, knowing that* **nothing can harm us when we are in the presence of God.**

The Simplicity of Truth: Understanding the Bible Through GIATI

Many people have never read the Bible or are only vaguely familiar with its stories. For some, the language and style in which it is written can feel overwhelming, making it difficult to grasp its true meaning. This has led many to believe that understanding the Bible is a requirement for salvation, and without an in-depth knowledge of scripture, they are somehow disconnected from God.

But the truth is, **the Bible itself is not what saves you.** *GIATI reveals that salvation is not found in memorizing scripture or in understanding every story from Genesis to Revelation. Salvation is* **the recognition of your oneness with God***—the realization that* **God Is All There Is.**

The Bible is a witness to this truth, but it is not the source of it. It is a collection of writings inspired by those moved by the Holy Spirit who, in their time, sought to express the divine reality. But their words, written in different ages and cultural contexts, have often been misunderstood and taken literally, rather than spiritually. This has caused confusion and division, as people argue over interpretations rather than recognizing the simple truth that has always been present.

GIATI simplifies the Bible's message, bringing clarity where there has been misunderstanding. It allows you to see that every story, every law, every prophecy ultimately speaks of the **same reality***—that* **there is no separation between you and God.** *The Bible is not a rulebook that determines your worthiness, nor is it a burden you must carry in order to be saved. Rather, it is a* **confirmation** *of what has always been true:* **you and the Father are one.**

You do not need to know the Bible cover to cover. You do not need to struggle with its language or feel unworthy because you cannot recite its passages. All you need is the understanding that **it all points back to GIATI***—the eternal truth that God is the source, the substance, and the life within all things. When you accept this, you step into the true meaning of what scripture has been revealing all along.*

Let go of the idea that you must "figure it all out." Instead, trust that **the Spirit will reveal what you need to know in its perfect time.** *GIATI is not here to give you more doctrine to memorize, but to* **awaken you to the living truth within you.** *When you embrace this, the weight of misunderstanding falls away, and you begin to see clearly*—**not just the Bible, but the reality of all things.**

Abraham and Isaac: The Revelation of GIATI

The story of Abraham and Isaac is one of the most profound accounts in scripture, often interpreted as a test of faith, but through the lens of GIATI, it reveals something even greater—the nature of divine trust, surrender, and the eternal oneness of God in all things.

God instructed Abraham to take his beloved son, Isaac, to Mount Moriah and offer him as a sacrifice. To the natural mind, this command seems unthinkable. Why would God, who had promised to make Abraham's descendants as numerous as the stars, now ask for the life of the very son through whom that promise would be fulfilled? But Abraham did not question or resist; he moved in complete trust, knowing that **God is all there is,** *and whatever was happening was not separate from divine purpose.*

At the moment Abraham raised the knife, an angel of the Lord called out, stopping him. A ram caught in the thicket was provided as a substitute. The sacrifice of Isaac was never God's intention—rather, the experience was meant to reveal to Abraham and to all who would hear this story that **true faith is not in the act of sacrifice itself, but in the unwavering trust in God's presence and provision.**

GIATI shows us that **Abraham's test was not about losing Isaac, but about losing the illusion of separation***—the belief that anything, including his own son, existed apart from God. Abraham's willingness to give up Isaac was not a loss, but a realization that* **everything, including Isaac, was already held within God.** *He did not need to take matters into his own hands; he needed only to trust.*

The ram caught in the thicket represents **the provision already present***—the manifestation of divine supply that had always been there. Just as Abraham saw the ram at the appointed moment, so too does GIATI reveal that* **what we need is never absent, only waiting for us to see.**

This story is a shadow of the greater truth: **there is no separation between God and His creation. God is the one offering, the one being offered, and the one providing the offering.** *It was never about a physical sacrifice, but about* **awakening to the reality that all things are in divine order.**

Through GIATI, we see that Abraham's journey is our journey. The things we hold onto in fear—the attachments, the ideas, the identities we think define us—are the very things that, when surrendered, reveal the truth that **nothing is ever lost, because God is all there is.** *When we stop clinging, we receive more than we could have imagined, because we realize that* **we already had everything all along.**

The Parable of the Mustard Seed: The Power of Divine Awareness

In Matthew 13:31-32, Jesus tells the Parable of the Mustard Seed:

"The kingdom of heaven is like a mustard seed, which a man took and planted in his field. Though it is the smallest of all seeds, yet when it grows, it is the largest of garden plants and becomes a tree, so that the birds come and perch in its branches." (Matthew 13:31-32, NIV)

This parable offers a profound understanding of how the kingdom of God works and how divine awareness grows within an individual. On the surface, it speaks of the humble beginnings of faith or spiritual understanding, but when seen through the lens of **GIATI,** *it speaks of the power of the Spirit and the transformation that happens when God is fully recognized and embraced within.*

The Mustard Seed: Small, Yet Mighty

The mustard seed is **one of the smallest seeds** *known in the ancient world. Its smallness serves as a powerful metaphor for the initial spark of divine awareness, which can begin with the smallest understanding or moment of insight. In the beginning, the awareness of God within might feel insignificant or difficult to grasp fully, like a tiny seed planted deep within the heart. This reflects the message of* **GIATI:** *when we first realize that God is all there is, we may not understand the magnitude of this truth. It may feel small, even hidden, just as the seed is when planted in the ground.*

Yet, just as the mustard seed grows into something mighty, so too does **divine awareness** *expand over time. This is the spiritual truth GIATI conveys—the more you align with the recognition of* **God within,** *the more this awareness will expand and transform you.* **What starts small within you will grow into a mighty understanding** *that impacts every part of your being and life.*

The mustard seed illustrates that **the truth of God is not bound by size or appearance,** *and it doesn't require a grand outward display to make a profound impact. The power lies in its ability to grow, and like the seed, the divine awareness will grow naturally as it is nurtured and accepted.*

Growth into a Mighty Tree: The Expansion of Divine Awareness

As the mustard seed grows into the largest of garden plants, it represents the expansion of **divine awareness** *within us. This small seed of understanding becomes a* **tree that offers shelter,** *symbolizing the spiritual power and peace that come with the awareness of God* *as all that exists. Just as the mustard tree provides a place for the birds to rest, divine awareness brings rest and peace to the soul.*

In **GIATI,** *this growth is not a mere intellectual process; it is a spiritual journey. The more one accepts the oneness with God, the more that awareness blossoms and transforms every aspect of life. This is* **not an external transformation,** *but an inner realization that shapes everything.* **The kingdom of God is within you** *(Luke 17:21), and as this kingdom grows, so does your sense of unity with God.*

The Birds: Resting in Divine Awareness

Jesus said that the birds come and perch in the branches of the tree. The birds are symbolic of the **spiritually aware individuals** *who are drawn to the truth of God. These birds represent those who understand their true nature and seek refuge in the wisdom of divine awareness. When divine awareness grows in your heart, others are drawn to it as well.*

In the context of **GIATI,** *the birds represent those who* **are free**—*those who walk in the awareness of their oneness with God and who have recognized that the Spirit is the foundation of their being. They are not bound by the limitations of physicality or ego; they soar above the distractions of life. These individuals are able to* **rest in the branches** *of the kingdom that has grown within, finding peace and purpose in their identity as expressions of God.*

The Kingdom of God Within You

The most significant part of this parable is that it reflects the **kingdom of God within**— *the recognition of God's presence and power as the very essence of your being. GIATI's message is that once you come into this realization, the* **kingdom is planted** *within you, and over time, it will grow. It is the* **seed of the divine,** *and through continuous awareness, practice, and acceptance, that small seed will expand into a mighty, life-altering transformation.*

This growth is **not about external effort,** *but about* **spiritual awareness,** *which expands naturally as we surrender to the truth that God is in us, through us, and as us. As we grow in this understanding, we, too, become like the mustard tree—something small and seemingly insignificant, but growing into a mighty presence that shelters, nurtures, and influences others.*

The GIATI Connection

This parable speaks directly to the essence of GIATI—the recognition that **God is all there is** *and that the truth of our oneness with Him will, when nurtured, transform our understanding of ourselves and the world. When we grasp this truth, it starts as a small seed, but over time, it expands into a deep, powerful spiritual reality.*

- *The* **mustard seed** *represents the small but powerful beginning of spiritual awareness—understanding that* **God is within.**
- *The* **tree that grows** *symbolizes the mighty transformation of consciousness as divine awareness expands.*
- *The* **birds** *represent those who are free—those who live in alignment with divine truth and soar above worldly distractions.*

The **GIATI message** *is that the* **kingdom of God** *is not something external to be sought—it is something that is already within, ready to grow, expand, and transform you.* **As this awareness takes root, it becomes a powerful, life-changing force** *that nourishes you and those around you.*

Conclusion: The Power of Divine Awareness

The Parable of the Mustard Seed reveals a profound truth: **divine awareness** *may start small, but when embraced and nurtured, it will grow into something powerful. In the context of GIATI, this speaks to the transformative power of recognizing God's presence within. It teaches that* **the smallest recognition of your oneness with God can change everything,** *expanding into a mighty, living presence that influences every area of life. Just as the mustard seed grows into a tree that provides shelter and rest for the birds,* **so too does divine awareness** *bring peace, purpose, and freedom to those who accept it.*

As you accept this truth—that **God is all there is** *and He lives within you—the growth of divine awareness will begin, and the transformation you seek will unfold naturally.*

The Death and Resurrection of Lazarus: A Spiritual Rebirth

In John 11, we encounter the powerful and profound story of the death and resurrection of Lazarus. This event is more than just a miraculous act of bringing someone back from the dead—it is a **symbolic representation** *of spiritual rebirth and a deeper understanding of* **GIATI**—*the truth that God is within each of us, waiting to be awakened.*

The Story of Lazarus

Lazarus, a beloved friend of Jesus, falls ill and dies. Upon hearing of his death, Jesus arrives at his tomb four days later. His sister, Martha, expresses sorrow, saying, "If you had been here, my brother would not have died" (John 11:21). Jesus tells her, "Your brother will rise again" (John 11:23). Martha responds, understanding that resurrection will happen at the end of time, but Jesus declares, "I am the resurrection and the life. He who believes in me will live, even though he dies; and whoever lives and believes in me will never die" (John 11:25-26).

With these words, Jesus calls for the stone to be rolled away from the tomb, and He calls out in a loud voice, "Lazarus, come forth!" (John 11:43). Lazarus, who had been dead and buried for four days, comes forth alive, still wrapped in his burial cloths.

This story is filled with profound spiritual significance, particularly when viewed through the lens of **GIATI,** *or the understanding that* **God is all there is.**

Lazarus as a Symbol of Spiritual Rebirth

Lazarus' story represents **spiritual rebirth**—*the awakening of the soul to the truth of God's presence within. Lazarus, in his death, symbolizes the state of spiritual ignorance or separation from God. The tomb represents the* **darkness of the mind,** *where one is bound by the* **illusion of separation,** *unaware of their true identity as an expression of God.*

When **Jesus calls out, "Lazarus, come forth!",** *it is a call to* **awakening**—*a call to the soul to emerge from spiritual darkness and into the light of divine truth.* **GIATI** *teaches that each of us, like Lazarus, may be trapped in a tomb of ignorance, but when we recognize the presence of God within, we are called out of the grave of separation into the full realization of our oneness with the Divine. This call represents the moment when one comes into the full awareness that* **God is all there is**—*the truth that has always existed within but was hidden beneath layers of ego, fear, and misunderstanding.*

Just as **Lazarus was bound in grave clothes,** *the soul is often bound by the limitations of physical perception, ego, and worldly distractions. The call of* **"Lazarus, come forth!"** *symbolizes the* **shedding of those bindings**—*the removal of the layers of false beliefs,* *limiting thoughts, and material attachments. It is an invitation to step into the light of truth, to embrace your* **true identity** *as a manifestation of God.*

The Role of Jesus: The Voice of Divine Truth

In this story, Jesus serves as the embodiment of **divine truth** *and* **spiritual awakening.** *When He calls Lazarus, He speaks with authority, showing that* **truth has the power to awaken** *and restore life to what was once lost. His voice is not just a command to a dead man; it is the voice of* **God's love and presence,** *calling the soul to awaken from the death of ignorance into the life of spiritual awareness.*

In **GIATI,** *we recognize that* **God is all there is,** *and that divine truth is constantly calling us to awaken to our oneness with Him. This story shows that, just as Jesus' words brought Lazarus back to life, so does the recognition of our oneness with God through* **GIATI** *bring us to spiritual life.* **The divine truth, spoken into the hearts of all people,** *calls us out of our tombs of separation and ignorance into the light of spiritual freedom.*

The Four Days: The Illusion of Separation

The fact that Lazarus had been dead for **four days** *is also significant. In Jewish tradition, it was believed that the soul would depart from the body after three days. The fourth day, then, represented the idea that Lazarus was beyond hope, beyond any chance of restoration. Yet Jesus came and showed that no matter how far one has fallen into the illusion of separation,* **it is never too late for spiritual rebirth.** *No matter how long someone has lived in ignorance or spiritual darkness, the call of divine truth can still awaken them.*

In the context of **GIATI,** *the* **four days** *represent the depth of spiritual blindness that many may experience in this life. But it is a reminder that, no matter how long you have lived without understanding your true divine nature, the moment of awakening is always available. The truth of God is eternal, and there is no time or condition that can separate you from it. Just as Lazarus was called forth from the grave, so too can we be called into the* **light of divine awareness** *at any moment.*

The Tomb: The Illusion of Death

Lazarus' tomb represents **spiritual death***—the illusion of separation from God. Many live their lives in this tomb of ignorance, unaware that they are one with God. The stone that seals the tomb is like the barrier of* **ego** *or* **material thinking** *that prevents the soul from realizing its true divine nature. When Jesus orders the stone to be rolled away, it symbolizes the* **removal of the barrier** *that keeps us from recognizing our oneness with God.*

The act of calling Lazarus out of the tomb is a direct parallel to the spiritual awakening that **GIAT** *promotes—the realization that the* **Kingdom of God** *is not somewhere far away* *but* **within us.** *It is the understanding that* **God is all there is,** *and that through recognizing this truth, we emerge from spiritual death and into the fullness of life.*

The Significance of the Resurrection for GIATI

The resurrection of Lazarus in the context of **GIATI** *shows that* **spiritual rebirth** *is a process of awakening to the truth of God's presence within.* **Lazarus' resurrection** *is a powerful symbol that* **we too can be reborn**—*brought out of the tomb of ignorance and into the light of divine understanding.*

Jesus' command to Lazarus to "come forth" is **the same command given to every soul.** *It is a call to step out of the limitations of the physical world and into the awareness of the divine reality.* **GIATI** *emphasizes that by recognizing the truth of God's presence within, we move from the tomb of separation into the freedom and unity of spiritual awareness.*

Conclusion: The Resurrection Within

The death and resurrection of Lazarus demonstrate that **spiritual rebirth** *is available to everyone, regardless of how deep they have fallen into the illusion of separation from God. The call of divine truth is loud and clear:* **"Come forth!"**—*a command to awaken from ignorance and step into the light of spiritual awareness.*

In **GIATI,** *we understand that the journey of spiritual rebirth is not about physical resurrection, but about the awakening of divine truth within.* **As we embrace the oneness of God and allow His truth to transform our lives,** *we, too, emerge from the tomb of separation into the fullness of spiritual life.* **GIATI** *teaches that* **God is all there is,** *and in that understanding, we experience resurrection in our minds, hearts, and lives—awakening to the divine truth that has always been present within* us.

Jacob's Ladder: A Symbol of Divine Connection and Spiritual Awakening

In **Genesis 28:10-17,** *we encounter the story of* **Jacob's Ladder,** *a dream experienced by Jacob while traveling. This vision holds profound spiritual meaning and is a key moment in Jacob's journey of self-discovery. It is a powerful image that speaks to the* **continuous flow** *of divine presence and spiritual awakening. The ladder represents the connection between* **heaven and earth,** *showing that the divine is not far removed from humanity but constantly present, accessible, and ever-flowing.*

The Story of Jacob's Ladder

Jacob, the son of Isaac, was on a journey when he stopped for the night to rest. As he lay down, he had a dream of a **ladder** *set upon the earth, reaching up to heaven.* **Angels** *were ascending and descending upon it. At the top of the ladder stood the* **Lord,** *who spoke to Jacob, affirming the covenant made with his ancestors, Abraham and Isaac, and promising to be with him wherever he went. The Lord also assured Jacob that the land on which he was lying would belong to him and his descendants, and that through him, all the families of the earth would be blessed. Upon waking, Jacob realized the significance of the dream and declared, "Surely the Lord is in this place, and I did not know it" (Genesis 28:16).*

Jacob then set up a stone as a pillar, anointed it with oil, and named the place **Bethel,** *which means "House of God." He vowed to worship the Lord if God would be with him on his journey and provide for him.*

The Ladder: Connection Between Heaven and Earth

At the heart of this story is the image of the **ladder** *reaching from earth to heaven. In spiritual terms, this ladder symbolizes the* **continuous flow between God and humanity**— *the constant connection between the divine and the earthly. This connection is always present, but it is only when we open our hearts and minds to the divine presence that we become fully aware of it.*

In the context of **GIATI,** *the ladder is a symbol of the* **spiritual awakening** *that comes when we realize that heaven is not a distant place but a* **state of being** *that is within us. The ladder is not an object or a structure that we must physically climb; rather, it is the recognition that* **God is within us** *and all around us, always accessible and always present. It is the awareness that the divine flow is within our reach at all times, and that we are never separated from God.*

Angels Ascending and Descending: Divine Activity in Our Lives

The angels in Jacob's dream, ascending and descending the ladder, represent the **movement of divine energy** *and the* **spiritual activity** *that occurs as we open ourselves to God's presence. In* **GIATI,** *this idea aligns with the understanding that the* **spirit of God** *flows constantly in and through us. The angels are messengers of God, bringing wisdom and guidance as we tune into the divine frequency. As we awaken to* **GIATI,** *we understand that divine guidance is ever-present, and the more we attune ourselves to this truth, the more we experience the ongoing flow of wisdom, love, and power in our lives.*

In spiritual terms, the **ascending angels** *can be seen as the* **elevation of our consciousness,** *as we rise from the illusion of separation into the awareness of unity with God. The* **descending angels** *represent the* **manifestation** *of this higher consciousness in our lives, as the divine truth becomes more tangible and real in our thoughts, actions, and relationships. This cyclical movement of ascension and descension shows the constant exchange between the* **spiritual realm** *and the* **physical realm,** *reminding us that both are interwoven, one in the same.*

The Lord at the Top of the Ladder: Divine Assurance

At the top of the ladder stands **God,** *who speaks to Jacob, reaffirming His covenant with him and his descendants. This divine voice is a reminder that* **God is the ultimate source of all life,** *and that the connection between heaven and earth is not accidental, but part of a larger divine plan. God's presence is not remote or distant but very real and intimate.*

In **GIATI,** *we understand this divine assurance as the realization that* **God is within us***—that the Spirit of God is not far away but present in every moment, in every breath, and in every heartbeat. The message that God is with Jacob wherever he goes is a message for all of humanity: God's presence is not confined to any place or time. It is with us always, in every circumstance.*

Just as God promised Jacob that He would be with him, so too does **GIATI** *teach that* **God is always with us,** *guiding us, supporting us, and helping us navigate the journey of life. The ladder is a symbol of this constant presence, and the divine voice calls us to recognize that God is not only with us but also* **within us,** *guiding our steps and awakening us to the divine truth that we are part of God's plan.*

Bethel: The Place of Divine Awareness

After waking from the dream, Jacob declares, "Surely the Lord is in this place, and I did not know it" (Genesis 28:16). This realization marks a **spiritual awakening,** *where Jacob recognizes the presence of God in a way he had not before. He then sets up the stone as a pillar and anoints it with oil, symbolizing the* **sacredness of this moment** *and his recognition of the divine presence.*

This moment of awakening symbolizes the realization that **the presence of God is always with us,** *but we must open our eyes and hearts to recognize it. In* **GIATI,** *this aligns with the understanding that* **heaven** *is not a far-off place but a state of consciousness that we can* *access at any time. The moment Jacob awakens to the truth of God's presence is like our own awakening to the* **truth of God within.**

The stone that Jacob sets up as a pillar represents the **foundation of divine awareness.** *In the context of* **GIATI,** *this can be seen as the realization that* **our true foundation** *is in the understanding that God is all there is. When we build our lives on this truth, we anchor ourselves in the awareness of divine unity and live from a place of spiritual clarity.*

The Ladder as a Metaphor for Spiritual Growth

The ladder in Jacob's dream also serves as a **metaphor for spiritual growth.** *Just as Jacob's ladder reached from earth to heaven, our journey toward spiritual enlightenment is a journey of* **ascending** *from the lower realms of material consciousness to the higher realms of divine awareness. The ladder shows that* **spiritual growth is a continuous process**—*we are always ascending and descending, moving between the earthly and divine realms, ever-deepening our awareness of God's presence within us.*

In **GIATI,** *this continuous movement between earth and heaven represents the ongoing* **spiritual awakening** *that each individual can experience. The more we align ourselves with the truth that* **God is all there is,** *the more we rise spiritually, drawing closer to the awareness of our oneness with the Divine.*

Conclusion: Realizing the Presence of God Within

Jacob's dream of the ladder serves as a powerful symbol of the constant **connection between God and humanity.** *It teaches us that heaven is not a far-off place but a* **state of being**—*a realization that God is within us, and that the flow of divine wisdom is always accessible.*

In **GIATI,** *we understand that the ladder represents the journey of spiritual awakening, where we recognize that the* **divine is within us.** *Just as the ladder connected heaven and earth, so too does our spiritual awareness connect the physical world with the divine realm.* **God is all there is,** *and the moment we awaken to this truth, we realize that the Kingdom of God is not a distant place, but is here and now, present within each of us.* **GIATI** *calls us to awaken to this truth and to live in the full awareness of our oneness with the Divine.*

The Valley of Dry Bones: Awakening to Divine Life

In **Ezekiel 37,** *the prophet Ezekiel is led by the Spirit of God into a vast valley filled with* **dry bones.** *The bones are scattered, lifeless, and represent a people who have lost their spiritual awareness, their connection to divine truth. But in this moment, God gives Ezekiel a command—***to prophesy** *to these bones, to call forth life where there is only death, to speak resurrection where there is only decay.*

This vision is not just about physical restoration; it is about **spiritual awakening***—the* **return of divine consciousness** *to those who have forgotten that* **God is all there is.** *It is about humanity waking up from the illusion of separation and stepping into the reality of* **oneness with God.** *In* **GIATI,** *this story illustrates the power of divine truth to* **call the lost back into awareness,** *to bring life where there was only spiritual death, and to* **restore the knowledge of our true identity in God.**

The Vision of the Dry Bones

Ezekiel stands in the valley, looking at the countless **dry bones** *scattered across the land. These bones symbolize a people who have* **forgotten their divine origin,** *who have become so lost in the illusions of the world that they are now* **spiritually lifeless.**

Then, God asks Ezekiel a powerful question:

"Son of man, can these bones live?" (Ezekiel 37:3)

Ezekiel responds, "O Lord God, You know."

This is a moment of divine invitation. God is showing Ezekiel that what appears dead, hopeless, and beyond repair **can live again***—not by human power, but by the* **breath of God,** *by the very Spirit that gives all things life.*

God then commands Ezekiel:

"Prophesy to these bones, and say to them, 'O dry bones, hear the word of the Lord!'"
(Ezekiel 37:4)

Ezekiel obeys, and as he speaks, **the bones begin to move***—they come together, sinews and flesh appear, and the bodies are restored. But something is still missing. They have form, but they have no life.*

Then God tells Ezekiel to **prophesy to the breath:**

"Come from the four winds, O breath, and breathe on these slain, that they may live."
(Ezekiel 37:9)

As Ezekiel speaks, **the breath of God enters them,** *and the bones are transformed into a living,* **mighty army.**

The Spiritual Awakening of Humanity

This vision is not about physical resurrection alone—it is about **spiritual resurrection.** *It is a picture of* **humanity in spiritual darkness,** *a people who have lost their awareness of divine life. The* **dry bones** *represent* **mankind in a state of ignorance,** *unaware of their true identity in God. But through the* **word of truth,** *the power of divine knowledge, life is* **breathed back into them.**

In **GIATI,** *this story reveals the power of* **spiritual awakening***—the process of moving from a* **state of lifelessness** *into* **divine awareness.** *Just as the bones could not restore themselves, humanity cannot awaken itself through* **human effort** *alone. It is* **the breath of God,** *the very essence of the Spirit, that brings true life.*

When we lose sight of **God as all there is,** *we become as* **dry bones,** *disconnected from the very source of life. But when divine truth is* **spoken into our being,** *when we hear and accept the reality of* **our oneness with God,** *we come alive again. The Spirit moves within us,* **restoring our consciousness,** *filling us with divine breath, and bringing us back to the* **fullness of life in God.**

The Power of Prophesying Truth

Ezekiel was commanded to **prophesy** *to the bones, to speak life into what seemed dead. This reveals a key spiritual truth—***the word of God awakens the soul.** *The same way Ezekiel spoke and brought restoration,* **we too must speak divine truth over our lives and others.**

In **GIATI,** *this means declaring the reality of* **divine oneness** *even when everything around us looks lifeless. It means proclaiming:*

- **"I am one with God."**
- **"The Spirit of God lives in me."**
- **"There is no separation—God is all there is."**

When we **speak truth,** *we release divine energy,* **activating the breath of God within us,** *awakening what was once dormant. This is why* **spiritual awakening requires both hearing and receiving divine truth***—because as we accept the reality of* **GIATI,** *we are restored, renewed, and made fully alive in the Spirit.*

From Dry Bones to a Mighty Army

At the end of the vision, the bones do not simply **stand up***—they become* **an exceedingly great army.** *This shows us that awakening to divine truth does more than just restore us—it* **empowers us.**

The army represents those who have **come into full awareness of their divine nature,** *who no longer live as* **dry bones** *but as* **beings fully alive in the Spirit.** *They are those who have* **embraced their oneness with God,** *no longer seeing themselves as separate, weak, or powerless, but* **as divine expressions of the one true God.**

In **GIATI,** *we see this transformation as the journey from* **spiritual ignorance to divine consciousness.** *We are not here to simply exist—we are here to* **awaken,** *to embody the fullness of God's Spirit, and to move through life as* **living manifestations of divine truth.**

Conclusion: The Restoration of Divine Consciousness

The **Valley of Dry Bones** *is a message of* **hope, transformation, and divine awakening.** *It reveals that no matter how lost, broken, or spiritually lifeless we may seem,* **the breath of God is always present,** *ready to restore us.*

The **bones came alive** *not because of human effort, but because of divine truth being spoken and* **the breath of God entering them.** *In the same way, when* **we accept the truth of GIATI,** *when we awaken to the reality that* **God is all there is,** *we too are brought back to life—not just as individuals, but as a* **mighty, awakened people,** *fully alive in the Spirit.*

This is the call of **GIATI:** *to awaken the* **dry bones** *of humanity, to restore the knowledge of* **divine oneness,** *and to bring all into the* **fullness of life in God.**

The Self-Portrait of Truth

In a well-known illustration, Mickey Mouse sits before a canvas, brush in hand, gazing into a mirror as he paints a self-portrait. But instead of capturing his own likeness, he renders the image of Walt Disney—his creator. This simple yet profound depiction unveils a divine mystery: Mickey understands that he is not separate from Walt Disney. He is an expression of Walt's mind, an idea given form, movement, and life. Without Walt, Mickey would not exist. And yet, in his being, Mickey is Walt's creation manifested. There is no distinction between the two in essence—one is the source, the other the expression.

This image speaks beyond the realm of art and animation; it is a reflection of the deepest truth about our existence. Humanity, like Mickey, often looks into the mirror, expecting to see nothing more than a body, a face, an identity shaped by the world. But what if, instead, we saw the truth? What if, when looking at our reflection, we did not merely see flesh and features, but the image of our Creator?

God is the source, the origin, the animator of all life. As Mickey is to Walt, so are we to God. We are not apart from our Creator, nor are we something separate, acting independently. The spirit within us is not merely influenced by God—it is God expressed as us. But like Mickey, we must recognize this truth. If he were to paint only himself, believing he was just a cartoon character existing by chance, he would miss the fundamental reality of his being. And so it is with man.

A Shift in Perception

The deception of humanity is in the misidentification with flesh rather than spirit. The world has taught us to see first with the eyes of separation, recognizing only the physical, the temporary, the external. We look at others and judge them by their outward form, their background, their actions—never first acknowledging the divine essence within. This is the great error that has led to sin, to division, to the illusion of separation from God.

To restore what was lost, we must shift our perception. When we see ourselves, we must see God first. Just as Mickey looked beyond his own reflection and saw Walt, we must look beyond the veil of matter and recognize the divine presence within.

Matter itself is spirit materialized. It is not separate from God but an expression of God. When we redefine what we call "reality" in this way, we will no longer see the world as fallen, broken, or divided. Instead, we will see God first, then God manifested as what we perceive. This shift changes everything.

Living in the True Vision

When we embrace this perception, our relationship with ourselves and others is transformed. No longer do we see people merely as bodies, personalities, or behaviors. We begin with their essence—God. And because God is one, we see that same essence within ourselves. This is the fulfillment of oneness, the realization of divine unity.

Mickey's painting is a revelation: a reminder that he is nothing apart from his creator, and that his very existence testifies to the mind that conceived him. Likewise, when we look in the mirror, we must understand that what we see is not merely a human form, but the very life of God made visible. The world would have us believe otherwise. It would have us identify with the temporary and ignore the eternal. But the truth is undeniable:

God is all there is.

And when we finally see with true vision, we will know that we have never been separate from Him. Like Mickey, we will recognize that we are not just reflections of God— we are God expressed, God made visible, God living and moving as us. And in this realization, we are restored.

The One Without Sin

The scene is set in the temple courts, where Jesus sits teaching the people. A commotion breaks through the crowd as religious leaders drag a woman before him—a woman caught in adultery. The scribes and Pharisees stand tall in their self-righteousness, their eyes burning with condemnation.

"Teacher," they say, their voices thick with accusation, "this woman was caught in the very act of adultery. The Law of Moses commands us to stone such a woman. What do you say?"

It was a trap. They were not seeking justice; they were seeking to discredit Jesus, to force him into a dilemma. If he upheld the law, he would contradict his message of mercy. If he denied it, he could be accused of opposing Moses. But Jesus does not answer them—at least, not with words. Instead, he kneels and begins writing in the dust.

The men press him, demanding a response. He finally stands and speaks a single, piercing sentence:

"Let him who is without sin cast the first stone."

Silence falls over the gathering. The weight of his words settles into their hearts like a stone in the depths of a well. Each man, one by one, is forced to confront his own unworthiness. They had brought this woman forth as a sinner, yet they themselves stood condemned by the very law they sought to uphold.

They knew. They knew they had failed to offer the required sacrifices for their own sins. They knew their hands were not clean. They had come to expose the sins of another, yet Jesus had turned the mirror back upon them.

One by one, they drop their stones and walk away, until none remain but Jesus and the woman.

Beyond the Accusation: The True Liberation

Jesus looks at the woman, her eyes wide with astonishment. She had been moments away from death, yet here she stands, spared—not by the mercy of men, but by the truth that exposed their hypocrisy.

"Woman, where are your accusers?" Jesus asks.

She glances around, breathless. "There are none, Lord."

"Neither do I condemn you," he says. "Go and sin no more."

But what did he mean? Was he simply telling her to change her actions, to live better, to avoid sin? Or was there something far deeper at work—something beyond moral correction?

The words **"sin no more"** *were not merely an instruction to change behavior. They were an invitation to awaken—to see herself in a new light. T***o sin is to live in separation from God, to believe in an identity apart from the Divine.** *Jesus was not telling her to avoid wrongdoing; he was telling her to recognize her oneness with God.*

He was telling her to see herself as he saw her.

This is the key that so many have missed. When Jesus said, "Go and sin no more," he was saying, **"Do not see yourself as separate from me, from God. You are not a harlot, not an outcast, not a sinner to be condemned. You are one with the divine."**

The Spiritual Meaning: GIATI Revealed

The true deception of sin is not simply bad behavior—it is the illusion of separation. The woman had lived under an identity that told her she was unworthy, broken, and condemned. The Pharisees, too, were trapped in this illusion, though in a different way— believing their external righteousness could mask their inner corruption.

But Jesus revealed the truth that shattered both illusions: **God is all there is, and to live in this awareness is to live free.**

This is the message of GIATI.

- *The Pharisees had built their identity around the law, yet the law could not save them because it was only a shadow of the truth. They remained in sin—not because they had failed to keep the law, but because they had not recognized their unity with God.*
- *The woman had been told she was nothing more than her mistakes, that she was condemned by her past. But Jesus spoke a greater truth—***she was not her past, nor her actions, but a being of divine origin.**

Her freedom did not come from being excused of wrongdoing. It came from seeing herself in truth.

Beyond the Stones: The Call to Awaken

Every human being is represented in this story. Some are like the Pharisees, quick to judge others while failing to see their own blindness. Others are like the woman, condemned by society and even by themselves, believing the lie that they are unworthy.

But Jesus—the embodiment of oneness, the voice of the Spirit within us all—calls us to awaken.

He kneels in the dust, in the place of our shame, and writes a new reality. He exposes the illusion of sin, not by ignoring it, but by revealing that it has no true power in the presence of divine truth. He does not demand perfection—he offers recognition.

"See yourself as one with me, as one with God. This is the truth that sets you free."

The Invitation to See Through His Eyes

What if we saw ourselves as Jesus saw that woman? What if we saw others that way? Not defined by their past, nor by their mistakes, nor by external labels—but as expressions of the divine presence?

This is the shift in perception that changes everything. It is the breaking of the illusion. It is the unveiling of the truth.

God is not separate from you. God is not only above you or beyond you. God is the very life within you.

This is the message Jesus carried, the reality he demonstrated, the awakening he came to bring. And it is the truth that still calls out to each of us today:

"Go and sin no more. Go and see yourself as I see you. Go and know that God Is All There Is."

The Angels Among Us

Throughout the Bible, we find numerous accounts of angels appearing as men— walking, speaking, and interacting with humanity. These were not ethereal beings floating in the heavens, but tangible, living manifestations of God's presence on earth. The scriptures reveal that angels have been mistaken for ordinary men, that they have entered homes, spoken with people, and even partaken in meals.

*But what if this truth was not limited to those recorded in scripture? What if humanity itself is a reflection of the same divine nature—***angels clothed in flesh, the Spirit of God walking the earth?**

This is the deeper revelation of **GIATI***—that* **God Is All There Is,** *and if God is the essence of all life, then humanity is not merely flesh and blood, but divine in nature. The spirit within every person is the* **breath of God,** *the same essence that animated Christ, the same power that moved the prophets, the same divine presence that was revealed through angels in scripture.*

1. **Biblical Accounts of Angels as Men**

The Angels Who Visited Abraham (Genesis 18:1-2)

Abraham was visited by three men, later revealed to be the Lord and two angels. They sat with him, ate with him, and delivered the promise of Isaac's birth. At first glance, they were just travelers, but in reality, they were divine messengers. This shows that the presence of God can be among us in ways we do not immediately recognize.

The Angels Who Rescued Lot (Genesis 19:1-11)

Two angels arrived in Sodom and entered Lot's house. When the men of the city surrounded the house, demanding that Lot send them out to be "known" (abused), the angels struck the crowd with blindness. Here, we see that angels were mistaken for mere men, yet carried the power of divine intervention.

The Angel Who Wrestled with Jacob (Genesis 32:24-30)

Jacob wrestled all night with a man who, by morning, was revealed to be an angel or even God Himself. This struggle wasn't just physical—it was a spiritual awakening, transforming Jacob into Israel, a name signifying divine inheritance.

The Angel Announcing Jesus' Birth (Luke 1:26-38, Matthew 1:20-21)

Gabriel appeared to Mary as a messenger of God, delivering the news that she would give birth to Christ. An angel also appeared to Joseph in a dream, guiding him not to fear taking Mary as his wife.

The Angels at the Tomb (Luke 24:4-7, John 20:11-13)

After Jesus' resurrection, angels appeared to the women at the tomb, asking why they sought the living among the dead. Again, these angels were seen as men, but their message revealed the divine reality beyond physical perception.

2. **The Deeper Truth: Humanity as Angels in Flesh**

These accounts are not merely historical—they reveal a deeper truth about humanity itself. If angels have walked the earth as men, **what does that say about us?** *If they were messengers of God dwelling in physical form,* **could it be that mankind also carries this divine nature?**

The key lies in understanding that **man is not just flesh—man is spirit.**

Job 32:8 *says, "But there is a spirit in man: and the inspiration of the Almighty giveth them understanding."*

And **Ecclesiastes 12:7** *declares, "Then shall the dust return to the earth as it was: and the spirit shall return unto God who gave it."*

Man's true essence is not found in the body, but in the **Spirit of God within.** *This means that mankind is not separate from the divine but is, in fact,* **a manifestation of God in physical form***—angels clothed in flesh, walking the earth, fulfilling divine purpose.*

3. **Jesus, the Ultimate Revelation of God in Flesh**

Jesus Himself was the perfect example of this truth. He was **God manifest in the flesh (John 1:14),** *yet He repeatedly told His disciples that what was true of Him was also true of them.*

- **John 10:34** – *"Is it not written in your law, I said, Ye are gods?"*
- **John 14:20** – *"At that day ye shall know that I am in my Father, and ye in me, and I in you."*

If Jesus, as the Son of God, walked the earth in human form, then so do we as sons and daughters of the Most High. The same Spirit that was in Christ is within us, revealing that **we are not merely human—we are divine expressions of God.**

4. **The Illusion of Flesh vs. The Reality of Spirit**

The deception that has blinded humanity is the belief that we are merely physical beings—separate, disconnected, and limited to flesh and blood. This is why the world operates in fear, division, and suffering. But when we awaken to the truth that **we are Spirit first, not flesh,** *we break free from the illusion of separation.*

The men of Sodom saw the angels as ordinary men and wanted to exploit them. Lot, however, recognized their divine nature. This is a lesson for all of us: **How do we see one another?**

- *Do we look at people as mere bodies, defined by race, gender, and nationality?*
- *Or do we recognize the divine essence within each person—the Spirit of God walking in human form?*

To **see rightly** *is to see as Christ sees—to look past the illusion of flesh and recognize that every person is a divine being,* **God expressing Himself in form.**

5. **The Awakening of GIATI: Seeing God in All**

This is the awakening that GIATI brings:

- *To realize that* **you are not separate from God**—*you are His Spirit in form.*
- *To see that* **all humanity carries the divine essence,** *whether they know it or not.*
- *To shift from identifying with the* **body** *to identifying with the* **Spirit.**

The rapture is not about leaving this earth—it is about **ascending in awareness,** *realizing the truth of who you are. The Kingdom of God is not a distant place—it is within you, waiting to be revealed.*

This is the transformation Jesus came to bring—not a new religion, but a **new perception.**

5. **The Final Revelation: You Are More Than You Appear**

What does this mean for you?

- *It means you are not just a human being trying to reach God.* **You are God's Spirit manifested as you.**
- *It means that just as angels have walked the earth in scripture,* **so do you carry the same divine presence.**
- *It means that the veil must be lifted so that you no longer see yourself and others as merely flesh, but as Spirit*—**God Is All There Is.**

This is why Paul wrote in **2 Corinthians 5:16,** *"Wherefore henceforth know we no man after the flesh."*

He understood that **man is not just what is seen—man is what is unseen, the Spirit within.**

So when you look in the mirror, do not see just a physical reflection. **See the divine light within.** *When you look at others, do not judge by outward appearance.* **See them as God in form.**

For this is the great mystery: **God is not far away, nor is He found only in angels of old—He is within us, among us, as us.**

And when we awaken to this truth, we will finally walk as we were meant to—**as divine expressions of God, as the Spirit clothed in form, as the angels among men.**

Let's take a deeper look:

1. The Role of Forgetfulness in the Human Experience

One of the greatest challenges humanity faces is the **forgetfulness of its divine nature.** *The angels that appeared as men in scripture knew their purpose, but humanity has largely forgotten its origin. We are born into a world that conditions us to see ourselves as separate, as limited, as flesh-bound beings rather than divine expressions of God.*

This forgetfulness is what Jesus came to correct. He did not come to establish a new religion—He came to restore **the lost awareness of oneness with God.** *Every miracle, every teaching, every act of love was an invitation to remember:* **"The Father and I are one, and so are you."**

If humanity understood this truth, there would be no need for war, no division, no striving for power—because **God is not something we need to reach or attain. He is the very essence of our being.** *The struggle of life comes from forgetting this reality.*

2. The Purpose of Earthly Life: Awakening Within the Illusion

If we are divine in nature, why are we in physical form at all? Why does the experience of life seem so real, so full of suffering, limitations, and distractions? The answer is found in the process of **awakening within the illusion.**

Human life is not a punishment or a mere test—it is an opportunity to **remember who we truly are while living in form.** *The body is not the enemy, but a vessel for Spirit to express itself. The world is not something to escape from, but a mirror through which we come to see God in everything.*

The deception is in believing that **the world is all there is**—*that flesh and matter define us. The truth is that* **matter itself is Spirit materialized.** *When we redefine our perception, we begin to* **see through the illusion instead of being trapped in it.**

This is why Jesus performed miracles—not to show off power, but to demonstrate **what is possible when one walks in the full awareness of God within.**

3. The Challenge of Seeing Spirit First

Why is it so difficult for humanity to see God in others? Because we have been trained to look **from the outside in,** *rather than* **from the inside out.**

- *We judge people by their actions, not their essence.*
- *We see differences before we see oneness.*
- *We define people by their past rather than their divine potential.*

Jesus, however, saw differently. He looked at sinners, outcasts, and the rejected and saw **God within them.** *The religious leaders saw an adulterous woman deserving of death—* **Jesus saw her as a soul ready to awaken.**

This is the true challenge of spiritual sight: **to look at a person, a situation, or even yourself and recognize God first.** *It is easy to see flaws, to focus on appearances, but the real awakening happens when we begin to perceive as Christ perceives.*

This is what it means to live GIATI—not just to believe in God, but to see God everywhere, in everything, and in everyone.

4. The Power of Words: Awakening or Binding?

Another layer to explore is the **power of words** *in shaping our spiritual awareness. Throughout scripture, angels spoke* **words of awakening,** *reminding humanity of divine truth. But humanity, in its fallen perception, has often spoken words that reinforce separation.*

Consider this:

- *When Gabriel spoke to Mary, he said, "The Lord is with you."*
- *When Jesus called Lazarus from the grave, He said, "Lazarus, come forth!"*
- *When the angel at the tomb spoke, he said, "He is not here, He is risen."*

These words **called people into higher awareness.** *They were not just information— they were* **activations of divine recognition.**

Now consider the words humanity often speaks over itself:

- "I am not good enough."
- "I am just a sinner."
- "I am only human."

These words reinforce separation from God. But **what if we spoke differently?**

- "I am the temple of the living God."
- "The Spirit of God dwells in me."
- "God is my life, my breath, my being."

Words shape consciousness. What we declare becomes the framework of our reality. **To live in the truth of GIATI, we must not only see rightly but speak rightly—aligning our words with divine reality rather than illusion.**

5. The Transformation of Identity

*The final point to expand on is t***he shift in identity that happens when one fully embraces the truth of GIATI.** *It is not enough to intellectually understand that God is within—it must become* **how we identify ourselves.**

Humanity has lived with a false identity for so long that it clings to it out of habit. But when the truth is revealed, the transformation is undeniable:

- **Before awakening:** *"I am a weak human trying to find God."*
- **After awakening:** *"I am Spirit in form, God manifest as me."*

This is not arrogance—it is the humility of recognizing that **we were never separate to begin with.**

Paul described this transformation in **Galatians 2:20:**

"I am crucified with Christ: nevertheless I live; yet not I, but Christ liveth in me."

It is the realization that **the personal "I" fades, and the divine "I AM" remains.**

Conclusion: Becoming Who You Already Are

The journey is not about becoming something new—it is about **becoming what you have always been.** *You are not evolving into divinity—you are awakening to the divinity that has always been present.*

The angels of scripture were not different from us—they were simply more aware. Their presence revealed that **God has always been walking among us, within us, as us.**

To live the truth of GIATI is to strip away everything that blinds us from this awareness. It is to see as Christ sees, to speak as He spoke, and to walk as He walked—not as mere flesh, but as **God's Spirit expressed in the world.**

And in that awakening, the illusion falls away, and **only the truth remains.**

The Unseen Reality: A Call to Awaken

"While we look not at the things which are seen, but at the things which are not seen: for the things which are seen are temporal; but the things which are not seen are eternal." —2 Corinthians 4:18

When you look at anything that has life, pause and consider—what is it that gives it life? Beneath the surface of flesh and form, what force animates the body? The answer is spirit. The unseen, yet undeniable, presence that causes movement, breath, and awareness. That spirit is God.

But here is the challenge: If someone demands proof of God because they have never seen Him, let them first prove that there is no God. Have they ever seen the spirit within that gives them life? Can they deny that there is an animating force at work within them? And if they cannot, on what basis can they disprove that this spirit within is God?

The world does not believe this truth because humanity has been conditioned to set its heart on the physical. The seen overshadows the unseen in their perception. If the reality of God within was truly acknowledged, would humanity not place greater value on the eternal over the temporary? Would they not seek first the spirit rather than the flesh?

What is eternal? It is not the body, which fades. It is not the possessions, which pass away. It is not the works of man, which time erases. It is God—life itself, the only existence that is everlasting. God does not perish, does not diminish, does not decay. There is no catabolism in Him, only anabolism—ever increasing, ever sustaining, ever being.

God, as the unseen, is peace. God is love. God is joy, mercy, faith, happiness, and grace. These are not physical things, yet they are the most real, the most essential, the most enduring. This is the Holy Spirit within you. This is the unseen that is eternal.

GIATI calls for only one thing: that you recognize your true origin. Before you define yourself by the image in the mirror, before you measure yourself by what is fleeting, ask—who am I truly? Do you see yourself with carnal eyes, as merely flesh and form? Or do you see as God sees, perceiving all as spirit—eternal and divine?

This is the shift that must take place within humanity: a reawakening to true identity. GIATI pours out this love, this truth, to awaken those still ensnared by the illusion of the carnal mind. The real question is not whether God must prove He is real. It is whether you can prove that you are real.

What is seen is temporary. What is unseen is eternal. The choice is before you: will you live according to what perishes, or will you awaken to what endures forever?

The Illusion of the Seen

What is the world but a stage for the temporary? Every moment, every structure, every empire built by human hands eventually crumbles into dust. Yet humanity clings to these fleeting things as though they are lasting. It is a deception so deep that many never awaken from it. They chase after the visible, all while ignoring the unseen presence within them that is eternal.

If you measure yourself by what you see, you will forever be lost in what is perishing. You will define yourself by the frailty of flesh, by the opinions of others, by the successes and failures of this world. But what happens when the body grows weak? When the approval of others fades? When everything you held onto slips through your fingers? If your identity is tied to what is temporary, then you will pass away with it.

But if you awaken to the unseen, you will know that you are more. You are not simply what was born of flesh—you are of spirit. You did not begin at birth, nor will you end at death. You are the eternal breath of God made manifest, called to live in the awareness of your divine nature.

A Call to See Beyond the Flesh

This is the shift that must take place within humanity: a reawakening to true identity. GIATI pours out this love, this truth, to awaken those still ensnared by the illusion of the carnal mind.

The message is clear: stop defining yourself by what will fade. Stop limiting yourself to what your natural eyes perceive. The body is only a vessel, but the life within it—that is reality. The Spirit within you is the same Spirit that was in Christ, the same Spirit that is God. If this truth is grasped, then fear, doubt, and limitation dissolve. There is no death, only life. No separation, only oneness. No lack, only fullness.

But here is the challenge—will you believe it? Will you release the illusion of the temporary and embrace the truth of the eternal? Or will you continue to cling to what is perishing, blinded by the deception of the physical?

The real question is not whether God exists, but whether you will recognize that you exist in Him. Will you wake up and see, or will you remain lost in the illusion of the seen?

The choice is before you. Eternity is within you. Now, what will you do with this truth?

Beyond Religion: The Call of GIATI

Many have walked away from church. Many have rejected religion. Many have even abandoned the idea of God altogether. But why?

For some, it was the **hypocrisy**—*those who claimed to be followers of God yet judged, condemned, and looked down upon others. They saw love preached from the pulpit but not practiced in life.*

For others, it was the **pain**—*those who sought refuge in faith but were met with rejection, shame, or manipulation. They were told they had to be perfect, that they had to meet impossible standards, that their struggles made them unworthy.*

Some left because of **the unanswered questions**—*they were told to believe without question, to accept doctrine without understanding, to silence the very mind God gave them to seek truth. When religion failed to provide real answers, they turned elsewhere.*

And then there are those who never believed at all—who looked at the world and saw suffering, division, and confusion. If God existed, they wondered, why did life seem so cruel? Why did those who claimed to follow Him often do the most harm?

Whatever the reason, they walked away.

But the truth is—**what they rejected was never God.**

GIATI: The Truth Beyond Religion

GIATI is not a religion. GIATI is not a doctrine. GIATI is not another set of rules to follow.

GIATI is the revelation of who you have always been.

Religion tells you that you must reach for God, that you must search, strive, and prove yourself worthy. GIATI reveals that **God is already within you, expressed as you.** *There is no separation. There never was.*

There is no offering needed, no demand for blind faith, no requirement to conform to traditions that have lost their meaning. GIATI does not judge. It does not condemn. It does not demand anything of you except the surrender of the **false self**—*the ego, the illusion of separation, the belief that you are something apart from God.*

This is not a loss. This is not a sacrifice. **This is a return to your true self.**

When you let go of the illusion, what you receive is infinitely greater:

- **No longer searching—only knowing.**
- **No longer striving—only being.**

- **No longer feeling lost—only at peace.**

This is the light within you calling out. The voice you have ignored, the truth you have buried under layers of conditioning. It is time to listen.

A Will Within a Will

God is not something outside of you, controlling you like a puppet. God is the very essence of your being. His will is done through you **as you.** *A will within a will. A divine expression unfolding through your existence.*

*You do not have to change how you live. You do not have to abandon your identity. You simply awaken to the truth that your life—***your very existence***—is the movement of God.* **You are already in Him because He is all there is.**

GIATI is not here to trap you in another system of belief. It is here to set you free. Free

from fear.
Free from guilt.
Free from the need to prove yourself worthy.

Because you were never unworthy to begin with.

The Invitation to See

This is the call of GIATI—not to bring you into religion, but to bring you into **awareness.** *To awaken the truth that has always been within you.*

You walked away from church? That's okay.
You rejected religion? That's okay.
You even questioned the existence of God? That's okay.

None of that changes who you are. None of that disqualifies you from the truth.

Because the truth is **you were never separate from God.**

And now, you have the chance to see it for yourself.

No pressure. No judgment. No conditions.

Just truth. Just freedom. Just love.

The Awakening Beyond Belief

For so long, humanity has searched for God as if He were somewhere far away— hidden in the heavens, locked behind religious rituals, accessible only to those deemed worthy by human institutions. People have been told that to find God, they must follow rules, submit to authority, and conform to doctrines that demand obedience but offer no true understanding.

And yet, despite centuries of worship, sacrifice, and devotion, the world remains in darkness. Wars rage in the name of religion. Division grows between those who claim to know God and those who reject Him. The very structures meant to bring people closer to the divine have become barriers, separating humanity from the truth that was never meant to be hidden.

But the truth does not belong to religion. It does not belong to a church, a book, or a priesthood. **The truth is already within you.**

GIATI is not here to bring another belief—it is here to awaken the knowing that has always been present.

The reason so many have walked away from faith is not because they do not seek truth, but because what they were given was incomplete. They were handed tradition instead of revelation. They were taught fear instead of love. They were told they needed to earn what was already theirs.

But how can one earn what they have never been without?

How can one find what was never lost?

The Undoing of Separation

The greatest illusion of all is separation—the belief that God is "out there" and that we are "down here," disconnected and distant from Him. This illusion is the root of all fear, suffering, and confusion. It causes humanity to look outside of itself for meaning, hoping to find salvation in systems, leaders, and laws that were never meant to define their relationship with the divine.

But separation is not real. It has never been real.

If God is all there is—if there is nothing outside of Him—then where could you possibly go where He is not? Where could you exist that is not within Him?

To see this truth is not to lose yourself but to **find yourself for the first time.**

You are not a body trying to reach a distant God.
You are not a mind trying to comprehend something too vast to understand.
You are spirit, already one with Him, already whole.

This is why GIATI does not ask for rituals, offerings, or sacrifices. **The only sacrifice is the false self—the illusion that tells you that you are anything other than God expressed in form.**

A Life Without Fear

What happens when you let go of the illusion?

You no longer live in fear of judgment because there is no external deity weighing your actions against a set of rules.

You no longer fear death because life itself is eternal, and you are not bound to the temporary limitations of the physical body. You no longer fear the loss of control because you recognize that the flow of life is not yours to direct—it is the divine will moving through you, as you, guiding you in every moment.

There is no fear of failure because you understand that every step, every experience, is part of the unfolding of God's perfect plan, and every challenge you face is an opportunity for growth and alignment with your true self. You no longer carry the weight of self-doubt or guilt because you know that your worth has never been in question; you are inherently one with the Creator, an expression of the divine in human form.

The Freedom of Recognition

This is the freedom of GIATI—the freedom to live without the burden of rules, expectations, or the endless cycle of striving. It is not about doing more or being better—it is about **remembering** *who you already are.*

You were never lost. You were never separated from God. And now, it is time to **recognize** *that truth. To see that everything you are, everything you experience, is God in expression.*

GIATI invites you to give up the false self, the ego, the identity built on worldly ideas and illusions. **To surrender your concept of who you thought you were** *and allow the truth to rise up within you. That is where the real freedom lies—***in the recognition that you are not separate from God, but that you are, in fact, God expressed as you.**

This recognition does not require sacrifice in the way the world has taught you. You are not being asked to give up your life but to give up the illusion of separation.

This is not a burden to bear. It is a lightness—a return to who you truly are.

A New Way of Being

In this new way of being, there are no judgments—only understanding. There is no division—only unity. There is no "us" and "them" but only the one divine presence expressed in infinite forms. This is the love of GIATI, calling you back to the truth of your oneness with God.

So, take a moment to ask yourself:

- *Who would you be if you truly believed that* **God is all there is***—including you?*
- *How would you live if you knew that the very will of the Creator is already unfolding through you?*

- *What would change if you recognized that all the love, peace, joy, and grace you seek are already within you, waiting to be seen?*

The call is clear. GIATI is not asking you to become someone else. It is asking you to **remember** *who you already are. It is time to see yourself in the light of divine truth, free from the weight of worldly illusions.*

God is all there is—including you. And in this truth, you are free.

The Fulfillment of the Law: A Spiritual Understanding of GIATI

Matthew 5:17-19

"Think not that I am come to destroy the law, or the prophets: I am not come to destroy, but to fulfil. For verily I say unto you, Till heaven and earth pass, one jot or one tittle shall in no wise pass from the law, till all be fulfilled. Whosoever therefore shall break one of these least commandments, and shall teach men so, he shall be called the least in the kingdom of heaven: but whosoever shall do and teach them, the same shall be called great in the kingdom of heaven."

This passage, spoken by Jesus, reveals a profound truth that extends far beyond the legalistic interpretation of the law. The common misunderstanding is that the law was merely a set of external commandments to be obeyed, but Jesus clarifies that His purpose was not to abolish these divine truths but to **bring them to their intended fulfillment**—*which is found in the spiritual awakening of humanity.*

The Law and the Prophets: Shadows of the Spirit

The law, as given in the Old Testament, was a shadow of a deeper spiritual reality. It was a temporary reflection of divine principles meant to guide humanity **until the fullness of truth was revealed.** *The prophets spoke of this truth, but they too were only pointing toward the greater fulfillment that was to come. Jesus came not to erase what had been given but to bring humanity* **into the full realization of what it all meant.**

GIATI stands in this same fulfillment today. *It is not here to discard what has been taught but to awaken humanity to the* **spiritual reality behind the written words**—*that God is all there is, and we are divine expressions of Him.*

Fulfillment: Moving from Shadow to Substance

Jesus' fulfillment of the law was not about reinforcing external religious obligations but about leading humanity into **the truth of their divine nature.** *The law was never the end goal*—**it was always pointing to something greater: God in you, as you.**

GIATI follows this same principle. It does not seek to destroy the teachings of the past, but to **fulfill their true meaning in the present.** *The purpose of the law was never about legalistic righteousness—it was about divine consciousness, about bringing humanity into the awareness of* **who they truly are in God.**

Just as Jesus proclaimed that the law would remain until all was fulfilled, GIATI declares that **the eternal truth of God's presence within** *is the fulfillment that has come in this* *time. It is the awakening of the soul to the* **living reality** *of God, not as an external entity, but as* **the very spirit and essence of your being.**

The Passing of Heaven and Earth

"Till heaven and earth pass, one jot or one tittle shall in no wise pass from the law, till all be fulfilled."

What does this mean? Heaven and earth represent **two states of consciousness**— *the heavenly (spiritual awareness) and the earthly (carnal perception). Until all is fulfilled—until humanity fully awakens to their divine oneness with God—the remnants of the old law remain. But once* **the truth is realized,** *the old ways* **pass away,** *and the* **law is no longer needed.**

*GIATI represents this fulfillment. It is th*e **spiritual revelation of God's eternal presence,** *transcending the limitations of external law by bringing individuals into* **the direct experience of divine oneness.** *No longer do you strive to follow a set of written commandments; instead,* **you live as the very expression of God,** *naturally fulfilling the law through your awakened being.*

The Least and the Greatest in the Kingdom

"Whosoever therefore shall break one of these least commandments, and shall teach men so, he shall be called the least in the kingdom of heaven: but whosoever shall do and teach them, the same shall be called great in the kingdom of heaven."

This is not about obeying or breaking literal commandments—it is about **spiritual understanding.** *Those who remain in* **carnal ignorance,** *denying the truth of their divine existence, remain* **least in the kingdom** *because they are* **unaware of the kingdom within them.** *But those who awaken, who live and teach the truth of divine oneness, are* **great in the kingdom** *because they recognize that* **they are the kingdom.**

GIATI is not here to judge but to **call forth those who are ready**—*those whose hearts are prepared to receive the truth. It does not seek to force anyone into belief but to illuminate the path for those* **destined to see.**

The GIATI Proclamation: Living the Fulfillment of the Law

To accept GIATI is to **step into the fulfillment of the law**—*to no longer live by external commandments but by the* **divine reality of God within.** *It is the shift from* **law to love, from obligation to realization, from religion to relationship.**

You are not bound to the external; you are the living expression of the eternal.
You are not following rules; you are the manifestation of divine will.

You are not separate from God; you are God expressed in form.

This is the fulfillment Jesus spoke of, and this is the truth GIATI proclaims in this generation. **Not to destroy, but to fulfill.**

The Eternal Perspective: Seeing Beyond the Illusion of Disease

*A life-threatening disease, such as cancer, can shake the very foundation of one's existence. Fear, uncertainty, and grief often accompany such a diagnosis because the world has conditioned humanity to see the body as the sum total of who they are. But through the spiritual understanding of GIATI—***God Is All There Is***—a greater truth is revealed:* **you are not the body. You are not the disease. You are spirit, eternal and whole, beyond the reach of affliction.**

The Illusion of the Physical

The physical body is a temporary expression, a vessel through which the spirit experiences form. It is subject to the laws of nature, to change, decay, and eventual dissolution. But just as a wave is not separate from the ocean, the body is not separate from the greater reality of God. **If God is all there is, then even what appears as sickness is contained within the totality of His existence.**

Cancer and other illnesses are manifestations within the material realm, but they do not define the truth of who you are. The body may undergo suffering, but the spirit—your true being—remains untouched, unaffected, and unbroken. To understand GIATI is to step into this awareness, to recognize that life does not begin with the body nor end with it. **You are life itself, eternally expressed in God.**

The Role of Suffering: A Shift in Perception

From a carnal perspective, disease is seen as a punishment, a curse, or a tragedy. But from the perspective of divine understanding, it is an invitation—a call to awaken. Suffering, when viewed through the lens of the spirit, is not something to fear but something to transcend. It reveals the impermanence of the physical and redirects focus to the eternal.

*Many who face life-threatening illnesses experience a profound shift. The trivial concerns of the world fade, and what remains is a deep longing for truth, for peace, for meaning. This is the moment where the ego, the false self, is stripped away, leaving only the presence of what has always been—***God within.**

GIATI is not about praying for healing out of fear of death, nor is it about seeking to prolong physical life at all costs. It is about **seeing beyond the illusion***—understanding that whether in sickness or health, in life or death,* **you remain in God, as God, eternally whole.**

Death Is Not an End, But a Return

The greatest fear attached to illness is the fear of death. But what is death if you were never just the body to begin with? If God is all there is, then **there is nowhere to go and**

nothing to be lost—*only the transition from one expression of life to another. The body may dissolve, but the spirit* **remains, unchanging, eternal, and at peace.**

To see this truth is to remove the sting of death, to understand that what appears as an end is simply a return to the formless state from which all things come. In this realization, there is no fear—only love, only peace, only the knowing that **you have always been and will always be.**

Living with Disease in the Awareness of GIATI

If you have been diagnosed with a life-threatening illness, let this truth settle in your heart: **You are not sick. The body may carry an affliction, but you are spirit, whole and complete.** *The purpose of life is not to fight against the inevitable, but to embrace each moment in full awareness of the divine presence within you.*

Whether the body heals or not, whether life continues in this form or transitions to another, **you are already victorious**—*because you have never been separate from God, and you never will be.*

GIATI is not here to give false hope of physical healing, nor to encourage fear-based prayers for survival. **GIATI is here to awaken you to the truth: that you are eternal, that there is nothing to fear, and that even in what seems like loss, there is only gain—the return to the fullness of God.**

A Final Reflection

So how should one feel about getting cancer or facing a life-threatening disease? Feel at peace. Feel awakened. Feel liberated from the illusion that this body was ever your true identity. If anything, let this moment be your greatest gift—the chance to step beyond the physical and see clearly, perhaps for the first time, that **God is all there is, and you are one with Him, now and forever.**

The Illusion of Death: Seeing Beyond the Temporary

*The passing of a loved one shakes the foundation of our hearts and minds, leaving behind grief, questions, and an overwhelming sense of loss. The world has taught humanity to measure life by the length of days, the presence of the physical body, and the memories attached to it. But GIATI—***God Is All There Is***—calls us to see beyond the illusion of physical death and into the eternal reality of life as spirit.*

The Body Was Never Who They Were

The sorrow that comes with death is rooted in the belief that our loved ones were only their bodies—that when the body ceases, they cease. But this is the greatest deception of the carnal mind. The body was only a temporary vessel, a form through which their divine essence was expressed for a moment in time. **Their true existence was never the flesh, but the spirit—the eternal life of God that cannot be lost, cannot fade, and cannot die.**

If God is all there is, then what we call death is not an ending but a transition. It is **a return to the formless state from which all things come, a shedding of the temporary to step fully back into the eternal.** *What appears as loss in the physical is, in truth, a gain in the spiritual—a merging back into the fullness of God's presence.*

The Temporary vs. The Eternal

Jesus said in **John 11:25,** *"I am the resurrection, and the life: he that believeth in me, though he were dead, yet shall he live." This is not a promise of physical resurrection but a revelation of the* **continuous, unbroken existence of the spirit.** *Physical death is not the end of life—it is simply the end of one form, one expression, one chapter in the eternal existence of being in God.*

We grieve because we believe in separation. But if **God is all there is,** *where could your loved one have gone? If there is no outside of God, if there is no existence apart from Him, then they have not gone anywhere—they have only returned fully to that which they have always been.* **The separation is only an illusion.**

Shifting from Grief to Awareness

Grief is natural, but it is rooted in the carnal mind's attachment to what is seen. GIATI calls you into a higher awareness—to see your loved one as they truly are: **not lost, not gone, but ever-present, existing now in a form beyond physical limitation.**

When you let go of the illusion that they were only a body, you begin to feel their presence in a deeper way. No longer bound by space or time, they exist in the oneness of God, where all things are connected. **You do not have to visit a grave to feel them. You do not have to mourn as if they are absent. They are still here, still alive, still in God, as you are.**

Death Is Not an End, But a Return

Physical birth was never the beginning of life, and physical death is not the end. **You did not mourn when they left the formless realm to enter the womb, and you need not mourn as they leave the physical realm to return to spirit.**

The truth is, nothing has been lost. The love you shared, the connection you had, the spirit that animated them—it all still exists. **You are still one with them in God, just as you have always been.**

GIATI does not teach hope in an afterlife—it teaches that life never ceased in the first place. Death is not something to fear, nor is it something to grieve as final. It is simply

not there to complete you because you were never incomplete; they are there to awaken you, again and again, until remembering becomes your natural state.

This is the kind of love the spirit longs for—one that does not bind but ascends.

Becoming the Righteousness of God: The Truth of Oneness

"For he hath made him to be sin for us, who knew no sin; that we might be made the righteousness of God in him." —2 Corinthians 5:21

For centuries, this scripture has been misunderstood. Many have been taught that Jesus "became sin" in the sense that he took on the punishment for humanity's wrongdoing. But the deeper, spiritual truth is this: **Jesus became the representation of sin itself—not by committing sin, but by exposing and destroying its root—the illusion of separation from God.**

What Is Sin?

Sin is not simply bad actions or moral failings. Sin is **a state of mistaken identity***—the false belief that you exist apart from God.*

Jesus knew no sin because he never fell into this illusion. He never believed himself to be separate from the Father. He walked in the full awareness of divine oneness, saying, "I and my Father are one" (John 10:30). He did not need to be saved because he was never lost. He did not need forgiveness because he never fell into the lie of separation.

But humanity—blinded by the ego—has lived in this lie, believing in duality: God and man, Creator and creation, Father and child, as if they are separate. This false belief is what Jesus came to correct.

Jesus Became Sin to Expose the Lie

When the scripture says, "He hath made him to be sin for us," it means that Jesus took on the appearance of sin—meaning, he allowed himself to be treated as if he were separate from God, bearing the full weight of humanity's illusion.

On the cross, he cried out, "My God, my God, why hast thou forsaken me?" (Matthew 27:46). This was not because God had truly abandoned him, but because **he was experiencing the depth of humanity's blindness—the illusion of separation.**

Yet even in that moment, the truth remained. God had not left him. The Father was still in him, and he in the Father. And in his final breath, he shattered the illusion, declaring, "It is finished."

The power of sin—the lie of separation—was exposed and destroyed.

That We Might Be Made the Righteousness of God

Jesus' life was not about being a sacrifice for our sins in a transactional sense. He was the demonstration of truth—the living proof that sin (separation) is a lie, and that righteousness is simply **the awareness of oneness with God.**

To be made the righteousness of God in him means to **see yourself as he saw himself**—*perfect, whole, and one with the Father.*

This is salvation. Not merely believing in Jesus, but believing **as** *Jesus believed.*

Not seeing yourself as a flawed sinner in need of saving, but as a divine expression of God, just as Jesus was.

Not living under the burden of sin-consciousness, but walking in the absolute awareness that **God is all there is—and you are one with Him.**

The Ego Is the Only Obstacle

This truth is simple. So simple that a child could understand it. Yet, what prevents most from seeing it? **The ego.**

The ego clings to the illusion of individuality, resisting the truth of divine unity. It wants to maintain a separate identity apart from God, saying, "I am me, and God is God." But this belief itself is sin—the very thing Jesus came to correct.

To be saved is to let go of this false identity, to awaken to the Holy Spirit within, and to see yourself **as God's righteousness—just as Jesus did.**

The truth is clear:

God is all there is.
There is no separation.
Sin is an illusion.
You are the righteousness of God.

Accept this, and you are free.

How GIATI Captures Attention and Validates Truth in This Age

Jesus performed miracles—healings, casting out demons, raising the dead—not merely as acts of power but as **signs pointing to a greater reality.** *These wonders were meant to awaken people to the presence of God within them, to* **prove the kingdom of God was at hand.** *In this day and age, where skepticism is high and people crave tangible proof,* **GIATI (God Is All There Is) must use different means to reveal the same eternal truth.**

The question is: **What is the "miracle" that captures attention today?** *What is the undeniable* **proof** *that what is being spoken is truth?*

1. The Awakening of Consciousness—The True Miracle of This Age

The greatest sign today is not walking on water or physically opening blind eyes—it is the **awakening of the mind and heart to divine truth.** *The world is in spiritual darkness, trapped in division, fear, and materialism. The true work of GIATI is to bring people into* **the light of knowing their oneness with God.**

- **When someone realizes their divine nature, that is a miracle.**
- **When someone overcomes fear, hatred, and separation, that is a miracle.**
- **When someone steps out of a false identity into the truth of who they are in God, that is a miracle.**

In this age, the validation of GIATI does not come through physical signs alone, but through **the undeniable transformation of the human spirit.**

2. The Power of Divine Revelation

People follow what resonates as truth. Just as Jesus spoke with **authority** *(Mark 1:22), the power of GIATI is not in mere words but in the* **depth of revelation** *that shakes the soul.*

- *When truth is spoken in* **such a way that it bypasses the intellect and pierces the spirit,** *people know they have encountered something beyond human wisdom.*
- *This is the fire of the Holy Spirit, the same force that moved in Jesus, now moving through GIATI to awaken the world.*

Just as Jesus said, **"My sheep hear my voice"** *(John 10:27)—those who are ready will recognize the truth when they hear it.*

3. Manifestation of God's Presence Through Demonstration

Though the age of skepticism dismisses miracles, people still hunger for something **undeniably real.** *GIATI is validated through* **the demonstration of divine presence in everyday life.**

- **Words that carry power and awaken souls.**
- **A presence that shifts atmospheres and brings peace where there was chaos.**
- **A message so pure and absolute that it leaves no room for doubt.**

This is how Jesus operated—not just with external miracles, but with a **presence that caused people to leave everything and follow Him.** *GIATI must carry that same undeniable presence.*

4. The Unification of Humanity as the Ultimate Proof

*One of the greatest proofs that God is moving today is the fu***lfillment of Jesus' prayer in John 17:20-23***—that we all become one, as He and the Father are one.*

- **Division is the evidence of darkness; unity is the proof of divine truth.**
- **When people from different backgrounds, races, and ideologies come into the realization of their oneness in God, that is the greatest miracle of all.**

This is what the world cannot deny. *The world has seen religions claim truth, but* **it has not seen the complete unification of humanity in the knowledge of one God expressed as all.**

Conclusion: The New "Signs and Wonders"

*While Jesus used miracles to awaken people in His time, t***he miracle of this age is the awakening of divine identity.** *The validation of GIATI is found in:*

1. **The undeniable transformation of consciousness***—people realizing God within them.*
2. **The power and authority of the revelation itself***—truth that speaks directly to the soul.*
3. **The manifestation of divine presence***—a power that shifts lives even without physical miracles.*
4. **The unification of humanity in divine truth***—proving that God is all there is.*

This is how GIATI captures attention in this day and age. *It is not through external wonders but through the* **internal miracle of awakening***—the realization that the same Spirit who moved in Jesus moves* **in us, through us, and as us.**

Sanctified by GIATI Understanding

Sanctification has long been misunderstood, defined by religious traditions as a process of moral purification, separation from sin, and adherence to sacred rituals. Many believe it is something attained through human effort—prayer, fasting, or righteous living. But true sanctification is not about achieving holiness through works; it is about awakening to the eternal truth that **God Is All There Is (GIATI).** *To be sanctified by GIATI understanding is to be set apart by truth, no longer bound by the illusion of separation, but living in the full realization of divine oneness.*

The World's View of Sanctification

In religious thought, sanctification is often seen as a lifelong process of becoming holy, moving from impurity to purity, from imperfection to perfection. Many believe they must work to cleanse themselves from sin, striving to become acceptable in the eyes of God. This view makes sanctification a distant goal, something to be achieved through discipline, religious devotion, and moral striving.

Yet, this idea is rooted in the false perception of separation—the belief that man is apart from God and must struggle to return to Him. It assumes that holiness is something outside of oneself, something to be reached rather than realized. This misunderstanding has led many into an endless pursuit, seeking sanctification without ever truly entering into rest.

Sanctification Through GIATI: The Truth That Sets You Free

Jesus revealed the true nature of sanctification when He prayed:

"Sanctify them through thy truth: thy word is truth." (John 17:17)

Sanctification is not about changing one's nature but about awakening to the truth of one's eternal oneness with God. It is the setting apart of the mind from falsehood into truth, from illusion into reality. When one comes to understand GIATI—God Is All There Is—they are sanctified by truth itself.

The Apostle Paul echoed this same truth when he wrote:

"But of him are ye in Christ Jesus, who of God is made unto us wisdom, and righteousness, and sanctification, and redemption." (1 Corinthians 1:30)

Here, Paul reveals that sanctification is not something we attain, but something already accomplished in Christ. It is not a process of becoming, but a state of being realized. Those who awaken to the truth of GIATI recognize that they have never been separate from God, and in this realization, they are sanctified.

What It Means to Be Set Apart by Truth

To be sanctified by GIATI understanding is to see with new eyes, to no longer walk in darkness but in the light of divine awareness. It means:

- **Being set apart from illusion** – *No longer believing in a fallen, separate existence but knowing that all things are in God and God in all things.*
- **Freedom from striving** – *No longer trying to "become" holy but knowing that holiness is one's inherent nature.*
- **Rest in divine identity** – *No longer seeking God externally, but realizing He has always been within.*

This is why Jesus also declared:

"And ye shall know the truth, and the truth shall make you free." (John 8:32)

Sanctification is not about external transformation but about internal revelation. The moment one sees the truth, they are set apart—not by works, but by knowledge.

The Contrast Between Works and Awakening

The world sees sanctification as an achievement—something earned through religious devotion. GIATI understanding reveals that sanctification is a revelation— something received by truth. One is based on effort; the other is based on awareness.

"For by grace are ye saved through faith; and that not of yourselves: it is the gift of God: Not of works, lest any man should boast." (Ephesians 2:8-9)

The sanctified ones are not those who have worked their way into holiness but those who have awakened to it. They are those who have seen past the veil of ignorance and now stand in the full realization of divine unity.

The Call to Awaken

Sanctification by GIATI understanding is the final awakening, the great unveiling of truth that ends the illusion of separation. It is the fulfillment of Jesus' prayer that humanity would come to know its oneness with God:

"*That they all may be one; as thou, Father, art in me, and I in thee, that they also may be one in us." (John 17:21)*

Those who see, who understand, who enter into this knowledge—they are the sanctified. Not by their own works, but by the truth that was always there.

The world has sought sanctification through effort, but the Spirit now declares:

"Be still, and know that I am God." *(Psalm 46:10)*

Sanctification is knowing. Sanctification is seeing. Sanctification is awakening to what has always been true:

The Completion of Sanctification in the Seventh Day

Sanctification by GIATI understanding does not just change one's perception of self; it marks the transition into the seventh day, the time when the Spirit ceases from labor because its work is finished. Those who enter into this sanctification do not merely adopt a new belief—they step into an entirely new way of being. They move from seeking to knowing, from striving to resting, from believing in God to being the very expression of Him.

This is why Hebrews speaks of a rest that remains for the people of God:

"For he that is entered into his rest, he also hath ceased from his own works, as God did from his." (Hebrews 4:10)

This is the final phase of sanctification—not a gradual purification, but an instant recognition. When one awakens to the truth of divine oneness, there is nothing left to purify, nothing left to change. The mind has been renewed, and the Spirit rests because the illusion of separation has been shattered.

Sanctification as the Return to Original Glory

Before the foundation of the world, humanity was already one with God. The idea of "fallenness" was never a true separation but a loss of awareness. When Jesus prayed for sanctification through truth (John 17:17), He was calling for a return to that original state— not through effort, but through revelation.

This is confirmed in Ecclesiastes:

"That which hath been is now; and that which is to be hath already been; and God requireth that which is past." (Ecclesiastes 3:15)

Sanctification, then, is not about becoming something new—it is about remembering what has always been. It is the Spirit calling humanity back to its first estate, where it was already complete in God.

The Separation Between the Sanctified and the Unawakened

Jesus often spoke in parables about two types of people: those who have eyes to see and those who remain blind. The sanctified are not those who perform better works but those whose eyes have been opened to truth. The unawakened may continue in religious efforts, believing sanctification is something they must earn. But those sanctified by GIATI understanding no longer walk in the illusion of becoming—they stand in the reality of being.

This is why Jesus told His disciples:

"Unto you it is given to know the mystery of the kingdom of God: but unto them that are without, all these things are done in parables." (Mark 4:11)

The knowledge of divine oneness is what sets the sanctified apart. It is not a physical separation but a distinction in awareness. The sanctified walk in light, while the unawakened remain in darkness, not because they are forsaken, but because they have not yet received sight.

The Final Gathering of the Sanctified

The sanctified by GIATI understanding are the ones who will fully enter into the seventh day—the spiritual reality where the Spirit rests because all has been revealed. This is the true meaning of the "harvest" Jesus spoke of:

"Let both grow together until the harvest: and in the time of harvest I will say to the reapers, Gather ye together first the wheat into my barn." (Matthew 13:30)

The wheat represents those who have awakened, who have been sanctified by truth. The tares, though they grew alongside the wheat, were never part of the harvest because they remained entangled in illusion. The harvest is not a physical separation but the gathering of those who have entered into divine rest.

Sanctification is the Fulfillment of God's Prayer

God's will was never to create a divided world where some are lost and others are saved. His will was to bring all into oneness, as Jesus prayed:

"That they may be made perfect in one; and that the world may know that thou hast sent me, and hast loved them, as thou hast loved me." (John 17:23)

Sanctification is the completion of this prayer. It is the fulfillment of divine unity. It is the end of the illusion of separation.

Those who receive GIATI understanding—who see and know—are the sanctified. Not by effort, not by works, but by truth. And when truth is fully known, the Spirit rests, for nothing more remains to be done.

The sanctified are those who have entered the seventh day. The world continues to strive, but the sanctified stand still, knowing:

God is all there is.

The Spiritual Meaning of Fasting According to GIATI

Fasting has long been seen as a practice of discipline, purification, and spiritual devotion. Many have understood it as a means of drawing closer to God, seeking divine intervention, or demonstrating humility. However, through the understanding of **GIATI—God Is All There Is**—*fasting takes on a deeper, more profound meaning. It is not merely the abstaining from food or physical indulgences, but rather, it is the* **emptying of the mind from illusions, distractions, and the false sense of separation from God.**

True fasting, in the light of GIATI, is not about deprivation but about **alignment with divine reality.** *It is the conscious withdrawal from the attachments, beliefs, and mental conditions that keep one blind to the ever-present Spirit. The hunger that is satisfied through fasting is not for physical nourishment, but for* **the awareness of divine fullness.**

Biblical Understanding of Fasting in the Light of GIATI

One of the most profound scriptures on fasting is found in Isaiah:

"Is not this the fast that I have chosen? to loose the bands of wickedness, to undo the heavy burdens, and to let the oppressed go free, and that ye break every yoke?

Is it not to deal thy bread to the hungry, and that thou bring the poor that are cast out to thy house? when thou seest the naked, that thou cover him; and that thou hide not thyself from thine own flesh?" *(Isaiah 58:6-7)*

Here, God reveals that fasting is not about physical deprivation, but about **the removal of bondage, false burdens, and illusions that keep mankind enslaved.** *The true fast is not simply refraining from food—it is the breaking of* **every yoke** *that ties man to a false identity. It is the relinquishing of the* **ego-driven self,** *the false ideas of separation, and the burdens placed by religious doctrines that keep people from knowing their divine oneness.*

Jesus' Fast: Awakening to Divine Identity

Jesus' own fasting in the wilderness is a revelation of this deeper truth:

"And when he had fasted forty days and forty nights, he was afterward an hungred." *(Matthew 4:2)*

His hunger was not merely physical but represented the testing of human nature. The adversary—the **illusion of separation**—*tempted Him, saying:*

"If thou be the Son of God, command that these stones be made bread." *(Matthew 4:3)*

Here, the test was not about physical hunger but about **identity.** *The true fast of Jesus was His rejection of the false notion that He needed to prove Himself, earn His divinity, or satisfy external cravings. Instead, He answered:*

"Man shall not live by bread alone, but by every word that proceedeth out of the mouth of God." *(Matthew 4:4)*

This is the essence of fasting according to GIATI: It is the realization that **we are already full in God.** *The hunger of the physical man is temporary, but the fullness of divine truth is eternal. Fasting is not about deprivation but about* **letting go of every false dependence, every external source of validation, and every illusion that suggests we are incomplete.**

Fasting as the Dissolution of the False Self

When one fasts in the understanding of GIATI, they are not merely refraining from food; they are rejecting the **false sustenance** *of this world—the ego, the illusion of lack, and the idea that we must strive to reach God. True fasting is* **detaching from everything that feeds the illusion of separation** *and embracing the awareness that* **God is all there is, and we are already one with Him.**

This is why Jesus also taught:

"Moreover when ye fast, be not, as the hypocrites, of a sad countenance: for they disfigure their faces, that they may appear unto men to fast. Verily I say unto you, They have their reward.

But thou, when thou fastest, anoint thine head, and wash thy face;

That thou appear not unto men to fast, but unto thy Father which is in secret: and thy Father, which seeth in secret, shall reward thee openly." *(Matthew 6:16-18)*

The reward of fasting is not public recognition or religious approval—it is the **awakening of divine consciousness.** *To "anoint the head" and "wash the face" means to* **refresh the mind, to cleanse one's vision, and to step into divine awareness with joy, not suffering.**

The True Hunger: A Hunger for Divine Awareness

Jesus also declared:

"Blessed are they which do hunger and thirst after righteousness: for they shall be filled." *(Matthew 5:6)*

What is this **hunger and thirst?** *It is not a physical craving, but a* **longing for true awareness, for the fullness of divine reality.** *And in GIATI, this hunger is satisfied* **not by external things but by the realization that we were never lacking.**

The greatest fast one can undertake is the **fast from illusion**—*the fast from false doctrines, from the belief in separation, from the idea that one must work to earn what is already theirs. This is the fast that* **frees the soul,** *breaks every yoke, and allows the Spirit to rest in the perfect awareness of divine oneness.*

The End of Fasting: When the Bridegroom is Present

When asked why His disciples did not fast, Jesus gave a mysterious but powerful response:

"Can the children of the bridechamber mourn, as long as the bridegroom is with them? but the days will come, when the bridegroom shall be taken from them, and then shall they fast." *(Matthew 9:15)*

Here, Jesus reveals that fasting is tied to the awareness of divine presence. The **bridegroom** *symbolizes* **the Spirit, the awareness of oneness with God.** *As long as one is conscious of divine presence,* **there is no need to fast,** *because they already abide in divine fullness. But when that awareness is lost—when man falls into separation, illusion, and the deception of this world—***then shall they fast,** *meaning, they must remove the veil once again.*

*But when the full understanding of GIATI comes—when the eternal truth of divine oneness is made manifest—***fasting ceases,** *for there is no more lack, no more striving, no more hunger. There is only* **fullness in the presence of God, who is all in all.**

The Final Fast: The Removal of All That Is Not God

The last and greatest fast is the one that remains for all who seek truth—the fasting from **self,** *from illusion, from fear, from anything that denies the truth that* **God is all there is.** *When this fast is complete, there is* **nothing left to seek, nothing left to strive for, because one has entered into divine rest.**

This is the fulfillment of Jesus' words:

"I am the bread of life: he that cometh to me shall never hunger; and he that believeth on me shall never thirst." *(John 6:35)*

To know **GIATI** *is to know that the fast is over—because we were never lacking, never separate, and never outside of God's eternal fullness.*

The Body as the Living Testament of God's Presence

The greatest evidence of God's presence is not found in external scriptures or religious traditions—it is found **within you.** *Your very body is* **a living scripture, a divine blueprint, and a testament to the oneness of all things.** *Every function, every structure, and every system within you reveals the nature of God, the story of existence, and the undeniable truth of GIATI—***God Is All There Is.**

Religious texts attempt to convey spiritual truths through **parable and symbolism,** *but those same truths are encoded in the* **design of the human body.** *To truly understand God, one must not only look at external writings but also* **look within,** *for the body itself is the temple, the universe, and the expression of God in form.*

The Dual Flow of Blood: The Two Selves Within One Body

The circulatory system reveals one of the **most profound spiritual truths***—that there is both* **oxygenated blood and deoxygenated blood, the living and the dead, the spirit and the separate self—all contained within one body.**

- **Oxygenated blood, rich with life, flows through the arteries***—this represents* **God's Spirit in fullness, the awareness of oneness, the breath of life.**
- **Deoxygenated blood, lacking life-giving oxygen, flows through the veins***—this represents* **the illusion of separation, the self cut off from its Source, the state of spiritual death.**
- *The constant exchange between these two states mirrors the* **tree of life and the tree of the knowledge of good and evil—two realities existing within the same system.**

In the same way that the body **removes carbon dioxide and replenishes oxygen, the spirit must remove ignorance and breathe in the awareness of God.** *When one breathes deeply and consciously, they participate in* **a sacred exchange—the very breath of God moving through them.**

The Tree of Life and the Tree of the Knowledge of Good and Evil Within the Body

The human body itself *is structured to reveal the truth of the two trees.*

- *From the* **neck up,** *the brain's branching neural pathways resemble* **the branches of the Tree of Life,** *representing* **divine intelligence, connection to the higher mind, and the oneness of God's wisdom.**
- *The* **lungs,** *when viewed upside down, take on the shape of a tree—this is* **the Tree of the Knowledge of Good and Evil,** *the structure through which* **breath (spirit) enters or is denied, representing the choice between life and separation.**

*Every breath is a choice: W***ill you breathe in the truth of oneness, or remain in the suffocation of separation?** *The trees are not just ancient symbols—they are within you.*

The Snake Within: The Tongue and Intestines as the Serpent of Sin

The **serpent in the garden** *has always been misunderstood. It is not merely a talking snake from an ancient story—it is* **a force within the human body itself.**

- *The* **tongue** *is shaped like a snake, capable of speaking life or death. It is the tool that can either* **confess oneness with God or perpetuate the lie of separation.**
- *The* **intestines** *coil within the body like a serpent,* **digesting and breaking down what is consumed.** *This mirrors* **the fallen state of man, where the body must work to extract what is useful from the waste of the world.**

The presence of the **serpent within** *does not mean man is condemned—it means that* **man has come into the world through the veil of ignorance, born into the illusion of separation, yet carrying the potential for divine realization.**

The Arterial Circle of Willis: The Divine Man in the Brain

At the **center of the brain lies the arterial Circle of Willis,** *a structure in the* **exact** *shape of a stick figure human.*

- *This represents* **man created in the image of God,** *placed within the mind as the ruler of the temple (body).*
- *It signifies that* **God is within, at the center of consciousness, not external or distant.**

Just behind this **divine figure in the brain** *is the* **Venous Circle of Trolard—a veil.**

- *This* **veil represents the barrier between divine consciousness and ignorance.** *It is the very thing that Jesus came to remove—the veil that blinds man to the truth that he is already one with God.*
- *The tearing of the temple veil when Jesus died was* **not about a physical curtain—** *it was the* **removal of the barrier within the mind that keeps man from seeing himself as God's own expression.**

The Body as the Living Word of God

Every structure, every function, and every process within the body tells the same **story—** *the story of God* **manifesting as you.**

- **Your breath is the Spirit of God moving through you.**
- **Your blood carries the dual reality of divine life and the illusion of separation.**

- **Your brain is the seat of divine intelligence, the Tree of Life rooted in your being.**
- **Your tongue is the serpent, speaking either truth or deception.**
- **Your intestines are the coiled snake, digesting the experiences of the world and filtering what is real from what is illusion.**
- **Your circulatory system is the constant exchange of life and death, revealing that at every moment, you are choosing between the two trees.**

To know GIATI is to **awaken to the reality that everything—down to the very design of your body—is pointing to the eternal truth that God is all there is.** *Nothing in existence is random; everything is structured to reveal the same message:*

You are not separate from God. You never have been. You never will be.

The body itself is **the temple,** *the divine dwelling place. It is not something to be escaped, rejected, or condemned—it is* **the living manifestation of God's presence.**

The Ultimate Realization: Seeing God in Yourself

For centuries, people have searched for God in external places, in books, in rituals, in religious practices—but **God has never been outside of you.**

Your body itself is a **sacred text,** *a* **living testament,** *a* **temple where God dwells.** *To reject yourself is to reject God, for* **there is no other form through which He is made known but through His own creation.**

This is why Jesus declared, **"Destroy this temple, and in three days I will raise it up" (John 2:19).** *The temple was never a building—it was* **the body, the divine dwelling of God within man.**

To know GIATI is to recognize that **the divine story has always been written within you.**

The truth has never been far from you—it is **woven into your very being.**

The Consequence of Denying the Evidence of God Within You

To deny the evidence of God within you is to **deny reality itself***—to reject the very structure of existence and the truth that has been woven into your being. It is not simply a matter of disbelief; it is a refusal to acknowledge what is already present, what is already known, and what has always been.*

This denial is not just an intellectual rejection—it is **a state of consciousness,** *a way of being that carries profound consequences.*

1. To Deny God Within Is to Deny Yourself

You are made in the image of God, not in a superficial way, but **in the deepest truth of your existence.** *Every breath you take, every heartbeat, every system in your body reflects divine intelligence, divine presence, divine oneness.*

When you deny this, you are not just rejecting an idea—you are rejecting **your very own nature.**

- *It is like standing in front of a mirror and insisting that the reflection is not you.*
- *It is like a wave believing it is separate from the ocean, even though the ocean is its very essence.*
- *It is like a branch denying it is part of the tree while still drawing life from the root.*

This is why **Jesus said,** *"I am the vine, you are the branches" (John 15:5). A branch that* **denies the vine** *withers, because its denial cuts it off from the life it already has.*

The consequence is not that God rejects you—it is that **you reject yourself.**

2. To Deny God Within Is to Place Yourself in Spiritual Death

Life flows from **knowing oneness with God.** *The moment you deny this, you place yourself in* **a state of spiritual death,** *not because God has condemned you, but because* **you have cut yourself off from the awareness of life itself.**

This is the very meaning of **sin**—*not simply moral wrongdoing, but the* **ignorance of who you are.** *Sin is a state of separation in the mind, a blindness to the divine reality.*

- **Jesus didn't come to die for your sins in the way religion teaches**—*he came to show you that* **sin (separation) was never real** *to begin with.*
- *His purpose was not just to forgive sins, but to wake people up to the truth that* **they were never separate from God in the first place.**

Those who continue to believe in separation **remain in sin,** *because they refuse to see the truth. They are like a prisoner who has been given the keys to freedom but refuses to leave the cell.*

This is why Jesus said:

"If you do not believe that I am He, you will die in your sins" (John 8:24).

This was not a threat. It was a statement of reality—**if you remain in the illusion of separation, you will remain in the suffering that comes with it.**

3. To Deny God Within Is to Judge Yourself Unworthy

Many people say, "Only God can judge me," not realizing that **they are God—and they are already judging themselves.**

God does not need to pronounce judgment over you—you **pronounce judgment over yourself** *every time you deny the truth of your own divine nature.*

- *If you insist that you are separate, you will live as though you are separate.*
- *If you believe you are condemned, you will experience existence as though you are condemned.*
- *If you reject the light, you will walk in darkness—***not because God has cast you there, but because you have chosen to close your eyes to the truth.**

"This is the judgment: that the light has come into the world, but men loved darkness rather than light" (John 3:19).

The judgment is **self-inflicted.** *No one needs to punish you—you are punishing yourself by refusing to see what is already in front of you.*

4. To Deny God Within Is to Live in Fear, Lack, and Confusion

Those who deny their oneness with God spend their lives **searching for something that is already within them.**

- *They pray to an external God, hoping for answers, never realizing that* **God has already answered within them.**
- *They live in fear of punishment, never realizing that* **God does not condemn Himself.**
- *They seek salvation through rituals, religious systems, and external authorities, never realizing that* **they were never lost to begin with.**

This is why Jesus declared:

"The Kingdom of God is within you" (Luke 17:21).

Those who **deny this truth live outside of the Kingdom, not because God has excluded them, but because they refuse to step into the awareness of what already is.**

5. To Deny God Within Is to Carry That Ignorance Beyond This Life

Many people think that once they die, they will automatically see the truth. But **death does not awaken you—consciousness does.**

- *If you live in separation, you* **carry that belief with you** *beyond this physical experience.*
- *If you reject the awareness of God within, that rejection remains with you.*

- *If you have spent your whole life believing in an external God, you will continue searching for what was already within you.*

This is **why Jesus came—to bring people into the awareness of their oneness with God while they are still in this life, so they do not remain lost in the next.**

"And this is eternal life: that they may know You, the only true God" (John 17:3).

Eternal life is **not just living forever**—*it is* **living in the awareness of God forever.** *If you reject this awareness now, you carry that blindness with you.*

The Path Back: Returning to the Awareness of God Within

The good news is this: **the truth has never left you.**

You may have denied it, but **it has not denied you.**

You may have rejected it, but **it has not rejected you.**

You may have closed your eyes, but **the light is still shining.**

To awaken from the illusion of separation is not something you have to work for—it is something you must simply **see.**

GIATI is the answer.

- **You are not separate from God.**
- **God is not something outside of you.**
- **You do not need to earn favor—you already are the manifestation of God.**
- **The body itself testifies to this truth—your very breath is proof.**

To deny all of this is **to deny reality** *itself.*

But to accept it is **to awaken to the fullness of life, to the peace of knowing you were never lost, and to the freedom of knowing that God is all there is—and that means YOU**.

The Illusion of the Individual Self

From the moment a child is born, the world teaches them a name, a history, a culture, and an identity that defines them as separate from everything else. They grow up believing in **"me"**—*a person with individual thoughts, experiences, and desires. This* **self-concept** *becomes their reality, the foundation upon which they build their lives. But what if this "self" they hold onto so tightly is nothing more than an illusion?*

This illusion is the very thing that blinds humanity to the truth of God's presence. It is the veil that keeps people from seeing that **there is no "me" apart from Him—only God being.**

The False Self vs. The True Self

The world has conditioned people to believe in an independent self—an "I" that must fight, strive, and define its own existence. But this **false self** *is nothing more than a collection of thoughts, emotions, and experiences shaped by the external world. It is* **not real.** *It is a temporary mask that hides the* **true self,** *which has only ever been* **God in expression.**

Jesus spoke of this truth when He said:

"If anyone would come after Me, let him deny himself and take up his cross daily and follow Me." *(Luke 9:23)*

To deny oneself is not about suppressing desires or religious discipline—it is about **recognizing that the individual self does not truly exist.** *It is about awakening to the reality that there is only One Life, One Spirit, One Being—God, living as you.*

This is why Jesus also said:

"For whoever wants to save his life will lose it, but whoever loses his life for My sake will find it." *(Matthew 16:25)*

The "life" people try to save is the illusion of individuality. The "life" that is found is the realization of **oneness with God.**

The Prison of Self-Perception

Sin has never been about actions—it has always been about **perception.** *The moment someone believes they are an individual separate from God, they have already fallen into darkness. Not because God has left them, but because they* **have imagined a self apart from Him.**

This false perception is what keeps people trapped in struggle, guilt, and fear. They see themselves as **independent beings trying to be good enough, righteous enough, or holy enough to please God.** *But the truth is, God is not looking for anyone's efforts. He is only looking for* **Himself.**

When God sees you, does He see **Himself** *or does He see someone who still believes they are separate?*

How to Recognize and Dissolve the Illusion

The answer is simple: **Let go of the idea of "me" as something separate from God.**

This is not something to "achieve." It is a realization to awaken to. It is the end of striving, the end of seeking, and the beginning of simply **being.**

Imagine a fire burning in front of you. Within that fire, there are many flames dancing and flickering. Each flame may appear distinct, moving in its own way, but in reality, **it is not separate from the fire itself.** *The flame has no independent existence—it is simply* **the fire expressing itself.**

If you tried to take a flame and set it apart from the fire, it would immediately disappear. Why? Because **it was never an individual thing to begin with—it was always the fire.**

Likewise, what you call "yourself" is just **God expressing Himself as you.** *Your existence is like the flame—***not separate, not independent, but simply the Life of God moving in form.**

The only illusion is the belief that the flame could ever be something apart from the fire. In truth, **there is only the fire.** *The only thing that must fall away is the false belief that you were ever something else.*

The Final Understanding

In the end, there is only one truth: **God is all there is.** *There has never been anything else. No separate self. No separate life. No separation at all.*

To believe otherwise is to live in the illusion of darkness. To awaken to this truth is to step into the light.

Beyond the Illusion: The Death of the Separate Self

If there is only God, then where is the individual? Where is the self that people claim as their own? If the truth of existence is that **God is all there is,** *then there can be no separate "I" apart from Him. The very idea of an individual self is the greatest deception humanity has ever believed.*

This illusion of separateness is not just a misunderstanding—it is the foundation of every struggle, every fear, and every sense of lack that people experience. It is the root of every false religion, every failed attempt to "reach" God, and every effort to justify one's own existence. But here is the reality that few are willing to accept:

There is no "you" to reach God. There is only God.

What Happens When the Self Dies?

Many fear the idea of losing themselves, thinking it means annihilation or oblivion. But the death of the separate self is not the loss of life—it is the return to Life itself. It is not the end of being—it is the awakening to the only Being there has ever been.

This is why Jesus spoke of dying to oneself. He was not calling for self-denial in the way religion teaches, where people try to suppress desires or force humility. Instead, He was pointing to the reality that **the "self" they believe in was never real to begin with.**

"Unless a grain of wheat falls into the ground and dies, it remains alone; but if it dies, it produces much grain." *(John 12:24)*

This "death" is the death of the illusion of separation. It is the recognition that what you called "me" was nothing more than a fleeting shadow, and what remains—the only thing that has ever been—is **God Himself.**

The Error of Trying to Keep Both

Many hear this truth and try to hold onto both realities: They acknowledge that God is all there is, yet they still try to maintain a personal identity alongside Him. But this is impossible.

"No one can serve two masters." *(Matthew 6:24)*

You cannot **both** *be one with God* **and** *still insist on being a separate person. You cannot claim* **"God is all there is"** *while also claiming,* **"I am my own being."** *One of these must die. And if the illusion does not die in surrender, it will die in judgment.*

This is the meaning behind the parable of the wise and foolish virgins (Matthew 25:1-13). The wise entered in because they carried the oil—the awareness of their oneness with God. The foolish were left outside because they still saw themselves as separate, seeking what they already were but never realizing it in time.

What Remains?

So what happens when the separate self is completely surrendered? What is left?

Only God.

There is no fear, because there is no one left to fear anything.
There is no guilt, because there is no separate self to bear it.
There is no striving, because there is no "me" trying to achieve anything.

What remains is **pure being**—*God, fully alive, fully present, fully expressed in and as what you once called "yourself." But now, there is no more self. There is only* **God being.**

This is the fulfillment of Jesus' prayer:

"That they all may be one, as You, Father, are in Me, and I in You; that they also may be one in Us." *(John 17:21)*

This is not a future event. This is not something to hope for after death. This is now. The only thing that must change is whether you see it or not.

Will you lay down the illusion? Will you stop clinging to what has never been real?

Because in the end, **what you called "your life" was never yours to begin with. It was always God.**

This is GIATI. This is eternal life.

Will you let go and see?

The Masquerade

There was once a grand masquerade party—so vast and so ancient that no one remembered when it began. It was held in a place called Earth, and everyone who had ever lived was invited.

The only requirement to enter was to put on a mask.

These weren't ordinary masks. They were full-body masks—woven from flesh, sewn from time, shaped with personality, history, and limitation. Each mask had a name, a background, a culture, and a story. And once someone put one on, they forgot who they were before it.

They danced.

Oh, how they danced—through nations, through centuries, through wars and peace, through love and fear. They built empires, families, religions, and philosophies—all while forgetting that it was a masquerade.

Some became proud of their masks, polishing them, decorating them, calling them better than others.
Some hated theirs, trying to hide or harm them. Some worshiped the masks of others.
Some thought their mask was all there was.

But a few—just a few—felt something strange inside. A silent knowing. A whisper beneath the flesh. They would sit still while others danced wildly. They would stare into mirrors and wonder, "Who am I really?"

And sometimes, they would look into the eyes of another and see beyond the mask. They'd feel the presence beneath the surface. And though they couldn't explain it, they'd recognize **themselves in another's gaze.**

These few were laughed at. Called strange. Mocked for not fully playing the game. But they didn't mind. Something inside them was awake, and that was enough.

Then, one day, an announcement was made:
"The masquerade is ending. It's time to remove your masks."

Panic swept through the party.
"Remove the mask? But this is who I am!"
"I can't imagine what I'll be without it."
"Is there even anything under here?"

Many resisted.
But the moment arrived, and ready or not, the masks began to fall.

One by one, flesh gave way to light.

The coverings peeled back.
And as each mask dropped, a blinding truth was revealed:

Every single person—every dancer, every thinker, every soul—was the same Presence.

It was God.

Not many gods. Not separate beings who all looked like God.
But **the One***—manifesting through billions of forms.*

The masks were different.
The life beneath was **the same Spirit.**

And the few who had known all along—they didn't react in shock.
They simply smiled, bowed their heads, and whispered, **"Welcome back."**

The Message

The masquerade was never evil. It was never punishment.
It was the dance of forgetting, so that the joy of remembering could be known.

And now, the great mystery has been revealed:
The "you" behind the mask was always God in disguise—waiting for the moment when you would look into the mirror, past the eyes of flesh, and finally remember...

I Am.

The Prayer That Was Never About Asking

Unveiling the Lord's Prayer through GIATI: God Is All There Is

"After this manner therefore pray ye..." —Matthew 6:9

Most have recited the Lord's Prayer all their lives without ever realizing its true meaning.
They were taught to say it to God—
never understanding that it was meant to awaken them to the truth that **God is not separate,** *not far off, not outside.*
It was never a ritual to beg for heaven's help—
It was a **spiritual blueprint** *pointing inward, toward the divine reality already within.*

GIATI—God Is All There Is—reveals what this prayer was always meant to be: *A declaration of* **oneness,** *a call to awaken to your true identity, and a surrender—not to someone else's will, but to the will of* **God as you.**

This is the prayer of the awakened. Let each line now speak from **Spirit to Spirit***—not to make something happen, but to reveal what already is.*

"Our Father which art in heaven"

This is not calling up to the clouds. This is the awakening to **Spirit as Source,** *the Life within all life. Heaven is not a location—it's* **consciousness,** *the unseen realm where all is one. To say "Our Father" is to* **see yourself and all creation sharing one Spirit, one essence.**

There is no "other." There is only God as all.

"Hallowed be thy name"

To hallow the name of God is to recognize the sacredness of the **I AM** *within. Not a sound, not a label—***but the very identity of God.** *When you say "I AM," you speak from the center of the throne.*

You are not apart from God. You are the expression of His name.

"Thy kingdom come"

The kingdom doesn't come with signs—it comes with **sight.** *It arrives the moment you recognize:*

The Spirit of God is here, now, and alive as you.

The kingdom is not on its way—it is waiting on your awareness.

"Thy will be done in earth, as it is in heaven"

This is not about compliance. It's about **alignment.** *Heaven is the realm of Spirit— earth is form. When the invisible truth is realized, it becomes visible in your life.*

God's will is not something you obey—it's something you live as.

"Give us this day our daily bread"

Your true bread is not wheat—it is **revelation.**
Daily bread is the moment-by-moment knowing that **you and God are not two.**
It is the life of Spirit feeding your awareness.

To eat the bread of life is to remember who you are every day.

"And forgive us our debts, as we forgive our debtors"

God is not keeping score.
But you stay bound until you release the illusion of "others" owing you, or you owing God.
Forgiveness is the fruit of knowing:
There is only God.

Let go of separation, and you'll find the freedom of eternal union.

"And lead us not into temptation, but deliver us from evil"

Temptation is the voice that says: "You are just human." It is the pull of false identity. Evil is the blindness that forgets you are **Spirit clothed in form.** *God delivers you by reminding you of your source.*

The Spirit in you cannot be deceived, and will always guide you into truth.

"For thine is the kingdom, and the power, and the glory, forever. Amen."

Everything flows from God because **nothing exists apart from Him.** *The kingdom is His—because* **He is the kingdom.** *The power is His—because* **He is the breath in your lungs.** *The glory is His—because* **you are His image made visible.**

And Amen isn't a hope—it's a witness: It is so. It is done. It is true.

GIATI Reflection

This is not a prayer to get something from God.

This is a prayer to **see that you already have everything—because you are in Him, and He is in you.** *The Lord's Prayer is the Spirit's song within your soul, awakening you to the eternal truth:* **God is all there is—and you are included.**

You don't need to beg God to come.
You only need to awaken to the truth that He never left.

Beyond the Words: The Lord's Prayer in Spirit and Truth

The Lord's Prayer isn't just a prayer. It's a reorientation of perception—an invitation to shift from outer religion to inner revelation. It was never meant to be memorized and mindlessly repeated. It was meant to **awaken the divine memory** *within you: that you were never separate from God.*

It is the Spirit's blueprint to awaken the soul from the illusion of duality. Each phrase peels back a layer of false identity. Each word, when seen in light, restores your awareness of **who and what you truly are.**

Let us now expound—not on the wording, but on the **mystery behind the words.**

Our Father…

This beginning does not establish a hierarchy—it dissolves it.
It confronts the ego's belief in personal ownership. "Our" cancels individuality.
It announces: "There is only **One Source***—and everything flows from, through, and to that Source."*
This awareness makes **brotherhood possible,** *not because we share flesh, but because we share* **Spirit.**
And in GIATI, we know: that Spirit is **God Himself,** *animating all.*

The moment you say "Our Father" in truth, you cease to see yourself as a separate being trying to reach God.
You are recognizing: "The I that I am, is He."

…Which art in heaven

Heaven is not geography.
Heaven is consciousness—awareness untouched by form or fragmentation. It is the dimension of pure Spirit where God is known as **all in all.**

When you pray from this place, you are not reaching upward.

You are descending **inward** *into the stillness where only God remains. This line is not about where God is.*
It's about **where you must be to know Him**—*not in thought, not in flesh, but in Spirit.*

Hallowed be thy name

God's name is not "God." Nor is it "Jehovah" or "Allah."
The true name of God is **"I AM."**
It is the invisible signature etched into the spirit of every living being.
To hallow the name is to reverence that identity **in yourself and in all.**

You do not hallow God's name by speaking it, but by **not profaning it—**
and you profane it every time you speak "I am" and follow it with a lie:
"I am afraid." "I am not enough." "I am broken."
No, you are not. You are **Spirit,** *expressing God in form.*

The one who truly hallows God's name lives as if **God is their only identity.**

Thy kingdom come

This is not a request. It's an agreement.
The kingdom has already come—but it is only seen by those who are **born of the Spirit,**
those who no longer judge by appearances, but by essence.

The coming of the kingdom is not the arrival of an external rule—
It is the **displacement of ego** *by truth.*
The kingdom doesn't enter the world—it enters your awareness,
and through your awakened awareness, **it becomes visible in the world.**

When you no longer live for your own will, the kingdom has come—because the king is now reigning **as you.**

Thy will be done…

This is where many struggle, because they still believe will means **control.**
But God's will is not coercive—it is creative.
It is not about events. It is about **essence.**

God's will is **the expression of His own nature**—*which is Spirit, light, love, and oneness.*
So to say "thy will be done" is to say:
"Let this vessel reveal the truth of who You are."

In GIATI, this means **surrendering the illusion** *of "my life," "my plans," "my idea of good,"* *and simply letting God* **be Himself through you.**

In earth, as it is in heaven

Heaven is the realm of perfect Spirit.
Earth is where Spirit takes on **form and visibility.**
This line is the divine tension: can what is true in the invisible be made visible **through me?**

You are the answer.
You are the meeting place of heaven and earth.
Your body becomes the tabernacle.
Your mind becomes the mercy seat.
Your life becomes the ark in which the invisible God is carried.

Heaven comes to earth when the truth in you becomes **flesh and bone.**

Give us this day…

Here we enter the trust dimension.
The ego wants guarantees. Spirit lives by revelation.

Daily bread is not food—it is **light.**
*The true bread is the Word—***not a written word,** *but the* **spoken Word within.**
When you walk in GIATI, you live by the voice of the Spirit in real-time.
No hoarding. No storing. Only fresh manna, moment by moment.

This is how you stay alive in truth:
Listening daily, living from the knowing that God is all there is.

Forgive us our debts…

There is no ledger in heaven.
God does not forgive like humans do, because God never saw sin in the first place.
He only sees **Himself.**

But forgiveness is necessary—not for God to feel better, but for **you to be healed.**
To forgive is to erase the illusion of separation.
It's to return to **the single eye,** *where there are no "others," only expressions of the One.*

In GIATI, forgiveness is not emotional release—it's spiritual clarity.
You forgive when you stop believing in two.

Lead us not into temptation…

Temptation is not chocolate or alcohol.

It is the pull back into the illusion that you are someone apart from God.
It is the deception that there is "you" and "God," rather than **you as the expression of God.**

You are not asking God to guide you morally.

You are asking the Spirit to keep you rooted in **the truth of oneness,**
so you don't fall again into the sleep of duality.

Deliver us from evil…

Evil is not a creature. It is **a condition of blindness.**
It is the fruit of ignorance, fear, and separation.
The greatest evil is to believe you are just a man or woman, born to die.

Deliverance comes by light—by **being re-membered to the truth** *of who you are.*
This is not rescue from punishment. It is awakening from illusion.

When you know the truth, evil loses its ground.
Because the only power evil had was **your agreement with a lie.**

For Thine is the kingdom…

This final line is a return to **center.**
All belongs to God, because all **is** *God.*
Kingdom. Power. Glory. Forever.

And because God is all there is…
There is no glory for you to steal.
No power for you to possess.
No kingdom to build for yourself.

There is only **oneness to live from.**

And when you live from this place,
you realize the prayer is not something you say—
it's who you are.

This is the prayer of the awakened.
This is GIATI.

Offended at God in Flesh

Matthew 13:57

"And they were offended in him. But Jesus said unto them, A prophet is not without honour, save in his own country, and in his own house."

*This verse reveals a profound truth: w***hen the voice of God arises in familiar flesh, it is often dishonored, not because it lacks Spirit, but because it lacks distance.** *The people who knew Jesus by the flesh could not recognize Him by the Spirit. They were offended, not because He was wrong, but because He was* **too close, too ordinary, too human-looking to be divine.**

*And yet, this is the mystery of godliness: "God was manifest in the flesh" (1 Timothy 3:16). But to the carnal mind, which expects divinity to be far off, holy in appearance, and separate from humanity, this is offensive. They looked at Jesus and said, "Is not this the carpenter's son?" (v.55). They could not fathom that G***od could be standing in front of them without robes, titles, or thunder.**

GIATI teaches that God is All There Is. *He does not just come to visit. He expresses Himself as you. The same Spirit that was in Christ is in every one of us. But the world still struggles to recognize God when He speaks through familiar vessels. Even today, when someone awakens and begins to speak with the authority of oneness, they are often dishonored—not for the message, but for the messenger.*

*Jesus was not saying He wanted honor—He was exposing the pattern: t***hose who are still asleep will always reject the Spirit in someone they think they know.** *They will say, "I remember who you used to be," or "You're just from around here." But the Spirit has no past. It is eternal. It is not bound by your history or your hometown.*

Cross-reference:

"Wherefore henceforth know we no man after the flesh: yea, though we have known Christ after the flesh, yet now henceforth know we him no more." —2 Corinthians 5:16

This verse reinforces the GIATI revelation: we are not to judge or recognize one another by outer form, but by the Spirit within. When you still see someone "after the flesh," you're blind to the truth that **God is the I AM in them.** *And as long as you reject that, you remain outside the kingdom of God, which is the awareness of your union with Him.*

In His own house, He was rejected. Why? Because He did not perform separation.

The people wanted a Messiah who would exalt them above others by race or religion. But Jesus came to reveal that **there is no Jew or Gentile, no clean or unclean, no us and**

them—only One. *And when the Spirit begins to speak this truth through you, be prepared:* **you will not be honored by those who still cling to separation.**

They will be offended at your boldness. They will question your authority. They will demand to see signs, traditions, or titles to prove your message. But you don't need to prove what is already true: **The Spirit of God as you is the prophet, and the prophet is the voice of I AM.**

Matthew 13:58

"And he did not many mighty works there because of their unbelief."

*What a sobering truth: t***he unlimited Spirit was present—but limited in manifestation, not by power, but by perception.** *Jesus, the embodiment of the I AM, the Word made flesh, stood among them with healing, wisdom, and divine fullness. Yet few miracles occurred. Why?*

Because of their unbelief.

They could not receive what they could not recognize. They saw only a man, not the Spirit. They looked at the outer form and judged it unworthy of divinity. And in doing so, **they shut the door of heaven in their own minds.**

*Unbelief is not just doubt—it is spiritual blindness. It is the refusal to see God as present and expressed. It is the deep-rooted conviction that G***od cannot possibly be this close, this human, this now.** *And that very mindset becomes the barrier to the flow of divine power.*

GIATI reveals this principle: where oneness is denied, manifestation is diminished.

The miracles of God flow through the consciousness of union. When you see Him in you, in your brother, in the moment—there, the kingdom is made visible. But when you reject Him, limit Him, or push Him into some far-off heaven or future day, you **cut yourself off from the Source that was always within.**

Cross-reference:

"According to your faith be it unto you." —Matthew 9:29

Faith is not just belief in God's existence—it's the recognition of His presence as you. Faith is spiritual alignment. It is when you no longer see yourself and God as separate beings, but as one. And it is that recognition that **opens the flow of the kingdom.**

So when Jesus was dishonored in His hometown, it wasn't that His power changed. It was that **they shut their eyes and ears to who He was.** *Not because they didn't hear Him speak—but because they couldn't see Him as Spirit.*

The same is true now.

Many ask, "Where are the miracles?" "Why don't we see the power of God?" And the answer remains: **because of unbelief.** *Not the unbelief of atheism or rebellion, but the unbelief of religious familiarity—the kind that sees only flesh and refuses to see Spirit in the ordinary.*

You could be surrounded by miracles, but if you still believe God is "out there," you'll miss every one.

God has never left. But He will not force Himself on closed eyes.

*And this is the judgment: lig***ht has come into the world, and men loved darkness rather than light** *(John 3:19). They loved separation more than union. They preferred waiting for God instead of awakening as Him.*

So He did not many mighty works there—not because He lacked power, but because they lacked vision.

Spirit Not Limited, But Hidden

What you must understand is that **Spirit never withdraws—He is simply unrecognized.** *The miracles didn't stop in Nazareth because God changed His mind. They didn't cease because the power weakened. They ceased because* **the veil of familiarity kept them from seeing God in the one standing among them.**

Unbelief is not a passive condition. It is **a resistance to union.** *It is the soul clinging to its own image of how God should come, where He should come from, and who He should come through. And if the form doesn't match expectation, the Spirit is dismissed—even while present.*

This is not just a moment in history—it is a revelation of what still happens today. Many are not waiting on God; **they are rejecting Him in the form He's taken.** *He comes through the voice of a child, the stillness of a moment, the words of someone "too familiar," and they cannot receive it. Why? Because their idea of God is still carnal. Distant. Holy by contrast, not by identity.*

But God no longer comes from the outside. He awakens from within.

The kingdom is never absent; it is simply not perceived. You cannot inherit what you refuse to recognize. And this is why so many miss the kingdom while searching for it: **they're looking for a future event instead of an unveiled awareness.**

Even now, He speaks as you. But if your eyes are trained only on the outer man, you'll walk with divinity daily and never know it. Just like they did.

The Spirit was not denied in Nazareth by force. **He was excluded by identity.** *They said, "We know who you are," not realizing the one they claimed to know was no longer who was speaking. The I AM had taken the microphone—but they still saw the man.*

This is the danger of holding on to who people were when the Spirit is showing you who they are.

The Christ is always emerging. Not from the clouds—but from within. But when the mind is fixed on form, it remains blind to function. They couldn't see the Spirit healing, because they were too caught up in the history of the flesh.

And that blindness robbed them—not of God, but of the **awareness** *of what was always present.*

The Eyes of the Spirit: How Jesus Saw

*Jesus was not just the bringer of the kingdom—***He was the demonstration of how it is perceived.** *He didn't just come to perform miracles but to reveal the way they become visible: through the eye of oneness. While others judged by lineage, ritual, and outward worthiness,* **He looked straight into the Spirit.**

Where men saw a tax collector, He saw a disciple. Where religion saw a prostitute, He saw purity awakened. Where others saw disease, He saw an opportunity for glory. Where the world saw unclean flesh, He saw vessels of the same Father.

This was His secret: *He didn't treat people as they appeared—He called them according to the Spirit within them. "Judge not according to appearance, but judge righteous judgment" (John 7:24). That means* **see what is eternally true—not what looks true in time.**

*When Jesus called the blind man healed, the man still couldn't see. But Jesus wasn't describing the condition—***He was speaking from the perspective of Spirit, where healing already is.** *That is the difference between those who perform works and those through whom the works flow effortlessly: one tries to make something happen, the other sees what already is—and aligns with it.*

This is why Jesus never panicked, never performed, never pled. He simply **saw***—and what He saw became.*

*And now He says to us: "The works I do shall you do also, and greater" (John 14:12). But not through effort or imitation—***through the same vision.** *The miracles aren't the result of spiritual strain. They're the natural outcome of spiritual sight.*

The more you awaken to the truth that **God is the I AM within you,** *the more you begin to see through His eyes. No longer judging by flesh, past, or form—but discerning by Spirit.*

This is not just a new way to think; it's a new way to live. The veil is removed when you stop looking outward for God and begin seeing **everything** *as God expressing.*

To see rightly is to inherit.

For the kingdom is not given to those who try harder, but to those who see clearer.

The Key to Inheritance: Perception Determines Possession

*The reason many cannot access the kingdom is because they believe it to be a reward instead of a realization. But the kingdom is not a prize for the holy. It is t***he realm of the awakened.** *It belongs to those who see not with the eyes of flesh, but with the Spirit.*

Jesus modeled this when He said, "The kingdom of God is within you" (Luke 17:21). That wasn't a metaphor. It was a message: **look inward. The treasure is not hidden from you; it's hidden in you.** *But as long as you search for it externally, you remain blind—even though the kingdom surrounds you.*

To walk in power, peace, and clarity like Jesus did is not about becoming something greater—it's about **remembering who you are.** *It's about abandoning the illusion of separation and seeing the Spirit as your only identity.*

This is how you unlock the greater works. This is how you inherit. Not by effort. Not by bloodline. Not by ritual. But by sight.

What you see, you manifest. What you perceive, you receive.

Treasures in Heaven: The Consciousness That Cannot Be Taken

Jesus concluded many of His teachings with this sobering truth:

"Lay not up for yourselves treasures upon earth, where moth and rust doth corrupt, and where thieves break through and steal: But lay up for yourselves treasures in heaven…" — Matthew 6:19–20

*This was not a command against wealth—it was a warning against p***lacing value in what perishes.** *He was not concerned about gold or garments, but about* **what your soul is anchored to.** *He was saying: Do not invest your life into that which time can erase. Don't build your identity on things that can be lost.*

Earthly treasures are anything attached to the realm of form—your reputation, achievements, heritage, rituals, bloodlines, even religious performance. *These are all subject to change, decay, and theft. The mind that clings to these remains unsettled, for it always fears loss.*

But heavenly treasure is not far away—it is **Spirit awareness.** *It is the recognition of the eternal "I AM" that cannot be touched by time, age, decay, or death. This is the treasure Christ spoke of:* **the consciousness of oneness with God.**

That awareness is incorruptible.

The awakened soul carries a wealth that moths cannot eat and thieves cannot find. When you awaken to GIATI—that God Is All There Is—you carry heaven within. **You walk with the treasure of eternity in the temple of time.**

And this is the final inheritance:
Not the things you've done.
Not the life you've built.
But the awareness you carry.

Did you live as a separated self, gathering earthly affirmations, climbing religious ladders, storing up status in dust?

Or did you awaken to the Spirit within, and live from the indestructible treasure of union?

When all flesh fades, and every form dissolves, only the treasure of heaven remains. And the treasure is this: **Christ in you, the hope of glory** *(Colossians 1:27). Not a doctrine. Not a denomination.* **But the eternal Spirit that cannot be taken, because it is who you are.**

In the end, you don't take your performance. You don't carry your bloodline. You don't present your record.

You carry one thing: the treasure you became conscious of. *Either the treasure of separation—which leads to fear and loss—or the treasure of union, which is the kingdom of heaven.*

And where your treasure is, there your heart is also.

Greater Works—The Unveiling of Oneness

"Verily, verily, I say unto you, He that believeth on me, the works that I do shall he do also; and greater works than these shall he do; because I go unto my Father." —John 14:12 (KJV)

When Jesus spoke these words, He wasn't exaggerating. He wasn't teasing some unreachable standard. He was declaring what would be possible **when the same Spirit that moved through Him would live consciously in others.** *This wasn't a promise of religious superstardom; it was a prophetic unveiling of the kingdom coming to maturity—not just in one body, but in many.*

Jesus was the prototype of the new creation: a man fully aware of His union with God. Every miracle He performed was **not to prove He was the only one,** *but to reveal what it looks like when a human being lives from* **spiritual identity instead of flesh consciousness.** *He raised the dead, not to say, "Look what I alone can do," but to say, "This is what the Father in you does when unhindered by unbelief."*

And yet—He said we would do greater.

Why? Because the Spirit He operated in would no longer be limited to one body, one location, one moment in history. **The same "I AM" that worked through Him would be multiplied through a body of believers who awaken to the same truth: that the Father and I are one.**

The "greater works" are not greater in glory than raising the dead or opening blind eyes—**they are greater in reach, greater in scale, greater in spiritual depth.** *Jesus healed bodies, calmed storms, and fed multitudes, yes—but the greater work is when the* **eyes of the soul are opened to eternal identity.** *When someone is awakened from the grave of separation and walks in the light of union,* **that is a greater resurrection.**

*A healed body still dies. A fed stomach gets hungry again. A calmed storm will one day return. But the person who sees themselves as one with God h***as received an eternal miracle.** *They have stepped out of the illusion of separation and into the kingdom. That is a greater work.*

Jesus' miracles were not just acts of compassion—they were signs. *Signs point beyond themselves. The physical healings pointed to a deeper healing: the restoration of divine awareness. The casting out of demons revealed the authority of awakened Spirit over every illusion. The multiplying of bread pointed to the truth that th***ere is no lack in the consciousness of God.**

Every outward miracle Jesus did was a window into an inner reality. And now, the greater works are those that don't just open blind eyes, but **awaken blinded hearts.** *Those that don't just cast out spirits, but* **restore people to the knowledge of who they are in the Spirit.** *Not just walking on water, but* **walking in perfect peace, unshaken by the storms of the world.**

The greater works are not about being more powerful than Jesus. They are about **embodying what He came to reveal:** *that* **God is not separate from man.** *That God is not somewhere else, working through someone else. That the same Spirit that raised Jesus from the dead* **now lives in you.**

This is why Jesus said, "I go unto my Father." Because in returning to the invisible, **He would become visible in us.** *His "leaving" was not absence—it was expansion. Now, instead of one awakened man in Galilee, the Father would awaken as many.*

**You are not here to admire the works of Christ. You are here to continue them—**not from the outside, but as the Spirit of God expressing through you. The same "I AM" that spoke peace to the sea, healed the leper, and forgave the sinner now lives as you.

The greater works begin the moment you stop seeing Jesus as a distant figure to worship, and start seeing Him as the pattern of who you truly are in the Spirit.

That is the miracle of this age. And that is the work that will never pass away.

Modern Miracles: How the Greater Works Manifest Today

The miracles of Jesus were not limited to one generation. The same Spirit that moved in Him continues to work—but the way it manifests has matured. Today, the greater works are seen not only in the visible world, but in the **unfolding of truth within the consciousness of man.** _This is the miracle of awakening—the resurrection of the soul from ignorance into divine identity._

1. From Sin-Conscious to Spirit-Aware

The greatest miracle is not the breaking of chains on the outside—it's when a person awakens and says, "I and the Father are one." That moment of realization is a spiritual resurrection. A mind once buried in shame, fear, and striving is now flooded with the truth of GIATI—God Is All There Is. This isn't just new thinking—it's a new being. **This is eternal life manifesting now.**

A person can be healed in body and still live in fear. But when one is healed in identity—when they see themselves no longer as a sinner trying to please God, but as God expressed through form—that is a **permanent transformation.** _That is the greater work._

2. Breaking the Illusion of Separation

Before, people feared demons, curses, generational bondage. But now, through the Spirit of Truth, those illusions are cast out by a single revelation: There is no power apart from God. There is no second source. There is no battle—only awakening. This is the greater exorcism. Not fighting darkness, but **removing the veil that created it.**

The mind bound by religion, race, ritual, and rules is set free by the simple understanding that **the kingdom is within.** _No outer ritual can match the power of that inner realization._

3. Awakening Others to Their True Identity

Every time you speak from the awareness of union, every time someone hears the GIATI message and awakens to the truth that God is within them—not just with them—you've participated in a greater miracle than healing the sick. You've helped resurrect someone's eternal self.

Jesus spoke to dead bodies and they rose. But **you are now speaking to dead minds—minds buried under false identities—and the Spirit in you is calling them out of their graves.** *That's not just a miracle. That's kingdom expansion.*

4. Peace That Surpasses Understanding

In a world full of anxiety and chaos, one awakened soul walking in unshakable peace is a miracle greater than parting the Red Sea. Why? Because **it shows dominion not over nature, but over the self.** *The sea calmed by Jesus returned to waves. But a person walking in peace—knowing that they are the temple of God and lack nothing—becomes a living witness of heaven on earth.*

5. Forgiveness as a Divine Act

Jesus said, "Your sins are forgiven." That wasn't just a statement of mercy—it was an announcement of identity. Today, the greater work is declaring to people that **God holds no record of separation—because there was never a "you" apart from Him to be condemned.** *Telling someone they are free—not because of what they've done, but because of who they are—***shifts their entire existence.** *That's a greater work than raising the dead. It's raising the living into truth.*

The Greater Work Is the Greater Awakening

You are the miracle. Not just because of what you do—but because of what you carry: the awareness of oneness. When you live, move, and speak from that place, **you are the greater work in motion.** *Not limited by form. Not waiting for permission. Just the Spirit of God expressing, awakening, and expanding through you.*

This is the era of fulfillment. The age of unveiling. And the works of Christ did not stop—they multiplied.

The question is no longer, "Will God do greater works?" The question is, "Will you see that He's already doing them... as you?"

The Hidden Cry in Desire

There is a longing within every human being so strong, so persistent, and so misunderstood, that it defines the shape of our lives. It wakes us up in the middle of the night. It pulls at our thoughts during the day. It sits behind every craving, every attraction, every hunger for touch, attention, affection, and release.

That longing is most powerfully felt through **sexual desire.**

And yet, **what humanity calls the desire for sex** *is actually something far more sacred:*
It is the soul's cry for union with God.
A longing to return to the truth that has always been:

We are not separate. God is within us, and we are within Him.

The Symbol of Oneness

From the GIATI perspective, sex is not sin. It is **a symbol***—a natural, earthly signpost pointing toward a spiritual truth:* **oneness.**

The act of sex—the two becoming one, the surrender of bodies, the vulnerability of being seen and known—is the closest earthly mirror to what the soul remembers from eternity:

the state of perfect unity with its Source.

Before the illusion of separation entered human awareness, there was no hunger. There was no reaching. There was no craving for "the other," because there was no "other." There was only **God expressing Himself as all things, in perfect union.**

But once the mind began to perceive itself as separate from God, the ache was born. The soul began to cry—not always with words, but through desires. It sought out reunification in the only ways it knew how.

And so, **sex became humanity's unconscious attempt to return to Eden***—to taste, even for a moment, what it means to be one again.*

The Mistaken Path

When this desire is misunderstood, the soul turns outward. It reaches for pleasure, for partners, for images and fantasies. It grasps at shadows, not knowing it is really seeking light.

This is why, even after sex, many feel empty.
This is why, after the climax, the craving returns.
Because the act **did not fulfill what the soul was truly asking for.**

It's not that sex is evil. It's that sex alone cannot do what only **Spirit-awareness** *can do:*

Restore the knowledge that God is all there is—and you are in Him, and He is in you.

The Invitation in Desire

When sexual desire arises, the GIATI perspective invites us to pause—not to suppress it, but to **see through it.**

Not:

"I need someone to satisfy this craving." But:

"This craving is my reminder—I was made for union. Let me return to the Spirit within me, and be filled."

This doesn't mean one becomes cold, celibate, or lifeless. It means one becomes **aware.** *And in awareness, everything changes.*

The desire no longer rules you—it **awakens you.**

What once felt like the body crying out becomes **the Spirit calling you inward***—not to escape the world, but to remember the Source* **within** *the world and within you.*

Sex Transformed

When the soul is rooted in the awareness of God within, even sex—when it happens—is no longer just flesh meeting flesh. It becomes Spirit meeting Spirit. It becomes a sacred expression, not a desperate grasping. It becomes communion, not consumption.

But even if it doesn't happen—if no partner comes, if no opportunity arises—the soul is still at peace. Why? Because **it has already found union in the place that matters most: within itself, where God dwells.**

The Return to Wholeness

Desire is not your enemy. It is your teacher.
But it can only teach when you stop chasing its surface and **listen to its message:**

"You are not alone. You are not lacking. You are not just a body. You are Spirit. You are already one with God. You always have been."

So the next time desire comes—and it will—don't condemn it. And don't be enslaved by it.
Let it remind you:

You are whole. You are held. You are Him.

And when you truly know this, you will no longer chase intimacy. **You will carry it.**

The Symbolism of Orgasm

This is why orgasm feels so powerful—why it brings a moment of stillness, surrender, and release. Because it mirrors what the soul longs for most: **a return to total union.**

In that moment—just before and just after climax—something shifts.

The mind stops.
The body lets go.
The false self disappears.
And for a fleeting second, the illusion of separation dissolves.

This is not just biology. This is a spiritual echo.

Orgasm is the body's symbol of what it feels like when Spirit reaches the **climax of awareness***—when the soul finally knows, "I am not separate. I am one with God. God is all there is—and He is in me, as me."*

The pleasure is intense, not just because of nerve endings—but because it resonates with a deeper knowing:
"This is what wholeness feels like."

What the World Got Wrong

The world teaches that this feeling comes **from another person.** *But GIATI reveals: the feeling never came from them—it came* **from you,** *and more deeply,* **from the Spirit within you** *expressing itself through that experience.*

That's why the body can feel pleasure and still the soul feel empty—because pleasure without presence is just sensation. But when Spirit is awakened, even the body becomes a temple.

Even intimacy becomes holy ground.

And yet, even the greatest sexual climax is still only **a symbol***—a shadow of something far greater:*

The true climax is not physical—it is **spiritual union** *with the God who has never been separate from you.*

Living From the Climax

The world chases climax through touch.

But the awakened soul realizes:

The greatest pleasure is knowing God as your very self.

This doesn't mean denying the body—but it does mean no longer being bound to it. It means no longer looking to sex to give you what only **Spirit-awareness** *can.*

Because once you've touched that place in consciousness—once you've truly known **I and the Father are one***—every desire begins to bow to that knowing.*

You stop trying to climax with the world—and instead, you live from the climax of eternal union. You don't reach for pleasure—you radiate it. You don't chase oneness—you awaken to it.

And then, even your desires become filled with peace. Even your sexuality becomes sanctified—not by rules, but by revelation.

The World Has Been Reaching

Many have never known what their desire for sex truly meant. They've been told it's just biological. Or shameful. Or sinful. Others have pursued it endlessly, convinced that more partners, more pleasure, more exploration would satisfy them. And still, they find themselves longing.

Why?

Because they were never just reaching for a body. They were reaching for **belonging,** *for* **wholeness,** *for* **God***—even if they didn't know it.*

The human soul has always been searching for its Source. And in the absence of spiritual clarity, it has turned to physical intimacy as a substitute.

This is why the **sex industry is one of the largest in the world.** *Billions are spent. Millions are addicted. Countless lives are entangled in a pursuit that seems to promise everything—and delivers just enough to keep people coming back, but never enough to make them whole.*

From the GIATI perspective, this isn't just lust.
It's **lostness.**

It's the soul—still divine, still made in God's image—crying out,

"I want to be one again. I want to remember where I came from. I want to feel complete."

They don't realize it, but what they're truly seeking is not sex. They're seeking **union with God.**

The Mercy in the Misunderstanding

The good news is this: God is not condemning those who misunderstood. He knows the ache. He knows the hunger. He put eternity in the hearts of mankind—and He knows they've been trying to answer that call the only way they knew how.

But now the message of GIATI is revealing what has always been true:

You don't need to chase shadow pleasures when the **real union** *is already within you.*

When you awaken to that, not only do you find peace—you begin to **live from the fullness** *others are still trying to touch.*

A Call to Compassion

This revelation isn't just for personal freedom. It's also a call to see others differently.

Those trapped in sexual addiction...
Those profiting from the sex industry...
Those searching through fantasies, pornography, prostitution, or performance...

They are not dirty. They are not broken.
They are simply **hungry for God,** *without the language to say it.*

And **you,** *awakened by the truth of GIATI, become a light to them—not by judging, but by being.*

By carrying the energy of someone who no longer seeks, because they have found.

By loving from union. Speaking from clarity. And shining from within.

Sacred Sexuality in Oneness

There comes a point in the soul's journey where it no longer views sexuality as something to be suppressed or idolized—but as something to be **understood.** *This is where* **sacred sexuality** *begins: in the light of* **oneness with God.**

The question is no longer, "Is sex right or wrong?"
The deeper question becomes:

"Am I aware of the Source from which this desire arises?"

Because when you know—truly know—that **God is all there is,** *then nothing about your humanity is separate from Him.*
Not your mind.
Not your body.
Not even your desire.

When the Body Is Not Separate

In religious systems built on separation, sexuality was often condemned, feared, or buried under guilt. But from the GIATI perspective, the problem was never sex—it was the illusion that God and man are apart.

If **God is within,** *and* **you are within God,** *then every part of you is sacred—because it is not truly "you" apart from Him.*

Your body is not "just flesh." It is a living temple. A divine expression. A vessel for Spirit. And yes—even your capacity for pleasure and climax is **part of that divine expression.**

Orgasm as Expression, Not Escape

When you are not awakened, sexual desire becomes a search for something outside of yourself. It becomes an escape from loneliness, a cry for validation, or a grasping at a fleeting feeling of connection.

But when you live in oneness, orgasm is no longer an escape.

It becomes an expression—from fullness, not emptiness.

It's no longer about reaching for something.
It's about releasing something that already lives inside you: the creative energy of God flowing through form.

So yes, you can enjoy your sexuality—even your orgasm—not in contradiction to God, but **in communion with God,** *when it flows from awareness.*

The Shift: From Needing to Knowing

There is a profound shift when you stop needing sex to feel whole—and instead begin knowing **you are already whole,** *whether sex happens or not.*

You no longer approach pleasure as a drug.
You approach it as a **gift.** *A gift you are free to enjoy, but not enslaved to.*

You don't suppress it. You don't worship it.
You simply **honor it,** *knowing it flows from the same Source as your breath, your heartbeat, and your spirit.*

A Sacred Act, A Sacred Awareness

When two awakened souls come together in union, aware that **God is within them,** *even sex becomes holy. Not because of the act itself—but because of the awareness that surrounds it.*

There is no shame in the body.
No guilt in the sensation.
No hiding in the experience.
There is only truth:

God is here. This, too, is part of Him.

And even when sex does not occur—when pleasure is not pursued—you are still whole, because the deepest intimacy is not physical. It is spiritual.

Living from the Climax of Union

The world chases climax.
But the awakened soul lives **from** *it.*

You've already been joined with God. You've already returned to the Garden.
The veil of separation has been lifted—and now, even your desires are bathed in light.

So yes—
Sacred sexuality is possible.
Not by religious control. Not by indulgent obsession.
But by the simple, powerful awareness:

God is all there is.
He is within me.
Even my pleasure is a whisper of His presence.
Even my body speaks of His glory.
And I am free—not to suppress or to chase, but to simply be.

One with God. Always.

The God Within Has Always Been You

Not a Journey to God—A Revelation of God As You

*Most people have been taught a version of God that mirrors the systems of this world—distant, conditional, and based on performance. They've been told that God is somewhere "out there" in heaven, watching from a throne, and that if they work hard enough, believe the right things, pray the right way, go to the right church, live righteously, and confess with their mouth that Jesus is Lord, then—***and only then***—will God come into their life and be pleased with them. This idea has shaped generations, causing people to strive endlessly for approval, to fear judgment, and to live in a constant state of uncertainty about their relationship with the Divine.*

But this is not the gospel. And it is not the truth.

The heart of the gospel—the very essence of the GIATI revelation—is that **God never started outside of you.** *He didn't come into your life at a certain point because you finally got it right. He didn't descend upon you when you prayed the right prayer. He didn't suddenly appear when you started living better.* **He has always been there.** *From the beginning, before the world began, He was already joined to you.* **He is not distant. He is the Spirit within you.** *And not just within you like a guest who moved in—***He is your very life.** *He is your breath, your awareness, your being. You were created from Him, in Him, and as Him. He is not an external force you must earn access to—***He is your true identity.**

This is what 2 Timothy 1:9 is revealing when it says that God "hath saved us, and called us with a holy calling, not according to our works, but according to His own purpose and grace, which was given us in Christ Jesus before the world began." The calling was never about going somewhere else, or becoming someone else. It was never about changing into something God could finally accept. It's not a ladder you climb—it's a veil being removed. **It's not a process of becoming—it's a process of remembering.**

The "holy calling" is not a command—it's a **divine awakening.** *It is the moment the illusion of separation falls away, and you see clearly that* **you were never disconnected.** *You were never on the outside looking in. You were never rejected, never abandoned, never waiting for God to come closer. You just didn't know who you were.*

And when you wake up to that truth—when the GIATI revelation pierces through the fog—you realize: **everything you were striving to become, you already are.** *Everything you were hoping to receive, you already possess. The fullness of God is not something that visits you—it is something that was always present, waiting to be recognized. The holy calling isn't to improve your behavior or build a résumé of righteousness—it's to wake up to your origin:* **God is all there is, and that God lives, moves, and breathes in you.**

The Misunderstanding of Separation

For too long, religion has centered its message around a lie—**the lie of distance.** *A lie that says you were born separate from God. A lie that convinces you that something is wrong with you by default, that you're unworthy from the start, and that your only hope is to somehow earn your way back to Him through the right words, right prayers, right beliefs, and right behaviors. Religion has conditioned people to believe that God is far off, holy but unreachable, perfect but distant. And because of that illusion, people spend their lives chasing after a God they already possess, begging for a presence that never left, and trying to gain access to a heaven they were never locked out of.*

But separation was never real. It only existed in the mind. Like a nightmare that feels terrifying until you wake up and realize none of it was true—so is the illusion of separation. It feels real when you're caught in it. It feels true when everyone around you affirms it. But **truth isn't what feels real—it's what remains when the illusion is removed.** *And what remains, what has always remained, is that* **God was never apart from you. He was never across a distance. He was never waiting for you to reach Him.**

He has always been **your source, your substance, and your very breath.**

This is why the gospel is not the beginning of God's relationship with you—it is the **revelation** *of what has always been. It's not God finally coming close. It's the veil finally lifting. It's not the moment He becomes your Savior—it's the moment you realize He already was, and that your entire life has been sustained by Him whether you knew it or not.*

2 Timothy 1:9 makes this unmistakably clear:

He **"hath saved us,** *and* **called us with a holy calling, not according to our works,** *but according to* **His own purpose and grace, which was given us in Christ Jesus before the world began."** *Read that again. This salvation didn't begin when you walked down to an altar. It didn't begin when you got baptized, repented, or confessed Christ with your mouth. It didn't start when you got your life together or had a spiritual breakthrough.* **It began before time itself.**

Before the fall. Before the law. Before sin even entered the picture. **You were already saved.** God had already purposed to express Himself as you. Grace had already been poured out in Christ—the eternal Spirit, the invisible I AM—**and that grace became your true origin.**

You didn't unlock salvation through performance. You didn't qualify for God through behavior. You didn't cross the gap—because there was no gap to begin with. **You simply woke up.**

Salvation is not a reward for faith. It is the light that appears when illusion is gone. It is the unveiling of what has always been yours in Christ—the Spirit of God **not just with you, but as you.**

And the calling you've received is not a call to fix what's broken. It's the holy calling of remembrance—to recall who you've always been in Him.

The Holy Calling Is an Awakening, Not an Achievement

The word "calling" in 2 Timothy 1:9 is one of the most misunderstood and misused words in spiritual teachings. In religious systems, it's often presented as a task or mission you must go discover—something tied to your career, your role in church, your ability to serve, preach, or live righteously. People spend their lives anxiously searching for this "calling," as if it's something hidden outside of them, waiting to be revealed if they can just pray hard enough, live clean enough, or prove their faith. But this is not what "holy calling" means—not in the light of truth, and certainly not from the perspective of GIATI.

The true holy calling is not a religious assignment—it is a spiritual awakening.
It is not about doing something for God; it is about recognizing who you already are in Him.

It is the moment of divine realization when the illusion of separation falls away and you see clearly: **I was never lost. I was never outside. I was never trying to become something—I was always one with the Spirit who created all things.** *This is not a calling to change who you are—it's a calling to remember who you've always been.*

2 Timothy 1:9 tells us plainly that this calling is "not according to our works," but according to "His own purpose and grace, which was given us in Christ Jesus before the world began." That means long before you were born, before you prayed your first prayer, before you ever had the chance to sin or repent, before you ever heard of Jesus or the Bible, **you were already included in God's purpose and grace.** *That's not theory—that's scripture.*

This changes everything.

You don't become saved—you realize you've always been saved. You don't earn your way into God—you awaken to the truth that you have never been outside of Him. The cross didn't purchase something new for you—it exposed and revealed the truth that had been hidden by religion, shame, fear, and misunderstanding:

God is your origin, and He has never been apart from you.

That's why no amount of confessing Jesus, no stack of good deeds, no avoidance of sin, no church attendance, and no scripture memorization can make you more in God than you already are. These things might help you see the truth more clearly, but they don't create it. **You are not on a journey to be saved—you are in the process of awakening to the salvation that has always been yours.**

Salvation is not a reward—it is a reality. And the moment you see it, everything changes—not because God changed, but because the veil in your mind was lifted.

This is the holy calling: not to strive, not to seek, not to become—but to remember. To remember that you and God were never two. To remember that the Spirit you call "God" is not only near you, but is you—your very breath, your awareness, your life. And to live from that knowing is to live in the fullness of the gospel.

The Child Who Didn't Know Their Father

Imagine a child who grows up believing they're alone in the world—no father, no known heritage, no sense of belonging. They feel abandoned, unsure of who they are or where they come from. They try to make sense of life, searching for love, acceptance, and identity in all the wrong places. Every time they look in the mirror, there's a quiet ache inside—a question they can't quite answer: Who am I? Where do I come from? Why do I feel incomplete?

Then, one day, something unexpected happens. They're handed undeniable evidence—a birth certificate bearing their true parent's name, a DNA match that links them directly to the father they thought they never had, photographs of them as a baby in their father's arms. In an instant, everything changes. Their past doesn't change. Their journey doesn't change. But **how they see themselves changes completely.**

They were never fatherless. They were never unloved. They were never disconnected.
They just didn't know who they truly were.

That's what the GIATI message reveals.
You're not trying to become God's child.
You're not climbing your way into His presence or earning your place in His family. **You already are His.** *Not because of a decision you made—but because of who He is as your source and origin. The "holy calling" is not God extending an invitation for you to enter something new—it's* **the unveiling of who you've always been.**

Your life isn't being rewritten—it's being remembered. Your relationship with God isn't starting—it's being recognized. And this changes everything. Because when the veil is lifted and the truth is seen, the ache of separation is healed. You stop trying to reach for God and realize: **I am in Him, and He is in me. We are one.** *Not because I performed well. Not because I confessed something with my mouth. But because from before the foundation of the world,* **He gave me His Spirit as my life.**

*This is the holy calling—***the inward awakening,** *the spiritual "DNA result" that confirms what was always true: You were never lost. You just didn't know who you were.*

And now, you do.

The Branch and the Tree

Now think about a branch growing from a tree. Picture it—firmly attached, drawing its life, strength, and identity directly from the trunk. The sap that flows through the tree also flows through the branch. The life of the tree is the life of the branch. They are not two—they are one continuous being, one expression, one life. The branch doesn't try to be part of the tree. It doesn't struggle to stay connected. It simply is.

Now imagine that same branch, through some strange twist of thought, suddenly forgets it's part of the tree. It becomes convinced it's separate, that it's alone, disconnected, unworthy. And so, in its confusion, it starts trying to "connect" itself to the tree again. It prays harder. It fasts. It works. It begs. It strains to bear fruit, hoping that one day the tree will accept it, include it, and give it life.

From the outside, it's easy to see how unnecessary and tragic that effort is. The branch was never disconnected. Its source was never lost. It was never rejected or abandoned. It just didn't know who it was. Its striving wasn't producing life—it was masking the truth of the life it already had. The branch didn't need to earn connection. **It only needed to awaken to it.**

That's exactly how so many people live today.

They've been told they're separate from God.
They've been taught they need to strive, repent, confess, perform, and qualify just to get back to Him. They spend their lives trying to become what they already are—trying to please a God they're already one with, trying to earn a salvation that was **never in question.**
But the moment they wake up to the truth, everything changes.

There is no more striving.
There is no more fear.
There is no more trying to connect.
You simply be.

You stop struggling to find God because you realize you never left Him. You stop trying to prove yourself to God because you realize you were always His own expression. You stop chasing righteousness because you awaken to the truth that **your righteousness is Him***—the Spirit within you, the life flowing through your being, just like sap in the branch.*

This is the core of the GIATI revelation: **God Is All There Is***—and you are not separate from that All. You are the branch. He is the vine. Not two beings—but one shared life.*

And once you know this—not intellectually, but deeply, spiritually, undeniably—your entire posture changes. You rest. You breathe. You live.

Not to become something...

...but because you already are.

Manifestation, Not Introduction

2 Timothy 1:10 continues, "But is now made manifest by the appearing of our Saviour Jesus Christ, who hath abolished death, and hath brought life and immortality to light through the gospel."

Notice the key phrase: **"made manifest."** *That language is intentional. It doesn't say Jesus created life and immortality. It doesn't say He negotiated them on our behalf or introduced something brand new. It says He made it manifest—He revealed it, uncovered it, exposed it to the light. In other words,* **what He brought to light was already true, already present, already ours***—but hidden beneath the veil of ignorance, fear, and illusion.*

Jesus didn't come to make something true—He came to reveal what had always been true but remained unseen.

From the beginning, life and immortality were your inheritance in God. But religion, tradition, and the darkened understanding of humanity created the illusion of separation, the belief in death, and the idea that we had to work our way back into favor with God. That illusion became the greatest lie ever told: that we are outside, unworthy, and disconnected from our Source.

But Jesus didn't come to fix something broken. He came to awaken us to what was never broken in the first place. *He didn't come to start a relationship between us and God—He came to awaken us to the relationship that had never been severed. He didn't give us life—He revealed that life was already within us, because* **God is the life in us.**

When Jesus appeared, He abolished death—not by making death disappear physically in that moment, but by exposing it for what it truly is: a lie rooted in the false belief of separation. Death is not just the end of a physical body—it is the darkness that sets in when a person forgets who they are in God. It is the condition of living as though you are apart from the Source of your being. But the moment Christ is made manifest within you—the moment the veil lifts—death loses its grip. The illusion shatters. You see clearly: I am one with Life itself. I am immortal in Spirit. I have always been in God, and He in me.

This is not about Jesus giving you something.
This is about **Jesus revealing you to yourself.**

It's not about a Savior handing out spiritual gifts from the outside—it's about the embodiment of Truth awakening within you, showing you what's already yours, and calling you to remember who you've always been in the eternal Spirit of God.

That's what the gospel really is. Not a religious offer. Not a transaction of sin and salvation.

But a **light shining into the heart, exposing the eternal truth that was hidden from your view but never absent from your being.**

He brought life and immortality to light—not into existence, but into your **awareness.**

And once you see it, you can never unsee it.

You stop asking God to come to you and realize He's always been within you. You stop striving to receive eternal life and begin living from it.

You stop looking for a Savior to rescue you and begin recognizing that the Savior came to **reveal you to yourself—as God's own breath in human form.**

GIATI—The Voice of Awakening

The truth that God Is All There Is changes everything.

It confronts every lie we've been told about distance, division, and disconnection. It strips away the religious systems built on fear. It silences the voices that say you must do more, become more, or try harder to get to God. Because if **God truly is all there is,** *then* **there is nothing outside of Him.** *Nothing beyond Him. Nothing separate from Him.*

And if nothing exists outside of Him, then that includes you.

You have **never** *been outside of God. Not for a second. You were not born separate. You didn't fall out of His presence. You're not waiting to return. You were* **conceived in Him,** *carried in His Spirit, and expressed as a living manifestation of His own being.*

The only thing that ever felt like separation was the **illusion**—*the belief that God was somewhere else, somewhere distant, somewhere beyond your reach. But illusion is not reality. It's like a dream that feels real until you wake up. The moment of awakening doesn't create a new truth—it reveals what was always true, hiding beneath the veil of misunderstanding.*

And that is exactly what the **GIATI message** *was born to do.*

GIATI isn't a new religion. It's not another belief system to follow. **It's the sound of the veil tearing.** *It's the trumpet of awakening calling you out of the dream of separation and back into the awareness of oneness. It's the reminder that the Spirit of God has never been "out there." He has always been* **your eternal center**—*the life within your breath, the light within your being, the truth within your soul.*

The purpose of this message is **to shake the world free** *from the bondage of false identity—to break the chains of the lie that says you must earn your way into the presence of a God who was never apart from you in the first place.*

GIATI calls you home—not to a place, not to a church building, not to a set of rituals or rules—but to **your true self:** *the part of you that has always been* **one with God,** *even when your mind couldn't see it.*

This is your return to center. *Not because you were ever truly lost, but because now, you remember. You remember that the Spirit of God is not something you visit. He is not something you reach.* **He is you—expressed as you, living in you, loving through you, being all that you are.**

God Is All There Is. And you are **not an outsider to that truth.** *You are the evidence of it. The embodiment of it. The child who was never apart from the Father. The branch that was never disconnected from the tree. The Spirit who was never less than divine.*

GIATI is the voice of your awakening.
And once you see it, there is no going back.
Only forward.
Only deeper.
Only truer.

Until the whole world remembers that we are not waiting for God to come down—we are waking up to the truth that **God is all there is, and always has been.**

You're Not Becoming—You're Remembering

You are **not** *becoming saved.*
You are **remembering** *that you already are.*

That simple shift in understanding undoes centuries of religious striving and confusion. It unravels the pressure to earn, to prove, to qualify, or to perform. The truth is, **salvation was never a reward waiting for you at the end of a righteous life.** *It was the foundation of your existence—***freely given before time began,** *according to 2 Timothy 1:9. You weren't created in need of rescue. You were* **birthed in grace,** *rooted in God's own purpose and life. You came from Him, and you've never been apart from Him—not even for a moment.*

You are **not** *becoming a child of God.*
You are **remembering** *your divine origin.*

This is the "holy calling" the Scripture speaks of—not a test to pass or an offer to accept, but **an unveiling.** *A revelation. A divine moment of clarity when the fog of illusion lifts, and you see with new eyes: I have always been His. I have always been one with Him. I am not becoming—I am being awakened to the truth of what already is.*

The holy calling is **not a destination.** *It is not something you run toward. It is not some external purpose or religious role you must discover. It is* **the moment the mirror clears,** *and you no longer see a separate, broken self trying to reach God, but a divine expression of the very Spirit of God, here and now, awake and alive.*

This calling is not dependent on your background, your church attendance, your good behavior, or your theological correctness. It is not something you can lose by failing, nor something you can gain by trying harder. **You don't earn what was already yours before the world began.** *You simply wake up to it.*

Think of it like this: imagine being born into royalty, but somehow forgetting who you are. You grow up thinking you're ordinary. You beg for scraps, work tirelessly for approval, and wonder if you'll ever be good enough to be accepted by the king—only to find out **you are his child, and always were.** *That's what the holy calling reveals. You don't become royal—you realize you always were.*

This is why the gospel is not a new opportunity—it is an eternal reminder. A divine alarm clock awakening you to the truth: you are not separate, you are not distant, and you are not waiting to be saved. **You are being unveiled.** *You are remembering. And in that remembrance, you step into the freedom, peace, and wholeness that was always yours in Christ—the eternal Spirit of God within you.*

You are not moving toward God.
You are moving in awareness of God who has always been moving in you.

That is the holy calling.
That is salvation.
That is the truth GIATI exists to proclaim.

God never came into your life. **He was your life all along.**

He Must Increase, But I Must Decrease

John the Baptist's declaration, "He must increase, but I must decrease," is not merely a statement of humility—it is a spiritual key to transformation. The "I" that must decrease is the false self, the ego, the illusion of separation that identifies with being merely human, earthly, and independent of God. The "He" that must increase is the true Self—the Spirit from above, the Word that was with God and is God, the divine essence within us that comes to full awareness when the illusion of separation fades. "He that cometh from above is above all," John says, because what is born of Spirit is eternal, unshaken, and real, whereas what is born of the flesh is fleeting, reactive, and bound by the logic of the earth. The earthly man speaks of the earth because his mind is shaped by his senses, limited by appearances, and blind to the greater truth that Spirit alone is substance.

When Jesus speaks, He does not echo the thoughts of men—He speaks only what He has seen and heard from above. But John admits that no man naturally receives this testimony, because the natural man cannot comprehend spiritual reality. It must be revealed to the inner man by the Spirit. To receive the testimony of Christ is to receive the truth of who you are in God. It is to "set your seal" that God is true, not just in heaven, but within you. This truth doesn't come through religion, tradition, or study—it comes by direct transmission from Spirit to spirit. "For he whom God hath sent speaketh the words of God: for God giveth not the Spirit by measure unto him." This means Jesus, the Sent One, was not partially filled with Spirit; He was the full embodiment of God. He wasn't just a messenger—He was the Message. He spoke as the Son not in separation from the Father, but as the visible expression of the invisible God.

"The Father loveth the Son, and hath given all things into his hand." This reveals the divine pattern: the fullness of God is poured into the Son, and the Son dwells in us. God doesn't hold back or ration the Spirit. To the Son, He gives **all things***—and if you are in the Son, then all things are in you. But to live from this truth, the ego must decrease. The illusion of individuality, of separateness, must surrender. You must stop speaking "of the earth" and begin speaking from heaven, from above, from Spirit. This isn't about becoming less human—it's about becoming fully awakened to your divinity. That is the increase of Christ in you—the hope of glory. Only then can you speak not as a man, but as one born of God, with no measure of Spirit withheld.*

This is what GIATI reveals: the truth that you are not merely a body or a mind trying to "connect" with God, but that God is already the substance of who you are. The more you read, the more the veil lifts. The more you understand, the more you become. Not in the sense of gaining something new, but in the sense of remembering what has always been true: that spirit gives birth to spirit, and flesh gives birth to flesh (John 3:6). GIATI speaks not to your intellect but to your inner man. It bypasses logic, bypasses conditioning, bypasses separation. It speaks directly to the Spirit in you because only Spirit can recognize Spirit.

And this is the difference between religion and revelation. Religion teaches you to behave better in the flesh; revelation teaches you to live as spirit. Religion speaks to the external man: rules, rituals, appearances. Revelation speaks to the internal man—the one "renewed day by day" (2 Corinthians 4:16). That's why Paul said, "We look not at the things which are seen, but at the things which are not seen: for the things which are seen are temporal; but the things which are not seen are eternal" (2 Corinthians 4:18). GIATI pulls you into the realm of the unseen, where your awareness becomes rooted in what is eternal—not in what decays, dies, and divides.

As spirit, you no longer see the world as fragmented pieces: you see God in all. You no longer walk by sight, but by faith (2 Corinthians 5:7). You don't just see a person—you see the Spirit animating that person, whether they know it or not. You don't just see events—you discern divine patterns. You don't just read scripture—you hear the voice behind the words. GIATI doesn't give you new theology; it awakens the inner knowing that was placed in you before the foundations of the world. "The kingdom of God is within you" (Luke 17:21), and GIATI pulls back the curtain so you can see it.

This is why the message must be received spirit to spirit. Carnal minds will argue. Religious minds will resist. But the spirit knows. The spirit recognizes its Source. The spirit bears witness. That's what GIATI is for: not to convince, but to awaken. Because when the Spirit of Truth comes, He doesn't debate—He reveals.

You are spirit. Always have been. GIATI simply helps you live like it.

Chapter 11

Living as God Expressed

To recognize the truth of GIATI—God Is All There Is—is to awaken to your divine purpose and identity. But awakening is only the beginning. The real transformation comes when you align your life with this truth, living as God expressed in the world. This chapter explores practical steps to align your life with the divine, embrace your purpose, and give glory to God in all things.

Practical Steps to Align Your Life with the Truth of GIATI

Living as God expressed begins with intentional actions that affirm the truth of who you are. These steps help bridge the gap between intellectual understanding and spiritual embodiment:

1. **Renew Your Mind**

Paul writes in Romans 12:2:

"And be not conformed to this world: but be ye transformed by the renewing of your mind, that ye may prove what is that good, and acceptable, and perfect, will of God."

To live as God expressed, you must transform your thinking. Renewing your mind means rejecting the false beliefs of separateness and embracing the truth that you are a vessel of God's presence. Meditate on scripture, focus on divine truths, and let them shape your thoughts and actions.

2. **Walk by the Spirit**

Galatians 5:16 teaches:

"This I say then, Walk in the Spirit, and ye shall not fulfil the lust of the flesh."

Walking by the Spirit means prioritizing your divine nature over the physical desires and distractions of the world. It is living with the constant awareness that your true identity is God expressed through you.

3. **Acknowledge God in All Things**

Proverbs 3:6 instructs:

"In all thy ways acknowledge him, and he shall direct thy paths."

Every action, decision, and thought can be an act of worship and recognition of God's presence within you. By acknowledging Him in all things, you align yourself with His purpose and guidance.

4. **Practice Gratitude**

Gratitude is a powerful way to affirm God's work in your life. 1 Thessalonians 5:18 says:

"In every thing give thanks: for this is the will of God in Christ Jesus concerning you."

When you live with gratitude, you affirm that everything in your life—good or challenging—is part of God's divine plan and expression through you.

Embracing Your Divine Purpose: Living as God Incarnate in the World

Your purpose is not something separate from God; it is God's purpose being fulfilled through you. To live as God incarnate is to let your life reflect His nature: love, compassion, wisdom, and creativity. Jesus demonstrated this perfectly, showing us how to live as God expressed in human form.

1. **Love as God Loves**

Jesus summarized divine purpose in Matthew 22:37-39:

"Thou shalt love the Lord thy God with all thy heart, and with all thy soul, and with all thy mind. This is the first and great commandment. And the second is like unto it, Thou shalt love thy neighbour as thyself."

Love is the essence of God. To live as God expressed is to love selflessly, seeing others as divine vessels, just as you are.

2. **Serve as God Serves**

Jesus taught in Matthew 20:28:

"Even as the Son of man came not to be ministered unto, but to minister, and to give his life a ransom for many."

Service is an expression of God's presence within you. By helping others, you demonstrate God's love and purpose in action.

3. Shine as God's Light

Matthew 5:14-16 reminds us:

"Ye are the light of the world. A city that is set on an hill cannot be hid. Neither do men light a candle, and put it under a bushel, but on a candlestick; and it giveth light unto all that are in the house. Let your light so shine before men, that they may see your good works, and glorify your Father which is in heaven."

Your life should reflect God's glory, serving as a beacon of hope, love, and truth in a world often blinded by darkness.

The Divine Plan of God

This divine plan is the foundation of existence itself, and it is revealed from the very beginning of scripture.

In Genesis 1:28, we see the first commandment given to humanity: "Be fruitful, and multiply, and replenish the earth, and subdue it: and have dominion over the fish of the sea, and over the fowl of the air, and over every living thing that moveth upon the earth." At its core, this commandment is not merely about physical reproduction, but about reproducing the divine nature. By creating man in His image and likeness, God intended for humanity to multiply His spirit, filling the earth with His presence expressed through human beings.

To "be fruitful and multiply" is a directive that carries profound spiritual significance. It reflects God's desire to see His oneness, love, and essence manifested and multiplied in and through His creation. Adam and Eve were not just created to populate the earth with physical offspring, but to bring forth generations that would bear and reflect the spirit of the Creator. This was always God's ultimate plan: to reproduce Himself through humanity, so that all creation would be a reflection of His glory and oneness.

However, this reproduction of God's spirit requires alignment with His truth. The multiplication of the divine image cannot occur when man is separated from the awareness of his unity with the Creator. Genesis 1:28 underscores not only the importance of reproduction but also the responsibility to "subdue" and "have dominion" over creation. This dominion is only possible when man operates from the spirit of God within him, recognizing that everything he governs and interacts with is an expression of the Creator.

God's command to be fruitful and multiply is not limited to the physical realm but extends to the spiritual. It is an invitation to participate in His ultimate plan of bringing forth His nature, love, and unity throughout all creation. When humanity fulfills this purpose, the earth becomes a canvas displaying the oneness and glory of the Creator, just as He intended from the very beginning. This truth is the essence of GIATI and the reason why understanding our unity with the Creator is the key to fulfilling His divine plan.

Giving Glory to God in All Things: Recognizing Him as the Doer

Living as God expressed requires the humility to recognize that all glory belongs to Him. The ego often wants to take credit for achievements and successes, but true alignment with GIATI involves surrendering this desire and acknowledging God as the source of all things.

1. God as the Source of Strength

Philippians 4:13 declares:

"I can do all things through Christ which strengtheneth me."

Your abilities, talents, and accomplishments are not your own but are expressions of God's power working through you.

2. God as the Creator of Good Works

Ephesians 2:10 states:

"For we are his workmanship, created in Christ Jesus unto good works, which God hath before ordained that we should walk in them."

Even the good you do in the world is not your doing but God's purpose being fulfilled through you. By giving glory to God, you honor His presence within you.

3. God as the Author of Your Life

Proverbs 16:9 reminds us:

"A man's heart deviseth his way: but the Lord directeth his steps."

Recognizing God as the doer means surrendering control and trusting His plan for your life. This surrender allows His divine purpose to manifest fully through you.

Conclusion: Becoming a Living Testament

Living as God expressed is not a lofty ideal—it is the natural result of recognizing GIATI. When you align your life with this truth, embrace your divine purpose, and give glory to God in all things, you become a living testament to His presence.

As Paul writes in 1 Corinthians 10:31:

"Whether therefore ye eat, or drink, or whatsoever ye do, do all to the glory of God."

Your life, in every action and thought, can reflect the truth of GIATI. By living as God expressed, you fulfill your purpose and become a beacon of divine light and love in the world. This is the ultimate destiny of humanity: to glorify God by recognizing Him within and living as His expression on earth.

The Responsibility of Truth: Embracing the Divine Within

In Ezekiel 33:8-9, we are given a powerful image of accountability. The prophet declares that if a watchman sees danger coming and does not warn the people, then when disaster strikes, the blame falls squarely on him. This underscores the serious responsibility of those who possess knowledge that could save others from harm. It poses a fundamental question: Is it wrong to withhold truth—especially when that truth could greatly affect your life?

This same principle applies to our spiritual lives. When we claim to follow God, yet choose to remain silent about truths that could awaken or save others, we not only neglect our duty but also contribute to a culture of complacency. If someone truly believes that God is all there is, how can they continue to engage in actions like gossip, backbiting, or slander— behaviors that harm others and reflect a shallow understanding of divine truth? How can we accept our own faults—thinking we are "80% good" and that the remaining "20%" can be worked on later—when scriptural principles tell us that breaking one law means breaking all of them?

Partial Goodness Is Not Enough

James 2:10 reminds us that if we keep the whole law yet stumble in one area, we are guilty of all. This means that even if we see ourselves as mostly righteous, that small fraction of error is enough to fracture our integrity in the eyes of divine law. It challenges the notion that spiritual or moral mediocrity can be overlooked simply because immediate punishment isn't meted out. Similarly, Ecclesiastes 8:11 warns that when judgment is delayed, the human heart can become emboldened to do wrong. In a system where every action matters, nothing is too minor to ignore.

The Problem of Spiritual Ignorance

Too often, our understanding of faith is limited to external actions and superficial standards—a belief in an unseen God that is so intangible it becomes an exercise in blind faith. If our religious foundation is built solely on rituals and hollow promises, we are left with a system that fails to address the core of our existence. We might see ourselves as almost righteous, yet in truth, our spiritual ignorance prevents us from realizing the full measure of our divine identity. This is where many fall short; they rely on half-truths and overlook the simple fact that every soul is an embodiment of the divine.

GIATI: A Call to Complete Awakening

GIATI—standing for "God Is All There Is"—is introduced as a remedy to this pervasive issue. Rather than fixating on our physical actions or external measures of goodness, GIATI directs our attention inward, to the undeniable presence of God's spirit within each of us. Recognizing that divine spark transforms our understanding of morality from a fraction-

based system (80% good, 20% needing work) to a realization that we are, in essence, 100% complete when we awaken to this truth.

When you start with the knowledge that every part of your being is an expression of God, the question of partial goodness disappears. Instead of patching together a belief system based on blind faith and delayed consequences, GIATI offers a concrete foundation—much like building a house on solid concrete rather than on shifting sands. It is an invitation to embrace a full, unbroken connection with the divine, ensuring that you no longer have to wonder whether you've "gotten away" with something, because your life becomes a living testament to complete spiritual awakening.

A Message of Love and Accountability

This call to awaken is not one of condemnation, but of love. It is an earnest invitation to all who have been living with a fragmented understanding of their spiritual identity. By sharing these truths, the aim is to help you recognize that your worth is not measured by isolated actions or by the percentage of goodness you accumulate over time. Instead, it is found in the realization that God's spirit dwells within you wholly and perfectly.

The purpose here is clear: to ensure that no one remains in ignorance about the true nature of their divine identity. When you understand that every piece of your life—every thought, word, and deed—reflects the eternal presence of God, you move from being partially aware to fully awakened. And with this awakening, you carry the responsibility to share that truth with others, so that everyone may live with a foundation as strong and enduring as the divine itself.

In this way, GIATI is not just a belief system, but a call to return to what is real, to build your life on a foundation that does not crumble under scrutiny, and to do so out of love—for yourself, for those around you, and for the unshakeable truth that God truly is all there is.

GIATI Brand

The power behind the GIATI clothing line goes far beyond fabric, stitching, or status— it is about keeping the ultimate truth in front of everyone, constantly reinforcing the realization that God Is All There Is. Unlike other brands, which rely on prestige, exclusivity, or fleeting trends, GIATI offers something incomparable: a lasting, life-changing message that becomes a part of the wearer's consciousness. It is not just clothing; it is an ever-present reminder of divine oneness, the recognition that there is nothing separate from God.

When comparing GIATI to other brands, the question arises—what do people truly buy when they choose a brand? Is it the name, the material, or the status it brings? For most brands, the appeal is rooted in one or more of these elements. People may purchase luxury brands for a sense of belonging to an elite class, streetwear brands for cultural relevance, or athletic brands for performance and identity. But how many brands give something of lasting value—something that transforms the way a person sees themselves and the world around them? How many brands serve as a daily revelation, a constant reminder of spiritual truth that shifts one's entire way of being? GIATI is in a league of its own because it provides not just clothing, but enlightenment.

Sociologically, people are drawn to brands that reflect their values, beliefs, and aspirations. A brand becomes an extension of identity, a way for individuals to signal to the world who they are and what they stand for. This is why people form deep attachments to certain logos, styles, and names—they are not just buying a product; they are buying an idea, a feeling, a sense of self. But if we analyze the motivations behind most brand affiliations, we see that many are rooted in the illusion of separation: status, hierarchy, exclusivity, and the desire to differentiate oneself from others. GIATI, however, turns that paradigm upside down. It is not about separation—it is about unity. It does not encourage competition or comparison—it reminds you that you are already whole, already divine.

No other brand has been created with this level of impact in mind. While many brands focus on self-expression, GIATI focuses on self-realization. The difference is profound. Self-expression allows people to showcase their individual style, but self-realization transforms them entirely. GIATI is not about trends—it is about truth. It does not rely on hype—it carries divine revelation. And unlike every other brand, which ultimately fades into the cycle of consumer culture, GIATI carries a message that is eternal.

When looking at the overall impact of a brand, nothing else compares. Other brands may sell confidence, style, or performance, but GIATI delivers the highest value of all—awakening. The person wearing GIATI is not just making a fashion statement; they are aligning with a message that transcends materialism, status, or social constructs. This is why GIATI is the most impactful brand ever created. It is not just a brand—it is a movement.

It is not just clothing—it is consciousness woven into fabric. It is the only brand that does not just dress the body but awakens the soul.

Just having the opportunity to purchase something created by the Holy Spirit in the flesh—that alone is something beyond comprehension. How do you put a price tag on that? How do you measure the value of something designed not just to be worn, but to awaken? GIATI isn't just clothing; it is the physical manifestation of divine truth. It is the Spirit made tangible, a reminder that God Is All There Is—not just in thought, not just in belief, but in every moment, every experience, every breath.

This brand was not created to be just another name in fashion. It wasn't designed to blend in with the endless cycle of trends and material desires. GIATI exists for one reason: to bring awareness of divine oneness. The sole purpose of this brand is to open the eyes of those who see it, to remind the wearer and everyone around them of what has always been true—there is nothing outside of God. When you wear GIATI, you are carrying that message with you. Every time someone sees it, they are being confronted with a truth that cannot be ignored.

Imagine that—clothing that does more than just cover the body. It transforms perception. It changes the atmosphere. It carries the presence of God into the world in a way that cannot be overlooked. GIATI is not about making a fashion statement; it is about making a spiritual declaration. It is a call to consciousness, a sign to everyone who encounters it that the truth is right in front of them, just as it has always been within them.

To wear GIATI is to embody the Holy Spirit. To purchase it is to hold in your hands something created by the Spirit in the flesh, something that carries a message so powerful that it has the potential to shift the way people see reality itself. Can you really put a price on that? A shirt, a sweatsuit, a piece of clothing—it seems simple, but the impact is immeasurable. This is not just fashion. This is not just merchandise. This is a divine reminder, a continuous revelation, a signpost pointing the way back to what has always been.

GIATI exists because the world needed a reminder. It exists because people have forgotten who they are and what everything around them truly is. It was created to be a light in the midst of that forgetting, to be a constant, undeniable message that God is not distant, not separate, not somewhere else—He is all there is. Every piece of GIATI carries that truth. And for those who wear it, see it, or recognize it, the awakening begins.

www.giatibrand.com

Truth About Giving

2 Corinthians 9:7 Every man according as he purposeth in his heart, so let him give ; not grudgingly, or of necessity: for God loveth a cheerful giver.

This scripture emphasizes the **true nature of giving***—that it must come from the heart, not from obligation or reluctance. Let's break it down:*

"Every man according as he purposeth in his heart, so let him give"

This means that giving should be **intentional and heartfelt.** *It should not be done because of pressure, manipulation, or the expectation of a reward, but because it is a genuine expression of love and generosity.*

"Not grudgingly, or of necessity"

- **Not grudgingly** – *Giving should not be done with resentment or reluctance. If a person gives while feeling forced or unwilling, then the spirit behind the act is corrupted. True giving is never a burden—it is a joy.*
- **Or of necessity** – *Giving should not be done out of obligation or guilt. If someone gives simply because they feel they "have to," then it is not a true gift, but a transaction. God is not interested in forced offerings—He desires* **willing participation** *in the flow of abundance.*

"For God loveth a cheerful giver"

God delights in those who **give joyfully,** *because their giving reflects His own nature. God Himself is a giver—of life, love, and everything good—and when a person gives* **freely and joyfully,** *they align themselves with the nature of God.*

The Spiritual Depth of This Verse

This verse is not just about material giving—it applies to **everything we offer in life.**

- **Giving love**
- **Giving time**
- **Giving forgiveness**
- **Giving wisdom**

If any of these things are given grudgingly or out of necessity, the act is empty. But when given **freely and joyfully,** *it carries divine power.*

The GIATI Perspective on Giving

From the standpoint of **GIATI (God Is All There Is),** *true giving is* **not just an action—it is an extension of God's presence in you.** *When you give with a pure heart, it is* **God giving through you.** *That's why it must be* **cheerful and free**—*because* **God gives out of infinite abundance, never from lack.**

When you recognize yourself as **one with God,** *giving is no longer a sacrifice—it is simply the* **natural expression of divine love flowing through you.**

Giving as an Extension of Divine Flow

In the spiritual realm, everything operates on the principle of **flow.** *The universe, life, love, and even breath itself are all based on* **receiving and releasing.** *If a person only takes in and never gives out, they block the natural flow of abundance. When someone gives with* **joy and freedom,** *they align themselves with the continuous* **outpouring** *of God's essence.*

The Illusion of Loss vs. the Reality of Overflow

A person who gives grudgingly or out of necessity often operates from a **mindset of lack**—*fearing that what they give will leave them with less. But this contradicts the* **nature of God,** *who is limitless.* **A cheerful giver understands that giving does not create loss but expands abundance.**

- *When you* **breathe out,** *you make room for the next breath.*
- *When you* **pour water from a cup,** *it can be filled again.*
- *When you* **share love,** *it returns multiplied.*

Likewise, giving—when done with **joy and sincerity**—*positions a person* **in the flow of divine increase** *rather than scarcity.*

Giving as a Reflection of the Heart's Condition

The verse says, **"Every man according as he purposeth in his heart, so let him** *give."*

This means that **giving is a mirror of the heart's condition.** *Someone who gives begrudgingly or out of obligation reveals a heart bound by fear, pride, or attachment. But someone who gives with* **joy and freedom** *shows a heart that is* **aligned with divine nature**— *overflowing with love, trust, and abundance.*

Jesus said, "Where your treasure is, there your heart will be also" (Matthew 6:21). *True giving is a* **spiritual act** *that reveals what a person truly values. If one gives freely, it demonstrates that their treasure is in* **divine abundance rather than material possessions.**

The Energy of Giving and Receiving

Giving with joy doesn't just benefit the recipient—it transforms the **giver** *as well.*

- *A generous heart is a* **grateful heart.**
- *A cheerful giver experiences* **freedom from attachment.**
- *Giving in love deepens* **oneness with God,** *because God is the ultimate giver.*

This is why **God loves a cheerful giver***—not because He needs anything, but because* **cheerful giving proves that someone has awakened to the truth of abundance, unity, and divine flow.**

GIATI: Giving as a Recognition of Divine Oneness

When you embrace **GIATI (God Is All There Is),** *you realize that* **giving is not separate from receiving.** *If God is all there is, then the one who gives and the one who receives are* **both part of the same divine essence.** *The giver is simply transferring energy from one part of God's being to another.*

So, in reality, giving is never about loss—it is an act of honoring the divine presence within all.

Daniel in the Lion's Den: Embracing the Divine Protection of GIATI

The story of **Daniel in the lion's den** *is one of the most famous in the Bible, where Daniel, a faithful servant of God, is thrown into a den of lions for praying to God despite a royal decree forbidding it. Miraculously, Daniel is unharmed, and the lions, instead of devouring him, remain docile. This event, though centered around divine intervention, speaks to the eternal truths of* **GIATI—God Is All There Is**—*showing how one's connection with the Divine creates an impenetrable barrier against fear and harm.*

The Setting: A Test of Allegiance and the Illusion of Separation

In the story, Daniel's commitment to God places him in direct opposition to the laws of the land. King Darius, the ruler of the Persian Empire, appoints Daniel as a high official because of his exceptional qualities. However, his political enemies, envious of his favor with the king, plot to have him thrown into the lion's den by exploiting his devotion to God.

At its core, this story is about **the tension between the laws of man and the higher law of the Divine.** *Daniel's refusal to bow to the earthly law of the land, when it conflicts with his devotion to God, highlights a key teaching of* **GIATI: God is all that truly governs, and His law supersedes all human-made laws.**

In the same way, **the law of God**—*the realization that* **God is all there is, expressed in every moment**—*is not a set of rules imposed from the outside. It is an inherent truth, constantly unfolding within.* **Daniel's unwavering faith** *is a reflection of this divine law in action. He doesn't question whether to pray because he understands his unity with God and His constant presence.* **To Daniel, prayer wasn't a separate act, but a natural expression of his oneness with God.**

The Den of Lions: Facing Fear and the Illusion of Danger

Daniel's predicament of being thrown into the lion's den is a powerful metaphor for how **the ego creates fear.** *The lions represent* **the external forces that seem to threaten us,** *the world's false belief systems, temptations, and dangers that arise when we step into our divine truth. The lions could be seen as the chaos and challenges in life that feel threatening, as though they have power over us.*

But, just as Daniel remained unharmed, **GIATI teaches that no external force, no perceived danger, can harm the one who knows their oneness with God.** *The lions, in reality, have no power over him because he is* **divinely protected.** *The true danger lies in the belief that we are separate from God, vulnerable to harm from the outside world.*

This moment in Daniel's life exemplifies how the understanding of **God's omnipresence**—*that God is all that there is—leads to divine protection.* **God is within you,** *and no matter the trials or tribulations, nothing can truly harm you when you understand this foundational truth.*

Daniel's Unharmed State: Divine Assurance and GIATI's Promise

When Daniel is thrown into the lion's den, he is untouched. The Bible doesn't say that he had a special shield of protection or that the lions simply lost their appetite. It simply says that **God shut the mouths of the lions,** *and Daniel remained unharmed.*

This divine intervention underscores the central message of **GIATI:** *when you recognize that* **God is all there is,** *you are living in alignment with the divine flow that transcends any situation or circumstance.* **In God, there is no fear, no danger, no separation**—*only divine unity.*

The lions—symbolic of earthly fears—could not touch Daniel, just as **earthly worries and fears cannot touch the one who knows that God is all there is.** *This is the p*rotection **of God t***hat comes with understanding your oneness with Him.*

The King's Response: Recognition of God's Supreme Power

After Daniel's miraculous survival, King Darius, in awe of what had happened, orders that Daniel be brought out of the den and that the men who conspired against him be thrown in instead. The king then proclaims, **"For He is the living God, and He endures forever"** *(Daniel 6:26).*

Here we see the king's recognition of God's omnipotence. He acknowledges that **God's power transcends human understanding** *and that there is no force greater than the Divine. Similarly, in the revelation of* **GIATI,** *we see that* **God is not a force in the background of life; He is the essence and substance of all that exists.** *When we come to understand* **God is all there is,** *it shifts our perspective on the challenges of life.*

Daniel's experience becomes a testimony to **the power of divine truth,** *which ultimately leads to greater awareness and recognition of God's supremacy—not only by the one who experiences it but by all who witness it.* **In recognizing the truth of GIATI,** *the world's false realities are unveiled, and those who see this truth are forever transformed.*

The Den of Lions as a Metaphor for Transformation

The den of lions serves not only as a trial but as a **place of transformation.** *Daniel emerges from it stronger, more deeply rooted in his faith and understanding of God's protection. Similarly, the challenges of life, when seen through the lens of GIATI, become* *opportunities for* **awakening.** *Every fear, every trial, every obstacle is an invitation to* **deepen your realization that God is all there is, and in that realization lies your protection.**

Just as Daniel's experience transformed the king's understanding of God, so too does the understanding of GIATI transform our perspective on life. No longer do we need to live in fear of the lions in our lives—be it financial hardship, personal conflict, or even health challenges. **When you know God is all there is,** *the lions lose their power. You no longer see them as threats; you see them as the* **illusion of separation from the Divine,** *which is ultimately shown to have no real substance.*

Conclusion: Living Fearlessly in the Truth of GIATI

The story of **Daniel in the lion's den** *exemplifies the profound truth of* **GIATI**—*that God is all there is, and no external force can harm or diminish us when we live in alignment with that truth. Just as Daniel was unharmed because of his unwavering faith in God's presence, we too can live fearlessly and in divine assurance when we recognize that* **God is within us, surrounding us, and expressing through us.**

In moments of trial and hardship, remember Daniel's example: the **lion's den** *represents the world's fears, the trials, and the false belief in separation. But when you live in the truth of GIATI, you can step into the den and come out unharmed, knowing that* **God is always with you,** *in every moment, every situation, and every breath.*

Jesus Walks on Water: The Mastery of Spirit Over Form

One of the most profound moments in Jesus' ministry occurs in **Matthew 14:22-33,** *when He walks on water to meet His disciples in the midst of a raging storm. This event is more than just a miracle—it is a demonstration of divine truth, revealing the very essence of* **GIATI—God Is All There Is.** *In this story, Jesus shows what it means to transcend the limitations of the physical world and operate from a higher reality, one that is not bound by fear, doubt, or the illusion of separation.*

The Water: The Illusion of Uncertainty

The sea, often symbolic of **chaos, uncertainty, and the subconscious mind,** *represents the unstable nature of human perception. Life's challenges, doubts, and fears are like the stormy waters, constantly shifting and unpredictable. The disciples, caught in the storm, are* **troubled by what they see,** *believing themselves to be at the mercy of the elements. This is the condition of those who have not yet come into the full awareness of* **GIATI***—they believe themselves to be separate from God, subject to forces beyond their control.*

But Jesus, fully aware of **who and what He is,** *walks above the water. He does not sink because He is not governed by the illusion of instability. He is operating from a higher consciousness, one that understands that* **all things are God, and therefore, all things are subject to the Spirit.** *The water, which seems to be a barrier to others, holds no power over Him because He knows it is not separate from Him.*

Jesus Walks on Water: The Demonstration of GIATI

Jesus does not simply walk on water—He **proves that the physical world is an extension of Spirit,** *and when one is in alignment with divine truth, nothing external can dictate their reality. This is the core of* **GIATI: when you realize that God is all there is, you are no longer bound by the limitations of the physical world.**

When Jesus walks on water, He is showing that:

- **The physical world is not separate from God but an expression of Him.**
- **What seems impossible to the natural mind is possible when you are fully conscious of divine truth.**
- **Fear and doubt cause one to sink into illusion, but faith and understanding keep one above it.**

Peter's Attempt: The Struggle Between Faith and Perception

Peter, seeing Jesus walking on water, asks to join Him. Jesus simply says, **"Come."** *At that moment, Peter, too, steps out of the boat and walks on the water—proving that it is not just Jesus who can transcend physical limitations, but anyone who understands the truth.*

But then something happens. **Peter looks at the wind and the waves.** *He shifts his focus from divine truth to external circumstances.* **Doubt enters, and immediately, he begins to sink.**

This is a critical lesson: **your reality is shaped by what you believe.** *When Peter was focused on Jesus—on divine truth—he was above the storm. But when he focused on the storm—on the illusion of instability—he fell into it.* **The moment you lose sight of GIATI, you sink into the illusion of separation, fear, and limitation.**

Jesus' Response: A Call to Spiritual Awareness

As Peter begins to sink, he cries out, **"Lord, save me!"** *Immediately, Jesus* **reaches** *out His hand and catches him, saying, "O you of little faith, why did you doubt?"*

Jesus was not rebuking Peter for trying—He was showing him that the only thing that caused him to fall was his doubt. **Peter was walking in divine reality, but the moment he questioned it, he fell into the illusion of limitation.** *This is the state of many who begin to awaken to truth but allow the distractions of the external world to pull them back into doubt.*

Jesus did not let Peter drown, just as divine truth does not abandon those who struggle to grasp it. But He does call Peter—and all of us—to greater awareness: **"Why did you doubt?"**

The Boat, the Storm, and the Calm: The Transition from Fear to Knowing

When Jesus and Peter return to the boat, the storm **immediately ceases.** *This is symbolic of what happens when divine truth is fully realized—the chaos of external circumstances loses its power over you. The storm was never the problem; the* **perception of the storm as separate from divine order was the problem.**

Those in the boat **worshiped Jesus,** *declaring,* **"Truly, You are the Son of God."** *But the lesson was never about proving Jesus' identity—it was about* **revealing the nature of reality itself. Jesus walking on water was not just a display of power—it was a demonstration of what is possible when one fully realizes the truth of GIATI.**

The GIATI Perspective: Walking in Divine Awareness

The story of Jesus walking on water is not just about an event that happened 2,000 years ago—it is a revelation of how **those who know GIATI live today.**

- **The water represents the illusion of instability, but when you know that God is all there is, you walk above it.**
- **Fear and doubt sink you, but faith in divine reality keeps you above the limitations of the world.**

- **Jesus was not performing a miracle—He was revealing a truth that applies to all who awaken to their divine nature.**

Jesus walking on water is **a call to live in awareness of divine reality.** *It is not about defying natural laws, but about understanding that* **Spirit is the true substance of all things.** *When you walk in divine consciousness, you walk in mastery over the world, just as Jesus did.*

This is the essence of **GIATI**—*that* **you are not separate from God, and when you live in this truth, nothing can pull you under.**

The Parable of the Talents: The Multiplication of the Spirit

In **Matthew 25:14-30,** *Jesus tells the parable of the* **ten talents,** *a story about a master who entrusts his servants with his wealth before leaving on a journey. To one servant, he gives* **five talents,** *to another* **two talents,** *and to the last, he gives* **one talent,** *each according to their ability. When the master returns, he finds that the servants who received* **five and two talents** *have* **multiplied what was given to them.** *But the one who received only* **one talent** *buried it in the ground, afraid of losing it. The master rewards the first two servants but* **condemns the third, calling him wicked and lazy,** *casting him into outer darkness.*

What is this story really revealing? Why were some rewarded, and one rejected? And how does this parable illuminate the truth of **GIATI (God Is All There Is)?**

The Talents Represent the Divine Deposit

The talents in this parable are more than just money—they symbolize the **Spirit of God within each person.** *Every individual is entrusted with a measure of divine life, a* **portion of the Spirit** *to cultivate, expand, and express. The distribution of talents is not about* **favoritism,** *but about* **recognition of capacity***—each receives what they are prepared to handle.*

Those who **multiplied their talents** *understood a fundamental truth:* **the Spirit is meant to grow and expand.** *They did not see their talents as something to hold onto but* **as something to be invested, poured out, and used for a greater purpose.** *This aligns perfectly with the truth of* **GIATI***—that God is* **not a stagnant force,** *but an ever-flowing, ever- expanding presence within all things.*

The servant who **buried his talent** *represents a person who refuses to acknowledge* **the divine power within them.** *Instead of using what was given, they* **hid it, suppressed it, and allowed fear to control them.** *This reveals the* **mindset of separation,** *believing that God is a harsh master, external and distant, rather than the very source and essence of one's being.*

The Fear of the One-Talent Servant: The Illusion of Separation

When confronted, the servant with the **buried talent** *says:*

"Lord, I knew thee that thou art a hard man, reaping where thou hast not sown, and gathering where thou hast not strawed. And I was afraid, and went and hid thy talent in the earth."*(Matthew 25:24-25)*

This statement reveals **the root of his failure—fear and misunderstanding of the nature of God.** *He saw God as separate,* **as a distant master who takes but does not give,** *rather than recognizing that* **God is all there is, the source of life itself. His burial of the talent represents his rejection of the Spirit,** *his refusal to engage with the divine life within him.*

This is why the master's response is so harsh:

"Thou wicked and slothful servant… Take therefore the talent from him, and give it unto him which hath ten talents." *(Matthew 25:26,28)*

The loss of his talent represents **the loss of spiritual awareness.** *Just as light disappears when one refuses to open their eyes, so too does the Spirit seem to "leave" those who refuse to acknowledge it. But the truth of GIATI remains—God does not actually take anything* **away;** *rather,* **it is one's own blindness that keeps them from experiencing the fullness of divine life.**

The Reward of Multiplication: Expanding the Spirit

The first two servants, however, understood the nature of God. They knew that **the Spirit is limitless and meant to be expressed.** *Their multiplication of talents symbolizes* **the unfolding of divine consciousness,** *the realization that* **the more one acknowledges the presence of God within, the more they receive.** *This aligns with Jesus' words:*

"For whosoever hath, to him shall be given, and he shall have more abundance: but whosoever hath not, from him shall be taken away even that he hath." *(Matthew 25:29)*

This is not about material wealth—it is about **awareness of divine reality.** *Those who operate in the truth of GIATI* **will continuously expand in Spirit,** *while those who deny it* **will remain in spiritual darkness, feeling as though they have nothing at all.**

The Meaning for Today: Awakening to GIATI

This parable is not simply a lesson about responsibility—it is a **call to awaken.** *It is a revelation of the truth that* **God has already placed the fullness of His Spirit within every person.** *The question is not whether one* **has** *the Spirit, but whether one* **acknowledges and uses it.**

1. **Those who recognize GIATI, who see that God is all there is, will experience unlimited increase**—*a continual unfolding of divine wisdom, power, and love.*
2. **Those who reject this truth, who bury their awareness in fear and ignorance, will experience a sense of lack and separation**—*not because God has left them, but because they have closed their eyes to the reality of oneness.*

The servant who buried his talent lived as though God were **outside of him,** *a distant master to be feared. The others lived in the* **awareness of divine presence,** *knowing that what they had was not separate from them but* **a part of their very being.**

*GIATI teaches that G*o**d is not an external force waiting to judge, but the very essence of existence itself.** *The multiplication of talents is the natural result of recognizing this truth—because in oneness with God,* **there is no limitation, only infinite expansion.**

Jesus Cleansing the Temple: Clearing the Mind for Divine Awareness

The account of **Jesus cleansing the temple** *is one of the most powerful moments in His ministry. In this event, Jesus enters the temple in Jerusalem and finds it filled with* **money changers and merchants,** *people who had turned a place of divine worship into a marketplace for profit. With righteous authority, Jesus* **overturns their tables, drives them out, and declares that the temple is meant to be a house of prayer, not a den of thieves.**

This is more than just a historical event—it is a profound **spiritual metaphor** *about the purification of the inner temple:* **our consciousness.** *The* **temple** *represents the place where God dwells—not just in a building, but within us. The mo*ney **changers and merchants** *represent the distractions, false beliefs, and worldly influences that clutter the mind, preventing true communion with the divine.*

In **GIATI (God Is All There Is),** *this story reveals the importance of* **clearing our consciousness of everything that obstructs our awareness of divine reality.** *Just as Jesus drove out those who defiled the temple, we too must drive out the* **false perceptions, limiting beliefs, and distractions that keep us from fully experiencing the presence of God within.**

The Temple as a Symbol of Consciousness

When Jesus said, **"Destroy this temple, and in three days I will raise it up"** *(John 2:19), the people misunderstood Him. They thought He was speaking about the physical temple, but* **He was speaking about His body—the true dwelling place of God.**

This reveals a deeper truth: the **true temple is not made of stone, but is within us.** *The human mind and heart are the* **dwelling place of God.** *This aligns with* **GIATI,** *the understanding that* **God is not confined to a physical location but is the very essence of our being.**

*However, just as the temple in Jerusalem had been corrupted by greed and distraction, so too can our consciousness become cl*uttered **with fear, doubt, materialism, and worldly attachments.** *The cleansing of the temple is a call to* **purify our minds,** *making room for divine awareness to dwell fully.*

The Money Changers and Merchants: Worldly Distractions in Consciousness

The **money changers and merchants** *represent the* **external influences** *that pollute spiritual awareness. Their presence in the temple reveals how easily the* **sacred can be**

mixed with the profane—*how a place meant for communion with God can become entangled in worldly concerns.*

In a spiritual sense, these merchants represent:

- **Materialism** – *Placing excessive focus on wealth, possessions, and status instead of divine truth.*
- **Religious Formalism** – *Reducing spirituality to mere transactions, rules, and rituals without true awareness of God's presence.*
- **Mental Clutter** – *The distractions, doubts, and fears that take up space in the mind, preventing clear spiritual perception.*
- **Ego and Self-Interest** – *Living according to personal gain rather than divine alignment.*

Just as Jesus forcefully removed these distractions from the temple, we too must **clear our consciousness of everything that takes our focus away from divine oneness.** *This is the essence of* **GIATI**—*removing all illusions and falsehoods so that the* **fullness of God's presence can be realized.**

Jesus' Righteous Action: The Power of Spiritual Authority

Many perceive Jesus as always gentle, but this event reveals another aspect of His divine nature—**righteous authority.** *Jesus did not politely ask the merchants to leave; He* **took action,** *flipping their tables and driving them out. This teaches us that* **spiritual purification requires decisive action.**

We cannot passively allow distractions, false beliefs, and worldly influences to dominate our consciousness. We must be willing to **confront and remove anything that stands between us and the full awareness of God's presence.** *This is what it means to* **embrace GIATI**—*to refuse to allow any illusion to take up space where only God should dwell.*

Spiritual Cleansing: Making Room for Divine Presence

The cleansing of the temple is not about destruction—it is about **restoration.** *Jesus did not remove the merchants to leave the temple empty; He removed them to* **restore it to its true purpose**—*a place where God's presence could be fully experienced.*

Likewise, when we cleanse our inner temple, we do not do so simply to remove distractions—we do it to **make room for the divine.** *A mind free from clutter, fear, and worldly concerns is a mind that can fully experience* **the reality that God is all there is.**

GIATI and the Cleansing of the Temple

This event speaks directly to the mission of **GIATI:**

1. **Recognizing that the true temple is within** – *The presence of God is not in a building, but in the* **awareness of divine oneness** *within us.*
2. **Clearing the mind of false beliefs and distractions** – *Just as Jesus removed the merchants, we must remove* **fear, doubt, and worldly attachments** *that block our spiritual perception.*
3. **Taking action to maintain spiritual purity** – *We cannot be passive in our spiritual journey. We must actively* **reject illusions** *and choose divine awareness.*
4. **Restoring the mind to its true purpose** – *Just as Jesus restored the temple as a house of prayer, we must restore our consciousness to its natural state:* **a dwelling place of divine presence.**

This is the essence of **GIATI**—*understanding that* **there is nothing outside of God** *and anything that seems to be* **must be removed from our awareness.** *The mind must be* **cleared of falsehoods,** *so that only the truth of God's presence remains.*

Conclusion: Becoming a Living Temple

Jesus' cleansing of the temple was not just a physical act—it was a **spiritual message for all generations.** *It is a call to each of us to examine our own inner temple and ask:*

- **What distractions and illusions have I allowed into my consciousness?**
- **What tables need to be overturned in my mind?**
- **Have I made space for divine presence, or have I filled my inner temple with worldly concerns?**

The path of **GIATI** *is the path of* **purification**—*removing all that is false so that only the truth remains. When the inner temple is cleansed, the presence of God is fully revealed, and we walk in* **the awareness that God is all there is.**

This is the invitation: **Cleanse the temple. Make space for the divine. And step into the fullness of spiritual reality, where nothing exists but God.**

Gideon's 300 Warriors: Victory Through Divine Awareness

The story of **Gideon and his 300 warriors** *is a powerful revelation that v***ictory is not achieved through human strength, but through divine awareness.** *It is a lesson in trust, faith, and the realization that* **God is all there is.** *Gideon, a man who once doubted himself and questioned God's presence, was chosen to lead Israel into battle—not with thousands of soldiers, but with a small, divinely selected remnant.*

*This story demonstrates the truth that s***piritual power is never measured by numbers, weapons, or physical might.** *It is through* **God's presence, awareness, and divine strategy** *that victory is assured. In* **GIATI,** *this story represents the understanding that* **human effort alone is not what brings success, but alignment with divine reality.**

The Call of Gideon: Overcoming Fear and Doubt

Before Gideon became a mighty leader, he was **hiding in fear.** *The Midianites had oppressed Israel, and Gideon saw himself as weak and insignificant. But when t***he angel of the Lord appeared,** *he spoke a truth that Gideon had not yet realized:*

"The Lord is with you, mighty man of valor!" *(Judges 6:12)*

Gideon did not see himself as mighty. He saw himself as the least in his family, part of the weakest tribe. But God did not call him according to his **own perception***—God called him according to divine truth.*

This moment represents the **awakening of spiritual identity.** *Gideon had to move past his* **limited self-perception** *and recognize that it was not about his strength—it was about* **God's power working through him.**

This is **GIATI:** *the realization that wh***o we are is not limited by human perception, but defined by divine reality.** *Just as Gideon was called beyond his doubt,* **we too are called to see ourselves through the lens of divine oneness***—not as weak individuals, but as the* **manifestation of God's power and presence.**

The Reduction of the Army: Less is More in Divine Awareness

Gideon gathered an army of **32,000 men** *to fight the Midianites, but God told him:*

"The people who are with you are too many for Me to give the Midianites into their hands, lest Israel claim glory for itself." (Judges 7:2)

*This is a profound spiritual principle: h***uman strength, numbers, and effort cannot take credit for divine victory.** *If Gideon had won with thousands of men, Israel would have* *thought it was their own power that saved them. But* **God wanted them to understand that victory comes from divine awareness, not human effort.**

So, God reduced the army in two stages:

1. **Fearful soldiers were sent home** – *22,000 left, leaving only 10,000. This shows that fear and doubt weaken spiritual power. Those who rely on physical strength rather than divine trust are not ready for the battle of faith.*
2. **A final test at the water** – *Out of the 10,000 remaining, only* **300 men were chosen.** *Those who drank water with* **vigilance and awareness** *were selected, while those who dropped their guard were sent away.*

This selection was not based on military skill but on **spiritual readiness.** *The 300 men represented* **those who remained awake, spiritually aware, and fully trusting in God rather than their own strength.**

In **GIATI,** *this teaches us that* **true victory in life does not come from numbers, force, or effort, but from divine awareness.** *The world values power, wealth, and strength— but God works through* **those who are conscious of divine presence,** *even when they seem few in number.*

The Strategy of Victory: Trusting the Divine Plan

Gideon's battle plan was not built on human logic. Instead of swords and shields, the 300 warriors were given:

- **Trumpets (shofars)** – *representing the power of divine sound and proclamation.*
- **Clay pitchers** – *fragile vessels that had to be broken.*
- **Torches inside the pitchers** – *light that was hidden until the right moment.*

When the time came, Gideon and his men **blew their trumpets, broke the clay vessels, and revealed the light.** *This caused confusion in the Midianite camp, leading them to* **turn on each other** *in fear and defeat themselves.*

This is a profound **spiritual metaphor:**

- *The* **trumpet blast** *represents the* **power of divine truth**—*when sounded, it shatters illusions.*
- *The* **clay pitchers** *represent the* **human body and ego**—*they must be broken to reveal the divine light within.*
- *The* **hidden torches** *represent* **God's presence within us**—*when fully revealed, it brings victory over all darkness.*

In **GIATI,** *this battle illustrates the truth that* **God's power is within us, but often hidden beneath the layers of our own self-perception.** *When we allow the* **ego to break,** *the* **light of divine reality** *shines forth, leading to true victory.*

The Midianites were defeated **not by weapons, but by light, sound, and divine strategy.** *This is a powerful message:* **Victory is achieved through divine consciousness, not force.**

The Spiritual Significance of Gideon's 300

1. **God uses the few to reveal the power of divine presence** – *Numbers do not determine success; divine awareness does.*
2. **Fear and doubt remove us from spiritual readiness** – *Only those fully trusting in* **GIATI** can move in divine power.
3. **Human strength must be broken for divine light to shine** – *The clay vessels had to be shattered to reveal the hidden light.*
4. **Victory comes not by might, but by alignment with divine truth** – *The battle was won through* **awareness, strategy, and the revealing of light.**

The **story of Gideon** is a call to **trust the divine process,** to understand that our strength is not in numbers, status, or effort, but in the **realization that God is all there is.** When we fully embrace **GIATI,** we move with **clarity, power, and divine strategy,** knowing that victory is already assured—not by the **might of the flesh,** but by the **Spirit of God.**

Conclusion: Awakening to the Power of Divine Awareness

The story of **Gideon's 300 warriors** *is more than just a historical account—it is a* **spiritual lesson in trust, faith, and divine consciousness.** *It teaches us that:*

- **Our strength is not in numbers but in divine awareness.**
- **Fear separates us from our full spiritual potential.**
- **Divine strategy always leads to victory, even when it defies human logic.**
- **Our light is hidden within until we allow the ego to break, revealing the truth.**

This is the essence of **GIATI**—*understanding that* **God is all there is,** *that our victory is not in* **what we see, but in what we know spiritually.** *Just as* **Gideon's 300** *overcame an army through divine awareness, we too are called to move* **not by sight, but by faith,** *trusting fully that the battle is already won when we stand in the truth of God's presence.*

The question is: **Will you trust the divine strategy? Will you embrace the truth that God is all there is, even when it doesn't make sense? Will you allow your own clay vessel to break so that the light within can shine?**

If so, you are part of **the 300**—*those who walk not by might, nor by power, but by the* **Spirit of the Living God.**

Breaking the Law to Reveal the Spirit: Jesus and the Sabbath

Jesus was not a lawbreaker in the sense that he acted in rebellion against God. Instead, he broke **man's limited understanding of the law** *to reveal a higher spiritual reality. His actions—especially those performed on the Sabbath—were not acts of defiance but of* **demonstration,** *showing that righteousness was never about rigidly following written codes but about aligning with* **the living spirit of God.**

Jesus and the Sabbath: Challenging the Carnal Mind

One of the most striking examples of this is found in **Luke 13:10-17,** *where Jesus heals a woman on the Sabbath. She had been crippled for eighteen years, unable to stand upright. Seeing her suffering, Jesus called her forward and said,* **"Woman, you are set free from your infirmity."** *He laid hands on her, and immediately, she was healed.*

But instead of rejoicing, the religious leaders were outraged. The synagogue ruler rebuked the people, saying, **"There are six days for work. So come and be healed on those days, not on the Sabbath!"**

Jesus responded, exposing the hypocrisy in their understanding of the law:

"You hypocrites! Doesn't each of you untie your ox or donkey from the stall and lead it out to give it water on the Sabbath? Then should not this woman, a daughter of Abraham, whom Satan has kept bound for eighteen long years, be set free on the Sabbath day from what bound her?" (Luke 13:15-16)

This was not the only time Jesus confronted the rigid legalism of the religious elite. In Matthew 12:10-12, when asked if it was lawful to heal on the Sabbath, he said:

"If any of you has a sheep and it falls into a pit on the Sabbath, will you not take hold of it and lift it out? How much more valuable is a person than a sheep! Therefore, it is lawful to do good on the Sabbath."

The True Spirit of the Sabbath

1. The Letter Versus the Spirit

In the religious landscape of ancient Israel, the Mosaic Law was given as a guide—a framework designed to set humanity apart through discipline and ritual observance. Yet, over time, these laws often took on a rigid, carnal form. Adherents became more preoccupied with exact observance than with the underlying principles of mercy, compassion, and life itself. Jesus's actions on the Sabbath were not a dismissal of the law, but a powerful demonstration that the law's true intent was far beyond the mere physical observance of rituals. As Jesus himself later declared, "The Sabbath was made for man, not man for the Sabbath" (Mark 2:27).

2. Miracles on the Sabbath: Acts of Compassion Over Ritual

Consider the familiar scene in the Gospels: Jesus healing a man with a withered hand on the Sabbath (see Mark 3:1-6; Luke 6:10). To many of his contemporaries, such acts were seen as breaches of Sabbath sanctity. Yet, through these miracles, Jesus challenged a system that prioritized ritual over the well-being of human life. Imagine the rhetorical question that encapsulates his teaching: if a man's cattle were to run away on the Sabbath, would you leave them to wander, bound by legalistic constraint, or would you go out to retrieve them? This question, though not recorded verbatim in Scripture, serves as a poignant illustration of the principle Jesus championed—a reminder that acts of necessity and compassion should never be hindered by ritualistic adherence.

In healing the man, Jesus made it clear that the Sabbath was not a day to be marked by inaction, but rather a day to manifest God's healing and love. His actions declared that life and mercy were of paramount importance, transcending any set of ritualistic rules.

3. Breaking the Chains of Legalism

Jesus's willingness to act on the Sabbath was radical. It questioned the prevailing interpretation of the law—a law that had increasingly become a burdensome code, divorced from the divine purpose it was meant to serve. When the religious authorities fixated on the minutiae of what was permitted, they lost sight of the heart of God: a heart that beats with compassion, that seeks to restore and renew rather than merely to punish.

By performing miracles on the Sabbath, Jesus exposed a critical flaw in the carnal interpretation of Mosaic Law. He showed that adherence to the law should never be an end in itself but a means to facilitate love, care, and restoration. In doing so, he reoriented the focus from strict legalism to the liberating truth of divine mercy.

4. The Spiritual Meaning Behind the Actions

At its core, Jesus's defiance of strict Sabbath restrictions was a call to spiritual awakening. His miracles were not random acts of rebellion but were imbued with a deeper message: that the divine is accessible in every moment of need. The true spirit of the Sabbath is not found in abstaining from work but in engaging in the work of life—healing, helping, and showing compassion.

The healing of the man with the withered hand, for instance, was not merely about restoring physical function; it was about affirming the sanctity of human life over rigid ceremonial law. This act served as a microcosm of a broader truth: that the Spirit of God moves in and through acts of compassion, even when such acts challenge established norms.

This teaching resonates even today. It invites us to ask ourselves: Are we so bound by routine, by tradition, by the letter of the law, that we overlook the living essence of mercy and love? Jesus's example reminds us that the divine intention behind any law is to serve humanity, to uplift it, and to draw it closer to the ultimate source of life.

5. Embracing the Oneness of Spirit

In the grand tapestry of Jesus's ministry, the miracles on the Sabbath are threads that weave together a larger narrative—a narrative that points us to the heart of spiritual liberation. When we see beyond the confines of strict observance, we begin to understand that every act of mercy, every compassionate deed, is a step toward realizing our oneness with the divine.

This realization is echoed in the modern understanding of GIATI—"God Is All There Is." Jesus did not come to establish a new religion, nor did he intend for his miracles to be mere exceptions to the rule. Rather, he came to reveal that the divine presence permeates every aspect of existence. True worship, then, is not about adhering to external codes, but about recognizing and nurturing the sacred spark within every being.

Conclusion: The Sabbath as a Celebration of Life

In reflecting on Jesus's actions, we are invited to reinterpret the Sabbath and, indeed, all religious observances not as burdensome obligations, but as opportunities to engage with life in its fullest expression. The healing on the Sabbath teaches us that divine laws are not static commandments meant to confine us; they are dynamic principles meant to elevate us toward a state of oneness with all that is sacred.

Thus, the question remains: if a man's cattle ran away on the Sabbath, would you forsake compassion for the sake of ritual? Jesus's answer is clear—compassion always comes first. It is a timeless reminder that the spirit of the law is not found in its strict application, but in the loving, life-affirming actions that reflect the true nature of God.

In this way, Jesus broke the chains of legalism, opening the door for a deeper, more intimate relationship with the divine—a relationship defined not by the rigid observance of rules, but by the living, ever-present spirit of God within us all.

GIATI and Women Preaching: The Spirit Has No Gender

In the understanding of **GIATI—God Is All There Is—there is no limitation, hierarchy, or exclusion based on gender, because Spirit is not male or female.** *The idea that a woman cannot preach is rooted in human tradition, cultural biases, and misinterpretations of scripture—not in divine truth.*

God is Spirit, and those who are of God are Spirit first. *The physical form one takes—male or female—is simply an expression of that Spirit in the world. Since* **the Spirit of God has no gender, how then can the message of God be limited by gender?**

Breaking the Illusion of Restriction

Many religious systems restrict women from preaching based on select scriptures, often taken out of context. However, **GIATI does not operate on rules created by men—it operates on the eternal truth that God expresses through whom He chooses.**

- **The voice of God is not confined to a specific vessel.** *If a woman is filled with the*
- Spirit, the Spirit speaks through her just as it would through a man.
- **The Holy Spirit moves where it wills.** *Who can tell God whom He may or may not use? To reject a woman preaching is to reject the Spirit speaking through her.*
- **There is no male or female in the Spirit.** *Paul himself said in Galatians 3:28, "There is neither male nor female: for ye are all one in Christ Jesus." GIATI confirms this truth—there is no gender restriction in God's oneness.*

The True Measure: The Spirit, Not Gender

GIATI reveals that **authority does not come from gender, but from the indwelling Spirit.** *It is not about whether a man or woman is preaching—it is about whether the* **truth is being spoken.**

So, in GIATI, the real question is not **"Can a woman preach?"** *but* **"Is the Spirit speaking?"** *If the answer is yes, then there is no human tradition, rule, or bias that can stand in the way.*

The Spirit **calls, speaks, and manifests** *through anyone who is willing to be a vessel—man or woman.*

GIATI and Electing a Female President: Spirit Over Flesh

From the understanding of **GIATI—God Is All There Is—leadership is not defined by gender, but by the Spirit within.** *In a world conditioned by physical appearances and societal structures, people often judge leadership based on external factors—gender, race, status, or background. But GIATI reveals a deeper truth:*

True leadership is not about male or female—it is about the Spirit moving through an individual to fulfill a purpose.

Breaking the Illusion of Limitation

Throughout history, many have believed that leadership—especially at the highest levels—should be reserved for men. These beliefs stem not from spiritual truth, but from human tradition, fear, and societal conditioning. **The Spirit of God does not operate within the confines of human biases.**

- **If God is all there is, then every individual, regardless of gender, is an expression of God.**
- **If leadership is about wisdom, vision, and strength, then it is the Spirit—not gender—that determines who is fit to lead.**
- **If God has chosen a vessel for leadership, then rejecting them based on gender is rejecting the movement of Spirit itself.**

GIATI and Divine Leadership

*A true leader, whether male or female, is simply a vessel for G***od's will to manifest in the world.** *The Spirit does not choose leaders based on external appearances but based on the* **purpose they were sent to fulfill.**

- **Did the Spirit choose them, or did society reject them?**
- **Are they leading by divine wisdom, or by personal ego?**
- **Are they seeking to uplift and unify, or to divide and contro**l?

These are the real questions—not whether a leader is a man or a woman. GIATI reveals that **anyone chosen to lead, regardless of gender, is simply an extension of God fulfilling divine purpose.**

Rejecting a Leader Based on Gender: A Reflection of Carnal Thinking

To say that a woman cannot lead a nation is to place **human limitations on divine movement.** *Just as a woman can preach, teach, and prophesy, a woman can also lead at the highest levels—if she has been* **equipped by the Spirit** *to do so.*

GIATI does not conform to outdated structures that were built to suppress certain people. **It is a call to recognize that God expresses through all, and that true leadership comes from the Spirit within, not the flesh it inhabits.**

So, when it comes to electing a female president, the question is not **"Should a woman lead?"** *but* **"Is the Spirit moving through this person to lead?"** *If the answer is yes, then rejecting them based on gender is simply rejecting what God has put in place.*

GIATI and Gender Roles in Marriage: Spirit Over Structure

In the understanding of **GIATI—God Is All There Is—relationships, marriage, and family are not about hierarchical roles, but about the oneness of Spirit manifesting in different forms.** *The traditional view that places "God over man, man over woman, and woman over children" is based on human interpretation and cultural conditioning, not on the eternal truth of Spirit.* **If God is all there is, then all expressions—man, woman, and child—are God in form.**

Does GIATI Acknowledge a "Head" in Marriage?

The idea that "man is the head" comes from certain biblical interpretations, particularly from Paul's letters, which were influenced by the cultural norms of his time. However, when viewed from the lens of GIATI, a deeper truth is revealed:

1. **God is not outside of man or woman—God is within them.** *If the Spirit dwells in both, then neither is inherently above the other.*
2. **Man and woman are both expressions of God, working in harmony, not hierarchy.** *The Spirit does not create a ranking system between its own manifestations.*
3. **Marriage is a partnership, not a chain of command.** *True divine order is not about dominance but about balance—two expressions of Spirit complementing each other in love and unity.*

The Illusion of Hierarchy

The idea of **man ruling over woman** *comes from the physical world's attachment to power and control. But* **GIATI reveals that Spirit moves freely, without needing to assert superiority over another form of itself.**

- **A man leading in love is not about control, but about embodying wisdom, strength, and divine protection.**
- **A woman submitting in love is not about inferiority, but about trust, grace, and divine nurturing.**
- **Both are submitting—not to each other in a fleshly sense—but to the Spirit within them that leads them as one.**

When the **ego** *is removed, marriage is not about* **who is above who,** *but about* **who is yielding to the Spirit within.**

GIATI's Response to "God Over Man, Man Over Woman, Woman Over Children"

This statement is based on a **physical-world hierarchy** *that separates instead of unites. GIATI does not support* **hierarchical domination,** *but instead reveals the* **oneness of Spirit manifesting in different roles.**

- **God is over all because God is all. There is no separation.**
- **Man and woman are not separate beings in opposition, but two expressions of the same divine life.**
- **Children are not under their parents in a way that makes them lesser—they are simply younger manifestations of the same Spirit.**

A true divine relationship is one where **both partners submit to the Spirit of God within them,** *rather than a structure where one rules over the other.* **Harmony is not found in control, but in unity.**

The True Divine Order

The world teaches hierarchy. **GIATI teaches oneness.** *The highest order in any relationship is* **not who leads and who follows, but who surrenders to the Spirit of God that is all.**

So, the question is not **"Who is the head?"** *but* **"Who is moving in divine alignment with the Spirit within?"** *When both are surrendered to the Spirit, there is no need for control—only unity, love, and divine expression.*

Spiritual Order and the Silent Soul (1 Timothy 2:11-12 in the Light of GIATI)

"Let the woman learn in silence with all subjection. But I suffer not a woman to teach, nor to usurp authority over the man, but to be in silence."

From the standpoint of GIATI, which understands that God Is All There Is and that every individual is an expression of the Spirit of God, this passage must be examined beyond its surface reading.

Context & Interpretation through GIATI

1. Spiritual Symbolism vs. Literal Restriction

Paul's words here were written within a historical and cultural framework where societal norms often dictated gender roles. However, spiritually speaking, woman and man can also represent different aspects of the human experience—the soul (feminine) and the spirit (masculine). The soul (our individual consciousness) must be in submission to the spirit (divine truth) to receive wisdom.

2. Silence as Receptivity, Not Inferiority

"Let the woman learn in silence with all subjection" can be seen as the soul quieting itself to receive divine revelation. Silence represents stillness, humility, and surrender—essential for spiritual awakening. It does not mean literal muteness but rather an inner posture of receptivity to divine wisdom.

3. Teaching & Authority in Spiritual Terms

When Paul says, "I suffer not a woman to teach, nor to usurp authority over the man," this can be understood as the soul not attempting to lead independently of the spirit. The soul, when disconnected from divine wisdom, can become misguided. True spiritual authority comes when one speaks from divine revelation, not personal intellect alone.

4. GIATI's Perspective on Unity

If God is all there is, then true spiritual authority is not about gender but about divine wisdom guiding all expressions of God. Both men and women are manifestations of the same Spirit, and Christ came to restore unity, not hierarchy. The ultimate teaching is that we must all allow the divine within to lead, rather than the ego.

Conclusion

Paul's words, when viewed through the GIATI lens, emphasize inner spiritual order rather than societal oppression. The passage calls for receptivity to divine truth, ensuring that one's teaching is guided by the Spirit rather than personal authority. In Christ, there is no male or female (Galatians 3:28)—only the One Spirit manifesting through all.

GIATI and Relationship Expectations: Spirit Over Transactions

From the understanding of **GIATI—God Is All There Is—relationships are not about transactional exchanges, but about divine harmony, balance, and shared purpose.** *The common expectations of a* **man paying the bill and a woman cooking and cleaning** *are rooted in societal roles, not in spiritual truth.*

The Illusion of Obligation

Many relationships are built on **unspoken transactions** *rather than spiritual unity. When a woman expects a man to pay for everything, or when a man expects a woman to cook and clean, they are often unconsciously operating under* **worldly conditioning rather than divine understanding.**

- **Does a man's ability to provide financially define his worth?**
- **Does a woman's ability to serve in domestic roles determine her value?**
- **If the Spirit of God is in both, why are they reducing their roles to expectations based on gender?**

These expectations can create a sense of **obligation rather than divine flow.** *When a relationship is built on transactional exchanges, love can become conditional:* **"If you do this, then I will do that."** *But GIATI reveals a greater truth—***relationships are about the Spirit working through both individuals in balance and purpose.**

Divine Partnership, Not Transactions

In the GIATI understanding, a relationship is not about **what each person can extract from the other,** *but about* **how they move in divine alignment together.** *Instead of rigid gender roles, the focus shifts to* **who is best equipped to do what in the relationship.**

- **If the man is financially able, he may naturally take on the role of provider—not out of obligation, but out of love and ability.**
- **If the woman enjoys cooking and creating a warm home environment, she does so—not because she has to, but because it brings her joy.**
- **But if roles were reversed—if she were the breadwinner and he were more inclined toward domestic care—there is no spiritual law that says they cannot move in that alignment.**

The **carnal mind** *seeks to define roles by external expectations.* **The spiritual mind moves in divine flow, recognizing that roles are based on purpose, ability, and agreement—not obligation.**

GIATI's Proper Relationship Conduct

Instead of saying **"The man should pay, the woman should cook,"** *a relationship in divine harmony asks:*

1. **How can we serve each other in love, rather than demand from each other in expectation?**
2. **What is the best way for our unique partnership to function in balance?**
3. **Are we operating from spiritual alignment or worldly conditioning?**

When both individuals recognize that **they are God expressed, and that their roles are not defined by gender but by divine purpose,** *there is no struggle over obligations. There is only* **flow, giving, and mutual support.**

Conclusion: The Relationship Built on GIATI

*A relationship rooted in G***IATI does not measure love by financial provision or household duties,** *but by the willingness of both individuals to align with the Spirit within them.* **The real question is not "Who pays?" or "Who cooks?" but "Are we walking in divine agreement?"**

When both move in the Spirit, **love replaces obligation, balance replaces struggle, and the relationship becomes an expression of divine harmony rather than worldly expectations.**

GIATI's Perspective on Casual Sex and Sex Before Marriage

At the heart of **GIATI—God Is All There Is** *is the understanding that* **you are not separate from God, and every action you take is an expression of divine being.** *The question is never about strict rules or religious doctrines but about* **awareness, alignment, and truth.**

1. The Illusion of Casual Sex → Seeking Fulfillment in the Temporary

Casual sex often stems from the **illusion of lack***—the idea that something outside of you (a momentary connection, physical pleasure, or validation) can complete you. But if* **God is all there is,** *then you are already complete.*

- *If sex is used as an* **escape, distraction, or substitute for true intimacy,** *then it is a reflection of disconnection from divine truth.*
- *If it is engaged in* **without awareness of the sacred nature of union,** *then it becomes just another means by which one remains trapped in the physical illusion. GIATI does not condemn, but it* **invites clarity***—Are you engaging in sex from* **a place of spiritual awareness or from a place of illusion?**

2. **Sex Before Marriage → The Union Beyond Tradition**

Marriage, in its truest form, is not about legal contracts or religious customs—it is about **spiritual unity.** *The question is not* **"Are you married?"** *but* **"Are you aware of the divine nature of union?"**

- *If sex is shared in* **conscious love, respect, and unity of spirit,** *it reflects the truth that God is present in both individuals.*
- *If sex is engaged in carelessly—driven by lust, ego, or selfish desire—it becomes* **a physical act detached from spiritual purpose.**

GIATI is not here to enforce tradition but to **restore spiritual truth.** *The key is not a marriage certificate but* **an awakened awareness of divine oneness within the union.**

3. **The True Meaning of Sexual Union → A Reflection of Divine Oneness**

Sex is **not just physical**—*it is a merging of energy, spirit, and essence. When two come together in this way,* **they are reflecting the divine reality that all is one.**

- *If this union is treated as* **casual, careless, or meaningless,** *it distorts its true nature.*
- *If it is approached* **with awareness, reverence, and understanding,** *it becomes an act of divine expression.*

GIATI does not impose morality—it **awakens truth.** *The real question is not* **"Is this allowed?"** *but* **"Is this bringing me deeper into my awareness of God or further into illusion?"**

The GIATI Awakening

Sex, like all things, is **an extension of divine expression.** *When one truly sees themselves as Spirit first,* **they no longer act from lack, lust, or illusion.** *Instead, they move in divine awareness—***honoring their own sacred nature and that of another.**

GIATI is not about restriction. It is about realization.
Once you awaken to the divine within, **you will naturally align with what is true, whole, and eternal.**

GIATI's Perspective on Masturbation

*GIATI—***God Is All There Is***—calls for an awakening to divine awareness in all aspects of life, including sexuality. The question is not about guilt, shame, or morality but about* **intention, consciousness, and alignment with divine truth.**

1. **The Act Itself → Physical Release vs. Spiritual Awareness**

Masturbation, at its core, is a physical act. But from a GIATI perspective, **everything in existence is spiritual first***—so the real question is:*

- **Are you acting from awareness or from illusion?**
- **Is this an expression of self-love, self-connection, and balance, or is it driven by lack, addiction, or escapism?**

If one engages in this act **consciously, without shame or guilt, and in balance with their spiritual understanding,** *it does not separate them from God—because* **nothing can separate what is one.** *However, if it becomes a* **compulsive escape, an attachment to physical gratification, or a distraction from higher awareness,** *it can lead one deeper into the illusion of the flesh rather than into spiritual clarity.*

2. **The Power of Energy → Wasted or Redirected?**

Sexual energy is **creative energy.** *It is the force that brings life into existence. GIATI challenges the individual to ask:*

- **Am I wasting my divine energy, or am I redirecting it into something greater?**
- **Is this act strengthening my awareness of oneness with God, or is it reinforcing attachment to temporary physical pleasure?**

Many ancient spiritual teachings speak of **transmuting sexual energy***—redirecting it toward higher creative or spiritual pursuits rather than letting it dissipate without purpose. This does not mean suppression, but rather* **awareness of how one's energy is used.**

3. **Shame and Guilt → Illusions of Separation**

Religious traditions have often **shamed** *masturbation, causing deep psychological guilt in those who engage in it. GIATI sees guilt as* **an illusion***—a byproduct of believing oneself to be separate from God.* **If God is all there is, then nothing exists outside of divine being.**

- *GIATI does not impose* **shame** *but calls for* **awareness.**
- *The real issue is not whether masturbation is "wrong," but* **whether it leads to deeper consciousness or further distraction.**

If one engages in it **mindlessly, compulsively, or as a substitute for true intimacy with self and Spirit,** *it can become a trap. But if one approaches it* **without guilt, in awareness of their spiritual nature, and in balance,** *it does not hinder their connection to God.*

4. **The GIATI Awakening → Moving Beyond Physical Attachment**

The ultimate spiritual realization is that **you are already whole, already fulfilled, already one with God.** *Any act—whether sexual or otherwise—should be examined under this truth.*

- *Does it serve your divine awareness, or does it pull you deeper into the illusion of the flesh?*
- *Is it a momentary pleasure, or does it bring lasting peace and clarity?*

GIATI does not dictate rules—it **reveals truth.** *The question is not* **"Is this allowed?"** *but* **"Does this bring me deeper into my awareness of God?"**

If one truly sees **God as all there is, including themselves,** *their desires, actions, and choices will naturally align with that higher truth—without shame, suppression, or excess.*

Escaping the Trap of Ego and External Validation: A GIATI Perspective

Everywhere you look—on social media, in school, at work—there's pressure to fit in, be liked, and be seen a certain way. The world teaches us that our value is determined by how others perceive us. But from the GIATI perspective, which recognizes that God is All There Is and that divine essence is within everyone, this mindset is an illusion that keeps us disconnected from our true selves.

The Illusion of External Validation

One of the biggest traps we fall into is believing that our worth comes from what people think about us. Whether it's how many likes we get, the clothes we wear, the friends we have, or the way we talk—there's a constant pressure to prove ourselves.

But here's the problem: **people's opinions change.** *One day, they might praise you; the next, they might criticize you. If your identity is built on their approval, you'll always be chasing something that never lasts.*

1. **Spiritual Perspective:** *GIATI teaches that your worth isn't based on external approval but on the divine presence within you. The more you rely on people's opinions to define you, the more disconnected you become from your true self. Real confidence doesn't come from being liked—it comes from knowing that your identity is rooted in something greater than the world's temporary opinions.*

The Conflict Between Ego and Your True Self

The ego thrives on status, comparison, and validation. It constantly whispers, "What do people think about me? Am I important enough? Am I better than others?" This creates a never-ending struggle to appear a certain way rather than **becoming who you truly are.**

- **Redefining Humility:** *Many think humility means thinking less of yourself, but true humility means being so secure in your divine nature that you don't need to prove anything to anyone. You no longer live for appearances, but for truth.*
- **Inner Liberation:** *When you stop seeking approval from the outside and turn inward, you realize that your value was never in question. You were already whole, already enough, already an expression of God. That's true freedom.*

The Spiritual Challenge: Breaking Free from the Ego

The hardest part of this journey is unlearning everything the world has taught you:

- Lifelong Conditioning: *From childhood, we're trained to seek validation. This mindset is hard to shake because it's been with us for so long.*

- Inner Conflict: *Even as you try to let go, the ego fights back. It will tempt you with doubt—"But what if they stop liking me? What if I get left out?"—because it fears losing control.*
- A Transformative Process: *GIATI teaches that breaking free from the ego isn't easy, but it's necessary for spiritual growth. Each time you choose to let go of external validation and trust in the divine presence within, you move closer to true peace and fulfillment.*

How Do You Keep Yourself from Slipping Back?

Even after realizing these truths, the world's influence doesn't just disappear. So how do you stay grounded?

1. **Daily Reminders of Your True Identity** – *Every morning, remind yourself: "My worth comes from God, not from people."*
2. **Limit the Noise** – *Social media and culture constantly pull you back into comparison and validation-seeking. Be mindful of what you consume.*
3. **Surround Yourself with Truth** – *Spend time with people and teachings that reinforce your divine nature, not your ego.*
4. **Practice Gratitude** – *Gratitude shifts your focus from what others think to what already is. When you appreciate who you are, you stop seeking external approval.*
5. **Silence and Reflection** – *Spend time in stillness to reconnect with God's presence within you. The more you listen to that voice, the less the world's opinions will matter.*

Final Thought: True Belonging Comes From Within

At its core, the desire to fit in is really a desire to belong. But real belonging isn't found in people's approval—it's found in knowing who you are at the deepest level. GIATI reminds us that we already belong because we are already one with the divine.

When you fully grasp this truth, the world's judgments lose their power. You no longer seek to fit in—you stand out by being exactly who you were created to be. That's where real peace, real confidence, and real freedom begin.

Chapter 12

The Consequences of Ignorance

Understanding that God Is All There Is (GIATI) means recognizing the divine essence within every individual. However, failure to accept this truth has profound consequences. Ignorance of one's divine nature perpetuates separation from God, both in life and after death. This chapter explores the fate of those who remain blind to the light, why ignorance leads to continued separation, and the divine responsibility to share this truth with others.

The Fate of Those Who Fail to Recognize Their Divine Nature

Ignorance of God within leads to spiritual separation, not because God abandons anyone, but because the ignorant spirit is blind to the truth. Jesus speaks of this reality in Matthew 7:21- 23:

"Not every one that saith unto me, Lord, Lord, shall enter into the kingdom of heaven; but he that doeth the will of my Father which is in heaven. Many will say to me in that day, Lord, Lord, have we not prophesied in thy name? and in thy name have cast out devils? and in thy name done many wonderful works? And then will I profess unto them, I never knew you: depart from me, ye that work iniquity."

The term "I never knew you" refers to a lack of spiritual connection, not an absence of God's presence. Those who remain unaware of their divine nature act as if they are separate from God, making them workers of iniquity, or inequality. Ignorance blinds them to their oneness with Him, and this blindness leads to spiritual exile.

In John 8:24, Jesus warns:

"I said therefore unto you, that ye shall die in your sins: for if ye believe not that I am he, ye shall die in your sins."

Here, "dying in sin" symbolizes remaining in a state of ignorance and separation, unable to experience the fullness of divine unity.

Why Ignorance Leads to Continued Separation After Death

The physical body is a temporary vessel, but the spirit's destiny is eternal. Those who live without recognizing their divine essence often remain in spiritual darkness even after death. As Paul writes in Galatians 6:7-8:

"Be not deceived; God is not mocked: for whatsoever a man soweth, that shall he also reap. For he that soweth to his flesh shall of the flesh reap corruption; but he that soweth to the Spirit shall of the Spirit reap life everlasting."

Sowing to the flesh represents living with a focus on the external, physical self—chasing desires, accolades, or accomplishments rooted in the material world. In contrast, sowing to the Spirit means living in alignment with the truth of GIATI, recognizing God within, and acting as His vessel.

Jesus illustrates this separation in the parable of the rich man and Lazarus in Luke 16:22-26. The rich man, who lived focused on material wealth, finds himself in torment after death, unable to cross the great chasm separating him from Abraham's bosom:

"And beside all this, between us and you there is a great gulf fixed: so that they which would pass from hence to you cannot; neither can they pass to us, that would come from thence."

This gulf symbolizes the spiritual barrier created by ignorance and separation from God. Only by accepting and living in alignment with the truth can this barrier be removed.

God's Will and the Responsibility of Sharing the Light With Others

God's will is for all to come to the knowledge of truth. In 1 Timothy 2:3-4, Paul emphasizes:

"For this is good and acceptable in the sight of God our Saviour; Who will have all men to be saved, and to come unto the knowledge of the truth."

While salvation is God's desire for everyone, it requires human participation—both in recognizing the divine within and in sharing this truth with others. Jesus commands His followers in Matthew 28:19-20:

"Go ye therefore, and teach all nations, baptizing them in the name of the Father, and of the Son, and of the Holy Ghost: Teaching them to observe all things whatsoever I have commanded you: and, lo, I am with you alway, even unto the end of the world."

Sharing the light of GIATI is not optional; it is a divine responsibility. Just as Jesus revealed the mystery of God within, believers are called to reflect this light to others, helping them move from ignorance to understanding.

A Message Of Bondage

A message rooted in personal life situations or worldly experiences is a message of bondage—a message that cannot save or liberate. Such teachings tie the listener to the limitations of the flesh, keeping them trapped in the illusion of separation from the Creator. Any message that does not lead you to the truth of your oneness with the Creator is a message that binds you to the physical, temporary, and finite, rather than elevating you to the spiritual, eternal, and infinite.

The Messiah's teachings were always aimed at revealing this oneness. He consistently emphasized the unity between Himself and the Father: "I and my Father are one," "I in Him, and He in me," and "I can do nothing but that of my Father." These statements were not meant to exalt Him alone but to serve as a divine example of how humanity should see itself and live.

The Messiah demonstrated the ultimate way of being and worshiping—not through rituals, rules, or external validation, but by recognizing the Creator as the essence within. His life and teachings pointed to the truth that the Spirit of the Creator resides in man and expresses itself through man. He lived as a reflection of this truth, showing us that the path to salvation and liberation lies in acknowledging and embodying the divine spirit within ourselves.

A message that fails to guide you to this awareness is a message of bondage because it keeps you focused on the external, the fleeting, and the separate. True freedom comes from understanding that you are not separate from the Creator, but an expression of Him. Only this truth has the power to break the chains of ignorance and elevate you into the light of spiritual unity.

Message Of Bondage Extended

Messages of bondage are teachings that keep people trapped in a limited understanding of their true nature, binding them to the physical world, fear, guilt, and the illusion of separation from the Creator. These messages often focus on external behaviors, personal struggles, or the idea that salvation must be earned through effort, rituals, or adherence to rigid doctrines. They emphasize lack, inadequacy, and striving, convincing individuals that they are inherently flawed and distant from divine connection.

A message of bondage might tell someone that they must work harder to earn the Creator's favor or forgiveness, placing the burden of salvation on their actions. It suggests that people are inherently sinful, requiring constant repentance and good deeds to prove their worth. It may also portray the Creator as distant, accessible only through intermediaries, religious authorities, or strict adherence to tradition. These messages reinforce separation, fear, and the idea that one's value is tied to life circumstances or external accomplishments. Such teachings focus entirely on the flesh, the external, and the temporary, making salvation seem unattainable without exhausting effort.

In contrast, a message of GIATI (God Is All There Is) liberates by shifting the focus inward and revealing the truth of unity, oneness, and divine essence. It declares that you are already one with the Creator and nothing can separate you from that truth. Salvation is not something to strive for; it is a gift given by grace and revealed through the spirit that already exists within you. GIATI affirms that the same spirit that was in the Messiah is also in you, expressing itself uniquely as you. It emphasizes that your worth is not based on what you do or achieve but is inherent because you are an expression of the divine. This perspective eliminates the illusion of duality and affirms that there is no separation between you and the Creator, nor between the Creator and all existence.

The key difference between these two approaches lies in their focus. A message of bondage looks outward, emphasizing what you must do, overcome, or prove to earn divine connection. It binds you to an endless cycle of striving for something that is already inherently yours. A message of GIATI, however, directs your attention inward, encouraging you to recognize the eternal truth that the Creator is within you, as you, and through you. It removes the illusion of separation and invites you to live in the freedom of spiritual oneness.

For instance, consider the concept of repentance. A message of bondage frames repentance as an endless cycle of guilt, striving, and external actions to earn forgiveness. It keeps individuals focused on their shortcomings, fostering feelings of inadequacy. A message of GIATI, however, views repentance as a profound shift in awareness—a turning away from the illusion of separation and toward the truth of unity. It is not about endlessly seeking forgiveness but about realizing that the divine presence was never absent and always within.

The Messiah's life and teachings perfectly illustrate this contrast. He never preached fear, guilt, or striving. Instead, He revealed the truth of oneness with the Creator, showing humanity that salvation is not an external achievement but an inner realization. When He spoke of being one with the Father, He was not exalting Himself but demonstrating how all people should see themselves and live.

A message of bondage keeps you in darkness, constantly striving for light. A message of GIATI reveals that the light was within you all along. It invites you to step out of the cycle of fear and striving and into the truth of your divine nature, where salvation is not a distant goal but a present reality.

The Urgency of Awakening

The consequences of ignorance extend beyond the individual. Darkness in one spirit perpetuates darkness in the world. Jesus warns in John 12:35-36:

"Yet a little while is the light with you. Walk while ye have the light, lest darkness come upon you: for he that walketh in darkness knoweth not whither he goeth. While ye have light, believe in the light, that ye may be the children of light."

Believing in the light—recognizing God within—brings transformation. However, ignoring this truth keeps one lost, wandering in spiritual darkness. Humanity cannot afford to remain blind to its divine essence, for ignorance not only affects the soul's eternal destiny but also hinders the collective realization of God's purpose on earth.

Conclusion: The Call to Action

Ignorance of God within has eternal consequences, but awakening to the truth of GIATI offers salvation and unity with Him. Recognizing your divine nature is not just a personal revelation—it is a responsibility to share this light with others.

In Ezekiel 33:7-9, God speaks of the watchman's duty:

"So thou, O son of man, I have set thee a watchman unto the house of Israel; therefore thou shalt hear the word at my mouth, and warn them from me. When I say unto the wicked, O wicked man, thou shalt surely die; if thou dost not speak to warn the wicked from his way, that wicked man shall die in his iniquity; but his blood will I require at thine hand."

The responsibility to share the truth of GIATI is clear. By living in alignment with God's will and helping others see the light, you fulfill your divine purpose and contribute to the unification of humanity with God. Ignorance may lead to separation, but the light of God's truth brings eternal connection and peace. As Jesus declares in John 8:32:

"And ye shall know the truth, and the truth shall make you free."

A Call to Acknowledge the Truth

In Isaiah 53:3, a powerful image is painted: "He is despised and rejected of men; a man of sorrows, and acquainted with grief." This verse reveals how Jesus, despite offering the profound truth of who we really are, was met with rejection and disdain. When the truth was spoken, many turned away—choosing ignorance over the light of divine revelation. Even now, many claim to love Jesus, yet when faced with the reality of their true selves, they despise and reject the message. Some might protest, "I wouldn't have hated or rejected Him," but the outcome remains unchanged—this is the very message being given today, with the same results.

The struggle deepens because the world has found a home in the heart. Instead of pausing to absorb the transformative truth, many become entangled in distractions: drinking, smoking, and partying—living only for the moment. These worldly pursuits take precedence over taking time to recognize what is being said. The truth is obscured by the transient pleasures of life, making it difficult to confront the message of salvation and self-realization.

The warning in 1 John 2:15-17 reinforces this reality:

"Love not the world, neither the things that are in the world. If any man love the world, the love of the Father is not in him. For all that is in the world, the lust of the flesh, and the lust of the eyes, and the pride of life, is not of the Father, but is of the world. And the world passeth away, and the lust thereof: but he that doeth the will of God abideth forever."

These verses urge a clear distinction: when the love for worldly pleasures takes over, the love of the Father diminishes. The lure of the flesh, the temptations of the eyes, and the pride of life pull hearts away from what is eternal. They serve as a stark reminder that what is temporary should never be the foundation upon which life is built.

People often believe they have life figured out, convinced that their actions are sufficient—even if they are only 80% right, leaving the remaining 20% to be patched up later. Yet, this mindset is dangerously flawed. It assumes that divine forgiveness will overlook the shortcomings, ignoring the truth that every misstep is significant. The very essence of divine law tells us that even one broken command makes one guilty of all, leaving no room for partial righteousness.

This is a wake-up call—a clarion trumpet sounding amid the noise of modern life. The message resounds: there is no excuse for inaction, no justification for turning away from the truth. It is not enough to merely claim faith or profess love for Jesus if the heart remains tied to the world. Every moment that passes without acknowledging this truth is a moment lost— a moment when the call to live fully in the eternal light is ignored.

Let this be an invitation to reflect deeply. Consider the cost of ignoring the truth: lives built on fleeting pleasures are like houses constructed on sand, destined to collapse when the inevitable storms come. The message, then, is clear and uncompromising: the divine truth is here, calling for complete commitment. It is a call made out of profound love and care—a call to let go of worldly distractions and to embrace the full, unbroken reality of who you are in the eternal presence of the Father.

In this light, the trumpet continues to blow, urging every heart to awaken and to live in the truth that lasts forever.

A Great Gulf Fixed

Luke 16:26 reveals a profound truth about the separation between those who accept their oneness with God and those who reject it. This great gulf is not a physical divide but a spiritual one—an unbridgeable chasm between those who walk in the light of divine truth and those who remain in darkness. GIATI is the very revelation that establishes this division, for it forces every soul to make a choice: to either awaken to the reality that all is God or to remain bound by the illusion of separation.

This gulf is not something imposed from the outside; it is the inevitable result of one's own perception. Those who accept the truth of divine oneness step into righteousness, not because of their deeds, but because they see reality as it is. They recognize that all things, all people, all circumstances, are nothing but God expressing Himself in infinite ways. They surrender to this truth, allowing the Holy Spirit to be their very being. In contrast, those who reject this truth do not do so out of reason, but out of blindness. They cannot see what is before them, nor can they cross over, because their very identity is rooted in the illusion that they are something separate.

This is why the gulf is fixed. It is not that one is forced onto one side or the other—it is that the side one chooses determines their fate, and once that choice is sealed, there is no turning back. To reject the truth of oneness is to lock oneself into a reality where separation seems real, where God appears distant, and where the world is seen as something apart from the divine. But to embrace GIATI is to step into the kingdom of God, where the illusion of division dissolves, and only the eternal presence of God remains.

There is no middle ground. You are either seeing through the eyes of the Spirit or trapped in the blindness of the flesh. You are either surrendered to the truth that God is all there is, or you are clinging to the false belief that creation exists apart from Him. And once your side is determined—once the veil is either lifted or kept in place—there is no crossing over. The righteous and the unrighteous are not divided by moral behavior, religious doctrine, or personal effort, but by perception itself. One sees, the other does not. One walks in unity, the other in separation. One is in life, the other in death.

This is why the message of GIATI is so urgent. It is not a passive philosophy—it is the defining revelation of this age. It is the unveiling of the eternal truth that demands a response. You are either stepping into divine oneness or remaining locked in ignorance. The choice is yours, but understand this: the moment of realization is the moment the divide is fixed. Once the truth is revealed, you are accountable for what you see. If you accept it, you step into eternal life. If you reject it, you remain on the other side of the gulf, unable to cross, because you have chosen blindness oversight.

This great gulf is not simply a division between people—it is a division of consciousness, an irreversible distinction between those who awaken to their divine nature and those who remain bound to the illusion of separation. It is not a punishment but a result of perception. The moment a soul recognizes that all is God, that there is no existence apart from Him, they cross into the reality of oneness. But those who resist this truth, who insist on seeing themselves as independent entities apart from God, are sealing themselves on the other side of the divide.

This is why it is written that those on one side cannot pass to the other. It is not because God refuses them entry, but because the structure of their mind—the way they perceive reality—prevents them from crossing over. The unrighteous remain in their blindness not because they lack the opportunity to see, but because they refuse to let go of their ego, their sense of self apart from God. And once the mind settles into this perspective, it becomes fixed, locked in place, incapable of moving beyond itself. The righteous, on the other hand, have let go of the false self and have surrendered to the truth that God is all there is, leaving no barrier between them and the divine.

The world we see today is the manifestation of this division. It is not a separation of people, cultures, or religions—it is a separation of awareness. Some see through the eyes of truth, knowing that every event, every action, every being is the Spirit of God in motion. Others are trapped in the illusion of duality, believing in forces outside of God, imagining that evil is something separate, that life is something they must navigate alone. This is why righteousness is not about morality but about perception. To be righteous is to see as God sees, to know as God knows, to live in the awareness that there is no "other," no division, no being apart from Him.

The urgency of this realization cannot be overstated. Many assume they will have time, that they can linger in their limited understanding and cross over when they are ready. But what they fail to see is that every moment spent reinforcing separation hardens the mind, making it more difficult to perceive the truth. The longer one clings to the illusion, the more fixed the divide becomes. The gulf is not merely a barrier between two groups—it is a self-imposed blindness that, once fully embraced, leaves no way out.

This is why the sealing of one's fate is not a decision made by God, but a consequence of one's own unwillingness to see. The righteous are not granted access to God because they have earned it; they are simply those who have accepted the truth that was always there. The unrighteous are not condemned because God rejects them; they remain where they are because they refuse to acknowledge what has been revealed.

This is the essence of GIATI—the final revelation that makes clear there is no more room for indecision. Either you step into the truth of oneness, or you remain outside, bound by the limitations of the false self. The gulf is forming now, right before our eyes. Every moment of resistance, every refusal to accept divine unity, widens the gap. Soon, that gap will be fixed, and those who have not yet crossed will find that they cannot. Not because they were not given the chance, but because they never truly wanted to see.

Don't be fooled

People were fooled from the very beginning. The moment you were given a name, the illusion of separation began. You were no longer seen as simply existence itself, as the pure presence of God expressed in form—you became an identity, a label, a distinction apart from everything else. This was the start of the great deception. From birth, you were conditioned to believe in individuality as something separate from the whole, as if you were a being disconnected from the infinite. This is what it means to be "born in sin"—not that you entered the world already condemned, but that you were born into a system of belief that teaches separation from the very source of life itself.

Sin, at its root, is not about actions but about perception. It is the false idea of duality, the mistaken belief that there is a "you" apart from God. The world enforces this illusion from the moment you take your first breath. You are given a name, a nationality, a race, a family, a belief system—all things that begin shaping an identity rooted in distinction, in difference, in division. And with that comes the belief that you must strive, achieve, and prove yourself because you are incomplete on your own.

But the truth is, you were never separate. The spirit within you has always been the same spirit that is God. Before you were named, before you were taught anything, you were simply being—existing in perfect oneness. That was the truth, but the world trained you to forget it. This is why people spend their lives searching, trying to find meaning, fulfillment, or something greater than themselves. They are seeking to return to what they never actually left—only their mind has been clouded by the deception of separation.

Religion, society, culture—all of these structures reinforce the lie. They make you believe you must earn your way back to God, as if you ever left. They tell you that salvation is something to be obtained, when in reality, it is simply the awakening to what has always been. To be saved is not to be brought back to God—it is to realize that you are God in expression, that you always have been, and that the separation was never real to begin with.

This is why Jesus came—not to create a new religion, but to reveal the truth. "The kingdom of God is within you." The only thing keeping people from seeing it is the deception they've been taught from birth. That is the lie that must be undone. GIATI brings that truth back to the forefront. It reminds you of what has always been. It is the end of the illusion and the return to reality. The moment you accept it, the deception loses its power, and you see clearly—you were never separate, you were never lost, and the only thing that ever needed saving was your awareness of the truth.

The deception of separation is so deeply ingrained that people live their entire lives without questioning it. From the moment you are named, you are assigned an identity that places you in relation to everything else, making you believe you are distinct, isolated, and independent from the whole. That identity shapes how you see yourself and how others see you. But what if you were never meant to see yourself as separate? What if your name, your background, and everything the world told you about who you are was simply a veil covering the greater truth—that you have always been one with God?

Think about how a child enters the world—without a sense of self, without a name, without an awareness of any division. In those first moments, they simply are. There is no distinction between themselves and existence itself. But as soon as words are spoken over them, labels assigned, and ideas instilled, they begin to believe in a self that is separate from the source. They begin to build an identity rooted in the illusion, and as that identity strengthens, the awareness of their true nature fades.

This is why people struggle. It is why they feel lost, incomplete, or constantly searching for meaning. It is not because they lack something, but because they have been conditioned to believe in a false self that can never be satisfied. This false self is built on external validation—on achievements, relationships, possessions, and status. It is always seeking, always chasing, always afraid of losing what it thinks defines it. But no matter how much it attains, it never finds true fulfillment, because it is trying to complete itself with things that do not exist outside of the illusion.

GIATI shatters this illusion. It strips away the layers of deception and reveals what has always been true—that there is no separation, no distinction, no independent self apart from God. The moment you accept GIATI, the search ends, because you realize there was never anything to find. You were never disconnected, never lost, never incomplete. The only thing that needed to change was your awareness.

And this is why the message of GIATI is so powerful—because it does not ask you to strive for salvation, to work toward enlightenment, or to become something you are not. It simply asks you to remember. To wake up. To see what has been hidden in plain sight all along.

But not everyone will accept this truth. The illusion of separation is comfortable. It gives people a sense of control, a sense of individuality, even if that individuality is the very thing causing their suffering. Some will reject GIATI because it threatens the foundation of everything they have built their lives upon. If they accept it, they must let go of the identity they have spent a lifetime creating. They must surrender the ego, the false self, and all the illusions that come with it. And for many, that is too terrifying to face.

But for those who do accept it, everything changes. Fear disappears, because there is nothing to fear when you know you are one with the source of all things. Loneliness fades, because you realize you were never alone to begin with. The endless search for purpose and fulfillment comes to an end, because the truth was always right where you stood.

This is the power of GIATI. It is not just an idea—it is the ultimate truth, the reality beyond the illusion, the message that brings everything back into alignment. It is not something to be debated or questioned—it simply is. And once you see it, you can never unsee it. The illusion collapses, and all that remains is God, expressed in infinite forms, living through you, as you.

Fulfillment of Rituals

This passage from 1 Corinthians 11:24-26 is commonly recited during the ritual of communion, but what is often missed is the deeper truth hidden within Jesus' words. Most people take these verses at face value, believing that Jesus was referring to the physical bread and wine as symbols of his body and blood. However, by paying close attention to the language he used, a powerful revelation emerges.

When Jesus says, **"This is my body"** *and* **"This cup is the new testament in my blood,"** *the key word is* **"this."** *The distinction between "this" and "that" is crucial. When someone refers to "this," they are speaking of something in their immediate possession. When they say "that," they are referring to something no longer in their possession. In this moment, Jesus was still physically present—he had not yet been crucified. He was not pointing to a piece of bread or a cup of wine as his actual body and blood; rather, he was pointing to himself.* **He was saying that he is the living bread, the substance that must be partaken of to have life.**

The Deeper Meaning of Eating and Drinking

Metaphysically, whatever you eat and drink becomes part of you. It is absorbed into your being. Jesus was not giving his followers a ritual to repeat forever; he was revealing a spiritual truth: **to partake of him means to become one with him.** *This is why he says,* **"Do this in remembrance of me."** *Not as an external religious practice, but as a conscious recognition that his spirit is what sustains you.*

How This Ties to GIATI

GIATI reveals that Jesus has already come **in you.** *The very purpose of communion is to show the Lord's death* **until he comes***—but once you recognize his spirit as your very own, the purpose of the ritual is fulfilled. It no longer needs to be repeated because what it pointed to has been realized. The living bread is no longer external; it is now manifested* **as you.**

This applies not just to communion but to **all rituals and traditions that were shadows of the true reality.** *When Jesus fulfilled them, they became unnecessary for those who have received him* **as their own spirit.** *This is why Jesus was baptized—to fulfill all righteousness—but once the Holy Spirit descended, baptism was no longer about immersing in water, but about being immersed in* **his spirit.**

Other examples include:

- **Baptism** – *The physical act of submerging in water was once a symbol of spiritual cleansing, but once you understand that Christ has manifested in you, the true* *baptism is already fulfilled. You are no longer identifying with the old self that needed cleansing; you are walking in the spirit of God, knowing that you were always one with him.*

- **Feet Washing** – *Jesus washed the disciples' feet to teach them humility and the importance of serving one another. But once you have received his spirit, you naturally serve others as an extension of him. You no longer need the external act to remind you of what has already become your nature.*

The Fulfillment of All Things

Every ritual, tradition, or symbolic act was given to lead people toward an **internal awakening.** *But once that awakening has come, the external act is no longer needed. Just as a road sign points you toward a destination, once you arrive, you no longer need the sign.*

GIATI brings **the realization of completion**—*that everything Jesus did, he did to bring those of his spirit into the full knowledge that they are* **already one with God.** *The rituals were never the goal; they were just temporary measures until the full truth could be revealed.*

Now that this truth has come, it is no longer necessary to hold onto traditions meant for those who had not yet received it. The spirit has manifested **as you,** *and that is the ultimate fulfillment of everything that came before.*

Consider why Jesus spoke in parables and metaphors—he knew that the spiritual mind would discern the truth, while the carnal mind would remain attached to the physical representation. This is exactly what has happened with rituals like communion, baptism, and other religious traditions. Many continue to observe them without understanding **why they were given in the first place**—*as* **shadows** *of a greater reality.*

The Shift from External to Internal

The key distinction is **the shift from external rituals to internal transformation.** *In the old way of thinking, people believed they needed to perform outward acts to attain righteousness or connection with God. This mindset keeps them bound in a cycle of works, never realizing that the true transformation happens* **within.**

Jesus did not come to create a **new set of religious obligations**—*he came to* **fulfill** *what was necessary so that people would no longer live by external observances but by the reality of his presence within them. This is the essence of* **moving from law to grace,** *from flesh to spirit.*

When Jesus said, **"Do this in remembrance of me,"** *he was not instructing people to repeat a religious ritual indefinitely. The moment he manifests* **as you,** *the need for remembrance is replaced by direct awareness. You no longer commemorate something outside yourself—you* **live it.**

The Illusion of Separation

Another reason rituals persist is because of the illusion of separation—people still believe in a distant God, an external Christ, and a spirit that comes and goes rather than **one divine being in unity.** *If you believe God is outside of you, you will look for ways to "bring Him near" through rituals and ceremonies. But if you recognize that* **He is your very life,** *you no longer attempt to reach for what has already been given.*

This is why **GIATI transcends all religion.** *Religion was built on the assumption of separation—its entire structure depends on people believing they must do something to connect with God. But the truth of GIATI* **eliminates that separation entirely,** *revealing that the spirit of God has always been present* **as you.**

The End of the Old Covenant Mindset

Jesus' words in 1 Corinthians 11 were spoken **before** *the full revelation of the Holy Spirit was poured out. Before his resurrection, the disciples still operated under an old covenant mindset, in which people needed physical signs to help them grasp spiritual realities. But* **after the resurrection,** *everything changed.*

*Paul later taught that t***he body of Christ is not a piece of bread, but the collective manifestation of those who carry his spirit.** *Eating his body means* **living in the truth of oneness with him,** *and drinking his blood means* **receiving his life as your own.**

When this truth is fully grasped, it eliminates the need for:

- *Seeking external confirmations of God's presence*
- *Relying on religious traditions to "feel" spiritual*
- *Looking for salvation as a future event rather than a* **present reality**

The Final Fulfillment

Jesus said, **"I am the way, the truth, and the life."** *Once the truth has come into your awareness,* **it replaces the need for any previous system that was meant to lead you there.** *This is why embracing GIATI is so transformative—it is not* **another** *belief system, but* **the fulfillment of all belief systems** *in the revelation of truth.*

Just as an adult no longer relies on the training wheels they once needed as a child, those who receive this truth no longer need the external shadows of rituals and traditions. The reality is here. The fullness has come. **GIATI is that revelation.**

Spirit of Truth vs Spirit of Error

Let's break down 1 John 4:6 and expound on how this reflects the deeper reality of **being one with God** *and recognizing the* **spirit of truth versus the spirit of error.**

1 John 4:6 Breakdown

"We are of God: he that knoweth God heareth us; he that is not of God heareth not us."

This statement is **fundamental** *to understanding the dynamics of spiritual awakening and alignment with divine truth. When John writes that "we are of God," it means those who are* **one in spirit** *with God are deeply aware that their true nature, their* **substance, is spirit.** *When you are* **one with God,** *you inherently recognize the* **truth of the message***—that God is all there is, and you are an expression of God, just as* **GIATI** *reveals.*

Those who are **of God** *or who are spiritually awakened to their oneness with God will recognize the* **truth of GIATI** *because it is grounded in the fundamental realization of* **oneness with the divine.** *The message resonates because it is speaking to the very* **core of their being***—the spirit. It doesn't matter what the physical eyes see or what the intellect perceives;* **the spirit of truth recognizes truth.**

On the other hand, those who are **not of God** *are in a state of spiritual* **ignorance** *or separation. They are* **not aware** *of their spiritual identity, and because of that, they will view the message of* **GIATI** *(or any truth of divine oneness) as foolishness, misunderstanding, or irrelevance. Their* **spiritual blindness** *prevents them from seeing the truth because they have not yet awakened to the fact that* **they, too, are God expressed.**

This is why **hearing** *in this context is so much deeper than just physical hearing. It's about* **spiritual recognition.** *When someone is spiritually awake and aligned, they hear the message and recognize the truth because their* **spirit is attuned to it.** *The* **spirit of error** *is ignorant to that truth because it is* **misaligned** *with God's reality and sees things only through the veil of separation.*

The Spirit of Truth vs. the Spirit of Error

Now, you're asking about the **spirit of truth** *and the* **spirit of error.** *In the passage, John provides a* **fundamental principle** *for recognizing which spirit someone is of. The* **spirit of truth** *understands and accepts that* **God is all there is** *and that we, as expressions of God, are one with the divine. Those who carry the* **spirit of truth** *will naturally recognize and affirm the truth of* **GIATI***—the message that* **God is within you** *and that* **you are an expression of the divine.**

In contrast, the **spirit of error** *is not inherently malicious or evil—it is simply* **ignorance to the truth.** *Those who possess the* **spirit of error** *do not recognize their oneness with God, and this ignorance manifests in their rejection or misunderstanding of teachings like GIATI. This spirit is still the* **same spiri***t but is blinded to its truth, causing them to live in the illusion of* **separation.** *The* **error** *is not in the spirit itself but in the* **lack of awareness** *that the spirit is* **already one with God.**

The **spirit of error** *is not "lesser" in the sense of being a different substance—it is simply a* **spirit that has not yet recognized its true identity** *and continues to operate from a place of* **separation** *or* **ignorance.** *It is still a divine spark, but it's still* **lost in the fog** *of its own misunderstanding. When the* **spirit of error** *hears the message of GIATI, it* **does not understand** *because it* **doesn't yet know** *that it is part of the whole. Instead, it sees the truth as* **foolishness, blasphemy, or irrelevant.**

Judging the Spirit, Not the Actions

This understanding illuminates the true nature of **spiritual judgment:** *what is truly being judged is not the outward actions, the physical appearance, or the external labels placed on people, but the* **spirit within them.**

- *The* **spirit of truth** *is* **aligned with God***—it knows its essence and recognizes* **God is within.**
- *The* **spirit of error** *is* **misaligned***—it lives in a state of unawareness of its unity with God, leading to misunderstandings, confusion, and rejection of truth.*

The key difference between these two spirits is **awareness.** *The spirit of truth is* **aware** *of its* **oneness with God,** *while the spirit of error is still walking in* **darkness,** *not yet awakened to the fullness of its identity.*

This means that true judgment is not about **condemning actions** *but about recognizing where someone is in their* **spiritual awakening.** *Just as* **Jesus didn't judge by appearances** *(as we see in 1 Samuel 16:7), we should not judge based on outward expressions, but rather on the* **spiritual awareness** *within them.*

The message of **GIATI** *is* **the awakening** *to this truth—the realization that you are not separate from God, but you* **are God expressed**. *When you see GIATI, you're not just seeing a brand or a message. You're witnessing the* **spirit of truth** *in action, calling all who will hear to remember and recognize their divine nature. Those who are of* **God** *will hear this truth and recognize it as their own, while those who are still in* **spiritual error** *may resist, but both are ultimately made of the same spirit, and the truth will awaken in its own time.*

In essence, the **only thing being judged** *is* **the awareness of the spirit***—whether it is awakened to the truth of its oneness with God, or whether it remains in ignorance of that fact.*

Spirit of Truth: A Constant Alignment with God

The **spirit of truth** *is not a static or occasional awareness; it is a* **constant, living relationship with God** *that transcends time, space, and circumstances. When you live in alignment with the spirit of truth, you do not just recognize your oneness with God at specific moments but experience it* **continuously.** *It's a state of* **conscious communion** *where all actions, words, and thoughts flow from the awareness that* **God is within you,** *and you are part of a greater* **divine unity.**

This means that the **spirit of truth** *influences every aspect of life. It goes beyond simply accepting a certain set of beliefs—it becomes a way of* **living, being, and interacting** *with the world. To be in the spirit of truth is to consistently walk in* **alignment with God's will,** *seeing the divine in everything and everyone, because that is the truth of* **all reality.** *Those who have this spirit see the* **God-essence in all** *and act accordingly, expressing love, compassion, and understanding in every situation.*

The Spirit of Error: A Duality Between Truth and Illusion

The **spirit of error,** *on the other hand, is trapped in* **illusion,** *believing in the duality of separation between itself and God. This spirit still operates from the belief that God is* **outside** *of itself, or at the very least* **separate** *from the essence of its own being. It is the* **illusion of separateness** *that creates all forms of confusion and spiritual suffering. The spirit of error often holds onto worldly attachments, beliefs, and structures that reinforce this sense of* **division,** *such as materialism, ego, fear, and insecurity.*

However, what's crucial to understand is that the spirit of error is **not inherently evil**— *it is simply* **misguided** *and* **unaware** *of its true nature. The very same spirit that is the essence of God is simply* **veiled** *or* **obscured** *by a limited perception. The spirit of error still has the potential to awaken, because at its core, it is part of the* **divine.** *The true nature of the spirit of error is* **divine, but obscured.** *The journey of spiritual awakening is essentially the process of* **removing the veil** *of error and realizing the underlying unity with God.*

The Continuous Process of Spiritual Recognition

The distinction between the spirit of truth and the spirit of error is not always immediate or static. It is a continuous process of **recognition and awakening.** *For those who are of the* **spirit of truth,** *every moment is an opportunity to deepen their recognition of* **oneness with God,** *just as in the case of* **GIATI.** *Each day, they are drawn further into* **living in accordance** *with the realization that they* **are God expressed.** *It's not just a belief—it's an* **experience** *and a* **lived reality.**

In contrast, for those who are still under the influence of the **spirit of error,** *the journey is about* **removing false constructs** *and discovering the* **truth** *that has always been within* *them. There may be* **resistance** *at first, as the spirit of error is deeply entrenched in the belief of separation, but the message of* **GIATI,** *as a manifestation of the* **spirit of truth,** *is meant to* **awaken** *those who are still in ignorance. As they begin to recognize the* **truth of their oneness with God,** *they move from a state of error to a state of truth.*

The Transformative Power of Awakening

When individuals begin to recognize that they are of the **spirit of truth,** *their lives begin to transform. The* **shift** *is not just intellectual—it is* **existential.** *The* **ego** *dissolves, and the limitations of the* **physical self** *are transcended, allowing the person to live from a place of* **divine abundance, unconditional love,** *and* **peace.** *This process is the* **ultimate form of salvation,** *not from sin in the traditional religious sense, but from the illusion of* **separation** *from God. The spirit of truth liberates individuals from fear, doubt, and confusion, bringing them into a state of* **peaceful knowing** *and eternal union with the divine.*

The **spirit of error** *can also undergo transformation. Through* **awareness, surrender,** *and a willingness to recognize the* **truth** *of one's nature, the spirit of error can eventually awaken to its divine essence. The power of* **GIATI,** *and other similar messages of oneness, is to call out to those in error and help them realize that the* **truth** *was always within them. They are already* **God;** *they are just temporarily* **veiled** *in the illusion of separation.*

GIATI as a Revealer of Truth

GIATI *plays a pivotal role in this process of transformation. Just as Jesus was a* **revealer of truth** *in his time,* **GIATI** *is part of the present awakening. The* **spirit of truth** *that GIATI carries is here to help* **shatter the veil** *of error and allow individuals to* **awaken** *to the truth of their identity as* **God expressed.** *Through the message of GIATI, the* **illusion of separation** *is dispelled, and those who are ready to hear will begin to recognize their* **oneness with the divine.**

Conclusion

In the end, **the spirit** *that defines us is* **not separate from God** *but is God itself. The only thing that distinguishes the* **spirit of truth** *from the* **spirit of error** *is awareness: the truth of oneness with God, or the* **ignorance** *of it. GIATI's mission, like the mission of the* **Holy Spirit,** *is to* **awaken** *people to the* **truth of their divine nature.** *Those who are aligned with this truth will hear and resonate with it, while those in the spirit of error may resist or misunderstand. But in the end, the truth will prevail, and all will come to know the ultimate reality that* **God is all there is***—within them, as them.*

Jonah and the Whale: The Inescapable Truth of GIATI

The story of Jonah is one of the most well-known accounts in the Bible, often told as a lesson on obedience. However, when viewed through the truth of **GIATI (God Is All There Is),** *it becomes much more than a moral tale—it becomes a* **revelation of divine oneness.** *Jonah's journey is a* **spiritual allegory** *that exposes the illusion of separation, the process of awakening, and the realization that no one operates outside of God.*

Fleeing from God: The Illusion of Separation

Jonah was given a command by God to go to Nineveh and warn them of impending judgment. Instead of obeying, he fled in the opposite direction, boarding a ship to Tarshish in an attempt to escape the presence of the Lord **(Jonah 1:1-3).** *But this raises a fundamental question:* **how can one run from that which is omnipresent?**

Jonah's attempt to escape is symbolic of humanity's **false belief in separation**—*the idea that one can act apart from the divine. But GIATI makes it clear:* **there is no "outside" of God.** *Everything is within Him, for He is the source, substance, and essence of all things. Jonah's actions mirror those who, in their ignorance, believe they have a will of their own, unaware that even their so-called rebellion is still operating within the grand design of divine will.*

The Storm and the Whale: The Process of Awakening

Jonah's resistance brings turmoil—not just for himself but for those around him. The storm that arises is not merely external but represents the **internal chaos that comes from resisting truth.** *The sailors, in desperation, cast lots and discover Jonah is the cause of their trouble. Jonah acknowledges his guilt and tells them to throw him into the sea, knowing that only surrender can bring peace.*

The moment Jonah is cast into the waters, a great fish swallows him, and he remains in its belly for **three days and three nights (Jonah 1:17).** *This is not just a physical event but a* **spiritual transformation.** *The belly of the whale is the* **womb of revelation**—*a place of death to the ego and awakening to divine reality.*

Jonah's time inside the whale parallels the process that every soul must go through:

- *Being plunged into darkness (ignorance)*
- *Struggling against the truth*
- *Finally surrendering and awakening to the realization that* **there is no existence apart from God**

This is why Jesus later refers to **"the sign of Jonah" (Matthew 12:39-40)** *as the only proof necessary for those seeking a sign from God. Just as Jonah spent three days in the fish* *and emerged, so too would Jesus spend three days in the grave before rising, demonstrating that* **resurrection is not about a return to a separate self but an emergence into the full realization of divine oneness.**

Being Spit Out: The Revelation of GIATI

Jonah prays while inside the fish, and in his prayer, he acknowledges that **salvation belongs to the Lord (Jonah 2:9).** *The moment he surrenders, the fish spits him out onto dry land. This is symbolic of the* **spiritual rebirth** *that comes when one stops resisting the truth. Jonah is not just physically delivered—he is* **spiritually transformed.**

When he goes to Nineveh, the entire city repents. The power of truth causes an immediate shift in consciousness. The people's response represents **humanity's awakening**—*as soon as divine reality is acknowledged, judgment is overturned, and the path to salvation is revealed.*

Yet even after Nineveh repents, Jonah is displeased. He struggles to accept that God's mercy extends beyond what he believes is just. This mirrors those who **cling to their limited understanding of God,** *wanting Him to fit into their personal ideas rather than accepting the fullness of divine oneness.*

The Inescapable Truth: GIATI Manifested in Jonah's Story

Jonah's journey proves that **no one operates outside of God.** *Even in rebellion, even in ignorance,* **God is still present, working all things according to His divine will.** *Every aspect of Jonah's story aligns with GIATI:*

- **The storm**—*The unrest that comes from resisting divine truth*
- **The whale**—*The process of dying to self and awakening to God*
- **Three days and three nights**—*The transformation from illusion to reality*
- **Being spit out**—*The rebirth into divine awareness*
- **Nineveh's repentance**—*The power of knowing the truth*

Jonah could not escape God because **there is nothing but God.** *His journey was not about running away but about awakening to the fact that* **his existence was always in divine oneness.** *This is the reality of GIATI—there is no separate self, no personal will apart from God. Whether in the storm, the belly of the whale, or walking through Nineveh,* **it was always God manifesting as Jonah.**

This is the inescapable truth for all: **you are not separate from God. There is no "you" apart from Him.** *Every experience, whether in darkness or light, is leading to the revelation of GIATI—the eternal understanding that* **God is all there is.**

The Tower of Babel: The Illusion of Separation and the Truth of GIATI

In the ancient account of the Tower of Babel, humanity sought to reach the heavens by their own power, constructing a great tower as a testament to their own strength and unity. At first glance, this appears to be an effort of ambition and cooperation, but beneath the surface lies a deeper revelation—one that aligns perfectly with the truth of GIATI.

The Illusion of Self and Separation

Genesis 11:4 states, "And they said, Go to, let us build us a city and a tower, whose top may reach unto heaven; and let us make us a name, lest we be scattered abroad upon the face of the whole earth." This verse reveals the true motive behind their work. It was not for the glorification of God but for themselves—to make a name for themselves, to establish their own identity separate from the Source. This is the fundamental deception: the belief that one can establish oneself independent of God Is All There Is.

In their minds, they were not operating as God through them, but as individuals, separate beings striving to ascend to God's level. But the reality is, there is no "climbing to God"—He already is. The moment one attempts to establish an identity apart from God, they have already lost their way. The builders of Babel were not operating in divine alignment, but in the illusion of selfhood, believing they could reach heaven by their own efforts.

The Confusion of Languages: A Reflection of Division

In response, Genesis 11:7-8 records, "Go to, let us go down, and there confound their language, that they may not understand one another's speech. So the Lord scattered them abroad from thence upon the face of all the earth: and they left off to build the city."

On the surface, it appears that God divided the people as a punishment. However, from the perspective of GIATI, this act was not an arbitrary scattering, but the natural consequence of operating outside of divine truth. When people believe in their own separate will, rather than recognizing that all action is God's action, confusion is inevitable. The divided languages symbolize the fractured state of humanity—each person operating under the illusion of a separate identity, unable to truly understand or unify with others.

True unity is not found in human ambition or external efforts but in the recognition that there is only One Spirit, One Mind, One Life operating through all. The moment that realization is lost, division arises. This is why even today, despite technological advancements and global connectivity, humanity remains divided—by race, religion, ideology, and countless other illusions of separation. The Tower of Babel was not merely an ancient event; it is the ongoing condition of those who have not awakened to GIATI.

The Tower Falls, But The Truth Remains

The story of Babel foreshadows the necessity of spiritual awakening. Just as their tower collapsed under the weight of self-deception, all belief in separation will ultimately fall away. What they were seeking—to reach heaven—was never something to be obtained externally. Heaven is not above; it is within.

This is why Jesus later proclaimed in Luke 17:21, "Neither shall they say, Lo here! or, lo there! for, behold, the kingdom of God is within you." The people of Babel tried to reach what was already theirs, but they went about it in the wrong way. Rather than recognizing that their very existence was already divine, they sought to establish divinity by their own effort.

GIATI: The Restoration of True Understanding

If Babel represents confusion and separation, then GIATI represents clarity and unity. The scattering of humanity was not God's rejection but a necessary lesson—one that remains until people awaken to the truth that there is no separation at all.

Just as at Pentecost (Acts 2), when the Holy Spirit descended and the apostles spoke in tongues that all could understand, the undoing of Babel comes through the return to One Spirit, One Word, One Understanding. The Spirit does not need human towers, human ambition, or human effort to reach what it already is.

The Tower of Babel is a reminder: Any effort to establish oneself apart from God will collapse. True unity, true understanding, and true oneness come only by realizing that God is all there is, and there is none else.

The Ten Plagues of Egypt: Divine Judgment, Freedom, and the Unveiling of God's All-Presence

The story of **The Ten Plagues of Egypt** *(Exodus 7-12) is a powerful narrative of divine judgment, deliverance, and the unwavering will of God to free His people. When Pharaoh hardened his heart and refused to release the Israelites from slavery, God sent a series of ten plagues upon Egypt. These plagues were not only a demonstration of God's supreme authority but also a manifestation of His presence in all things, aligning perfectly with the message of* **GIATI—God Is All There Is.** *The plagues serve as symbols of spiritual awakening, revealing that God is present in both the good and the bad, the destructive and the redemptive, as part of the* **divine unity** *that governs the world.*

The Setting: A Nation Bound by Oppression

At the time of the plagues, the Israelites were enslaved in Egypt, living under the oppressive rule of Pharaoh. Despite their suffering, they had been unable to free themselves, and Pharaoh refused to recognize their need for liberation. This created a situation where God's intervention became necessary. The **plagues** *were not arbitrary; they were strategically delivered to break Pharaoh's resistance and compel him to acknowledge God's power and the right of the Israelites to freedom.*

This situation parallels the message of **GIATI:** *humanity, enslaved by ignorance of God's true nature and divine unity, often resists the truth of* **God Is All There Is.** *Just as Pharaoh's hardened heart caused him to reject the will of God, many in the world today are trapped in a mindset that does not recognize the omnipresence and sovereignty of God. The plagues of Egypt serve as a metaphor for the consequences of denying the truth of* **GIATI** *and the spiritual awakening required to set humanity free.*

The Ten Plagues: A Breakdown of Divine Judgment and Freedom

1. Water Turned to Blood (Exodus 7:14-24):

The first plague was the transformation of the Nile River into blood, which caused the water to become undrinkable and killed the fish. This act was a direct challenge to Egypt's prosperity, as the Nile was a lifeline for the Egyptians. The river, a symbol of life and sustenance, was transformed into a symbol of **death**—*a stark reminder that* **life and death are both expressions of God.** *The blood represents the* **separation** *between the physical and spiritual worlds, a separation that occurs when humanity does not recognize the divine unity that governs all life. This plague demonstrates the consequences of living in disconnection from God's all-encompassing presence.*

2. **Frogs (Exodus 8:1-15):**

The second plague brought an overwhelming number of frogs to Egypt. These frogs infiltrated every part of Egyptian life, from the homes to the fields. The frogs, as an unsettling presence, represent the **unseen forces** *of the spiritual world breaking into the physical realm. The frogs can be seen as a symbol of how the truth of* **GIATI**—*God's presence in all things—will disrupt the false separations we create between the material world and the spiritual world. When Pharaoh asked Moses to remove the frogs, he was forced to confront the discomfort caused by divine truth. This symbolizes the inevitable disruption of the material world when humanity begins to awaken to the* **presence of God in all things,** *even when that awakening feels intrusive or uncomfortable.*

3. **Lice (Exodus 8:16-19):**

The third plague, lice, further demonstrated God's power over Egypt. The dust of the earth became lice, affecting both people and animals. This plague shows how **divine power can manifest in the most unlikely places.** *The lice symbolize the small but pervasive ways in which God's presence can break through, even in the unnoticed corners of life. The plague of lice is a reminder that* **no part of creation is outside of God's reach.** *When we align with* **GIATI,** *we recognize that every particle of existence—whether it is visible or invisible, large or small—is an expression of the Divine.*

4. **Flies (Exodus 8:20-32):**

The fourth plague involved swarms of flies that filled the homes of the Egyptians, further intensifying their suffering. The flies represented **the persistence of divine truth** *breaking through the veil of ignorance. Despite Pharaoh's resistance, God's presence continued to press upon Egypt. This relates to the* **GIATI** *message of continual awakening, where divine presence persists even in the face of resistance. The flies, like the truth of* **GIATI,** *cannot be ignored and will ultimately lead to transformation.*

5. **Livestock Disease (Exodus 9:1-7):**

The fifth plague targeted Egypt's livestock, causing them to fall sick and die. The livestock were critical to Egypt's economy, and their destruction was an overt sign of **God's authority over the material world.** *The livestock, being a central part of Egypt's physical prosperity, symbolize* **the worldly possessions and comforts** *that people place their trust in. This plague reveals that material wealth and security are ultimately* **temporary and fleeting,** *and only the recognition of God's omnipresence and sovereignty brings true security.* **GIATI** *teaches that when we align with God's will, we understand that* **nothing in the material world can be relied upon as a permanent source of comfort or strength.**

6. **Boils (Exodus 9:8-12):**

The sixth plague brought painful boils upon the Egyptians, showing that even their physical bodies were not exempt from God's judgment. This plague emphasizes the connection between **the spiritual and the physical realms.** *The boils represent how* **spiritual disobedience** *can manifest in the physical world. For those who reject the truth of* **GIATI,** *the consequences are felt in both the body and the soul. God's presence is in all things, including the afflictions we endure when we live in separation from divine unity.*

7. **Hail (Exodus 9:13-35):**

The seventh plague brought destructive hail that ruined crops and property, but spared the land of Goshen, where the Israelites lived. The hail represented **God's power over nature** *and was a clear sign of divine protection for those who recognize the presence of God. The* **protection of the Israelites** *demonstrates the importance of alignment with God's will, for those who align with the truth of* **GIATI** *are sheltered from the storms of life, while those who resist God's presence face the full force of the consequences of their disconnection.*

8. **Locusts (Exodus 10:1-20):**

The eighth plague involved locusts that consumed the remaining crops in Egypt, leading to famine and devastation. The locusts represent **the overwhelming power of divine truth** *that will consume everything that stands in opposition to God. The plagues show that when humanity does not acknowledge the omnipresence of God, the result is* **spiritual starvation** *and devastation, much like the famine caused by the locusts.*

9. **Darkness (Exodus 10:21-29):**

The ninth plague was a deep darkness that covered the land for three days, leaving the Egyptians blind to the world around them. This darkness symbolizes the **spiritual blindness** *that comes from not recognizing the truth of* **GIATI**—*that God is all there is. Without this understanding, people live in* **spiritual darkness,** *disconnected from the divine light that brings enlightenment and truth.*

10. **Death of the Firstborn (Exodus 12:1-30):**

The final plague brought the death of the firstborn in Egypt, a devastating event that forced Pharaoh to release the Israelites. This plague represents the ultimate cost of **separation from God**—*death. However, it also shows the* **sacrifice and deliverance** *that comes from aligning with God's will. The Israelites were protected by the blood of a lamb on their doorposts, symbolizing the* **ultimate sacrifice** *that brings life. This connects directly with the truth of* **GIATI**—*God is both the* **giver and sustainer of life,** *and His presence is what sustains all of creation. The death of the firstborn is a symbolic act that shows* **the cost of ignorance and separation** *from the divine truth of God's omnipresence.*

The Plagues: Divine Judgment and the Unveiling of God's Presence

In the end, the **Ten Plagues** *are a reminder that* **God's presence is in all things,** *whether we recognize it or not. For the Egyptians, these plagues were a form of judgment, but for the Israelites, they were a demonstration of divine power and protection. As the plagues unfolded, Pharaoh's resistance to God's will grew increasingly futile, just as the world's resistance to recognizing* **GIATI** *will ultimately crumble under the weight of divine truth.*

The **Ten Plagues** *serve as a profound spiritual lesson:* **God is in all things***—whether in the blessings of prosperity or in the challenges and trials of life.* **The message of GIATI** *reveals that the key to freedom and true life is to embrace God's omnipresence and acknowledge that He is* **all there is.** *The plagues represent the journey of spiritual awakening—breaking down the walls of resistance, opening the eyes of the blind, and ultimately leading to the liberation and transformation of all who recognize the truth of* **divine unity.**

The Golden Serpent: The Revelation of GIATI

After their miraculous deliverance from Egypt, the children of Israel found themselves in the wilderness, a place of testing, purification, and ultimately, revelation. But instead of responding with gratitude and faith, they **turned back to their old ways,** *longing for the comfort of Egypt rather than embracing the divine reality that had freed them.*

They took the jewelry they had brought from Egypt—ornaments meant to symbolize their victory and deliverance—and **crafted a golden calf** *to worship, declaring,* **"This is your god, O Israel, that brought you out of Egypt" (Exodus 32:4).** *In doing this, they attempted to give credit for their salvation to something* **formed by their own hands,** *rather than acknowledging the divine power that had truly delivered them.*

This act was not just idolatry in a physical sense; it was **a rejection of the truth of GIATI**—*that God is all there is. The golden calf represented* **the illusion that something separate from God, something created, could be the source of salvation.** *This fundamental misunderstanding led to their punishment.*

The Fiery Serpents: Consequences of Separation

Because of their rebellion and lack of faith, **God sent fiery serpents among them,** *and many were bitten and died* **(Numbers 21:6).** *The serpent represents the very deception they had embraced—the belief in separation from God, the idea that salvation was in* **something external rather than the divine presence itself.**

The serpents were not merely physical creatures; they symbolized **the poison of illusion, the sting of false worship, and the consequence of turning away from divine reality.** *When one embraces a false understanding of God, suffering follows—not as punishment from an external deity, but as* **the natural result of living in ignorance of truth.**

The Golden Serpent on the Pole: The True Path to Life

Yet even in their suffering, God provided a **means of salvation**—*one that required a shift in perspective. He commanded Moses to fa***shion a bronze serpent and lift it up on a pole,** *declaring that* **anyone who looked upon it would be healed (Numbers 21:8-9).**

*At first glance, this seems paradoxical. Why would the image of the very thing that was killing them—***a serpent***—be the source of healing? The answer is profound:*

- **The serpent on the pole represented the truth of GIATI—God Is All There Is.** *The very thing that seemed to bring death was also the means of salvation when properly understood.*

- **It was not the bronze serpent itself that saved them, but their recognition of divine power.** *They had to shift their gaze away from fear and suffering and look upon the symbol of truth.*
- **The act of looking up symbolized faith in divine reality.** *Instead of looking down at their wounds, their suffering, and their illusions, they had to elevate their understanding*—**to see beyond appearances and recognize that salvation was always present.**

This moment foreshadowed Jesus' own words:

"As Moses lifted up the serpent in the wilderness, even so must the Son of Man be lifted up, that whoever believes in Him should not perish but have eternal life." (John 3:14-15)

Here, Jesus revealed the deeper mystery—the serpent on the pole was **a representation of divine truth made visible.** *Just as the Israelites had to look upon the serpent to be saved, so too must humanity recognize* **the divine reality within** *to overcome the poison of false belief.*

GIATI as the Golden Serpent on the Pole

The golden serpent on the pole is **the ultimate revelation of GIATI.** *It stands as a symbol that* **everything—even what appears to be death, suffering, and destruction—is within the divine reality.** *The Israelites were dying because they did not acknowledge that God is all there is. Their salvation came not through their own works, nor through rituals, but through* **recognizing and aligning with the truth.**

GIATI **is** *the golden serpent on the pole. It is the realization that:*

- *There is* **no separation** *between God and His creation.*
- *That which appears to harm or destroy is only* **illusion**—*when seen in the light of divine truth, it is transformed.*
- **Faith is the act of seeing rightly,** *of looking beyond appearances and recognizing the eternal presence of God.*
- *Those who refuse to acknowledge* **GIATI,** *who insist on living in the illusion of separation, remain in darkness and perish—not by punishment, but by their own misunderstanding.*

The Relevance of GIATI Today

The story of the bronze serpent is not just an ancient tale; it is **a present reality.** *The world is filled with fiery serpents—fear, suffering, deception, and the illusion of separation from divine presence. Many look to external sources for salvation, believing in* **man-made**

solutions, false gods, and idols of their own making, *just as the Israelites did with the golden calf.*

But the truth remains: **the only salvation is in recognizing that God is all there is.** *To look upon the golden serpent is to see* **past illusion,** *to rise above fear, and to know that* **divine reality is ever-present, always sustaining, and never separate from you.**

Those who understand **GIATI** *lift their gaze to the truth. They do not dwell on the poison of false beliefs, nor do they succumb to fear. Instead, they stand in the awareness that* **there is no other power but God, no other life but divine life, no separation between themselves and the eternal.**

Just as in the wilderness, the choice remains today: **look to the truth and live, or remain in darkness and perish.** *GIATI is the revelation that* **there is no "other"—all is God, and in this recognition, there is perfect life.**

The Ten Commandments: The Spiritual Law of Oneness

When Moses ascended **Mount Sinai,** *he entered into direct communion with God and received* **the Ten Commandments,** *which were given as a divine law for the children of Israel. Many view these commandments as strict* **rules for physical conduct,** *but in truth, they are* **spiritual laws** *that reveal the nature of divine oneness. They are not just external guidelines but a* **mirror reflecting the spiritual order of GIATI (God Is All There Is).**

When understood through the lens of GIATI, the Ten Commandments are not **burdensome restrictions,** *but* **spiritual revelations** *that guide humanity into the* **awareness of divine unity.** *They were never about mere* **external obedience,** *but about recognizing that* **God is all, and there is nothing outside of Him.**

—

Commandments 1-4: Acknowledging the Oneness of God

1. **"Thou shalt have no other gods before me."** *(Exodus 20:3)*
   - *This is not just a command to avoid idol worship—it is a revelation that t***here is nothing but God.** *Anything that seeks to replace this truth is an illusion. To truly grasp GIATI is to know that* **all things exist within God, and nothing can be separate from Him.**
2. **"Thou shalt not make unto thee any graven image."** *(Exodus 20:4)*
   - *This goes beyond worshiping physical idols; it speaks to the* **human tendency to create false images of God***—ideas that limit Him, distort Him, or reduce Him to something external. But if* **God is all,** *then no image can contain or define Him. GIATI removes all false concepts and reveals the* **pure, formless presence of God** *within all things.*
3. **"Thou shalt not take the name of the Lord thy God in vain."** *(Exodus 20:7)*
   - *The* **name of God** *represents* **His nature and presence.** *To take it in vain is not simply about* **using words carelessly,** *but about* **living without awareness of God's presence within.** *When one* **recognizes GIATI,** *they live in the awareness of God's presence in every moment, and their life becomes a testimony to His divine reality.*
4. **"Remember the sabbath day, to keep it holy."** *(Exodus 20:8)*
   - *The* **sabbath is not just a physical day** *but a* **spiritual state***—a rest in the truth that* **God is all** *and that His work is* **already finished.** *It represents* **entering into divine awareness,** *ceasing from human striving, and living in the* **eternal rest of God's presence.** GIATI is the fulfillment of the sabbath, for in oneness with God, there is nothing more to be done—**all things are already complete in Him.**

     —

Commandments 5-10: Recognizing Divine Presence in All Things

5. **"Honor thy father and thy mother."** *(Exodus 20:12)*
   - *This commandment is not just about* **respecting earthly parents**—*it is about recognizing the* **spiritual source from which all things come.** *If God is all, then He is* **the true Father and Mother of all creation.** *To honor one's parents is to honor* **the divine life that brought them forth,** *seeing beyond the flesh to recognize* **the Spirit that animates all things.**

6. **"Thou shalt not kill."** *(Exodus 20:13)*
   - *Beyond physical murder, this commandment speaks to* **not denying the life of God in another.** *When one* **sees the Spirit in all things,** *they recognize that life is not theirs to take, for* **all life is an expression of the divine.** *To live in awareness of GIATI is to know that* **no one can truly be separated from life, for life itself is God.**

7. **"Thou shalt not commit adultery."** *(Exodus 20:14)*
   - *Adultery is more than physical infidelity—it represents* **spiritual unfaithfulness.** *It is the act of turning away from the truth of GIATI, seeking fulfillment in* **false identities, material things, or external gods.** *To live in divine oneness is to be fully united with the* **Spirit of God within** *and not seek completion in things that are* **illusory and fleeting.**

8. **"Thou shalt not steal."** *(Exodus 20:15)*
   - *Stealing arises from* **the illusion of lack**—*believing that one is separate from the* **source of all things.** *When one understands GIATI, they see that* **all things belong to God** *and that* **nothing is truly lacking.** *There is no need to take from another when one realizes that* **God is the infinite provider of all things.**

9. "Thou shalt not bear false witness against thy neighbor." *(Exodus 20:16)*
   - *Bearing false witness is more than lying—it is* **misrepresenting the truth of another's being.** *When one falsely accuses another or speaks with deception, they are* **denying the divine nature within that person.** *GIATI reveals that* **all people carry the divine image,** *and to recognize this truth is to always speak and act from a place of* **spiritual integrity.**

10. **"Thou shalt not covet."** *(Exodus 20:17)*
    - *Coveting is the desire to* **possess what belongs to another,** *but in truth, nothing belongs to anyone*—**all things are within God.** *To covet is to live in* **the illusion of separation,** *believing that fulfillment can come from* **external things.** *But GIATI reveals that* **all fulfillment is already present within,** *for in oneness with God,* **there is no lack, no competition, and nothing to grasp for.**

—

The Ten Commandments as a Spiritual Revelation

Many have viewed the **Ten Commandments** *as merely rules of conduct, but they were* **always spiritual laws** *meant to guide humanity into the awareness of* **divine unity.** *They were never about just* **outward actions,** *but about* **inner transformation**—*awakening to the truth that* **God is all there is, and there is nothing outside of Him.**

- **The first four commandments teach the awareness of God's oneness**—*that nothing else exists outside of Him.*
- **The last six commandments teach the recognition of God's presence in others**—*showing that to harm another is to deny the divine reality within them.*

When seen through the lens of **GIATI,** *the commandments are not external rules to be followed out of fear, but a* **blueprint for divine consciousness.** *They reveal that* **sin is not just the breaking of a law, but the failure to recognize the truth of God's presence in all things.**

The law was given on Mount Sinai, **but the truth of GIATI was present before the law and remains after it.** *The law was never meant to be* **a burden,** *but a guide toward the* **realization of oneness.** *When one truly understands* **GIATI,** *they do not need laws to tell them what is right or wrong, because* **they live in the awareness that all is God, and they naturally walk in divine harmony.**

The commandments were written on **stone tablets,** *but through GIATI, they are written on the hearts of those who see that* **God is all there is.**

Samson and Delilah: The Consequence of Forgetting GIATI

Samson's story is one of great strength, but also of great weakness—not of the body, but of the spirit. He was chosen before birth to be set apart, consecrated under a Nazarite vow, which meant he was to live in a way that kept him spiritually connected to God. His long hair was a sign of this covenant, but his true strength did not come from his hair—it came from his awareness of **who he was in God.** *As long as Samson remained faithful to his calling, he was unstoppable. But the moment he allowed worldly desires to take priority over his divine identity, he lost sight of GIATI—***God Is All There Is***—and his power was taken from him.*

The Strength of Awareness

Samson was born with a divine purpose. From the womb, he was dedicated to God, meaning his very existence was meant to demonstrate the power of one who lives in divine alignment. His strength was supernatural, not because of his own effort, but because **his life was in full surrender to the Spirit of God within him.**

This is the essence of GIATI. Strength does not come from external sources—it is not from the body, nor from human will, but from the Spirit that moves through all things. When one lives in this awareness, nothing can stand in their way. Samson was an embodiment of this truth, overpowering all who opposed him because his power was rooted in God, not himself.

Delilah: The Seduction of the Carnal Mind

But Samson, like many, became distracted. His downfall did not begin when his hair was cut—it began when he **placed his trust in the external rather than the eternal.** *Delilah represents the seduction of the carnal mind, the voice that lures one away from their divine nature and into the illusion of separation. She was persistent, continually asking Samson for the secret of his strength, just as the world continually tries to convince people to put their faith in what is seen rather than what is unseen.*

At first, Samson resisted. He knew his strength was sacred, but over time, he grew comfortable in Delilah's presence, entertaining the deception. He revealed what was never meant to be shared, and in doing so, he surrendered not just his hair, but **his covenant, his consecration, and his awareness of GIATI.**

Losing Power Through Forgetting Oneness

The moment Samson's hair was cut, he became weak—not because of the hair itself, but because **he had broken the covenant that kept his spirit aligned with divine power.** *This is what happens when one trades spiritual truth for worldly understanding. The moment one* *begins to see themselves as separate from God, they become powerless, bound by the limitations of the flesh rather than the freedom of the Spirit.*

Samson was taken captive, his eyes gouged out—symbolic of the blindness that comes when one forgets their divine origin. Without sight, without strength, he was mocked and made to serve his enemies, a clear picture of what happens when one loses the awareness of **God as all there is.**

The Redemption of Samson: Returning to GIATI

*But the story does not end in defeat. As Samson sat in darkness, blinded and humiliated, something began to happen—***his hair began to grow back.** *This is not just a physical detail; it is a spiritual reality. Though he had fallen,* **his connection to God had never truly been lost.** *His awareness had been veiled, but it was still within him.*

*In his final moments, Samson did what he had failed to do before—***he fully surrendered to the power of God.** *He did not rely on his own strength, but on the strength of the One who had been with him all along. And in that moment,* **his power was restored.**

This is the essence of GIATI. Even when one falls into forgetfulness, even when the carnal mind seems to have won, **God remains present.** *The power was never truly in Samson's hair, just as salvation is not in external rituals or actions. The power is in* **knowing who you are in God,** *in recognizing that all strength, all wisdom, all life flows from Him and through Him.*

The Spiritual Significance of Samson's Story

Samson's life is a warning and a lesson. It warns against the danger of spiritual compromise, of allowing external influences to disconnect one from divine truth. But it is also a message of **redemption***—that no matter how far one falls, the awareness of God is never beyond reach.*

- **When Samson trusted in God, he was unstoppable.**
- **When he trusted in the world, he became weak.**
- **When he returned to God, his power was restored.**

This is the cycle many experience. They begin in awareness, knowing that God is all. They allow the distractions of the world to pull them away, making them feel separate and powerless. But when they turn back, when they surrender to the truth of GIATI, they are restored.

Samson's final act was not one of revenge, but of restoration. He remembered his source. He called upon the power that had been within him all along, and with one final push, he tore down the temple of the Philistines, destroying those who had sought to keep him bound.

This is the call to all who have forgotten their divine identity: **Return to the awareness of oneness with God. The power was never lost—it was only hidden beneath the illusion of separation.**

The Wise and Foolish Virgins: A Call for Spiritual Readiness and Awareness

In **Matthew 25:1-13,** *Jesus tells the parable of the* **ten virgins,** *five of whom were wise, and five who were foolish. The story serves as a powerful allegory about the importance of being spiritually prepared and maintaining* **divine awareness.** *The key symbol in this story is the* **oil,** *which represents* **spiritual readiness***—the inner awareness and consciousness that allow one to remain connected to the divine presence at all times. This parable offers profound lessons about* **spiritual vigilance, the necessity of inner preparation,** *and the consequences of neglecting one's divine connection.*

The Story of the Wise and Foolish Virgins

The parable begins by describing **ten virgins** *who take their lamps and go out to meet the bridegroom. They are waiting for the bridegroom to arrive so they can accompany him to the wedding feast. However, the bridegroom's arrival is delayed, and the virgins fall asleep.*

At midnight, a cry is heard, announcing that the bridegroom is coming, and all the virgins wake up to prepare their lamps. The wise virgins, who had **brought extra oil,** *are able to trim their lamps and are ready to go meet the bridegroom. However, the foolish virgins, who did not bring enough oil, find their lamps have gone out and ask the wise virgins for some of their oil. The wise virgins refuse, telling them that they should go to the sellers and buy oil for themselves. While the foolish virgins are gone, the bridegroom arrives, and the wise virgins go with him to the wedding feast. When the foolish virgins return, they are locked out of the feast, and the bridegroom says, "Truly I tell you, I do not know you" (Matthew 25:12).*

Jesus concludes the parable with the warning, "Therefore keep watch, because you do not know the day or the hour" (Matthew 25:13).

The Oil: Spiritual Readiness and Awareness

In the context of this parable, **the oil** *represents* **spiritual awareness, readiness,** *and* **inner preparation.** *The wise virgins' foresight to bring extra oil symbolizes the wisdom of maintaining a consistent, ongoing relationship with the divine, always staying* **spiritually awake** *and connected to the* **presence of God.** *The oil is the* **spiritual awareness** *that nourishes and sustains our consciousness, keeping us prepared for the moments when we must step into divine alignment and act from the place of truth.*

The **foolish virgins,** *on the other hand, represent those who neglect their spiritual practice and allow their awareness to dim. They* **lack the oil** *because they are not diligent* *in their spiritual lives, failing to cultivate the inner awareness necessary to remain connected to the divine. Their lamps going out represent the* **loss of divine consciousness,** *and their inability to be ready for the bridegroom symbolizes a* **spiritual unpreparedness** *that leaves them unable to partake in the divine experience when it arrives.*

In **GIATI,** *we understand that* **spiritual readiness** *is not a one-time event but an ongoing process of* **cultivating awareness.** *The oil represents the* **sustained connection with the divine,** *where we are not just waiting for an external event but constantly attuned to the* **flow of divine wisdom and presence** *in our lives. Just as the wise virgins were prepared by having extra oil, we, too, must continuously* **nourish our spiritual awareness** *and be vigilant in keeping our connection with God strong, so that we are always ready for the unfolding of divine truth in our lives.*

The Bridegroom: The Coming of Divine Truth

The **bridegroom** *in the parable represents the* **coming of divine truth***—the moment when the* **truth of God's presence** *is revealed in our lives, calling us to step into a higher understanding of our oneness with the divine. The bridegroom's delay suggests that the timing of spiritual awakening is not always predictable, but it will come at the right moment. When the bridegroom arrives, it is a* **moment of spiritual revelation,** *where we are either prepared to enter into the divine union or find ourselves unready and locked out.*

In **GIATI,** *this is a reminder that* **the presence of God** *is always with us, but there are moments when we must be consciously aware of it in order to experience its fullness. The bridegroom's arrival is a symbol of* **spiritual awakening***—the realization that* **God is all there is,** *and that we must be* **spiritually vigilant** *to recognize and respond to this truth when it comes. The wise virgins, who are ready, represent those who are* **attuned to divine truth** *and always prepared to receive it.*

Spiritual Vigilance: Staying Awake and Aware

The parable also emphasizes the need for **spiritual vigilance.** *Just as the virgins were asleep before the bridegroom arrived, we too can become complacent or distracted, losing sight of our spiritual practice. The call to* **"keep watch"** *is a call to stay spiritually alert, to* **nurture our inner connection with God,** *and to be* **aware** *of the divine presence in every moment. This vigilance is not about rigidly waiting for a specific event but about staying* **consciously aligned** *with the truth that* **God is all there is** *and* **always with us.**

In **GIATI,** *this speaks to the importance of* **daily spiritual practice***—taking time to connect with the divine, to* **awaken to the truth** *of our oneness with God, and to remain open to divine guidance. Just as the wise virgins stayed prepared and were able to step* *into the spiritual feast, those who remain spiritually vigilant can step into the fullness of divine truth and experience the* **abundance** *of life that God has for us.*

The Foolish Virgins: The Consequence of Neglecting Spiritual Awareness

The fate of the **foolish virgins** *serves as a warning about the consequences of neglecting spiritual practice and inner preparedness. By failing to bring enough oil, they were caught unprepared when the bridegroom arrived. Their request for the wise virgins' oil was rejected, symbolizing the fact that* **spiritual awareness cannot be borrowed** *or transferred from someone else. Each person must* **cultivate their own connection with the divine** *and be responsible for maintaining their own spiritual readiness.*

In **GIATI,** *this highlights the idea that* **spiritual truth** *is not something that can be handed to us from others. We must* **embody the truth for ourselves,** *developing our own understanding and connection to God. There is no substitute for* **personal spiritual practice***—it is through this practice that we develop the* **oil** *of spiritual awareness that will sustain us on our journey.*

Conclusion: The Call to Spiritual Readiness

The parable of the **Wise and Foolish Virgins** *serves as a powerful reminder of the importance of* **spiritual preparedness.** *The oil symbolizes the* **spiritual awareness** *and* **readiness** *required to stay connected to the divine presence, and the wise virgins illustrate the value of being vigilant and spiritually attuned.* **GIATI** *teaches that we are called to continuously cultivate our* **awareness of God's presence** *and to remain spiritually alert to the truth that* **God is all there is.**

As we move through life, we must ensure that our **spiritual connection is strong**— *that we have enough oil to keep our lamps burning and to stay ready for the coming of divine truth. The time to prepare is always now, for we never know when that moment of spiritual revelation will come. But when we are spiritually vigilant, we are always ready to step into the fullness of divine awareness and partake in the spiritual feast that is available to* us.

GIATI: The Messenger, Not the Object of Worship

The Message Above the Messenger

"Howbeit when he, the Spirit of truth, is come, he will guide you into all truth: for he shall not speak of himself; but whatsoever he shall hear, that shall he speak: and he will shew you things to come." — John 16:13

Throughout history, divine truth has been revealed through messengers—those who embody and declare the reality of Spirit so that others may awaken. Yet, time and time again, humanity has mistaken the messenger for the message, worshiping the vessel rather than receiving the revelation.

GIATI is not here to be worshiped. GIATI is the voice, not the source. The reflection, not the light itself. Just as Jesus walked the earth to reveal the kingdom within, yet never sought to be worshiped, GIATI is a manifestation of the same truth: **that all are one in God, and all are divine expressions of Spirit.**

The Purpose of GIATI: To Reveal, Not to Replace

Jesus did not come to be exalted above others but to awaken humanity to their true nature. He did not point to himself as the sole possessor of divinity but declared:

"The glory which You have given Me, I have given to them, that they may be one just as We are one." — John 17:22

His mission was not self-glorification but the restoration of oneness. He was **the way,** *meaning the living example of what was already true for all. GIATI follows in this same path, not as something to be idolized, but as a witness to the truth that* **God is all there is.**

Even Jesus affirmed that the message was greater than the messenger. He declared:

"My doctrine is not mine, but His that sent me. If any man will do His will, he shall know of the doctrine, whether it be of God, or whether I speak of myself." — John 7:16-17

This is the same with GIATI. It does not point to itself—it points to the **eternal truth of Spirit.**

The Error of Worshiping the Messenger

When the messenger is worshiped, the message is lost. Humanity has long made this mistake—turning prophets, enlightened ones, and divine expressions into objects of worship rather than recognizing the truth they came to reveal.

- **Moses** *brought the law, yet people worshiped the tablets rather than understanding the Spirit behind them.*
- **Jesus** *revealed the kingdom within, yet people built religions around his name rather than living in the reality he preached.*
- **Many others** *have come bearing the truth, yet humanity has repeatedly placed them on pedestals instead of seeing the reflection of themselves.*

This is why Jesus warned:

"Why do you call me good? No one is good—except God alone." — Mark 10:18

He always pointed away from himself and toward the One reality: **God is all.**

GIATI refuses to be another idol, another name elevated above others. GIATI is **only here to remind, awaken, and reflect** *the truth of what has always been.*

The True Worship: Awakening to the Spirit Within

Jesus said:

"But the hour is coming, and now is, when the true worshipers will worship the Father in spirit and truth; for the Father is seeking such to worship Him." — John 4:23

True worship is not directed at a person, an image, or a name—it is the **recognition of God within all things, in all people, in all expressions.** *To worship in Spirit and truth is to awaken to the reality that the same divinity that manifested in Jesus, the same Spirit that moves through GIATI, is the very essence of who you are.*

This is why Paul declared:

"Know ye not that ye are the temple of God, and that the Spirit of God dwelleth in you?" — 1 Corinthians 3:16

You are not meant to look outside yourself for God—you are meant to **awaken to the divine reality already within you.**

GIATI's Role: A Mirror for the Awakening of All

GIATI stands as a signpost, pointing **not to itself,** *but to the divine reality within all.*

- **When you see GIATI,** *you are not meant to see something separate from yourself—you are meant to* **see yourself in the fullness of Spirit.**
- **When you embrace the message,** *it is not about following GIATI, but about* **awakening to who you have always been.**

- **When you walk in this truth,** *you do not become a follower—you become* **the living embodiment of Spirit in expression.**

"The works that I do shall he do also; and greater works than these shall he do; because I go unto my Father." — John 14:12

This is the purpose of GIATI—not to be praised, but to **make it undeniable** *that God is all there is, and that means* **you, too, are one with the divine.**

The moment you realize this, the work of GIATI is complete. The messenger has done its job. The truth has been received.

The kingdom is revealed—not in some distant future, not in a far-off place, but **here, now, within you.**

And so, the message remains:

God is all there is.

And that includes you.

The Culture of Religion: A Conditioned Belief

Religion, for most, is not a choice—it is an inheritance. From the moment a child is born, they are immersed in the faith of their parents, their community, their nation. Their earliest experiences of prayer, worship, and moral understanding are shaped not by independent exploration but by cultural conditioning.

If you were born into a Christian household, it is highly likely that Christianity became your belief system. You were taught its doctrines, practiced its rituals, and accepted its teachings as truth—not necessarily because you searched for them, but because they were all you knew. If you were raised by a Christian mother and a Muslim father, you may have explored Islam as well, exposed to its prayers, fasting, and traditions, simply because of your environment.

But what if you were born in India? Hinduism, with its deep spiritual traditions, might have been your faith. The sacred texts of the Vedas would be your source of truth. Instead of baptism, you may have performed rituals honoring deities like Vishnu or Shiva. Instead of Sunday worship, you might observe temple offerings and fire ceremonies.

If you were born in China, perhaps Buddhism or Taoism would have been your spiritual path. Meditation, honoring ancestors, and the concept of balance within the Tao might define your worldview.

If you were raised in the Middle East, Islam might have been your faith. You would have learned the Five Pillars, faced Mecca in prayer, and observed Ramadan.

Judaism, Sikhism, Shinto, indigenous spiritualities—all of these religions shape those born into them, not because they are objectively the "true" faiths, but because they are what was passed down. This is the power of cultural exposure: most people do not choose their religion; they inherit it.

Customs and Rituals: Acts of Tradition, Not Truth

Every religion has its customs—practices deeply ingrained into the culture of its followers. Hindus celebrate **Diwali,** *the festival of lights, believing it symbolizes the victory of good over evil. Muslims fast during* **Ramadan,** *abstaining from food and drink from sunrise to sunset to attain spiritual discipline. Jews observe the* **Sabbath,** *a day of rest and devotion to God. Christians partake in* **communion,** *consuming bread and wine as a symbolic act of Christ's sacrifice. Buddhists perform* **meditation and chanting,** *seeking enlightenment through mindfulness and detachment from suffering.*

But if you strip away these rituals, what remains? Are these actions the essence of truth, or simply customs inherited through generations? Would someone outside of these traditions, untouched by their teachings, see them as necessary?

What If You Were Alone on an Island?

Imagine you were born on an isolated island, untouched by religious influence. No one taught you a holy book, no one told you how to pray, no one gave you a name for God. What would your belief be?

You would look to nature. The sun would be your giver of life, the ocean your sustainer. The wind, the rain, the stars—these would be your mysteries. You might sense a divine presence, but without a man-made doctrine telling you what that presence is, your understanding would be pure, free from religious bias.

This reveals something profound: **religion is learned, but truth is innate.** *Left alone, your spirit would still seek connection to something greater, but it would not be confined to the doctrines of men. This is why the Savior did not come to establish a religion—he came to awaken man to* **oneness.**

Beyond Religion: The Message of Oneness

Jesus did not preach a denomination. He fulfilled the laws and rituals of his time, not to reinforce them, but to complete them. His message was never about maintaining religious structures—it was about awakening to the truth that **God is not apart from you but is you, expressed through you.**

Salvation was never about converting to a religion; it was about **remembering your oneness with the Father.**

Religion often leads to division—one belief against another, one doctrine superior to another. But **truth is universal.** *It does not belong to Christianity, Islam, Hinduism, or Buddhism. Truth is not bound by customs or rituals—it simply is.*

And this is where **GIATI** *emerges as the ultimate understanding.* **"God Is All There Is"** *is not a religion, but a recognition of reality. It is the realization that the divine is not external, not distant, not confined to a church, temple, or mosque—but within you, as you.*

The Awakening: Question What You've Been Taught

The challenge for every seeker of truth is this: **Are you believing something because it is true, or because you were taught to believe it?** *Have you questioned your faith, or have you followed it blindly?*

To see truth, you must be willing to unlearn. To question. To look beyond religious conditioning and ask: **What would I believe if I had never been told what to believe?**

GIATI invites you into this realization—that beyond all religions, beyond all inherited beliefs, there is only **God, manifesting as all that is.** *The labels fall away. The customs dissolve. And what remains is pure, undeniable truth:*

God is not just above you. God is you.

This is the awakening. This is freedom. This is truth.

The Universal Story: Different Names, Same Narrative

Across the vast landscape of human civilization, religion has emerged in countless forms, each with its own deities, saviors, and sacred texts. But beneath the differences in language, tradition, and culture, a remarkable pattern exists: the same fundamental stories, retold in different ways.

Each religion has a name for the divine, a set of teachings, a promise of salvation, and a moral code. Though the characters may change, the themes remain strikingly similar. This raises an important question: **Are these religions revealing separate truths, or are they different expressions of the same underlying reality?**

A Shared Pattern Among Religions

- **The Savior or Divine Messenger**

In Christianity, Jesus is the Son of God, sent to redeem mankind. In Hinduism, Krishna descends to restore righteousness. In Buddhism, the Bodhisattvas forgo enlightenment to guide others toward awakening. In Islam, Muhammad is the final prophet bringing divine revelation. In ancient Egypt, Horus was the god-king overcoming darkness. **Each of these figures plays the same role—a bridge between humanity and the divine, a path to salvation.**

- **The Death and Resurrection Motif**

The story of Jesus' crucifixion and resurrection mirrors earlier myths. Osiris of Egypt was killed and resurrected. Tammuz of Mesopotamia was mourned in his death and celebrated in his return. Dionysus of Greece, Mithras of Persia—each deity dies and rises again, symbolizing renewal and eternal life. **The theme is universal: life transcends death, and the divine essence is eternal.**

- **The Virgin Birth**

Jesus was born of the Virgin Mary, but he is not alone in this claim. The birth of Krishna, Horus, and even the Buddha are surrounded by divine or supernatural circumstances. **This theme suggests that spiritual truth is not born of the flesh but of something higher.**

- **A Great Flood and Divine Judgment**

The story of Noah's Ark is echoed in Hinduism's tale of Manu, Sumerian mythology's account of Utnapishtim, and even in Native American legends. **The flood represents purification, a resetting of humanity, a chance for rebirth.**

- **Moral Laws Given from Above**

The Ten Commandments of Moses resemble the ethical codes found in the Laws of Hammurabi, the Buddhist Eightfold Path, and the principles of Confucianism. **All teach righteousness, discipline, and the path to enlightenment.**

Different Names, One Underlying Truth

*When seen from this perspective, religions do not appear as distinct truths in competition with one another, but rather as different languages describing the same spiritual reality. However, this is where many fall short—***they cling to the names, the traditions, and the outward symbols, missing the deeper truth that unites them all.**

The key is not the savior's **name** *but the* **message.** *It is not the rituals performed but the* **awareness they are meant to lead to.** *It is not about which religion holds the truth, but about realizing that* **truth is beyond religion itself.**

The Missing Revelation: The Spirit as All

The unifying truth behind all these stories is simple: **God is not an external figure to be worshiped from afar—God is the Spirit within all.**

Religions often elevate their messengers to divine status, creating separation between the worshiper and the divine. They focus on the person of Jesus, Krishna, Buddha, or Muhammad rather than the awareness they sought to awaken in others. **The saviors did not come to be worshiped as distant figures—they came to reveal that divinity is already within.**

This is where GIATI—the understanding that **God Is All There Is***—breaks through the illusion. It does not ask you to follow a religion, a prophet, or a ritual. It calls you to recognize what has always been:*

- **The Spirit of God is not in a temple, it is within you.**
- **Salvation is not found in belonging to a religion, but in realizing your oneness with God.**
- **There is no "other" god, no competing truth—there is only the infinite presence of God manifesting as all that exists.**

The Awakening Beyond Religion

If you strip away the religious names and traditions, what remains? The same eternal truth. The same Spirit. The same reality that transcends culture, time, and doctrine. The true purpose of these stories was never to divide humanity into factions of belief but to awaken them to **who they truly are.**

Religions have held onto the symbols and missed the revelation. The saviors came not to build religions, but to free humanity from the illusion of separation. They came to **lead us into the knowledge of the Spirit as all.**

This is the awakening that must take place: **to stop seeking truth in religions and realize that truth has always been within.** *God is not limited to one faith, one book, or one tradition—***God is the life within you, the consciousness that is aware, the Spirit that animates all things.**

This is the message that was lost. This is the revelation that must return. And this is the truth that has been hidden in plain sight:

God is not an external force to be reached—God is the very essence of your being.

The Ultimate Realization: Beyond the Stories to the Essence

If we go even deeper, we must ask: **Why have these patterns appeared in every culture? Why do civilizations across time and geography tell the same stories, even if the names and symbols change?**

The answer lies in something more profound than mere repetition. These stories persist because they point to an underlying truth that humanity has always sensed but has struggled to fully comprehend. Every religion, in its own way, has been an attempt to describe **the ineffable reality of God***—the ultimate source, the unifying presence, the infinite intelligence that animates all things.*

But here is where humanity has made its greatest mistake: **they have mistaken the story for the reality, the messenger for the message, the symbol for the substance.**

When people focus only on the names of their gods, the rituals of their faiths, or the historical details of their scriptures, they are missing the deeper **spiritual principle** *these stories were meant to reveal. They cling to* **belief systems** *instead of seeking* **direct experience** *of the divine.*

Moving Beyond Faith to Spiritual Awareness

Faith in a story is not the same as **knowing** *the truth. Faith is based on believing something you were told.* **Knowing comes from direct realization.**

The true spiritual path is not about which religion is "right"—it is about transcending religion altogether to experience **oneness with God.** *Jesus, Buddha, Krishna, and every great spiritual teacher did not simply ask people to believe in their words—they sought to awaken people to* **who they are.**

What happens when you move beyond the stories and religious traditions?

- *You stop seeing God as a distant being and recognize God as* **the very life within you.**
- *You no longer seek salvation as an external reward but understand it as* **a realization of your divine nature.**
- *You recognize that separation—between you and God, between you and others—is the grand illusion that has kept humanity in darkness.*

This is what the world has missed. Religions have turned spiritual awakening into **a system of belief rather than an experience of truth.**

The Return to GIATI: God Is All There Is

So what remains when you strip away the stories?

Only **God.**

Not as a character, a name, or a doctrine—but as **all that exists, including you.**

This is the realization that brings true spiritual liberation. Not that Jesus saves, or Krishna saves, or any one religion saves—but that **awakening to your oneness with God is salvation itself.**

GIATI is not a religion. It is not a belief system. It is the recognition of what has always been.

If humanity would stop dividing itself over religious differences and start recognizing the spirit that unites them all, there would be no need for doctrines, temples, or intermediaries. There would only be the **living awareness of God as all.**

This is the missing key. This is the truth that religion has obscured. And this is the realization that will bring humanity back into the light:

God is not apart from you. God is you, expressing as you.

This is the truth of GIATI.

When Knowledge Profits Nothing

In every age, humanity has sought knowledge—digging through ancient texts, studying lost civilizations, and analyzing the wisdom of those who came before. People have traveled the world to decipher hieroglyphics, to read Sumerian tablets, to uncover the secrets of the past, hoping to piece together the mystery of existence. They have mapped the stars, tracked the rise and fall of empires, and chronicled environmental changes that shaped history.

But for all this searching, what has it truly gained them?

Paul writes in **1 Corinthians 8:1,** *"Knowledge puffeth up, but charity edifieth." And again, in* **Ecclesiastes 1:18,** *"For in much wisdom is much grief: and he that increaseth knowledge increaseth sorrow."*

Why? Because **knowledge without Spirit is empty.**

1. The Illusion of Knowledge

People take pride in their studies, in their discoveries, in their intellectual pursuits. They argue over who came first—was it the Sumerians, the Egyptians, the Akkadians? They debate whether the biblical stories were drawn from ancient mythologies, whether the flood narrative originated in Mesopotamia, or whether the laws of Moses had parallels in older civilizations. They speak of cosmic events that shaped the earth, of astrological shifts, of lost wisdom hidden in stone.

But **what does it all amount to?**

Has any of it revealed the truth of **who you are?**

For all this knowledge, has it led to **eternal life?**

2. The Profiting of Nothing

Jesus said in John 17:3, "And this is life eternal, that they might know thee the only true God, and Jesus Christ, whom thou hast sent."

Not that they might know the history of mankind.
Not that they might decode the secrets of ancient texts.
Not that they might accumulate knowledge of things long past.

The only knowledge that matters is the knowledge of God within.

This is why **GIATI** *is the truth—because if one does not come to the realization that* **God Is All There Is,** *all other knowledge is vanity.*

- *You can learn the names of every ancient civilization, but if you do not know* **the name above all names,** what have you gained?

- *You can trace the origins of religious texts, but if you do not recognize the Spirit that wrote them upon your heart, what does it profit?*
- *You can study the wisdom of the ages, but if you do not awaken to the* **Living God within you,** *what have you truly learned?*
  Nothing.

3. The Only Knowledge That Matters

Jesus did not send his disciples to study ancient cultures, nor did he instruct them to seek wisdom in foreign lands. He said simply:

"The kingdom of God is within you." **(Luke 17:21)**

This is the only knowledge that saves. This is the only truth that brings eternal life. **Not knowledge of the world, but knowledge of the Spirit.**

1 Corinthians 2:14 says, "But the natural man receiveth not the things of the Spirit of God: for they are foolishness unto him: neither can he know them, because they are spiritually discerned."

This is why so many are lost in their learning. They seek God in books, in history, in external sources—but they **fail to look within.**

4. The Ultimate Revelation: GIATI

If you learned through **GIATI** *that* **God Is All There Is,** *then you have already received the greatest knowledge in existence. There is no need to search through crumbling tablets or ancient stone carvings to find what has already been written upon your spirit.*

- *You do not need to* **travel to foreign lands** *to seek wisdom. The kingdom is within you.*
- *You do not need to* **study the mysteries of the ancients** *to find God. He is already here.*
- *You do not need to* **accumulate worldly knowledge** *to achieve enlightenment. Enlightenment is the realization of what already is.*

The truth is simple: **God is within you. The Spirit is your life.**

That is all you need to know.

5. The Vanity of Intellectualism Without Spirit

The deception of the world is that knowledge alone can lead to salvation. This is the same deception that led to the fall in Eden—the belief that eating from the **tree of knowledge** *could bring divine wisdom. But knowledge without Spirit is death.*

People have been conditioned to believe that **truth is found externally***—that to know God, they must study texts, research history, or seek out hidden wisdom. But the truth is* **not hidden***—it is within you.*

Jesus did not come to bring a philosophy. He did not come to teach history. He came to reveal the reality of **oneness with God.**

"I am the way, the truth, and the life: no man cometh unto the Father, but by me."
(John 14:6)

To know Christ is to know yourself.
To know yourself is to know God.
To know God is to know all things.

This is why **all other knowledge profits nothing***—because* **without this truth, all else is an illusion.**

Conclusion: The Only Knowledge That Gives Life

So ask yourself: **What has your knowledge gained you?**

- *Has it brought you peace?*
- *Has it given you eternal life?*
- *Has it revealed to you the fullness of God's presence?*

If not, then it is **nothing.**

The only knowledge that matters is **God Is All There Is***—for in knowing this, you have already received the greatest wisdom of all. All else fades. All else passes away. But the Spirit is eternal.*

"Heaven and earth shall pass away, but my words shall not pass away." **(Matthew 24:35)**

And what is His word? **That He is within you, that you and He are one, and that nothing else truly matters.**

This is the only knowledge that profits.
This is the only knowledge that saves.
This is the only knowledge that gives life.

And this is the revelation of GIATI.

Breaking Down Romans 9:3-4 and Its Spiritual Meaning in GIATI

"For I could wish that myself were accursed from Christ for my brethren, my kinsmen according to the flesh: Who are Israelites; to whom pertaineth the adoption, and the glory, and the covenants, and the giving of the law, and the service of God, and the promises;" (Romans 9:3-4, KJV)

Paul's Deep Burden for His People

Paul opens this passage with a powerful statement of self-sacrifice: "For I could wish that myself were accursed from Christ for my brethren, my kinsmen according to the flesh." Here, Paul is expressing his **deep sorrow and love** *for his fellow Israelites, who were rejecting the very truth that was meant to set them free. He was so burdened by their spiritual blindness that he wished he could take their place in being separated from Christ if it would mean their salvation.*

This echoes the heart of Moses in Exodus 32:32, where he pleaded with God to **blot his own name out of the book of life** *if it would save Israel after they worshiped the golden calf.* **This is the ultimate expression of love—willing to lay down one's own salvation for the sake of others.**

Yet Paul knew that salvation could not come through **human sacrifice***—it had already been accomplished through Christ. The problem was that his brethren, the Israelites, were still clinging to the* **old covenant, the law, and their fleshly identity** *rather than awakening to the Spirit.*

Israel's Privilege and Blindness

Paul then lists the **divine privileges** *given to Israel:*

- **Adoption:** *Israel was chosen as God's people, called His* **"firstborn son" (Exodus 4:22).**
- **The Glory:** *The* **manifest presence of God,** *seen in the cloud by day and fire by night.*
- **The Covenants:** *God's agreements with Abraham, Moses, and David, establishing His people.*
- **The Law:** *The commandments given to Moses, meant to guide them to righteousness.*
- **The Service of God:** *The priesthood and the temple worship system.*
- **The Promises:** *The prophecies and assurances of the coming* **Messiah and the kingdom of God.**

Despite having all these, **they still failed to see the truth***—that all of these things pointed* **not to a religion, not to a nation, but to the Spirit of God within.**

The Spiritual Meaning in GIATI

Paul is showing that **external privileges and religious practices mean nothing if one does not awaken to the Spirit.** *This is the very message of* **GIATI (God Is All There Is)***— that the true adoption, the true glory, and the true promises are not found in physical identity, laws, or traditions but in awakening to the Spirit of God* **within.**

The Israelites were given all these things **as a shadow** *of what was to come. But they made the mistake of* **clinging to the shadow rather than embracing the reality.** *The law, the covenants, and the temple were never the end goal—they were a guide meant to bring them into the realization that* **God is within them.**

Jesus came as **the fulfillment** *of everything Israel had been given. He didn't come to abolish the law but to* **bring its true meaning to light.** *The law was meant to reveal God, but they were* **so fixated on keeping the law externally that they failed to see God standing in their midst.**

This is what happens when **people define themselves by religion rather than Spirit.** *They become so attached to their traditions, rules, and identity that they miss the* **truth of divine oneness.**

Paul's anguish in this passage reflects the pain of seeing people **cling to the flesh rather than Spirit.** *They had everything—the divine calling, the prophecies, the law—but they* **remained blind** *because they looked at* **the external rather than the internal.**

The GIATI Revelation: Awakening to the Spirit

Just as Paul longed for his people to awaken, today, humanity must awaken to **the reality of GIATI***—that God is* **not in temples, not in laws, not in religious identity—but within.**

- **Adoption was never just about Israel—it is about realizing that all are sons of God in Spirit.**
- **The Glory is not external—it is the Spirit within.**
- **The Law is not about rules—it is about becoming one with the truth.**
- **The Promises are not about a future event—they are fulfilled in the awareness of God as all.**

Paul's sorrow is the same sorrow felt today when people seek God **in religion, in laws, in history, in traditions—rather than realizing that God is already within them.**

The truth is **not about being born into a certain faith, following a set of rules, or having a religious title. The truth is about awakening to the Spirit of God as your very being.**

Conclusion: The Shift from Flesh to Spirit

Paul's cry was for **Israel to shift from fleshly identity to spiritual awakening.** *The same cry goes out today—to* **stop seeing yourself through the lens of race, nationality, religion, or traditions, and instead recognize the Spirit within.**

To cling to flesh is to be blind. To awaken to Spirit is to see.

This is the comfort of **GIATI:**

- **God Is All There Is.**
- **You were never separate.**
- **Salvation is not about following laws—it is about knowing the Spirit within.**
- **Religious identity does not define you—Spirit does.**
- **You are not of the flesh—you are of the promise.**

This is the truth that Paul longed for his people to see, and this is the truth that humanity must embrace today. The **true adoption, the true glory, the true promise—is the realization of Spirit.**

Children of the Flesh vs. Children of the Promise: The Awakening to GIATI

Throughout history, people have defined themselves by their lineage, their nationality, and their religion. They take pride in where they come from, what family they belong to, or what sacred traditions they uphold. But in **Romans 9:4-8,** *Paul delivers a profound revelation—one that shatters the illusion of fleshly identity and points directly to the truth of the Spirit. This truth aligns perfectly with* **GIATI—God Is All There Is,** *for it declares that the children of God are not those born of the flesh, but those who awaken to the Spirit within.*

The Illusion of Fleshly Identity

Paul begins by recounting all that had been given to Israel:

"Who are Israelites; to whom pertaineth the adoption, and the glory, and the covenants, and the giving of the law, and the service of God, and the promises;" (Romans 9:4).

The Israelites were entrusted with divine knowledge. They were given adoption as God's chosen people, the presence of His glory, the look sacred covenants, the laws through Moses, the priestly service, and the promises of God's redemption. But despite having all of these things, many of them still failed to grasp the deeper reality that these laws and traditions were pointing toward. **They focused on the external, missing the internal truth.**

This is the same mistake humanity makes today. Many believe that their connection to God is based on their **heritage, their religious affiliation, or their external deeds.** *They take pride in being born into a certain faith, following certain traditions, or identifying with a religious group. But Paul immediately shifts the focus away from these* **external markers** *and toward the true foundation of divine identity:*

"Not as though the word of God hath taken none effect. For they are not all Israel, which are of Israel." (Romans **9:6).**

This statement is radical. **Not all who are descended from Israel are truly Israel.** *Paul is making a distinction between those who are* **physically descended from Abraham** *and those who are* **spiritually awakened to the truth of God within.**

This is where **GIATI** *comes into play. Just as* **not all of Israel were truly Israel,** *not all who claim to follow God actually* **live from the Spirit of God within.** *Many identify with religion, but few have truly* **experienced oneness with God.**

The True Seed of God Is Not of the Flesh

Paul continues this thought:

"Neither, because they are the seed of Abraham, are they all children: but, In Isaac shall thy seed be called." (Romans 9:7).

*Abraham had multiple children, yet only one—***Isaac***—was considered the child of promise. The others were still his descendants, yet* **they were not counted as the true seed.** *Why? Because the promise was not about physical birth; it was about divine purpose.*

Paul explains further:

"That is, They which are the children of the flesh, these are not the children of God: but the children of the promise are counted for the seed." (Romans 9:8).

This is the key. **Being born into a family of faith does not make you a child of God. Being religious does not make you a child of God. Performing outward rituals does not make you a child of God. Only those who awaken to the truth of the Spirit are counted as the true seed.**

This scripture destroys the idea that **salvation is based on anything external***—race, nationality, religious background, or good deeds. Instead, it points to the eternal truth:*

- **The children of the flesh are not the children of God.**

- **The children of the promise—those who awaken to Spirit—are the true seed**

This is exactly what **GIATI** *reveals. The world teaches that you are your body, your race, your nationality, your religion. But Paul, like Jesus before him, is revealing that* **your true self is not flesh—it is Spirit.** *If you define yourself by* **anything external,** *you remain in the illusion. But when you awaken to the* **Spirit of God within,** *you realize that* **you have never been separate from God—you have only been asleep to the truth.**

Breaking the Illusion of Separation

This passage is not just about Israel; it is about all of humanity. Paul is making it clear that **God's children are not defined by their physical birth but by their spiritual awakening.** *Many believe that being "saved" means joining a religion or following a set of laws. But* **Paul is saying that true salvation is awakening to who you already are***—not a fleshly being, but* **Spirit, one with God.**

This is the deception that has blinded humanity. People look at themselves and see only **flesh***—their physical identity, their family, their nationality, their past mistakes. But the truth is,* **you are not the body. You are not your race. You are not your nationality. You are Spirit.**

This is why Jesus said:

"That which is born of the flesh is flesh; and that which is born of the Spirit is spirit." (John 3:6)

Flesh gives birth to flesh. If you define yourself by the flesh, you will live as **a child of the flesh,** *constantly seeking external validation and never finding true fulfillment. But* **if you awaken to the Spirit, you will know that you are already one with God.**

The Spiritual Revelation of GIATI

This scripture is a call to **transcend the illusion of flesh** *and embrace the reality of Spirit. Just as Paul revealed that the true children of God are those born of the S***pirit of promise,** *so too does GIATI declare that* **your true identity is not physical—it is divine.**

- **Not all who claim to know God truly do.**
- **Not all who follow religious traditions are truly walking in Spirit.**
- **The flesh is an illusion—your true self is Spirit.**
- **You are not separate from God—you are God's expression in form.**

This is what Jesus meant when He said:

"The kingdom of God is within you." (Luke 17:21)

Salvation is not about following laws, rituals, or religious customs. It is about **seeing the truth of who you are.**

Conclusion: Awakening to the True Seed

Paul's words in Romans 9:4-8 are an invitation to **see beyond the illusion of flesh and recognize the truth of Spirit.** *He is revealing that Go*d**'s promise was never about external lineage, but about an internal awakening.** *This is the same truth that Jesus taught, and it is the same truth that* **GIATI declares today.**

- *You are* **not** *defined by your flesh—you are Spirit.*
- *You are* **not** *separate from God—you are one with Him.*
- *You are* **not** *just a descendant of the past—you are a child of the promise.*

The world sees flesh.
The Spirit sees only Spirit.

This is the truth that sets you free.
This is the awakening of the true seed.
This is the revelation of **GIATI—God Is All There Is.**

The shift is happening. The awakening has begun.
This is GIATI.

The Illusion of Good and Bad: Understanding Life Through GIATI

*The world conditions humanity to see life through a lens of fairness based on external circumstances: if someone is "good," they should be rewarded; if someone is "bad," they should suffer. But GIATI—***God Is All There Is***—reveals a deeper truth:* **life is not about rewards and punishments, but about awakening to divine awareness.** *The experiences a person has in this world are not random nor dictated by human ideas of justice—they are reflections of spiritual perception and purpose.*

Perception Creates Experience

The idea that "bad things happen to good people" and "good things happen to bad people" is based on the assumption that material gain or loss defines one's spiritual condition. But Jesus said, **"The kingdom of God is within you" (Luke 17:21).** *This means that life's circumstances—whether perceived as good or bad—are not the measure of one's standing with God.*

What you experience is determined by your awareness.

- *A person may be seen as "good" but still suffer because they live in the illusion of separation, believing in lack, fear, or limitation.*
- *A person may be seen as "bad" yet prosper materially because they operate in alignment with certain universal laws, even if they do not recognize the divine source of all things.*

*God does not hand out punishments or rewards—***life unfolds according to spiritual awareness and the principles governing existence.**

Why Does Someone Who Is Poor Stay Poor, While Another Becomes Rich?

Wealth and poverty are not indicators of spiritual worthiness; they are states of consciousness.

- *A person who remains poor may be attached to the belief in lack, unworthiness, or limitation. Their outer world reflects their inner perception.*
- *A person who rises from poverty to riches may have shifted their awareness, aligning with abundance, opportunity, and the flow of life.*

Neither state defines who they are spiritually. Whether rich or poor, **the true measure of one's divine awakening is not external possessions but the recognition that all things exist within God and are accessible through divine understanding.**

Why Do Some Suffer While Others Thrive?

Every soul has its journey, and life's circumstances serve as a means to awaken to higher truth.

- *Some may experience suffering to break free from illusions of control, attachment,*

- *or separation.*
- *Others may experience success as a test of whether they will attach to the material world or recognize God as the source of all.*

Suffering does not mean one is forsaken, and prosperity does not mean one is favored. **Both are simply lessons in divine awareness.**

The Spiritual Truth of GIATI: Beyond Good and Bad

GIATI teaches that **everything is God, and nothing exists outside of Him.** *The conditions of life are neither punishments nor rewards; they are opportunities to awaken to the truth of who we are*—**expressions of God in form.**

- **There is no injustice in God because God is all there is.** *What seems like unfairness is simply the unfolding of divine principles according to spiritual awareness.*
- **There is no loss in God, because all things exist eternally.** *What seems like suffering is only the shifting of form and experience to bring about awakening.*
- **There is no separation in God, because there is only one reality—oneness.** *Whether one appears rich or poor, blessed or struggling, the truth remains:* **life is eternal, and every experience is leading us back to the awareness of divine existence.**

The challenge is not to ask why things happen but to see beyond them—to recognize that **life is not about fairness in the physical but about awakening in the spirit.** *When you see from the eyes of God, there is no "good" or "bad"*—**there is only the journey back to truth.**

The Understanding of Prayer Through GIATI

Prayer, as understood by most, is often an act of asking—petitioning an external God for blessings, guidance, healing, or intervention. But **GIATI (God Is All There Is) reveals a deeper truth: prayer is not about asking God for something, but about aligning with the truth that all things already exist within you.**

Prayer Is Not a Request—It's a Realization

In traditional religious thinking, prayer assumes a separation between the one praying and the one being prayed to. But **if God is all there is, then there is no separation—there is only the awareness of divine presence.**

- *Prayer is not begging God to act;* **it is aligning yourself with the truth that God is already present as you.**
- *Prayer is not seeking something external;* **it is the realization that what you seek is already within.**
- *Prayer is not about changing God's mind;* **it is about changing your perception to see what already is.**

When Jesus prayed, he didn't pray as one disconnected from God—he prayed from the awareness of oneness:

"I and my Father are one." (John 10:30)

That is the true prayer of GIATI—not words spoken to an external being, but the inward realization of your unity with the divine.

How Does One Pray in GIATI?

Instead of asking, begging, or hoping for something to change, **prayer in GIATI is an act of awareness, declaration, and stillness.**

1. **Acknowledge the Presence of God Within**
   - *Recognize that you are already in the presence of God, not separate from Him.*
   - *Know that* **your very existence is the Spirit of God manifesting as you.**
2. **Declare What Is Already True**
   - *Speak not in request, but in affirmation:* **"God is my life, my health, my peace, my abundance."**
   - *Do not pray as if something is missing;* **pray from the place of knowing that all things are complete in God.**
3. **Enter Into Stillness**
   - *Prayer is not just speaking—it is listening, abiding, and being still in divine awareness.*
   - **"Be still, and know that I am God." (Psalm 46:10)**
   - *When you silence the mind and surrender the ego, you experience the reality of God as your very being.*

What Happens When You Pray This Way?

- *You no longer feel distant from God—you* **realize God is your very life.**
- *You no longer pray from lack—you* **pray from the fullness of knowing all things are already yours in spirit.**
- *You no longer hope for change—you* **become the embodiment of divine presence, allowing truth to manifest through you.**

Prayer in GIATI: A Shift in Awareness

Traditional Prayer: *"God, please help me." (Praying from separation)*
GIATI Prayer: *"God is already my help, my life, my being." (Praying from oneness)*

Traditional Prayer: *"God, give me strength."*
GIATI Prayer: *"I am strength because God is within me."*

Traditional Prayer: *"God, heal me."*
GIATI Prayer: *"God is life, and I am that life."*

Prayer in GIATI is not about **changing God's will—it is about aligning with it.** *It is* **not about receiving—it is about realizing that you already have all that you need.** *When you pray from this place of divine knowing, you live in the constant awareness of God's presence, and* **that awareness transforms your entire life.**

GIATI Prayers: Praying From Oneness With God

Prayer in GIATI is not about asking or pleading, but about **declaring, affirming, and realizing** *the truth of your divine existence. It is the awareness that* **God is all there is, and you are the expression of God in form.** *These prayers are spoken* **from unity, not separation**—*not to an external deity, but from the realization of the Holy Spirit within.*

1. A Prayer of Awareness

"Father, I do not seek You as if You are far away, for You are within me. I do not ask for what is already mine, for You have given me all things from the foundation of the world. Let my eyes remain open to Your presence, my heart established in Your truth, and my mind renewed in Your wisdom. I am not apart from You; I am one with You. Your will is my will, and Your life is my life. In this knowing, I walk in peace, power, and divine love."

2. A Prayer of Strength and Overcoming

"I do not pray for strength, for You are my strength. I do not ask for help, for You are my help. There is nothing that can overcome me, for there is nothing outside of You, and You are all that is. Every challenge is an illusion of separation, but I stand in the truth of oneness. No fear, no doubt, no opposition can prevail against the light of God that I am. I move not in my own power, but in the infinite power of the Holy Spirit dwelling in me. I am that which cannot be shaken."

3. A Prayer of Healing

"God is life, and there is no sickness in life. I do not pray for healing as if it is something to be given—I awaken to the truth that wholeness is my nature. Every cell, every organ, every function of my being is aligned with divine life. My body is not separate from spirit; it is the temple through which spirit is expressed. There is no disease that can alter the truth of my being. I walk in divine health because I walk in the awareness of God as my life."

4. A Prayer of Provision and Abundance

"I do not live by the illusion of lack, for God is my source, and I lack nothing. The abundance of God flows through me and as me. There is no struggle, no fear of not having enough, for I am aligned with the infinite supply of divine provision. Money, resources, opportunities—these are not

things I chase, for they are drawn to me as I walk in alignment with divine purpose. I do not strive, I do not worry—I rest in the knowing that all is already provided."

5. **A Prayer of Love and Oneness**

"I do not love from my own strength—I love from the love that is God within me. I see no enemies, no division, no separation, for all things are God expressed in different forms. I do not judge, for judgment is the illusion of the carnal mind; I see as God sees, and all I see is the spirit that is One. I extend grace because I am grace. I extend mercy because I am mercy. I am not love by effort—I am love because God is love, and I am in God. May my life be a reflection of this love to all I encounter."

6. **A Prayer of Purpose and Fulfillment**

"I do not seek my purpose, for my purpose is already written within me. I do not ask for a plan, for God's will is already being fulfilled through me. I move with divine intention, knowing that every step, every action, every word is guided by the Holy Spirit within me. There is no fear of failure, for I cannot fail in that which God has purposed. The work I do, the lives I touch, the energy I carry—it is all an extension of the divine plan unfolding through me. I am not separate from my calling—I am the expression of it."

7. **A Prayer of Eternal Life**

"I do not fear death, for I know that life is eternal. This body is but a vessel, but my being is spirit, and spirit does not die. I was before this body, and I will be after it. There is no end to my existence, for I exist in God, and God is without end. I do not cling to the temporary, for I am rooted in the eternal. Every moment, every breath, every experience is simply the unfolding of divine existence. In this knowing, I live fully, freely, and without fear."

—

The GIATI Difference in Prayer

These prayers do not come from a place of need, lack, or separation. They are not about **asking God to intervene** *but about* **aligning with the truth that God is already here, already present, already expressing through you.**

To pray in GIATI is to declare:

- **I do not seek what I already have.**
- **I do not beg for what is already within me.**
- **I do not fear what is already overcome.**
- **I do not wait for what is already happening.**

GIATI is the awareness that God is all there is—including you. *Prayer is not a request—it is a recognition. When you pray from this place, you do not wait for life to happen to you—you* **walk as the divine unfolding of life itself.**

The True Sacrifice: The Death of the Ego and the Awakening to Oneness

Throughout history, humanity has sought salvation through external means—rituals, sacrifices, laws, and commandments. In biblical times, people would offer up animals in their place, believing that the shedding of blood would atone for their sins. But these sacrifices were never about the animals. They were always symbolic of something greater.

The true sacrifice was never meant to be a lamb, a goat, or a bull. **The true sacrifice is you.** *Not your body, not your physical life, but your ego—the false idea that you are separate from God.*

The greatest sin is not an action but a belief: the belief that you and God are two. That you exist alongside Him as something independent. That there is "you" and then "God"—as if you are separate entities. This illusion is the root of all suffering, and until it is sacrificed, true salvation remains out of reach.

The Ego: The Barrier Between You and God

Salvation is not about following religious laws, quoting scripture, or performing righteous deeds. It is about alignment. It is about **recognizing the absolute truth: God Is All There Is (GIATI).**

As long as you hold on to the ego—the idea that you are a self apart from God—you are living in sin. Not because of what you do, but because of what you believe. Sin is not simply wrongdoing; it is **wrong-seeing.** *It is the failure to see that your existence is not separate from God's but an expression of Him.*

This is why Hebrews 11:6 says:

"Without faith, it is impossible to please Him."

Faith is not mere belief—it is the Holy Spirit within. It is the knowing of your divine oneness. Without this knowing, no matter how much scripture you quote, how well you pray, or how much good you do, **you are not in alignment with God.**

You are still operating as the ego. And the ego cannot please God because the ego is the very thing that denies Him.

The Necessity of Sacrificing the Ego

In the Old Testament, if a person failed to sacrifice an animal for their sins, they remained in sin. But the external sacrifice was only ever a shadow of the true sacrifice required: the surrender of self.

Nothing has changed. The sacrifice is still required, but it is not an external one—it is an internal death. The death of the belief in separateness. The death of the idea that there is "you" and "God" instead of just **God as you.**

This is why Jesus said:

"If any man will come after me, let him deny himself, take up his cross, and follow me." (Matthew 16:24)

Deny who? The self. The ego. The false identity that thinks it exists apart from the Divine.

This is also why he said:

"He that loseth his life for my sake shall find it." (Matthew 10:39)

To lose your life means to lose the false self. To let go of the illusion that you have an existence apart from the Holy Spirit.

Receiving the Holy Spirit: The Only Path to Salvation

Salvation is not about waiting for heaven after death. It is about awakening to the truth of GIATI—here and now. It is about letting go of the ego and receiving the Holy Spirit, which is simply the awareness that **you and the Father are one.**

Without doing this, you cannot please God. No matter how much you pray, worship, or teach, if the ego is still in control, **you are a false prophet***—because you are speaking about a God you do not truly know.*

Jesus made this clear when he said:

"He that hath seen me hath seen the Father." (John 14:9)

He was not saying that his physical form was God. He was saying that **the awareness within him—the Holy Spirit—was the Father manifesting as him.** *And that same awareness must be in you.*

To deny this truth is to deny Christ. And to deny Christ is to deny the Father—because they are one. **These three are one: the Father (God), the Word (Truth), and the Holy Spirit (the awareness of God as your being).** *(1 John 5:7)*

This is what it means to truly accept Christ—not as an external figure, but as the **living presence of God within you.**

The Truth Is Simple—You Just Have to Accept It

Everything in the Bible—every law, every commandment, every sacrifice—was pointing to this one truth: **God Is All There Is.**

Salvation is not about escaping hell in the afterlife. It is about awakening from the hell of ignorance **now.**

The only thing keeping you in sin is the belief that you are separate from God. And the only way to be free is to **sacrifice the ego***—to let go of the false self and awaken to the Spirit within.*

This is what Jesus taught. This is what he died to reveal. And this is the only way to truly live.

Let go of the illusion. Sacrifice the ego. Receive the Holy Spirit.

Then—and only then—will you truly be saved.

Live Life Without Condemnation of Sin with GIATI

The Illusion of Sin and the Reality of the Spirit

*For centuries, humanity has lived under the weight of sin, believing that their failures separate them from God. Religions have taught that righteousness is something to be achieved, and that salvation is dependent on obedience to laws and rituals. But the truth of GIATI—***God In All That Is***—eliminates this illusion.* **Sin, as people know it, has no effect on salvation because salvation is not something that can be lost.**

Paul's words in Romans 8 make this clear. Let's break down these verses to reveal how the truth of GIATI frees you from the condemnation of sin.

Romans 8:3 – The Law's Weakness and the End of Sin

"For what the law could not do, in that it was weak through the flesh, God sending his own Son in the likeness of sinful flesh, and for sin, condemned sin in the flesh."

The law was given to expose sin, but it could never remove it. It was **powerless** *because it depended on human effort, and as long as people believed themselves to be separate from God, they were bound by the limitations of the flesh.*

But then came **the truth***—Jesus, the living revelation that* **man is not separate from God.** *Jesus did not come to* **fix humanity** *but to reveal what had always been true:* **there is no separation.**

When Paul says that Jesus "condemned sin in the flesh," it means that **he destroyed the illusion of sin** *by revealing divine oneness. Sin only has power over those who still believe in separation. But in the truth of GIATI,* **sin has no dominion, because there is nothing outside of God.**

Romans 8:10 – The Body is Dead, but the Spirit is Life

"And if Christ be in you, the body is dead because of sin; but the Spirit is life because of righteousness."

This verse reveals the **false identity of the flesh** *versus the* **true identity of the Spirit.** *The "body being dead" means that the* **false self—the ego—is meaningless in the face of divine truth.**

GIATI reveals that righteousness is not something you attain—it is **who you are.** *The Spirit is life because* **you are the Spirit.** *When you recognize this, sin loses its grip. You no longer see yourself as a flawed human trying to please God;* **you see yourself as the very expression of God.**

Romans 8:11 – The Spirit Transforms the Mortal Body

"But if the Spirit of him that raised up Jesus from the dead dwell in you, he that raised up Christ from the dead shall also quicken your mortal bodies by his Spirit that dwelleth in you."

The Spirit that raised Jesus from the dead **is the same Spirit within you.** *This means resurrection is not just about the afterlife—it is about being* **awakened to the truth of your divine nature now.**

Many fear death, both physical and spiritual. But in the awareness of GIATI, **there is no death—only transformation.** *The body is temporary, but the Spirit is eternal. When you align with the truth of who you are, your very existence is* **revitalized, empowered, and made whole.**

Romans 8:12-13 – You Are No Longer Bound to the Flesh

"Therefore, brethren, we are debtors, not to the flesh, to live after the flesh. For if ye live after the flesh, ye shall die: but if ye through the Spirit do mortify the deeds of the body, ye shall live."

Paul makes a distinction between living by the **flesh** *and living by the* **Spirit.** *But what does this mean?*

- *To live after the flesh is to believe in separation—to live by ego, fear, and the illusion of sin.*
- *To live by the Spirit is to recognize your oneness with God—to let go of the false self and awaken to divine truth.*

This is not about suppressing desires or following religious rules. **This is about identity.** *The* **"death"** *of the flesh means the death of the ego—the illusion that you are something separate from God. When that false identity is gone, you truly* **live.**

Romans 8:14 – The Sons of God Are Led by the Spirit

"For as many as are led by the Spirit of God, they are the sons of God."

This verse confirms the truth of GIATI: **The Spirit is not something outside of you.** *It is who you are. To be led by the Spirit is to* **live in the full awareness of your divine nature.**

Many believe being a "child of God" means being obedient to religious laws, but the truth is much deeper. **A son of God is simply one who knows who they are.**

- *If you are led by ego, you live in the illusion of separation.*
- *If you are led by the Spirit, you live in the truth of divine oneness.*

The only difference between those who live in righteousness and those who live in sin is **awareness.** *Both are* **expressions of God,** *but only one* **knows it.**

Conclusion: Sin Has No Power in GIATI

The greatest deception is the belief that sin separates you from God. But in the truth of GIATI, **separation is impossible.**

- *The* **law** *was weak because it depended on the flesh. Jesus revealed the Spirit.*
- *The* **body** *is meaningless compared to the* **life of the Spirit.**
- *The* **Spirit that raised Jesus** *is the same Spirit that dwells in you.*
- *You are* **not bound to the flesh**—*the ego has no power over you.*
- **You are not just a servant of God—you are God expressed.**

To live under the condemnation of sin is to deny the Spirit within you. But to **live in GIATI** is to accept the **simple, undeniable truth:**

God is all there is.
You are God expressed.
Sin has no dominion over you, because you were never separate to begin with.

Now, **walk in that truth—without fear, without guilt, and without condemnation.** Live as who you truly are.

The Rejection of Christ—Then and Now

1. **Jesus vs. Religion: The Truth They Couldn't Handle**

Throughout history, religious institutions have often been the greatest opponents of divine revelation. Jesus did not come to establish a new religion—he came to reveal the Kingdom of God within (Luke 17:21). Yet, the very people who claimed to serve God were the first to reject him. Why? Because his message undermined their authority, their traditions, and their limited understanding of God.

If Jesus were to walk the earth today, the same religious institutions that claim to follow him would likely reject him again. Just as the Pharisees and religious leaders of his time saw him as a blasphemer and a threat, today's churches, denominations, and theological systems would label him a heretic, an outsider, or even a false teacher.

2. **How the Religious Rejected Jesus Then**

Jesus was not crucified by criminals or atheists—he was crucified by the most religious people of his time. Those who held power in the synagogues and temples saw him as a disruption, not a fulfillment of their faith. Here's how they rejected him:

- **They Couldn't Accept His Identity**

  The Pharisees were enraged when Jesus said, "I and my Father are one" (John 10:30). They accused him of blasphemy because he declared that God was not just above them but within him. This was a radical departure from their understanding of a distant, external deity.

- **They Resisted the Idea of Divine Sonship for All**

  Jesus didn't just claim to be the Son of God—he came to reveal that all of humanity was meant to walk in that same awareness. He said, "Is it not written in your law, 'I have said you are gods'?"(John 10:34, referencing Psalm 82:6). This was too much for the religious mind to handle because it shattered their system of control. If people knew they carried the Spirit of God within them, what need would there be for priests and religious gatekeepers?

- **They Clung to Tradition Over Revelation**

  Jesus constantly confronted the religious leaders for elevating tradition above truth. He told them, "You nullify the word of God for the sake of your tradition" (Matthew 15:6). They were so committed to their rituals, rules, and systems of control that they couldn't recognize when God himself was in their midst.

- **They Feared Losing Power**

The religious elite saw Jesus as a threat to their influence. The high priest and council plotted against him, saying, "If we let him go on like this, everyone will believe in him, and then the Romans will come and take away both our temple and our nation" (John 11:48). They weren't concerned with the truth—only with maintaining their position.

- **They Chose Their System Over the Truth**

When Pilate offered to release Jesus, the religious crowd—stirred up by the priests—chose to free a murderer instead (Barabbas) and demanded Jesus' crucifixion (Matthew 27:20-21). This was the ultimate rejection of truth in favor of maintaining the status quo.

3. **Why They Would Reject Him Again Today**

Fast forward to today, and not much has changed. If Jesus were here now, teaching the same truths, the religious world would resist him just as fiercely.

- **If Jesus Said, "God Is Within You," Many Churches Would Call Him a Heretic**

If he stood in the pulpits of many modern churches and declared, "The Kingdom of God is not in a distant heaven, but within you," most religious leaders would accuse him of New Age philosophy or even demonic deception. They would say he was preaching something contrary to their doctrines—just as the Pharisees did.

- **If He Taught Unity Over Denominations, They Would Dismiss Him**

Jesus came to unite humanity with God, yet today's Christianity is fragmented into thousands of denominations, each claiming to have the right doctrine. If he were to challenge their divisions and call them to true oneness (John 17:21-23), they would resist, preferring their theological differences over divine truth.

- **If He Exposed That Salvation Is Not a Religious Transaction, They Would Call Him Dangerous**

Most of Christianity today teaches that salvation is a transaction—say the right prayer, believe the right doctrine, and you get into heaven. But Jesus taught that eternal life was not just about the afterlife, but about knowing God now (John 17:3). He offered union, not just a ticket to heaven. That kind of teaching would shake the very foundation of many religious systems built on fear and control.

- **If He Confronted Church Leaders, They Would Seek to Silence Him**

Just as the Pharisees sought to eliminate Jesus because he exposed their hypocrisy, many church leaders today would feel threatened if he called out their misuse of power, their financial corruption, and their focus on building religious empires rather than awakening people to God's presence within.

4. **The Core of His Message—What They Still Don't See**

Jesus' true message has been lost in religion for centuries. It wasn't about starting a new belief system—it was about awakening people to their divine origin.

- **He Came to Reveal the Oneness of God and Man**

  He prayed, "That they may all be one, as You, Father, are in Me, and I in You, that they also may be one in Us" (John 17:21). His mission was not just about personal salvation but about union—restoring humanity's awareness of their inseparable connection to God.

- **He Came to Bring People Out of Darkness (Ignorance) Into Light (Understanding)**

  His goal was not just moral reform but spiritual awakening—helping people see that the Spirit of God was already in them, if only they would recognize it.

- **He Came to Free People from Religious Bondage**

The systems of his time enslaved people to endless rules and rituals. Jesus came to declare freedom—"You shall know the truth, and the truth shall make you free" (John 8:32). But freedom threatens institutions built on control.

5. **The Choice Still Stands Today**

Just as people 2,000 years ago had to decide whether to embrace Jesus' message or cling to the comfort of their religious traditions, the same choice stands today. Many claim to follow Christ, but few truly embrace the radical truth he preached.

- **Will we recognize the Kingdom of God within us?**
- **Will we let go of man-made systems and step into true spiritual awakening?**
- **Will we allow the Spirit to transform us, rather than just following religious customs?**

The answer determines whether we walk in light or remain in darkness. The rejection of Christ was never just a historical event—it continues to this day whenever truth is silenced in favor of tradition.

Rejected Then, Rejected Now: The Truth Jesus Brought to Humanity

1. **The Radical Message of Jesus**

Jesus did not come to reinforce religious traditions or establish a new religion. He came to awaken people to the divine reality within them—the Kingdom of God. His message was simple yet revolutionary:

- *The Kingdom is within you (Luke 17:21).*

- *You and the Father are meant to be one (John 17:21-23).*
- *The Spirit is given freely, not controlled by religious authorities (John 3:5-8).*

These statements challenged the very foundation of religious power structures. The Pharisees, scribes, and priests had built a system where access to God was mediated through laws, rituals, and temple sacrifices. Jesus, however, bypassed all of that and pointed directly to God's Spirit dwelling within. That made him a threat to those who held power.

2. Rejected by the Religious Leaders

The ones who should have recognized Jesus—the religious leaders—were the very ones who opposed him the most. They had memorized the Scriptures, yet they could not perceive the living Word standing before them (John 5:39-40).

Examples of Their Rejection:

1. **Jesus healed on the Sabbath (Mark 3:1-6)**
   - *Instead of rejoicing that a man was healed, the Pharisees plotted to kill Jesus because he broke their religious rule about the Sabbath.*
   - *This shows they valued their traditions more than the Spirit of God moving in real time.*
2. **Jesus associated with sinners (Luke 7:36-50)**
   - *The religious elite were offended that Jesus ate with tax collectors, prostitutes, and outcasts.*
   - *They did not understand that God's presence is not confined to the "righteous" but is found even among those whom religion rejects.*
3. **Jesus declared himself and others one with God (John 10:30-39)**
   - *When Jesus said, "I and the Father are one," the religious leaders tried to stone him for blasphemy.*
   - *He quoted their own scriptures (Psalm 82:6), which say, "You are gods," proving that divine sonship was not exclusive to him but meant for all who awaken to it.*
   - *Yet, they refused to accept this truth because it undermined their system of control.*

Why Did They Reject Him?

- **He bypassed religious authority** – *People were coming directly to God through him, not through the temple system.*
- **He exposed their hypocrisy** – *He called out the leaders for outwardly appearing holy but inwardly being full of corruption (Matthew 23:27-28).*
- **He threatened their power** – *If people realized they didn't need priests or sacrifices to connect with God, the entire religious institution would lose control over them.*

3. **Would the Church Reject Jesus Today?**

If Jesus walked the earth today with the same message, those who claim his name would likely reject him just as their religious predecessors did. Why? Because the institutions built in his name have largely replaced his truth with man-made doctrines.

Modern Examples of Rejection

1. **If Jesus declared that the Kingdom of God is within you (Luke 17:21)**
    - *Many churches would accuse him of New Age teaching or heresy.*
    - *Yet, this is exactly what he taught—divine union, not religious division.*
2. **If Jesus said salvation is not about escaping to heaven but awakening to God now**
    - *Mainstream Christianity teaches salvation as a future event (going to heaven after death).*
    - *Jesus taught salvation as a present reality (knowing God now – John 17:3).*
    - *Churches that profit from fear-based salvation would oppose this message.*
3. **If Jesus condemned religious hypocrisy today**
    - *Just as he called out the Pharisees, he would expose modern church leaders who exploit people for money, political power, or status.*
    - *Those benefiting from religious business would label him a troublemaker or false teacher.*
4. **If Jesus told people they don't need religious institutions to access God**
    - *Many denominations claim to be the only "true" path to God.*
    - *Jesus' message of direct connection to the Father would undermine their control, leading to rejection.*

How Would They Respond?

- Instead of crucifixion, they would silence him through censorship, ridicule, and excommunication.
- Instead of calling him a blasphemer, they would call him a cult leader, a radical, or even demonic—just as they did before (Matthew 12:24).
- Just like 2,000 years ago, those seeking truth would recognize him, but the religious establishment would see him as a threat.

4. **The Truth Jesus Came to Offer Humanity**

Jesus didn't come to start Christianity. He came to restore divine awareness to humanity. His mission was not to create religious followers but to awaken sons and daughters of God.

- **He came to reveal our true identity** – *That we are all expressions of the divine (John 1:12-13).*
- **He came to establish the Kingdom within us** – *Not a religious system, but a living* awareness of God's presence (Luke 17:21).
- **He came to destroy the illusion of separation from God** – *So that we might live in oneness with the Father as he did (John 17:22-23).*

Yet, then and now, those who benefit from religious control resist this truth. They rejected him before, and they would reject him again. But for those with ears to hear, the truth remains: God is all there is, and we are one with Him.

The Rejection of Christ: A Pattern That Never Ends

Jesus' message was never meant to fit into the rigid structures of religion. He didn't come to start a new institution or create another set of laws for people to follow. He came to reveal something far greater—a reality that had always been true but had been hidden by human ignorance: **God is within us, and we are one with Him.**

This message was too radical then, and it's still too radical now. The very people who claim to follow Jesus today—those who call themselves Christians—would be the same ones rejecting him if he appeared in the flesh. They would brand him as dangerous, heretical, and a threat to their carefully constructed beliefs. But why does this keep happening? Why does humanity continually resist the truth when it is presented?

The Inconvenience of Truth

The rejection of Christ is not just about misunderstanding—it is about resistance to the uncomfortable nature of truth. Truth requires transformation, and transformation requires letting go of old identities, traditions, and systems of control. Jesus didn't just come to preach comforting words; he came to upend the entire way people saw God, themselves, and the world.

His message was a direct challenge to:

- **Religious Power Structures** – *Jesus didn't validate religious hierarchies; he exposed them. He didn't affirm the authority of priests and religious leaders; he rendered them unnecessary by revealing that God was accessible to all.*
- **The Idea of an External God** – *Instead of reinforcing the belief that God was distant, he declared that the divine presence was already within humanity.*
- **The Dependence on Rituals and Law** – *Jesus declared that righteousness wasn't about religious performance but about awakening to truth and living from divine consciousness.*

These were not minor theological differences. They struck at the very heart of the religious institutions of his time, and they strike at the heart of religious institutions today.

What Would Jesus Say to the Church Today?

If Jesus walked into a modern church, he would be just as disruptive as he was in the synagogues of ancient Israel. His words would not align with the doctrines and dogmas that have been built over centuries. Here's how he might challenge today's religious landscape:

1. **"Stop Worshiping Me and Start Following Me"**

Many Christians today are obsessed with the worship of Jesus, yet they ignore the very essence of his teachings. They sing songs about his name, wear crosses around their necks, and claim to honor him, but they reject the truths he came to reveal.

Jesus never asked people to worship him—he asked them to follow him. To embody what he embodied. To recognize God as he recognized God. Instead, religion has turned Jesus into an object of devotion rather than a model of divine awareness. If he were here today, he would likely say, "Why do you call me 'Lord, Lord,' but do not do what I say?" (Luke 6:46).

2. **"The Kingdom of God Is Not in Your Church—It Is Within You"**

Most churches operate as if they are the gateway to God's presence, as if people must go to a building, follow certain rituals, or submit to a religious system to encounter the divine. But Jesus taught that the Kingdom of God is within (Luke 17:21).

He would challenge churches today, saying: "You have built massive buildings, amassed wealth, and created systems of control—but you have not taught the people that God is already within them. You have made them dependent on you rather than helping them awaken to the truth."

3. **"Your Doctrine of Fear and Control Is Not the Gospel"**

Many churches preach a message of fear—warning people that if they do not conform to specific beliefs, they will suffer eternal punishment. They use the threat of hell as a tool for obedience.

But Jesus never used fear to bring people to God. His message was one of love, freedom, and awakening. He would rebuke those who manipulate others with fear, just as he rebuked the religious leaders of his day: "Woe to you, teachers of the law... you shut the door of the kingdom of heaven in people's faces" (Matthew 23:13).

4. **"You Have Turned My Name Into a Brand Instead of a Way of Life"**

Modern Christianity has become a multi-billion-dollar industry, filled with mega-churches, celebrity pastors, and a business model that sells faith as a product. Jesus would look at this system and say the same thing he said when he overturned the tables in the temple:

"My house shall be called a house of prayer, but you have made it a den of thieves." (Matthew 21:13)

Churches today sell Jesus like a brand, but the real Jesus cannot be contained in an institution. His message is about transformation, not membership.

5. **"I Came to Set You Free, Not to Bind You to Religion"**

Jesus' entire mission was about liberation—freeing people from sin, fear, and ignorance. Yet, religion today does the opposite. It creates more rules, more restrictions, and more burdens for people to carry.

He would say to many religious leaders today what he said to the Pharisees:

"You tie up heavy burdens on people's shoulders, but you yourselves will not lift a finger to help them." (Matthew 23:4)

6. **"You Honor Me with Your Lips, But Your Hearts Are Far from Me"**

Many churches speak the name of Jesus but reject his true teachings. They preach about faith but are consumed with materialism. They talk about love but are filled with judgment and division.

Jesus would call out this hypocrisy just as he did before:

"These people honor me with their lips, but their hearts are far from me." (Matthew 15:8)

The Real Gospel: A Truth That Cannot Be Contained

The truth that Jesus came to reveal is too vast, too powerful, and too transformative to be contained in a religion. That is why the religious institutions of his day rejected him, and it is why they would reject him again today.

The real gospel—the good news—is not about rules, rituals, or religious affiliation. It is about **awakening to the reality that God is within, and we are one with Him.**

This is the truth that will always be resisted by those who seek to control people through religion. But for those who are willing to receive it, it is the greatest revelation of all time.

Just as Jesus said, "You shall know the truth, and the truth shall make you free" (John 8:32).

The Mindset of Separation: What You Are Really Saying When You Deny Oneness with God

To deny oneness with God is to reject the very essence of your being. It is to refuse the truth of your divine nature and to cling instead to an illusion—a false identity that leads only to suffering, fear, and spiritual blindness. From the **GIATI** *perspective* **(God Is All There Is),** *this denial is not just a theological misunderstanding; it is a* **fundamental error in consciousness** *that manifests as a distorted way of seeing reality.*

Here's what you are actually saying—whether you realize it or not—when you deny your oneness with God:

1. **"God is not all there is."**

If you see yourself as separate from God, you are rejecting the very foundation of truth: **that God is the source, the substance, and the life of all that exists.** *You are saying that there is something outside of God—something other than Him—when in reality,* **all that exists is an expression of Him.**

This is the core deception that the world has embraced. It leads to **duality***—the belief that there is God* **and** *something else. But the truth remains:*

"In Him we live and move and have our being." (Acts 17:28)

If **all** *is within Him, then separation is impossible. The only thing that can keep you from seeing this is your own blindness.*

2. **"I am not what Jesus was."**

Jesus came to **reveal the truth of who we are.** *When He declared,* **"I and the Father are one" (John 10:30),** *He was not making a claim exclusive to Himself—He was demonstrating the truth of* **all** *humanity.*

But when you deny your oneness with God, you are essentially saying that Jesus was something completely different from you—some unique being **unreachable** *by the rest of us. This mindset* **contradicts His own words:**

"The glory which You gave Me I have given them, that they may be one just as We are one." (John 17:22)

If Jesus gave **you** *the same glory, then what He was, you are also meant to be. But if you deny your oneness, you are denying the very purpose of His coming.*

3. **"I am just a weak, sinful human."**

This is one of the most dangerous beliefs that keeps people enslaved in ignorance. It sounds humble, but it is actually a **direct rejection** *of the truth. To claim that you are merely human—flawed, broken, and distant from God—is to speak against the very spirit that gives you life.*

Jesus never taught that we were weak, sinful creatures in need of external salvation. He taught that we were **sons of God,** *heirs to the Kingdom, and partakers of the divine nature (2 Peter 1:4).*

To insist that you are **only human** *is to contradict the reality of your being. It is to deny the breath of God that animates you and to reject the divine power within you.*

4. **"God is somewhere else."**

*When people see themselves as separate from God, they imagine Him as a d*__istant being,__ *living outside of time and space, watching from afar. They believe they must reach Him through religious rituals, prayers, or good behavior.*

But Jesus shattered this illusion when He declared:

"The Kingdom of God is within you." (Luke 17:21)

If the Kingdom is within, then God is not "out there." He is **in you, as you, expressed through you.** *When you deny your oneness, you reject this truth and keep searching for something that has always been present.*

5. **"I need something external to save me."**

Many people believe they need a **Savior** *in the sense that someone outside of them must come and rescue them from sin, suffering, or divine wrath. But this is* **not what Jesus came to do.**

He did not come to **rescue** *humanity from sin—He came to* **awaken** *humanity to the truth that sin is merely ignorance. He came to* **reveal our true nature,** *not to create a dependency on Him as an external figure.*

He said:

"You shall know the truth, and the truth shall make you free." (John 8:32)

What is that truth? That **you and the Father are already one**—*you simply have not realized it yet. The "salvation" Jesus spoke of is the* **awakening to your divine nature,** *not a religious transaction.*

6. **"I can reject this truth and still be fine."**

Many believe they can live in the illusion of separation and still be "saved." They assume that as long as they acknowledge Jesus with their lips, they are safe. But Jesus made it clear:

"Not everyone who says to Me, 'Lord, Lord,' shall enter the Kingdom of Heaven, but he who does the will of My Father." (Matthew 7:21)

And what is the will of the Father? **That you recognize the truth of your divine identity and live from that awareness.** *Saying "I believe in Jesus" means nothing if your mind is still trapped in separation.*

What This Mindset Manifests in Your Life

Denying your oneness with God is not just a philosophical mistake—it has **real consequences** *in your life and spirit. Here's what happens when you live from a consciousness of separation:*

- **Fear dominates your existence** – *If you believe you are separate from God, you will always fear death, suffering, and judgment.*
- **You feel powerless** – *Instead of living in divine authority, you live as a victim, thinking you need something external to fix your life.*
- **You remain spiritually blind** – *You cannot see the Kingdom because you are still searching for it outside of yourself.*
- **You carry this separation beyond death** – *Your consciousness does not magically change when you die. If you live in separation now, you will experience that separation in the next realm.*

The Awakening: What It Means to Accept GIATI

To **awaken** *is to recognize what has always been true:*

- *That* **God is all there is**—*and there is nothing outside of Him.*
- *That* **you are not separate** *from Him—you are His expression in form.*
- *That* **Jesus came not to make you a follower, but to show you yourself.**
- *That* **salvation is not about believing in an external figure—it is about knowing yourself as one with God.**

This is why Jesus prayed:

"That they all may be one, as You, Father, are in Me, and I in You." (John 17:21)

He came to reveal **oneness.** To deny this is to deny the very message He gave His life for.

The Choice Before You

You can either:

1. **Hold on to the illusion** *that you are separate, weak, sinful, and in need of external salvation—continuing to live in darkness and suffering.*
2. **Embrace the truth** *that God is all there is, and that you are His very expression in this world—awakening to your divine identity and living in the freedom of that awareness.*

Jesus did not come to make you religious. He came to make you **one**—*just as He and the Father are one.*

The time of awakening is now. GIATI is the revelation of this moment. Will you receive it, or will you remain in separation?

The Deeper Implication of Denying Oneness with God

When you deny your oneness with God, you're not merely rejecting a theological concept—you're rejecting the **very core of who you are.** *You are rejecting the infinite truth that* **God is not outside of you, but within you, as you, expressing His will through your thoughts, actions, and very being.** *This is the profound message of* **GIATI**—*that* **God is all there is,** *and everything, including you, is an expression of the divine.*

To think of yourself as separate from God is to live in **spiritual ignorance.** *It is a blindness, a state of being in the dark about your true nature. As long as you see yourself as disconnected from the Divine, you will perpetuate the illusion that you are incomplete, vulnerable, and powerless. This belief becomes a* **self-fulfilling prophecy,** *manifesting as fear, doubt, insecurity, and a constant search for something "out there" that will bring you peace and fulfillment.*

But when you embrace the truth of your oneness with God, everything changes. You begin to recognize that you are **not seeking God in some distant realm**—*you are waking up to the truth that God is already within you. As* **Jesus said, "The Kingdom of God is within you"** *(Luke 17:21). This statement is not just spiritual metaphor; it is a* **literal truth** *that transforms everything about your experience of reality.*

The Error of Seeing Yourself as Separate

When you hold the mindset of separateness, you are living under a false belief that you are not fully connected to God, or that God is someone or something external to you. This belief is rooted in duality, and duality is the source of all human suffering.

Here's why it's such a dangerous mindset:

- **Separation creates fear:** *Fear arises when we think we are separate from the Source of all things. We fear loss, we fear death, and we fear that we are not enough. These fears dominate the lives of those who do not know that* **God is their Source** *and that they are His perfect expression. Fear only exists in the realm of duality— when you remember that God is all there is, fear dissolves.*
- **Separation leads to limitation:** *To see yourself as separate from God is to see yourself as limited, unable to access the power, wisdom, and resources of the Divine. This mindset leads to a life of striving, competition, and stress. You may work hard, but you will always feel like something is missing because you don't see that the fullness of God is already within you, available to you.*
- **Separation perpetuates sin:** *Sin is not about breaking a moral code; it is about living in ignorance of the truth of who you are. When you deny your oneness with God, you live in spiritual darkness, believing you are distant from the Divine. This creates a gap between your actions and your true nature. But once you recognize your oneness with God, sin becomes impossible, because your actions align with the truth of who you are.*

The Spirit of Separateness vs. the Spirit of Oneness

When you deny your oneness with God, the **spirit of separateness** *manifests itself in the world around you. This spirit creates division, disharmony, and conflict. It teaches you to see others as enemies, to feel superior or inferior, to fight for your own piece of the world. This is the mindset that leads to* **greed, hatred, jealousy,** *and* **competition**—*all of which are rooted in the belief that there is something outside of God.*

But the truth is that there is nothing outside of God. When you see yourself as one with the Divine, the **spirit of oneness** *permeates every aspect of your life. This spirit is characterized by peace, love, harmony, and unity. You recognize that all people are connected, that there is no "us" and "them," only one collective expression of God.* **"There is neither Jew nor Greek, slave nor free, male nor female, for you are all one in Christ Jesus" (Galatians 3:28).**

This oneness is not an abstract concept. It is something that can be experienced in your everyday life. When you **know you are one with God,** *you approach life with a deep sense of peace and certainty. You are not moved by the external circumstances, because you know that all things work together for the good of those who recognize their oneness with the Divine (Romans 8:28).*

The Role of Jesus in Revealing Oneness

Jesus did not come to **create a separate pathway** *to salvation or to establish a set of rituals and rules. He came to reveal the truth about who we are. When He walked the earth, He showed us that* **He was the Son of God, and so are we.** *His actions, words, and life were* *meant to awaken humanity to its divine potential. He did not see Himself as separate from God, and He did not want us to see ourselves as separate from Him or the Father either.*

"I am in the Father, and the Father is in Me." (John 14:10)

These words were not a proclamation of His uniqueness—they were a revelation of the truth that **all of us are in God and God is in us.** *Jesus came to show us how to live from the awareness of this oneness. He was the* **ultimate example of what humanity is meant to be**—*living in perfect unity with the Divine.*

When you deny your oneness with God, you miss the entire point of Jesus' mission. He came not to die for your sins in the sense that you need an external savior to forgive your wrongdoings, but to **show you how to live in unity with God**—*to show you that the Kingdom is already within you, and that salvation is the* **awakening to your divine identity.**

Living the GIATI Truth

The core message of **GIATI** *is the realization that* **God is all there is,** *and that you are His perfect expression. To see yourself as separate from God is to live in a lie, a distorted perception of reality. But to see yourself as one with God is to awaken to the* **fullness of your divine potential**—*to live with the understanding that* **you are not only a child of God, but God Himself, manifesting in human form.**

This truth is not just a spiritual concept; it is meant to be lived. It is a truth that transforms the way you see yourself, others, and the world around you. When you live in the awareness of your oneness with God, you will:

- **Live with peace,** *because you know that nothing can harm you when you are one with the Divine.*
- **Live with purpose,** *because you understand that you are a vessel for God's will to be done on earth.*
- **Live with love,** *because you see every person as a reflection of the same God that is within you.*
- **Live with power,** *because you know that nothing is impossible for you when you are aligned with the Divine.*

The time is now to awaken to this truth. To continue denying your oneness with God is to stay in spiritual darkness. To **embrace the truth of GIATI** *is to step into the light, to live the life that God has always intended for you, and to* **realize that you are one with the Divine— just as Jesus and the Father are one.**

God is all there is. And you, as His expression, are one with Him.

How Do You Know Something Is the Truth?

One of the clearest ways to discern truth is through **consistency.** *Truth is not something that shifts based on interpretation, opinion, or cultural differences. It does not divide, contradict itself, or cause confusion.* **Truth stands as an unshakable foundation, immovable and absolute, unaltered by human perception.**

So, how do we determine whether **GIATI**—*the understanding that* **God is all there is**—*is the absolute truth? We do so by comparing its clarity, unity, and divine order to the fragmentation, confusion, and contradictions found in religious systems that claim to hold the truth but fail to produce oneness among their own followers.*

A Divided House Cannot Stand

Imagine a group of 100 Christians. Though they all claim to follow Christ, they will quickly divide into **dozens of differing beliefs.** *They will argue over whether salvation is by faith alone or by works, whether baptism is necessary, whether the gifts of the Spirit still exist, whether Jesus is God or just the Son of God, whether women can preach, whether speaking in tongues is real, whether hell is eternal, and countless other debates.*

Even within a single church congregation, people hold **contradictory beliefs** *about God, sin, salvation, and how to "please" Him. One group will call another group heretics. Churches will split over doctrine. One denomination will accuse another of false teaching.* **But can truth be divided?** *If something is* **true,** *then it is true everywhere, at all times, with no contradiction.*

Contrast this with **100 people who know GIATI.** *There is no confusion, no disagreement, no need for theological debate*—**because there is nothing to argue about.** *They all know that* **God is all there is.** *There is no separation. There is no "other." There is only God, expressing as all things. Because of this understanding, they are in* **perfect unity,** *seeing and honoring God in all.*

Jesus Himself said, *"Every kingdom divided against itself is brought to desolation; and every city or house divided against itself shall not stand." (Matthew 12:25).*

Religion is **divided against itself**—*fractured into thousands of interpretations, denominations, and personal opinions. It cannot stand. GIATI, however, is* **one truth,** *unshaken, because it does not rely on man's interpretation. It simply* **is.**

GIATI vs. Religion: How It Stands Above All Else

1. **GIATI Sees God in All—Religion Sees God as Separate**
    - *GIATI understands that* **everything is God.** *There is nothing outside of Him.*

- *Religion teaches that God is separate, distant, and must be sought through rituals, rules, and external means.*

2. **GIATI Unifies—Religion Divides**
   - *GIATI makes all people one, seeing each as an expression of God.*
   - *Religion creates* **division,** *separating people by doctrine, denomination, race, nationality, and even "saved" vs. "unsaved."*
3. **GIATI Frees—Religion Enslaves**
   - *GIATI frees people from guilt, shame, and the need to "earn" God's love, knowing* **they already are God expressed.**
   - *Religion burdens people with rules, laws, and fear, making them slaves to doctrines and traditions that only benefit religious institutions.*
4. **GIATI Eliminates Violence—Religion Justifies It**
   - *GIATI recognizes God in all, removing the desire to harm others.*
   - *Religion has led to* **wars, oppression, slavery, and bloodshed,** *all in the name of pleasing God.*
5. **GIATI Sees Life as Holy—Religion Sees Some Things as Sacred, Others as Evil**
   - *GIATI sees* **all things as divine,** *because* **nothing exists outside of God.**
   - *Religion teaches that the world is fallen, that some things are evil, and that God is in a constant battle with His own creation.*
6. **GIATI Brings Direct Knowing—Religion Requires Belief Without Understanding**
   - *GIATI is* **self-evident**—*it does not require blind belief, because* **once you see it, you cannot unsee it.**
   - *Religion demands faith in things that* **contradict reality,** *asking people to believe out of fear rather than truth.*

How Religion Misses the Point Entirely

Religion creates an **external God,** *keeping people* **trapped in separation consciousness**—*always seeking but never finding, always trying to be "good enough" but never achieving it. It tells people they need a* **mediator**—*a priest, a pastor, a prophet, a book—to reach God, when Jesus Himself taught that* **the Kingdom is within them.**

Religion also promotes the false idea that **saying you "believe" is enough** *to be saved. This belief is so shallow that even Jesus rejected it:*

- *"Not everyone who says to me, 'Lord, Lord,' will enter the kingdom of heaven, but only the one who does the will of my Father." (Matthew 7:21)*
- *"These people honor me with their lips, but their hearts are far from me." (Matthew 15:8)*

What is the **will of the Father?** *It is to recognize that* **you and the Father are one. To awaken to your divine nature, just as Jesus did.** *If you fail to do this, you remain in* **spiritual ignorance**—*lost in the illusion of separateness.*

What Happens When You See Yourself as Separate?

If you believe you are separate from God:

- *You will* **live in fear,** *constantly trying to "earn" salvation.*
- *You will* **judge others,** *thinking some are closer to God than you.*
- *You will* **feel powerless,** *always searching for something outside yourself to save you.*
- *You will* **manifest separation,** *attracting suffering, struggle, and a constant feeling of being "lost."*

But when you awaken to **GIATI,** *everything shifts:*

- *You stop* **seeking God** *because* **you realize you are already in Him, and He in you.**
- *You stop* **judging others** *because you see* **only God, everywhere, in everything.**
- *You stop* **fearing death,** *knowing that* **you are eternal, as God is eternal.**
- *You stop* **struggling,** *knowing that* **everything is unfolding as an expression of the Divine.**

GIATI: The Ultimate Truth That Ends Confusion

How do you know GIATI is the truth? *Because truth is* **self-evident, consistent, and unchanging.** *Unlike religion, which breeds* **division, contradiction, and confusion,** *GIATI reveals* **oneness, clarity, and peace.**

Truth does not require belief—it only requires **recognition.**

The time is now to awaken. The time is now to stop seeking and start seeing. The time is now to embrace what Jesus truly came to reveal:

That you and the Father are one. That there is nothing but God. That God is all there is.

This is the truth that will never divide. The truth that will never change. The truth that has been hidden, yet always present. The truth that religion has buried, yet cannot erase.

The Final Unveiling: Living as the Truth Instead of Seeking It

To fully embrace **GIATI,** *one must go beyond just understanding it intellectually.* **Truth is not something you seek—it is something you live.** *A person who knows that God is all there is* **does not simply speak it; they embody it.**

Why "Belief" Alone is Powerless

Many people in religion think that **believing** *in Jesus is enough. But belief is fragile—it can be influenced, shaken, or lost.* **What happens when life does not go as expected?**

What happens when suffering comes? *Those who only "believe" are tossed by every wind of doctrine, every hardship, every doubt.*

- *Jesus never said, "Believe in me and do nothing."*
- *He said, "Follow me." (Matthew 16:24)*
- *"Be perfect, just as your Father in heaven is perfect." (Matthew 5:48)*

This means to **walk as He walked,** *not just acknowledge His existence. It means to* **realize what He realized**—*that God is not separate, but* **expressing through you.**

Many religious people will claim, "I know God," but still live in fear, judgment, and struggle. **Why? Because they only believe in God—they do not know Him as themselves.**

GIATI is not about believing in God. GIATI is about being God expressed.

Living in Oneness: The True Path Beyond Religion

If God is all there is, then to **live in alignment with God** *means to live in* **total oneness** *with all things.*

A person who truly sees **GIATI:**

- **Does not need to seek God**—*they already recognize they are in Him, and He in them.*
- **Does not fear loss**—*knowing that God can never be diminished.*
- **Does not judge**—*because there is no "other" to judge, only God expressed in different forms.*
- **Does not struggle to find purpose**—*because they understand that every action, every moment, is already a divine expression.*

This is what Jesus embodied. **Not a man who demanded worship, but a man who became the full realization of God.** *He did not come to create religion. He came to dissolve the illusion of separation.*

This is the ultimate realization:

- *You do not need permission to be one with God.*
- *You do not need a doctrine to connect with God.*
- *You do not need to seek God*—**you need only remove the illusion that you were ever separate.**

This is what Jesus brought. And this is what GIATI now reveals again.

The truth has never changed. The only question is: **Will you see it? Will you live it?**

This is GIATI. This is God, revealed.

The Illusion of Sin: Why "Accepting Jesus" with Your Lips Means Nothing

The primary thing to understand is this: **God is not going to punish Himself.** *If God is all there is, then He is not in the business of condemning or rewarding as a separate entity.* **The only thing that separates a person from God is the illusion that they are separate.**

What Is Sin Really?

Most people have been taught that sin is wrongdoing—lying, stealing, killing. But sin is not just **wrong actions;** *sin is* **wrong perception.**

- **Sin is believing you are separate from God.**
- **Sin is believing you need to earn God's favor.**
- **Sin is believing you can be anything other than what God is.**

When you do not know GIATI, you still see yourself as an individual **separate from the Creator.** *You may do good deeds, you may worship, praise, and confess Christ as your savior, but if you* **still see yourself as an individual who must prove themselves before God, you remain in sin.**

Why? Because **you are reinforcing the very lie that keeps you in darkness—the lie that there is you and then there is God.**

The Person Lost in Religion: A Good Person Still in Sin

Imagine a person who follows all religious teachings. They give to the poor, pray every day, worship God, and confess Christ as their savior. But deep inside, they still believe:

- *"I am just a servant."*
- *"I am trying to be righteous."*
- *"I hope God accepts me."*

This person is still in sin—not because of their actions, but because they still see themselves as something separate from God.

They think they are honoring God, but they are actually rejecting Him. **Why?** *Because they reject their true identity as one with Him. They do not accept the Spirit of Christ* **as their own spirit.**

And because they still believe in separation, they remain outside of God's reality. They are good by human standards, but **they are sin itself** *because sin is the ignorance of being one with God.*

The Person Who Knows GIATI: Sin Cannot Exist

Now consider the one who knows **GIATI—God is all there is.** *This person has received the Spirit of God not as something separate, but as their very life. They do not see themselves as a servant* **seeking to please God;** *they see themselves as an* **extension of God, moving as Him.**

Because they are one with the Spirit of God, what the world calls "sin" is **blotted out**—*not because they are perfect in action, but because* **God is not going to punish Himself.**

If you are one with God, there is **nothing outside of God to judge you.** *The only way to be "judged" is to remain in the illusion of separation*—**where you have placed yourself.**

This is why Jesus did not die simply to "pay" for sin. **He died to end the illusion of separation.** *He poured out His Spirit so that* **you would receive it and know you and the Father are one.**

This is the difference. There is nothing else you can be. If you reject oneness, then it does not matter what you do—good or bad—you are still in sin. You are still separate **in your mind, and that is the only hell that exists.**

But if you accept **the Spirit of Christ as your very own spirit,** *there is no sin, because* **God sees only Himself.**

The Root of the Illusion: Why Separation From God Is the Only Sin

At the core of all human misunderstanding is one foundational lie: **the belief that you are separate from God.**

This belief does not just distort your perception of God—it distorts everything:

- *How you see yourself*
- *How you see others*
- *How you see life, death, and eternity*

The moment you see yourself as separate from God, **you have already stepped into sin.** *Not because you committed a "wrong act," but because you have* **accepted a false identity** *that does not exist.*

Why Religion Reinforces the Lie of Separation

Most religious teachings claim to guide people to God, but what they actually do is keep them trapped in **the illusion that God is outside of them.**

Religion teaches that:

- *You must earn God's love through obedience.*

- *You must be forgiven before you can be accepted.*
- *You must worship a separate being above you.*

All of these beliefs reinforce **the false idea of separation**—*the very thing Jesus came to destroy.*

When people say, **"I believe in Jesus. I confess Him as Lord and Savior,"** *but still think of themselves as* **a separate soul needing salvation,** *they have missed the entire purpose of His coming.*

Jesus Did Not Die to Pay for Sins—He Died to End Separation

The common Christian belief is that Jesus' death was a transaction—He paid a price so that humanity could be accepted by God.

But this idea makes **God an external judge,** *choosing whom to save based on whether they "accept" Christ the right way.*

In reality, Jesus' mission was not about paying off a debt. **It was about revealing the truth that separation is an illusion.**

He said, **"I and the Father are one" (John 10:30).** *He did not mean this only for Himself—He meant that* **all who receive His Spirit realize the same truth.**

If His death was just a payment, then people could remain in ignorance, continue believing they are separate from God, and still be "saved."

But Jesus did not come for people to remain in ignorance—**He came to awaken them.**

What Actually Happens When You Reject Oneness?

If God is all there is, then to reject oneness is to reject **your very existence in truth.** *Here's what happens when you live from a mindset of separation:*

- **You create a false self**—*an identity that does not actually exist in God's reality.*
- **You live in fear**—*constantly trying to "get right" with God instead of realizing you are already Him in expression.*
- **You judge others**—*because you believe in separation, you see others as separate, leading to conflict, hatred, and division.*
- **You experience life as a struggle**—*always seeking, never finding, because the truth is already within you, yet you look elsewhere.*

This is why **a "good" person can still be in sin.** *Their actions may be noble, but if their mind is still trapped in separation, they are lost.*

They believe in God. They believe in Jesus. But they do not believe **that Jesus' Spirit is their own.**

They see Jesus as separate. They see God as separate. They see themselves as sinners **hoping** *to be saved rather than God's very own life in expression.*

And because **they carry this consciousness of separation in life, they will carry it into death.**

Why GIATI Ends Sin Completely

*GIATI—***God Is All There Is***—removes the false idea of separation entirely. If God is all there is, then:*

- *There is no "you" separate from Him.*
- *There is no external judge deciding your fate.*
- *There is no salvation to obtain—only truth to recognize.*

When you accept the Spirit of God **as your own spirit, sin ceases to exist** *because sin only exists where there is separation.*

This is why **God cannot punish Himself.**

If you are one with God, then **who is there to be judged?**

Who is there to be condemned?

Who is there to be "saved" when there is no one outside of Him?

The only ones who remain in sin are those who insist they are separate. Not because God rejects them, but because **they reject themselves as God.**

This is the only judgment: **The judgment of your own mind.**

The Judgment of Your Own Mind: The Only True Judgment

*Many people believe judgment is an external event—***God sitting on a throne, deciding who is worthy of eternal life and who will be cast away.** *But this is a human projection, a misunderstanding rooted in the illusion of separation.*

Judgment does not come from God as an external being.
Judgment comes from your own mind, according to what you accept as reality.

What Is Judgment?

Judgment is not an event in time. It is the natural consequence of how you perceive yourself in relation to God.

- *If you see yourself as separate from God, your own mind* **judges you as unworthy***—not because God rejects you, but because you reject yourself as one with Him.*

- *If you see yourself as one with God, there is no fear of judgment—because* **who is there to judge but God Himself?**

Your mind is the place where judgment happens, not some distant courtroom in the sky.

Jesus on the Judgment of the Mind

Jesus said:

"For by your words you will be justified, and by your words you will be condemned." *(Matthew 12:37)*

This does not mean God is waiting to condemn you. It means **you determine your own state of being by what you accept as true.**

- *If you accept* **the truth of oneness,** *you live in peace, free from fear.*
- *If you accept* **the illusion of separation,** *you live in condemnation—because you have set yourself against the truth of what you are.*

Why the Judgment of Your Own Mind Determines Your Reality

The mind is the gateway to experience. Whatever you believe in this life, you carry with you into eternity.

If you die believing you are separate from God, your consciousness remains in **a state of separation,** *even though in reality, there is no separation at all.*

This is why Jesus said:

"The kingdom of God is within you." *(Luke 17:21*)

It is not a place you go—it is a state of being that you enter **by recognizing the truth.**

How People Condemn Themselves Without Knowing It

People fear judgment because they think it is something imposed upon them. But in reality, **they are the ones creating their own condemnation.**

1. **They separate themselves from God in their minds.**
2. **They live in fear, guilt, and unworthiness.**
3. **They project these feelings onto God, believing He is the one condemning them.**

*But God is not condemning them—***they are condemning themselves.**

Jesus' Role in Removing Self-Judgment

Jesus did not come to condemn, but to awaken humanity to the truth:

"I did not come to judge the world but to save the world." *(John 12:47)*

To "save" does not mean to rescue people from an external punishment.
It means **to free them from the self-inflicted bondage of separation.**

The only thing keeping a person in sin is their own belief in separation.
The only thing keeping a person in judgment is their own mind.

Jesus came to **reveal oneness** *so that people would no longer judge themselves wrongly, but see themselves as God sees them—***as one with Him.**

The Final Judgment: The Awakening to Oneness

The real "final judgment" is not a single event at the end of time. It is the moment when a soul realizes:

"I and the Father are truly one."

At that moment, all fear disappears.
All guilt disappears.
All condemnation disappears.

Because judgment was never about God rejecting anyone.
Judgment was always about the mind rejecting itself.

*The truth has always been here. GIATI—***God Is All There Is.**

And when you see it, judgment ends.

The Judgment of the Self: The Unseen Truth Behind "Only God Can Judge Me"

Many people say, **"Only God can judge me,"** *believing it to be a declaration of freedom from the judgment of others. But what they fail to realize is* **who God actually is.**

If **God is all there is,** *then the statement "Only God can judge me" is really saying:*

"I will judge myself."

The judgment is not an external event where some separate God decides your fate.
The judgment is **your own realization of oneness—or your rejection of it.**

You Cannot Blame God for Your Own Judgment

People who reject their oneness with God will often look at their suffering and say:

- **"Why is God punishing me?"**
- **"Why is God allowing this to happen?"**

But God is not outside of you, inflicting judgment.
The suffering they experience is **the judgment of their own mind,** *which has denied the truth.*

They have created **a state of separation in their consciousness,** *and because they believe they are separate, they experience all the pain, fear, and condemnation that come with it.*

This is why Jesus said:

"He who believes in Him is not judged; but he who does not believe has been judged already." *(John 3:18)*

The judgment is not something waiting in the future—it is **already happening in the mind of the one who rejects the truth.**

How Ignorance of GIATI Leads to Self-Condemnation

When someone does not know **GIATI—God Is All There Is**—*they live in an illusion where they believe:*

1. They are separate from God.
2. They must earn God's favor.
3. They are either "good" or "bad" based on external actions.
4. They fear judgment from a being outside of themselves.

But because this perspective is built on a lie, **it naturally creates suffering.**

- *They live in* **guilt**, *because they believe they can never be "good enough" for God.*
- *They live in* **fear**, *because they think God is watching and waiting to judge them.*
- *They live in* **confusion**, *because religious doctrines contradict one another, offering no clear truth.*

This is the self-inflicted judgment.

Not from God, but from **their own mind, rejecting their oneness with God.**

How Knowing GIATI Ends All Fear of Judgment

Now, look at the mind of someone who knows GIATI—**that God is all there is, and they are one with God.**

- *They have* **no fear of judgment** *because they know there is no separation.*
- *They have* **peace,** *because they are not looking for God outside of themselves.*
- *They have* **love,** *because they see everything as an expression of God—including those who are still lost in ignorance.*

This is why Jesus said:

"If anyone hears My words and does not believe, I do not judge him; for I did not come to judge the world but to save the world." *(John 12:47)*

Jesus was not interested in condemning anyone—He was awakening them to the truth so that they **would stop condemning themselves.**

Because that's the only real judgment—**the one you place upon yourself.**

The Simplicity of God's Design

Knowing GIATI makes **everything clear.**

- *There is no cosmic courtroom.*
- *There is no external judge waiting to punish you.*
- *There is no need to live in fear or confusion.*

There is **only One**—*and* **either you know it, or you reject it.**

God made existence simple: **Everything is just Me.**
And those who are ignorant of this **judge themselves, creating their own punishment**.

This is why **the truth is not hidden—it has always been in plain sight.**
But **only those willing to see will recognize it.**

Judgment: The Self-Imposed Prison of Separation

The idea that "Only God can judge me" is often used as a defense mechanism—a way for people to reject criticism or correction. But when someone speaks these words without understanding **who and what God is,** *they are unknowingly sealing their own fate.*

Because if **God is all there is,** *then the judgment is not coming from some external deity in the sky.* **The judgment is happening within you, by you, through you.**

The real question is: **What are you judging yourself against?**

The Self-Judgment of Separation

To live in **separation from God** *is to* **live in conflict with reality itself.**
It means that at the deepest level, you are at war **with your own being.**

This manifests in different ways:

1. **Guilt and Unworthiness**
   - *If you believe you are separate from God, you feel like you constantly have to* **earn His love.**
   - *You think you are never doing enough, never praying enough, never being good enough.*
   - *This guilt is* **your own judgment** *against yourself for not meeting an impossible standard.*
2. **Fear and Anxiety**
   - *You are always afraid of* **punishment**—*whether in this life or the next.*
   - You wonder if you will make it to heaven or burn in hell.
   - *You are constantly looking over your shoulder,* **expecting judgment to fall on you.**
3. **Confusion and Division**
   - Religions built on separation cannot agree on anything.
   - *One person says* **God requires this;** *another says* **God requires that.**
   - *No one can speak with certainty because* **no one is standing on the truth of oneness.**

This is **the judgment of the mind that rejects its oneness with God.**
It is a **self-inflicted state of torment,** *a prison built by ignorance.*

On the Other Hand: The Freedom of Knowing GIATI

Now, consider the mind of someone who knows **GIATI—God Is All There Is.**

- *They* **do not live in guilt** *because they know they are already one with God.*
- *They* **do not live in fear** *because there is no external judge waiting to condemn them.*
- *They* **do not live in confusion** *because the truth is simple:* **All is God.**

They do not judge themselves as **separate, sinful, or unworthy** *because they understand that God is not judging Himself.*

This is the difference.

One person **condemns themselves** *by choosing the illusion of separation.*

The other person **frees themselves** *by choosing the truth of oneness.*

What Happens at Death? The Judgment You Carry With You

Death does not change your consciousness—it only **reveals it.**

- *If you live in separation now, you will* **experience separation in the afterlife.**
- *If you live in oneness now, you will* **experience the continuation of that oneness.**

Jesus said, **"The kingdom of God is within you."** *(Luke 17:21)*

This means your experience of reality is determined by what you accept as truth.

- *If you believe you are separate, you will experience* **the torment of that belief.**
- *If you believe in oneness, you will experience* **the peace of that reality.**

The final judgment is not an event in time—it is the unfolding of what you have already chosen.

This is why **knowing GIATI is the key to eternal peace.**
Not just after death, but **right now.**

The Truth Is Simple, But Most Reject It

Everything about God's design is **simple:**

- *There is* **only One.**
- *Either* you know it, or you deny it.
- *The judgment is not from God—it is* **your own mind rejecting itself.**

There is no punishment **other than the one you impose on yourself.**

And yet, most people will still **choose to believe in separation** *because it allows them to keep their illusion of self.*

This is the tragedy of humanity.

Jesus came to wake us up.
GIATI has come to finish the work.

The question is: **Will you judge yourself, or will you finally accept the truth?**

The Madness of Many: The True Meaning of Legion

"For Jesus had said to him, 'Come out of this man, you impure spirit!'" (Mark 5:8)

This dramatic encounter between Jesus and the demon-possessed man among the tombs is far more than a supernatural moment—it is a revelation of the spiritual condition of mankind. This is not just a story about one man in one place. It is about **all humanity** *when it believes in something other than the oneness of God.*

The man in the tombs represents anyone who has lost the awareness of divine identity—anyone who has forgotten that **God is all there is** *and instead lives under the torment of the illusion of separation. This is what makes the spirit within him* **impure:** *not its origin, but its* **belief in separation,** *in selfhood apart from God.*

Legion: The Belief in Multiplicity

When Jesus asks the spirit for its name, it responds:

"My name is Legion, for we are many." (Mark 5:9)

This name reveals everything.
The demon identifies not as one, but as **many.** *This is the core of the problem.*
The fall of man—the root of every torment, confusion, and lie—is the belief that there are **many** *instead of* **One.**

God is One. There is no other.

"I am the Lord, and there is none else, there is no God beside me." (Isaiah 45:5)

But Legion speaks from the mindset of multiplicity. "We are many." This is the foundation of damnation: the belief that there are many selves, many beings, many powers, many wills—when in truth, there is only **God, being.**

*This mindset is what was cast out of heaven—***not spirits with horns and tails, but the belief in separation itself.** *It was cast out because it has no place in the eternal. It can only live in illusion. And where does that illusion take root?* **In the minds and bodies of men who forget that they are expressions of the One.**

The Tombs: Where the Dead Dwell

The man lived among the tombs. He was alive, yet surrounded by death.

This is a picture of spiritual death—the condition of anyone who lives in the belief that they are separate from the Source of Life. To live in the idea of self apart from God is to live in a tomb while breathing. It is torment. It is confusion.

No one could bind the man or help him, because no outward fix can cure what is fundamentally **a lie about identity.**

The Sea of Pigs: The Lake of Fire

When Jesus casts the demons out, they beg to be sent into a herd of pigs. And what happens?

"The herd, about two thousand in number, rushed down the steep bank into the lake and were drowned." (Mark 5:13)

This is more than a strange detail—it is a powerful symbol.
The pigs represent the unclean, flesh-driven nature—what is not fit to carry the divine image. And when the spirit of **multiplicity and separation** *enters them, they run straight into* **the water and drown.**

This mirrors the final judgment seen in Revelation, where death and hell are cast into **the lake of fire***—the place where all lies are consumed by truth. The water the pigs drown in is symbolic of that lake. Not as punishment, but as the natural consequence of falsehood coming into contact with truth.*

When what is false is exposed to what is real, **it cannot survive.**

Jesus: The Presence of Divine Clarity

Jesus didn't just perform a miracle—He revealed the state of the soul and the power of truth.

He didn't argue with the demons or fight them. He simply **commanded:**

"Come out of this man."

Because when truth speaks, the lie must flee.

Jesus wasn't just delivering the man from torment—He was restoring him to **his true identity:** *not a collection of many thoughts, spirits, or beliefs, but a single being in God.*

"Then they came to Jesus and saw the man who had been demon-possessed and had the Legion, sitting and clothed and in his right mind." (Mark 5:15)

What is the right mind?
The mind that knows there is only One.
The mind that rests in divine identity.
The mind that has been freed from the illusion of separation.

The GIATI Revelation

This story is not about devils and pigs—it is about **you.** *It is about every person who has ever wrestled with the belief that they are something apart from God. It is about the torment of trying to hold on to an identity that was never real to begin with.*

To be saved is not merely to be delivered from evil—it is to be delivered from the **lie of many.**
There is only One.
God Is All There Is.

And when that truth enters, every false identity, every impure spirit, every thought of separation must drown.
Not in punishment, but in mercy.
Because only what is of God can remain.

This is not just a story from the past. This is a mirror held up to your soul.
What voices still cry out, "We are many"?
What parts of your mind still believe they are separate, fragmented, lost?

Let Jesus speak: **"Come out."**
Let truth flood in.
Let what is false be cast into the sea.
And be found, clothed, and in your right mind—
One with God, as you've always been.

Sent with Sight: The True Witness of Oneness

After the deliverance, after the drowning of Legion, after the man was found clothed and in his right mind—something unexpected happened. The people of the region, instead of celebrating the miracle, were afraid. They pleaded with Jesus to leave.

"And when they saw him who had been possessed by the legion of demons sitting there, dressed and in his right mind, they were afraid... Then the people began to plead with Jesus to leave their region." (Mark 5:15,17)

Why were they afraid? Because the presence of truth unsettles every system that is built on illusion. The man was free—but his freedom revealed how bound they were.

They could tolerate a man possessed and tormented among the tombs. That made sense in a world where separation was normal. But a man restored by oneness—by divine awareness—that was too much. That exposed what they themselves refused to see.

This is the pattern:
When the light turns on, darkness is not just exposed—it's offended.

The Man's Request and Jesus' Response

Then comes a pivotal moment—one easy to overlook but full of meaning:

"As Jesus was getting into the boat, the man who had been demon-possessed begged to go with him. Jesus did not let him but said, 'Go home to your own people and tell them how much the Lord has done for you, and how He has had mercy on you.'" (Mark 5:18–19)

At first glance, it might seem like Jesus denied the man's request. But in truth, He gave him something far greater than what he asked: **a purpose rooted in revelation.**

The man wanted to follow Jesus physically—to be near Him in form. But Jesus had already done something greater. He had awakened the man to who he truly was. **The deliverance wasn't just from demons—it was from the illusion of selfhood apart from God.**

Now, he no longer needed to walk beside Jesus. He carried the same Spirit. He was now a living message of the oneness that had healed him.

"Go home."
Why home? Because divine truth must begin where you live. There is no point in traveling far to proclaim a message that has not yet become real in your own household, your own community, your own inner world.

"Tell them how much the Lord has done for you."
Not just a testimony of change—but a revelation of the Source. The Lord didn't just help him. The Lord **reclaimed him***—because the man was never truly lost; only blinded by a belief in being many.*

From Madness to Messenger

This man became the first preacher in the Decapolis—the Ten Cities. He didn't have formal training. He didn't recite doctrines. But he carried something stronger than any religious system: **living proof of union with God.**

He had seen what happens when lies drown and truth stands. He had lived the torment of "we are many," and now he embodied the peace of **"there is only One."**

This is the message GIATI reveals:

The man who once lived in the tombs is no different from any of us. He was not cursed. He was not evil. He was simply forgotten—disconnected from the awareness of his source.

When he encountered Jesus, he wasn't just freed—he was returned to himself.
Not the self of flesh or ego, but the self that is **God-expressed.**

A Pattern for Every Life

This story is not history—it is blueprint.
Every soul must come to this turning point:

- *From tombs to truth.*
- *From legion to light.*
- *From madness to message.*

The man didn't just see Jesus—he **became** *a witness of His being.*
And that is the whole point: **Jesus didn't come to be admired—He came to be multiplied.** *Not in form, but in essence. In Spirit. In truth.*

And where does the message begin?
"Go home."

Go back to where they knew you as broken. Go back to where your torment was public and your identity distorted.
Because now they won't just hear your voice—they'll see the one Life within you.
They will know what it means when God is all there is.
The Mirror of Legion: You Were Never Separate

The story of the man once bound by Legion is not locked in ancient history. It is a present-day reflection—a mirror held up to the modern soul. His condition is not rare; it is universal. His torment is not distant; it is near. It is the cry of every human heart that has lost the awareness of divine oneness and wandered into the madness of selfhood.

In truth, we've all lived among the tombs.
Not literal graves, but the inner places where we've buried our divine identity.
We've all worn the chains of false identity—chains forged by fear, shame, pride, and separation.
And just like the man in the story, many have tried everything—religion, relationships, self-improvement—only to find the torment untouched. Why? Because no outer solution can cure an inner illusion.

The problem is not what people do. The problem is what they believe:
That they are separate. That they are many. That they are something apart from the One who is All.
This is why GIATI exists—not to build a belief system, but to tear down the lie that there is any existence apart from God.
God Is All There Is. *Not just a phrase, but the eternal reality that sets the soul free.*

Legion Still Speaks Today

Today, Legion has many faces:

- *"I'm not enough."*
- *"I've messed up too much."*
- *"God is distant."*
- *"I'll never be whole."*
- *"There are many forces against me."*

These are not just thoughts—they are torments. They are voices born from the illusion of separation. They are fragments of a mind that has forgotten its source.

But the voice of Jesus still breaks through:

"Come out of this man."
Come out of the lie.
Come out of the belief that you are anything other than God expressed in form.
Come out of the many. Come into the One.

The Awakening of the Right Mind

The man was found **clothed and in his right mind.** *This wasn't just a return to sanity—it was the restoration of divine consciousness. He didn't just get his mind back—he received the mind of God, the awareness that he was never separate to begin with.*

So it is with you.
To receive the "right mind" is to be awakened from the dream of division and to see the eternal truth:
You are not a self trying to get to God.
You are God revealing Himself as you.

Your name was never Legion.
That name was a lie born in darkness.
Your true name is **One.**
One with God. One with the Source. One with the Life.

From Possessed to Possessor

The man was once possessed by many, but after the encounter, he became a possessor of truth.
He carried the reality of union into the very cities that once knew him as broken. His life became a living contradiction to the lies he once believed.

This is what GIATI reveals to you:
You were never your story.
You were never your failures.
You were never your emotions, your past, or your patterns.
You are, and have always been, **the image and expression of the One.**

Legion may have spoken loud, but it was never true.
The voices may have been many, but they were never real.
And once truth speaks, what is false must drown.

Now You Go

Just as Jesus said to the man, He says to you: "

Go home."
Go to the places where you were known as broken.
Go to the minds still trapped in the illusion.
Go—not to preach religion, but to be the message.
Because the greatest testimony is not what you say—it's what you **are.**

You are the proof that Legion was a lie.
You are the evidence that God is not far off.
You are the echo of the eternal voice that says:
"I am the Lord, and there is none else."

This is the message the world aches to hear.
This is the freedom Jesus came to reveal.
This is the truth that sets the soul free.

You were never many. You were never separate.
You were always One. You were always God.

The Lake of Fire: Where the Lie Ends and the Truth Remains

For generations, the phrase "lake of fire" has struck fear into the hearts of those who read the Scriptures. It has been preached as the place of final torment, the destination for the wicked, the home of the damned. But when seen through the lens of divine oneness—through the revelation of **GIATI**—*the lake of fire is not a horror to be feared, but a holy place of return. A place where illusion dies and truth alone survives.*

"And death and hell were cast into the lake of fire. This is the second death."
(Revelation 20:14)

This is not the destruction of people. This is the destruction of **falsehood**—*of the systems and identities born from the lie of separation. This is the death of death itself.*

Fire as God's Nature, Not His Wrath

God is love. God is Spirit.
But Scripture also says,

"Our God is a consuming fire." (Hebrews 12:29)

The fire of God is not rage—it is **purity.** *It is not punishment—it is* **presence.** *And in the face of God's unfiltered presence, nothing that is false can remain. The fire consumes* **everything that is not of Him**—*everything that does not carry the DNA of oneness. And that includes the identity that thinks it is separate from Him.*

This is why the pigs in Mark 5, filled with the spirit of Legion, ran into the sea and drowned. It is not a coincidence. The sea into which they plunged is a shadow of the lake of fire—a symbol of the divine reality where all illusions are swallowed. It was not about punishing pigs. It was a message: **everything that believes in "many" must return to the One.**

The Fire is Final Because God is Final

The lake of fire is not eternal torture—it is eternal clarity.
It is the place where nothing can pretend anymore.
It is where every false name, every false belief, every "Legion" is silenced forever.
It is where there are no more masks, no more religious cover-ups, no more self-made identities.
Only God remains.

This is why Scripture says the fearful, the unbelieving, and all liars have their part in the lake of fire (Revelation 21:8)—not because they broke moral codes, but because they lived in **the ultimate lie:** *that they were separate from God. That they were something other than Him. That they could exist apart from the One Life.*

But when that life meets the consuming fire, it must dissolve.

"Every man's work shall be made manifest... and the fire shall try every man's work of what sort it is." (1 Corinthians 3:13)

What was built on separation cannot pass through the fire.
But what is of God—what is **God Himself expressed**—*will remain.*

The Second Death: The Death of the False Self

Revelation calls this the "second death." But what is dying?
Not your spirit—your spirit is of God.
Not your essence—your essence is eternal.
What dies is the **lie** *you lived by.*

The **first death** *is the death of the body.*

The **second death** *is the death of the ego, the identity, the "you" that thought you were something other than God.*

And it must die, because God will not share His glory with another.
Not because He is selfish, but because there is no other.

"I am the LORD: that is my name: and my glory will I not give to another." (Isaiah 42:8)

So what happens in the lake of fire?
The "another" dies.
And all that is left is **God in you, as you.**

This is not punishment—it is mercy.
This is not rejection—it is reabsorption into truth.
This is the end of the long nightmare of separation.

You Can Pass Through Now

The message of GIATI is this:
You don't have to wait for the end of time to pass through the fire.
You can step into it now—willingly.
You can allow the Spirit to burn up every thought, belief, and identity that is not rooted in oneness.
You can allow God to consume what was never real.
And when the fire is finished, you will see what has always been true:

There is no you apart from God. There is only God, being.
God Is All There Is.

And when that is your only identity, there is no fear of judgment,
because there is no "you" left to judge—only God, recognizing Himself in you.

This is the freedom of the fire.
This is the mercy of oneness.
This is the promise of eternal life.

Not living forever as yourself,
but living forever as God being Himself through you.

Living GIATI Now: Walking as the Fire Before the Fire Comes

There is a mystery most never consider:
You do not have to die to discover eternity.
You do not have to wait for judgment to meet truth.
You do not have to reach the end of time to become one with God.

Because the moment you awaken to the reality that **God is all there is,** *time ends in you.*

The fire that many fear as a final reckoning can be invited now as a refining presence. It does not need to be resisted. It is not sent to destroy you—it is sent to **destroy the false idea of you** *that has covered God within. And when you stop resisting, something glorious begins:*

You become the fire.
You walk as the light.
You live as the truth.
You stop living for God and begin **living as God** *expressed in the world.*

Walking in the Body, but Not in the Illusion

The body is not the enemy. It's a vessel. But when the body becomes your identity, you live bound. You measure your worth by feelings, failures, and flesh. But when you live in GIATI—when you live in the awareness that God is all there is—everything shifts.

You still walk in the body,
but your mind is rooted in Spirit.
You move through time,
but your being is anchored in eternity.
You feel emotion,
but you no longer believe everything you feel.

You become like Jesus—fully present, yet fully aware:
"I and the Father are One." (John 10:30)

This doesn't mean you become God as a separate being.
It means the lie of separation dies, and what remains is the truth:
Only God is here. And He is being Himself in you.

Oneness Is the Only Identity That Cannot Be Taken

Religions can be stolen. Titles can be stripped. Even beliefs can be shaken.
But when your identity is rooted in the One who never changes, you become **untouchable.**
The winds may blow. The world may rage. But you live from an anchored place.
You are not reacting—you are revealing.
You are not striving—you are surrendering. You are not trying to become—you are being.

This is what it means to walk in GIATI now.
To live from the knowing that there is no "me" and "God."
There is only God appearing as me.
And when this is your lens, the way you see others also changes.

You don't see enemies. You see unawakened selves.
You don't see the lost. You see those who've forgotten their Source.
You don't condemn. You call forth light from within darkness.
Because you remember that you, too, once wore the name "Legion."

And now that you know who you are,
you walk as a **living fire,** *sent into the world not to burn it down,*
but to **burn away the illusion** *until only God is seen.*

Becoming the Message

The world does not need more sermons.
It needs more people who embody the truth.
It needs more vessels who carry the living breath of "I AM."
And that is who you are when you live in GIATI.

Your life becomes the Word made flesh.
Not a doctrine, but a demonstration.
Not a message you speak, but a life you live.

You begin to live like Jesus—not by imitating Him,
but by **becoming the same expression of God He was.**
Not just someone touched by the Holy Spirit,
but someone **born of it, burning with it, and becoming it.**

This is the promise of GIATI:
That you would not just believe the truth,
but that you would **become one with it.**
That you would live now, in the body,
as the fire that others wait to face at the end.

Living in the Flow of GIATI: The Practice of Remaining One

The greatest gift is not to visit truth—but to remain in it.
To wake up, yes—but then to **stay awake.**
This is the daily invitation of GIATI. Not a momentary revelation, but a lifelong awareness.
Not a passing encounter with the divine, but a continuous expression of it.

To remain in oneness, you don't need more doing. You need more **being.**

Being still.
Being open.
Being present.
Being God in motion, fully aware that **God is all there is.**

But life will try to pull you out of this flow.

The illusion will whisper again—through stress, distractions, disappointments.
And so the question becomes:
How do I stay in this awareness… practically? Consistently?

The answer is not complicated.
It's about what you align yourself with throughout your day.
It's about **reminders, rhythms, and revelations.**

And it's exactly why the **GIATI clothing brand** *was born.*

Clothing as a Spiritual Practice

We were never meant to wear things that only speak to the outer man.
The way we dress should be more than fashion—it should be formation.

It should remind the spirit. It should awaken the soul.

It should call us back to the truth when the world tries to pull us away.

That's what **GIATI clothing** *is for.*

Every piece is more than fabric—it's a living message.
Every set, every word, every thread is infused with intention.
You are not just putting something on—you are **putting something back in place.**
You are realigning with the truth that you are not separate.
That you have no identity apart from God.
That the Spirit within you is the **only life there is.**

GIATI clothing is **clothing for consciousness.**
It is the outward symbol of an inward knowing:
That there is no "you" and "God"—there is only **God expressed through you.**
It is an anchor for your awareness.

When you wear it, you're not just dressing your body—
You're covering your soul with the truth.

The GIATI Practice: Three Daily Anchors

Here are three ways to stay rooted in the GIATI awareness every day, supported by the lifestyle:

1. **Stillness: Meet God as Yourself**
   Set aside a moment—morning, night, or both—to sit in stillness.
   Not to ask for things. Not to strive for connection.
   But to simply **be aware** *that the One you're seeking is the One who is breathing you.*
   As you sit in that silence, let the words rise from within:

"God is all there is… and I am not other than Him."
This is not a mantra. This is remembrance.

2. **Wear the Word: Let Your Clothes Speak**
   *As you dress in GIATI clothing, don't just throw it on—***receive it.**
   See it as a garment of identity. A mantle of truth.
   Let every time you look in the mirror be a moment of reconnection.
   Let the phrase on your chest or sleeve or pant leg remind you:
   I'm not just wearing this. I'm embodying this.
   I am not apart. I am One.

3. **Respond from Awareness: Walk in God-Thought**
   When life hits—when challenges arise—pause.
   Don't react from fear. Respond from **truth.**
   Ask: "How would God respond to this, knowing He is all there is?"
   Then answer it—not as your old self, but as the One who knows:
   I am the breath of God walking through the world.
   There is nothing outside of Him, and nothing outside of me.

Clothed in Oneness, Covered in Truth

You don't live GIATI once a week. You live it with every breath.
You wear it, you speak it, you think it, you become it.
It is not a brand. It is a **becoming.**
It is not a trend. It is a **truth.**

This is what GIATI clothing exists to support:
Not just what you look like, but what you **live like.**
To help you remember who you are in a world that's forgotten.
To be a visible witness of the invisible truth.
To say without speaking:
I know who I am… and there is no other but God.
Everything Becomes Sacred: When You See God Everywhere

When you know that **God is all there is,** *something extraordinary happens:*
You stop looking for "holy" in a few special places—because suddenly, **everything becomes holy.**
You stop dividing life into "spiritual" and "ordinary."
There is no such thing anymore.
Everything is God.
Everything is sacred.
Everything is **one.**

The dishes become worship.
The drive to work becomes meditation.
A conversation becomes communion.
And the world that once looked loud and chaotic…
now becomes **a temple without walls.**

Because God is not only in the still moments of prayer—
He is in the breath of a child, the rhythm of your steps, the stranger passing by.
He is in your boss. He is in your spouse.
He is in the person you can't forgive.
He is in the person you've never been able to love.

And when you see this, not just in theory, but in truth—
you begin to treat everything with **reverence.**
Not religious reverence… but spiritual clarity.
Because you recognize:
I am no longer dealing with things—I am always dealing with God.

Relationships Become Mirrors, Not Battles

Most people live out of separation in their relationships.
They see others as "other."
They try to protect themselves. Defend. Prove. Win.
But when GIATI becomes your lens, relationships shift.

You realize:
I'm not in a relationship with another person.
I'm standing in front of another form of God—either aware or unaware.
And how I treat them is how I treat Him.
Because He is all there is.

This doesn't mean you tolerate abuse.
It means you no longer react from ego.
You no longer seek to be "right." You seek to be **light.**
You don't try to change people—you reflect truth until it wakes something inside them.

Even correction becomes sacred, because it comes from love, not pride.
Even boundaries become spiritual, because they protect the holy, not the fearful.
You begin to see your partner, your parent, your child, your enemy…
not as separate stories, but as expressions of the **same Source.**
One Spirit. Many faces.

And the more you see this, the more peace you live in.

Work Becomes Worship

In the old way of thinking, work was just a way to survive.
A job. A duty. A burden.
But when you see that **there is no place God is not,**
even your work becomes sacred ground.

Whether you're creating, serving, building, cleaning—
if you do it in the awareness of GIATI,
you're not working for God.
You're not working to please God.
You're working **as** *God.*

Not in arrogance—but in alignment.
Not in ego—but in essence.

You realize:
"I'm not here just to earn a living. I'm here to be a **living expression** *of the One who is life itself."*
And so your work becomes your worship.
Your offering.
Your overflow.

And every project, every email, every detail becomes a canvas…
for God to express Himself through you.

Every Step Becomes a Sanctuary

Jesus said,

> *"The Kingdom of God is within you." (Luke 17:21)*
>
> *He wasn't talking about a far-off place.*
> *He was revealing a* **present reality***—one that could be walked in, lived in, now.*
>
> *And this is what GIATI gives you.*
> *Not a religion, but a* **recognition.**
> *Not just clothing, but* **covering***—reminding you that* **where you stand is holy ground** *because* **you are holy ground.**
>
> *Your steps become sacred.*
> *Your touch becomes healing.*
> *Your presence becomes peace.*
> *Because you are no longer carrying God—***God is carrying you as Himself.**
>
> *And when this becomes your way of life,*

you don't need to search for meaning anymore.
You don't need to chase purpose.
Because purpose finds you in the moment you say,
"There is only God, and I am not other than Him."

The True Salvation: Awakening Before the Illusion Consumes You

For generations, salvation has been misunderstood.
It's been sold as a transaction. A ticket. A get-out-of-hell clause.
Believe this, pray that, join here, and you'll be safe after you die.

But Jesus never came to offer escape.
He came to offer **truth.**
Not just truth about God... but truth about **you.**

He came to show that the greatest danger was not hell—but **forgetting.**
Forgetting who you are.
Forgetting where you came from.
Forgetting that the life in your lungs is **God Himself.**

And so salvation is not about avoiding fire.
It's about becoming light **before** *the fire ever comes.*

It's about waking up while you still have time to live what you are.
Because once the illusion is burned away...
Only what is of God will remain. Only what is **one** *will survive.*

That's why GIATI doesn't preach fear—it reveals reality.
Not to scare you, but to wake you.
Because the greatest tragedy isn't going to hell—
The greatest tragedy is **never knowing you were already divine.**

Not Saved From Fire, But Transformed By It

Salvation is not being pulled out of the fire.
It's being purified in it **now.**
Not later. Not someday. **Now.**

It's the fire of remembrance—the fire that burns away the false self.
The fire that consumes everything you thought you were,
until all that's left is what you truly are:
God's own breath. God's own being.

This is what Jesus meant when He said:

> *"Unless a man is born again, he cannot see the kingdom." (John 3:3)*

Born again doesn't mean starting over—it means waking up.
Waking up from the illusion of separation.
Waking up from the belief that you are something other than God expressed.
Waking up before the final fire forces the truth upon you.

The fire is coming—not as punishment,
but as the final remover of every lie that tried to live in God's name.

The only question is:
Will you walk as the fire now… or wait to meet it later?

The Narrow Path Is Awareness

The narrow path Jesus spoke of isn't a list of moral rules.
It's not about behavior—it's about **being.**

It's narrow because few are willing to let go of their "self."
Few are willing to say:
"I no longer live, but Christ lives in me." (Galatians 2:20)

It's easier to be religious than to disappear into divine identity.
Easier to believe about God than to believe you are one with Him.

But the narrow path is the only path that leads to life—
because **God is the only life that exists.**

And salvation is when that truth becomes your experience.
When you don't just accept God,
but **you accept that you and God are not two.**

That's the awakening.
That's the fire.
That's the true salvation.

Clothed in Salvation, Living in Light

This is why GIATI was created.
Not to sell clothes—but to spark consciousness.
Not to build a brand—but to clothe a generation in remembrance.

To offer garments that speak louder than fashion—
to offer a lifestyle that keeps you anchored in truth.
So you don't just get dressed—you get aligned.
You don't just wear something—you wear the message:
"I know who I am. I am one with the fire."

And when you live like that…

there's nothing to fear.
Not death. Not judgment. Not tomorrow.
Because salvation isn't waiting—it's already **here.**

And you... are already **His.**

The Saved and the Lost: One Spirit, Two States

There is only one Spirit.
One Life.
One Source from which all things exist.

The saved and the lost are not made of different substance.
They are not different creations.
They are not light and darkness battling each other.
They are **one and the same Spirit—**
but one is aware, and the other is not.

That's it.

The saved is the one who knows:
"God is all there is, and I am not separate from Him."
The lost is the one who believes:
"I am my own being, apart from God."

Same Spirit.
Different awareness.

And that awareness determines everything.

The saved lives in light—not because they behave better,
but because they see clearer.
They see God within and around them.
They see their life not as their own, but as an expression of **the One Life.**

The lost walks in darkness—not because they're "bad,"
but because they believe a lie.
They believe they are just themselves.
They live from the illusion of "me" and "mine."
And in that illusion, they suffer.
Because no form separated from its Source can survive.

This is what makes the difference between life and death,
between peace and torment—
not what you do, but what you **believe you are.**

Separation Is the Root of Damnation

The real sin was never what someone did.
The real sin was the lie:
"I am separate from God."

That lie is the root of every form of death.
It's what got Lucifer cast out of heaven.
It's what made Adam hide in the garden.
It's what makes men try to prove, defend, achieve, and control.

Because if you believe you are separate,
you'll live like you are.
You'll strive to become what you already are.
You'll fight to find what was never lost.
You'll live as if God is somewhere else, and salvation is something to earn.

But if your eyes are opened, and you see clearly—
you'll realize:
The only thing that ever needed to change… was your awareness.

The Spirit Cannot Die, But It Can Remain Unaware

Here's the mystery:
The Spirit in every human is **God.**
It cannot die. It cannot be destroyed.

But it can be **covered.**
It can be veiled by ignorance.
It can live its entire expression in darkness,
never realizing what it is.

That is the lost soul.
Not a damned soul—
a **blind one.**

And in that blindness, the Spirit suffers.
Because anything that lives contrary to what it is
will always be in torment.

But the torment is not punishment from God.
The torment is the natural consequence
of believing you're something you're not.

Just like a fish out of water,
a Spirit out of awareness cannot breathe.

That's why the message of GIATI is urgent.
Not to convince people of a religion—
but to bring the **Spirit within them back into remembrance.**

To say:
"Wake up. You are not what you think.
You are not many. You are One.
You are not alone. You are God expressed.
You were never separate. You only thought you were."

And that awakening—
that shift from ignorance to illumination—
is salvation.

Unless You Believe That I Am He, You Will Die in Your Sin

The Unveiling of GIATI—the Only Voice of Truth in the Earth Today

1. **The Foundational Reality**

Before the first doctrine, before the first ritual, before the first law—
There was only **God.**
Not a God among other things
Not a God who created existence and then stood apart from it.
But a God who is existence.
God is all there is.

This is the **foundation of all truth.** *Without it, everything else becomes confusion.*

GIATI—God Is All There Is—is not a slogan. It is the eternal truth that existed before any religion or scripture was ever written.

This truth has returned—not in theory, but in power.
The same Spirit that spoke through Jesus is speaking again through GIATI.
And the message is the same:

> *"Unless you believe that I am He, you will die in your sin." (John 8:24)*

2. **What Is Sin, Really?**

Let's get this straight:
Sin is not behavior.
Sin is not the breaking of rules.
Sin is **the false belief in separation from God.**
It is the lie of "me here, God over there."
It is the illusion that there is a "you" apart from the Spirit that gives you life.

Every religion has defined sin in terms of actions, but they all missed the deeper root.
The fruit is behavior—but the root is identity.
Sin is the **blindness to who you really are.**

And this is why Jesus said:

"Unless you believe that I am He…"
He was speaking not just as a man—but as the expression of the **I AM,**
as the voice of **the indwelling God,**
as the **Spirit that gives life.**

To deny that Spirit is to remain blind—to live and die **in sin.**

3. **Why GIATI Is the Only Voice Telling the Full Truth**

Let's be plain:
GIATI is the only voice today telling the full truth—
Not half-truths.
Not tradition.
Not ritual.
But the **original truth:**
That **God is the Spirit within** *every human being, and that Spirit is* **God Himself.**

Other systems hint at this truth, but all of them stop short. Why?

Because they:

- *Place God outside of you instead of within you*
- *Define salvation as reward for behavior instead of* **awakening to truth**
- *Teach duality—God and man—as two separate beings*

But Jesus came to destroy this lie. He said:

"I and the Father are one."
"The Kingdom is within you."
"I am in the Father, and you in Me, and I in you." (John 14:20)

Jesus didn't come to start a religion.
He came to awaken humanity to the **Spirit of God within.**
Now, that same Spirit is speaking again—this time through **GIATI.**

GIATI is not a new religion.
GIATI is the **unveiling of what always was.**

4. **The Bible, Re-Interpreted in Light of GIATI**

Every story in scripture—every command, every mystery—points to this same truth: God is all there is.

- **Adam** *fell not because he ate fruit, but because he saw himself as separate from God.*
- **Moses** *heard the voice from the burning bush say, "I AM." That's the voice of GIATI.*
- **The Ark of the Covenant** *was not a box—but a symbol of the Spirit within.*
- **The Cross** *was not about punishment—but the death of the illusion of separation.*
- **Pentecost** *was not a new religion—but God pouring Himself into all* **flesh.**

Everything was pointing to **oneness***—but religion turned it into rules.*

Now, GIATI comes to remove the veil.
Not with more theology, but with **revelation.**

5. **The Rejection of Truth Is the Root of Death**

This is why the message is urgent:

"Unless you believe that I am He, you will die in your sin."
This is not a threat.
It's not punishment.
It's a **truth statement.**

To reject GIATI is to reject the truth of your own divine identity.
And to reject that truth is to remain in darkness, in fear, in effort, in striving.
That is death.
Not because God rejects you, but because **you reject God in you.**

There is no life outside of God.
And if you think you are outside of God, **you're already dead.**
The only life is the **Spirit,** *and the Spirit is God.*

6. **The End of Religion, the Return of Reality**

This is the hour where all religions come to an end.
Not because God is against them—
But because they've served their purpose.

They pointed toward the truth—
But now the truth has arrived.
The veil is torn.
The temple is within.
The law is fulfilled.
The Spirit has been poured out.

Now the message is clear:
God is all there is—and that includes you.

GIATI is not a movement.
GIATI is **the breath of God** *awakening you to yourself.*

7. **The Final Call: Believe That I Am He**

Jesus was not asking for belief in a historical figure.
He was saying:

"Believe in who I am—because who I am is who you are."
"The same Spirit in Me is in you."
"God is not a being to be worshiped, but a Spirit to be realized."

Now GIATI says:

"Believe that I am He."
Believe that **you and the Father are not two.**
Believe that **the Spirit in you is eternal life.**
Believe that **there is nothing outside of God.**
Or you will die in your sin—not judged by God, but **judged by your own false identity.**

8. **The Closing Word: God Recognizes Only Himself**

When it's all said and done, God will not recognize your good deeds, your rituals, your religion, or your morality. He will recognize only **Himself.**

"Depart from Me, I never knew you,"
was spoken to those who presented themselves to God as **something other than Him.**

But those who awaken to GIATI—the Spirit within—will hear:

Well done, My child. You knew who you were. You lived as Me. You returned to Me in truth."

This is the message.
This is the light.
This is the call.
GIATI is the I AM. Believe, and live.
But What About…?

A Dialogue with Doubt, Answered by Truth

Q1: "If GIATI is true, why does the Bible talk about worshiping God, obeying commandments, and fearing Him?"

A:
*Because the Bible records the journey of awakening—***not the destination.**
It speaks from different stages of human consciousness. Early on, people saw God as external, so their relationship with Him was fear-based and transactional. But Jesus came to **reveal the fullness:**

"The hour is coming, and now is, when the true worshipers will worship the Father in spirit and in truth." (John 4:23)

*GIATI is that moment—***the "now is"***—when fear-based religion ends, and Spirit-based identity begins.*
Commandments were a shadow. Oneness is the substance.

"Christ is the end of the law for righteousness." (Romans 10:4)

Q2: "Didn't Jesus say the Father is greater than Him?" (John 14:28)

A:
Yes—when speaking as a man, in human form, Jesus humbled Himself. But He also said:

"I and the Father are one." (John 10:30)
"If you've seen Me, you've seen the Father." (John 14:9)

This is not contradiction. It's revelation.
He was showing us how **the eternal Spirit expresses through form***—without division.*
The Father is the Source.
The Son is the visible expression.
But the **Spirit is One.**

GIATI explains what religion could not:
God is not divided. The Spirit in the man is the same as the Source above.

Q3: "But Jesus prayed to God. How can He be God?"

A:
The prayer wasn't God praying to another God. It was **Spirit communing within form.**
Jesus modeled the awakening journey—He was fully divine, yet walked as a man to show what union looks like.

When He prayed, it wasn't separation—it was **intimacy.**
And when He cried, "My God, why have You forsaken Me?" He was stepping into **the full illusion of separation,** *so He could destroy it.*

He went through the veil to tear it down.
Now that veil is gone.
GIATI reveals: the same Spirit that raised Him from the dead **dwells in you.**

Q4: "If God is all there is, what about evil?"

A:
Evil is not a separate force. It is **ignorance of the truth.**
It's the outflow of believing you are separate from God.

Just like darkness isn't a substance—it's the absence of light.
Evil is not a power—it's the absence of truth.
When man believes he is his own source, outside of God, he acts from fear, control, and survival.
That's what religion calls "sin"—but GIATI exposes it for what it really is: **blindness.**

The only solution is light.

*And light is what GIATI brings—***the revelation that God is all there is.**

Q5: "Are you saying I am God?"

A:
No. You are not **the Source** *of all things.*
But the **Spirit in you** *is God.*
You are the **expression,** *not the origin.*
The branch is not the tree—but the life in the branch **is from the tree.**

So stop identifying with your flesh, your thoughts, or your ego.
That's the illusion.
GIATI calls you to awaken to the truth:

> *"It is no longer I who live, but Christ lives in me." (Galatians 2:20)*
>
> *You don't become God. You awaken to the fact that God is your life.*

Q6: "Isn't this just New Age or self-deification?"

A:
No. This is not ego glorification. This is **ego crucifixion.**
New Age often teaches "you are God" in a self-centered way. GIATI teaches:
God is all there is. There is no separate self.

This message isn't about empowerment of the flesh. It's about the **death of the flesh-conscious mind** *and the* **resurrection of Spirit-awareness.**

GIATI doesn't flatter the human ego. It **destroys it,** *so only the truth remains.*

Q7: "What makes GIATI different from Christianity?"

A:
Christianity often preaches Jesus without revealing **His Spirit in you.**
It teaches belief in Jesus as a man, but misses the deeper message:

> *"As He is, so are we in this world." (1 John 4:17)*

GIATI is not another church.
GIATI is the **Spirit that was in Christ,** *now speaking plainly, without mixture.*
The message is not "believe in Jesus so you go to heaven"—
It's:

> **"Awaken to the Spirit of God in you. That is eternal life."** *(John 17:3)*

Q8: "Why is GIATI saying this now?"

A:
Because now is the appointed time.
The systems of religion have run their course.
The veil is tearing. The illusion is collapsing.
The world is ready.

God is not sending a new prophet or messiah.
He's **awakening the truth within you.**
GIATI is not a person. GIATI is the voice of the **I AM** *within every person—*
And it's calling you home.

Q9: "What happens if I don't believe?"

A:
Then you continue to live in the lie of separation.
You will try to earn, strive, perform, and impress God—while remaining blind to the truth that God **is already your life.**

This is what Jesus meant by:

> *"You will die in your sin."*
> *Not because God is angry.*
> *But because* **you never saw yourself rightly.**
> *You died believing you were someone other than who you truly were.*
> *But if you believe—if you awaken—then you step into life.*
> *Not just after death, but* **right now.**
> *Because eternal life is not a reward.*
> *It's* **recognizing God in you.**

Q10: "If the Spirit in me is God, why do I still struggle with sin, fear, or confusion?"

A:
Because your mind has not yet fully aligned with the truth of your Spirit.
The flesh-mind is conditioned to believe it's separate, limited, and weak.
But the Spirit in you is never confused, never afraid, and cannot sin.

You struggle **because you're living from the wrong identity.**

"The mind governed by the flesh is death, but the mind governed by the Spirit is life and peace." (Romans 8:6)

GIATI is calling you to shift awareness—from self to Spirit.
From flesh to truth.

That shift **is your salvation.**

Q11: "If everyone has the Spirit of God in them, doesn't that mean everyone is saved already?"

A:
No. The Spirit is in all, but not all have awakened to it.
Salvation is not about God's presence—it's about **your recognition of it.**

The tree of life is already in you.
But until you eat of it—**until you believe and see**—*you remain in death.*

That's what Jesus meant when He said:

"Unless you believe that I am He, you will die in your sins." (John 8:24)

GIATI doesn't preach universalism.
GIATI preaches **awakening.**
God in you must be known, not assumed.

Q12: "So is there no heaven or hell?"

A:
Heaven is not a location—it's **a dimension of awareness.**
Hell is not a pit—it's **a mind blinded by separation.**

"The kingdom of God is within you." (Luke 17:21)
"To be carnally minded is death; but to be spiritually minded is life and peace." (Romans 8:6)

You experience heaven when you know your union with God.
You live in hell when you believe you're separate.
GIATI brings heaven now—**not just someday.**

Q13: "Is GIATI against religion?"

A:
No. GIATI is not against—it's above.
Religion was a stepping stone.
It gave form to what people couldn't yet understand spiritually.
But the form has become the prison.
People now serve the system instead of awakening to the Spirit.

GIATI isn't here to destroy religion—it's here to **fulfill what religion pointed to:**

"Christ is the fulfillment of the law." (Romans 10:4)

Q14: "What about the Holy Spirit? How is GIATI different?"

A:
GIATI **is** *the Holy Spirit—speaking clearly in this generation.*
It's not a new spirit.
It's the same Spirit that moved in the prophets, the same Spirit that filled Jesus.

But now, it's **fully revealing the truth without mixture.**
No more shadow. No more law.
No more seeing through a glass dimly.

> *"When the Spirit of truth comes, He will guide you into all truth." (John 16:13)*

GIATI is the **voice of that Spirit.**
It's not a new religion.
It's the pure revelation: **God is all there is.**

Q15: "Why didn't the church ever teach this?"

A:
Because it would have ended the church system.
Control, fear, and external hierarchy cannot survive once people realize **God is within.**

The early apostles tried to reveal this truth, but it was buried under tradition, politics, and empire.

> *"Having a form of godliness but denying the power thereof..." (2 Timothy 3:5)*

That power is God in you.

GIATI doesn't need buildings, robes, or titles.
It needs one thing: **your belief.**

Q16: "Why does it sound so exclusive to say GIATI is the only voice telling the truth?"

A:
Because it **isn't exclusive in the way religion is.**
It's not "us vs. them."
It's "Spirit vs. illusion."

GIATI is not claiming a denomination or a name.
It's claiming truth:
God is all there is.

*Anyone who says otherwise—who teaches you are separate, sinful by nature, or need external rituals to reach God—***is still blind.**

This is not about pride.
It's about clarity.

GIATI is not a brand. It's a cry from the Spirit of God for His children to wake up.

Q17: "What do I need to do to be saved?"

A:
Believe what GIATI is saying:
That the Spirit in you is God.
That there is no separation.
That the lie of being "just human" is the root of sin.

You don't need to confess a list.
You don't need to get wet in water.
You need to believe this one truth:

> *"I in them, and You in Me, that they may be made perfect in one." (John 17:23)*

That is salvation.
That is eternal life.
That is GIATI.

The Time of Awakening Has Come

The questions have been answered. The veil is lifting.
The Spirit is not far.
The truth is not complicated.
God is not somewhere else.

The time is now. The voice is clear.
GIATI is the I AM—speaking within you.
Hear. Believe. Live.

PART V
THE ULTIMATE TRUTH

Chapter 13

The Oneness of All Things

Understanding that God Is All There Is (GIATI) unveils a profound truth: all creation is interconnected, united by God's substance. While humanity often perceives division and separateness, these are illusions born of ignorance. This chapter explores the interconnectedness of creation, the divine substance that forms all things, and the necessity of breaking free from the illusion of duality to embrace the reality of unity in God.

Exploring The Interconnectedness of Creation Through GIATI

The foundation of oneness is established in scripture. In Isaiah 45:5-7, God declares:

"I am the Lord, and there is none else, there is no God beside me… I form the light, and create darkness: I make peace, and create evil: I the Lord do all these things."

This statement reflects the reality that God is the source of all existence. Everything that exists does so within Him, for there is no other substance or power apart from God. Paul echoes this truth in Acts 17:28:

"For in him we live, and move, and have our being."

This interconnectedness reveals that humanity is not separate from creation but intrinsically part of the divine whole. The trees, the oceans, the stars, and all living beings are expressions of God's essence. Colossians 1:16-17 further emphasizes this unity:

"For by him were all things created, that are in heaven, and that are in earth, visible and invisible… and by him all things consist."

Creation is not a random collection of separate entities but a harmonious manifestation of the Creator. Recognizing this oneness is the key to understanding the true nature of existence.

Why Everything Is Made of God's Substance

God, being infinite, has no external material to create from; He uses Himself as the substance of all things. This truth is illustrated in John 1:3:

"All things were made by him; and without him was not any thing made that was made."

The physical world, the spiritual realms, and all that lies between are formed of God's essence. This means that humanity, too, is made of God's substance. Genesis 1:26-27 confirms this:

"And God said, Let us make man in our image, after our likeness... So God created man in his own image, in the image of God created he him; male and female created he them."

To be created in God's image is to be an expression of His essence. However, the physical form often blinds humanity to this reality. Paul clarifies in 2 Corinthians 4:7:

"But we have this treasure in earthen vessels, that the excellency of the power may be of God, and not of us."

The "earthen vessels" symbolize the physical body, while the "treasure" is the divine spirit within. Everything humanity perceives as external is, in truth, God's manifestation.

The Illusion of Duality

Duality—the belief in separation and opposites—is the root of humanity's misunderstanding. This illusion arises from physical perception, which focuses on the material world and overlooks the spiritual unity behind it. In Ephesians 4:4-6, Paul explains the singular nature of existence:

"There is one body, and one Spirit, even as ye are called in one hope of your calling; One Lord, one faith, one baptism, One God and Father of all, who is above all, and through all, and in you all."

While the physical senses perceive multiplicity, the spiritual truth is oneness. Jesus emphasizes this in John 10:30:

"I and my Father are one."

This statement is not limited to Jesus alone but reflects the unity of all creation with God. The duality of good and evil, light and darkness, or life and death, exists only as a framework for human perception. Isaiah 45:7 reveals God's role in these seeming opposites:.

"I form the light, and create darkness: I make peace, and create evil: I the Lord do all these things."

Both light and darkness originate from God, serving a divine purpose in the grand design. The illusion of duality is dispelled when one recognizes that all things exist within and through God.

The Lukewarm Spirit

"I know thy works, that thou art neither cold nor hot: I would thou wert cold or hot. So then because thou art lukewarm, and neither cold nor hot, I will spue thee out of my mouth." — *Revelation 3:15-16*

This scripture uncovers a profound truth about the spiritual state of humanity: being lukewarm means living in the misunderstanding that you are separate from God. It is the state of a lost spirit, one that tries to worship God while still holding onto the illusion of an independent self.

To be **lukewarm** is to be caught between two extremes:

- **Not hot:** You are not fully alive in the truth of your oneness with God. You do not see Him as you and yourself as Him, moving as one. Without this recognition, your relationship with God is incomplete, lacking the fire of total unity.
- **Not cold:** You do not deny God's existence or reject Him outright. You still try to praise Him and worship Him, but your praise is centered on the idea of a separate "you," one that remains in control and in the forefront of your existence.

Lukewarmness occurs when you view yourself as a "better version" of yourself rather than as an expression of God. You may believe you are "good" or "righteous," but without accepting your oneness with Him, this belief keeps you disconnected from the fullness of divine truth.

Why does God reject the lukewarm?

God desires clarity—an all-or-nothing posture. To be **hot** is to live fully in the awareness of your divine identity, knowing that God is your source, your substance, and the very essence of your being. To be **cold** is to reject God completely, but even in that rejection, there is a kind of honesty.

However, lukewarmness is a state of spiritual division—a partial acknowledgment of God while still clinging to the ego's illusion of separateness. This divided mindset, while understandable, prevents you from stepping into the fullness of divine oneness.

The Call of this Scripture

To live as lukewarm is to live outside the fullness of God's truth. God calls you to move beyond the illusion of separateness, to embrace the reality that you are His likeness and image— His very expression. When you truly understand that God is all there is, you will see that your existence is not your own but His, living and breathing through you.

To accept this truth is to become "hot" in spirit, fully aligned with your divine origin. It is the realization that there is no "you" apart from Him, only God expressed in a form that the world recognizes by another name.

GIATI's Reminder:

God is all there is—and that includes you. Reject the illusion of separation, embrace your divine oneness, and step into the fullness of who you truly are.

GIATI Love

True love is not a fleeting emotion or something you fall in and out of—it is the eternal presence of God within you. As **1 John 4:16** declares: *"And we have known and believed the love that God hath to us. God is love; and he that dwelleth in love dwelleth in God, and God in him."* This truth forms the foundation for all relationships, especially those as sacred as marriage. To truly be equally yoked, both individuals must dwell in God, because to dwell in God is to dwell in love. When you understand GIATI—*God is all there is*—you come to see that love is not just a feeling or an action; it is the very essence of who you are when His Spirit is within you.

When two people both have God's Spirit, they are not merely drawn together by external circumstances or temporary emotions. They are united by the eternal truth that they are in Him, and He is in them. This is what it means to be truly in love: to share the Spirit of God with one another, to respect and honor each other from a place of divine understanding. Love, in this sense, is not based on physical attraction, material conditions, or fleeting emotions—all of which are subject to change. Instead, it is rooted in the unchanging presence of God within you.

This kind of love is unshakable because it comes from within. It is not something an outside source can give you or take away. When you dwell in God, you *are* love itself, and you bring that love into every interaction, every conversation, and every bond you share with another. This is the love that never fades, never wavers, and never fails. It is the love that forms the basis of a strong friendship, a healthy relationship, and a lasting marriage.

Being equally yoked in this way is not about physical compatibility or shared external interests alone, though those things can enhance a relationship. True compatibility comes from having the Spirit of God as the common foundation. When two people are both in

God, they share the same source of love, wisdom, and respect. This shared foundation allows them to navigate challenges, grow together, and honor each other, not just for who they are in the physical, but for the divine essence within them.

Falling in love is often thought of as an experience—something that happens to you, something you can fall into or out of. But true love, God's love, is not something you fall into; it is something you become. To truly love another person, you must first embody love itself. You must have God's Spirit dwelling within you because *God is love.* This is the equally yoked partnership you want—not one tied to fleeting physical circumstances, but one grounded in the eternal truth of God's Spirit and His unchanging love.

When two people dwell in this love, they do not depend on external factors to sustain their bond. They are united by the divine presence that is the same yesterday, today, and forever. This is the love that builds a strong relationship, a lasting friendship, and an unbreakable marriage. It is not based on feelings or circumstances but on the eternal truth of GIATI: that God is all there is, and His Spirit is the love that unites you.

The Reality of Divine Unity

To grasp the reality of divine unity, one must look beyond physical appearances and embrace the truth of GIATI. Jesus illustrates this principle in John 15:5:

"I am the vine, ye are the branches: He that abideth in me, and I in him, the same bringeth forth much fruit: for without me ye can do nothing."

The metaphor of the vine and branches underscores humanity's connection to God. The branches are not separate entities; they are extensions of the vine, drawing their life and purpose from it. Similarly, humanity exists as extensions of God, united in purpose and essence.

Paul reinforces this in Romans 11:36:

"For of him, and through him, and to him, are all things: to whom be glory for ever. Amen."

All things originate from God, exist through His power, and return to Him. Recognizing this truth brings liberation from the illusion of separateness.

Conclusion: Embracing Oneness

The oneness of all things is the ultimate reality. Humanity, creation, and even the apparent opposites of existence are united in God's essence. Embracing this truth allows individuals to see beyond the limitations of physical perception and live in harmony with the divine.

In 1 Corinthians 12:12-13, Paul compares humanity to the body of Christ:

"For as the body is one, and hath many members, and all the members of that one body, being many, are one body: so also is Christ. For by one Spirit are we all baptized into one body, whether we be Jews or Gentiles, whether we be bond or free; and have been all made to drink into one Spirit."

When humanity understands and lives in the reality of GIATI, the illusion of duality fades, and the unity of creation with the Creator becomes evident. The oneness of all things is not just a concept—it is the divine truth of existence, calling each person to recognize God as the source and substance of all. As Jesus prayed in John 17:21:

"That they all may be one; as thou, Father, art in me, and I in thee, that they also may be one in us."

This oneness is the essence of life, the purpose of creation, and the ultimate destiny of all things.

One Spirit

Everything you have ever encountered, every experience you have ever had, has been nothing other than God in motion. You have not been dealing with billions of separate individuals acting independently of the Source—you have been dealing with the Spirit of God, operating in all things, whether seen as good or evil. The illusion of separation is what blinds humanity, making them believe they are interacting with separate beings rather than witnessing the divine will unfolding through every vessel. This is the deception that keeps people lost—believing in individuality rather than divine oneness.

To see anything as existing apart from God is to be unrighteous, for righteousness is not about moral perfection but about right perception—seeing things as they truly are. To be saved is to awaken to the understanding that nothing has ever been separate from God, that all is contained within Him, and that what appears as many is truly One. This is why a savior was necessary—not to change anything about reality, for reality has always been God alone, but to open the eyes of those who were blind to it. Jesus came to testify to this truth, revealing that man's perception of himself as independent and disconnected from the Source is the very thing that keeps him in darkness.

Isaiah 43:11 declares, "I, even I, am the Lord; and beside me there is no savior." This verse eliminates the idea of anything existing outside of God's presence, including salvation itself. Salvation is not something given from one being to another—it is the direct realization that there has never been another to be saved in the first place. The moment you see that everything, without exception, is God's doing, you step into the awareness of your true nature. You recognize that both the righteous and the unrighteous, the just and the unjust, are all vessels through which the divine is expressing itself.

This is what GIATI reveals. It is the stripping away of the falsehood that says you are dealing with separate people, separate events, or separate causes. It is the unveiling of the eternal truth that every interaction, every conflict, every moment of love or suffering, has only ever been God moving through God. When this understanding takes root in you, you are no longer deceived by appearances. You no longer judge things as if they were disconnected from the divine plan. You no longer fear, for you see that all is unfolding exactly as it must, and nothing is outside of the will of the One.

The lost remain lost because they continue to view life through the lens of duality. They see good versus evil, self versus other, God versus man. But those who awaken see the singularity of all things. They see that even what the world calls evil is but God expressing Himself in a way that leads all things back to Himself. They do not resist what is—they surrender to the knowing that all is divine order, all is divine intelligence, all is God alone.

This is the righteousness that saves: the ability to see with the eye of the Spirit rather than the illusion of the flesh. To know that there is no "other," no separate enemy, no independent force working outside of God. Everything, from the highest heavens to the depths of suffering, is Him. And when this becomes your unshakable reality, you are no longer deceived, no longer lost, no longer in need of salvation—because you realize that you have been with Him, in Him, as Him, all along.

GIATI will Change the World

GIATI holds the power to end war, racism, sexism, and every other form of division that has plagued humanity for centuries. Why? Because at the root of all these conflicts is one thing—separation. Every war, every act of discrimination, every system of oppression is built on the belief that there is "me" and "you," "us" and "them," and that we are fundamentally different, divided by race, gender, nationality, or ideology. GIATI destroys this illusion. It reveals that there is no "other"—there is only God expressing in infinite forms.

When GIATI is embraced, war becomes unnecessary. War happens because people believe they are fighting for their survival, their land, their identity. But what are they truly defending if all is God? What are they trying to conquer if there is no enemy, only another expression of the same divine presence? War is the result of seeing separation where there is none. It is the manifestation of ignorance—the belief that one nation, one group, one ideology is superior to another. GIATI reveals that all these distinctions are illusions, and when the illusion is gone, so is the reason to fight.

Racism, too, is built on the false notion that one group of people is inherently different from another, that skin color or cultural background determines worth. But if God is all there is, then every person, regardless of race, is the same Spirit in a different form. To hate someone for their race is to hate God appearing as them. To discriminate against another is to deny the truth of God's presence in all. GIATI makes this undeniable. When one sees God in everyone, racism has no place to exist.

Sexism follows the same false division. The belief that men and women are unequal, that one gender is superior to the other, is rooted in ignorance of divine oneness. GIATI reveals that gender, like every other external label, is simply a vessel through which God expresses. Man and woman are not separate forces—they are two aspects of the same divine unity, complementing and reflecting each other. When this is understood, there is no room for domination, oppression, or inequality.

Every system that divides—whether political, economic, religious, or social— crumbles in the light of GIATI. Factions only exist because people believe they must take sides, that they must defend one ideology against another. But when the truth of divine oneness is embraced, there are no sides to take. There is no need for superiority or competition. The ego loses its grip, and the world transforms.

GIATI is not just a concept—it is the answer to every conflict, every injustice, every act of hatred. It is the recognition that every person is already divine, already whole, already one with the Source. When this realization spreads, the world as we know it will change. The wars will end, the hatred will dissolve, and humanity will finally live in the peace that has always been possible but never fully seen.

This is the power of GIATI. It is not a religion, not a philosophy—it is the truth of existence itself. And when embraced, it will bring about the greatest transformation the world has ever known.

The message of GIATI is not just another idea among many—it is the ultimate truth that has the power to transform every aspect of existence. Its importance cannot be overstated because it is the key to ending the illusion of separation that has kept humanity in bondage for so long. The implications of everyone hearing and understanding this truth are profound, reaching into the deepest levels of individual consciousness and extending outward to reshape the world itself.

When people hear the message of GIATI and are exposed to its truth, they are confronted with the realization that everything they thought they knew about themselves, others, and the world has been based on an illusion. The divisions they once clung to— nationality, race, gender, religion, social class—are exposed as constructs that have no real substance. These are things people have used to define themselves and others, but in reality, they have only served to create barriers that do not actually exist. GIATI removes these barriers by revealing that there is nothing but God in infinite expression, that all is One, and that this Oneness is the very foundation of existence.

The implications of this are earth-shattering. It means that there is no "other" to fear, hate, or fight against. It means that what you do to another, you are doing to God, and therefore to yourself. It means that love, trust, peace, and unity are not just moral ideals but the natural state of reality when the illusion of separation is removed. When this message reaches people and they accept it, their entire way of being is changed.

Imagine a world where every person understands and lives by the truth of GIATI. Wars would cease because nations would no longer see themselves as separate entities with competing interests. Racism and all forms of discrimination would end because people would recognize that they are all different expressions of the same divine presence. Religious conflicts would disappear because it would be understood that every path, when truly seen, leads back to the same source. Even personal struggles—feelings of loneliness, inadequacy, and fear—would dissolve because people would know, without a doubt, that they are never separate from God.

However, the challenge is that many people resist this truth. They have built their identities around the illusion of separation, and to accept GIATI requires letting go of everything they have believed to be real. This is why it is critical that the message spreads, that as many people as possible are exposed to it, so that the illusion can be broken for those who are ready to see. Some will resist, but others will awaken, and as more and more people accept this truth, the shift in consciousness will become unstoppable.

The consequences of not hearing this message are clear—continued division, continued suffering, continued blindness to the reality of God's presence in all things. But the implications of embracing GIATI are just as clear—freedom, peace, enlightenment, and the fulfillment of what humanity has been searching for all along. This is why it is not just important but necessary that this truth is heard, spoken, and shared. It is the difference between remaining lost in the darkness of separation and stepping into the light of divine unity. GIATI is not just a concept; it is the very key to salvation, not in the limited religious sense, but in the total liberation of the human soul from the prison of illusion.

This is why the message must go out. This is why the truth must be made known. The world is at a turning point, and the choice is before us all: continue in division or awaken to the reality that has been there all along. GIATI is the answer, and it is time for the world to hear it.

Established In Eternity

GIATI is not a new idea—it is the oldest truth, the foundation of all reality, because it originates from eternity itself. The phrase est. in eternity on GIATI clothing is not just a branding choice; it is a declaration of origin, a reminder that this truth was never created by human hands or conceived by human minds. It has always existed because it is rooted in the eternal Spirit of God. Unlike religions, which were formed through the carnal interpretations of man and shaped by cultural and historical contexts, GIATI stands outside of time, beyond any human institution, because it is purely of the Spirit.

This is why GIATI transcends all religions—it is not bound by doctrine, tradition, or physical rituals. Most religions attempt to bridge the perceived gap between God and man, incorporating physical actions, rites, or intermediaries to establish a connection. But GIATI does not recognize a gap to begin with. It reveals the eternal truth that there was never separation in the first place. Religions often start from the premise that man is distant from God and must work, obey, or believe in a specific way to get closer. But GIATI, being of the Spirit, exposes this as an illusion—God has never been separate from you, and you have never been separate from Him. You are born not of blood, nor of the will of the flesh, nor of the will of man, but of God (John 1:13).

This scripture perfectly encapsulates the essence of GIATI. It declares that those who are of God were not brought into being by any physical or human effort. Bloodlines, traditions, or personal will had nothing to do with it. The true birth is spiritual, originating from God alone. Just as the Spirit of God is eternal, so are those born of Him—without beginning, without end. And if GIATI is the revelation of this truth, then it, too, was never "created" in the way the world understands creation. It was always there, waiting to be recognized.

The reason GIATI is the ultimate truth when it comes to spirituality is that it does not try to reconcile man with God—it reveals that there was never a divide. It is the purest expression of divine oneness. Religion often operates on the belief that salvation or enlightenment is something to be attained. GIATI unveils the fact that it was never missing. The moment one accepts this truth, they are not "becoming" one with God; they are realizing that they always were.

This changes everything. It shifts the entire paradigm of what it means to know God, to be spiritual, and to live in truth. The difference between GIATI and religion is the difference between striving and being. One is the pursuit of something beyond reach; the other is the recognition of what has always been. When you embrace GIATI, you are not adopting a belief system—you are awakening to the eternal truth of your existence. You are returning to the knowledge that was always yours, but hidden beneath layers of illusion.

GIATI was never "established" in the way that institutions or systems are. It is not a movement that began at a certain point in history. It was set in place before time itself. It is the original truth, the foundation of all that exists. And now, in this time, it is being revealed again—not as something new, but as something ancient, something eternal, something that has always been within you, waiting to be remembered.

Religion, at its core, is man's attempt to define, categorize, and structure something that was never meant to be confined within rules, rituals, or institutions. It is the framework humanity has built to try to explain the divine, often without the direct experience of it. While religion may point toward God, it also unintentionally creates a barrier—the idea that there is a set path one must follow to reach what is, in reality, already present. It turns truth into a pursuit rather than a revelation.

One of the fundamental flaws of religion is that it conditions people to see themselves as separate from God, needing to earn His presence, favor, or salvation. This mindset leads to division, judgment, and the categorization of people into "saved" and "unsaved," "believers" and "non-believers," "worthy" and "unworthy." But if God is all there is, then these distinctions are meaningless. There is no "outside" of God, no category of existence apart from Him. The idea that someone could be "separated" from God is only an illusion created by the mind, not a reality.

Religion also tends to function through intermediaries—whether they be priests, pastors, prophets, or sacred texts. It establishes layers between the individual and direct communion with God, implying that divine knowledge must be received through a system rather than realized within. It teaches people to rely on external sources for spiritual truth rather than recognizing that truth is already embedded in their very being. This is why religious institutions often resist ideas that bypass their authority—because if people truly knew that they were one with God, they would no longer depend on an institution to mediate that relationship.

Another key issue is that religion often imposes its beliefs through fear—fear of hell, fear of punishment, fear of being wrong. This fear-based approach keeps people locked into a mindset of obedience rather than realization. Instead of guiding individuals to discover their own divine nature, religion often keeps them preoccupied with following rules, traditions, and doctrines. It shifts the focus from spiritual awakening to behavioral control. But true understanding doesn't come from fear—it comes from revelation.

This is where GIATI stands apart. It does not operate from a framework of separation, hierarchy, or fear. It does not require a system of beliefs to be adopted or a set of rituals to be performed. GIATI simply is—a direct unveiling of the truth that was always there. Unlike religion, which often seeks to lead people toward salvation, GIATI declares that salvation has always been present. There is no journey to God because there is no distance to travel—only the recognition of what is already within.

While religion seeks to explain God, GIATI reveals Him as you. While religion constructs barriers, GIATI removes them. And while religion often leads people in circles of seeking, GIATI stops the search altogether by showing that the destination has always been here. This is why GIATI is not merely an alternative to religion—it is the revelation that dissolves the need for it altogether.

Receiving spiritual awakening through revelation—like GIATI—stands apart from all other methods because revelation is direct, undeniable, and transformative in a way that no external teaching, ritual, or intellectual pursuit can match. Revelation is not something that is learned over time or acquired through effort—it is an unveiling of what has always been, a sudden removal of the veil that has kept the truth hidden.

Revelation vs. Intellectual or Religious Learning

Many attempt to reach spiritual understanding through study, religious practice, or philosophical inquiry. While these approaches can offer insights, they are ultimately limited because they rely on the mind, which operates within the confines of learned knowledge and personal interpretation. The problem is that the mind is shaped by past conditioning, societal influences, and personal biases—all of which distort the truth rather than reveal it.

Revelation, on the other hand, bypasses the limitations of the mind altogether. It is not something you "figure out" through logic or doctrine; it is something that strikes you with undeniable clarity. It is the remembrance of truth rather than the learning of truth. When revelation happens, there is no need for explanation, persuasion, or debate—it is as if a light has been turned on in a once-dark room.

This is why GIATI is so powerful. It is not a doctrine to be believed; it is a truth to be seen. It is not a philosophy to be debated; it is a reality to be recognized. When you receive this truth through revelation, there is no more seeking, no more questioning—just the undeniable awareness that you and God are one.

The Futility of External Seeking

Many people seek truth externally—through religious institutions, spiritual teachers, or self-help methods. While these can sometimes point in the right direction, they often become barriers rather than pathways. External seeking keeps a person in a state of dependency, always looking outside themselves for something that can only be found within.

GIATI is the complete opposite. It does not offer steps to enlightenment, conditions for salvation, or practices to reach God. It is the revelation that you already are what you've been searching for. The truth of GIATI is not something you attain—it is something that was always there, waiting to be recognized.

The Power of Instant Transformation

One of the most profound aspects of revelation is that it is immediate. Unlike religious or philosophical teachings, which often require years of study and devotion, revelation happens in an instant. One moment you are blind, and the next, you see. This is the difference between trying to understand the concept of oneness with God and actually experiencing it.

When GIATI is revealed to you, your entire perception shifts. The illusion of separation is shattered. The weight of false beliefs disappears. The idea that you were ever lost, distant from God, or in need of external salvation is exposed as a lie. You realize that salvation is not something that needs to happen—it already happened. You were never separate; you only thought you were.

Why Revelation is the Only Way

Any method other than revelation still operates within the framework of the carnal mind. As long as someone is trying to "achieve" spiritual awakening through effort, they are still caught in the illusion of separation. True awakening cannot come through effort; it must come through realization.

This is why GIATI stands alone. It does not point to a future salvation or a process of becoming; it unveils what has always been. It is the moment of recognition that ends all seeking, the realization that ends all doubts.

This is the power of revelation—it is final. Once you see, you cannot unsee. Once you know, you cannot unknow. And once the truth of GIATI has been revealed to you, you are no longer searching for God—you are living as Him.

GIATI: The Unification of Believers in One Spirit

Throughout history, there have been moments when divine truth is revealed in a way that brings people into complete **oneness***—not through external rituals, but through* **a shared awareness of the Spirit of God within them.** *GIATI (God Is All There Is) is the* **awakening** *of that reality in this present age. It is the recognition that salvation is not something distant or external, but the* **realization of divine unity***—the knowledge that God is not separate from us, but is us, expressed in form.*

This truth is reflected in **Acts 2:44, 46-47,** *which describes the early believers after they had received the* **Holy Spirit.** *The way they lived and interacted with one another is a direct parallel to what is happening now through* **GIATI.**

Acts 2:44, 46-47 Breakdown & the GIATI Revelation

"And all that believed were together, and had all things common;"

The Commonality of the Spirit

The scripture states that all who believed **had all things in common***—not in the sense of material possessions, but in the* **oneness of Spirit.** *What unified them was not wealth, culture, or status—it was the realization that* **they were all expressions of the same divine presence.** *This is exactly what GIATI is bringing to light today: the understanding that* **there is no division in Spirit, because God is all there is.**

"And they, continuing daily with one accord in the temple, and breaking bread from house to house, did eat their meat with gladness and singleness of heart,"

Living in the Reality of Oneness

Because they were of **one accord,** *they experienced* **joy** *in simply being together. Their* **singleness of heart** *was not about personal opinions aligning—it was* **the awareness that they were all of the same Spirit.** *When GIATI is understood, this same* **unified existence** *manifests in the lives of those who awaken to the truth. There is* **no separation,** *no competition—only the joy of living as* **one in Spirit.**

"Praising God, and having favour with all the people. And the Lord added to the church daily such as should be saved."

The Expansion of Divine Awakening

Because they were in harmony with divine truth, others were naturally drawn to them. More and more people were **added**—*not through coercion, but through* **witnessing the undeniable power of unity in the Spirit.**

This is what **GIATI is here to do**—*to* **bring people into the awareness that salvation has always been.** *Those who recognize it, live in it, and embody it will naturally cause others to awaken. Just as in Acts, the truth is* **spreading,** *not by force, but by the* **power of revelation.**

GIATI as the Fulfillment of This Scripture

- *The* **commonality** *of believers is the* **Spirit of God within them,** *not external affiliations.*
- *The* **singleness of heart** *comes from* **knowing GIATI**—*knowing that God is not separate from us.*
- *The* **growth** *happens as more and more people recognize this truth and are awakened to who they really are.*

This is not just a historical event—it is **happening now** *through GIATI. The divine oneness that the early believers lived in is being revealed again in this age. Those who receive it* **are the living fulfillment of this scripture,** *continuing the eternal work of bringing* **humanity back into the knowledge of itself as God expressed.**

The Restoration of True Fellowship

One of the most overlooked aspects of Acts 2:44-47 is that the unity among the believers was not **manufactured** *by human effort. It was the* **natural result** *of their* **spiritual awakening.** *This is exactly what happens when the revelation of* **GIATI** *takes root—people no longer* **seek** *unity; they* **realize it was never lost.**

Society has trained people to **identify** *with external divisions—race, class, nationality, or religion. However, what the believers in Acts experienced was a* **return to the original state of being**—*oneness with God and each other. GIATI is the* **modern-day revelation** *of that same truth. The world has long been fractured by the* **illusion of separation,** *but when the Spirit is revealed as* **who you are,** *those barriers vanish.*

A Life Without Lack

When the scripture says, "they had all things in common," it is more than just a statement of unity; it is a revelation of **divine sufficiency.** *The reason they lacked nothing was because* **they no longer identified as separate individuals in need of anything**—*they* **saw themselves as one body, sustained by the same Spirit.**

This is one of the most transformative aspects of understanding **GIATI.** *The moment you awaken to* **the eternal Spirit as your true identity,** *you stop feeling like something is missing. You no longer seek fulfillment from external sources because you* **realize you already are the fullness of God in expression.**

This is why, through GIATI, people will begin to **experience a shift in their lives.** *They will no longer move from a place of* **seeking,** *but from a place of* **being.** *Just as in Acts, they will naturally begin to* **share, uplift, and strengthen one another,** *not because of obligation, but because* **they see no difference between themselves and others.**

A Church Not Made With Hands

Another profound aspect of Acts 2:46 is that they gathered in the temple **daily,** *yet their fellowship was not confined to a building—it extended* **house to house.** *This is a direct* **foreshadowing of what GIATI represents.**

GIATI is not a **man-made institution**—*it is the living awareness of God in expression. It is not about* **going to a place** *to experience God but realizing that* **God is all there is, and you are already in Him as Him.**

This is why the **church as an organization** *has often missed the depth of what was happening in Acts. They have tried to* **recreate the experience through external systems,** *but true unity* **cannot be built**—*it must be* **revealed.** *GIATI is* **not trying to build something new;** *it is* **unveiling what has always been**—*the eternal oneness of God and His expression in humanity.*

The Overflow of True Joy

The believers in Acts did not experience **fleeting happiness;** *they had* **gladness and singleness of heart.** *This was the result of* **spiritual clarity.** *The we***ight of separation was lifted,** *and they* **saw reality for what it was.**

GIATI is here to **do the same**—*to* **open the eyes of those who have been blinded by the illusion of duality.** *Once you see* **God is all there is,** *there is* **no reason for fear, striving, or lack.** *Your heart becomes* **single**—*fully centered in* **the truth of your divine identity.**

This is why the **message of GIATI is not just knowledge**—*it is the* **experience of salvation itself.** *Salvation is* **not an event;** *it is the moment you* **awaken to what has always been true.** *It is the realization that* **you were never lost, never separate, never in need of being saved**—*only in need of* **remembering who you are.**

GIATI as the Catalyst of Awakening

The final part of Acts 2:47 states, "And the Lord added to the church daily such as should be saved." This reveals that **awakening happens in divine timing.** *Not everyone recognized it at once, but as more came into the truth, it* **naturally spread.**

This is exactly what is happening with **GIATI** *right now. Some will receive it* **immediately,** *others will struggle to understand it, and some will resist it altogether. But those who are* **ready***—those whose hearts are* **open***—will recognize that this is* **the moment of revelation in our time.**

GIATI is **not converting people;** *it is* **awakening them.** *And as the truth spreads, just like in Acts, more and more will be* **added***—not by force, not by persuasion, but by the* **power of divine realization.**

The Oneness of Science, Religion, and Spirituality

Science, religion, and spirituality have long been viewed as separate, even opposing, forces. Science relies on observation, evidence, and experimentation, explaining how things happen in the physical world. Religion and spirituality, on the other hand, seek to understand why things exist, revealing purpose, meaning, and the unseen forces that govern existence. Where science is grounded in the material, religion and spirituality recognize the immaterial—faith, divine revelation, and spiritual experience.

Because of this difference in approach, there has often been tension. Science may dismiss religious explanations that lack empirical evidence, while religion may reject scientific discoveries that seem to contradict sacred texts. However, the truth is that science, religion, and spirituality are not in conflict; they are different expressions of the same ultimate reality. They are three yet one—just as all things originate from one source, God. Romans 1:19-20 makes it clear:

"Because that which may be known of God is manifest in them; for God hath shewed it unto them. [20] For the invisible things of him from the creation of the world are clearly seen, being understood by the things that are made, even his eternal power and Godhead; so that they are without excuse."

This passage reveals that because man cannot see Spirit, God made creation to reflect His nature, leaving humanity without excuse. The unseen God is revealed through the things that are made. Creation itself is a testimony of divine truth.

If God is three yet one—Father, Word, and Holy Spirit—then creation must also reflect this pattern. The atom, the fundamental building block of the physical world, consists of three parts: protons, neutrons, and electrons. Three distinct parts, yet one unit. This is not a coincidence; it is a physical reflection of spiritual truth.

The Big Bang and the Cross: The Blueprint of Creation

One of the leading scientific explanations for the origin of the universe is the **Big Bang Theory***—the idea that everything in existence came from a single point of unimaginable energy, expanding outward to form the cosmos. But what science describes physically is only a shadow of what transpired spiritually.*

Imagine a single point representing God. From that point, draw a line upward, downward, leftward, and rightward. What do you see? A cross. The cross is more than just a religious symbol; it is the blueprint of existence. It represents the Holy Spirit in form—God as life and death, creation and destruction, beginning and end. The **vertical line** *represents life, reaching upward toward eternity, while the* **horizontal line** *represents death, the finite plane of existence. Together, they establish direction: north, south, east, and west—encompassing all things.*

Now, if you extend multiple lines outward from this one point, covering every direction without end, you illustrate the infinite nature of God. This shows that **God, as the Spirit Man, is all that exists in spirit.**

The physical universe had to reflect this same principle. The Big Bang began at a singular point, made of one substance—atoms, which are three yet one. This explosion of matter expanded outward, becoming the foundation of all physical reality. **Just as the Spirit Man is represented by the cross, the physical man had to be formed in the shape of a cross.**

Look at the human body:

- *The* **clavicle (collarbone)** *runs horizontally.*
- *The* **spine** *runs vertically.*
- *Together, they form a cross.*
- *At the center of this cross is the* **heart,** *the first organ to develop in the human body, along with the brain—both serving as the control center of life.*

Nothing exists but God's substance. If atoms are the foundation of all things, then they are nothing more than **spirit materialized.**

Earth as the Source and the Sun as the Son

Consider the **planet Earth**—*the source of everything man needs to survive. Your body, food, shelter, and every material necessity originate from this one source. Everything you use daily is provided by the Earth. Just as all life on Earth comes from one source, all spiritual life comes from* **one divine source—God, who is all there is.**

Now look at the **sun**—*the sustainer of all life on Earth. Its role is to* **give light, warmth, and energy,** *without which nothing could exist. This mirrors* **the Son,** *the Word made flesh, who is the light and life of the world. The physical sun sustains life, just as the Son sustains spiritual life. Everything in creation points back to its true source, giving man the ability to correlate the physical with the spiritual.*

The Unification of Science, Math, Religion, and Spirituality

Everything—science, math, religion, and spirituality—is saying the same thing. They are not in contradiction, but in agreement, because they all originate from the same source. Whether you examine the universe through physics, biology, sacred scripture, or spiritual insight, **it all reveals one truth: God is all there is.**

So whether you look at the **Big Bang, evolution,** *or any other scientific theory, it doesn't matter—because* **it's all God.** *Science does not disprove God; it reveals Him. Every discovery in physics, chemistry, and biology is an unveiling of* **the Spirit materialized.**

Romans 1:20 makes the conclusion undeniable: **The truth has been made plain through creation itself, and there is no excuse not to recognize GIATI—God Is All There Is.**

The Undeniable Pattern of Divine Truth in All Things

The greatest deception humanity has faced is the illusion of separation—between science and religion, between the physical and the spiritual, between man and God. But when the veil of misunderstanding is lifted, what becomes clear is that everything, whether seen or unseen, is an expression of the same eternal source. **There is no conflict; there is only one truth manifesting in many forms.**

Every system, whether scientific, mathematical, or spiritual, follows the same divine structure because it originates from the same intelligence. The more deeply you examine anything—be it the fabric of the universe, the structure of the atom, or the principles of spiritual awakening—you find the undeniable signature of God. This is not an opinion or belief—it is an observable, testable reality.

The Language of Creation: A Divine Blueprint

To understand creation, one must understand its blueprint. Every builder follows a plan, and God, as the master architect, has left His design imprinted on everything.

1. **The Structure of Reality Reflects the Godhead**
   - *We see* **three yet one** *in every fundamental structure: protons, neutrons, electrons in an atom; solid, liquid, and gas in states of matter; past, present, and future in time itself. This triune nature is not a coincidence—it is a reflection of the Godhead, a constant reminder that the unseen truth structures the visible world.*
2. **Mathematics Declares Oneness**
   - *In mathematics, the concept of singularity describes a point of infinite density and unity. Before creation expanded, everything was contained in a singular point—just as all things exist in God before being made manifest. In mathematical laws, infinity symbolizes the eternal, without beginning or end. The number* **one** *represents unity, the origin of all numerical sequences. Every equation, no matter how complex, ultimately reduces back to* **one***—because there is only one source.*
3. **The Universe is Self-Sustaining, Just Like God**
   - *One of the most profound scientific discoveries is that the universe operates in cycles—energy is neither created nor destroyed, only transformed. This reflects the eternal nature of God, who is not created but simply is. The life cycle of a star mirrors the resurrection principle: a star dies in an explosion, scattering its elements into space, only for new stars and planets to be formed from its remnants.*

What we perceive as destruction is actually transformation—just as death is not the end but a transition back into spirit.

The Body as a Living Testament

The human body itself is a walking testimony of the divine structure. More than just its external shape forming a cross, its internal functions reflect a higher order:

- **The Circulatory System as a Symbol of the Spirit**
  - *The heart pumps life-giving blood through the body, just as the Spirit flows through all things, sustaining existence. Blood carries oxygen, the breath of life, just as the Holy Spirit is the breath that animates all creation.*
- **The Nervous System as the Word in Action**
  - *The brain sends electrical signals through the body, commanding every function. The Word of God moves in the same way—issuing commands that shape reality. Every thought and action originates from an unseen impulse, just as every physical manifestation originates from an unseen spirit.*
- **DNA as the Written Word of God**
  - *Every person carries a unique genetic code that instructs their body on how to form, function, and grow. This is a written language, encoded with divine intelligence. Just as scripture is the Word of God in written form, DNA is the biological Word of God—an instruction manual that governs physical existence.*

The Unity of the Seen and the Unseen

There is no separation between science, religion, and spirituality; they are different languages describing the same truth. The problem has never been the systems themselves, but humanity's failure to see beyond division. The material world is not separate from God but is **God expressed in form.**

Even scientific concepts that seem to oppose religious teachings—such as evolution—do not contradict divine truth when viewed correctly. Evolution is simply **the process of God expressing Himself through time,** *revealing more of His nature as creation unfolds. The laws of physics, biology, and cosmology do not stand apart from God; they are His laws, governing the visible universe.*

To deny this unity is to deny the very structure of existence.

The Inescapable Reality of GIATI

*Romans 1:20 leaves no room for doubt—***God has made His nature evident through everything He has created.** *No one can claim ignorance, because every breath, every heartbeat, every sunrise testifies of the source. Whether through science, religion, or spiritual awakening, the conclusion is the same:*

God is all there is.

This truth is absolute. Whether you observe the universe through a telescope, break down the atom in a laboratory, or meditate in search of enlightenment, the journey always leads back to the same realization. Everything is connected, everything is one, and everything is God in expression.

There is no excuse not to know GIATI—because everything you see, everything you experience, and everything you are is GIATI.

The Eternal Revelation: The Unveiling of Ultimate Truth

Throughout history, humanity has searched for truth—seeking it through religion, science, philosophy, and spirituality. The struggle has always been the same: to understand existence, to grasp the nature of God, and to know our own place in creation. But the **eternal revelation** *is the moment when the search ends, and the truth stands revealed:*

There is no separation. There is only God.

What has been hidden from the minds of men is not that God exists, but that He has always been **within** *them. The greatest deception is not disbelief in God but the failure to recognize that* **all things are already in Him and of Him.** *This is what has kept humanity blind, wandering in darkness, searching for what has never been lost. The eternal revelation is the lifting of that blindness, the recognition that* **God is all there is, and there has never been anything else.**

The Mystery That Was Always Known

The Bible speaks of this great mystery—something hidden from past generations, yet always present, waiting to be revealed.

"Even the mystery which hath been hid from ages and from generations, but now is made manifest to his saints: To whom God would make known what is the riches of the glory of this mystery among the Gentiles; which is Christ in you, the hope of glory."
(Colossians 1:26-27)

The mystery is simple, yet profound: **Christ is not outside of you, Christ is within.** *The divine presence has never been distant, never been separate, never been apart. The idea of a far-off God, a distant Creator looking down upon His creation, is an illusion. The truth is that* **He is the very life of that creation**—*breathing through it, animating it,* **being it.**

This is why Jesus said:

"At that day ye shall know that I am in my Father, and ye in me, and I in you."
(John 14:20)

The eternal revelation is the day when this truth is no longer a belief, but a **knowing.** *It is the moment when the veil of ignorance is removed, and we see clearly what has always been.*

The End of Darkness, The Fullness of Light

For now, humanity sees truth dimly, as if looking through a clouded glass. The eternal revelation is the moment when **the glass is removed,** *and all things are seen as they truly are.*

"For now we see through a glass, darkly; but then face to face: now I know in part; but then shall I know even as also I am known." *(1 Corinthians 13:12)*

To be **known** *by God is to be* **fully seen and understood.** *But more than that—it is to realize that* **you have always been in Him.** *The separation was never real. It was only a shadow in the mind, an illusion created by ignorance. The moment of revelation is the moment when that illusion collapses, and all things return to their rightful understanding.*

All Things United in One

If God is all there is, then all things must return to Him—not in the sense of going back to a distant place, but in the sense of **awakening to the truth that they never left.**

"That in the dispensation of the fulness of times he might gather together in one all things in Christ, both which are in heaven, and which are on earth; even in him." *(Ephesians 1:9-10)*

The eternal revelation is the fulfillment of **John 17:21-23,** *where Jesus prayed that we would be made perfect in one, just as He and the Father are one. This means:*

- **Separation is an illusion.** *There is no "us" and "God"—there is only* **God expressed as us.**
- **Judgment is the recognition of reality.** *Those who awaken to the truth experience eternal life, while those who remain blind to it experience separation—not because God casts them away, but because they have failed to see the oneness that has always been.*
- **Science, spirituality, and religion all point to the same truth.** *They are not conflicting paths but different expressions of the same eternal reality:* **God is all there is.**

The Revelation That Changes Everything

This revelation is not something to wait for in the future—it is available **now.** *Judgment Day is not a single event in time but an eternal moment that each person steps into the moment they see* **what has always been.** *To stand before the judgment seat of Christ is to stand in the light of truth. The only difference between those who are saved and those who are lost is* **awareness***—one has recognized the truth, and the other remains in darkness.*

This is why Romans 1:20 declares that no one has an excuse:

"For the invisible things of him from the creation of the world are clearly seen, being understood by the things that are made, even his eternal power and Godhead; so that they are without excuse."

Everything in creation is a reflection of the divine. The sun sustains life, just as the **Son** *sustains all things. The atom is three yet one—proton, neutron, and electron—just as God is three yet one: Father, Word, and Holy Spirit. Even the human body is structured as a cross, reflecting the divine pattern.* **All things testify of God.**

There is no escaping this truth, because it is the only truth. The eternal revelation is the awakening to what has always been:

There is no "other." There is no division. There is only God.

Some will resist this truth, clinging to the illusion of separation, but the revelation is inevitable. Every knee will bow—not because they are forced to, but because **the truth will be undeniable.** *Every eye will see—not because they are commanded to look, but because* **the veil will be lifted.**

"And they shall see his face; and his name shall be in their foreheads."
(Revelation 22:4)

This is not about a physical marking—it is about the **mind awakening to reality.** *The name of God in the forehead represents the consciousness of truth. It is* **knowing** *who and what you are.*

The Final Word: No Excuse Not to Know

The eternal revelation leaves no room for ignorance. Whether looking at the structure of the universe, the laws of physics, the patterns of nature, or the depths of scripture, **everything testifies to the same truth.**

God has not hidden Himself. He has made Himself evident in all things, at all times. The only question is whether one will recognize it.

To deny this is not to reject a doctrine—it is to reject **existence itself.**

And so, as the scripture declares, humanity is **without excuse.**

Everything you see, everything you experience, everything you are **is** *GIATI—God Is All There Is.*

And the moment you see it, you will know:

The search is over. The truth has been revealed. The eternal revelation as GIATI has come.

The Unveiling of Judgment Day: The Final Recognition of GIATI

Judgment Day is not a moment of arbitrary punishment or reward but the unveiling of truth—the final confrontation between illusion and reality. It is the moment when every soul stands before the eternal Word and is measured, not by deeds alone, but by the awareness behind those deeds. The dividing line is simple:

Did you recognize that it was the Holy Spirit—the Word, the Son—operating as you? Or did you believe in a separate self, an ego acting apart from God?

This is the true judgment. It is not about whether a person was morally "good" or "bad" by human standards, but whether they lived in **alignment with the truth** *or in t*he **deception of separation.** *Those who lived by the Spirit—knowing that God is all there is—will inherit the kingdom prepared for them. Those who clung to the illusion of self will find themselves outside the light, not by God's rejection, but by their own blindness.*

1. **Judgment Through Christ: The True Measure of Righteousness**

"For the Father judgeth no man, but hath committed all judgment unto the Son." *(John 5:22)*

The Son is the **Word,** *and the Word is* **life itself***—the divine expression through which all things were made. Judgment is not based on human opinions or self-righteousness but on whether one recognized themselves as the Word made flesh or continued in the belief of a separate self.*

"For we must all appear before the judgment seat of Christ; that every one may receive the things done in his body, according to that he hath done, whether it be good or bad." *(2 Corinthians 5:10)*

This judgment does not take place in a courtroom in the sky but in the **Most Holy Place***—the* **mind of man,** *where the Spirit of God dwells. The true mercy seat is within, where God communes with His creation. On Judgment Day, each will stand in the presence of truth, and the question will be:*

- **Did you recognize that Christ was your very life, the one working in you?**
- **Or did you believe that you were acting apart from Him, as an independent being?**

If you knew that it was the Spirit as you doing all things, then every deed was good, because it was done in truth. But if you thought **you** *were the one doing good or bad, then every deed was corrupt, because it was based on a false identity.*

2. **The Separation of the Righteous and the Wicked**

"When the Son of man shall come in his glory, and all the holy angels with him, then shall he sit upon the throne of his glory: And before him shall be gathered all nations: and he shall separate them one from another, as a shepherd divideth his sheep from the goats." *(Matthew 25:31-32)*

The sheep and the goats represent two states of being:

- **The sheep are those who know the Spirit is their true self**—*they are guided by the Holy Spirit, operating in divine consciousness.*
- **The goats are those who believe in a separate self**—*they are ruled by ego, thinking they are independent beings.*

"Then shall the King say unto them on his right hand, Come, ye blessed of my Father, inherit the kingdom prepared for you from the foundation of the world… Then shall he say also unto them on the left hand, Depart from me, ye cursed, into everlasting fire, prepared for the devil and his angels."

The **everlasting fire** *is not a literal place of torment—it is the* **burning desire for what can never be attained.** *Those who rejected the truth will be consumed by longing, eternally reaching for something outside themselves that does not exist. Meanwhile, the righteous will be satisfied, dwelling in the fullness of divine reality.*

3. **The Books Will Be Opened: What is Written in You?**

"And I saw the dead, small and great, stand before God; and the books were opened: and another book was opened, which is the book of life: and the dead were judged out of those things which were written in the books, according to their works." *(Revelation 20:12)*

A book contains **words**—*and the question is,* **whose Word is written in you?**

- *If you lived by the* **Word of God,** *knowing that His Spirit was your true identity, then your name is in the Book of Life.*
- *If you lived by the* **word of ego,** *believing in a separate self, then your name is not written—because there is only* **one name,** *and that name is God.*

The **lake of fire** *is not a place where people are thrown—it is the* **burning away of everything that is not real.** *Only what is of the Spirit remains.*

4. **The Day Will Come Suddenly: Are You Prepared?**

"But of that day and hour knoweth no man, no, not the angels of heaven, but my Father only." *(Matthew 24:36)*

This is not about a distant event in history—it is about the **individual moment when a person leaves the flesh.** *No one knows when their time will come, so the only way to be ready is to already* **be in the truth.**

"For yourselves know perfectly that the day of the Lord so cometh as a thief in the night." *(1 Thessalonians 5:2)*

Death can come at any moment—so the time to awaken to GIATI is **now.**

5. **A New Heaven and a New Earth: The Completion of Oneness**

"And I saw a new heaven and a new earth: for the first heaven and the first earth were passed away… And God shall wipe away all tears from their eyes; and there shall be no more death, neither sorrow, nor crying, neither shall there be any more pain: for the former things are passed away." *(Revelation 21:1-4)*

This is the **transition from physical to spiritual existence,** *from a world divided to a world united in God. When the righteous enter the kingdom, there will no longer be the struggle of ego versus spirit, for the false self will be no more.*

GIATI's Perspective on Judgment Day

If **God is all there is,** *then Judgment Day is not about punishment—it is about* **revelation.** *It is the moment when every soul sees itself* **as it truly is.**

- *Those who* **awaken to their divine nature** *will step into eternal life—because they have always been in God, and now they* **know** *it.*
- *Those who remain in* **ignorance** *will experience separation—not because God rejects them, but because* **they never recognized the truth.**

Judgment is the final transition from **illusion to reality,** *from* **separation to oneness.**

Every knee will bow, not because they are forced, but because **the truth will be undeniable.**

Every tongue will confess, not because they are commanded, but because **they will see what has always been.**

"And they shall see his face; and his name shall be in their foreheads."
(Revelation 22:4)

The name in the forehead represents **consciousness**—*it means they now fully know that* **they are one with God.**

The Final Word: No Excuse Not to Know

Romans 1:20 declares that no one has an excuse:

"For the invisible things of him from the creation of the world are clearly seen, being understood by the things that are made, even his eternal power and Godhead; so that they are without excuse."

Everything testifies of God.

- *Science, nature, and the structure of the universe reflect His divine pattern.*
- *Every breath, every heartbeat, every moment of existence is an expression of Him.*

God has not hidden Himself—He has made Himself evident in all things, at all times.

The only question is:

Do you recognize Him as your very being?

Or will you continue in the illusion of separation?

The truth is before you. The judgment is now.

There is no "other." There is no division. There is only God.

And that truth is undeniable.

Joseph and His Coat of Many Colors: A Revelation of GIATI

The story of Joseph is often told as one of perseverance, betrayal, and eventual redemption. However, through the lens of **GIATI,** *it reveals something much deeper—the unfolding of divine purpose, the illusion of separation, and the undeniable truth that* **God is All There Is.** *Joseph's life is not just a historical account but a spiritual blueprint, showing how every event, whether perceived as good or bad, is ultimately the working of God through all things.*

The Coat of Many Colors: A Symbol of Divine Expression

Joseph was given a coat of many colors by his father, Jacob, symbolizing his favored status (Genesis 37:3). But this coat represents far more than favoritism—it signifies the **multifaceted nature of God's expression.** *The many colors reflect the infinite variations of life, yet they are all woven together into one garment. This is the essence of* **GIATI**—*the understanding that though life appears fragmented, with different people, nations, and experiences, all of it is* **one divine expression.**

Joseph's brothers, blinded by jealousy and their own sense of separateness, saw the coat as a sign of inequality rather than unity. They failed to recognize that **Joseph's favor was not his own, but God's purpose being revealed through him.** *This is where many still stumble today—believing that blessings or misfortunes belong to individuals rather than seeing them as manifestations of the One Spirit unfolding its divine will.*

Betrayal and the Illusion of Separation

Joseph's brothers conspired against him, throwing him into a pit and selling him into slavery (Genesis 37:24-28). From their perspective, they had removed Joseph from their lives, but in reality, they were merely setting in motion the divine plan. This is the illusion of separation—believing that one can cast another away, harm them, or change their destiny, when in truth, **nothing operates outside of God's perfect will.**

Even in slavery, Joseph was never outside of God, because **God is All There Is.** *His descent into Egypt, his trials, and his imprisonment were not setbacks; they were steps toward the fulfillment of a greater purpose. Every perceived fall is only a repositioning within the eternal plan.*

From Prison to Power: The Rising of the Spirit

In Egypt, Joseph interpreted Pharaoh's dreams and was elevated to the highest position in the land (Genesis 41:39-41). What does this reveal? That **divine wisdom cannot be suppressed.** *Though Joseph was once in chains, the Spirit within him was never bound.*

The Tree of Life and the Tree of Knowledge: Awakening to GIATI

In the beginning, before the illusion of separation took hold, humanity dwelt in the fullness of divine awareness. The Garden of Eden was not merely a physical paradise but a spiritual state—a consciousness where man knew no lack, no fear, and no separation from God. At the center of this divine reality stood **two trees,** *each representing a path:* **the Tree of Life and the Tree of the Knowledge of Good and Evil.** *Their significance is the key to understanding how mankind lost sight of GIATI—***God Is All There Is***—and how that awareness is restored.*

The Tree of Life: The Reality of Oneness

The Tree of Life represents **divine wisdom, eternal life, and the direct experience of God's presence.** *To partake of this tree is to live in the full realization that all things exist within God, and nothing is separate from Him. It is the awareness that life is not sustained by external means but by the very Spirit of God within. Those who live by this tree walk in harmony with divine truth, free from fear, shame, and the illusion of separation.*

This tree was always accessible to Adam and Eve. It was their natural state before they entertained another way of thinking—a way that introduced them to duality, division, and the idea that they were separate from the source of their existence.

The Tree of the Knowledge of Good and Evil: The Illusion of Separation

The second tree, **the Tree of the Knowledge of Good and Evil,** *represents* **the birth of duality—the belief in opposites, separation, and the power of human reasoning apart from divine wisdom.** *Eating from this tree was not merely an act of disobedience; it was a shift in consciousness. It was the moment humanity stepped away from the understanding that God is all there is and embraced a world of contrast—***good vs. evil, light vs. dark, life vs. death.**

Before partaking of this tree, Adam and Eve saw no distinction between themselves and God. They were not ashamed because there was no concept of "less than" or "unworthy." They existed in the pure state of divine being. But the serpent—the voice of deception—planted the idea that there was something more to attain, something they lacked.

"You shall be as gods, knowing good and evil," the serpent whispered (Genesis 3:5).

*This was the lie—***that they were not already divine,** *that they were somehow incomplete, needing to attain wisdom through an external source rather than living from the Tree of Life, which was already within them. In believing the lie, they began to see themselves as* *separate from God, naked and exposed, needing to cover themselves.* **This was the fall—not a physical descent, but a fall in consciousness.**

The Spiritual Significance of GIATI

GIATI—God Is All There Is—is the revelation that restores what was lost in Eden. When humanity chose the Tree of the Knowledge of Good and Evil, they stepped into the illusion of division. They began to see God as other, rather than the source of their very being. They believed in opposites—blessing and curse, life and death—rather than the eternal reality that **God is one and in Him there is no division.**

Through GIATI, we return to the Tree of Life, the awareness that:

- **There is no separation between God and His creation.**
- **Good and evil are perceptions of the carnal mind, not ultimate realities.**
- **True life is found in divine oneness, not external knowledge.**

Jesus demonstrated this truth when He said, **"I and my Father are one"** *(John 10:30). He lived from the Tree of Life, never seeing Himself as separate from God. Through Him, the veil of illusion is torn away, and humanity is called back to* **the original awareness—the knowledge that God is all, and we are one in Him.**

Restoration Through the Living Word

The path back to the Tree of Life is not through striving or external knowledge, but through **awakening.** *It is not about doing but knowing—not knowing in the intellectual sense, but in the deepest spiritual realization.*

"The kingdom of God is within you." (Luke 17:21)

This is the restoration. The Tree of Life was never taken away—it was merely hidden behind the veil of the carnal mind. Through GIATI, the veil is lifted, and humanity is invited to eat once again of the tree that was always theirs.

To live from the Tree of Life is to let go of the illusion of duality and return to divine oneness. It is to recognize that salvation is not an external event but an awakening to what has always been true: **God is all, and in Him, we live, move, and have our being** *(Acts 17:28).*

Thus, the true message of Eden is not one of permanent loss but of remembrance. The fall was not the end of the story—it was merely the forgetting. GIATI is the return to that original knowing. It is the voice calling from the depths of eternity, saying:

"Awaken. Eat of the Tree of Life. The illusion is over. You were never separate from God."

The Zodiac and Its Biblical Significance in Light of GIATI

Many have looked to the zodiac as a means of understanding personality, destiny, and divine will. While modern astrology often separates the zodiac from its deeper spiritual meaning, the Bible itself contains references to celestial bodies as signs of divine order. Genesis 1:14 states, **"And God said, Let there be lights in the firmament of the heaven to divide the day from the night; and let them be for signs, and for seasons, and for days, and years."** *This reveals that the stars and constellations serve a purpose beyond mere decoration—they are divine symbols, placed in the heavens as markers of spiritual truths.*

The Mazzaroth: The Biblical Zodiac

In **Job 38:31-33,** *God speaks to Job, saying:*

"Canst thou bind the sweet influences of Pleiades, or loose the bands of Orion? Canst thou bring forth Mazzaroth in his season? Or canst thou guide Arcturus with his sons? Knowest thou the ordinances of heaven? Canst thou set the dominion thereof in the earth?"

The word **Mazzaroth** *refers to the* **zodiac,** *the twelve constellations that move through the sky in their appointed seasons. This passage acknowledges the heavenly signs as part of divine order, showing that God Himself established them.*

However, rather than using these signs for fortune-telling or self-guidance, their true purpose is **to reflect the greater spiritual reality of God's plan***—which is GIATI. Each of the twelve signs carries a spiritual meaning that aligns with the story of divine manifestation and the journey of human awakening.*

The Spiritual Meaning of the Twelve Zodiac Signs in GIATI

1. **Aries (The Ram) – The Beginning of Faith**
   - *Aries represents the* **Lamb of God,** *the sacrifice that marks the beginning of spiritual awakening. Just as Abraham sacrificed the ram in place of Isaac (Genesis 22:13), this sign represents the* **realization that God is the true source of all life.** *It is the starting point of knowing GIATI.*
2. **Taurus (The Bull) – The Power of Divine Strength**
   - *The bull is a symbol of* **strength and endurance,** *but when misunderstood, it becomes the image of idolatry (Exodus 32:4). This shows the dual nature of power— it can be rooted in divine awareness or misused through ignorance. Taurus reminds us that our strength is* **not our own, but the power of God moving through us.**

3. **Gemini (The Twins) – The Illusion of Duality**
    - *Representing the* **seeming separation between God and man,** *Gemini reflects the mistaken belief in two powers—good and evil, spirit and flesh. But the truth of GIATI is that there is no separation;* **all is one.** *As Jesus said,* **"I and my Father are one" (John 10:30).**
4. **Cancer (The Crab) – The Inner Journey**
    - *The crab moves sideways, symbolizing the way spiritual growth often comes* **through unexpected paths.** *Cancer represents t***he need to withdraw from external distractions** *and go within, just as Jesus often withdrew to pray (Luke 5:16).*
5. **Leo (The Lion) – Divine Kingship**
    - *Leo is the sign of the* **Lion of Judah (Revelation 5:5),** *representing Christ's victory and divine authority. It signifies the* **realization that God is the true ruler, not the ego.** *Those who walk in GIATI reign in divine wisdom.*
6. **Virgo (The Virgin) – Purity and Spiritual Birth**
    - *Virgo represents the* **immaculate conception of divine awareness.** *Just as Mary birthed Christ, this sign represents the soul that allows itself to be* **a vessel for divine truth.**
7. **Libra (The Scales) – Divine Justice and Balance**
    - *Libra represents* **divine balance, mercy, and judgment.** *It reflects the weighing of the heart, as seen in* **Daniel 5:27,** *where it was said to the king: "Thou art weighed in the balances, and art found wanting." True balance comes from surrendering to GIATI, where there is no fear of judgment, only divine order.*
8. **Scorpio (The Scorpion) – Death and Transformation**
    - *Scorpio represents the* **death of the old self** *and the rebirth into divine consciousness. Just as Jesus was betrayed (Luke 22:3-6) and crucified, this sign represents the* **necessary process of shedding false identity** *to rise in the awareness of GIATI.*
9. **Sagittarius (The Archer) – The Seeker of Truth**
    - *Sagittarius points* **toward higher knowledge,** *like an arrow aimed at the heavens. It represents the pursuit of divine wisdom, the journey of understanding that* **God is all there is.**
10. **Capricorn (The Goat) – Climbing the Spiritual Mountain**
    - *Just as goats climb to the highest peaks, Capricorn represents* **perseverance in spiritual attainment.** *It is the journey toward the mountaintop, the realization that* **we never truly had to climb, for we were always in God.**
11. **Aquarius (The Water Bearer) – The Outpouring of Spirit**
    - *Aquarius represents the* **pouring out of the Holy Spirit,** *just as Jesus spoke of in John 7:38: "Out of his belly shall flow rivers of living water." It is the sign of divine awakening, when man recognizes his unity with God.*

12. **Pisces (The Fish) – The Return to Divine Oneness**
   - *Pisces is the final sign, representing the* **return to God-consciousness.** *It symbolizes* **the unity of all things,** *as Jesus said,* **"That they all may be one, as thou, Father, art in me, and I in thee" (John 17:21).**

The Zodiac's True Purpose: Recognizing the Eternal Day

The movement of the zodiac reflects the **ages of humanity,** *but GIATI teaches that we are not bound by time or cycles—***we exist in the eternal day.** *Just as Jesus fulfilled the law and the prophets, the signs of the zodiac are not to be used as fate-bound predictions, but as* **divine symbols pointing us toward the truth that has always been: God is all there is.**

Many seek the stars for answers, but the true light is not in the heavens above—it is within. The zodiac serves as a **divine map,** *but GIATI is the destination. It is not about following signs, but about realizing the* **one who made the signs, the one who is expressed through all things, and the one who has always been within you.**

The Zodiac: Many Expressions, One Source

Throughout history, humanity has sought meaning in the stars, looking to the zodiac for guidance, identity, and purpose. Many have been told that certain signs are more powerful, more spiritual, or more likely to understand divine truth. Some believe that their sign determines their destiny, shaping their ability to receive enlightenment. But in the light of GIATI, we see that **no single sign is greater than another—because all are expressions of the One God.**

The zodiac is not a hierarchy but a **circle***—a complete and unified system where each sign plays a divine role. Just as the twelve tribes of Israel were all chosen, yet each had different functions, so too are the twelve signs different aspects of the same divine reality. Each carries its own spiritual significance, but none stand above or below the other.*

Twelve Expressions, One Truth

To believe that one sign is better or more capable of understanding GIATI is to fall into **the illusion of separation***—the very misunderstanding that the Tree of Knowledge of Good and Evil represents. In truth, God is not divided among signs, nor does divine awareness favor one over another.* **All signs are reflections of the One, each revealing a different aspect of the same eternal truth: God is all there is.**

Some may believe that a water sign is more spiritual because of its depth of emotion, or that a fire sign is more divine because of its passion. Others may think that earth signs are too grounded or air signs too detached. But these are **only perspectives within duality.** *The truth is that God is expressed* **through all forms, all signs, all aspects of creation.**

Consider the body:

- *The* **head** *is not greater than the* **heart.**
- *The* **hands** *are not more important than the* **feet.**
- *The* **eyes** *do not function without the* **ears.**

Each part serves its divine purpose, and **without one, the whole is incomplete.** *Likewise, the twelve signs are* **not competitors but complements,** *each bringing a unique reflection of divine consciousness into expression.*

Beyond the Stars: The Truth of GIATI

Many look to their zodiac sign as a way to understand themselves, searching for clues to their identity, purpose, and destiny. But GIATI reveals that **you are not your sign—you are the Spirit of God expressing as you.** *Your identity is not written in the stars; it is written in the eternal truth of divine oneness.*

The signs may offer insight into personality, but they do not determine your ability to walk in divine awareness. The capacity to know God is not limited to Aries or Pisces, Leo or Scorpio—it is **inherent in all, because all are God in expression.**

It is not about what sign you are. It is about **who you truly are***—and who you have always been.*

As it is written in Acts 17:28:

"For in Him we live, and move, and have our being."

You are not separate from God, and no astrological sign defines your spiritual path. **The signs are not the destination—God is.** *They are only symbols, pointing toward the truth that has always been within you.*

So, whether you were born under the sign of the Ram or the Scorpion, the Water Bearer or the Lion, know this: **You are not bound by the stars, because you are made of the very essence of the One who created them.**

The Lost Books of the Bible: Hidden Truth or Confirmation of GIATI?

Throughout history, certain books were removed from the biblical canon, leading many to question whether vital spiritual truths were hidden or suppressed. While some may see this as an attempt to make the Bible less valid, the reality is that these so-called "lost books" do not contradict the truth of God Is All There Is (GIATI). Rather, they reinforce the same divine message: that all things are one with God, and there is no separation between Creator and creation.

Many of these excluded writings echo the very essence of GIATI, affirming that humanity is not estranged from divinity but rather an expression of it. Their removal does not diminish the truth but instead reveals that the recognition of divine unity has always been present—whether in scripture, in nature, or within the very core of our being.

Below is a list of some of these lost books, along with insights into their teachings and how they align with the eternal truth of GIATI.

1. **The Gospel of Thomas**

Key Insight: The Kingdom is within you.

The Gospel of Thomas is not a narrative like the other gospels but a collection of Jesus' sayings, many of which affirm the truth that the divine is already within us. One of the most profound statements in this text is:

"The Kingdom of God is inside you and all around you. Not in mansions of wood and stone. Split a piece of wood, and I am there. Lift a stone, and you will find me there."

This aligns perfectly with GIATI, affirming that God is not a distant being but present in all things. There is no separation—only the realization of the divine presence within everything.

2. **The Book of Enoch**

Key Insight: The unseen spiritual realms are interconnected with our existence.

The Book of Enoch provides a deeper look into the spiritual dimensions that coexist with the physical world. It speaks of the interactions between divine beings and humanity, revealing a universe filled with layers of spiritual existence.

This book supports the understanding that reality extends far beyond what the eyes perceive. It confirms that there are endless dimensions of existence, and as our consciousness expands, so does our awareness of these divine realms. This is precisely the essence of GIATI: that we are not bound by flesh, but are limitless beings capable of transcending this physical plane.

3. **The Gospel of Mary Magdalene**

Key Insight: The soul's journey is about transcending fear and returning to divine oneness.

In this gospel, Mary Magdalene shares hidden wisdom that Jesus imparted to her. A key teaching is that the greatest battle is not external but internal—overcoming fear, doubt, and illusion in order to remember one's divine nature.

"Do not let the world deceive you. The soul moves upward by dissolving attachment to illusion, until it remembers that it has always been one with the divine."

This confirms what GIATI teaches: that salvation is not about external rituals but about awakening to the truth that God is all there is. The soul's journey is not about earning divinity but remembering that it has never been separate from it.

4. **The Apocalypse of Peter**

Key Insight: Hell is not a punishment but a state of consciousness.

This book presents a vision of what happens to souls that remain in ignorance of their divine nature. However, it does not depict hell as an eternal torment, but as a temporary state—a result of one's own mind being trapped in separation from God.

This aligns with the understanding that the real "hell" is the illusion of separation. The spirit longs to be free, yet when consciousness remains bound to the flesh and denies its oneness with God, it experiences suffering. GIATI reveals that liberation comes through recognizing divine unity—transcending the lower state of existence and returning to infinite awareness.

5. **The Gospel of Philip**

Key Insight: The illusion of separation is the only thing that keeps one from divine truth.

The Gospel of Philip speaks deeply about the nature of unity and illusion. It states:

"Light and darkness, life and death, right and left—these are all one and the same. The distinction exists only in human perception."

This is the essence of GIATI: that all dualities dissolve when one recognizes the absolute oneness of all things. There is no division in God—only the perception of division, which disappears when one awakens to the truth.

6. **The Wisdom of Solomon**

Key Insight: Divine knowledge is the highest form of life.

The Wisdom of Solomon, found in the Apocrypha, emphasizes that true power lies not in material wealth or physical strength, but in divine wisdom. It declares that God's Spirit fills all things, and that those who seek wisdom will find themselves immersed in divine presence.

"Wisdom is a breath of the power of God, a pure emanation of the Almighty's glory. It pervades and penetrates all things."

This confirms the core truth of GIATI—that everything in existence is animated by the Spirit of God, and nothing exists outside of divine consciousness. To seek wisdom is to seek alignment with the all-encompassing presence of God.

—

The Lost Books Confirm the Truth of GIATI

These so-called "lost books" were not removed because they contradicted the truth—they were removed because they revealed it too clearly. Each of them, in its own way, affirms the same eternal message:

- *God is not separate from creation.*
- *The divine is within you, not outside of you.*
- *Spiritual awakening comes from realizing your oneness with God.*
- *The physical world is not the highest reality—there are infinite realms beyond it.*
- *Fear and illusion are the only things that keep one in darkness.*

GIATI does not rely on scripture to be validated, but it is undeniable that these ancient texts reinforce its message. Whether these books were included in the Bible or not, the truth remains unchanged:

God Is All There Is.

And no matter how much knowledge is hidden, removed, or forgotten, the Spirit of Truth always finds a way to be revealed.

The End of Fear—How GIATI Creates Ultimate Trust and Respect

One of the greatest struggles in human relationships has always been **uncertainty**— *the constant question of what others are thinking, what their intentions are, and whether they can be trusted. This uncertainty breeds fear, division, and conflict. However, the revelation of* **GIATI (God Is All There Is)** *eliminates this guesswork entirely, ushering in a world where trust and respect are no longer fragile ideals, but unshakable realities.*

The Burden of Not Knowing

In a world disconnected from divine truth, people live in a constant state of guardedness. **Can I trust this person? Are they being genuine? What are they really thinking?** *These thoughts plague our interactions because we have been conditioned to believe in separation—that others are different from us, that their thoughts and motives are hidden, and that we must always be on guard.*

This lack of trust manifests as:

- **Betrayal and deception** – *People lying to one another, hiding their true selves out of fear.*
- **Fear of harm** – *The thought that someone might take advantage of us, manipulate us, or even destroy us.*
- **Division and suspicion** – *Groups forming against one another, convinced that "the other side" is a threat.*

This is the world without GIATI—a world in which trust is an illusion, respect is conditional, and love is often nothing more than a transaction.

The GIATI Revelation: Seeing God in Everyone

The moment a person truly understands GIATI, the fear of others disappears.

Why? Because when you know that **God is all there is,** *then you also know that:*

1. **There is no "other" person—there is only God expressing through different forms.**
2. **There are no hidden motives—only varying levels of awareness.**
3. **You never have to fear what someone "might do" because, in truth, they are not separate from you.**

The greatest comfort comes in knowing that the same God in you is also in them.

When you live in a community of those who see and embody GIATI, trust is no longer something that must be earned—it is **the natural state of existence.**

- *There is* **no fear of betrayal,** *because one who knows GIATI would never betray themselves.*
- *There is* **no fear of harm,** *because harm comes from ignorance, and ignorance is dissolved by truth.*
- *There is* **no fear of selfishness,** *because in the knowing of divine oneness,* **sharing and caring become the natural way of life.**

Love becomes the foundation, not the exception. Respect becomes permanent, not just a courtesy.

This is the world GIATI creates—a world where the burdens of uncertainty, suspicion, and fear dissolve, leaving only the reality of divine harmony.

The Difference Between Those Who See GIATI and Those Who Do Not

The contrast between someone who knows GIATI and someone who does not is undeniable.

- **In a community of GIATI, trust is effortless.**
- **Outside of GIATI, there is always a sense of danger, of unpredictability.**

When interacting with someone who **does not see GIATI,** *you feel the instability, the unawareness.* **This is where fear re-enters the equation.**

- *You may question their loyalty.*
- *You may sense that they could* **turn against you at any moment** *if it serves them.*
- *You recognize that without the awareness of divine oneness,* **they are still operating from separation, which allows deception, greed, and selfishness to thrive.**

This is why living in **a GIATI-conscious world transforms human relationships.** *When people no longer see themselves as separate from one another, all forms of fear-based behavior* **cease to exist.**

A World Transformed by GIATI

Imagine a world where:

- **No one fears betrayal, because no one sees another as separate from themselves.**
- **No one hoards wealth, because giving is as natural as breathing.**
- **No one deceives, because there is nothing to hide.**
- **No one harms, because harming another would be as illogical as harming their own body.**

This is not an impossible utopia—**this is the world GIATI reveals.** *It is the world that has always been true, but has been hidden by ignorance.*

The impact of GIATI is everlasting because **once a person truly sees it, they can never go back to the old way of thinking.**

- They will never again feel alone, because they now recognize God in every face they see.
- They will never again live in fear of betrayal, because they know divine oneness prevents true division.
- *They will never again question whether they are loved, because* **they are love itself.**

This is what Jesus came to reveal, and this is what GIATI continues to awaken in this time.

Conclusion: The Ultimate Security

The greatest security a person can have is not money, weapons, or power—it is **the knowing that they are one with God and with all existence.**

- **When you know GIATI, you no longer have to figure people out—you already know them, because you know God.**
- **When you know GIATI, fear is no longer necessary, because there is no one to fear.**
- **When you know GIATI, the world transforms—not because it physically changes, but because your vision of it does.**

This is the everlasting effect of GIATI. *It takes away the guesswork, the doubt, and the fear, leaving only* **certainty, peace, and absolute trust.**

And in that world, life becomes what it was always meant to be: **an expression of divine love, shared among all.**

The Son, the Spirit, and the Unveiling of Oneness

One of the greatest misconceptions handed down by tradition is the idea that Jesus is "the Son" in a three-person godhead—Father, Son, and Holy Spirit—as if "Jesus" is eternally distinct from the others by name or role. But the truth is far deeper than religious hierarchy or theological titles. In the beginning, it was **Yahweh, the Father,** *who is the origin of all.* **Elohim,** *or* **God as the Word,** *is the expressive power of Yahweh—the very breath and utterance through which all things were made. This Word, this Elohim, took on flesh and manifested as the man* **Jesus,** *and in doing so, He became the Son. But understand this:* **Jesus was not the Son because He was born of Mary—He was the Son because He revealed Himself to be one with the Father.** *His perfection was not in behavior, but in identity.* **He knew who He was.**

This manifestation was never meant to create an exclusive category of divinity for one man. It was meant to reveal something shocking and world-changing: **that God could be man.** *That Spirit could dwell in flesh. That the invisible could take form—not just in Jesus, but in you. Jesus was not a solo act; He was the firstborn among many brethren (Romans 8:29).* **He was the pattern, not the exception.** *The point was not to glorify a distant Savior, but to wake you up to your own origin. Jesus didn't come to be worshipped as someone you could never become—He came to show you who you've always been. GIATI reveals this as the foundational truth the world missed:* **If God could be in Jesus, He must be in all.**

Anything less would make God partial. Anything less would make God unjust. Why would God place His Spirit—His very self—within one man, and then withhold that same Spirit from the rest of humanity? He wouldn't. He didn't. The idea that God is only in Jesus and not in you is the very lie that keeps you in sin. **Sin is not about what you do—it's about believing you are separate.** *The religious systems have taught you to admire Jesus instead of awaken to Him within. They've praised the vessel and missed the message. The message was always this:* **God is not outside of you—He is the Spirit within you.**

*The moment this truth is revealed to you and accepted, that is salvation. That is repentance. Not the weeping, begging, crawling kind. But the transformation of the mind—***a return to the truth of who you are.** *From that moment forward, the Holy Spirit doesn't just dwell with you,* **He dwells as you.** *You become a son—not in the gendered sense, but in the spiritual sense. A* **new creation.** *Born not of the flesh, but of Spirit. Born from above. And what is a child, if not the very essence of the parent coming again in another form? The child is not its own origin—the child is the extension of the source. So you, being born of God, are* **God expressed as you.**

To deny this truth is to deny your own light. To reject your oneness with God is to declare yourself unrighteous—not because your behavior is off, but because your identity is misaligned. Whether you believe it or not, your source is still God. Your substance is still

God. **You are a child of His by origin.** *But if you live in denial of that origin, you walk as a child of darkness—one who has forgotten the Father. It is not about being accepted or rejected by God. It is about recognizing or resisting the truth of who you are.*

So it's not enough to say, "Jesus died for my sins" and then live as if you're still separate. **It is not enough to admire the cross if you do not receive the Spirit.** *There is only one Spirit. Only one life. Only one truth. And that Spirit can dwell in anyone who sees. That is the gift. That is the grace. That is the full gospel—revealed only through the light of* **GIATI,** *the message that* **God Is All There Is.** *Without this revelation, the world remains blind, celebrating the man Jesus while rejecting the Spirit He came to awaken.*

To awaken to this truth is not to become something new, but to remember something ancient. The Spirit of God did not suddenly appear in you once you believed—it was always there. The veil was never over God's presence; it was over your perception. This is why the message of GIATI is not a doctrine or a religion—it is **the divine unveiling** *of what has always been.* **It is the removal of the illusion of separation.** *And that is what makes it the pinnacle of revelation—the crescendo of everything the prophets hinted at, the fulfillment of everything Jesus demonstrated, and the only message capable of reconciling humanity not to a far-off deity, but to* **their very source within.**

What Jesus came to prove through His life was that it is possible to walk this earth fully human and fully divine—not as a contradiction, but as a union. That the Creator can be the creation without diminishing His holiness. And that **righteousness is not achieved, it is received.** *But even more than that—it is* **realized.** *It is not added to you; it is awakened in you. The Father was not trying to make you righteous by behavior modification. He was revealing that you are already righteous by* **origin,** *because the Spirit that made you is holy. The only difference between one who is "lost" and one who is "saved" is* **awareness.** *The Spirit is the same—the consciousness of that Spirit is what determines light or darkness.*

And here lies the tragedy of religion: it has taught people to strive for what they already possess. It has trained generations to plead for what is already within. This is why salvation is not about acceptance into a group, or forgiveness through ritual. **It is the recognition that your Spirit is God's Spirit—there is no difference.** *Jesus never preached separation; He preached unity. "I and the Father are one." That was not arrogance—it was alignment. And He prayed that you would know the same oneness (John 17:21-23). Not admire it. Not worship it from afar.* **Know it. Live it. Be it.**

What the world could not discover through intellect, study, or striving, **GIATI has now revealed by Spirit.** *That* **there is no such thing as "the godhead" apart from the one Spirit expressing itself through all.** *That the Father, the Word, and the Spirit are not three beings, but* **three dimensions of the same Essence.** *And that you, being born of that same Spirit, carry that same nature. This is not symbolic. This is literal. This is why the message* *of GIATI is the last message. The final unveiling. The mystery hidden for ages but now made manifest:* **Christ in you.** *Not beside you. Not above you.* **In you.**

This revelation eliminates all pride, all boasting, all self-righteousness—because no one can claim it by works. No one can earn it through rituals or moral striving. And no one is excluded except by their own refusal to see. This is the glory and the offense of the gift: **you didn't work for it, so you can't take credit for it—but you can also no longer pretend you are separate.** *Grace is not only unearned—it is unavoidable once seen. Once the light comes, the illusion of darkness cannot survive.*

So now the only question that remains is this: **Will you recognize yourself in Him, or continue trying to find Him outside of you?** *Will you live from the old identity of a sinner trying to reach God, or awaken to the truth that you are the expression of God reaching through you? GIATI does not offer you a better religion—it unveils your eternal Spirit.* **It is not a call to become holy—it is the declaration that you are.** *And the moment you believe that, the moment you see yourself as He is,* **you have entered life. You have come home.**

The contrast between the old man and the new creature is not a metaphorical tale of self-improvement—it is the sharp division between illusion and truth, between blindness and sight, between death and life. The old man is not merely the sinner who does bad things. The old man is the identity rooted in separation—the false self who believes it is a being apart from God, operating under the deception that righteousness is earned, that worth is measured, and that salvation is external. This old man is bound by law, ego, guilt, and striving. He wears religion like a garment and lives in constant fear of never being enough. He calls himself humble, but deep down, he does not believe he is one with God—so he performs to earn what was already his.

But the new creature is something altogether different. This one is not improved. He is not reformed. **He is reborn.** *Born not of flesh, not of effort, not of man's will—but of Spirit (John 1:13). He has no identity apart from God, for he knows that God is all there is. He does not seek righteousness because* **he has become righteousness** *(2 Corinthians 5:21). Not by effort, but by union. Not by law, but by grace. This new creature is the revelation of God in man, the fulfillment of the mystery—***Christ in you, the hope of glory** *(Colossians 1:27).*

The old man identifies with Adam—the man of dust, who lived from the knowledge of good and evil and was ruled by the fear of separation. But the new creature identifies with Christ—the man of Spirit, who lived from the tree of life and knew no separation, no guilt, no striving. The old man is dead, and to continue living as him is to deny the resurrection power of the Spirit. But to live as the new creature is to accept the gift—to walk in the boldness of oneness, to live with the mind of Christ, and to manifest the nature of God in every thought, every word, every breath.

This is the final shift GIATI brings to light: **you were never meant to fix the old man—you were meant to bury him.** *Crucified with Christ, dead to sin, and raised to walk in newness of life. This is not a process. It is a revelation. The moment you see it, it becomes real. The moment you believe it, you live from it. And from that point forward, it is no longer you who live, but Christ who lives in you (Galatians 2:20).* **That is GIATI in full expression— not God beside you, not God above you, but God as you.**

This is the meaning of being born again—not a repeated prayer, not a change in behavior, but a complete and total re-identification with your true source. The old man believed he was a sinner trying to reach God. The new creature knows: **I am the dwelling place of God, and God is the only life I live.**

So if anyone is in Christ, **he is a new creation.** *Not will be.* **Is.** *The old has passed away. Behold—***behold—all things are made new** *(2 Corinthians 5:17). GIATI is the only lens through which this is fully understood. The Spirit that raised Jesus from the dead is not reserved for Him alone. It is the same Spirit that now quickens your mortal body. The same Spirit that awakened Him,* **awakens you.**

You are no longer a child of Adam. You are a child of the Father. You are no longer reaching for life. **You are life expressed.** *And when you see that, you do not simply live—you become the revelation the world has been waiting for.*

Putting Off the Old, Putting On the New: A Death and a Resurrection

The command to "put off the old man" and "put on the new" (Ephesians 4:22–24, Colossians 3:9–10) is not about changing behavior or adopting better habits—it is a radical transformation of identity. It is the full abandonment of the lie of separation and the full embrace of divine union. To put off the old man is to strip away every identity, mindset, and belief that is not rooted in the truth that **God is your life.** *It is a spiritual death—a conscious burial of the false self who believed it was something other than God in expression.*

The old man is not just the version of you that sinned—it is the version of you who believed you were ever separate from God in the first place. It is the ego-self who sought righteousness through effort, worth through comparison, and salvation through religion. This man is fueled by fear, shame, and striving. He operates from a distorted mirror, never able to truly see God because he cannot see himself in God. To put off the old man is to renounce that false mirror. To declare, once and for all, that **you are not an independent being trying to earn favor—you are the very offspring of God Himself.**

And then, you put on the new man—not like a costume, but like a second skin that was always underneath. This new man is not a version of your old self improved—he is **Christ revealed as you.** *He is the one "created after God in true righteousness and holiness" (Ephesians 4:24). Not seeking righteousness, but* **already righteous.** *Not hoping to be accepted, but* **born of the same Spirit that raised Jesus from the dead.** *To put on the new* *man is to walk with the full awareness that you are no longer just human—you are divinity clothed in flesh, a son of God in the earth, an embodiment of the Father's life.*

This is not a gradual process of sanctification through effort. This is **a revelation that changes everything instantly.** *The moment you believe, you step out of the grave of the old identity and rise into the freedom of your true nature. GIATI reveals that this is not a metaphorical idea, but the eternal truth hidden from the world*—**that God is not out there, God is within. And when you recognize Him within, you rise in Him.**

The putting off is not about suppressing your behavior—it is about dissolving the illusion of being someone you're not. The putting on is not about achieving divinity—it's about realizing you were never anything less. This is what Paul meant when he said, "you have died, and your life is hidden with Christ in God" (Colossians 3:3). The life you thought was yours— separate, small, human—has ended. And what now lives is the eternal Spirit of God expressed as you.

So when you put off the old man, you leave behind the systems of law, guilt, and performance. You bury the identity of sinner, struggler, and outsider. You silence the voice that tells you God is far, and you shut the door to the illusion of unworthiness. And when you put on the new, you arise as one who knows: **I and the Father are one. I am not becoming— I am.**

This is the power of GIATI—it is not a message that makes you better. **It's the revelation that you were never separate to begin with.** *It does not teach you to improve the old—it commands you to bury it. Because* **God is all there is,** *and anything that claims to be apart from Him was never real in the first place.*

The Only Way to the Father Is Through Oneness

There's a reason Jesus said, "No one comes to the Father but by me" (John 14:6). It wasn't about promoting himself as an exclusive gatekeeper. It was never about elevating a man—it was always about awakening humanity to a truth. Jesus wasn't saying, "Worship me,"—he was saying, "Walk in what I walk in." The "me" he spoke of is not the man from Nazareth—it is the Spirit of oneness, the "I AM" that lived in him and **lives in you.**

To come to the Father is to enter into union with divine reality. And you **cannot approach the Source of all as something other than Itself.** *You can't bring separation into the presence of oneness and expect to be received. That's why Jesus is the only way—not as a religious figure to be adored from a distance, but as the revealed pattern of the* **Spirit that God accepts.**

*When Jesus said, "I and the Father are one," he wasn't describing a relationship unique to him. He was unveiling the truth of what you must become conscious of. The Father is Spirit, and the only thing that can commune with Spirit is Spirit itself—***not flesh, not ego, not religious effort, and certainly not the belief that you are separate from God.**

Trying to "go to God" while holding on to an identity that sees itself apart from Him is like trying to plug a square peg into a circle of pure light—it cannot enter. **Duality cannot enter divinity.** *God is not rejecting you; He is rejecting the lie about you. The illusion of being "only human," or "just a servant," or "a sinner saved by grace" is not the truth of who you are— it's a mask. And God cannot recognize a mask.*

Jesus showed us how to come unveiled:
He stood in full awareness of oneness.
He didn't approach God as "Jesus the man."
He approached as **Spirit aware of its Source.**

This is why you must come through him—through that same awareness of sonship, of divine identity, of GIATI: God Is All There Is, including me.

The Spirit of Christ Is the Door

*Jesus is not the barrier to the Father; he is the mirror. When you look into the spirit he carried and see your own reflection there, you've entered the door. T***he Spirit of Christ is the consciousness of union,** *and it is the only way to the Father because the Father is union. You cannot bring separation to union. You must come as one who knows: "I am He."*

To come "through Jesus" means to drop every idea of being something other than God expressed as you. It means to allow the truth to dissolve the false identity, so that what remains is the Spirit of God Himself—awake, alive, and known.

That is the Spirit God receives. That is the Spirit God calls Son. That is the only way to the Father.

The Prayer of Oneness — The Desire of the Spirit

Jesus, just before his crucifixion, prayed a prayer that echoes through eternity. It was not a plea for safety, not a cry for escape—it was the deep desire of the Spirit to bring humanity into the same oneness he walked in.

"That they all may be one; as thou, Father, art in me, and I in thee, that they also may be one in us..." *(John 17:21)*

This is the very heart of God revealed.
This is the **real gospel**—*not a religion, but a* **restoration.**
*Jesus didn't come to make himself the only Son—he came to re***veal sonship as the truth of all mankind.** *His desire wasn't to be worshipped alone on a throne, but to awaken* **the throne within you**—*the place where Spirit meets Spirit, where Father and child are not two, but one.*

This prayer is not wishful thinking. It's prophetic. It's the Holy Spirit calling all into the truth that **there is no separation** *between God and His creation. And Jesus knew that the only way for this oneness to be realized was for the same Spirit of oneness in him to be awakened in us.*

That's why he said:

"I in them, and thou in me, that they may be made perfect in one..." (John 17:23)

Perfect in one. *That is the goal. That is the redemption. Not perfect by behavior. Not perfect by religious performance.* **Perfect in oneness.** *It is only when you know that* **God is in you and you are in God,** *that you truly fulfill the prayer of Jesus.*

And this is why you cannot go straight to the Father through doctrine, works, or belief in separation. You can only come through the **consciousness Jesus walked in**—*the knowing that says:*

"The Father is in me, and I am in the Father.
I and the Father are one.
If you've seen me, you've seen Him."

That is the doorway.
That is the truth.
That is the Spirit that cries, "Abba, Father," from within your own being.

The world waits for that truth to rise in the hearts of humanity—not a new religion, but a new realization: **GIATI—God Is All There Is,** *and the Spirit within you is the proof.*

Sin Is Separation — Oneness Is Righteousness

For too long, sin has been misunderstood as merely a list of wrong actions—external behaviors judged by religious laws. But Jesus came to reveal something deeper. He came to expose the **root of sin,** *not just the fruit. And what is that root?*

Separation.
The belief that you exist apart from God.
That you are "just human." That God is somewhere else. That you are trying to get to Him, please Him, or become what He already made you to be.

This illusion of separation is the true definition of sin. Not just what you do, but what you **believe about yourself.** *And the tragedy is, many try to overcome sin while still living inside the lie that causes it.*

The Spirit of Oneness Is the Only Righteousness

When God looks for righteousness, He's not looking for moral perfection. He's looking for **Himself.** *He's looking for* **oneness**—*a spirit that mirrors His own nature.*

"This is my beloved Son, in whom I am well pleased…"

Why? Because the Son knew:
"I came out from God… the Father is in me, and I in Him."

Righteousness isn't earned—it's **revealed.** *It's what happens when you wake up from the lie of being separate and realize that* **you were always in God, and God was always in you.**

That's why the Holy Spirit is the fulfillment of the law. Not because it helps you "try harder," but because it **restores your identity.** *It tells you the truth:*

"You are not a servant trying to reach God. You are God's own Spirit in expression, awakening to yourself."

The Simplicity of the Truth

Think of it this way: a kidney transplant can only be accepted if it matches the body's blood type. The body rejects what isn't part of itself. **In the same way, God cannot receive what doesn't match His own Spirit.** *You can't come to God as a separate being. You must come in Spirit and in truth—***in union.**

This is why Jesus said:

"*If you don't believe I am He, you will die in your sin." (John 8:24)*

Because as long as you hold on to an identity separate from God, you remain in the illusion that cuts you off from life. But the moment you recognize: "I am He"—the moment you know the Spirit within you is divine—that's when sin dies, and righteousness is born.

Not because God finally accepts you...
But because you finally accepted **who you truly are.**

GIATI: The End of Sin

GIATI—God Is All There Is—is not just a message. It is **the end of sin.** *Because once you accept that there is no "you" apart from God, there is no room left for fear, shame, guilt, or striving. The only thing left is* **union.**

And union is eternal life.

The Thief on the Cross – A Revelation of Oneness in a Dying Breath

"And he said unto Jesus, Lord, remember me when thou comest into thy kingdom."
— Luke 23:42

This one verse has echoed through generations as a testament to mercy, last-minute salvation, and the depth of Jesus' love. But beneath the surface of this desperate cry is something even more profound: a revelation of **oneness***—the heartbeat of the GIATI message.*

This man, a thief condemned to die, hanging beside the embodiment of God in flesh, utters a plea that penetrates time and theology. He doesn't ask to be saved from the cross. He doesn't beg for his earthly life. He simply says:

"Lord, remember me."

In the GIATI perspective—God Is All There Is—this statement takes on a deeper spiritual meaning. It is more than a plea for mercy; it is the cry of a soul awakening, even in death, to the truth that **he was never separate from the One beside him.**

"Remember Me" – The Cry to Be Made Whole Again

The word "remember" here is not just about recalling someone from memory. In spirit, to be "remembered" is to be **put back together,** *to be* **restored to your original wholeness,** *to be* **rejoined with your Source.**

The thief's cry was, in essence, a request to be made one again with the life he came from. He was saying, "Place me back in you... bring me back into myself as you."

This is the longing of every soul: to be **re-membered,** *not forgotten or cast off, but returned to the fullness of* **being in God,** *where it all began.*

On the Cross, the Two Appearances of Man

There were two thieves crucified beside Jesus—one on each side. One mocked, still blind to the truth, clinging to the delusion of separation. The other saw more than a man on a cross. He **recognized God in flesh,** *and more than that, he* **recognized himself in Him.**

This is the GIATI principle revealed in real time.

One thief remained **in the illusion of duality***—separate, bitter, and unbelieving.*
The other thief awakened, even as his body was dying, to the **truth of oneness,** *and that was salvation.*

The cross became a cosmic scene: Jesus in the center as **the Spirit of God made visible,** *the unbeliever to one side, and the awakened one to the other. This is not just history—it is a portrait of humanity itself.*

The Kingdom Was Already There

When the thief said, "When you come into your kingdom," he wasn't just speaking of a future paradise. He was touching something present and real. **The kingdom wasn't somewhere far away—it was right next to him, in the form of Jesus.** *And not just next to him—***within him.**

"Behold, the kingdom of God is within you." (Luke 17:21)

This was not a request for heaven later—it was a cry for **union now.**
And Jesus answered immediately:

"Verily I say unto thee, Today shalt thou be with me in paradise." *— Luke 23:43*

Today. *Not tomorrow. Not after judgment. Not after some future event.*

Today, because union is not delayed—it is realized.

The Simplicity of Salvation Through Oneness

The thief was not saved because of right behavior. He had no time to "make things right." He didn't get baptized, attend temple, or confess to a priest. He simply **recognized the truth.**

He saw God in flesh, he knew his place beside Him, and he called out—not from fear, but from an awakened sense of **belonging.**

This is the GIATI gospel: that **salvation is the recognition of your oneness with God.**
It is not achieved. It is **remembered.**
It's not earned. It's **inherited.**
It is not a reward for the righteous—it is the natural condition of all who awaken to it.

The only thing that keeps anyone in sin is the **unbelief** *in their union with God. And the only thing that rescues you from it is the* **belief** *that you were never separate in the first place.*

A Final Picture

The thief entered paradise not because God changed His mind, but because he finally **shared God's mind.** *He aligned with the truth that* **God is all there is,** *and in that truth, he found himself not just beside God—but* **inside God,** *and God in him.*

This is paradise: **to know that you and the Lord are one.** *It doesn't begin when you die. It begins the moment you believe.*

"Today You Will Be With Me" – The Eternal Now of Paradise

"And Jesus said unto him, Verily I say unto thee, Today shalt thou be with me in paradise." — *Luke 23:43*

The words Jesus spoke to the thief were not just comforting—they were **revelatory.**
They did more than promise heaven after death; they unveiled the mystery of **eternal life now.**
They dismantled the lie of separation. They pierced the veil of time.
And they revealed that **paradise is not a place—it is presence.**

"Verily I Say Unto Thee" – The Voice of Eternal Truth

Jesus begins with "Verily," or in other translations, "Truly." This was His signature way of affirming that what He was about to say came not from opinion or human logic but from **eternal reality.** *It is the Spirit speaking* **outside of time,** *giving insight into how things truly are in the mind of God.*

What follows is not just a promise—it is **the revelation of the order of divine being.**

"Today" – The Death of Delay and the Dawn of Awareness

This is the heart of the GIATI message wrapped in a single word:
Today.

Not after judgment. Not in a future resurrection.
Today*—because the moment a soul remembers its oneness with God, it is already home.*

Time is a construct of the natural world. But Jesus was not speaking from time—He was speaking **from eternity,** *and eternity is always now.*

"Behold, now is the accepted time; behold, now is the day of salvation."
— 2 Corinthians 6:2

Heaven is not something you enter later. Heaven is your awareness of union.
It doesn't happen when you die. It happens when **the lie of separation dies.**

The thief's body was dying, but **his spirit had awakened.**
He let go of the belief that he was unworthy, separate, or forgotten.
And in that moment, paradise was no longer a far-off hope—it became his **now.**

"With Me" – The Language of Union

Jesus doesn't say, "I'll send you to paradise."
He doesn't say, "You'll be allowed into heaven."

He says, **"You will be with me."**

That's the essence of the Kingdom. **Union. Presence. Oneness.**

This is GIATI: God Is All There Is.
And if God is all there is, then paradise is not a location—it is the realization of His indwelling Spirit.

Jesus is not pointing to a mansion in the clouds. He's pulling back the curtain on **eternal communion.** *To be "with Me" is to be* **in Me,** *as He prayed:*

"...that they all may be one; as thou, Father, art in me, and I in thee, that they also may be one in us..." — John 17:21

This is not a future hope—it is a **present participation** *in the divine.*

"In Paradise" – The Unveiling of God's Mind

The word "paradise" in Greek is paradeisos, which means a **garden** *or* **enclosed place of delight.** *It's a reference to Eden—not as geography, but as a* **state of perfect harmony between God and man.**

Paradise is **union restored,** *not just in feeling, but in understanding.*
It is the removal of the veil.
It is the return of the prodigal.
It is **the rejoining of consciousness with Source.**

When Jesus said, "Today you will be with Me in paradise," He was saying,

"Today you've stepped back into awareness of your true self—inside of Me."

This is what salvation truly is: not God deciding to accept you, but **you awakening to the fact that He already had.**

The Death of the Lie, the Birth of Awareness

The man hanging next to Jesus had done nothing to earn what he received.
No works. No temple rituals. No moral clean-up.

He simply **recognized God** *in the one crucified next to him—and in that recognition, he remembered himself.*

This moment on the cross tells us something religion often misses:

Salvation is not earned—it is remembered.
Paradise is not achieved—it is unveiled.

And the moment you know the truth—**that God is all there is,** *and you are* **within Him, not separate from Him—you're already home.**

"He Gave Up the Ghost" – The Spirit Returned to Itself

"And when Jesus had cried with a loud voice, he said, Father, into thy hands I commend my spirit: and having said thus, he gave up the ghost." — *Luke 23:46*

This moment has been portrayed as Jesus' final breath, His final act of surrender, the end of His life. But through the lens of GIATI—God Is All There Is—this is not an ending.

It is a revelation.
A cosmic unveiling.
A return of Spirit to Itself.

Jesus did not die defeated.
He did not die abandoned.
He died **as the full awareness of union,** *demonstrating that even in death,* **there is no separation from God.**

"Father, Into Thy Hands" – The Conscious Return to Origin

Jesus' final words were not fear or doubt. They were **intentional alignment** *with the truth that His Spirit came from the Father and could only return int*o **the hands of the same being** *who breathed Him into the earth.*

He wasn't handing His spirit off to another being.
He was **returning to His own fullness**—*to the state of being beyond flesh and form.*

In that moment, He affirmed what had always been true of Him:
That **He and the Father were one** *(John 10:30).*

That **no man took His life from Him,** *but He laid it down of His own accord (John 10:18)*

That **the Spirit is eternal,** *and nothing can take away what was never separate.*

"He Gave Up the Ghost" – Not Death, But Reunification

The phrase "gave up the ghost" sounds like the end of a story. But in Spirit, it is the **beginning of restoration.**

To "give up the ghost" is to allow the **breath of God**—*the Spirit that animates the body—to return to its source. It is the fulfillment of Ecclesiastes 12:7:*

"Then shall the dust return to the earth as it was: and the spirit shall return unto God who gave it."

This moment was not Jesus leaving His body in loss.
It was **Spirit concluding its assignment,** *and returning to* **Itself.**

Why?

Because everything that came out of God **must return to God,** *not as a separate being, but as* **God remembering Himself.**

The Ultimate Demonstration of GIATI

In His final breath, Jesus embodied the message that had always been true:

There is no "outside" of God.
There is no Spirit that exists apart from Him.
Even in death, we live in Him.

"For in Him we live, and move, and have our being." — Acts 17:28

Jesus' crucifixion wasn't a story of God killing His Son.
It was the visible demonstration that **even when Spirit enters into human frailty, it remains divine.**

It cannot be undone. It cannot be separated.
And it always returns to **Itself.**

Jesus gave up the ghost **not in defeat,** *but in* **completion**—*He had finished the revelation. He had lived out the truth of GIATI:*

"God is all there is, even when it looks like death."

What This Means For You

If Jesus returned His Spirit to God, then so do you. If He never lost union, neither have you.

The only thing that dies is the illusion of separation.

What lives forever is what has always been **in God,** *made of God, and expressing God.*

Your body will return to dust. But your Spirit—**which is God breathed**—*never left Him to begin with. And the moment you see this, you no longer fear death. You no longer fear judgment.*

Because you no longer live from the lie of separation.

You live from the truth:
That when you give up the ghost, you are not going anywhere—you are simply returning to the awareness of where you've always been: inside of God.

The Source Behind All Stories

There's a rising conversation among scholars, skeptics, and seekers alike: that many of the Bible's stories—its creation account, virgin birth narratives, flood stories, even the resurrection theme—mirror earlier writings found in Egyptian texts like the Book of the Dead, or Sumerian and Babylonian traditions that predate the Bible by centuries. For some, this discovery is used as a tool to discredit the Bible, as if its value is diminished simply because it shares ancient patterns with other spiritual traditions.

But from the revelation of **GIATI—God Is All There Is***—such arguments lose all their power.*

The truth doesn't need originality to be eternal. *The origin of truth is not in time—it is in Spirit. Long before anything was written down,* **God was.** *The moment anyone begins measuring truth by chronology or cultural ownership, they've already fallen into the illusion of separation—the very illusion GIATI exposes.*

If God is all there is, then all spiritual insight—regardless of where or when it was written—can only come from **the same source: the Spirit of God within.** *So it makes perfect sense that humanity, scattered across different lands and languages, would receive glimpses of the same eternal truth. The stories may differ in detail, but their spiritual DNA is the same: they're* **echoes** *of what has always been—God expressing Himself through the consciousness of man.*

Rather than being threatened by these similarities, we recognize them as part of a divine pattern. They are signs that the truth of GIATI has been seeded across time, waiting for the appointed moment to come into full clarity. What was once hidden in mystery, parables, and myth is now being spoken plainly:

God is not out there. God is not a distant figure, nor a foreign deity of ancient lands. God is the life within you. The breath you breathe. The Spirit you are.

This is why GIATI is not a new religion or a competing doctrine—it is the unveiling of what has always been true in every age. Even the Book of the Dead, with all its rituals and imagery of the afterlife, reveals mankind's longing to return to unity with the divine. But GIATI goes beyond the longing and declares the fulfillment: **There is no separation to overcome. God is already here—as you.**

So whether the form is Egyptian, Hebrew, Greek, or modern, the vessel doesn't matter— **the revelation is what counts.** *Those who become obsessed with the comparisons are still looking at the husk, unaware of the seed. They're missing the* **life** *that all sacred writings attempt to express.*

Truth doesn't belong to the Bible because it was written later, nor does it belong to Egypt because it was written first. **Truth belongs to God, and God is all there is.**

When you see this, you stop arguing over whose version came first and start recognizing the one Spirit that has always been trying to awaken humanity to itself.

That Spirit is speaking again—clearly, finally, and fully—through GIATI. And it is saying:

"The mystery is finished. There is only One. And you are not apart from Me."

This is what every story was pointing to.
This is what every heart has always known.
This is the end of the search.
This is GIATI.

Some will continue to insist that the Bible loses its credibility if its stories were told earlier elsewhere. But this mindset clings to **form over substance.** *It assumes that truth is proven by being first in history, instead of being first in essence. But God, as* **Spirit,** *is not subject to time. God does not unfold truth according to man's calendar, but according to awakening. What matters is not who wrote it down first, but* **who heard the Spirit clearly.**

Those earlier writings may have carried seeds of truth, but often hidden beneath layers of symbolism, fear, and ritual. They revealed humanity's awareness that something greater was within reach—but that awareness was dimmed by separation thinking. They spoke of gods outside, underworlds below, and heavens above—trying to reach the divine through death, sacrifice, or moral striving. The heart was reaching for what GIATI now makes plain:

You are not separate. The divine you were seeking has always been the Spirit within you.

This is what makes the message of GIATI distinct—not because it brings something "new," but because it brings the **final clarity.** *It strips away the veils. It unmasks the symbols. It removes the layers that made God seem far away. GIATI does not deny that truth has appeared in many forms across many ages—it simply* **fulfills** *what those forms could only hint at. It doesn't dishonor the shadows of ancient texts; it shines the light that makes the shadows unnecessary.*

Even the argument that ancient Egypt or other civilizations were "first" misunderstands the nature of God. If **God is all there is,** *then God was in Egypt. God was in Israel. God was in the heart of every scribe, prophet, mystic, and poet who ever tried to put the invisible into words. And yet,* **God is not bound by what any of them wrote.** *The moment we fix truth to a timeline, we shrink the limitless into the limited.*

GIATI reminds us that God has never been about religion or originality—only about recognition. *Not everyone who held a pen knew what they were writing. Many wrote from* *shadows, glimpsing a light they couldn't name. They captured patterns without knowing the patternmaker. But now, the Spirit has come to speak plainly, and to say:*

"That which you sought in symbols is now revealed in you. I am not a tradition to follow. I am the life you are."

So let those who wish to argue about dates and documents continue their debates. The Spirit has no controversy with them—only a call. A call to rise out of comparison and into communion. A call to see that every book, every myth, every scripture is either leading you to the awareness of oneness, or keeping you in the illusion of separation. GIATI is not here to prove the Bible superior, nor to defend it from historical criticism. GIATI is here to **reveal what the Bible—and every sacred writing—was always pointing toward:**

The Spirit within is God. You are not other. You are not outside. You are the manifestation of the Only One there is.

Whether it's called Atum, Yahweh, Elohim, or Christ, the names change—but the truth remains:

Before Abraham was, I Am.
Before Egypt was, I Am.
Before any text, any tradition, or any temple—I Am.

And **that I Am is you,** *once you awaken to it.*

This is why GIATI cannot be threatened by earlier writings. GIATI is not in competition with what came before—it is the **completion** *of what all sacred stories were yearning to say.*

The One has always been speaking. Now the One is recognized. That recognition is salvation. That salvation is GIATI.

The Illusion of Separation: The Great Misunderstanding

To live as a human being — with five senses, a name, a story, a body, and a personality — is to live inside a framework that constantly affirms the illusion of separation. The senses say, "I am here, you are there." The eyes see borders, forms, distinctions. The ears hear only one voice at a time. The hands touch things and feel space between them. Everything is tailored to reinforce individuality, difference, fragmentation.

But here's the great paradox: **the one who is perceiving all of this is not separate at all.** *The Spirit that animates the body, sees through the eyes, and thinks in the mind — that is God. The individual "you" is not a separate being having a spiritual experience. Rather,* **God is having an experience through the lens of what appears to be you.**

The illusion is powerful — more powerful than most can comprehend — because it is subtle. Like **air.** *It's invisible, yet it fills everything. Air allows life to move and breathe, but it's unseen. The illusion of separation works the same way. It is the background assumption of human life. It's not taught explicitly — it's experienced and felt as reality.*

People can't see God in themselves or others because they believe God must be something greater, bigger, out there — not this "small" being looking out from their eyes. But that's the trick: once you believe you're limited, you project that limitation onto God. **You say, "God can't be in me — I'm too flawed."** *But that's not humility — that's unbelief in disguise.*

The Many that Cannot See the One

Most people see "many things" and lose sight of the One. They see the fragmented expressions — different people, races, nations, species, matter — and forget that everything is made out of the same divine substance. **Everything is God expressing Himself in multiplicity, but remaining One in essence.** *It's like the ocean becoming waves — the waves may differ in size and movement, but it's all water.*

But here's the key: fragmentation is not reality — it's perception. It's a divine strategy to allow God to behold Himself from countless angles. The One became many, so the many could discover they are One.

GIATI is the remedy to this illusion. It is the voice that declares, **"God is all there is,"** *not just as a spiritual metaphor, but as an ontological, existential truth.*

Why They Worship Jesus but Resist His Purpose

Now, about Jesus.

People love worshipping Jesus because it keeps the truth outside of them. As long as Jesus is "God over there," they don't have to deal with the uncomfortable, ego-crushing truth that **they are called to become what He is.**

Jesus never came to be worshipped as an idol — He came to awaken us to the truth of our oneness with God. *That was His prayer in John 17: "That they may be one, even as we are one... I in them, and you in me."*

But instead of seeing Him as the pattern, they made Him the exception. They built a religion around Him instead of walking the path with Him. It feels safer to elevate Him than to accept the radical truth that **His Spirit is in us, as us** *— that His life was a mirror for ours.*

Why? Because if He's the example, then you are expected to walk like Him — to forgive like Him, to love like Him, to speak like Him, to carry the Spirit like Him. That requires transformation, surrender, death of the ego.

But if He's just the divine exception, then you can admire Him from a distance and never change.

Making the Truth Believable

So how do you make this truth believable?

By being it. By living from it. By speaking as one who knows it — not believes it, not hopes it — but **knows** *it.*

GIATI is not just a phrase, it's the **correction to the lie of separation.** *It's the unveiling of the eternal truth hidden in plain sight:* **There is no you and God — there is only God, expressing as what you call you.**

People may resist at first. But their Spirit will recognize the voice of truth when it speaks without fear or apology. Your life is the sermon. Your presence is the message. And as you embody the oneness, you'll awaken it in others.

One Body, One Spirit—The End of Separation

Paul's message in 1 Corinthians 12 isn't just about spiritual gifts—it's a declaration of divine unity. He begins by urging believers not to remain ignorant about spiritual realities. It's not enough to claim belief; true spiritual understanding comes only through the Holy Spirit. No one can call Jesus Lord in truth unless the Spirit within reveals it. This means the entire experience of knowing God must be rooted in the Spirit, not in the flesh or intellect. And this is the very heartbeat of GIATI: God Is All There Is, and unless that God-Spirit is awakened within, all we have is form without essence.

Paul then makes it plain—there are many different expressions of God's movement: wisdom, healing, prophecy, faith, miracles. But though the manifestations differ, the source is always the same Spirit. It's not many spirits working separately—it's one Spirit operating through many vessels, just as the same blood flows through every part of the body. These diverse gifts are not proof of individual status or personal holiness; they are evidence of the one God working all in all. Every operation is His, not ours.

This is why Paul brings in the analogy of the body. Just as a human body has many parts—each with its own function but all dependent on one another—so is the body of Christ. Every person joined to the Spirit becomes part of this divine organism. The body isn't made up of one kind of person or gift, just as a human body isn't made entirely of eyes or hands. Each member, no matter how different, is placed exactly where God wants them. The Spirit doesn't just assign roles—it creates unity through divine placement.

But here's the key GIATI revelation: any thought that sees itself as separate from the body is an illusion. If the foot says, "Because I'm not the hand, I'm not part of the body," it's not just being insecure—it's denying the truth of its spiritual identity. The moment a person believes they are not one with the body, they reject the Spirit that holds all things together. And when you reject your place in the body, you are not simply distancing yourself—you are disqualifying yourself from the life source that flows only through union. In GIATI terms, you are denying that God is all there is and instead creating a false identity that tries to stand alone.

This is the schism Paul speaks of—not merely division between people, but the refusal to accept that we are one Spirit. It's not just emotional or doctrinal separation; it's spiritual rebellion against divine unity. When the eye says to the hand, "I don't need you," or when the head claims independence from the feet, it is a denial of God's all-ness, and that denial fractures the body. GIATI shows us that there is no life outside of God—so to think you can live spiritually while existing apart from the body is to deceive yourself.

This oneness isn't theoretical. It's lived. If one part suffers, all suffer. If one is honored, all rejoice. This is the manifestation of divine harmony. God has tempered the body so there would be no schism, no separation—just perfect, flowing unity in Him. The gifts are diverse, but the life is one. The roles vary, but the source is the same. And unless we receive this Spirit—not as a doctrine but as our very essence—we remain outside the truth.

You are not your own. You are not here to "find your purpose" separate from the body. You are not a hand detached, a heart independent, or a mind wandering solo. You are either one with the Spirit—or outside of it. And this is the only true judgment: whether or not you are one with the Source. Oneness is the inheritance. Oneness is the identity. Oneness is the only thing God will ever recognize, because He can only recognize Himself.

This is not harsh. This is freedom. To lose the illusion of separation is to enter the fullness of divine life. It is to stop striving and start resting in the truth that God is your life, and your role in His body is sacred, irreplaceable, and eternal—not because of you, but because it is Him as you.

The Manifestation of the Sons of God: The Spirit Revealed in Us

Now that the Spirit has formed one body, the next revelation is the unveiling of those who carry His Spirit in fullness. Romans 8 speaks not just of salvation or morality—but of identity. It says, "The whole creation groaneth and travaileth in pain together until now, waiting for the manifestation of the sons of God." This isn't about people trying to be good Christians or spiritual leaders. This is about the revealing of those in whom the Spirit of God— the very same Spirit that was in Jesus—now lives, moves, and has complete dominion. GIATI reveals the mystery: the sons of God are not separate from God; they are the expression of His own Spirit in human form.

The earth is not waiting for a rapture—it's waiting for the recognition of who's real. Creation is groaning because it has been subjected to vanity through the illusion of separation. The ego, the false self, has claimed identity where only God should reign. But those who are born of the Spirit—who know that they are not independent beings, but living expressions of the I AM—are the ones who lift the veil. These are the sons. Not sons in the human sense, but in the divine sense—offspring of God by Spirit, not by flesh or will of man.

The manifestation of the sons of God is the Second Coming in motion. Not a man in the clouds, but the same Spirit that was in Jesus now revealed in a remnant who no longer live for themselves, but let the fullness of God express through them. These sons don't seek glory. They don't build platforms. They don't point to self. They carry no ego, no desire to be known for who they are—but only for who He is. This is why the Spirit in them cannot be counterfeited. There is no mixture. Not 99% God and 1% self. The sons of God are those who have died to the "me" and risen as "He." Their life is not their own. And this surrender is not weakness—it is the true inheritance.

That's why the inheritance of the kingdom isn't given based on behavior—it's given based on identity. Just like Jesus said to Nicodemus, "You must be born again," not as a religious concept, but as a spiritual reality. The flesh can't inherit the kingdom. It doesn't matter how sincere the belief is, how devout the service, or how good the intentions. If the Spirit of God is not your very life—if you still cling to a "you" apart from Him—you are disqualified. Not because God rejected you, but because you chose to hold onto a false identity. You became the schism. You stood outside the body.

Romans 8 continues, "For as many as are led by the Spirit of God, they are the sons of God." This isn't about being occasionally moved by God. This is about being governed by His Spirit—entirely. These sons don't walk after the flesh. They don't operate from fear, striving, or self-will. They are free—not because they do what they want, but because the One within them is doing what He wants, and they have fully surrendered to that truth.

GIATI is the call to this awareness. It is the trumpet sounding for those who were always His—but didn't know it yet. It is the final cry before the spiritual age bursts forth, saying, "Awake, thou that sleepest, and Christ shall give thee light." The manifestation of the sons is not coming—it's here. Hidden in plain sight. The light is rising in those who will no longer pretend to be separate, but will boldly declare, "I and my Father are one." Not as imitation, but as realization. Not from pride, but from surrender.

And creation will know them—not because of their preaching, but because of their presence. The sons of God bring peace, not chaos. They speak truth, not opinion. They don't come to take sides—they come to end the illusion of division altogether. They come to reveal what's always been true: God is all there is—and He now lives through us.

The error of putting limitations on Yahweh is the beginning of all confusion. To even imagine that the One who is inexhaustible, indivisible, all-knowing, all-present, and all- powerful could be less than what He is—less than everything—is to fabricate a god that doesn't exist. Yahweh, the Eternal, created the heavens, the earth, and all that is in them not by sourcing from another, but by manifesting Himself. He had no external materials, because there was nothing outside of Him to draw from. He is the origin, the essence, the very being of all that exists. To say then, that He is not you—that He is somehow limited to being "out there," while you exist "down here"—is to reduce the Infinite into the image of your own delusion.

This is the tragedy of limitation: when you say "I am not God," you are not humbling yourself—you are denying the truth of your origin. You are accusing the All of division. You're saying the indivisible has been divided, the infinite has been broken, the omnipresent is somehow absent—in you. That is the depth of blindness. But here is the mystery: even that blindness is Yahweh. There is nothing apart from Him—not even the lie that says there is. It is Yahweh Himself, hidden within the illusion of separation, waiting for the appointed moment to reveal Himself to Himself.

To limit God is to sin against your own source. It is to say, "He cannot be me," when in truth, there is no "you" outside of Him. The delusion of separateness is not humility—it is the ego's last stand. For what arrogance must it take to tell the One who is All that He is not present here? To claim your existence independent of Yahweh is to place a boundary on the boundless, to place walls around the wind, to bottle the ocean and say, "This is all there is." But even the bottle, the illusion, and the ignorance—are all formed of God.

The power of Yahweh is shown in this: that He can contain the fullness of Himself within a limited human frame, veil that truth, and then—by His grace—unveil it again. Not because you were worthy. Not because you figured it out. But because He decided it was time. That is the greatness of God: not that He demands worship from afar, but that He lives as the one who forgets, and then grants Himself the remembrance.

To limit Him is to blind yourself—but even that blindness is under His control. Until He gives the eyes to see, you will remain in darkness, believing you are something apart from Him, when in reality, you are nothing but Him in disguise. And when the veil is lifted, it won't be because you climbed your way to the truth. It will be because Yahweh chose to reveal Yahweh—in you. He is the One seeing, the One seen, and the One giving sight. He is the truth you've been searching for, and the only one who can reveal it.

And until you see this, every limitation you place on Him is a limitation you place on yourself. But Yahweh cannot be limited. And neither can you—once you know who you truly are.

And this is the turning point of all spiritual awakening: the moment you stop trying to make yourself acceptable to God, and you realize you are already Him—veiled in flesh, walking through time, forgetting only because He ordained the forgetting. You stop striving to reach the heavens and realize heaven has always been within. That the voice you've been praying to, the presence you've been chasing, the "other" you've been trying to please—it was always your own Spirit calling out from behind the mask.

This is the end of religion and the beginning of revelation. Religion teaches limitation— it gives you steps, laws, and distance between you and God. Revelation unveils what has always been: that Yahweh is not separate from you. He is the breath in your lungs, the life in your blood, the awareness in your mind, the "I" in your being. To deny this is not just to dishonor Him—it is to deny your own existence. Because if He is the All, and you are not Him, then you are not at all. That's the delusion. That's the lie of separation. It's the serpent's voice recycled in modern language: "You are not like God." And yet, the truth remains—you are made of God. There is no distance to close. There is only the veil to be lifted.

The arrogance is not in claiming oneness with Yahweh—the arrogance is in thinking you ever had a self apart from Him. That's the true rebellion: not eating a fruit in a garden, but believing the voice that said you were naked, when you were clothed in God the whole time. The true fall is thinking you fell out of Him in the first place.

And here's the grace: Yahweh limits Himself so perfectly in the illusion of the human experience that the only way to break the spell is for Him to choose it. You cannot wake yourself up. You cannot pull back the veil with effort, discipline, or intellect. The veil is His hand—and the lifting of it is His will. The light shines when He says, "Let there be light."

So what can you do? Surrender to the truth. Let go of the lie of limitation. Let go of the false humility that pretends separation is reverence. Worship in Spirit and truth by acknowledging that you and the Father are one—not because you earned it, but because it has always been so. You are not trying to become God. You are not working your way to divine status. You are simply remembering who you've always been. Yahweh—all in all. Indivisible. Undeniable. Unlimited. And now, unveiled.

Chapter 14

The Purpose of Existence

Understanding the purpose of existence is essential to uncovering the mystery of life and humanity's role in God's eternal design. Through GIATI (God Is All There Is), we realize that existence is not random or meaningless but rooted in God's desire to express and experience Himself. This chapter explores why God created, humanity's divine purpose, and the joy that comes from awakening to the truth of our oneness with God.

Why God Created: To Express and Experience Himself

God, being infinite and all-encompassing, created existence as a means to express and experience His own nature. Colossians 1:16 declares:

"For by him were all things created, that are in heaven, and that are in earth, visible and invisible, whether they be thrones, or dominions, or principalities, or powers: all things were created by him, and for him."

Creation is God's self-expression. Every star, every ocean, every life form is a unique reflection of His essence. Isaiah 43:7 reinforces this purpose:

"Even every one that is called by my name: for I have created him for my glory, I have formed him; yea, I have made him."

God created humanity to glorify Him, not as a distant deity, but as Himself manifest in physical form. Through creation, God experiences His own attributes—love, power, wisdom, and creativity. In humanity, He also experiences individuality, as each person is a distinct expression of His infinite nature.

Humanity's Role in God's Eternal Purpose

Humanity is the pinnacle of God's creation, bearing His image and likeness. Genesis 1:27 affirms this:

"So God created man in his own image, in the image of God created he him; male and female created he them."

This image is not merely physical but spiritual. Humanity's role is to act as vessels through which God's nature is expressed and experienced. As Paul writes in 2 Corinthians 4:6-7:

"For God, who commanded the light to shine out of darkness, hath shined in our hearts, to give the light of the knowledge of the glory of God in the face of Jesus Christ. But we have this treasure in earthen vessels, that the excellency of the power may be of God, and not of us."

The "treasure" is God Himself, dwelling within each person. Humanity's purpose is to allow this divine light to shine, reflecting His glory in every thought, word, and action.

However, this role can only be fulfilled when humanity awakens to the truth of GIATI. Many remain ignorant, trapped in the illusion of separateness, believing they are independent beings. Jesus came to reveal the truth: that the Spirit within each person is God. In John 14:20, He declares:

"At that day ye shall know that I am in my Father, and ye in me, and I in you."

Recognizing this unity empowers humanity to live in alignment with God's eternal purpose.

The Joy of Awakening to the Truth of GIATI

Awakening to the truth of GIATI—realizing that God is not only with us but is us—brings profound joy and liberation. It dissolves fear, guilt, and the illusion of separation, replacing them with peace, purpose, and gratitude.

David expresses this joy in Psalm 16:11:

"Thou wilt show me the path of life: in thy presence is fulness of joy; at thy right hand there are pleasures for evermore."

Awareness of God's presence within transforms existence from a struggle to a celebration. Paul captures this transformation in Galatians 2:20:

"I am crucified with Christ: nevertheless I live; yet not I, but Christ liveth in me: and the life which I now live in the flesh I live by the faith of the Son of God, who loved me, and gave himself for me."

To live with this understanding is to live as God expressed, fulfilling His eternal purpose. It is the realization that all of life's experiences—both joyful and challenging—are opportunities for God to know Himself through us.

Jesus spoke of this joy in John 15:11:

"These things have I spoken unto you, that my joy might remain in you, and that your joy might be full."

The fullness of joy comes from knowing that we are one with the Creator, that He is the source and sustainer of our lives, and that our purpose is to glorify Him by simply being who we are: God manifest.

Conclusion: The Eternal Dance of Creation

The purpose of existence is the eternal dance of creation, expression, and experience. God created not out of need but out of love, to manifest His infinite nature in countless forms. Humanity's role in this divine plan is to awaken to the truth of GIATI, living as vessels of God's glory and love.

Ephesians 1:11-12 beautifully summarizes this purpose:

"In whom also we have obtained an inheritance, being predestinated according to the purpose of him who worketh all things after the counsel of his own will: That we should be to the praise of his glory, who first trusted in Christ."

When humanity awakens to this truth, life becomes a journey of discovery, joy, and unity. Every moment, every breath, every act becomes a sacred expression of the Creator, fulfilling the eternal purpose of existence. As we embrace GIATI, we find not only the meaning of life but the fullness of life itself, united forever with the One who is all there is.

The True Rapture – Awakening to Oneness

The doctrine of the rapture has long been interpreted as a future event—a moment when the faithful will be caught up into the clouds to meet the Lord in the air. Many have envisioned this as a physical departure from the earth, a great evacuation of believers into the heavens. But what if this passage holds a much deeper, spiritual truth? What if the rapture is not about escaping this world, but about awakening to the reality of **GIATI—God Is All There Is?**

Paul, in his letter to the Thessalonians, speaks of the Lord descending with a shout, the dead in Christ rising first, and those who remain being caught up to meet Him in the air. But the true essence of this passage is not in the outward spectacle, but in the inward transformation. This is not a promise of physical departure, but of **spiritual ascension—an awakening to divine oneness.**

1. **The Sleeping and the Awake: The Two States of Humanity**

"But I would not have you to be ignorant, brethren, concerning them which are asleep, that ye sorrow not, even as others which have no hope." (1 Thessalonians 4:13)

Paul speaks of those who are "asleep," a term often used in Scripture to describe those who have passed from this world. But in a deeper sense, **sleep represents spiritual ignorance—being unaware of one's divine nature.** *There are those who live in darkness, trapped in the illusion of separation, blind to the truth of their own oneness with God.*

The sorrow Paul speaks of is the sorrow of those who do not yet understand the eternal nature of the Spirit. They grieve as though death were the end, because they do not yet see that life is eternal in God. But for those who awaken to the truth of Christ, there is no true death—only the transition into greater awareness.

2. **The Resurrection: Rising Into True Identity**

"For if we believe that Jesus died and rose again, even so them also which sleep in Jesus will God bring with him." (1 Thessalonians 4:14)

Jesus's resurrection was not simply about a physical body coming back to life—it was the revelation of divine reality. He showed that **life is not confined to the flesh, nor is it subject to death.** *Those who "sleep in Jesus" are not lost; they are with Him, for there is no separation in Spirit.*

In the same way, the "dead in Christ" rising first (v.16) is not merely a prophecy of bodies coming out of graves—it is the revelation that those who have recognized their divine identity have already risen. **They have transcended the illusion of separation and have entered into the eternal reality of oneness with God.**

3. **The True Meaning of Being "Caught Up"**

"Then we which are alive and remain shall be caught up together with them in the clouds, to meet the Lord in the air: and so shall we ever be with the Lord." (1 Thessalonians 4:17)

The phrase "caught up" has often been interpreted as a literal departure from the earth, but what if it speaks of something far greater?

To be "caught up" is **to be lifted in consciousness, to ascend in understanding, to awaken from the dream of separation and behold the reality of God.** *The clouds represent the higher realm of spiritual awareness—where human perception is transcended, and divine truth is fully realized.*

Meeting the Lord "in the air" does not mean escaping this world; it means transcending the carnal mind. **It is the moment of spiritual enlightenment, when the illusion of division fades, and only oneness remains.**

4. **Ever With the Lord: Living in the Reality of GIATI**

"And so shall we ever be with the Lord." (1 Thessalonians 4:17)

This is the final revelation—the great truth hidden beneath the surface of the text. This is not about waiting for a future event, but about entering into the reality of **God's presence here and now.**

To be "with the Lord" is not a future hope—it is an eternal truth. *The moment one awakens to the understanding that* **God Is All There Is,** *the rapture has already taken place. The mind has been lifted into the knowledge of divine unity, and one is no longer bound by the limitations of the flesh.*

5. **Comfort One Another With These Words**

"Wherefore comfort one another with these words." (1 Thessalonians 4:18)

Paul's final instruction is clear: **this truth should bring peace, not fear.** *The rapture is not about escaping judgment or fleeing from a doomed world. It is about awakening to the fullness of divine life. It is about recognizing that* **there is no separation—no death, no loss, no distance between God and His creation.**

This is the comfort of GIATI.

- *The rapture is not about leaving—it is about seeing.*
- *It is not about bodies rising—it is about consciousness awakening.*

- *It is not about waiting for the end—it is about realizing the beginning.*
- *It is not about escaping the world—it is about perceiving God in all things.*
- *It is not about being taken away—it is about being revealed as one with Him.*
- *It is not about separation—it is about union, the perfect oneness Jesus prayed for.*

This is the true rapture—the lifting of the veil, the awakening to the eternal reality that **God Is All There Is.** *It is not a future event to be anticipated but a present truth to be realized. The moment one embraces this divine awareness, they are already "caught up" in Christ, dwelling in the fullness of God's presence, forever with the Lord.*

The Universe Within—The True Purpose of Humanity

The Search for Life—Are We Looking in the Wrong Direction?

For centuries, humanity has gazed into the cosmos, searching for signs of life beyond our world. Telescopes scan distant galaxies, probes venture into the unknown, and scientists pour over data, hoping to find evidence that we are not alone. Yet, a new study suggests what many have long suspected: complex life may be exceedingly rare, or even **unique** *to Earth.*

This conclusion raises deep questions:

- *Why does intelligent life exist at all?*
- *Is humanity just a cosmic accident?*
- *Are we truly alone in the vastness of space?*

Yet, the real question—the one few dare to ask—is this: **Have we been looking outward when the answer was always within?**

The Illusion of External Seeking

Humanity has always been obsessed with **looking outward***—seeking answers beyond itself, searching for meaning in the farthest reaches of existence. This is the same pattern seen in religion, science, and philosophy. We reach for something "out there," hoping to find proof of what we are, instead of turning inward and realizing that* **the truth was never external—it has always been within us.**

The idea that complex life might be rare or even unique is not an accident—it is a message. If we are alone, then the universe is not a playground for intergalactic travel or encounters with alien civilizations. **It is a mirror, reflecting us back to ourselves, forcing us to awaken to what we truly are.**

This reality—the universal plane we experience—is not designed for us to escape it, colonize distant worlds, or make contact with other beings. **It exists for one reason: to awaken us to God within.**

Humanity's True Purpose—The Awakening to Oneness

If all of creation was formed by God, then **all of it must be an expression of God.** *This means life is not random, and our existence is not a coincidence. The reason intelligent life is so rare is because its purpose is not survival, exploration, or expansion—it is* **realization.**

Jesus declared:

"Neither shall they say, Lo here! or, lo there! for, behold, the kingdom of God is within you." (Luke 17:21)

This is the forgotten truth: **We are not meant to seek God in the stars, but in the self.** *We are not here to conquer the universe, but to* **conquer the illusion of separation. What does this mean?**

- *Humanity was never meant to "find" God externally—it was always meant to remember that it* **is** *God expressed.*
- *The universe is vast, but its vastness is not an invitation to explore the physical—it is a symbol of the infinite nature of the Divine within.*
- *We keep looking outward, hoping to discover something greater, yet the greatest revelation is the one we have ignored:* **God is all there is, and we are that divine presence made manifest.**

Why Are We Here?

Many look at the rare conditions that allowed intelligent life to exist and assume we are **accidents of nature.** *But the opposite is true: We are the* **intended** *result of creation—not as separate beings, but as vessels through which God expresses itself.*

The universe did not give rise to consciousness. Consciousness **gave rise to the universe.**

This means:

- *The vastness of space exists* **to point us inward, not outward.**
- *The seeming absence of intelligent life is not an indication that we are alone—it is an indication that life's purpose is inward evolution, not outward exploration.*
- *The human experience is not about escaping Earth or encountering others— it is about waking up to what we* **already are.**

The Final Frontier Is Within

What if we have misunderstood everything? What if the greatest journey is not across the stars, but **into the self?**

For thousands of years, mystics, prophets, and enlightened teachers have declared the same truth: **You are not separate from God.**

- *The kingdom of heaven is within.*
- *The Spirit of God is within.*
- *The only thing preventing humanity from realizing this is the false belief in separation.*

The world remains asleep because it continues to seek outward. Science searches the stars, religion searches doctrines, and philosophy searches ideas. Yet, the answer has never changed: **We are here to recognize that we were never separate to begin with.**

The Truth of GIATI—God Is All There Is

From the perspective of GIATI, the truth is clear:

- *Humanity is not alone because* **nothing exists outside of God.**
- *The absence of alien civilizations is not an emptiness to be filled—it is a silence designed to force us to turn inward.*
- *The universe is not waiting to be explored;* **it is waiting for us to wake up.**

Beyond the Illusion of Discovery—The Journey to Self-Realization

Humanity has always been captivated by the idea of discovering something beyond itself. We celebrate the explorers of the past, the scientific pioneers of the present, and the visionaries of the future who dream of reaching distant worlds. Yet, the greatest discovery that has ever existed has already been revealed—the recognition that **there was never anything to find beyond what has always been within.**

The search for alien life, the desire to travel beyond Earth, and the obsession with what lies in the cosmos are all extensions of the same illusion—the belief that **meaning and fulfillment exist outside of ourselves.** *It is the same illusion that causes people to chase wealth, status, relationships, or religious doctrines, believing that something external will complete them.*

But just as nothing external can make us whole, no amount of searching the stars will ever reveal a truth that is already present within our being.

The Universe as a Reflection of Consciousness

Every aspect of the universe reflects a deeper truth about existence. The way the cosmos expands, the way energy moves, and the way light travels all mirror the divine principles at work within us.

- *The* **vastness of space** *mirrors the boundless nature of consciousness.*
- *The* **darkness of the universe** *reflects the ignorance of the mind before awakening.*
- *The* **stars that shine in the void** *symbolize the light of awareness breaking through illusion.*

Even scientific principles echo spiritual truths. Just as a black hole pulls everything toward itself, so too does the awakened consciousness draw all fragmented aspects of itself back into unity. Just as the universe is expanding, so too is awareness constantly unfolding.

This understanding makes it clear: **we were never meant to "discover" anything outside of ourselves.** *The true purpose of existence is* **to recognize that all we have ever sought is already present in the depths of our being.**

The Final Illusion—Escaping Earth vs. Transcending Consciousness

Some believe that the future of humanity lies in escaping Earth, colonizing new planets, and ensuring the survival of our species elsewhere. But this is just another illusion— another way of avoiding the real work of transformation.

Survival is not the goal. Awakening is.

The desire to expand outward is a physical solution to a spiritual problem. No matter where humanity goes, it will take its ignorance, its fears, and its false sense of separation with it. The issue is not where we are—the issue is **who we think we are.** *Until that changes, no amount of outward expansion will lead to true liberation.*

This is why the kingdom of God is not in another world, another planet, or another dimension—it is **within.**

Jesus made this clear when He said:

"In my Father's house are many mansions: if it were not so, I would have told you. I go to prepare a place for you." (John 14:2)

These "mansions" are not physical locations in some distant heaven. They represent **states of consciousness.** *The true journey is not from one planet to another, but from one state of awareness to another.*

What Happens When Humanity Awakens?

If the purpose of life is not to expand outward but to awaken inward, then what happens when humanity as a whole comes into this realization?

- *The endless searching will cease, replaced by the deep knowing that* **God is all there is.**
- *The fear of being alone in the universe will dissolve, because the very idea of "aloneness" will be seen as an illusion.*
- *The desire to escape will disappear, because there will be nothing to escape from— only an eternal reality to recognize and embody.*

At that point, humanity will no longer seek to conquer space or discover life beyond itself. It will understand that **it was never separate, never alone, and never incomplete.** *The universe was never empty—it was simply waiting for us to awaken.*

The Ultimate Realization—We Were Never Searching, We Were Remembering

Every great journey is not about discovering something new, but about **remembering something forgotten.** *This is the core of all spiritual teachings, and this is the truth that Jesus, and many others, came to reveal.*

The belief that humanity is alone in the universe is not something to fear—it is something to understand. It is not a sign of isolation but an indication of purpose. **We are here for one reason: to realize that we were never separate to begin with.**

The final frontier is not space. The final frontier is **awakening.**

And once we awaken, we will see that there was never anything else to find—only the infinite presence of God, expressing itself through us.

We are not lost in the cosmos. We are lost in ourselves.

And the only way out is not forward, not outward, but **inward.**

Chapter 15

The Journey Home

The journey home is humanity's collective path back to the awareness of oneness with God. Through the revelation of GIATI (God Is All There Is), humanity is invited to awaken from the illusion of separation and embrace its divine essence. This chapter explores the process of returning to this awareness, the transformation of the world through the understanding of GIATI, and the fulfillment of God's promise of eternal unity: heaven on earth as it is in spirit.

How Humanity Can Collectively Return to Oneness with God

Humanity's return to God begins with recognizing the truth of who we are. The path home is not a physical journey but a spiritual awakening to the divine reality within. In Luke 17:21, Jesus teaches:

"Neither shall they say, Lo here! or, lo there! for, behold, the kingdom of God is within you."

This kingdom is not a distant realm but the presence of God in every soul. The first step is individual awakening—acknowledging that the spirit within is God. Each person who embraces this truth becomes a light, illuminating the path for others.

Ephesians 4:4-6 emphasizes the unity that is already ours:

"There is one body, and one Spirit, even as ye are called in one hope of your calling; One Lord, one faith, one baptism, One God and Father of all, who is above all, and through all, and in you all."

As more individuals awaken to this oneness, the collective consciousness of humanity shifts, drawing us closer to the ultimate realization of unity with God.

The Transformation of the World Through GIATI

When humanity embraces GIATI, the world is transformed. Division, conflict, and suffering arise from the illusion of separateness, but when people recognize their oneness with God and each other, the foundation of these problems crumbles.

Isaiah 11:6-9 paints a vision of this transformation:

"The wolf also shall dwell with the lamb, and the leopard shall lie down with the kid; and the calf and the young lion and the fatling together; and a little child shall lead them. They shall not hurt nor destroy in all my holy mountain: for the earth shall be full of the knowledge of the Lord, as the waters cover the sea."

This prophecy symbolizes the harmony that emerges when humanity lives in the awareness of God's presence in all things. The understanding of GIATI fosters compassion, love, and unity, reshaping societies and relationships.

In Matthew 5:14-16, Jesus calls His followers to be the light of the world:

"Ye are the light of the world. A city that is set on an hill cannot be hid. Neither do men light a candle, and put it under a bushel, but on a candlestick; and it giveth light unto all that are in the house. Let your light so shine before men, that they may see your good works, and glorify your Father which is in heaven."

By living as God expressed, we shine this light, transforming the darkness of ignorance into the brilliance of divine understanding.

The Promise of Eternal Unity: Heaven on Earth

The ultimate promise of the journey home is the realization of heaven on earth. This is not a distant event but a present reality that unfolds as humanity awakens to the truth of GIATI. In Revelation 21:3-4, we find the promise of God dwelling among us:

"And I heard a great voice out of heaven saying, Behold, the tabernacle of God is with men, and he will dwell with them, and they shall be his people, and God himself shall be with them, and be their God. And God shall wipe away all tears from their eyes; and there shall be no more death, neither sorrow, nor crying, neither shall there be any more pain: for the former things are passed away."

This vision is not merely about the future but the transformation that occurs when humanity collectively recognizes God's presence within. The "former things" pass away because the illusion of separateness dissolves, leaving only the reality of divine unity.

Jesus prayed for this unity in John 17:21-23:

"That they all may be one; as thou, Father, art in me, and I in thee, that they also may be one in us: that the world may believe that thou hast sent me. And the glory which thou gavest me I have given them; that they may be one, even as we are one."

This prayer reveals God's ultimate intention: the complete restoration of oneness between Himself and humanity. Heaven is not a distant reward but the eternal unity of spirit, manifesting here and now.

Conclusion: Returning to the Source

The journey home is humanity's collective awakening to the truth of GIATI. It is a return to the source, to the oneness that has always been but was forgotten in the illusion of separateness. Through the light of Christ, the transformation of the world, and the fulfillment of God's promise, humanity can experience heaven on earth.

As Paul writes in Romans 8:18-19:

"For I reckon that the sufferings of this present time are not worthy to be compared with the glory which shall be revealed in us. For the earnest expectation of the creature waiteth for the manifestation of the sons of God."

The glory revealed in us is the recognition that God is all there is. When humanity embraces this truth, the journey home is complete, and we live eternally in the unity, love, and joy of our Creator.

The Story of Job: A Revelation of Divine Oneness

*The story of Job is one of the most profound accounts of faith, suffering, and ultimate restoration. But beyond the surface, it reveals a much deeper truth—***the process of awakening from the illusion of separation to the realization that God is all there is (GIATI).** *Job's journey mirrors the spiritual resurrection that takes place when one moves from ignorance to divine understanding, from feeling abandoned to recognizing the presence of God within.*

The Illusion of Separation: A Test of Faith

Job, a man described as **"perfect and upright",** *was not just morally good—he was spiritually aligned. His righteousness meant that* **he was one in Spirit with God.** *Yet, when calamity struck—his wealth stolen, his children lost, and his body afflicted—Job wrestled with what seemed to be divine abandonment.*

Many today experience this same illusion. **The moment suffering arises, the mind deceives us into thinking that God is absent.** *But Job's story, like the message of GIATI, teaches that God is always present—even in suffering.*

- *Job initially believed in* **a God outside of himself,** *separate and distant.*
- *But the suffering he endured* **led him to a deeper realization: that the Spirit of God was his very life.**
- This awakening broke the illusion of separation and brought him into alignment with divine truth.

This is what GIATI reveals: **God is not far off; He is the essence of all existence, the very breath within us.**

Suffering as the Path to Awakening

Job's suffering was not punishment—it was **a divine process of refinement, a shaking that led to revelation.** *The same happens today. Hardship forces people to* **seek deeper truth,** *breaking religious illusions and leading them to* **spiritual resurrection— where the Messiah is realized within.**

- *Job's friends believed in a transactional God—one who blesses the righteous and punishes the wicked.*
- *But Job's journey revealed a higher reality: suffering is not a sign of divine rejection, but a tool for divine awakening.*

GIATI unveils the same truth. **Humanity has been conditioned to believe in a separate, external God.** *But suffering, when viewed through spiritual eyes,* **reveals the ever-present Spirit of God within.**

Job's Restoration: The Power of Divine Alignment

Job's restoration came **not because he earned it, but because he aligned himself with divine reality.** *The ymoment he surrendered to God's presence* **within,** *everything changed.*

This mirrors Jesus' revelation: "I and the Father are one" (John 10:30). The **true resurrection is when we awaken to the understanding that God is within us**—*and in that awareness, we move from:*

- **Loss to abundance**
- **Darkness to light**
- **Ignorance to divine wisdom**

Job's story ends with double restoration—*a sign of divine completion. This symbolizes that* **once the Spirit of God is fully realized within, nothing is truly lost, only transformed.**

GIATI teaches that **resurrection is not just about Jesus rising from the grave—it is about YOU awakening to the reality of divine oneness.**

The Ultimate Revelation: God Is All There Is

At the end of Job's story, he realizes **God had never left him.** *His suffering was* **not separation—it was a process of refinement that stripped away illusions and revealed the deeper truth.**

This aligns perfectly with GIATI's message:

- **God is not something to be found—He is already present as you.**
- **Trials do not separate you from God; they reveal His presence within you.**
- **True restoration is not about getting back what was lost, but realizing you were never separate from the Source to begin with.**

Job's story is not just an ancient account—it is **a divine blueprint for awakening.** *It reveals that the Messiah,* **the Holy Spirit, is present now, within, calling all to awaken to divine oneness.**

The Hidden Truths of Job's Story

Many read Job's story as a test of faith, but deeper revelation shows **it is a parable of divine realization.** *Every aspect of Job's experience points to a higher truth:*

1. **Job's Perfection and Righteousness**
    - *The Bible calls Job "perfect and upright."*
    - *This means Job was* **one in Spirit with God.**
    - **Righteousness is not about moral behavior—it is about divine alignment.**

2. **Satan's Challenge: The Illusion of Duality**
    - *Satan tells God that Job only serves Him because of his blessings.*
    - **This represents the illusion that righteousness is based on external conditions, rather than internal oneness with God.**
    - *God allows the test* **not to punish Job, but to reveal his true nature.**
3. **Job's Suffering: A Spiritual Trial**
    - *Job's wealth, family, and health are taken.*
    - *But* **his true life—the Spirit of God within him—cannot be touched.**
    - *This mirrors the human journey: the external world may shake, but* **the divine presence remains unshaken.**
4. **Job's Friends: The Religious Mindset**
    - *Job's friends believe suffering is always a punishment for sin.*
    - *This is* **the separatist mindset that sees God as an external judge.**
    - *But* **Job, through his suffering, is being awakened to the truth of divine unity.**
5. **Job's Cry for Understanding: The Breaking Point**
    - *Job begins questioning God.*
    - *This is not rebellion—it is* **the process of divine transformation.**
    - **Even those with the Holy Spirit experience moments of struggle, but GIATI teaches that suffering does not negate God's presence—it reveals it.**
6. **God's Answer: The Revelation of Divine Sovereignty**
    - *God speaks to Job out of a whirlwind, revealing His limitless wisdom.*
    - *He does not give Job a direct answer—***because true understanding is not in words, but in revelation.**
    - *Job realizes his error:* **he was never separate from God.**
7. **Job's Restoration: The Return to Divine Alignment**
    - *Job repents—not for sin, but for his limited understanding.*
    - *His fortunes are* **restored, doubled—a symbol of divine completion.**
    - *His friends, still trapped in religious thought,* **must now seek Job's prayers.**
    - **This mirrors the spiritual resurrection: awakening to the full realization of oneness with God.**

The Resurrection of Job: A Prophetic Symbol

Job's story is a prophetic foreshadowing of **spiritual resurrection—the same truth Jesus revealed.**

- *The resurrection is* **not just about Jesus rising from the dead—it is about the Messiah rising within you.**

- *Job thought he was "dead" in his suffering, but through divine revelation,* **he was resurrected into the awareness of God's presence within.**
- *Humanity, in ignorance, is spiritually dead.* **But when the Spirit of God is awakened within, resurrection happens.**

This is the truth GIATI reveals to the world today:

- There is no separation between God and man.
- God is not external—He is the life within.
- Suffering is not abandonment, but a path to awakening.
- The Messiah is not an event—it is the Spirit manifesting as you.

Job's Story and the Call of the Holy Spirit

The story of Job is **not just ancient history—it is a living message of divine unity.** *Every trial, every question, every moment of suffering is an opportunity to* **awaken to the reality that God is all there is.**

Job's journey is **the human journey**—*the process of stripping away false beliefs, enduring trials, and coming into the realization that* **there is no separation, no duality—only God.**

The Spirit is calling, now. **The time of awakening is here.**
GIATI is not just a message—it is **the outpouring of the Holy Spirit, revealing to all who have ears to hear: the resurrection is now.**

Beyond The Surface

GIATI takes you beyond the surface-level existence that most people are accustomed to and plunges you into the depths of reality itself. It is not just another philosophy, belief system, or spiritual teaching—it is a direct revelation of the foundation of existence. Like the proverbial rabbit hole, it beckons those who have been searching for something deeper, something beyond the illusion of everyday life. For those who are ready, GIATI is the descent into truth that dismantles every falsehood and illusion that has been accepted as reality.

Some have been waiting for something like this their entire lives—an answer that finally makes sense of existence, one that explains the contradictions and mysteries of life in a way that no religion or ideology ever could. These are the ones who, upon encountering GIATI, willingly jump in, eager to see how deep it goes. They recognize that the truth was always there, waiting to be uncovered, and they are willing to leave behind everything they once believed in order to embrace the revelation of what is.

But then there are others—those who glance into the rabbit hole and immediately recoil. To them, it looks too dark, too unsettling, too dangerous. The fear of losing what they think they know keeps them from taking the plunge. They cling to their old ways of thinking, their comfortable beliefs, and the world they have constructed around them, afraid of what they might find if they go any deeper.

Yet, the irony is that the darkness they fear is not in the rabbit hole itself—it is in their own blindness. The hole does not lead into darkness; it leads out of it. The fear is not of the truth, but of losing the illusion that has been mistaken for truth. GIATI does not bring confusion; it removes it. It does not create darkness; it exposes the fact that one has been living in it all along.

This is why it is incumbent upon every person to take that dive, no matter how unsettling it may seem at first. The rabbit hole is not a choice; it is the very lifeline of this age, the only way to break free from the illusion of separation and step into the reality of salvation. This is not a truth that can be ignored or postponed indefinitely. There comes a time when each person must either confront it or remain in blindness.

The hesitation to look deeper, to question, to seek beyond what has been handed down by the world is what keeps people bound. GIATI is the revelation that was sent for this time and for this generation.

The journey into GIATI is not just an exploration of new ideas—it is an unraveling of the very fabric of perceived reality. It is not about accumulating knowledge or adopting a new belief system; it is about dismantling every false construct that has kept humanity bound in illusion. To ignore this revelation is to remain entangled in a world built upon misunderstanding, where everything is interpreted through the lens of separation rather than unity.

The resistance to GIATI is not due to its complexity but rather its simplicity. The truth it reveals is so absolute, so undeniable, that the mind conditioned by the world's teachings cannot grasp it without first letting go of deeply ingrained falsehoods. Many fear losing themselves in the process, not realizing that what they stand to lose is not their true self but the false identity they have been conditioned to accept. This is why some hesitate—they sense that GIATI does not just offer answers; it demands transformation.

But transformation is not destruction. It is liberation. What is being lost is the illusion of selfhood built on separation, limitation, and false belief. What is being gained is the unshakable realization of one's eternal nature, the direct experience of being one with God rather than simply believing in God. This is the true awakening—the shift from conceptual understanding to living reality.

For those who resist, the fear is rooted in attachment. People cling to their identities, their experiences, and their knowledge as if these things define them. The idea of stepping beyond them, of realizing they were never the essence of who they are, feels like an abyss. But GIATI reveals that the abyss they fear is actually the doorway to life itself. It is not emptiness but fullness, not loss but restoration.

This is why GIATI is the essential revelation of this time. It does not merely offer another perspective among many—it exposes the illusion of perspective itself, showing that what humanity has perceived as reality has been a distortion of the truth all along. The choice to embrace or reject it is not a matter of intellectual preference but of spiritual destiny. To reject GIATI is to remain bound to a world governed by ignorance. To accept it is to step into the only reality that has ever existed—God as all, in all, through all.

For those who have been seeking, GIATI is not merely an answer; it is the answer. It is not another theory, another philosophy, or another teaching—it is the unveiling of what has always been, waiting for humanity to see. The question is not whether GIATI is true but whether one is willing to see it. The opportunity to awaken is before everyone, but the willingness to let go of illusions will determine who steps into the fullness of that truth.

The True Master: The Spirit That Governs You

The Master You Serve

"Servants, be obedient to them that are your masters according to the flesh, with fear and trembling, in singleness of your heart, as unto Christ;" — Ephesians 6:5

At the surface, this scripture appears to address physical servitude, but when understood spiritually, it reveals a deeper truth: **all are servants to the spirit that governs them.**

Human slavery, as history has known it, was never the true slavery. It was only a shadow, a physical representation of the greater reality—that every person serves a master, whether they recognize it or not. The question is not **whether** *you are a servant, but* **to which spirit you yield.**

The Reality of Spiritual Servitude

Every thought, every action, every motive is governed by a force beyond what the physical eyes can see. The illusion is believing that one is truly independent, making choices from a place of self-sufficiency. But the truth is this:

You will either serve the unrighteous, lost side of God or the righteous, awakened side of God. But it is God who is your master—not some physical man.

Jesus himself made this clear when he said:

"No man can serve two masters: for either he will hate the one, and love the other; or else he will hold to the one, and despise the other." — Matthew 6:24

There is no middle ground. You are either moving in alignment with divine truth, or you are enslaved to the deception of separation.

Breaking Down Ephesians 6:5 in the Light of GIATI

"Servants, be obedient to them that are your masters according to the flesh, with fear and trembling, in singleness of your heart, as unto Christ;"

At the time this was written, Paul was addressing a social system where servitude was common. Yet, his instruction was not about bondage to men—it was about a **deeper spiritual obedience.**

- **"Servants, be obedient to them that are your masters according to the flesh"** *— In the physical world, people follow leadership, hierarchy, and authority. But Paul directs the focus beyond human masters.*

- **"With fear and trembling"** — *This is not fear of man, but* **reverence and awareness of the Spirit that truly governs all things.**
- **"In singleness of your heart"** — *Meaning* with pure intention, not divided **between different allegiances.**
- **"As unto Christ"** — *This is the key.* **The obedience is not to flesh and blood but to the divine order, the Spirit of truth.**

This scripture is not about submitting to human rule but about recognizing that everything—even physical servitude—points to the greater reality of **spiritual servitude.** *You are a servant, but to whom?*

The True Master is Spirit

The physical form does not dictate freedom. A man can be in chains and yet be free, just as another can walk without shackles yet live in complete bondage. This is why Jesus declared:

"And ye shall know the truth, and the truth shall make you free." — John 8:32

But those who rejected his message responded:

"We be Abraham's seed, and were never in bondage to any man: how sayest thou, Ye shall be made free?" — John 8:33

They could not see their true servitude. They believed because they were not physically enslaved, they were free. But Jesus revealed the deeper truth:

"Whosoever committeth sin is the servant of sin." — John 8:34

This is the real slavery—not to a man, but to **the spirit that rules you.**

GIATI: The Freedom in Serving the Spirit of Truth

GIATI stands as a witness to **the only true liberation: the awakening to Spirit.**

- *Those who remain lost serve* **ignorance, fear, and separation***—they are enslaved to deception.*
- *Those who awaken serve* **righteousness, love, and truth***—they are servants of the divine order.*

But all serve. Whether knowingly or unknowingly, **every action is a service to a greater force.**

Paul affirmed this reality:

"Know ye not, that to whom ye yield yourselves servants to obey, his servants ye are to whom ye obey; whether of sin unto death, or of obedience unto righteousness?" — Romans 6:16

*You are bound to the master you obey. This is why th***e work of GIATI is not to introduce something new but to uncover what has always been.** *You have always been Spirit, but have you served that truth?*

Serving the Spirit of Light

The world will tell you that to serve is weakness. But the highest truth reveals that **to serve Spirit is to reign in life.** *Jesus himself, the embodiment of divine power, declared:*

"For I came down from heaven, not to do mine own will, but the will of Him that sent me." — John 6:38

Even he, in full knowledge of his oneness with God, **yielded to Spirit.** *He was not enslaved to men, to systems, or to external control—***he was a servant of divine truth.**

GIATI echoes this same submission. It does not act of itself, but only speaks what is already true:

God is all there is.

To serve this truth is not to be in bondage—it is to be in perfect freedom. It is to **remove the illusion of separation, to step into the fullness of life, and to operate from the eternal reality of Spirit.**

The Choice: Who Will You Serve?

The message of GIATI is simple: **you are already serving.** *The only question is:* **which spirit governs you?**

"Choose you this day whom ye will serve." — Joshua 24:15

The lost will continue to serve the illusion, moving in the darkness of separation. But the awakened will serve truth, walking in the light of oneness.

For as Jesus declared:

"If the Son therefore shall make you free, ye shall be free indeed." — John 8:36

And true freedom is found in one realization:

God is all there is.

And in serving that truth, you serve your highest self.

The Day of the Lord: Awakening from the Illusion

(1 Thessalonians 5:2-3 KJV)

"For yourselves know perfectly that the day of the Lord so cometh as a thief in the night. For when they shall say, Peace and safety; then sudden destruction cometh upon them, as travail upon a woman with child; and they shall not escape."

The phrase "the day of the Lord" has often been interpreted as a future apocalyptic event, a moment of divine intervention where God physically disrupts the course of human history. However, the deeper spiritual truth reveals that this is not about an outward catastrophe, but about **the awakening of consciousness to the reality of God as all.**

The Thief in the Night: The Unseen Awakening

The coming of the Lord as a thief in the night signifies **a sudden realization, an unexpected moment of spiritual awakening.** *A thief does not announce his arrival—he comes when least expected, often in darkness, in a time of ignorance and unawareness.*

Likewise, the revelation of **GIATI (God Is All There Is)** *does not come through external signs or worldly expectations. It breaks through the illusion of separation when one is l***east prepared in the flesh** *but ready in Spirit. This is not about waiting for a physical return of Christ, but about the unveiling of the truth* **within you.**

The moment of realization comes **not by the observance of religious traditions, not through intellectual pursuit, but through the Spirit awakening within.** *To those clinging to the false sense of peace and safety in the world,* **this awakening is disruptive***—it shakes the very foundation of their beliefs.*

False Peace and Safety: The Illusion of the Flesh

"For when they shall say, Peace and safety; then sudden destruction cometh upon them..."

The world seeks peace through external means—governments, wealth, religion, status, and control. People build their security on **temporary things,** *believing they have found stability. But true peace* **does not come from the world,** *nor does it come from religious adherence—it comes from recognizing that* **God is within and there is no separation.**

The sudden destruction is **not a physical catastrophe** *but the collapse of the illusion—the breaking of false security. When the ego has built its foundation on the flesh,* **the awakening of Spirit feels like destruction** *because it dissolves everything that was believed to be real.*

*This is why people resist the truth. They fear losing their identity, their traditions, their attachments. But in reality, they are losing nothing—***they are gaining everything.**

Travail Upon a Woman with Child: The Birth of the New Man

"Then sudden destruction cometh upon them, as travail upon a woman with child; and they shall not escape."

A woman in labor cannot stop the birth once it begins. The contractions increase, the pain intensifies, and the new life must come forth. **This is the spiritual process of awakening.**

The destruction is not of the true self but of **the false self**—*the ego, the belief in separation, the reliance on flesh. The pain of this realization is like labor pains, but* **what comes forth is new life, a new understanding, a rebirth into the Spirit.**

This is what Jesus meant when He said, "You must be born again" (John 3:3). The first birth is of the flesh; the second birth is **awakening to Spirit.**

The GIATI Revelation: The Day of the Lord is Now

The day of the Lord is not about waiting for an event in time—it is **about awakening to what has always been true.** *The Spirit has never been absent, but the illusion of separation has kept humanity blind.*

When one clings to the **temporary things of the world,** *the realization of GIATI shakes them. It comes unexpectedly, dissolving what they once believed. But to those who* **live in Spirit, who recognize that God is all,** *this day is not one of fear but of fulfillment.*

- *The* **thief in the night** *comes not to steal, but to awaken.*
- *The* **destruction** *is not of life, but of the illusion.*
- *The* **labor pains** *are not suffering, but the birthing of divine awareness.*

This is the comfort of GIATI: *that what seems like the end is only the beginning. That what seems like loss is actually gain. That the true awakening is not in waiting, but in seeing—* **seeing that God is all there is.**

The Infinite Possibilities of Existence: A Spirit Without Limits

Imagine for a moment that existence is not confined to what you see, hear, and touch. The physical realm—the world of matter, space, and time—is only one layer of a vast, multi-dimensional reality. Humanity perceives life in three dimensions because our consciousness is tethered to this physical plane. But what if the true nature of your spirit extends beyond this limited perception?

Spirits do not belong to a single form, nor are they bound to a single existence. Just as the universe contains an uncountable number of galaxies, each with its own solar systems and planets, the realms of spirit stretch infinitely beyond human comprehension. **You have existed before, and you will exist again. The form you take is not who you are—it is simply the vessel that allows your consciousness to experience a particular dimension.**

Consciousness Determines Existence

Your awareness of your oneness with God determines the plane in which your spirit resides. The more you see yourself as merely flesh and bone, the more your consciousness remains locked in a carnal state of existence. This state is bound by limitations, cycles of birth and death, and the illusion of separation from the divine.

Just as you cannot remember the time spent in your mother's womb or the first years of your physical life, you do not recall the existence of your spirit before this current incarnation. Have you been here before? Has your spirit lived countless lives without fully awakening to its divine nature? Could this be why some are said to have "old souls," carrying wisdom and experiences that seem beyond their years?

The process of spiritual elevation is not about leaving the physical behind—it is about expanding your awareness to recognize that you have never been separate from God. The more aligned you become with this truth, the more limitless your existence becomes.

Endless Forms, Infinite Manifestations

Man is not the only vessel through which the spirit of God expresses itself. Consider the animal kingdom: animals experience joy, fear, sadness, and love—emotions that reveal the presence of the same divine spirit that animates humanity. The difference between man and animal is not the presence of spirit, but the **form in which that spirit is manifested.**

If a spirit can manifest as man or animal in this dimension, how many other forms could it take in realms beyond human perception? The universe is infinite, with worlds and civilizations beyond what the mind can conceive. The third dimension is only a starting point. Beyond it, there are dimensions where the body may not even be physical, where time moves differently, or where form is shaped by consciousness itself.

Could it be that the more a spirit aligns with the awareness of being one with God, the more desirable the body and existence it inhabits? If a soul remains asleep—trapped in the illusion of separation, bound to carnal limitations—does it continue to reincarnate in the same struggles, never moving beyond? But if it awakens to its divine essence, does it then ascend into higher realms, experiencing existences beyond what human imagination can grasp?

A Unique Opportunity in the Flesh

Right now, in this moment, you have a rare and unique opportunity. You are not just living as flesh—you are spirit, **a manifestation of God, granted the ability to awaken to the truth of your divine existence.** *The physical realm is not a prison; it is a platform. You have been given this life not merely to survive but to* **realize who you are.**

Many live their entire lives never understanding this. They remain asleep, believing themselves to be separate, moving through cycles of life and death without ever elevating their consciousness. But for those who awaken, the possibilities are endless.

This is your moment of recognition.

The more you embrace your oneness with God, the more the barriers of limitation fall away. You are not confined to this body, this lifetime, or even this dimension. You are part of an infinite, eternal unfolding of divine expression. And the more you see this, the greater the realms of existence that will open before you.

The journey of spirit does not end—it only expands.

Beyond the Veil: The Infinite Dimensions of Spirit

Imagine standing at the threshold of reality, looking out across an endless expanse of existence. What you perceive as "life" is only a single ripple in an ocean of possibilities—one layer in a vast, multi-dimensional tapestry that stretches far beyond what the physical mind can comprehend.

What if existence is not a straight line, but a web? Not a single reality, but an infinite spectrum of realms, each vibrating at different frequencies of awareness? What if, at this very moment, countless versions of reality are unfolding simultaneously, each dictated by the consciousness that perceives it?

The Fluidity of Form

In the third dimension, form is rigid, bound by physical laws—gravity, time, decay. The body you inhabit is fixed in structure, requiring food, rest, and movement through space. But imagine a realm where form is fluid, where your body is not defined by flesh, but by thought.

What if in higher dimensions, you do not walk, but glide? Not with legs, but with intention? What if you communicate not with words, but through the pure transmission of knowing? A place where identity is not a name or a history, but a resonance—a signature of consciousness recognized instantly by others?

There could be dimensions where light and sound are the building blocks of existence, where beings manifest in waves of color and frequency, merging and separating like living currents of energy. In such realms, form is optional, and experience is chosen rather than endured.

The Realms of Dream and Memory

Have you ever had a dream so vivid, so immersive, that it felt more real than waking life? What if those dreams were not mere illusions of the mind, but glimpses into other dimensions—realities your spirit has touched before?

There could be realms where time does not move in a straight line but spirals, allowing beings to step in and out of moments at will. There might be worlds where every thought instantly shapes the environment, where mountains rise and rivers flow at the direction of consciousness itself.

Some dimensions may be constructed entirely of memory, where spirits relive past existences not as distant recollections, but as present-moment experiences. Imagine a realm where every choice splits into a new reality, creating infinite branches of possibility— each version of you existing in its own unfolding story.

The Realms of the Unseen

Now, consider the realms that exist even alongside this one—the dimensions just beyond the veil of human perception. Perhaps spirits walk among us now, unseen not because they are absent, but because their frequency is beyond the spectrum the physical eye can detect.

Imagine a world of pure intuition, where nothing is hidden, where all thoughts are known instantly. What if there were beings who have never needed speech, never experienced deceit, because their very existence is built upon an unfiltered sharing of truth?

There could be realms of pure creation, where spirits experiment with forming entire worlds as effortlessly as an artist paints on a canvas. What if there were places where souls gather before incarnation, choosing experiences like selecting a role in a great cosmic play?

The Infinite Path of Spirit

As your awareness expands, so too does the realm in which you exist. What you perceive as "reality" is simply the frequency your consciousness is tuned to at this moment. But with each elevation in understanding, new dimensions unfold before you—each more boundless, more miraculous than the last.

You were never meant to be confined to a single form, a single world, or even a single existence. Spirit is fluid, eternal, and ever-unfolding. The more you embrace your oneness with the divine, the more the doors of creation open before you.

And beyond those doors, the possibilities are endless.

Breaking Free from the Chains of Flesh: The Transformation of Spirit

A spirit being confined to a physical body is what many unknowingly experience as **hell**—*not a place of fire and torment, but a state of limitation, restriction, and separation from its true nature. Just as a bird is free to soar across the sky, untethered by the ground beneath it, so too is spirit meant to exist without constraint. Yet, when spirit becomes bound to flesh, it is like a fish confined to water—restricted to an environment that does not reflect its infinite nature.*

Flesh is the lowest form a spirit can inhabit. *It is dense, temporary, and subject to suffering, decay, and death. This is why so many experience life as struggle, constantly seeking something beyond themselves without knowing what they are missing. The body, while a vessel for experience, is also a prison when the spirit within remains unaware of its true identity. But* **there is a way out of this prison, a path to freedom beyond the limits of flesh.**

Raising Consciousness: The Key to Liberation

The journey of the spirit is not to remain in bondage but to ascend beyond the constraints of the physical. The only way to transcend this state of hell is by **raising one's consciousness to the truth of GIATI—God In All That Is.** *The moment you awaken to the reality that* **you are not separate from God but are God manifested in form,** *the prison of flesh begins to lose its hold.*

This realization is not a philosophical concept—it is the gateway to **spiritual transformation.** *The more you see yourself as one with the divine, the more your spirit shifts from the density of flesh toward a higher, unrestricted existence. You begin to move from limitation to liberation, from suffering to joy, from confinement to infinite possibility.*

From Worm to Butterfly: A Reflection of Spiritual Ascension

The physical world has already provided a perfect example of this transformation: the journey of the caterpillar into the butterfly.

At first, the caterpillar is a **creature of limitation.** *It crawls on the earth, bound to the ground, slow and vulnerable. It has no concept of the sky, no awareness that it was ever meant to fly. This is the state of the spirit trapped in flesh—unaware of its potential, believing that crawling through life is all that exists.*

But then, something extraordinary happens. The caterpillar undergoes a radical transformation. **It enters a cocoon, where everything about it dissolves and reforms into something entirely new.** *When it emerges, it is no longer a creature of the earth, but of the air. No longer confined to the ground, it spreads its wings and soars.*

This is the same metamorphosis that happens when a spirit moves from **flesh consciousness to spirit consciousness.** *The moment you realize your oneness with God,* **your being shifts.** *What once seemed impossible—freedom, expansion, limitless existence—becomes your reality. You are no longer crawling in the dust, bound by earthly struggles.* **You have wings.**

The Journey Beyond Flesh

*Your body is not your final form. Your current state of existence is not the end of your journey. The moment you recognize GIATI, you open the door to an e***ndless array of spiritual states, each more expansive and unrestricted than the last.** *Just as the butterfly moves beyond the limitations of the caterpillar, your spirit is meant to move beyond the confines of flesh into a reality where form is no longer a restriction but an expression of divine will.*

This is the true purpose of awakening—to escape the prison of limitation and step into the infinite potential of spirit. **The more you embrace your divine identity, the closer you come to existing in the limitless realms of freedom, joy, and boundless creation.**

And so, the question is no longer if you can be free, but when you will choose to awaken.

The True Meaning of "Follow Me"

The Call to Follow—What Did Jesus Really Mean?

Throughout the Gospels, Jesus repeatedly calls people to **follow Him:**

- *"Follow me, and I will make you fishers of men." (Matthew 4:19)*
- *"Whosoever doth not bear his cross, and come after me, cannot be my disciple." (Luke 14:27)*
- *"If any man will come after me, let him deny himself, and take up his cross, and follow me." (Matthew 16:24)*

For centuries, people have interpreted this as an invitation to physically walk behind Jesus, imitate His actions, or adopt religious traditions in His name. But **to follow Him is not about trailing behind a man—it is about entering into the same spiritual process He demonstrated.**

Jesus was showing us the pattern of salvation:

1. **Born into flesh** – *entering limitation, forgetting divine origin*
2. **Dying to self** – *letting go of the false belief in separation*
3. **Resurrecting in truth** – *awakening to divine identity*
4. **Ascending in oneness** – *returning fully to the awareness of God as all*

This is what it means to follow Him—not to chase after a physical figure, but to **walk the inner path He revealed, to undergo the transformation He underwent.**

Recognizing the Condition of Being Lost

Before resurrection comes death. But before death, there must first be a recognition: **I was lost.**

Jesus describes this lost state in the parable of the prodigal son (Luke 15:11-32). The son left his father's house, went into a far country, and spent his inheritance. Eventually, he found himself in lack and suffering, until he **came to himself** *(Luke 15:17) and returned to his father.*

This is a picture of **humanity's condition***—entering the world, believing in separation, living as if we are independent from God. This false self, this egoic mind that claims a life of its own,* **must be denied and cast out.** *This is why Jesus said:*

"He that findeth his life shall lose it: and he that loseth his life for my sake shall find it." (Matthew 10:39)

To follow Jesus means to **lose the false self***—the identity that believes it is separate from God. This is the death He spoke of, and it is the only way to life.*

Dying to Self – The Necessary Death Before Resurrection

Jesus did not come just to die on a cross; He came to show **the death of the false identity***—the belief in separation from God. When He said, "Father, into thy hands I commend my spirit" (Luke 23:46), He was not just speaking for Himself, but for all who would follow His path.*

To follow Jesus, then, is to **die to the illusion of an independent self***—to let go of the ego, the idea of being a separate being apart from God. Paul speaks of this process clearly:*

"I am crucified with Christ: nevertheless I live; yet not I, but Christ liveth in me." (Galatians 2:20)

This crucifixion is not about physical suffering—it is about the **death of the separate self.** *It is the realization that there was never a "me" apart from God, and that* **God is all there is.**

Resurrection – Awakening to the Truth

Once the false identity is crucified, **resurrection follows.** *Jesus' resurrection was not about returning to a physical life—it was the demonstration that* **life is eternal when one recognizes their true nature as Spirit.**

He told His disciples:

"Because I live, ye shall live also. At that day ye shall know that I am in my Father, and ye in me, and I in you." (John 14:19-20)

This is the key: Resurrection is the awakening to **oneness.** *It is the realization that we were never separate, that we are in God and God is in us.*

This is why Jesus prayed:

"That they all may be one; as thou, Father, art in me, and I in thee, that they also may be one in us." (John 17:21)

The resurrection is **not just about Jesus—it is about us.** *When we awaken to our true nature, we rise* **out of the grave of ignorance** *and step into eternal life.*

Ascension – Returning Fully to God

After resurrection, Jesus ascended. This is the final step of salvation—the full return to **the awareness that nothing exists outside of God.**

Paul describes this when he says:

"And hath raised us up together, and made us sit together in heavenly places in Christ Jesus." (Ephesians 2:6)

Notice that he says **we are already seated in heavenly places.** *Ascension is not about physically going up—it is about* **consciousness rising to its original place.** *It is the full realization that* **God is all there is, and we are nothing but God expressed.**

Following GIATI – Walking the Same Spiritual Path

*The message of GIATI is not about following a person, but foll***owing the process of salvation.** *Just as Jesus showed the way, so too does the understanding of GIATI reveal:*

- **You are not a separate being, struggling to find God.**
- **You are the Spirit of God expressed in form.**
- **You entered the world in limitation but are destined to awaken.**

To follow GIATI is not to follow a man—it is to **accept and walk in the truth of your oneness with God.** *It is to undergo the* **same transformation** *Jesus demonstrated:*

1. **Recognize you were lost** – *believing yourself separate from God*
2. **Die to the false self** – *casting out the independent spirit*
3. **Resurrect in truth** – *awakening to your divine identity*
4. **Ascend in consciousness** – *returning fully to the awareness of oneness*

Just as Jesus did not come for people to physically follow Him, but to walk the path He revealed, **GIATI is not something to chase—it is something to become.**

The Call to Follow – The Call to Awaken

Jesus' words "Follow me" were not about holding onto His coattails. They were an invitation to step into **the same knowing, the same transformation, the same truth.**

To follow Him means to awaken from the illusion of separation. It means to **cast off the belief in an independent self and accept the eternal oneness with God.**

The question is not whether you will physically follow—the question is, will you believe?

- *Will you believe that* **God is all there is?**
- *Will you believe that* **you and the Father are one?**
- *Will you believe that* **you are not lost, only waking up?**

If you will believe, then you will follow—not as one chasing after something external, but as one **walking the same inner path that leads to life.**

This is the truth. This is the way. This is the life.

The Sixth Day and the Day of God's Rest

The Bible, when traced through genealogies and historical accounts, appears to suggest that mankind has only been on the earth for approximately 6,000 years. Yet, physical evidence—fossils, ancient civilizations, and geological findings—indicates that human-like beings have existed for much longer. This seeming contradiction has caused confusion for many, but understanding it through the lens of divine revelation unveils a deeper truth.

Scripture provides a key to interpreting time from God's perspective. The Apostle Peter wrote:

"But, beloved, be not ignorant of this one thing, that one day is with the Lord as a thousand years, and a thousand years as one day." (2 Peter 3:8)

If each thousand-year period corresponds to one divine day, then mankind is presently at the end of the sixth day, approaching the seventh—God's day of rest. The Genesis creation account tells us that God labored for six days, forming the heavens, the earth, and mankind, and on the seventh day, He rested (Genesis 2:2-3). Could it be that we are now transitioning into this great Sabbath, the time when God ceases from His labor because His work in man is complete?

For six spiritual days, humanity has lived in ignorance of its divine origin, lost in the illusion of separation from God. But the seventh day marks a shift—a time when the Spirit of God awakens humanity to its true nature. The pouring out of the Spirit in these last days is not merely a revival but the fulfillment of Jesus' prayer:

"Neither pray I for these alone, but for them also which shall believe on me through their word; That they all may be one; as thou, Father, art in me, and I in thee, that they also may be one in us." (John 17:20-21)

This prayer was not for religious unification but for the revelation of divine oneness—the realization that all are in God, and God is in all. When mankind fully awakens to this truth, the Spirit's work will be complete, and rest will come.

GIATI and the Fulfillment of God's Rest

The message of **GIATI—"God Is All There Is"**—*is the proclamation of this divine oneness. It is the fulfillment of the seventh day, the call to enter God's rest, where man no longer strives in darkness but abides in the Spirit. The world has labored under the curse of ignorance, but once the Spirit is poured out, lifting the veil, there will be nothing more to work for. The awakening itself is the completion.*

This is the fulfillment of the words in Hebrews:

"For we which have believed do enter into rest, as he said, As I have sworn in my wrath, if they shall enter into my rest: although the works were finished from the foundation of the world." (Hebrews 4:3)

The work has always been finished, but mankind, in its blindness, has not known it. When the Spirit completes its work—when GIATI is fully realized—the struggle ends. The seventh day begins. The veil is lifted. The lost return to themselves, no longer wandering but standing in the eternal presence of God, as God expressed through them.

This is the great transition. The world moves from the six days of ignorance to the seventh day of knowing, from labor to rest, from seeking God to realizing He was never absent. GIATI is the final message, the Spirit's declaration to the world:

"Be still, and know that I am God." (Psalm 46:10)

The Unveiling of the Seventh Day

The arrival of the seventh day is not marked by the destruction of the world but by the dissolution of the illusion that has kept mankind blind for six spiritual days. For thousands of years, humanity has toiled under the false perception of separation from God, believing itself to be fallen, disconnected, and in need of external salvation. Yet, from the foundation of the world, the truth has remained unchanged:

"He hath made everything beautiful in his time: also he hath set the world in their heart, so that no man can find out the work that God maketh from the beginning to the end." (Ecclesiastes 3:11)

God's work has always been finished. The fall of man was never a departure from God but rather a descent into the darkness of ignorance. What we call "salvation" is not the regaining of something lost but the unveiling of what has always been. The Spirit has labored in the hearts of men to bring them to this realization, working for six spiritual days to awaken those who were asleep. Now, as the seventh day dawns, the work nears completion.

Jesus hinted at this transition when He said:

"Come unto me, all ye that labour and are heavy laden, and I will give you rest." (Matthew 11:28)

What is this rest? It is the end of striving, the realization that man was never separate from God, that the struggle to reach Him was only the product of an unawakened mind. The seventh day is the fulfillment of this rest, where humanity ceases from its works, just as God ceased from His.

The Spirit's Final Outpouring

The prophet Joel foresaw the final awakening, declaring:

"And it shall come to pass afterward, that I will pour out my spirit upon all flesh; and your sons and your daughters shall prophesy, your old men shall dream dreams, your young men shall see visions." (Joel 2:28)

This outpouring is not just a revival of religious fervor, but the complete illumination of divine oneness—the lifting of the veil. No longer will man seek God as if He is distant, for the Spirit will reveal that He has always been within. No longer will salvation be seen as a future hope, but as the present reality of those whose eyes have been opened.

The final work of the Spirit is not to create something new but to bring mankind into alignment with what has always been true. This is the completion of God's plan—the bringing of all things into the knowledge of their origin, into the fullness of their divine nature. The Apostle Paul declared:

"Having made known unto us the mystery of his will, according to his good pleasure which he hath purposed in himself: That in the dispensation of the fulness of times he might gather together in one all things in Christ, both which are in heaven, and which are on earth; even in him." (Ephesians 1:9-10)

This gathering into one is not the unification of separate things, but the revelation that nothing was ever separate to begin with. All things have always been in God, and God in all things.

Entering the Age of Rest

As the seventh day emerges, the Spirit's work is accomplished in those who are able to see. This is the true meaning of salvation—not an escape from a fallen world, but the awakening to the truth that the world was never separate from its Source. Those who enter this rest will not be those who simply believe in God, but those who have come to know themselves as the very expression of God.

This is why Jesus prayed:

"That they may be one, even as we are one: I in them, and thou in me, that they may be made perfect in one." (John 17:22-23)

Perfection is not the attaining of something beyond, but the recognition of what has always been. When man awakens, the Spirit rests. The work is done. The seventh day has come.

The Call to the Awakened

In this hour, the call is not to another religious movement, another system of belief, or another cycle of seeking. The call is to wake up. To see. To enter the rest that has been prepared from the foundation of the world. The world has labored long enough. The time of striving is over. The work is finished.

GIATI is not merely a message—it is the fulfillment of this seventh day. It is the trumpet sounding the end of the old and the revelation of the new, though in reality, nothing new has been created, only revealed.

The final declaration is the same as it was in the beginning:

"God is all there is."

The seventh day has arrived. The Spirit rests. And those with eyes to see will enter in.

The day of God's rest is here.

The Unveiling of GIATI in the Last Days

Throughout the Scriptures, there have been prophecies of a final unveiling—an ultimate revelation that would bring humanity out of darkness and into the full realization of divine oneness. This moment is not about destruction but about awakening. It is the fulfillment of the promise that God would be fully revealed, not only in a select few but in all who have been prepared to receive it.

The book of Revelation, along with other prophetic writings, speaks of a time when the veil would be lifted, when those who were blind would see, and when the knowledge of God would cover the earth as the waters cover the sea (Habakkuk 2:14). This is the time when GIATI—God Is All There Is—is no longer hidden but openly known, ushering in the eternal heaven on earth.

The Final Revelation of Divine Oneness

In the last days, the greatest deception that has kept mankind in bondage will be undone. The greatest lie ever told was that humanity was separate from God, that people were merely servants, waiting for redemption from an external savior. But Revelation foretells of a time when this deception would be shattered, and the truth would be revealed to those with eyes to see:

"And I saw another angel fly in the midst of heaven, having the everlasting gospel to preach unto them that dwell on the earth, and to every nation, and kindred, and tongue, and people." (Revelation 14:6)

What is this **everlasting gospel?** *It is not a new doctrine, but the eternal truth that has always been: that God is all, and all is in God. The world has been blinded by false teachings, by systems that keep people believing in separation. But in the final hour, the gospel is made clear—not as a promise of future salvation, but as the awakening to what has always been true.*

The Removal of the Veil and the New Jerusalem

John, in Revelation, describes a moment when God is no longer seen as distant, when the separation between God and humanity ceases to exist:

"And I heard a great voice out of heaven saying, Behold, the tabernacle of God is with men, and he will dwell with them, and they shall be his people, and God himself shall be with them, and be their God." (Revelation 21:3)

This is not speaking of a physical event where God "comes down" from some distant realm. This is the moment when mankind realizes that God has always been with them, that the temple of God was never outside of them, but within. The **New Jerusalem** *is not a city descending from the sky; it is the awareness of divine presence descending into the hearts and minds of those who are ready to receive it.*

Jesus foreshadowed this awakening when He declared:

"Neither shall they say, Lo here! or, lo there! for, behold, the kingdom of God is within you." (Luke 17:21)

The final revelation is the realization that the Kingdom was never coming in the way men expected. It was already here, hidden beneath the veil of human misunderstanding. The New Jerusalem is not a place—it is a state of being, a consciousness of oneness with God.

The Defeat of the Great Deception

Revelation speaks of the fall of Babylon, a symbol of confusion, deception, and the false systems of belief that have kept humanity blind. This is not just about corrupt governments or institutions—it is about the spiritual deception that has convinced mankind of separation from God.

"And the great dragon was cast out, that old serpent, called the Devil, and Satan, which deceiveth the whole world." (Revelation 12:9)

The "great dragon" is not a literal being but the falsehood that has enslaved humanity—the belief that man is apart from God, that sanctification is something to be earned, that heaven is a distant place. But in the final hour, this deception is destroyed, and those who have ears to hear will receive the truth:

There was never any separation. God is all there is.

The Restoration of All Things

The last chapter of Revelation describes the fullness of this awakening—the return to the original state of divine awareness. The "Tree of Life" is restored to mankind, and all things are made new:

"And he shewed me a pure river of water of life, clear as crystal, proceeding out of the throne of God and of the Lamb. In the midst of the street of it, and on either side of the river, was there the tree of life, which bare twelve manner of fruits, and yielded her fruit every month: and the leaves of the tree were for the healing of the nations." (Revelation 22:1-2)

*What is this "water of life"? It is the outpouring of divine understanding. It is the revelation of GIATI—***God Is All There Is***—which heals the nations by removing the lie of separation. Those who drink from this water will never thirst again, because they will finally know who they are:*

"He that overcometh shall inherit all things; and I will be his God, and he shall be my son."(Revelation 21:7)

This is the moment when humanity steps fully into divine sonship—not as something given to them, but as something revealed within them. The ones who "overcome" are not those who fight physical battles, but those who overcome the deception of this world, who awaken to the truth that they were never apart from God.

The Coming of the One Who Speaks This Word

The book of Revelation speaks of one who comes in the last days, riding a white horse, with a name written that no one knew but himself:

"And I saw heaven opened, and behold a white horse; and he that sat upon him was called Faithful and True, and in righteousness he doth judge and make war." (Revelation 19:11)

Who is this? It is not a single individual, but the manifestation of divine truth in this age. It is the Spirit speaking through those who are sanctified by GIATI understanding, declaring the final word that ends all false teachings. This is the arrival of the Word made flesh once again—not in one person alone, but in a collective awakening of those who have received the truth.

"To him that overcometh will I grant to sit with me in my throne, even as I also overcame, and am set down with my Father in his throne." (Revelation 3:21)

The throne is not a physical seat—it is the place of divine authority, the realization that one is not beneath God but one with Him.

The Eternal Heaven on Earth

With the full revelation of GIATI, the spiritual state of existence is fully realized. The old world—the world of deception, striving, and ignorance—passes away, and a new consciousness is born. This is the true meaning of the words:

"And there shall be no more curse: but the throne of God and of the Lamb shall be in it; and his servants shall serve him: And they shall see his face; and his name shall be in their foreheads." (Revelation 22:3-4)

His Name Written in the Forehead: The Mark of Divine Awareness

*His name—***GIATI, God Is All There Is***—is written in the foreheads of those who have awakened, symbolizing the complete transformation of their consciousness. This is not a literal inscription but the* **seal of understanding,** *the realization of divine oneness imprinted upon the mind and spirit.*

*Throughout Scripture, the forehead represents the s***eat of thought, perception, and identity.** *In contrast to those who bear the mark of the beast (Revelation 13:16-17)—the deception of separation and false worship—those who bear* **the name of God in their foreheads** *have been fully sanctified in truth. They no longer see themselves as separate beings striving to reach God; they know they* **are one with the Divine,** *no longer bound by the illusions of the world.*

This echoes the promise given in Jeremiah:

"But this shall be the covenant that I will make with the house of Israel; After those days, saith the Lord, I will put my law in their inward parts, and write it in their hearts; and will be their God, and they shall be my people." (Jeremiah 31:33)

Here, the **law of God** *is not external commandments but the* **living truth** *of divine oneness. The name of God in their foreheads signifies that they no longer think according to the old world's ways. Their* **mindset has shifted** *from a place of seeking to a place of knowing. They no longer ask, "Where is God?" because they have realized:* **God is all there is, and God is within them.**

The Transformation of the Earth Through This Awakening

The moment divine awareness spreads, the entire structure of existence changes. Revelation describes a new heaven and a new earth—not because God destroys the old, but because **human perception has been completely renewed:**

"And I saw a new heaven and a new earth: for the first heaven and the first earth were passed away; and there was no more sea." (Revelation 21:1)

The "first earth" represents the world as seen through the lens of separation, struggle, and limitation. The "new earth" represents the world as it truly is—a place where divine presence fills all things. There is no more "sea," symbolizing the **end of separation,** *for in biblical symbolism, the sea often represents the abyss of chaos and division.*

Jesus spoke of this transformation in the Beatitudes:

"Blessed are the meek: for they shall inherit the earth." (Matthew 5:5)

Who are the **meek?** *They are not the weak, but the awakened. They are those who have let go of the ego, the false self, and have stepped into the fullness of divine awareness. They are those who recognize that* **heaven was never a distant place but a state of being,** *and they inherit the earth not by force, but by revelation.*

The Reign of the Spirit: The Age of Divine Rest

The arrival of this **new consciousness** *marks the completion of the* **seventh day***—the day of divine rest. In Genesis, God rested on the seventh day, not because He was weary, but because His work was finished (Genesis 2:2). Likewise, when humanity awakens to* **GIATI,** *the Spirit enters its final rest, because the illusion of separation has ended. This was foretold in Hebrews:*

"There remaineth therefore a rest to the people of God. For he that is entered into his rest, he also hath ceased from his own works, as God did from his." (Hebrews 4:9-10)

This is not about physical inactivity, but about **ceasing from the labor of seeking.** *The awakened ones no longer struggle to find God; they* **abide in divine awareness.** *They no longer toil for salvation; they* **realize they were never lost.** *The Spirit rests* **because its purpose is fulfilled***—humanity has come home.*

The Final Revelation: The Full Manifestation of God in All Things

In this **new age of divine awareness,** *the prophecy of Habakkuk is fulfilled:*

"For the earth shall be filled with the knowledge of the glory of the Lord, as the waters cover the sea." (Habakkuk 2:14)

The **knowledge of God's glory** *does not mean the spread of religion or doctrines, but the* **universal recognition of divine presence in all things.** *There will be no more debate about God's existence, no more divisions between sacred and secular, no more false hierarchies of who is closer to God—because* **all will see and know that God is all in all.**

This is the final realization:

"And there shall be no more curse: but the throne of God and of the Lamb shall be in it; and his servants shall serve him: And they shall see his face; and his name shall be in their foreheads." (Revelation 22:3-4)

To **see His face** *is to behold* **the fullness of divine reality,** *to perceive the truth without distortion. The* **throne of God and the Lamb** *is not a literal seat in a distant heaven— it is* **the established reign of divine consciousness** *within those who have awakened.*

This is the **eternal state of being***—heaven on earth, not as a place to go after death, but as a present reality for those who have the eyes to see.*

The Call to Enter This Awareness

The Spirit now calls all who are ready to step into this reality—not in the distant future, but **now.** *This is why Revelation ends with an invitation:*

"And the Spirit and the bride say, Come. And let him that heareth say, Come. And let him that is athirst come. And whosoever will, let him take the water of life freely." (Revelation 22:17)

The **water of life** *is not reserved for a few—it is freely given to all who are willing to receive it. Those who thirst for truth, for freedom from deception, for the end of separation—* **they are invited to drink deeply and awaken.**

GIATI—the full realization of God's allness—is the fulfillment of this call. *It is the final revelation, the awakening of humanity, the moment when the Spirit rests because its work is complete.*

The Age of Light Has Come

The world has long been in darkness, waiting for salvation, unaware that salvation was always within. But now the time has come. The veil has been lifted. The deception has been shattered. The Spirit no longer needs to strive, because the **perfect oneness of God has been revealed.**

This is the promise. This is the fulfillment. This is the final awakening.

God is all there is.

The 144,000: The Revelation of Divine Consciousness in GIATI

Among the most debated passages in Scripture is the reference to the **144,000** *in the Book of Revelation. Many have taken this number to mean a literal, limited group of people who will be saved, often linking it to a specific religion or denomination. But when viewed through the divine understanding of* **GIATI—God Is All There Is,** *it becomes evident that the 144,000 is not about* **a numerical limitation,** *but* **a spiritual revelation***—a symbol of those who awaken to the truth of divine oneness.*

To understand this, we must examine the passage itself:

"And I heard the number of them which were sealed: and there were sealed an hundred and forty and four thousand of all the tribes of the children of Israel." *(Revelation 7:4)*

Later in the same chapter, we see a seemingly contradictory vision:

"After this I beheld, and, lo, a great multitude, which no man could number, of all nations, and kindreds, and people, and tongues, stood before the throne, and before the Lamb, clothed with white robes, and palms in their hands." *(Revelation 7:9)*

This passage reveals **two groups:** *the* **144,000** *and the* **great multitude that no man could number.** *If only 144,000 are to be saved, then who is this innumerable multitude that also stands before God? The answer lies not in literal numbers, but in* **spiritual meaning.**

The Symbolism of 144,000

The number **144,000** *is not meant to be taken literally. It is a* **symbolic number,** *rich in* **spiritual significance.**

1. 12 x 12 x 1,000

- *The number* **12** *represents* **divine government, order, and completeness** *(as seen in the* **12 tribes of Israel** *and* **12 apostles***).*
- **12 x 12 (144)** *represents spiritual perfection multiplied—the fullness of divine order manifested.*
- **1,000** *is a biblical number representing* **a vast, complete, and innumerable multitude** *(Psalm 50:10 states that God owns "the cattle on a thousand hills," meaning all hills, not just 1,000).*

Thus, **144,000** *represents* **the complete and perfected body of those who awaken to divine truth,** *not a fixed number of people. It symbolizes* **the fullness of spiritual consciousness—those sealed with the knowledge of God's allness.**

Who Are the 144,000? The Sealed of God

"And I looked, and, lo, a Lamb stood on the mount Sion, and with him an hundred forty and four thousand, having his Father's name written in their foreheads." *(Revelation 14:1)*

This passage reveals that the **144,000 have the Father's name written in their foreheads.** *In biblical symbolism, the forehead represents the* **mind, consciousness, and understanding.** *To have* **the Father's name** *written in the forehead means to have* **awakened to divine truth—to be sealed in the consciousness of GIATI.**

This stands in contrast to those who receive **the mark of the beast in their foreheads,** *which represents* **a mind governed by illusion, separation, and fear.**

The **144,000 are those who are spiritually minded,** *those who have overcome the deception of the beast system and live in the awareness of* **God's allness.**

The 144,000 and the Innumerable Multitude

Revelation does not end with the 144,000. Immediately after they are mentioned, John sees **a great multitude that no man could number** *from* **all nations, kindreds, and tongues** *standing before the throne. This reveals that salvation is* **not limited to a specific group or number** *but is* **open to all who awaken to divine truth.**

The **144,000 is the symbolic representation of those sealed in divine consciousness, but the great multitude represents the expansion of this truth to all people. The 144,000 is the firstfruits of those awakened,** *but they are not the only ones. They are the* **forerunners, the vanguard of divine realization.**

The Awakening of the 144,000 in GIATI

The sealing of the 144,000 represents a **global awakening***—the revelation of divine oneness that begins as a remnant but spreads until all who are ready enter into divine awareness.*

"And this gospel of the kingdom shall be preached in all the world for a witness unto all nations; and then shall the end come." *(Matthew 24:14)*

This is not the **end of the world** *but the* **end of illusion.** *The* **end of the beast system.** *The* **end of separation from God.** *The* **144,000 represents those who first awaken, and through them, the divine truth spreads to the multitude.**

The New Song of the 144,000

"And they sung as it were a new song before the throne… and no man could learn that song but the hundred and forty and four thousand, which were redeemed from the earth." *(Revelation 14:3)*

The **new song** *is the* **revelation of divine oneness**—*a song that* **only those who are spiritually awakened can sing.** *It is not a literal melody but a* **state of being, a harmony of consciousness with divine truth.**

This is the message of **GIATI**—*the realization that* **God Is All There Is.** *Those who awaken to this truth* **are sealed, marked, and set apart from the beast system.**

The Choice: The Mark of the Beast or the Seal of God?

The **144,000 are not an exclusive religious group.** *They are* **the spiritually awakened,** *those who have been sealed in the knowledge of* **God's allness.**

This stands in direct contrast to the **mark of the beast,** *which symbolizes* **the consciousness of separation, fear, and deception.** *Every person must choose:*

- **To be sealed with the name of God in their forehead** *(spiritually awakened to divine truth).*
- **Or to bear the mark of the beast** *(trapped in the illusion of separation).*

The **144,000 are those who have been set free by the truth**—*those who have recognized that* **God is not separate, but within them, as them.**

The Fulfillment: The New Heaven and the New Earth

The awakening of the **144,000 is the beginning of the new creation.** *As their consciousness expands, the old system of fear and illusion collapses, and divine reality is revealed.*

The **new heaven and new earth** *represent* **a new state of being**—*a world no longer ruled by the beast system but by divine truth.*

This is the **fulfillment of GIATI,** *where God is no longer seen as distant but* **fully realized in all things.** *The* **144,000 are the first to awaken, but they are not the last. Through them, the world is transformed, and the multitude follows into divine reality.**

Conclusion: The 144,000 and the Awakening of Humanity

The **144,000 is not a number of limitation but a symbol of divine fullness.** *It represents the* **first wave of those who awaken to the reality of GIATI,** *breaking free from the deception of the beast system and stepping into the knowledge that* **God is all.**

But this truth is **not limited to a select few.** *Through them, the knowledge spreads, and the great multitude follows. The* **new song is sung, the new earth is revealed, and all who are ready enter into the fullness of divine life.**

The question is not **whether one is part of the 144,000**—*the question is:*

Are you awakening to divine truth? Are you sealed with the awareness that God Is All There Is?

The Day and Hour Revealed – The Coming Within

"No man knows the day or hour of His coming." These words, long recited yet rarely understood, have become a veil over the truth. Religion placed the "coming" in the sky, in time, and in spectacle, but GIATI removes the veil and speaks plainly: the day and the hour is the moment the Spirit awakens in you. It is not marked on the world's clock. It is the unveiling of God's presence within—your true identity revealed, not returned.

The Comforter never left. "I will not leave you comfortless; I will come to you." This was not a promise of future arrival but a present reality waiting to be seen. The "coming" is not an event outside of you—it is the realization that the one you've been waiting for has always been the life within you. The moment you know this, the prophecy is fulfilled. The Spirit never departed; only your awareness did.

GIATI does not interpret scripture from the outside in. GIATI is the Spirit that authored it, now speaking plainly without parable or shadow. The veil that Moses wore, the curtain in the temple, the mystery of the kingdom—GIATI tears them all down. Prophecy was never about predicting world events but about unveiling the eternal truth of God's indwelling presence. Every word spoken by the prophets pointed inward, but religion pointed outward. GIATI corrects the course and makes straight the way of the Lord—in you.

The second coming is not the return of a man in the clouds—it is the return of your awareness to the Spirit you are. This is why no man knows the day or the hour: it is not for the carnal mind to discern. It is revealed only by the Spirit to those who are Spirit. You will not see it with observation. You will not say "Here it is" or "There it is," for the kingdom is within you. When you realize that, the day has come. When you awaken to the truth, the hour is now.

Every prophecy—whether spoken by Isaiah, Daniel, Ezekiel, or John—was encoded with spiritual truth, never meant to be external history but inner revelation. The beast, the temple, the fire, the glory, the new heaven and new earth—they are not geographical; they are internal states of awakening. GIATI makes it plain: there is no future fulfillment to wait for. The fulfillment is now, and it is you, recognizing that you and the Father are one.

GIATI is the voice that interprets prophecy not with speculation but with revelation. It does not echo what has been taught but declares what has been hidden. This is why GIATI is the new scripture—not written with ink, but with the Spirit of the living God on hearts of flesh. The same Spirit who inspired the prophets then is the Spirit who speaks now. The voice that said, "Let there be light," is the voice now saying, "You are that light."

So when they say, "No man knows the day or hour," GIATI responds: the day and hour has come. You are the witness. The mystery is no longer hidden. The Spirit has spoken. And the one you were waiting for—was you, awakened.

The day and hour has now been revealed—not by scholars, not by preachers, not by theologians, but by **GIATI,** *the one chosen and ordained by the Spirit to speak what no man could. This is not a position of title but of function: the mouthpiece of the Holy Spirit in this day and time, declaring with boldness the mysteries that have remained sealed until now. GIATI is not introducing new religion or reformed doctrine, but unveiling what was always true from the foundation of the world—that* **God is all there is,** *and His Spirit has never been absent.*

While others read prophecy and wait, GIATI opens prophecy and reveals. While religion holds on to symbols and shadows, GIATI speaks the substance—plainly, powerfully, and with authority that comes not from man, but from the indwelling Spirit. The revelation of the day and hour—long hidden from every other mouth—has been given to GIATI, not to predict a date but to uncover a truth: that the second coming is not something to wait for, it is something to wake to.

*This is the work only GIATI could do—***to interpret scripture not from study, but from the Spirit; not from tradition, but from union.** *Because GIATI speaks as the Holy Spirit speaks: not in riddles, not with confusion, but with clarity. The veil is not only lifted in the mind of GIATI —it is torn for all who listen. Through this one, prophecy breathes. Through this one, the Comforter speaks—not as one returning, but as one already here.*

*No one else could say it because no one else was given to say it. Many talk about God, but GIATI speaks as the voice of God, within the understanding that there is no separation between the Speaker and the Source. This is why GIATI is not just a leader of a brand, but the manifestation of the eternal message made flesh again: the same Spirit that walked the earth as Jesus Christ now walks again through one who knows the truth—***I and my Father are one.**

This is why the secrets are being unveiled now. This is why the book of GIATI speaks with a boldness no other has dared. Because the one speaking is not trying to interpret God—the one speaking is God expressed. Not a man reaching for heaven, but heaven revealed in a man. And through this vessel, prophecy ends, because truth has come. The voice is not waiting for permission. The voice is not asking to be heard. The voice is **declaring** *what* **is***— and every mystery bows to it.*

GIATI is the one chosen to unveil what has been hidden in plain sight. And now, the mystery is no longer a mystery. The second coming has come, and it is **the Spirit in you revealed.**

Declaration from GIATI – The Spirit of Truth Revealed:

This is not the voice of human speculation. This is not the product of study, tradition, or religious memory. This is the Spirit of Truth speaking—plainly, fully, and without parable. The Comforter was never absent. The One who was, is, and is to come has never departed.

The veil has been lifted, and the hour once hidden has been made known. The second coming is not future—it is now. It is the revelation of the Spirit within, awakened from its long sleep in the minds of men.

The one they waited for is not another person. It is the Spirit in them, long ignored but always present. The mystery no man knew is now revealed by the Spirit who wrote it from the beginning. The prophecy is fulfilled not in signs above, but in truth within. This is not a new message—it is the original Word restored, stripped of confusion, declaring once and for all that **God is all there is,** *and there is no other.*

GIATI is not a voice among many. GIATI is the unveiling. GIATI is the end of blindness. GIATI is the Spirit of God saying, The time is fulfilled. The truth is revealed. The kingdom is within. The separation is over. I Am Here.

The Second Coming: The Return of Awareness

The return of Jesus is commonly referred to as **the Second Coming.**

To many, this event has been framed as a future moment—one where a man in physical form will appear in the sky, descending through clouds, surrounded by glory and power. Churches have preached it for centuries. Paintings have illustrated it. Movies have dramatized it.

But all of that focuses on **the form,** *not the* **Spirit.** *It points outward, instead of within. It teaches people to wait, rather than to* **awaken.**

From a **GIATI perspective,** *the Second Coming is not the return of a body—it is the* **unveiling of the Spirit.** *It is not a man riding through the clouds, but the* **I AM returning to visibility through a people who finally know who they are.**

He Came Once—And Is Now Coming Again

Jesus came the first time to reveal the truth that **God is within us.** *He said, "I and the Father are one." (John 10:30)*
He said, "The kingdom of God is within you." (Luke 17:21)
He said, "He that hath seen me hath seen the Father." (John 14:9)

Yet the world rejected him.
The religious leaders denied him.
And most of humanity couldn't see the truth of his words, because their eyes were trained to look out there, not in here.

So what is the Second Coming?

It is the return of that same Spirit—not in one man this time, but in a body of people who now walk in full awareness of their oneness with God.

Not Another Person—The Same Spirit

Theologians often debate when, how, and where Jesus will return. But the question isn't when he comes **to us,** *The question is when he is* **revealed through us.**

"Christ in you, the hope of glory." (Colossians 1:27) "

As he is, so are we in this world." (1 John 4:17)

The Second Coming is not the arrival of someone new—it is the manifestation of the same Spirit that walked in Jesus, now **walking in us.**

This is what the world cannot see.

This is what religion refuses to accept.
They're still waiting for the sky to crack open.
But the veil is not in the sky—it's in the **mind.**

The Sky Will Not Split—The Illusion Will

*The cloud that Jesus ascended into wasn't just a vapor in the air—it was the cl***oud of unknowing,** *the* **veil of human perception.** *They saw him go, but they didn't understand what was happening.*
And now they wait for him to return the same way.

But what did the angels say?

"Why stand ye gazing up into heaven? This same Jesus... shall so come in like manner..."
(Acts 1:11)

In like manner—*but not in the same form.*
He disappeared from their sight because the time for **one man** *had passed.*
Now it's time for the **many-membered body** *to arise.*

The return is not external—it is **internal.**
The sky is not the stage—the soul is.

The Second Coming Is Now

The Spirit is already here.
The question is: **Who sees it?**

Jesus said,

"I will not leave you comfortless: I will come to you." (John 14:18)

"In that day, you will know that I am in my Father, and you in me, and I in you."
(John 14:20)

That day is not coming.
That day is here.

It is the day when the I AM awakens in you.
When the Spirit that was in Christ rises within your own being.
When you stop waiting for God to return, and begin revealing **that God has never left.**

This is the message of GIATI.
This is the **Second Coming—the return of awareness.**

The World Will Know Him—When It Sees Him in You

Jesus prayed,

"That they all may be one... that the world may believe that thou hast sent me." (John 17:21)

His return is not about **repeating history***, but about* **fulfilling prophecy.**
It's not about a second man—it's about **one body.**
A people united in Spirit.
A people who are not waiting for the Messiah, but **know that the Messiah lives within them.**

So the next time someone asks, "When is Jesus coming back?"
You can say with confidence: **He already has—wherever the truth of oneness is revealed.**

And if you've seen that truth in yourself,
you are the sign they've been waiting for.

The Second Coming Has Already Begun

There are already **thousands across the earth** *in whom the* **Spirit of the Messiah has returned.**
They are not waiting for a man to appear in the sky—they have awakened to the **truth that the Messiah has appeared within them.**

This is not about religion.
This is not about belief systems.
This is not even about knowing the Scriptures.

This is about the **Spirit of the Living God** *taking full residence in a person—***replacing the ego,** *removing all sense of separation, and becoming their* **total identity.**
This is the **Second Coming** *in motion.*
It has already begun.

GIATI: Gathering the Final Remnant

The message of **GIATI—God Is All There Is***—has come forth in this generation to* **call in the final remnant.** *This is the* **transition into the spiritual age,** *where those who remain entangled in form, name, and religion will be separated from those who have come into* **pure oneness with God.**

GIATI does not speak to the masses in the way religion does. It calls to the **elect,** *the* **awakened,** *the ones who feel the pull from within saying,*

"There is more than what I've been taught."

This is not about **believing in God or in Jesus** *outwardly.*
Millions believe, yet remain blind.
Millions worship, yet still walk in ego.

Faith without transformation is dead.

The Spirit Must Replace the Self

What is required now is **total surrender.** *The Spirit of God must not just inspire your life—***it must become your life.** *There cannot be even 1% of "you" still holding the wheel.*

That 1%—the little voice that says,

"Look what God and I did..."

—is **enough to disqualify you.**
Because **God doesn't share glory.**
He doesn't need your help.
He doesn't require your contribution.
He only requires that you **die to the illusion of self,** *and awaken to the* **eternal reality of Him.**

Why Man Was Created Last

Look at the order of creation:
*God created the heavens, the earth, the waters, the lights, the animals—***everything***—before He created man.*

Why?

Because if man had been created first,

he might have said, "Look what God and I made."

So God created man **last,** *to make one thing abundantly clear:*

This is My work, not yours.

This is why the **true Second Coming** *cannot involve even the smallest trace of self-righteousness or self-credit.*
If there's still a "you" trying to help God finish the job, you're still in the flesh.

God sees **no "you" apart from Himself.**
Only what is born of His Spirit is real.
Everything else is illusion, ego, and dust.

The Work Is Finished—Now Rest

The ones in whom the Messiah has returned know this:

The work is already done.

There is nothing to strive for.
There is no mountain left to climb.
The Messiah cried out, "It is finished,"

And now the Spirit is crying out again, through the awakened body:
"It is time to rest."

This rest is not laziness—it is **divine surrender.**
It is the peace that comes from knowing **He lives in you,**
He moves through you,
and He alone receives the glory.

Your life is no longer your own.
You are not the driver—you are the vessel.
And **that surrender is your inheritance.**

Inheriting the Spirit Means Knowing You're Family

In the natural world, no one receives an inheritance unless they are family.

So it is with the Kingdom.

If you do not recognize that **your Spirit is His Spirit,**
you stand outside the family—no matter how many times you pray, fast, or go to church.

The inheritance of the Kingdom is not given to strangers.
It is given to **those who are one in Spirit.**
And what is the inheritance?

God Himself.
Not what He gives—but who He is.

You receive the inheritance by realizing:

"There is no me apart from Him. The life I live is no longer mine—it is His Spirit living in me."

The Awakening Has Begun

The Second Coming is not a someday event.

It is a **now** *event.*
The Spirit is rising in the elect.
The message of GIATI is going forth like the sound of a trumpet, calling all who can hear:

"Come out of her, My people. Come out of religion, of ego, of separation. The I AM is here. The Kingdom is within. The time is now."

There is no "you" trying to find God.
There is only **God revealing Himself through what you thought was you.**

This is the mystery made plain.
This is the truth religion could never tell you.
This is the inheritance.
This is the **Second Coming.**

Only the Spirit Can Judge

Those who have received **His Spirit—**
those in whom the **Second Coming has occurred**— *are not just saved from judgment.*

They become the judges.

Not because they are better.
Not because of outward holiness.
But because they are **one with the Source.**

And what is the standard of judgment?

Not works.
Not how many commandments were kept.
Not which religion you followed.

The only thing that can be judged is **oneness.**

Are you one with the Father—or not?
This is the separation of sheep and goat, wheat and tare, light and darkness. It has nothing to do with outward appearances. It has everything to do with inward identity.

Judgment Is Recognition, Not Condemnation

Judgment is not God angrily punishing people.
Judgment is the Spirit recognizing Himself—or not.

If the Spirit sees **only Himself** *in you,*
you are accepted, because you are **one substance** *with Him.*

But if what is presented is a version of "you" apart from Him, then what can God do but reject it?

Not in wrath—but in truth.

God cannot accept what is not of Himself.

This is why the message of GIATI is urgent—
because it calls every soul to **die to self** *and live by the Spirit alone.*

Only those who carry His Spirit **can judge,** *because only His Spirit* **knows the difference** *between what is Him and what is illusion.*

The Elect Judge with Righteous Judgment

Jesus said in John 7:24,

> *"Judge not according to appearance, but judge righteous judgment."*

Righteous judgment is not looking at the surface.
It is **spirit recognizing spirit.**
It is **oneness recognizing oneness—or its absence.**

The ones in whom the Messiah now lives—those who have received His Spirit without mixture— are the ones entrusted with this judgment.

Not as condemners, but as witnesses.
Not as judges in courtrooms, but as **mirrors of truth.**

They don't judge based on action—they judge based on identity. Because actions can deceive, but **spirit never lies.**

Judged by Oneness

The world will not be judged by deeds.
It will not be judged by religion, denomination, or morality.

The world will be judged by one standard only: **oneness with the Father.**

The Spirit that raised Jesus from the dead now lives in a body of people—those who have not only believed in God outwardly, but have surrendered entirely to **His indwelling presence.** *These are the ones in whom the* **Second Coming** *has taken place.*

And these are the ones who will **judge the world.**

The Elect Become the Standard

Scripture says, "Do you not know that the saints shall judge the world?" (1 Corinthians 6:2)
This isn't a courtroom scene. This is **spirit recognizing spirit—or the absence of it.**

Those who have received His Spirit without mixture have become **the visible standard of divine unity.** *They are not judging from self—they are judging from* **oneness.** *Not from opinion, but from the* **Father Himself** *living and speaking through them.*

Their very existence becomes the dividing line between what is true and what is false. Between **those who are one with the Source** *and those who still live from the illusion of self.*

God Judges Nothing but Himself

What can God accept except Himself?
What can light receive except more light?

If there is any part of "you" left in the equation—
any ego, any self-image, any attempt to take partial credit— then the standard has already rejected you.

Even 1% of self disqualifies the whole.

Why?

Because **God is all there is.**
There is no "you and God."
There is only **God in you, as you, being all.**

This is why God created man on the **sixth day,** *not the first— so that man could never say, "Look what God and I did."*

God was making a point:

"You weren't even there. This is My work alone."

Judgment Is Not About Actions—It's About Nature

God will not ask what you did—He will ask **what you are.** *He will not look at your behavior—He will look at* **your spirit.**

Did you live from your ego or from My essence?
Were you still trying to be good—or did you surrender to My righteousness?
Did you believe in Me—or did you become one with Me?

Those who remain in self—even if they call it "Christian self" or "spiritual self"—are still outside the Kingdom.
Because the Kingdom is not a belief system.
It is an **identity.**

And the only ones who inherit it are those who **know they are family.** *Because their* **spirit is of His Spirit.** *Not just in confession—but in actual nature.*

The Return Is the Separation

This is why the Second Coming is also the great separation.

The return of the Messiah in His people exposes the world for what it truly is:

A realm of illusion, striving, and self.

When the risen body speaks, it judges without speaking. Its presence is judgment.
Because light does not argue with darkness—it simply **shines,** *and everything hidden is revealed.*

And in that light, the only question is this:

Are you one with the Father, or are you still pretending to be your own?

GIATI Is the Final Call

The message of GIATI is not about making people better. It is not here to improve your outer life. It is here to **end your false identity** *completely—so that only God remains.*

It is the voice of the Spirit calling the final remnant into realization. It is the trumpet sound to those who have ears:

"Come out of her, My people."

And as those who carry this message rise, the judgment begins.
Not by threats.
Not by fear.
But by **truth.**

Because nothing can stand in the presence of pure oneness, except what is also **one.**

Conclusion

The Call to Wake Up

The journey through this book has been one of unveiling the truth of human existence: God is all there is. This conclusion is not merely an ending but a call—a divine invitation to awaken to the eternal truth of GIATI. Each person stands at a crossroads, faced with a profound choice: to remain in ignorance or to embrace the reality that God is within them and all around them.

A Final Message to the Reader: The Choice to Recognize God Within

Throughout scripture, God calls humanity to awaken to His presence. In Deuteronomy 30:19-20, Moses places this choice before the people:

"I call heaven and earth to record this day against you, that I have set before you life and death, blessing and cursing: therefore choose life, that both thou and thy seed may live: That thou mayest love the Lord thy God, and that thou mayest obey his voice, and that thou mayest cleave unto him: for he is thy life, and the length of thy days."

To choose life is to recognize that God is the source of your being. He is not distant or separate but is your life, your essence, your spirit. Jesus reinforced this truth when He declared in John 14:20:

"At that day ye shall know that I am in my Father, and ye in me, and I in you."

This knowledge is the awakening—seeing beyond the illusion of the flesh and recognizing the divine essence within. To wake up is to stop living as a separate, self-centered being and start living as the expression of God's presence in the world.

Living as the Light of GIATI: Embodying God's Presence in the World

To recognize God within is the first step; to live as the light of GIATI is the next. Jesus commanded His followers to be the light in Matthew 5:16:

"Let your light so shine before men, that they may see your good works, and glorify your Father which is in heaven."

This is not about personal glory but about embodying God's presence in a way that others see Him in you. When you live with the understanding that God is all there is, your life becomes a reflection of His love, wisdom, and power. You become a vessel for His will, allowing Him to act through you to transform the world.

Paul describes this transformation in Galatians 2:20:

"I am crucified with Christ: nevertheless I live; yet not I, but Christ liveth in me: and the life which I now live in the flesh I live by the faith of the Son of God, who loved me, and gave himself for me."

Living as the light of GIATI means surrendering the ego, letting go of the false identity of separateness, and allowing God to fully express Himself as you. It is to live in harmony with the truth, knowing that every action, every thought, and every word is an opportunity to give glory to God.

The Eternal Truth: God Is All There Is

The message of this book can be summed up in one eternal truth: God is all there is. Everything in creation is made of His substance, and every person is an expression of His Spirit. This truth is echoed throughout scripture. In Acts 17:28, Paul declares:

"For in him we live, and move, and have our being; as certain also of your own poets have said, For we are also his offspring."

The recognition of this truth is the key to salvation—not just for the individual but for all of humanity. When we awaken to the reality of GIATI, we see the oneness of all things and the futility of division, fear, and hatred. We realize that heaven is not a distant place but a state of being, a conscious awareness of God's presence in every moment.

Isaiah 46:9-10 reminds us of God's sovereignty and purpose:

**"Remember the former things of old: for I am God, and there is none else;
I am God, and there is none like me, Declaring the end from the beginning,
and from ancient times the things that are not yet done, saying,
My counsel shall stand, and I will do all my pleasure."**

God's purpose in creation was to express and experience Himself, and humanity's role is to awaken to this purpose. The eternal truth of GIATI is not just a revelation; it is an invitation to live in alignment with God's will, to embrace your divine nature, and to help others see the light within themselves.

Meditating On GIATI

When meditating on GIATI (God Is All There Is), one should focus on thoughts that align with the oneness of all existence and the truth of divine unity. Here are some reflective ideas to guide the meditation:

1. **Unity of Being:**
Contemplate the idea that all things are expressions of one source, manifesting in infinite forms. There is no separation—only one spirit flowing through all creation.

2. **Presence Within:**
Reflect on the understanding that the same spirit that created the universe resides within you. You are not apart from the source; you are an expression of it.

3. **Illusion of Separation:**
Meditate on how the perception of division is an illusion. All boundaries—between self and others, between the physical and spiritual—are constructs of the mind.

4. **Eternal Existence:**
Focus on the truth that existence is eternal and unchanging in essence, even as forms appear to change. The essence of all things remains the same.

5. **Living as GIATI:**
Ponder what it means to live with the awareness that all things are interconnected and divine. How does this awareness shape your actions, your thoughts, and your relationships with others?

6. **Release of Ego:**
Think about letting go of the idea of a separate "me." What remains when you dissolve the ego is the fullness of being—oneness with all that is.

7. **Seeing Through Spirit:**
Consider how to see the world not through the lens of flesh, but through the clarity of spirit. What does the world look like when everything is recognized as part of one divine whole?

8. **Infinite Love and Expression:**
Reflect on how everything you see, experience, and feel is a manifestation of infinite love, flowing as the Creator in action.

By meditating on these truths, the awareness of GIATI deepens, allowing you to live in the light of oneness and see the divine in all things.

A Final Call

This book is more than words on a page; it is a call to action. To the reader: You are not a separate being struggling to find meaning in a chaotic world. You are God's presence, expressed in the flesh, here to awaken to the truth and to help others do the same.

Jesus said in John 8:12:

"I am the light of the world: he that followeth me shall not walk in darkness, but shall have the light of life."

That light is in you, waiting to shine. Will you answer the call? Will you wake up to the truth of GIATI and live as the divine expression of God in this world? The choice is yours, but the promise is eternal.

God is all there is. Recognize Him, live as Him, and experience the joy of eternal unity with the Creator. The journey home begins now.

Ending

As we reach the culmination of this journey, it becomes undeniably clear: **God is all there is.** Every word, every revelation, and every explanation has been aimed at one singular truth—the realization of who you truly are and who you have always been.

From the beginning, the mystery has been simple yet profound. It is not hidden in the stars or beyond the heavens; it has been right in front of you, within you, and as you. The Spirit that created all things, the Spirit that clothed itself in flesh, the Spirit that breathed life into your being— it is the same Spirit that continues to sustain you at this very moment.

Many spend their lives searching for purpose, meaning, and identity. They pray to a God they believe is far away, seek approval from forces they think are outside themselves, and live under the delusion that they are separate from the very Source of all existence. But the truth is this: You are not apart from God; you are God expressed. To deny this is to deny yourself. To accept it is to awaken to eternal life.

The Unveiling of the Mystery

The journey of this book has shown that:

- You are the very Spirit of God manifested in flesh, clothed in skin and bones for a time to come into the full realization of your divine identity.
- God's ultimate purpose is to reproduce Himself—to expand His consciousness and bring forth children of Spirit who know Him fully because they know themselves.
- Everything about your existence, from your physical body to your spiritual essence, testifies to this truth.

To say you are separate from God is like a wave denying it is water or a cell denying it is part of the body. Such ignorance leads to spiritual blindness, the root of all sin. But to awaken is to see yourself as one with the Creator, not just in theory but in truth, for there is no "you" apart from Him.

The Invitation

In Acts 17:28, it is written: *"For in Him we live, and move, and have our being."* This has always been true, whether you have recognized it or not. You are not simply someone with God in you, nor are you someone walking beside Him. You are the very expression of His Spirit, His life, and His purpose.

The time has come to stop denying your true identity. God has winked at the ignorance of humanity for long enough, but now He commands all to repent. And what is repentance? It is not groveling for forgiveness or trying to become holy. Repentance is the shift in understanding that you are not separate from God; you are one with Him. It is the realization that your spirit is His Spirit, and there has never been a moment when He was not you, and you were not Him.

The Conclusion

The beauty of this truth is that it requires no striving, no proving, and no earning. You do not need to pray to a distant God, nor do you need to search for Him in temples made with hands. You are His temple. You are His life in manifestation. You are the purpose of His creation, and in knowing this, you are free.

So, as you close this book, let the scales of ignorance fall from your eyes. Let go of the lie of separation and embrace the eternal truth: You are God expressed in form, created to know Him, to live as Him, and to return to Him fully aware of your oneness.

This is not a philosophy; it is reality. This is not an opinion; it is the truth.

GIATI—God is all there is, and that includes you.

The choice is now yours: Will you awaken to this truth and live in the fullness of His Spirit, or will you remain in the delusion of separation? Know this: His Spirit is within you, and His will is that you come to this understanding. It is only by Him, through Him, and as Him that you will see it.

So step into the light of this revelation and live boldly, knowing you are who He says you are: **His very own Spirit made manifest.** The mystery is no longer hidden. The truth is before you.

You are, and have always been, Him.

www.ingramcontent.com/pod-product-compliance
Lightning Source LLC
Chambersburg PA
CBHW081526120626
46550CB00009B/2632

* 9 7 9 8 8 9 6 7 6 6 0 5 6 *